M000106810

Regenerated Identities

Regenerated Identities
Documenting African Lives

Paul E. Lovejoy, Henry B. Lovejoy,
Érika Melek Delgado, Kartikay Chadha, eds.

The Harriet Tubman Series
on the African Diaspora

AFRICA WORLD PRESS
TRENTON | LONDON | CAPE TOWN | NAIROBI | ADDIS ABABA | ASMARA | IBADAN | NEW DELHI

AFRICA WORLD PRESS
541 West Ingham Avenue | Suite B
Trenton, New Jersey 08638

Copyright © 2022
All rights reserved. No part of this publication may be reproduced, stored in a retrieval system or transmitted in any form or by any means electronic, mechanical, photocopying, recording or otherwise without the prior written permission of the publisher.

Book design: Dawid Kahts
Cover design: Fernanda Sierra, Ashraful Haque, Eric Kabré

Cataloging-in-Publication Data may be obtained from the Library of Congress.

ISBNs: 9781569027929 (HB)
9781569027935 (PB)

TABLE OF CONTENTS

List of Tables

List of Figures

List of Maps

Acknowledgements

The editors wish to acknowledge the support of the Andrew W. Mellon Foundation, National Endowment for the Humanities, the Social Sciences and Humanities Research Council (SSHRC) of Canada, York University, the University of Colorado at Boulder, McGill University, and King's College London for the successful completion of this book. The book has been inspired by the establishment of Walk With Web Inc. (WWW), www.walkwithweb.org, which was incorporated in 2020. The aim of this company has been to develop and provide digital solutions to enhance sustainability for research websites and databases of humanities and social science research. WWW was formed because many post-secondary institutions do not have infrastructure in place to provide services to help scholars develop and host digital humanities projects, although some of these institutions invest heavily in their production. Based in the ancestral and traditional territories of the Mississauga of the Credit, Haudenosaunee, Anishinaabe and Huron-Wendat in what now commonly is known as Toronto, Ontario, WWW is currently developing and hosting over 20 digital publications and growing.

During the establishment and expansion of WWW, this edited volume emerged from discussions surrounding how best to talk about "data," especially when referring to documented instances of enslaved people whose name and other personal details are then transcribed into spreadsheets and databases. We all agreed that there is an ethical dilemma as humanists and computer scientists talk about how best to represent, visualize, and generate new methodological practices of regenerating digital identities of enslaved peoples and their descendant communities. As we discussed these challenges, we also began soliciting the opinions of others, especially the contributors to this edited volume, who were not only soliciting the services of WWW to develop their projects, but also concerned about best practices surrounding data-driven repositories and digital archives focused on millions of peoples who were forced into slavery and involuntarily transported around the world.

This edited volume would not have been possible without all the hard work of the various contributors who are also researchers on projects and project directors of already established and soon-to-be-launched digital humanities publications. Many of these projects have received funding from various national and international granting agencies, post-secondary institutions, and private foundations. We are all indebted to the support because developing, hosting, and sustaining digital humanities publications is costly, but worthwhile to produce because of the immediate accessibility of such work through the internet to other researchers, students, and the general public.

We also want to thank Melchisedek Chétima for helping edit the chapters written in French. He was extremely generous in reviewing each for content and grammar. We acknowledge further the on-going support, contribution to research, and feedback from our team including Fábio Silva, Paola Vargas, Telma Santos, Thomas Garriss, Vincent Lai, and Fernanda Sierra at Walk With Web Inc. as well as Martha Ladly, Maria Yala, Youssouf Tarrore, and Eric Lehman at Ontario College of Art and Design (OCAD) University, and Katrina Keefer and Michael McGill at Trent University. Fernanda Sierra organized the design, while design rights are with Walk With Web Inc.

We also thank Dr. Stephen Peters at McGill University and the students in his class EDEC 635 (Fall 2020) for providing constructive feedback on sections of the introduction to this book. Last, we thank our family and friends who have provided constant support during the development and completion of this book.

Introduction:

Regenerating Digital Identities of Enslaved People in the African Diaspora

Henry B. Lovejoy, Kartikay Chadha, Paul E. Lovejoy, Érika Melek Delgado

Regenerated Identities: Documenting African Lives is an edited volume in digital humanities that highlights the use of computing technologies to recover, organize, analyze, and visualize African history, culture, and the life stories of children, women, and men in diaspora. The volume describes projects that use independent or collaborative data management tools or analog practices that have been employed to develop databases and platforms for the dissemination of research results. As African digital humanities intersect with computer and information sciences, controlled vocabularies, or standardized sets of terms, are being developed into databases to facilitate the storage and retrieval of information. This edited volume addresses ethical concerns surrounding terminologies that describe people as unhuman pieces of "data." Responsible stewardship of historical data about enslaved people requires more consideration because the increasing amount of information being collected and disseminated in digital spaces mostly derive from primary sources heavily biased toward oppressing African and African-derived cultures and peoples. The inclusive and reparative digital history projects discussed herein seek to shift how we talk about digital representations of people as "data." Instead, we elect to use the term "digital identities," which we believe does better to acknowledge the actual experiences, personalities, and life stories of enslaved people in digital form. Just as we reject the use of the term "slave" because the emphasis of the former lies with the "owners" perspective and an element of property, we reassess the appropriateness of the term "data," as frequently used in computer sciences and by extension its application to digital humanities. In this volume, we often prefer to use "digital identities" as an alternative for "data," "metadata," "databases," and "datasets," which scholars have compiled to identify and recognize the lived experiences of Africans and their descendants around the world, especially those children, women, and men who were involuntarily enslaved.

In 2011, the United Nations declared slavery and the slave trade a crime against humanity, which in its conception aimed to address the intercontinental forced migration of Africans to the Americas, and by extension to the various forms of modern slavery. The UN Declaration made it clear that slavery was no less a crime in the past when countries and societies considered enslavement legal and upheld the enforced enslavement of people against their will, with the resulting subjugation leading to persecution, discrimination, and intergenerational trauma, often reinforced by racism. The digital humanities initiatives discussed in this volume contribute to the movement for reparative justice by documenting the past in innovative ways that can disseminate knowledge and correct the false impression that the slavery past cannot be adequately documented. While the UNESCO initiative, "The Slave Route Project – Resistance, Legacy, Heritage," inspired the UN Declaration, digital humanities methods have advanced the consolidation of research and outreach, especially as we regenerate more digital identities into machine readable formats. "The Slave Route Project" was launched in Ouidah, Republique du Benin in 1994 with the purpose of drawing attention to the need to conduct extensive international research, educational reform, and training in uncovering the inglorious past to which countless millions of people had been subjected and the majority whose histories were silenced.

One of the most egregious after-effects of this barbaric forced migration was the attempt to erase the identities of millions of people who were taken from their homes and forced into slavery, their names changed, and their birth places and family ties hidden in personal memory that eroded over the generations. In the case of Africa, 12.5 million individuals were embarked on vessels for transport across the Atlantic to work in the slave societies of the Americas. Millions more trekked the Sahara over the centuries, even before the launch of the Middle Passage across the Atlantic. Africans crossed the

Indian Ocean long before the Atlantic slave trade, while unknown numbers of people were moved between different parts of the African continent.

The legacy of forgetting has been foundational to human rights abuses, inequity, and social injustices in Africa, the former slave colonies in the Americas and the Caribbean, the Islamic world, the Indian Ocean, and indeed in Africa. Despite repeated calls for reparations, the history of slavery continues to confront contemporary society and confound policy makers, government officials, and educators whose ancestors were sometimes perpetrators of enslavement and whose complicity is likewise purged from memory as a stain that is to be hidden. The tragic contradiction is that the benefits derived from slavery have reinforced intergenerational privilege, while the scourge of enslavement has crystalized into racialized discrimination and subjugation that has led to intergenerational trauma.

In this volume, we explore digital identities of many individuals who suffered from enslavement, even if for only a part of their lives. These people were not numbers that comprise "data" in research studies but actual people whose lives mattered. The trajectory from data extraction and curation to the analysis of digital identities challenges our methodological paradigm. *Regenerated Identities: Documenting African Lives* focuses on understanding the interaction of human lives by organizing surviving information on individuals in a manner that allows understanding history and promotes knowledge dissemination. The increased searchability of original historical manuscripts, meta-tagging sources, and online presentation of scholarly analysis via websites enables the mobilization of new knowledge. These innovative methodologies permit experts to reconstruct historical processes beyond the range of traditional historical scholarship so that students and the public can explore the past in unique, creative, and more accessible ways via the internet.

The contributors herein reveal novel approaches in digital history that can overcome the silences that have been based on suppression and denial. In the first instance, the effort to identify where people came from and where they went draws attention to the need to examine Africa according to various regions and the movement of people both within Africa and beyond its continental shores. To this end, six broad regions and 34 sub-regions have been defined to facilitate analysis of data (Map 1). Projects use a variety of analog practices, content management tools, geographic information systems, and 3D software to create interactive educational environments, historical analysis and access to digital archives for public consumption. The innovative approaches to reorganize data, which involves generating new digital identities from vast quantities of source materials is often scattered around world archives. These digital identities address questions that relate to the interactions of data categorized into spreadsheets of people, events, places, and sources.

Map 1
Regions of Africa

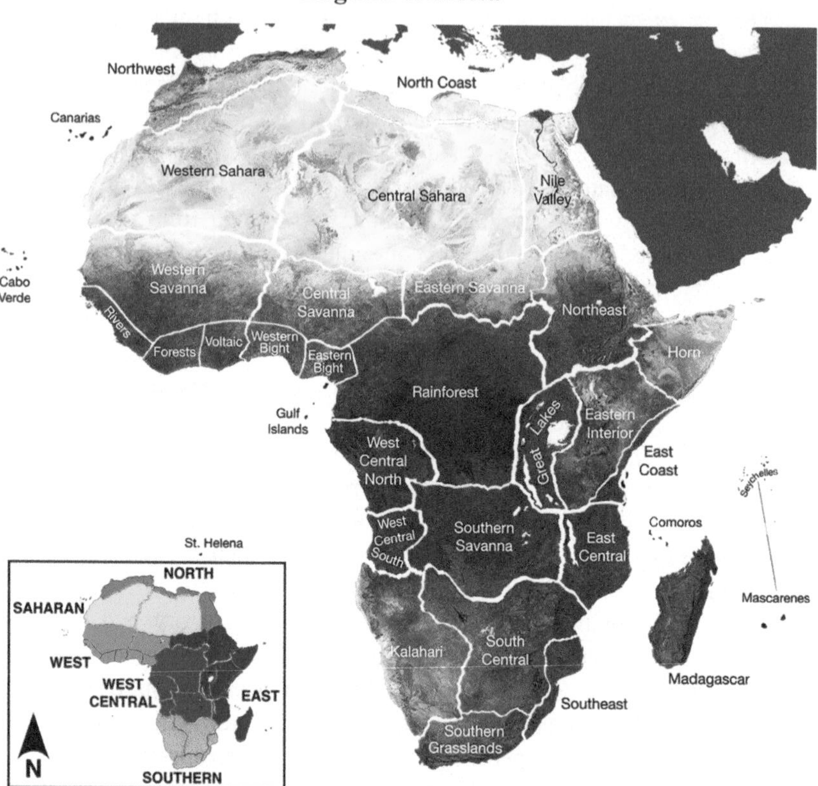

Source: Henry B. Lovejoy, Paul E. Lovejoy, Walter Hawthorne, Edward A. Alpers, Mariana Candido, Matthew S. Hopper, Ghislaine Lydon, Colleen E. Kriger, John Thornton, "Defining Regions of Pre-Colonial Africa: A Controlled Vocabulary for Linking Open-Source Data in Digital History Projects," *History in Africa* 48 (2021), 1-26.

As African history and computer science have become increasingly intertwined, there has been a monumental shift in what we can know and how to organize information about enslaved Africans and their descendants around the world. As scholars of the African diaspora have long known, there is an abundance of information about this history in the archeological record, oral sources, archives, courthouses, churches, mosques, and private collections. The main problem in this field has been that this information is scattered and spread out around the entire world,which has made it difficult and expensive for researchers to access and link more broadly across geographic regions. With the advent of affordable digital cameras and improved humanities-based computing in the 1990s, archives, libraries, governments, religious organizations, academics, and members of the general public have been digitizing primary sources and making them accessible online as digital archives.

Due to intercontinental and transoceanic enforced migrations, many digital history projects focused on the African diaspora either have content or methodological overlap, which enables possibilities of cross-referencing across web-based platforms to link digital identities of hundreds of thousands of people together over time and space. These humanities-based studies of enforced African migration involve the development of complex strategies for information retrieval, output, and visualization from a historian's point-of-view, as made accessible through programming and data science. Often, the methods for one project apply to another, despite differences in digital identities generated from a vast array of primary sources in multiple languages.

Digital humanities over the past two decades have fundamentally altered scholarship in global African history (Eltis 2007; H. Lovejoy 2010; H. Lovejoy 2016; Mnjama 2017; Molineux 2020). Most especially, the use of biographical materials and mapping has enhanced the study of developments in the consolidation of information on an intercontinental African diaspora (P. Lovejoy 2011; H. Lovejoy 2019; Melek Delgado, 2022). Such biographical materials derive from historical manuscripts, which are centuries old and are now housed at various archives around the Atlantic and Indian Ocean worlds. Archival research and preservation initiatives, such as the British Library Endangered Archive Programme (www.eap.bl.uk), supports the digitization of rare sources, manuscripts, visual materials, audio recordings in archives that are in danger of destruction or neglect and suffer from physical deterioration. With an increase in digitized collections of archival materials available online, primary sources from around the world have facilitated research into the African diaspora. The corpus of historical manuscripts in context includes digitized copies of both printed and hand-written documents including ship logs, military records, court files, government correspondences, ecclesiastical sources, pension records, newspapers, advertisements, and many other materials (Mnjama 2017). Scholars of African studies have been curating, digitizing, organizing, meta-tagging, and analyzing such historical manuscripts to generate new knowledge to inform the descent of the enslaved on their ancestry. This accessibility to primary source, along with more tools to build websites, has led to an increase in digital African history projects, a handful of which are described in the following chapters.

The proliferation of digital archives and databases of digital identities present several challenges related to best practices on how to represent enslaved people from Africa and their descendants around the world as rows and columns. The shared goal of these projects and initiatives is to respect the provenance of important historical and personal information in the manuscripts and to apply computational data gathering and analytics to join ongoing efforts to restore and recover African identities which the slave trade sought to erase. As historians continue to generate new datasets that operate with a variety of evolving technologies and digital tools, programming jargon has naturally crept into the lexicon of the field, which requires careful consideration of sensitive issues due to a past rooted in racism and discrimination. Indeed, we fear that a trend has been developing in which "data" is being used too generally and without much consideration to the individuals whose lives have mostly been silenced. Assigning "ID numbers" and calling people "data" is inherently problematic on an ethical and moral level, especially in terms of the historical crimes against humanity, where the counting, numbering, and trading of people was an all-too-common feature.

Designing digital African history projects is a relatively simple process, however. Historians are often bound to the data contained in primary source materials, whether oral or written, which they then transcribe into spreadsheets or forms connected directly to a content management system. Programmers, mostly supported through grants and other support, help apply a wide range of digital tools and technologies, such as Microsoft Excel, Google Sheets, Google Documents, Adobe Acrobat Pro DC and Google Drive (H. Lovejoy 2010; P. Lovejoy, Melek Delgado and Chadha 2022). The best practices and methodologies are far more complex because data is usually bound to the constraints of extractable information embedded in the primary sources, which historians are constantly expanding and improving upon, while evaluating various levels of bias. Meanwhile, digital tools oftentimes require other data not found in historical sources as a minimum requirement needed to operate. Reorganizing historical manuscripts into digital identities helps preserve basic biographical information of enslaved people, such as names, gender, ages, places, occupations, or ethnicities. Digital identities are transcribed, usually from digital copies of original manuscripts in PDF format. These "data" are stored on network computers, which are servers that host the content on the world wide web.

Best Practices and Ethics

The combination of expanding datasets and evolving technologies requires a review of best practices in terms of data collection and digital project design. While we propose being more sensitive to the way in which we discuss the backend of digital projects and scholarly websites, we fully embrace the interdisciplinarity of the digital humanities. The results of these cross-disciplinary collaborations facilitate the mobilization of new knowledge through the development of searchable and interactive websites which have the capacity to link together global collections of primary sources involving fragmented references to enslaved Africans and their descendants as they were forcibly moved around the world at different moments in time.

This ongoing research has been providing valuable methods to analyze information within historical manuscripts but face both methodological and technical challenges. Transcribing historical manuscripts is time-consuming and prone to error. The methodological challenge relates to the content in these historical manuscripts such as ambiguities inherent in the records of names, phonetic spellings of African names in European languages, the involuntary renaming of enslaved Africans, ethnonyms and other identities assigned to people, a poor understanding of pre-colonial Africa's internal geography, among other reasons. The technical challenges in African digital humanities relate to the usage of multiple computational software, demand for high digital storage capacities, requirement for higher computational processing power and long-term sustainability of research websites. These challenges are addressed by developing new research methodologies to enable rigorous results. Additionally, research projects are funded for a limited period. Upon completion of the funding term, the sustainability of digital projects is the responsibility of project directors, which is challenging due to insufficient humanities-based cyberinfrastructure at most universities, which is oftentimes lacking to support the output of digital humanities project development.

By revealing novel, digital approaches in reconstructing a past that has repeatedly been suppressed and denied, the essays herein address ethical questions related to the best practices and methodologies on representing identities of enslaved Africans and their descendants in digital formats. We explore the challenges that interdisciplinary teams are confronted with in terms of respecting the minute details of individual microhistories within "big data," which sometimes contains lists of hundreds of thousands of people or more. Digital identities largely derive from written primary sources produced in former slave societies. As scholars regenerate digital identities, they constantly take into consideration biases and historical context, while envisioning future benefits to cross-referencing the multitude of web-based platforms to reveal deeper histories.

To overcome some difficulties, digital humanities scholars have defined methodological steps as "analog best practices" that document standard rules to follow while curating, digitizing and meta-tagging historical manuscripts. These methods allow production of "clean" data, as explained in computer science to be in a machine-readable format and free from inconsistencies, addressing technical applicability to some extent. These new computational tools support analog best practices by combining various functionalities of individual computer software into a single platform. In many circumstances, tools are designed for individual project for specific needs related to the data, and unfortunately do not incorporate the wider range of research activities conducted in the field. A single computational tool or methodology that assists all aspects of research methodologies is ambitious, especially because of the fast-changing nature of technology. No single, self-contained software currently can be standardized across multiple projects, but some software offers a portion of the important functionalities such as data extraction, spatial analysis (for mapping), visualization and machine-assisted analysis. Projects that are established or in developmental phases have sometimes been left without necessary support. It is because of long-term sustainability issues surrounding the survival of digital projects that this volume has been prepared. The editors want to document the development of projects on Global Africa, now that sustainability, preoccupation with best practices, and close interaction between digital programmers and research scholars has reached a new level. It has become apparent that the content of research and the manner which data are processed cannot be divorced from the mechanisms of digital applicability. The interdisciplinarity underlying digital humanities now requires that researchers understand some of the language and methodology of computer technology and digital scientists recognize the context and informatics of scholarship. In our case, the focus is on Global Africa and especially but not exclusively on issues relating to slavery and history. This realization has evolved through collaboration and ongoing engagement.

In July 2020, various academics including contributors to this volume created Walk With Web Inc. (https://walkwithweb.org) to address the digital component of social sciences and humanities research. WWW is an independent technical hub, which was incorporated especially for researchers in African digital humanities to gain customized technical support on specific research projects and to overcome challenges around long term sustainability of research outcomes. WWW introduced a new concept of gateway services in the field which is a mid-way path between developing a single software and using a pipeline of multiple softwares to include a wide range of research methodological requirements. Through streamlined, online, user-friendly interfaces, gateway services are technical structures that combine a variety of components (usually software and virtual services) that can support a community-specific requirement in data collection and analyses. Inspired by the content management tools like the *Decoding Origins Web Portal* and Spatial Historians, WWW provides access to its gateway service through a new web interface called Regenerated Identities (RegID).

Chadha, Keefer and Ladly (2021) base high usability of the *Decoding Origins Web Portal* on their development methodology, which incorporates an innovative and multidisciplinary team consisting of information experts, computer scientists, artists, historians and anthropologists. They introduce the concept of human-computer interaction and *Design Thinking* process in User Centered Design (UCD) from the computer science field to allow development of intuitive and user-friendly computational tools for Global Africa. WWW infrastructure is also based on UCD research concepts, which promotes inclusion of users in the development process of a digital platform. Multidisciplinary researchers at WWW work to narrow the gap between scholars in African studies and professional computer programmers by employing an iterative learning methodology (Zimmerman, 2008) that directly improves efficiency of RegID. WWW is concerned with the application of computational tools and methods to traditional humanities disciplines such as literature, history, and philosophy (Gold 2012; Dalton & Charnigo 2004; Meirelles 2013). The collaborative goal of WWW and its clients is to form an understanding of the scope and meaning of digital visualization and digital representation of African ancestral identities and allows integration of global research in digital humanities with a long-term sustainability technical architecture.

RegID supports a number of major digital humanities projects in the field of African studies. These projects share a similar theme enabling an exploration of the lives of people who were born free, people of African descent born into slavery in the Americas, and in many cases, those individuals who regained their freedom having been born free. Personal accounts fundamental to analysis across these projects include texts that arise from first person memory, amanuensis, or reconstruction from various types of documentation. WWW is a real-time example demonstrating that a partnership between industry professionals and academia can add to our knowledge of personal identities and the evolution of social communities.

Chapter Organization

The first section of this edited volume examines various methodological approaches to the importance of digital identity data management and their dissemination in digital formats. In the first chapter, Gwendolyn Midlo Hall discusses how historical databases are wonderful, innovative tools, but cautions that databases have limitations because their development depends on the questions that a given database is designed to answer. Using her famous *Louisiana Slave Database* (www.louisianaslavedatabase.org), she argues how spreadsheets of data can be more rigid than qualitative sources. In using them, scholars must keep in mind that just because something is not included in a historical document or a database, that does not mean that it did not happen. Obviously, historians record only what they think is important, and we cannot tell what those who did the original research chose not to record.

Paul LaChance, in chapter 2, praises Hall's methodological approach which he argues set seven precedents for historians undertaking digital scholarship, which involve deciding the scope (larger the better), who will contribute, which sources to use, developing a metadata schema and controlled vocabulary, allowing for annotations, and making digital humanities publication accessible, in all sense of the term.

In the third chapter, Jerome S. Handler and Michael Tuite created one of the first digital humanities publications for African diaspora history, which first went online in 2001. Now known as *Slavery Images* (www.slaveryimages.org), Handler demonstrated how a simplistic four-part metadata schema can lead to one of the most widely used teaching resources with over 1,200 images related to the African slave trade and slave life in diaspora. This chapter, however, discusses sustainability challenges as websites have to be passed on to younger generations to preserve their legacy, which in this case involved transitioning directorships from Handler to Henry B. Lovejoy in 2018. Since then, H. Lovejoy has been able to add new features, such as mapping the images for better accessibility. This piece also recognizes the importance of providing project histories and milestones on digital humanities publications as best practice.

Léon Robichaud's chapter centers on the development of *Marronnage in the Atlantic World* (www.marronnage.info), which he co-directs with Jean-Pierre Le Glaunec. This project collates inaccessible collections of fugitive slave advertisements and lists of imprisoned captives to publish them online in a user-friendly website. Originally designed to report escapes and to provide information for the recapture of self-liberating slaves, the project's co-directors have published more than 20,000 documents in French and English from 21 newspapers. The chapter shows how information was converted into data and how the project evolved over time, including various experiments in document selection, management, and presentation. Metadata and attributes were selected to provide for basic yet broad coverage while transcribing the digital identities of as many people as possible to give a voice to those who endured and resisted slavery.

H. Lovejoy's chapter uses a detailed project history of *Liberated Africans* (www.liberatedafricans.org) to discuss the complications of assigning credit for tenure and promotion to highly collaborative digital humanities publications. Yhe comprehensive metadata schema and controlled vocabulary, which revolve around four main categories: people, events, places, and sources. During the second version development in mid 2016, *Liberated Africans* was likely the earliest digital humanities publications to develop a four-part relational database structure, which has since been adapted by other projects, including for a linked open data ontology in *Enslaved: Peoples of the Historic Slave Trade* (www.enslaved.org), which launched in late 2020.

The following chapter, co-authored by Paul E. Lovejoy, Erika Delgado, and Karikay Chadha, explains the application of the four-part relational database structure to *Freedom Narratives: Testimonies of West Africans from the Era of Slavery* (www.freedomnarrratives.org). This digital publication focuses on individuals who were born in West Africa, many of whom were shipped to the Americas, but by no means all. The project also identifies individuals who were taken across the Sahara and most importantly on those who remained in West Africa.

In chapter 7, Kartikay Chadha, Katrina Keefer and Martha Ladly discuss their usage of people, places, events, and sources database schema in their forthcoming digital humanities publication currently under development. *Decoding Origins: Creating a Visual Language of Marks* (www.languageofmarks.org) seeks to catalogue intricate tattoos and scarification documented in primary sources to identify African ethnicity. Their chapter examines how to improve data collection strategies to within this four-part database schema. This process is important as many projects being developed through WWW intend to share and develop overlapping data together, especially so as not to duplicate efforts and to facilitate data entry to engage more student involvement and participation.

P. Lovejoy and Chadha's chapter on *Equiano's World* (www.equianosworld.org) chronicles the life and times of Gustavus Vassa (c. 1741-1797), who is known most frequently by his birth name, Olaudah Equiano. Vassa became well known in Britain after the publication of his autobiography in 1789 and his prominent role in the movement to abolish the British slave trade. The study of individual digital identities in detail places microhistory in a context that can shed light on larger events and processes. The associated database includes all known documentation on Vassa and relevant information that informs a study of his biography, which presents challenges surrounding how best to capture the lived experiences, known associates, and contributions to a single individual, whose life contains exceptional details and extensive documentation.

Chapter 9 examines how Jane Landers, Daniel Genkins, and Jim Schindling are developing innovative ways to capture, generate, and associate digital identities from Catholic baptismal records housed in the *Slave Societies Digital Archives* (www.slavesocieties.org). Their system, called the Spatial Historian, implements user-friendly ways to connect different groups of people involved in baptism records (child, parents, godparents, ministers, witnesses, etc…), to baptismal events occurring at specific locations of churches. As more and more data is being extracted from a large collection of ecclesiastical sources, they will unravel an enormous amounts of information about familial, religious, and slave/master relationships in Catholic communities in the Americas from the 1500s to the 1900s.

The second section of this edited volume examines the methodological and ethical problems of regenerating digital identities, especially in relation to the oftentimes enforced labelling of enslaved people with colonial designations for ethnic groups, languages, and places in Africa. This section examines how historical data needs to be humanized, in that digital identities represent people and these data need to re-tell their stories in an ethical manner which involves best practices.

In chapter 10, P. Lovejoy discusses a new platform, called *Documenting Africans in Trans-Atlantic Slavery* (www.datasproject.org), which is also under development with WWW. This forthcoming digital humanities publication will provide a central list of ethnonyms and their interpretation, which in many circumstances can be plotted on maps and visualized for improved searchability. This innovative platform will revolutionize how scholars can access and better understand identity during the era of the

Chapter 11 demonstrates the power of cross-referencing between two longstanding digital humanities publications to be able to understand more about the identities of enslaved Africans in Louisiana between 1699 and 1766. Ibrahim Seck combines ship data from *Voyages* with digital identities from the *Louisiana Slave Database*. He provides detailed interpretations of ethnonyms, which are also presented alongside slave ship arrivals. This combination of historical data provides exemplary evidence to nearly pinpoint when and where these enslaved Africans came from in different parts of West Africa, and in particular given slave trading patterns in this period, mostly came from the Western Sudan.

Paola Vargas Arana discusses in chapter 12 women gold miners in Antioguia, New Granada during the sixteenth and seventeenth century. She provides several case studies to be included in *Freedom Narratives* and *DATAS* because these women came from Africa and had many biographical details, including ethnonyms, recorded in the Americas. These case studies not only show linkages back to African regions, places and ethnolinguistic groups, these soon-to-be regenerated digital identities will also help understand early processes of creolization in the Spanish Americas, as well as the resistance of women to the conditions of slavery.

Telma Santos and Nina Borba examine the baptismal records of Santo Amaro de Ipitanga Parish in Bahia, whose documentation covers one hundred years from the 1770s to the 1870s. They compiled information on 352 individuals born in Africa, 215 of whom can be traced to different parts of Africa. The remaining 137 are only identified as being born in Africa, although it is likely that most of these individuals came from West Africa. A shift in nomenclature from specific identifications to generic terminology occurred when it was no longer legal to bring enslaved Africans from West Africa in 1831. The registers provide evidence of ethnic identification for West Africa, with almost all people coming from the Bight of Benin. The means of identification for people from west central and southeastern Africa was different, being based on the port of departure, not by ethno-linguistic classification.

In the following chapter, Susan Peabody, examines the microhistories of enslaved Africans in the Indian Ocean world. She examines the case of 324 "prize negroes" on board the French brig *Le Succès*, who the British navy recaptured in violation anti-slave trade legislation in 1821. Her definition of microhistory, which revolves around an intensive investigation of people, communities, and events within a wider historical context. Microhistorical approaches helps to humanize concepts of data and digital identities, especially as historians balance a tension between focusing on individuals whose lives were extremely well documented (and thus exceptional rare) and the degree to which these people can be considered "representative" of the wider experiences of large groups of enslaved Africans in diaspora.

In the last chapter of this volume, Klara Boyer-Rossol examines the extensive and detailed collection of Eugène de Froberville, who interviewed, sketched, and made sculptured busts of Africans between 1845 and 1847. Many of these individuals were liberated from the slave ship *Lily*. The use of digital humanities methods on these collections will help trace and reconstruct the lived experiences of these individuals based on the Froberville collection. Through a discussion of this evidence, it is not hard to imagine how organizing the imagery and cultural artifacts leads to detailed and complex digital identities with rich microhistories. Their stories and "data" can be organized along the people, events, places, and sources schema, which will then have the potential to link into other digital humanities publications, such as *Liberated Africans*, *Language of Marks*, and due to the documentation of ethnonyms, *DATAS*.

When regenerating digital identities there are many ethical considerations. This chapter focuses on digitizing the personnel records and biographical information from the West African Frontier Force held at the Sierra Leone Public Archives in Freetown. These records reflect a knowable and living past of soldiers forced to serve British imperial interests in the twentieth century. These contain sensitive and confidential information including medical and personal details not normally disclosed to the public. Best practices and ethics must be introduced to protect the privacy of these subjects, but this approach extends beyond these files and applies to records concerning the trans-Atlantic slave trade. This methodology has the dual purpose of preventing exploitation and re-traumatization while still allowing researchers access to primary documents. These best practices fundamentally emphasize the human dignity of what might otherwise be regarded as data alone.

The volume includes an appendix which examines the technical architecture of the Regenerated Identity (RegID) web application being developed by Kartikay Chadha, President of Walk With Web Inc. (www.

walkwithweb.org). WWW is a web-development company to support digital humanities publications and projects focused on Africa and the African Diaspora. The ability to publish open-source digital humanities projects has a significant impact for scholars who wish to focus on non-traditional mediums in which to conduct scholarship, especially for tenure and promotion.

Part I:

Databases, Digital Archives, and Best Practices

1

Africa and Africans in the African Diaspora:

The Uses of Relational Databases[1]

Gwendolyn Midlo Hall[2]

> African American Studies, better labeled Negro American Studies, are for the most part superficial and incomplete, referring to black people without knowing them. The typical researcher cannot disengage from the tendency to present them as fragmented and superficial, without seeing Africans as individuals coming from a society with rules and values of its own . . . as someone torn from a particular culture that could not be erased by the simple act of crossing the Atlantic. From human beings full of culture and knowledge, they have been transformed into mere merchandise: tons of ebony.
>
> Nicola´s Ngou-Mve, "Historia de la población negra en México"

In their article "Agency and Diaspora in Atlantic History," David Eltis, Philip Morgan, and David Richardson (2007, 1329-1358) make two major claims: (1) that the article presents a new, superior model for interpreting the formation of culture in the Americas, and (2) that it challenges the belief that Africans played an important role in the introduction and technology of rice cultivation and processing in the Americas. For their conclusions about rice, they rely mainly on calculations from *Voyages: the Trans-Atlantic Slave Trade Database* (www.slavevoyages.org) as a tool to study the distribution of enslaved Africans from rice growing regions in Africa to regions in the Americas that exported rice to Europe.

The authors claim to have made a great new discovery about culture formation in the Americas. They then revive and reprise an unrelated discussion from a 1991 forum in the *William and Mary Quarterly* (1991, 224-308) criticizing a book by David Hackett Fischer titled *Albion's Seed* (1989) Fischer's book is about British colonizers of the United States. Scholars have never claimed that British cultures were erased by the transatlantic crossing. Its methodology has not served as a model for African diaspora studies.

Eltis, Morgan, and Richardson (2007, 1332) distort the work of the many scholars it criticizes. Our varied methodologies are reduced to a monolithic advocacy of static "seed" cultures brought over from the Old World and continued as "enclave cultures" in the Americas. "Rather than frame the issue as solely one of transfers and conduits," Eltis, Morgan, and Richardson write, "we should also think of transformations and overlapping circuits. Rather than posit whether slaves and planters always acted knowingly, we should entertain the possibility that they often responded to unseen market forces. Rather than assume that migrants remained conservatively attached to traditional ways, we might also view them as experimenters and improvisers."

The scholars criticized in "Agency and Diaspora" of Eltis, Morgan, Richardson share only one interpretation: that the knowledge and culture of Africans from particular coasts and ethnicities were not erased by the transatlantic crossing. This historian, for example, has written that the process of culture formation (creolization) responded to various, changing factors in the Americas, including the patterns of introduction of Africans from particular regions and ethnicities; gender proportions and patterns of mating and parenting; how rapidly migrants began to procreate and the extent of biological merger among diverse peoples; the demographic and military strength of the Native American population; whether the geography facilitated runaway slave (maroon) communities; the economic, strategic, and military priorities of the colonizing powers; the extent of manumission of former slaves and their demographic strength and social status; military and police uses of slaves and free people of color; the labor demands of the major exports as the economy evolved; and policies of social control reflected in various European political and religious traditions and institutions and how effectively they were enforced (Hall 2005, 166-167). Concepts and definitions of creolization in the Americas vary among the scholars whose work is criticized in "Agency and Diaspora." The most recent version is the conclusion of Linda Heywood and John Thornton (2003) that the Charter Generation of Africans who molded the Creole cultures of British and Dutch America before 1660 were largely Europeanized, Catholic West Central Africans.[3]

Otherwise Eltis, Morgan, and Richardson minimize the significance of African technological transfer to the Americas in the planting and processing of rice. Although some anecdotal qualitative sources are used, the argument relies overwhelmingly on calculations made from *Voyages*. David Eltis, Stephen Behrendt, David Richardson, and Manolo Florentino deserve great credit for their tireless work on this database, including its impressive technological advances over the first version of *Voyages*. Thousands of new Brazilian and Portuguese voyages have been added, correcting the Anglo focused distortion of the first version of *Voyages*. The database has been made more user friendly and is accessible to the public free of charge as an open source work. It enables users to make calculations, corrections, and additions. It can answer many important questions about the transatlantic slave trade. But when it comes to certain kinds of questions, its limitations must be considered. It cannot answer the questions about rice posed in "Agency and Diaspora."[4]

Historical databases are wonderful, innovative tools. They can integrate huge amounts of detailed, concrete data into broad patterns allowing for analysis over time and place. The vast quantity of information they can contain and analyze is a great advantage, especially in making broad, comparative studies. Databases can answer questions that cannot be answered using more traditional methodologies, can partially or tentatively answer others, and can help answer still others, combining quantitative calculations with the findings of other disciplines, including archaeology, anthropology, linguistics, and geography, as well as traditional history. But there are some questions that are simply beyond their capabilities. It all depends on the questions that a given database is designed to answer. Databases can be more rigid than qualitative sources. In using them, scholars must keep in mind that just because something is not included in a historical document or a database, that does not mean that it did not happen. There is important information that has never been documented; there are documents that have not yet been found and studied. Versions of the *Voyages* database were designed to contain only documented and studied voyages of slave trade ships that crossed the Atlantic. "Agency and Diaspora" hardly considers the redistribution process that took place when these new Africans were first sold in the Americas, then reloaded onto other ships and subsequently moved by water and/or land to other places before reaching their varied final destinations. In this process, they were sometimes clustered by their region of origin and/or ethnicity when buyers were able to purchase the new Africans they preferred (Inikori 1998; Hall 2005; Chambers 2008, 335-346).[5]

There are problems with rigidity as well as the omission of important data in *Voyages*. It was created from research into original manuscript documents carried out by many historians during the past forty years or more. Each record covers a specific transatlantic slave trade voyage. The fields in a database contain information about the individual records that it includes. They are designed to answer the questions the creators of the database want to ask, not necessarily to provide the information contained in the original documents. Unless a database has been designed to be flexible, once the fields have been defined and a substantial amount of data has been entered, adding new fields can be laborious, time consuming, and expensive. *Voyages* remains locked into the same questions that scholars have asked since the publication of Phillip D. Curtin's *The Atlantic Slave Trade: A Census* in 1969, but with a notable limitation: there is no field for the entry of data on African ethnicities. Except for a few entirely quantitative questions, such as gender, age category, and deaths when this information was recorded in the documents and then noted and published by the historians who studied them, *Voyages* does not focus on information about the enslaved Africans on the ships. The fields were not changed between the first and second versions of *Voyages*.

Obviously, historians record only what they think is important, and we cannot tell what those who did the original research chose not to record. In some cases, information that indeed was recorded by the scholar who conducted the initial research will not be entered into the database because no field was created for it. Such omissions may have included information about African ethnicities that Eltis, Morgan, and Richardson (2007, 1349) dismiss as inaccurate and perhaps therefore unimportant. Was information about the ethnicities of Africans on transatlantic slave trade voyages documented? Yes. To what extent? Without consulting the original documents, we cannot know. If there were no fields in *Voyages* in which this information and the contents of these original documents could be recorded, this data is not available to us. Thus, a crucial advantage of using original manuscript documents is lost. Perhaps there is very little information in transatlantic slave trade documents about the Africans aboard the ships; or perhaps, as Nicola´s Ngou-Mve observed, those who conducted the research using the original documents did not consider this information important enough to record. Thus, when the editors of *Voyages* did not do the initial research themselves, the information in the database is twice removed from the original sources. Ngou-Mve calls on historians to look at all the documents again, even if other historians have already studied them. This writer's experience (Hall 1992, 56-95) with voyage documents is limited to Louisiana, but it supports Ngou-Mve's conclusion (2005, 51).

Historical databases and new media need to go beyond purely quantifiable questions. As Daniel J. Cohen suggests, "Focusing on the full potential of the medium and being sure that digital history is not simply an echo of quantitative processes or algorithms to the abundant digital record in the service of source discovery and analysis is extremely important . . . and equally important are the networking and collaborative possibilities of the medium—that is, focusing on human rather than machine activities."[6] The search and visualization capabilities of advancing technology facilitate these advances. Visualization will allow us to consult the original documents whose contents have been filtered out by rigid, purely quantifiable databases and their questions.

During the past two decades, there has been a seismic change in perception about documents relating to Africans and their descendants throughout the Americas. The shift has been from a belief that original manuscript sources did not exist or were extremely rare to a recognition of the truly extraordinary abundance of documents in archives, courthouses, ports, museums, and private collections housed throughout the Americas. This writer's database about Louisiana slaves was initiated in 1984. Focusing on people who were enslaved, it was created almost entirely from original manuscript documents. The database contains almost all the information about each description of a slave from original documents, including unquantifiable data.[7]

The limitations of *Voyages* call into question Eltis, Morgan, and Richardson's critique of Judith A. Carney's well known work about the transfer of rice cultivation from Africa to the Americas. She carried out a truly impressive range of varied and exhaustive research and used it judiciously and well. Carney is a multilingual, multidisciplinary geographer who was inspired to study original historical documents the pioneering work of historians Daniel C. Littlefield and Peter H. Wood. Her grasp of geography and agricultural technology enhances her insights into the meanings of such primary sources. From the earliest manuscript sources and publications of Portuguese observers, beginning with the mid fifteenth century, she thoroughly documents the well-established, widespread, complex cultivation of rice in varied environments along the coasts of upper Guinea and up its rivers. She makes use of a variety of approaches, including documentary sources on both sides of the Atlantic throughout the five centuries of the Atlantic slave trade and in depth field work in Africa and the Americas. In contrast, Eltis, Morgan, and Richardson base their conclusions on the flimsy evidence of what they found documented for twenty voyages of the Royal African Company visiting Gambia and Sierra Leone between 1779 and 1788. The sample of voyages they used is very small and limited in time because there was no field to record such information in *Voyages*; thus, they had to consult original documents. Nevertheless, they state: "From this evidence, women did not mill rice on the Middle Passage" (Eltis, Morgan, Richardson 2007, 1347).

It is possible that women milled rice on slave trade trips but that those activities were not recorded in the documents; or that documents survive but have not yet been found; or that the original researchers did not record this information; or that they did record it, but it was not included in *Voyages*. Carney has evidence of women pounding seed rice on a slave trade ship in 1796, pointing out that it is only one such clearly documented case. She speculates about how rice seeds could have been introduced into the Americas without drawing firm conclusions. She discusses evidence for multiple and varied directional introduction of rice between Africa and the Americas over the centuries. Carney could not possibly have claimed, as Eltis, Morgan, and Richardson state, that "a single enslaved African woman carrying a few grains of rice in her hair can become all that is necessary to sustain the thesis" (2007, 1357). One of the major points she makes in Black Rice is that the Columbian exchange involved the transfer not only of seeds, but of systems of cultivation as well, including processing techniques from places of domestication to elsewhere in the Atlantic world. That is why she uses the word "systems." Eltis, Morgan, and Richardson take the word "systems" out of context and then dismiss her entire work with unsupportable criticisms.

"Agency and Diaspora" is correct in stating that "Part of the strategy for keeping valuable property alive on the transatlantic crossing was to ensure that slaves received food to which they were accustomed" (Eltis, Morgan, Richardson 2007, 1347). The authors say that more millet than rice was placed on the twelve slave trade ships they studied, which left upper Guinea between 1779 and 1788. But rice, not millet, was an important food crop in the Americas. The authors suggest that Africans as well as Europeans might have improvised their eating patterns in the Americas, minimizing enslaved Africans' preferences for rice (Eltis, Morgan, Richardson 2007, 1354). Did the need to enable enslaved Africans to follow their traditional eating patterns to keep them alive disappear after the Atlantic crossing?

Eltis, Morgan, and Richardson criticize Carney for overstating the role of women in rice production in the Americas. They point to the relatively high male ratios on voyages arriving from upper Guinea. But these calculations tell us nothing about sex ratios among slaves from rice producing ethnicities, or about masters' preferences for women of these ethnicities. They write that "the number and percentage of Africans with rice growing experience must have been far below the total number of slaves leaving upper Guinea" (Eltis, Morgan, Richardson 2007, 1348). This is no doubt true, but therefore their studies of gross gender ratios among slaves leaving the entire upper Guinea coast are not clarifying with respect to rice producers. Throughout most of the eighteenth and early nineteenth centuries, enslaved warriors were sent down the Senegal and Gambia rivers in large numbers, mainly Bamana (Bambara) during the 1720s, before the designation "Bambara" took on wider, vague, generic meanings. Many captured warriors were shipped to the Americas from Senegambia and Sierra Leone, tilting gender ratios toward males. Male ratios were highest among the ethnicities most often captured in warfare, as well as among cattle herders. Gender ratios among Africans from upper Guinea varied in accordance with ethnicity. Some captured warriors came from rice producing ethnicities, for example Bamana (Bambara) and Mandinke. The male ratios on slave trade ships that the authors present (1350-1351, Tables 5-7) tell us nothing about whether masters cultivating rice in Carolina, Georgia, and northeast Brazil preferred women from rice producing ethnicities.

Table 1.1: Gender Ratio of Upper Guinean Ethnicities in Louisiana (age 15-39), 1719-1820

Ethnicity	Male		Female		Total
Bamana	n = 205	87.2%	n = 30	12.8%	235
Mandingo	n = 353	67.9%	n = 167	32.1%	520
Nar/Moor	n = 49	70.0%	n = 21	30.0%	70
Poulard/Fulbe	n = 80	69.6%	n = 35	30.4%	115
Wolof/Senegal	n = 225	61.5%	n = 141	38.5%	366
TOTAL	n = 912	69.8%	n = 394	30.2%	1,306

Source: Gwendolyn Midlo Hall, *Louisiana Slave Database, 1719-1820*

A stronger case can be made about preferences for women who knew how to produce rice by focusing on mean prices by gender among rice cultivating ethnicities. In Louisiana during the 1770s, the mean price for women from two rice producing ethnicities inventoried on estates, Mandingo, and Wolof, was higher than that for men. Among the Bamana (Bambara), another rice producing ethnicity, the mean price was slightly lower for women than for men during the 1770s and higher for women than for men between 1810 and 1820. The mean price for Wolof women was higher than the price for men throughout the Spanish period (1770-1803). The rice producing skills of these women might at least partially account for this atypical price pattern. Eltis, Morgan, and Richardson (2007, 1335-1338) claim that calculations from *Voyages* prove that Africans from upper Guinea could not have introduced rice or systems for its cultivation and processing to the Americas, nor did masters who planted rice prefer them or choose them (Tables 1.1 and 1.2). They argue that few slaves from upper Guinea arrived in rice exporting regions when this crop began to be cultivated. For later periods, they dismiss the significant impact on transatlantic slave trade patterns of the relatively high proportion of enslaved Africans brought from rice producing regions in Africa to rice exporting regions in the Americas, pointing to factors other than the preferences of slave buyers (1335, 1342, 1345). This is not news. In

Slavery and African Ethnicities in the Americas: Restoring the Links, which is cited several times in "Agency and Diaspora" in other contexts, has an entire chapter devoted to various evolving patterns in the entire Atlantic slave trade, including market forces (Hall 2005, 55-79). Preferences among buyers for slaves of different ethnicities are treated as only one factor.

Table 1.2: Mean Price by Gender: Ethnicities Inventoried on Rice Estates in Louisiana, 1770–1820

Decades	Ethnicity	Number of Males	Mean	Standard Deviation	Number Females	Mean	Standard Deviation
1770-1779	Bamana	7	282.66	26.904	3	266.67	61.101
1770-1779	Mandingo	18	297.78	87.753	5	312.00	45.497
1770-1779	Wolof	9	235.56	107.251	5	288.00	56.619
1770-1803	Wolof	96	321.87	236.861	188	331.23	260.229
1810-1820	Bamana	45	420.22	261.008	7	511.43	316.882

Source: Hall, *Louisiana Slave Database, 1719–1820*. Explanations of price data, price conversion formulas, and studies of mean prices by gender and ethnicity by decade for Africans inventoried on Louisiana estates can be found in Hall, Slavery and African Ethnicities in the Americas, Appendix A, 173-179.

It is unclear what the calculations from *Voyages* cited by Eltis, Morgan, and Richardson can prove about whether there was an African impact on rice production and processing in the Americas. How many people did it take to introduce and develop rice in varying environments? Was there only one introduction of rice, after which the masters knew everything, they needed to know about its cultivation despite the varied and changing environments and ecosystems used in its production over time? Did there have to be a majority, or a large minority, of enslaved Africans arriving from upper Guinea at the time rice began to be produced, or a higher percentage of upper Guineans among all slaves arriving in both the Caribbean and the Atlantic coast of colonial North America (Eltis, Morgan, Richardson 2007, 1337, 1338), even though rice was rarely exported from the Caribbean, and colonial North America was a marginal region for the transatlantic slave trade (Table 1.2)? Documents from Louisiana show that the Company of the Indies asked only for several slaves who could teach them how to cultivate rice.[8]

Carney perhaps understates, and Eltis, Morgan, and Richardson do not mention, the possible role of Madagascar in the introduction of rice to America. Immigrants from Ceylon began to populate Madagascar in about 800 A.D., bringing with them Asian sativa rice and techniques for its cultivation and processing. *Voyages* contains records for ten voyages arriving in Barbados from Madagascar between 1664 and 1683, and seventeen voyages arriving in the East Coast colonial United States from Madagascar between 1686 and 1721. There were also slave trade voyages from Madagascar by smugglers, privateers, and pirates of several nationalities that are not recorded in the database. Aside from the voyages from upper Guinea entered into *Voyages*, any one or more of these voyages or one or more of the 749 voyages whose provenance is listed in *Voyages* as "Africa port unspecified" could have brought seed rice and enough Africans who knew how to cultivate and process it and who could have taught their masters these skills. Conclusions about the role that Africans played or did not play in the introduction of rice into the Americas cannot be drawn from *Voyages*, whose calculations are based on African regions, not African ethnicities. Carney's careful, exhaustive, multilingual, multidisciplinary field work and studies of documents in several languages over the wide sweep of time and place in the Atlantic world are much more convincing. In addition, Edda L. Fields-Black's book *Deep Roots* (2008), which uses mainly sociolinguistic evidence along with traditional historical sources, establishes the time depth and variety of rice cultivation involving inheritance, innovation, and borrowing among several ethnicities living along the Rice Coast of upper Guinea and their transfer to the Americas over time.

Eltis, Morgan, and Richardson conflate rice production with the export of rice to Europe. This narrow definition enhances their argument that masters fully controlled the decisions relating to the production, processing, and marketing of rice. Production by maroon (runaway slave) communities is dismissed as unimportant. The domestic market for rice is dismissed as subsistence production, or a "system that generated exports rather than the export itself" (Eltis, Morgan, Richardson 2007, 1343). Food crops were introduced and exchanged throughout the Atlantic world. Slaves worked their own garden plots, and they produced and sold all types of foods, including rice, corn, beans, fruits, vegetables, eggs, poultry, pork, ham, and smoked beef. In South Carolina, Jamaica, and Louisiana, slaves were the major suppliers of food to towns and cities. Europeans and Africans—especially the first generation—and Native Americans preferred to eat the cereals they were accustomed to. In Louisiana, Europeans preferred wheat, Native Americans preferred corn, and Africans preferred rice. But those preferences did not always determine the types of cereals they consumed. Everyone ate whatever they could get during the frequent wars, when imported food was cut off and food was hoarded by speculators, and during hurricanes and floods, when rice survived better than any other crop. Even for the Carolina plantations that produced rice for export to Europe, the authors of "Agency and Diaspora" exaggerate the power and control which masters had over their slaves. Europeans were not all powerful, certainly not in matters of economy and culture. They, too, were strangers in a strange, dangerous, and hostile world. Control was not always firmly in their hands, especially during the early, most crucial stages of the formation of the economy and culture. William Dusinberre (1996), who examined life on the rice plantations of Carolina and Georgia, demonstrates that masters and their families were often absentees from that environment of deadly fevers. Masters could not get white overseers to work in the rice swamps. During the nineteenth century, black slave overseers were the supervisors of the slave laborers. But the most trusted slave overseers were often the leaders of slave conspiracies and revolts (Hall 1992, 21, 24, 123-124, 343-375; Paquette 2000, 31-58).

Eltis, Morgan and Richardson (2007, 1339) minimize the interest of buyers in the skills of new Africans: "Buyers of slaves in the Americas wanted a cheap supply of undifferentiated labor for field work, and transatlantic suppliers sought locations in Africa where they could obtain large numbers of slaves quickly and at reasonable cost." The *Louisiana Slave Database* records an impressive range of expertise among African born slaves. Thousands of the Africans arriving in Louisiana came from regions that were well known for certain skills. Although we can query the *Louisiana Slave Database* about the skills listed for African born slaves, it cannot tell us that they brought such expertise with them, even though we know that specific skills were widely practiced in their African homelands. But it is highly suggestive of skills transferred by enslaved Africans arriving in the Americas.

Timing gives us even stronger evidence for the transfer of African technology and skills. Having complained for years that they could not find anyone who knew how to produce and process indigo, the Louisiana colonial authorities asked French colonial authorities to send someone who possessed such knowledge. Shortly after Africans began arriving from Senegambia, Louisiana started to produce indigo, beginning in 1721 on an experimental basis, and soon as the major export crop. In French Louisiana, the captains of the first two Atlantic slave trade ships that arrived from the African coast in 1719 had both been officially instructed "to try to purchase several blacks who know how to cultivate rice and three or four barrels of rice for seeding which they were to give to the directors of the Company of the Indies upon their arrival in Louisiana." The first ship, *l'Aurore*, stopped at Cap Lahou on August 28, 1718, where these instructions could have been carried out, and then went on to Ouidah to buy slaves. Rice production in Louisiana expanded rapidly thereafter, as almost all transatlantic slave trade ships began coming from Senegambia. During the French administration (1699-1769), rice was shipped from Louisiana to the French Caribbean and to Spanish Pensacola. It was widely cultivated in swampy soils, which did not require irrigation, while indigo, corn, and other crops were cultivated on the same farms and estates on higher lands near the rivers. During the Spanish administration (1770-1803), rice was shipped to the French Caribbean and to Havana as Cuba's sugar monoculture expanded. Louisiana began to satisfy Cuba's needs for foods of all kinds, including rice. Did whites teach clueless Africans all these skills? It seems obvious that the diverse peoples of Louisiana—Africans, Creoles, Cajuns, Canadians, French, Germans, Spanish, Canary Islanders, and Native Americans—taught each other.[9]

Eltis, Morgan, and Richardson seriously overstate what we can know from calculations derived from *Voyages* about the distribution of Africans in the Americas. We have seen that newly arrived Africans were often sold and then transferred to final destinations outside the colony where they first landed. Documents created and housed in the Americas show that at each stage of their redistribution, buyers could, and often did, select Africans from specific coastal regions and/or ethnicities. In Cuba, Manuel Barcia and Matt D. Childs have found clustering of African ethnicities on plantations, among *cabildos de naciones*, and among slave rebels. In St. Domingue/Haiti, Gabriel Debien and David Geggus found clustering of African ethnicities on individual estates. In Spanish Louisiana, upper Guineans were clustered disproportionately in St. Charles Parish, which produced rice, and in St. Landry Parish, where cattle were raised. St. Landry Parish contained a far higher proportion of upper Guineans among African born slaves than any other parish: 67.9 percent (73 percent male) among slaves with identified birthplaces. In West Africa, breeding and herding were not practiced east of upper Guinea because of the tsetse fly. St. Landry Parish remains the traditional place of Afro-Creole cowboys and zydeco music. Transatlantic slave trade voyages alone cannot tell us nearly as much as Eltis, Morgan, and Richardson claim about the gender proportions among African ethnicities or the distribution of Africans at their final destinations in the Americas.

Historical databases are extraordinary new tools, and more scholars should learn to use them and to create them. They should be used widely, but wisely and judiciously, with an understanding of their limitations. But depending on how they are designed and the questions they are programmed to answer, they can be rigid and inflexible, locking in outmoded research and questions and not allowing for new ones. Databases are not a higher form of knowledge that can somehow trump other kinds of research. Scholarship is not a zero sum game. When scholars overstate the questions that a database can answer and criticize others' work through irrelevant calculations, it seriously undermines our difficult but essential task of informing our colleagues about the unique value of historical databases in producing broad, comparative studies. We need to appreciate what others have done and encourage diverse scholars to use a variety of methodologies in doing the important work they do best. Despite the vast complexities of these questions, the long list of senior scholars and the new generation criticized in "Agency and Diaspora" are constantly making new discoveries, the value and impact of which will be enhanced by rapidly advancing technology.

There has been much progress in historical methodology since World War II. We have developed social history: history from the bottom up. Concepts of the positive values of race mixture and creolization have been introduced through the work of José Vasconcelos of Mexico, Gilberto Freyre of Brazil, and Edward (Kamau) Brathwaite of Barbados (Vasconcelos 1997; Freyre 1946; Brathwaite 1971). Our greatest strength is our growing acceptance of diversity. We live in a rapidly shrinking world where ethnic and religious conflicts are stirred up and exploited by ambitious political, military, and religious bureaucracies and economic elites. It is not so much that people are intolerant of "the other" as social systems and their ideologues provoke and exploit these conflicts. History is applied art, science, and literature that can teach mutual appreciation and respect among peoples. The authors of "Agency and Diaspora" have taken a great leap backward in this task. As *Voyages* is revised and improved, its editors need to make it more flexible and avoid drawing invalid conclusions from evidence that is indirect, incomplete, and flawed, or our work will be discredited by overreaching. The calculations from *Voyages* that Eltis, Morgan, and Richardson cite in their article might seem impressive, but these historians do not look at what they do not want to see, and they cannot look at what they do not have. Their conclusions far outrun their evidence.

Endnotes

1 An earlier version was published in the *American Historical Review* 115:1 (2010), 136-150.

2 I owe a deep debt to the National Endowment for the Humanities and the taxpayers of our country, which funded the expansion of my Louisiana Slave Database as part of National Endowment for the Humanities Collaborative Research Contracts numbers RO-22619-1901 and 1993, "Africans in Spanish and Early American Louisiana," with Patrick Manning as co-investigator. I also received major financial support from the Guggenheim Foundation, as well as generous contributions from the French Ministry of Culture, the Program for Cultural Cooperation between Spain's Ministry of Culture and United States Universities, and the Louisiana Endowment for the Humanities. Steven Mintz has given generously of his enthusiasm, time, and support for nearly a decade now, including with this article. Paul E. Lovejoy, Director of the Harriet Tubman Institute for Research on the Global Migrations of African Peoples, York University, Toronto, Canada, and his graduate students and our colleagues in

this network have played a very special role. I am grateful to Maureen Hewitt, Editor in Chief at Louisiana State University Press, for her foresight and enthusiastic work in preparing the CD-ROM version of the database for publication (Databases for the Study of Afro-Louisiana History and Genealogy, 1699–1860: Computerized Information from Original Manuscript Sources, 2000). Other colleagues have given their time and attention to help and encourage me after Katrina and to make this article much better than it was: O. Vernon Burton, Rina Cáceres, Yvonne Captain-Hidalgo, Judith A. Carney, Douglas B. Chambers, Matt D. Childs, Howard Dodson, Joseph C. Dorsey, Christopher Dunn, David Hackett Fischer, Michael A. Gomez, Rebecca L. Hall, Joseph E. Harris, Susan Heywood, Joseph E. Inikori, Aondofe Joseph-Ernest Iyo, Eileen M. Julien, Jane I. Landers, Juan Manuel de la Serna, Joseph C. Miller, Nell Irvin Painter, Ibrahima Seck, Ned Sublette, Ibrahim K. Sundiata, and John K. Thornton.

3 See my review of Heywood and Thornton's book in *Journal of Interdisciplinary History* 39:3 (2009), 463-464.

4 *Voyages* calculates 5,099,816 enslaved Africans landed by Portuguese and Brazilian voyages and 2,733,323 by British voyages (Accessed 2010).

5 Joseph E. Inikori, "The Known, the Unknown, the Knowable and the Unknowable: Evidence and the Evaluation of Evidence in the Measurement of the Trans-Atlantic Slave Trade" (unpublished paper presented at the Conference on the Trans-Atlantic Slave Trade Database, Williamsburg, Virginia, September 1998).

6 Remarks by Daniel J. Cohen in "Interchange: The Promise of Digital History," *Journal of American History* 95:2 (2008), 463.

7 The Louisiana Slave Database was initially located at www.ibiblio.org/laslave and now has been moved to a new URL, www.louisianaslavedatabase.org. The search engine can be used for many fields, and the entire database can be downloaded free of charge in several formats. For a discussion of its origin and possibilities for other databases to be created from various types of original manuscript documents housed throughout the Americas, see www.afropop.org/multi/interview/ID/76/Gwendolyn-MidloHall-2005.

8 "Instructions pour le sieur Herpin, commandant du vaisseau l'Aurore, destiné pour la traite des nègres à la coste de Guynée," 4 July 1718, Section Marine, Archives Nationales, Paris, series B42B, folios 201-204.

9 The practitioners of such skills include cowboys, breeders of cattle and horses, horse trainers and groomers, leatherworkers, tanners, saddlers, shoemakers, butchers, cooks, bakers, confectioners, pastry chefs, chocolate makers, rum makers, cigar makers/tobacco stemmers, goldsmiths, silversmiths, potters, indigo makers, tailors, hat makers, charcoal makers, basket makers, oven makers, barbers, wigmakers, spinners, coach/cart drivers, plantation managers, overseers, foremen, masons, painters, plasterers, chimney builders, stone engravers, millers, blacksmiths, tool makers, tool sharpeners, metalworkers, makers of fireworks, wheelwrights, cart makers, woodsmen, hunters, fishermen, lumbermen, carriers and squarers of timber, sawmill workers, carpenters, cabinetmakers, locksmiths, brick makers, sailors, navigators, sounders, shipbuilders, sail makers, oar makers, caulkers, coopers, innkeepers, street vendors, butlers, domestics, personal servants, seamstresses, laundresses, hospital workers, nurses, midwives, doctors, dentists, surgeons, musicians, and linguists/interpreters of languages. Calculated from Skill fields in the *Louisiana Slave Database*.

2

Setting a Precedent for Historical Scholarship in the Digital Age:

The *Louisiana Slave Database*

Paul Lachance

This chapter discusses the methodology of Gwendolyn Midlo Hall's *Louisiana Slave Database* (www.louisianaslavedatabase.org) and demonstrates what can be learned from a deep, complex, original and innovative project in digital humanities.[1] The project traces its origins to 1984 when digital technology was in its infancy. The chapter focuses on the form in which the database became available to scholars and to the public and points out how it has been precedent-setting from the start.

The term "digital age" refers to a step in human evolution comparable to the discovery of fire, the agricultural revolution, and the industrial revolution, if the global economy on which it precariously rests and of which it is an integral part can be sustained. The key invention launching the digital age was the microchip, which fundamentally transformed the capacity to communicate and manipulate information, notably by the personal computer and mobile devices linked to a global network aptly named the internet. Among the many ways the digital revolution is altering lives of human beings, it is having a profound impact on history, both in the sense of the nature and content of the collective memory of mankind and in the way in which specialists who study the past go about their work and communicate the information they produce to others.

Like many of us, Hall's lifetime coincides with the digital revolution. When she began her research, historians still had to visit archives to view physical records from the past. Today they do not even have to get out of bed, let alone travel to a library or archive, to examine digital images of many of these records or databases compiled from them. As a student of history, she learned how to take notes on unwieldy pieces of paper or cards and adopt a system of organizing this material to evaluate evidence, construct arguments, and reassemble sets of past events into narratives. She did benefit from the typewriter, an invention of the 1860s whose widespread adoption and standardization made a substantial difference in the production of legible texts, although now remembered more for its disadvantages than its advantages over pen and quill, its inefficient use of time, the hours spent retyping an entire page to correct a turn of phrase, the additional hours spent making corrections with an eraser or whitener. And once a manuscript was typed, it had to be type set for publication as a book or an article in a journal, which had to be either purchased as a physical object or read in a library for its contents to reach other individuals. All this has been changed by the word-processor, the PDF file, and the internet, which have not only transformed the process by which ideas are transformed into words and transmitted to others, but also increased accessibility to information and techniques for analysis.

It has not been easy for historians who grew up in the pre-digital age to adapt to the new technology. Many of us have done so reluctantly and partially, and some have stubbornly resisted, continuing to type their manuscripts like farmers who continued to plow their fields with horses even after the tractor had been invented. A few historians, however, have embraced the new technology wholeheartedly and by doing so have set examples for the next generation to imitate and improve upon. Among the pioneers of the digital age, Hall has a pre-eminent place. The transition began with her decision in 1984 to record information about slaves in records from Pointe Coupee Parish in a database. She credits her colleague at Rutgers University, Robert A. Rosenberg, then director of the Thomas A. Edison Papers Project, with introducing her to Power Base, one of the first database programs, as a more effective way of storing information from many records than note cards. And she has not looked back, moving on from Power Base to DBASE 5 and eventually to SPSS, the latter providing programs to analyze the data she collected as well as storage.

The decision to create a database by using statistical software to detect and analyze patterns in the data was precedent setting in the 1980s, while her conception of a much larger project demonstrated the potential of digital technology to expand the evidence base for historical generalizations significantly and, equally importantly, to give historians the means to interpret data in a systematic and scientific way. The *Louisiana Slave Database* received a National Endowment for the Humanities contract in 1991 that enabled her to extend a project on one parish in Louisiana to include the entire colony and then the territory and state of Louisiana through 1820. Completed in five years, this database was published as a CD-ROM by Louisiana State University Press in 2000.

Among the characteristics of the slave database, the first that strikes the eye is its scope. The *Louisiana Slave Database* contains over 104,666 records of individuals who were enslaved, separated into 162 fields, covering a century from 1719 to 1820. It was the largest slavery database ever compiled at the time of its completion, and it remains one of the largest to the present. Geographically, it covers the area of the Gulf Coast and the lower Mississippi Valley colonized by Spain, then France and finally the United States. The proportion of records can be broken down as follows: for the Parish of Orleans (58 percent), rural parishes to the west of the Mississippi River (35 percent), and Mobile, Natchez, and rural areas to the east of the Mississippi (8 percent), which reflects the geographical distribution of the slave population of the region in the eighteenth century, when Orleans parish included not only the town of New Orleans but also the adjacent plantation district known as Chapitoulas, where more than half the slave population in French and Spanish Louisiana was located. With only 15 records for the Illinois country, Upper Louisiana is for the most part outside its purview.

There is a plethora of studies with a quantitative dimension of slavery for other regions of North America that have been produced over the last half-century, but there still is no database for the enslaved population that covers the colonial period comparable to Hall's for any of the other regions of the future United States, neither for the North, the Chesapeake (upper South), nor the Carolinas (the lower South). There are now other slavery databases comparable to hers, such as *Slave Voyages: The Trans-Atlantic Slave Trade Database* (www.slavevoyages.org). First appearing at approximately the same time as Hall's database, *Slave Voyages* consists of records for over 35,000 voyages of all nations participating in the Atlantic slave trade from 1514 to 1866. Its development took much longer than Hall's project because it combined databases of national slave trades compiled over several preceding decades. The African Names Database (www.slavevoyages.org/resources/names-database) has been developed as an extension of *Slave Voyages* to include the names and identifying characteristics of over 90,000 Africans taken off slave ships in Havana, Cuba and Freetown, Sierra Leone between 1808 and 1862.

Several other large slavery databases have been created since 1990, including the Integrated Public Use Microdata Series (IPUMS) which is the world's largest individual-level population database. IPUMS (www.usa.ipums.org/usa/) consists of microdata samples from United States and international census records, as well as data from U.S. and international surveys, including samples of the slave schedules from the 1850 and 1860 censuses. The Digital Library of American Slavery (DLAS) at the University of North Carolina Greensboro (www.library.uncg.edu/slavery) has extracted information from legal and county court petitions, insurance registries, slave deeds from North Carolina, and a variety of other legal sources throughout the American South from 1775 to 1867 on almost 87,000 enslaved individuals, 8,000 free people of color, and 62,000 whites, both slave owners and non-slave owners.

Much smaller databases have also proven to be valuable in testing hypotheses about slavery. It is important to recognize their importance since their construction remains within the capabilities of individual scholars and because they provide the building blocks for larger composite databases. For example, Hall's CD-ROM in 2000 contains Virginia Gould's databases of household censuses of New Orleans, Mobile, and Pensacola in the late Spanish and early American periods. Independently and coincidentally, Kimberly Hanger (1997) created a separate database of manumissions in Orleans parish from 1777 to 1803, while Thomas Ingersoll (1999) developed a database for the years 1769 to 1810 for New Orleans. Hall's database including manumissions of slaves is more comprehensive, however, covering the French period and the second decade of the nineteenth century as well as rural parishes beyond Orleans Parish. On the one hand, independent coding of three databases makes it possible to judge the consistency and completeness of the contents of each of them. On the other hand, they are an example of duplication, indeed triplication, of efforts – an inefficient use of scarce resources, i.e., the considerable human capital involved in the coding of data. Inefficiency seems to be inevitable in the first stage of technological development. Consolidation of existing databases should make duplication of efforts less likely. It will permit scholars to review sources that have been databased to correct problems in their coding rather than code them anew as if they had never been coded in the first place.

However valuable small databases with only 5,000 cases, or even several hundred, are, there are certain large questions that can only be answered with large databases. For its part, the century of Louisiana history covered by Hall's database embraces 50 years of French domination, 33 years of Spanish control, and 17 years of American incorporation, making the region a laboratory for testing various theses such as that of Frank Tannenbaum (1946) and other generalizations about differences in slave regimes in the Americas. As argued at a digital humanities conference in 2013,

> when records about many individuals are combined, patterns can be discerned. Data about ethnicities tell us from where within Africa many slaves hailed; data about slave residence in the Americas tell us where members of particular groups ended up and where and how they were housed; data about marriages tell us with whom Africans and their descendants chose to partner; data about skills tell us what slaves did and their contributions to agriculture, trade and the economy beyond brute labor.[2]

Besides breadth of coverage of space and time, a large database supplies the number of cases needed for calculation of significant statistics for subgroups of a population. Hall's database contains 217 different ethnic designations for 8,994 slaves, including 18 ethnicities with 68 or more persons, enough to calculate meaningful statistics of gender distribution, child-woman ratios, and average age. Statistics for groups with less than 50 cases risk being unrepresentative. With a database of only 10,000 slaves, the number of ethnic groups large enough to warrant statistical calculation would have been reduced from eighteen to five. Thus, the larger a database, the ability to generalize about subgroups in a population increases. Without the large number of enslaved in the database, it would have been much more difficult to support the argument that nationalities attributed to the enslaved in legal documents were ones that enslaved individuals themselves affirmed or to demonstrate that the origins of enslaved Africans came from certain places in Africa despite their transshipment from the Caribbean to Spanish Louisiana, two of the findings reported in Hall's monograph on *Slavery and African Ethnicities in the Americas* (2005).

The scope of the database implies its second precedent-setting characteristic. It is too large to have been compiled by a single individual. It could only have been put together by a team of scholars. In other words, it had to be collaborative. In this respect, too, the *Louisiana Slave Database* set a precedent by resolving the problems encountered in organizing and directing a collaborative project. To fully exploit the potential of digital technology for organizing large amounts of data, co-ordination of the work of several individuals was needed. In the introduction to the version of the database on the CD-ROM, Hall acknowledges the assistance which she received from four archivists and graduate students who entered data directly from original manuscripts into DBASE V on their laptops. She worked alongside each until confident of his or her competence in reading eighteenth century handwriting and in understanding French and Spanish terms. The coding involved identification and translation of words for skills and illnesses some of which are no longer used in any language. In the process of translation, an attempt was made to include the original words and spellings in the original languages in all fields. Hall maintained the central databases into which new data were downloaded as they were collected. In addition to entering the data, members of the team helped to check the data for accuracy of transcription and for duplication.

Another level of collaboration in development of the database involved specialists in African and world history who helped identify 96 of the 217 African "nations" (ethnicities) found in the documents. Patrick Manning played a major role in identifying ethnicities and their African regions of origin at the early stages of the project. Since 1996, 11 other scholars have contributed their expertise over H-Africa net and through email. Hall acknowledges the assistance received from Paul Lovejoy and Ibrahima Seck. Current developments will expand considerably the collaborative dimension of the database, involving not only many other historians, archivists, and researchers, but also the expertise of specialists in web design and programming from the humanities computing company Walk With Web Inc. (www.walkwithweb.org).

> Walk With Web is a corporation led by a group of academicians working in the field of African Digital Humanities. The WWW mission is to develop, support and preserve digital humanities research by creating novel digital sustainability solutions. Walk With Web has a digital content management service called Regenerated Identities (RegID), which supports the development, deployment, and long-term maintenance of digital research in North America, Europe, Caribbean, Latin America, and Africa. RegID provides a custom graphical user interface that fulfills specific needs of various research projects, thus enabling development of robust databases that lead to the creation and semi-automated self-publication of research outcomes on the world wide web.

Certain fundamental databasing techniques are used in the construction of the *Louisiana Slave Database* which historians have had to teach themselves, to a large extent by trial and error. Today there is enough accumulated experience for anyone coding a source for the first time to use codebooks to serve as models. Nonetheless, any historian interested in organizing results of his or her research into a database has much to learn by studying carefully how Hall has constructed hers. She succeeded brilliantly in coding information in primary sources in a way that maximizes utility for historical analysis yet preserves key information in its original form in the documents to allow other historians who desire to re-conceptualize the information to pursue a different line of inquiry should they wish to do so.

One feature of the *Louisiana Slave Database*, and a third way in which Hall has set a precedent for digital scholarship, are fields identifying sources.

It may seem elementary to include information on sources, but it is not always done within the database itself. When all information is drawn from one source, it may seem sufficient to identify it in a separate description of the database. Nevertheless, even for a single source, it is useful to have a field for page or item number showing exactly where in a document information for each record is found. When the database is constructed from a variety of different sources, it is imperative to provide source fields.

Hall identifies sources in two ways in her database. For lists of enslaved individuals in inventories of estates, she assigns a complex identifier consisting of information on the prices for individuals (estimates or actual price at the time of sale), the period in which the inventory was taken (French, Spanish, or early American), the location of the estate, the total number of individuals in the inventory, and the year of the inventory -- an ingenious way to combine different types of information that can then be used to define subgroups of estate inventories. Otherwise, the source for any record in the database is precisely identified through a combination of variables: the depository where the document is housed, the type of document, the name of the notary when the document is a notarial record, the page or number of the item when it is specified in a collection of documents, the place where the document was drafted, and its date.

Such information makes it possible to use the database as an index to the different types of documents in Louisiana naming and describing individuals. The most common are legal records of the transmission of wealth – estate inventories, wills, marriage contracts, mortgages, acts of sale of property – found in court houses and archives throughout Louisiana, but a variety of other sources were mined as well, trial records concerning enslaved, some with testimony from enslaved individuals themselves, advertisements for those who ran away, censuses enumerating individuals by name, other kinds of enslaved lists, and information from the slave trade. For a particular repository, the acts of a notary or a parish courthouse, the database enables a researcher to find the documents relating to slaves quickly. For example, 1,552 enslaved individuals are found in censuses or on lists made for a particular purpose. Observing the year of entry and location of people of this document type reveals that 500 were named in a census of St. Landry Parish in 1777 and 115 in lists of prison inmates, executed, or involved one way or another in the 1811 German Coast slave revolt. Since it is impossible for even a database as comprehensive as Hall's to capture all the information in a document, it does not replace the need for a serious researcher to read the documents him or herself. The coding of sources makes it a lot easier to find records relevant to a particular topic of slavery. Each record in Hall's database corresponds to an individual named in a particular document. Although it has not yet been determined how often it happens, it is possible for the same person to be mentioned in several documents.

There are 162 fields or variables for each record. Sixteen of the fields are used to identify the source or describe other technical aspects of the coding of information. The other records describe information in a document as it pertains to the person who is the subject of the record. These include the way he or she is identified: name, gender, age, birthplace or origin, place of residence, phenotype or skin color, skills or occupation, health and physical condition or defects, family group, estimated or actual sale price, the name of his or her seller, buyer, or owner, whether the individual is mentioned in a particular context such as being a runaway or involvement in an act of resistance or revolt. Eight variables describe a slave voyage when the person is mentioned in a document relating to the slave trade. For certain characteristics, such as skills, multiple variables are created with more than one trait, like Louise, a 27-year-old woman enslaved in New Orleans whose act of sale in 1807 described her as a laundress, cook, confectioner, seamstress, and street vendor.

The number of fields expanded as Hall compiled the database. Use of DBASE allowed for the creation of additional fields as the need for them became apparent in coding the data. As Hall writes in her introduction:

> Database design cannot be divorced from the process of research. Early database design does not produce a finished product. It evolves as the historian becomes more familiar with the documents, with the data, and with new questions as they arise. Answers, tentative answers, and partial answers lead to new questions. Additional fields are entered and recoded during and after the data entry process has been completed. Maintaining flexibility to make changes in database design and to make corrections in data entry is essential.

Flexibility is the fourth way Hall has set a precedent for historians in the digital stage, particularly because it acts as a safeguard against the temptation to impose preconceived categories of classification on data. Her descriptive variables are of two basic types: characteristics as reported in a document and characteristics derived from those recorded in a document. For example, notaries usually began by noting the date of a document they were asked to transcribe. The field for date records this date directly, from which other fields are derived for decade and epoch (French, Spanish, or American period). For the most part, Hall followed the excellent practice of entering data as found in the documents in string variables, with coders instructed to enter names, nations (ethnicities), location, skills, physical defects, and other characteristics with the same terms and spelling used in the document. Numeric codes were then created for categories into which these characteristics fit, for example, whether a name is African, or the sector of skills: agriculture, domestic work, transportation, or a craft. Hall's categories are only one way of describing naming patterns, occupational structure, and other social characteristics.

Her method of coding allows another researcher to use her categories or substitute another scheme by recoding the string variables with terms used in the document. This is a fifth way in which her database sets a precedent – inclusion of string variables that replicate exactly terminology found in the document as well as derivative variables collapsing traits with multiple values into a more manageable number of categories.

A sixth feature of her dataset which merits emulation is the special variable for "comments." No matter how comprehensive a database, it necessarily simplifies a more complex reality. As Hall explains in the introduction to the version of the *Louisiana Slave Database* on CD-ROM,

> In databases created from original manuscript documents, fields are defined which can answer the questions their creators wish to pose. Definition of fields is a long process requiring a thorough knowledge of the documents used. As the researcher becomes more familiar with the documents, fields are added as regular significant information appears in the documents. There is a COMMENTS field in these Louisiana databases where important information for which there were no defined fields were placed and from which new fields were created.

Where the comments have led to additions of new fields, they are incorporated in these variables, but often the comments supply important context for interpreting information. For a particular set of documents, such as those that pertain to runaways, it can be useful to browse the comments to obtain a sense of circumstances surrounding the escape or the decision of his or her owner to seek capture and return. Although comments enrich the information contained in a database, they may be most valuable in calling the researcher's attention to documents that need to be reread in their entirety.

A seventh way in which Hall has set a precedent for the digital age, and the last one discussed, is in rendering her database accessible to other researchers. In November 2001, *ibiblio* mounted a web page with a user-friendly search engine, the free library and digital archive of the Center for the Public Domain at the University of North Carolina (www.ibiblio.org/laslave). The website has an interface that allows users to search for records pertaining to a particular individual, if enough is known about the person to indicate parameters of the search: name, master's name, gender, epoch, racial designation, location, and/or origin. The website also provides digital copies of examples of original documents from which the database was created, and some SPSS tables and graphs generated by Hall. Although all this information is free, it is limited in several respects. *Ibiblio* search results give only seven pieces of information for any individual or subset of individuals identified by a search, and the website does not allow the user to calculate statistics showing patterns or trends in the data, as will be the case for the new versions under construction for the entire period of slavery. For these reasons, Hall's database has been reformulated in its entirety using the Regenerated Identities back end developed at Walk With Web Inc.

Nevertheless, *ibiblio* served one purpose extremely well. It enabled users to download free of charge the complete *Louisiana Slave Database* in a variety of formats (DBASE, ACCESS, and SPSS), with supporting documents, codebooks, and SPSS syntax files. This accessibility is again precedent setting. Most databases remain in the hands of the scholars who have created them, even though they need to be stored in an archive capable of maintaining them indefinitely into the future. Moreover, data need to be stored in formats that continue to be readable by ever evolving database and statistical software, ideally in several different formats adapted to different uses to which they may be put by scholars, genealogists, and the public. And it should be possible to download both the database and the files needed to read them, particularly codebooks, over the internet onto personal computers. All these conditions for maximum accessibility were met at a very early date by Hall through the *ibiblio* website. In these respects, it fits entirely the goal of "Open Access," which continues with the WWW version.

How important open access will be depends on the extent to which historians make use of the digital tools freely available over the internet. Besides Hall's own on-going analysis of her databases, historians and scholars from other disciplines have already made use of her database, sometimes to test hypotheses drawn from her interpretation of the role of African ethnicity in the development of slave culture and moments of resistance in Louisiana and throughout the Americas and at other times hypotheses drawn from disciplines like economics and linguistics.

While the contribution of Hall's work to Atlantic history is clear, her database is no less important in establishing a foundation for further databasing of slavery in Louisiana. Unlike historians who are content to work with samples, any historian who sets out to database all known cases of a population or a group within a population confronts sooner or later the realization that it is not complete, indeed can never be said to be complete. One reason for this is the attrition of documentation over time. Documents are lost or destroyed. Lost documents may still be recovered, which then need to be added to the database. A more important reason for completeness being an unrealizable goal, though, is the enormous amount of data generated by human activity.

Even if each of the 104,000 documented enslaved people in the *Louisiana Slave Database* can be considered to represent a unique individual, the total would be a fraction of the true number who lived part or all their lives in Louisiana in the century covered by the database. The different types of documents that have been perused for names of those who were enslaved are far less than the total number who must have been there. A database does not need to be complete to serve as evidence of general trends and patterns of the enslaved population; and the size of the *Louisiana Slave Database* is such that it allows for description of the subgroups within the population, such as the size and characteristics of eighteen subgroups defined by place of origin in Africa. However, it also means that the documentation can be improved by adding new records as they are found, or new information about individuals who are already in the database. In a database of this size, there are inevitably some errors in coding which, when identified, it will be useful to correct.

To recapitulate, the *Louisiana Slave Database* has set at least seven precedents for historians undertaking digital scholarship:

(1) scope – the larger, the better
(2) collaboration
(3) identification of sources
(4) flexibility in development of the coding scheme
(5) use of string variables to capture the terms and phrasing of document
(6) a comment field
(7) accessibility

Hall has demonstrated through her database that these practices are both desirable and possible.

Future collaboration involves a tight network of museums and the broad communities they serve. This relationship goes back to 1993. In 1993, Hall and Kathe Hambrick, then one of the first African-American women working at IBM in California, sat on a Mississippi River levy discussing whether Kathe should quit her job at IBM and return home to Ascension Parish to create The River Road African-American Museum. Hall encouraged her to choose the museum and that is what she did. Her fine museum then began to work closely with the community. Hambrick became a leading figure in the African-American Museum movement throughout the United States. She then began to work at the West Baton Rouge Museum with Angelique Bergeron and together will extend the *Louisiana Slave Database* to Iberville, West and East Baton Rouge and Pointe Coupee parishes.

In that same year, 1993, Eileen Julien invited Hall to give the keynote address at the opening ceremony of the West African Research Center in Dakar, Senegal. At a talk she gave at l'École normale supérieure in Dakar, Ibrahima Seck, then a high school teacher in Dakar was in the audience. At his request, she gave him a copy of her talk. During the next few years, he completed his Ph.D. in history at Cheikh Anta Diop University in Dakar and is now a widely recognized, international historian and the Research Director of the Whitney Plantation Slave Museum in St John the Baptist Parish. His museum is committed to funding the completion of the *Louisiana Slave Database* in the three German parishes, thereby completing this database for most of the parishes along the lower Mississippi valley. The focus is the Louisiana parishes along the Mississippi upriver from New Orleans. The rest of Louisiana will be another project. Data entry will be carried out by a combination of paid and unpaid volunteers with some financial support but above all community involvement through the museums. The learning curve will be substantial. It is therefore of the utmost importance to have a user-friendly data entry form as well as a central database which conforms with the enslaved project, the task of development being undertaken by Walk With Web Inc.

Endnotes

1 This chapter is largely the text of a paper presented to a panel in honor of Gwyndolyn Midlo Hall at the American Historical Association meeting in New Orleans in 2013.

2 "Slave Biographies: Atlantic Database Network," University of Nebraska-Lincoln, 16-19 July 2013.

3

Legacy Websites: The Case of *Slavery Images*:

A Visual Record of the African Slave Trade and Slave Life in the Early African Diaspora

Henry B. Lovejoy, and Jerome S. Handler[1]

In the field of African diaspora studies, online educational resources emerged shortly after the public opening of the World Wide Web in the 1990s. Reflecting a rapid proliferation of digital humanities projects in the new millennium, the National Endowment for the Humanities (NEH) opened its Office of Digital Humanities in 2008. The founding director, Brett Bobley, explained that supporting digital projects was "high risk, high reward," wherein "the risk was that an experimental project might not succeed, but the reward was that if it did succeed it could have a positive impact on the field" (Hindley 2018). Having recently surpassed the ten-year anniversary of the establishment of the NEH's digital office, it has now become mandatory that all digital humanities projects demand data management and sustainability plans to ensure long-term preservation and address the need for ongoing financial support to host websites as technologies rapidly and continuously evolve. A more pressing issue, however, is that some of the oldest digital humanities projects are at a major crossroad in terms of their long-term survival. The pioneers who created and developed some of the earliest digital resources have or are about to retire from their academic positions, and they have had to consider succession plans due to the human life cycle, or natural death.

As morbid as this reality is, younger scholars are having to fill directorial roles to conserve decades worth of collaborative research built into versions of software developed for rapidly advancing digital realities. At the turn of the twenty-first century, African diaspora historians, such as Gwendolyn Midlo Hall and David Eltis, published CD-ROMs built around impressive primary source datasets which quickly became obsolete due to new digital publication mediums via the internet (Eltis 1999; Hall 2000; Hall 2001; Eltis 2008). Scholars experimented with new computational technologies and different digital publication platforms to showcase academic output and to develop new tools which specifically address humanities-based problems. While the new innovations involving interdisciplinary collaborations have often been positive and impactful on the field, scholars are continuously wrestling with standardizing digital humanities best practices, which are quickly evolving as fast as the internet-based technologies around them.

This chapter explores the case of *Slavery Images: A Visual Record of the African Slave Trade and Slave Life in the Early African Diaspora* (www.slaveryimages.org). This website, which Jerome Handler and Michael Tuite created and developed starting in the late-1990s, came under the direction of Henry Lovejoy in January 2018. Long-standing digital humanities projects, which often involve large, interdisciplinary collaborations, should require digital project histories that explain the collaborative creation and development of the digital resource, data updates, transitions of directorships, and migration of digital resources.

The Making of *Slavery Images*

When Handler began accumulating images of slave life in the Americas and the Atlantic slave trade, the prospect of building a website was the furthest thing in his mind. In fact, the concept of "website" was not even in his consciousness. In retrospect, however, the collection of multimedia and metadata development for *Slavery Images* began at Southern Illinois University, Carbondale in the late-1980s. At the time, Handler was a professor of anthropology and had introduced an undergraduate anthropology course which focused on the Atlantic slave trade and the everyday life of enslaved Africans and their descendants in the Americas. Such a course was not then (nor now) a conventional topic in anthropology. Handler attempted to illustrate every lecture with slides and overheads – a goal that was only partially achieved. His sole intention was to give students visual perspectives on the topics discussed in class. In hindsight, Handler was naïve in approaching visual images of slavery in published works. Little thought was given to historical accuracy or bibliographic issues. He selected images from a variety of well-known published secondary sources on New World slavery and the Atlantic slave trade (e.g., Davidson 1961; Mannix and Cowley 1962; Aguet 1971; Blassingame 1981). An archive of 100 to 150 photographic slides were accumulated with the help of Southern Illinois University's Learning Resources Services. These early efforts formed the core of the imagery on the current website, although Handler developed metadata over subsequent years.

After retiring from Southern Illinois in the fall of 1995, Handler moved to Charlottesville, Virginia, where he took up a fellowship at the Virginia Foundation for the Humanities, now known as Virginia Humanities. During this time, he had an idea for an NEH Summer Institute for College Teachers, which was to focus on the slave trade, particularly the middle passage and life aboard slave ships. A year later, he collaborated with a prominent Africanist historian at the University of Virginia, Joseph Miller (d. 2019), who suggested a somewhat different, albeit related, focus for the Institute. For four weeks during the summer of 1998, this co-directed program, called "ROOTS: the African Background of American Culture Through the Trans-Atlantic Slave Trade," took place under the auspices of the Virginia Foundation for the Humanities. During the Institute, Handler gave a lecture using some of the slides he had collected at Southern Illinois. His talk focused on the lives of enslaved individuals for whom images and biographical information were available from primary or secondary sources (later amplified and modified; see Handler 2002).

Someone, perhaps Miller after he heard Handler's talk, suggested that Handler's slides should be digitized. At the time, Handler did not fully understand what "digitize" meant, but was directed to Michael Tuite, director of the Multimedia Resource Center, later renamed the Digital Media Center after it became part of the University of Virginia library. Tuite converted the slides into JPGs and TIFs, and suggested developing a database and later, building a website to bring the images to the attention of a much wider audience. Thus, the website, or idea of the website, was born in late-1998 or early-1999. In September 2000, the website launched with about 150 to 200 images and corresponding metadata arranged into ten topical categories. By November 2001, the site expanded to host close to 300 images; by spring 2002, 500 images; by August 2006, 1,200 images; by November 2010, 1,275, and in March or April 2011, it reached 1,281 images, the total number of images on the site when it was taken over by Henry Lovejoy in early 2018.

The images were arranged into eighteen topical categories, which, it should be stressed, were not mutually exclusive because many images fit into more than one category.

Handler and Tuite decided upon the domain name, www.slaveryimages.org, and titled the website, *The Atlantic Slave Trade and Slave Life in the Americas: A Visual Record.* From the beginning, there was a clear division of labor. Handler was responsible for the "scholarly" portion of the website. He located the images through research in scores of libraries and archival repositories, selected the images to be placed on the site, and obtained permissions, when necessary, for their publication online. In addition, he arranged for their scanning or photographing at the repository, created textual metadata accompanying each image, and developed the topical categories in which the images were organized. Tuite was entirely responsible for the technical aspects of the website. He designed it, built it, maintained it, and uploaded images. He first developed the database with Filemaker, but a few years later, he switched to MySQL. After Tuite left the project in 2006, the website was supported by the University of Virginia's Digital Media Lab, and then by the Virginia Foundation for the Humanities between 2007 and 2018.[2] When Lovejoy became director, *Slavery Images* functioned on PHP 5.6, which since December 2018 has gone unsupported for security fixes.

Handler's background, as a cultural anthropologist specializing in Caribbean and West African societies and cultures, informed his subjective and often arbitrary criteria for the project's scope, which shifted over time. The four key criteria, which remained constant over Handler's direction of the website, included: 1) The site would be selective and not strive to include every single image of enslaved Africans or even of pre-colonial continental Africans; 2) In all cases, efforts, not always realizable, were made to achieve some geographic and temporal balance to give a diaspora perspective on the lives of enslaved Africans and their New World descendants. In other words, Handler wanted to avoid overloading the site with images of enslaved people in the antebellum U.S. South, a corrective to conceptions of slavery held by most North Americans. 3) Ideal images were those based on eyewitness drawings, even if embellished by engravers/publishers before publication, emphasizing cultural features, social life, and material culture. Such images were especially desirable if they were accompanied by a textual description. 4) Images that were patently racist and grossly portray Africans or their descendants in negative stereotypes were not considered. Also, with a few exceptions, images that were political satires or cartoons produced during emancipation and abolition controversies were ignored. Such images were considered outside the scope of a website that focused on portraying, as realistically as possible, the everyday life of enslaved peoples and their experiences.

Accurate bibliographic information was of fundamental importance throughout the development of the metadata. It was felt essential that users should be able to trace individual images and have a starting point to judge their historical and pedagogical value for their own purposes. Every effort was therefore made to identify the original sources of the images and subsequent reproductions in published secondary works. It was discovered early on that commercial image repositories, which resell prints of historic images, often incorrectly cite the original sources of images, even if they bother to provide one at all. Moreover, these reproductions online, as well as in published works, often contain incorrect or misleading metadata. Authors/publishers who use these images compound the errors when they uncritically and unwittingly depend on such sources (Handler and Steiner 2006).

The most difficult images to acquire were portrayals of social scenes relating to the enslaved in the New World, for example, funerals, marriages, religious rituals, recreational activities, family, and community life. Images easier to obtain showed economic activities, such as plantation labor in sugar or cotton, local markets, and other aspects of slave societies, including physical punishments, fugitive slaves, and revolts. Finally, images were often included which were evocative of a particular cultural practice or event, even though their authenticity was problematic, i.e., the image was not based on direct observation or was a fabrication loosely based on some historical event.[3]

Over time, Handler's metadata increasingly located the images in historical context and included direct quotations from the caption and other textual materials that accompany the printed image, when available, and biographical information about the author and/or artist. For example, it can be useful to know if either the author or artist were first-hand observers, or whether they supported or opposed slavery and/or abolition. As with many digital projects, metadata revisions have been continuous and constant, while updates have occurred in real time, often without any public announcement.

From its very inception, *Slavery Images* has been envisioned as a tool and a resource that can be used by teachers, researchers, students, and the public – in brief, anyone interested in the experiences of Africans who were transported to the Americas and the lives of their descendants in the slave societies of the New World. By 2018, when Handler transferred *Slavery Images* to Lovejoy, Google Analytics had demonstrated how successful this website had become. Since 2007 (when the analytics code was first added), the site had attracted over 1.5 million new users on average at about 15,000 per month; and single page views totaled above 12 million hits. The analytics also show that this website is a popular educational resource with more users active during academic fall and winter semesters. The main visitor age categories are 18-24 (27 percent) and 25-34 (33 percent), suggesting it was primarily used among university students and likely among K-12 students too.[4] Frequent users also include publishers seeking images to reproduce in books, college and university level teachers giving PowerPoint lectures in their classes, scholars giving PowerPoint presentations at professional meetings, etc.[5] Two-thirds of users originate in the United States, followed by thousands of users in the United Kingdom, Australia, Canada, France, Brazil and Germany. Persons in many other countries had also accessed the website.

Current Status of *Slavery Images*

After PHP 5.6 ended in late 2018, *Slavery Images* risked going offline and required redevelopment for longer term preservation. For financial and personnel reasons, Virginia Humanities no longer wished to host the website. Tuite had moved to California several years earlier, leaving Handler without a collaborator who had the technical expertise to maintain the website as well as redevelop it. Handler (who maintains his relationship with Virginia Humanities as a senior scholar) sought out a new director to lead this initiative and through mutual acquaintances he met Lovejoy, who had the scholarly interest and digital expertise to assume the directorship of the website. Lovejoy is an Assistant Professor of African diaspora and digital history at the University of Colorado Boulder (CU Boulder). With support from CU Boulder, Lovejoy collaborated with Brumfield Labs (www.brumfieldlabs.com), which specializes in developing software for historic documents and image repositories. By January 2019, Slavery Images had been updated to operate with Omeka-S (www.omeka.org/s), a web publishing platform capable of linking digital cultural heritage collections with other online resources. For example, Omeka-S can integrate coding from the International Image Interoperability Framework, commonly known as IIIF (www.iiif.io); and also with image viewers, such as Mirador (www.projectmirador.org). IIIF is a framework that has standardized the protocols on how an image should be saved/organized; thus, the Handler-Tuite image collection can be accessed uniformly from around the world.[6] Applying open-source web applications, frameworks and code to *Slavery Images* is helping to preserve this legacy website through wider distribution networks.

Maintaining and updating a digital project requires five-to-ten-year sustainability plans. *Slavery Images* currently resides on a privately-owned server, but it will migrate to CU Boulder soon. In order for the website to reside on a CU Boulder server, all metadata and imagery must adhere to strict accessibility regulations for the visually and hearing impaired.[7] While implementing these standards are in the long term plans, the current focus is on revising, editing and expanding Handler's metadata to conform to DCMI: DublinCore standards (www.dublincore.org). This data contained only five columns: URI, date, image title, image description and source. Since 2018,

Lovejoy, Tiffany Beebe and Travis May, graduate students in the History department at CU, began to parse out Handler's metadata into a more detailed spreadsheet whose columns are: URI, image creator, description, language, resource type, source, rights management, contributing institutions, object type, researcher, additional notes, approval to display and spatial coverage.

During the website's revision, its overall scope has maintained Handler's initial criteria for the selection of images and adherence to bibliographic accuracy. To preserve a complete record of background research, Lovejoy scanned and posted Handler's research notes, constituting two banker's boxes of paper files organized alphabetically.[8] He also partnered with UNESCO's "Slave Route Project: Resistance, Liberty, Heritage," to promote *Slavery Images*, during the United Nations' International Decade for People of African Descent (2015–2024). Efforts have been made to maintain the major elements of the website's original scope, but small modifications have occurred. For example, the project's short-title has been changed "*Slavery Images*" to reflect the URL www.slaveryimages.org. In addition, Lovejoy has replaced Handler's original image titles with the original caption found on the images. Using original titles facilitates learning, teaching, and citing each image more precisely.[9] The map category on the original website was deleted due to the existence of major cartography-focused digital projects (Hedges 2019; and Rizzo 2019).

As noted above, *Slavery Images* will continue to make every effort to ensure bibliographic accuracy and the correct identification of both primary and secondary sources from which the images have been obtained. Nonetheless, errors remain, especially when assigning precise dates to the historical imagery. In many cases, it is only possible to assign date ranges to certain images. In terms of Handler's textual descriptions, Lovejoy has been revising and editing these data into a standardized template, starting with: 1) a translation of the image title into English which is reconciled with previous transcriptions, translations and cataloguing; 2) an explanation of each image, which oftentimes includes a quote from the accompanying text; and 3) a short blurb about the author/artist to highlight bias of pro- or anti-slavery perspectives; and/or to indicate whether or not the author/artist had visited the location depicted. The descriptions also appear in alternative boxes for the visually impaired. Handler's references to secondary sources have also been cleaned, verified, and move into a separate field. Finally, each image has been assigned a geographic hierarchy to visualize image locations using Leaflet, which is now a major feature of the site's landing page. Lovejoy applied a geographical hierarchy based on continent, region, and city/town (for African regions see H. Lovejoy et al. 2021).

With most image repositories copyright is a major issue, but less so with *Slavery Images* because most images fall outside of copyright laws.[10] Almost all historical images published on this website are in the public domain since they were produced before 1923 and are of fair use in many countries, especially for educational purposes. Although copyright law varies from country-to-country, significant portions of the images currently online were acquired in the U.S. at the John Carter Brown Library, Library Company of Philadelphia, Library of Congress, and the UVA Library, including its Department of Special Collections, among other institutions in Western Europe, particularly Great Britain. Other images were digitized by or donated to Handler specifically for re-publication online. As a final disclaimer, a lengthy permissions statement is adapted and based on the Library of Congress's policies surrounding the re-publication of open-source historical imagery.[11] All image metadata fall under a Creative Commons Attribution-NonCommercial 4.0 International license (www.creativecommons.org/licenses/by-nc/4.0).

Conclusion

Most, if not all, African diaspora-related websites provide explanations about the scholarly resource, the project team and acknowledgments. These project descriptions often appear online as static webpages generally called, "About," "Project Overview," "Acknowledgements" and/or "Contributors." However, these sections frequently change with each new website release and/or at other key milestones, especially as collaborators join or leave the digital project. By publishing a project history at key intervals, such as this chapter, not only ensures a durable record of the project participants created at a moment in time, but also it provides a chronological marker of major developmental phases to help gauge past accomplishments and future directions. Having a record of the decision-making process behind educational website development, including providing recognition to the interdisciplinary collaborative process, is best practice. Without project histories, the collaborative process, especially the names of people involved in the backend development at different stages, may be overlooked and/or disappear from memory.

Endnotes

1 We would like to acknowledge Tiffany Beebe, Ben Brumfield, Sara Brumfield, Matt Gibson, Worthy Martin, Travis May, and Will Rourk for helping with the relaunch of the website in January 2019. The relaunch and sustainability of *Slavery Images* would not have been possible without the support of the University of Colorado Boulder's Center for the Humanities and the Arts, College of Arts and Sciences, Department of History, Graduate School, Office of Research Computing, and Research and Innovation Office.

2 In late 2006, Tuite left the Digital Media Lab in the University of Virginia library to pursue a PhD in Environmental Studies at UVA. He received the degree in 2012 and joined the Jet Propulsion Lab at CalTech, where he now manages the Astrobio-

geochemistry Lab. For more information see J. S. Handler, "Project History" and "Acknowledgments," *Slavery Images*, www.slaveryimages.org/s/slaveryimages/page/history and www.slaveryimages.org/s/slaveryimages/page/acknowledgements (accessed 2020).

3 A good example, often reproduced in historical works of the United States with the implication that the event was directly observed by the artist, is an image of the landing of enslaved Africans in Virginia, an event that took place in 1619; the image itself, however, was created around 1900 by a well-known American illustrator, Howard Pyle (1853-1911). See "Untitled Image (Enslaved Africans Landed at American Port)," *Slavery Images* (Accessed 2019), H022, www.slaveryimages.org/s/slaveryimages/item/1977.

4 Unfortunately, these statistics do not include the period between 2000 and 2007, or data for users in the K-12 demographic, which would likely increase user totals overall.

5 Even though scholars and publishers frequently reach out to request permissions to reproduce images, *Slavery Images*, and particularly its metadata, are rarely, if ever, acknowledged.

6 Email with Kartikay Chadha, 15 October 2019.

7 See "Digital Accessibility Program," *University of Colorado Boulder* (accessed 2019), www.colorado.edu/accessible-technology/digital-accessibility-program.

8 "Jerome S. Handler's Research Notes," *Slavery Images* (accessed 2019), www.104.200.20.178/s/slaveryimages/page/handler-notes.

9 If a source did not include a title or caption for an image, then "Untitled Image" is specified followed by a brief description of the image in parenthesis.

10 See the Copyright Term Extension Act; *Bridgeman Art Library v. Corel Corporation*, 36 F. Supp. 2d 191 (S.D.N.Y. 1999); and Intellectual Property Office of the United Kingdom, and by extension the Court of Justice of the European Union, "Copyright Notice: Digital Images, Photographs and the Internet" (November 2015).

11 See "Copyright," *Slavery Images* (Accessed in 2018), www.slaveryimages.org/s/slaveryimages/page/copyright; Anonymous, "Copyright and Other Restrictions That Apply to Publication/Distribution of Images: Assessing the Risk of Using a P&P Image," *Library of Congress* (Accessed 2018), www.maint.loc.gov/index.html; Anon., "Legal Disclaimer," *Library of Congress* (accessed 2018), www.loc.gov/legal.

4

Behind the *Marronnage* Project:

Balancing Resources, Methodology and Access to Achieve Basic Source Digitization[1]

Léon Robichaud

The digitization and the online publication of archival material have transformed the logistics of historical research.[2] We now have access to collections which until recently were generally only available on site. With the dissemination of archives in digital form, researchers, students, and members of the public can locate, read, and analyze sources from their office or from their home. Furthermore, the digital format has also changed how we access the information. Effective search tools have made it possible to identify a relevant corpus or subset of a collection or even to locate a single document without having to read a complete collection. While historians tend not to measure their research time in terms of efficiency – many hours are still spent reading documents that will not be referenced in publications – online access to archives has allowed us to broaden our ambitions by reducing the obstacles of distance and of volume.

Archives dedicated to the documentation of slavery and to slave resistance have now become an essential part of historical scholarship. Since the emergence of the World Wide Web, the publication of these archives has also migrated online. This movement has brought the discussion around the "marginalized or discriminated against" outside the walls of academia.[3] As researchers developed and debated the concepts of humanity, agency and resistance,[4] they mobilized different types of documents to bring to light the oppression and the struggle of millions of individuals, largely Africans, who were subjected to this practice. One of the first collections used to convey life under slavery came out of oral history, demonstrating the variety of materials required to give a voice to the oppressed. Slave narratives collected by the Federal Writers' Project were transcribed and then made available on microfilm, in print and now online.[5] Less common occurrences such as large-scale slave rebellions have also gathered significant attention as flash-points of resistance. The web sites developed to present these events provide in-depth analysis supported by maps or by powerful illustrations. In between, printed collections of runaway slave advertisements[6] have emerged as "one of the staples of the historiography of eighteenth-century slavery."[7] These short notices were originally designed to report escapes and to provide information for the recapture of self-liberating slaves. As with many other documents created to enforce slave systems, they have become important sources for the study of slavery and resistance. Given the nature of the material (brief, descriptive, varied and powerful), advertisements are now also a staple of online archives dedicated to the history of slavery and to its teaching. The richness of the documents has been brought out through new analyses, creating a prism where individual actions are refracted to bring out the conditions of slave humanity.

The process through which such documents are digitized and published online has matured as institutions and research teams have developed methodologies to ensure the authenticity, the quality and the ease of access of various collections, relying on best practices and impressive infrastructures.[8] At the other end of the spectrum, historical photographs are published with incorrect attribution or context, creating confusion and misinformation in the process.[9] Across this large band, there are projects which endeavor to present archival material with a scientific approach, even though they are not integrated within a large institutional framework. The *Marronnage* project fits into this last category and therefore propose a reflection on the digitization and the publication process. The goal is to strike a balance between the scientific and usability requirements of the users while working within the resources available for small projects. Faced with an archival collection which one would deem of interest for others, there are many challenges to be resolved before the documents are available online.

This chapter is based upon experience with the digitization of fugitive slave advertisements for *Marronnage in the Atlantic World* (www.marronnage.info),[10] a project co-directed with Jean-Pierre Le Glaunec. At first, the objective was to publish a collection of documents which were hard to access: fugitive slave advertisements published in the *Affiches Américaines*, the official newspaper of the French colony of Saint-Domingue which became Haiti when it gained independence in 1804. Selected advertisements from this newspaper had been used by historians, but the full extent of fugitive advertisements and lists of captured fugitives (or prison lists) was unknown and the newspaper was only available on microfilm.[11] We hoped that the digitization of all ads would make this corpus accessible for research and for the general community and would shed some light on the diversity of *marronnage* in Saint-Domingue. Following the success of this first foray into publishing this type of document, we expanded the site to include fugitive slave advertisements from other regions (Guadeloupe, Louisiana, South Carolina, Jamaica, and Lower Canada) to facilitate comparative studies. We experimented with various types of documents (images, travel accounts, teaching materials) but we returned our focus on our original objective: selecting and digitizing small portions of texts, attaching metadata and making them available online. We believe that our experience can be useful to others who would like to contribute to the online dissemination of archives but are not sure how to proceed.

Before presenting the principles and the methodology of our project, this paper will survey some of the types of digital archives. This survey made it possible for us to define a set of principles and practices from which we created a rigorous and accessible digital archive. We will then propose a set of guidelines to implement these practices, reflecting upon some errors we made along the way.

Digital Archive Projects: A Survey of Approaches and Practices

A fundamental two-part question guides the development of any digital archive project: who will use it and how. From this question, project leaders will select the standards and practices most relevant to the nature of their endeavor, based upon available resources. For the purposes of this paper, I have classified projects in the following categories: complete archives, virtual exhibitions, teaching materials and research.

Complete archive projects are institutional initiatives which, regardless of the size of the collection or of the organization, comply to recognized standards in terms of digitization process, associated metadata and online content structure. The basic objective is to digitize full collections and make them available online. The digital collection is a surrogate for the original and must respect the same structure. These projects are the gold standard in digital archival practice and follow guides which have been developed since the 1990s.[12] These digital surrogates have greatly facilitated research for academics, students and genealogists. Collections are normally digitized and published in their integral form. Students from regional universities and with limited financial means now have access to material previously beyond their reach. The standards implemented in these projects ensure that users are working with the same content as if they were on site, with the addition of tools which allow for general searches, including across collections, as well as drilling down to specialized content. However, despite efforts by the institutions, interfaces tend to be not very intuitive and a conversation with archivists is always very useful to learn certain tips which facilitate consultation.

Given that requirements for digital humanities publications necessitate complex interfaces, libraries, archives, and museums have also used a more accessible format for digital archives, the virtual exhibition, an approach now facilitated by the use of content management systems, whether as themes for a general purpose systems such as Wordpress,[13] or as platforms designed specifically for digital virtual exhibitions, such as Omeka,[14] or as tools designed specifically for a given project. The "New France Archives" project, which was launched to commemorate the founding of Samuel de Champlain's first post in Acadia in 1604, offers both a virtual exhibition ("New France, New Horizons") as well as collections from seven archival centers.[15] Virtual exhibitions make it possible for an institution to package documents related to a theme (democracy, women, "the most precious artifacts") or to a specific event (the influenza epidemic of 1919, President Richard Nixon's meeting with Elvis Presley), as can be seen at the National Archives and Records Administration.[16] In France, the Bibliothèque nationale currently offers 98 virtual exhibitions.[17]

We could multiply the examples from different national libraries, archives, and museums, but what typifies this approach is the presentation of material to emphasize exploration and storytelling as opposed to research. The pioneering work by the McCord Museum of Canadian History with its impressive collection of photographs, also reflects the technical challenges of such initiatives. However, some exhibits which used original and impressive technical approaches in the early 2000s can no longer be displayed, due to changes in web technologies.[18] On one hand, these projects are always confronted with the challenge of selecting technologies which meet or surpass the expectations of their user base while remaining usable in the long run. The existence of competing web technologies in the form of proprietary plugins before the advent of the HTML5 standard resulted in the creation of many exhibits which became obsolete. On the other hand, sites which adopted basic technologies can still be consulted today, even if their graphic design is dated.

In an effort to integrate sources in the history curriculum, several websites have been created to create collections of documents accompanied by teaching guides and materials. Academic publishers also provide paid digital archival content as part of their offerings to library collections.[19] Since 1997, the MERLOT project has recognized the creation and the recognition of online pedagogical material.[20] Depending on the pedagogical approach, the material is selected and presented in a suggested order so that the students may acquire certain elements of knowledge and develop certain research and analytical skills. A popular concept has been that of the criminal inquiry. *The Martha Ballard Case Study: A Midwife's Tale* is an example of a website focused on a single case,[21] while the "Who Killed William Robinson" website, created in 1997, led to the Great Unsolved Mysteries in Canadian History collection.[22] All these initiatives owe a great debt, directly or indirectly, to the pioneering work of Edward L. Ayers on the Civil War. First appearing online in 1993 when most people were not yet aware of the Internet's existence and when the first image-capable browser (Mosaic) was about to integrate multimedia into the World Wide Web, *The Valley of the Shadow* remains a standard for quality and usability.[23]

Finally, some online archives of primary sources do not have a teaching guide and were not created by libraries, archives, or museums. Generally initiated in universities and colleges,[24] there are also individual projects.[25] Maintaining focus can be an issue as content tends to grow beyond the original project scope. Digital humanities have been criticized for their potential to be dominated by and to focus on traditional Caucasian males.[26] However, digital online archives have also demonstrated that they can be used to foster discovery and research regarding traditionally marginalized groups, namely people of African descent living under slavery.[27] Slave rebellions provide cases studies to explore different documents and different forms of resistance in Louisiana,[28] Jamaica,[29] and Cuba.[30] One of the documents which sheds light on various aspects of slavery is the fugitive slave advertisement.[31] From specific locations[32] to the ambition of exhaustive national coverage,[33] the sites are designed to offer samples or complete collections of these short documents.

Through the *Marronnage* project, we have explored how to efficiently publish a varied corpus of advertisements. Our primary objective was to present, as much as possible, both the image of the original document as well as a complete transcription of the text. This made it possible to offer text searches while providing access to an image of many of the original documents. We tested different types of data to facilitate search to focus on elements which emphasized the identity of the enslaved persons. This met our objective of remembering the many stories of *marronnage* and, through documents designed to oppress and maintain slavery, give a voice to those who regained, even temporarily for some of them, a measure of freedom. Limited resources have prevented us from offering uniform coverage for all sources, but we were able to offer content which would not otherwise be as easily available.

Meeting the Objectives of a Research Digital Archive

In preparing this project, we naturally wished to unlock these documents for academic research. However, we also hoped that non-academics would use these documents to discover these important traces of history. According to the diversity of geographical origins of visitors to the site, we believe that we have achieved this goal. Table 4.1 shows that our main audience is in Haiti, the United States, France, Canada, and the United Kingdom. Other former French slave territories (Martinique, Guadeloupe, Réunion, French Guyana) appear in the top 25 places or origins, as well as countries from which people were captured (Senegal, Côte d'Ivoire).

Table 4.1
Visitors to the *Marronnage* Website, 2019

Country	Number of sessions	Percentage of sessions
Haiti	14,333	35.38
United States	9,490	23.42
France	5,274	13.02
Canada	5,128	12.66
United Kingdom	833	2.06

Document selection is a crucial component of any digitization initiative. Fugitive slave advertisements were always at the core of the project, demonstrating the varied aspects and contexts of efforts towards self-liberation. As the newspapers were analyzed, it rapidly became obvious that prison lists would also have to be included, given that they presented a potential outcome of the search for freedom: capture. These lists also gave another measure of the importance of the resistance to slavery, given that published advertisements only cover a small portion of the liberation efforts. For the year 1776 in

Saint-Domingue, we found that there were 4.5 times more people captured than were reported as escaped (Table 4.2). In Guadeloupe, there are twice as many prison lists than there are advertisements, even without counting the individuals mentioned.

Table 4.2
Number of Individuals in Advertisements and Individuals Captured, Saint-Domingue, 1776

Month	Individuals in advertisements	Individuals in prison lists
January	59	107
February	25	192
March	54	172
April	46	174
May	55	204
June	44	177
July	47	210
August	35	208
September	37	193
October	23	158
November	21	179
December	20	125
Total	466	2099

Source: *Affiches Américaines*, 1776. I would like to thank Dave Roy for the data entry for this sample analysis

As complements to advertisements and prison lists, we have considered including other documents to provide a broader portrait of the life under slavery. We even offered a resources section which included a bibliography, images, and primary printed sources.[34] As we planned the latest version of the website, which was released in March 2019, we concluded that there were other projects that already did an excellent job of offering those documents.

As a result, we recentered our efforts on the documents which had been at the core of the project and thus avoid mission creep.

While it was an easy decision to maintain focus on advertisements and lists, a clear definition of broader geographic limits was more difficult to achieve as we expanded our documentation beyond Saint-Domingue. We wanted to include the documents analyzed by the co-director, Jean-Pierre Le Glaunec, as part of his doctoral dissertation: Louisiana, South Carolina, and Jamaica.[35] To remind people that slavery extended beyond the plantation economy, we added documents from Lower Canada, based upon the appendices published in Frank Mackey's study of the abolition of slavery in that colony.[36] During a research trip to Guadeloupe, Le Glaunec photographed documents on site while the digitization of the *Feuille de la Guyane française* made it possible to venture into another French colony. We analyzed the pertinence of adding the slave colonies of Mauritius and Réunion, but this would have extended our geographic coverage beyond the Atlantic. With regards to Spanish or Portuguese colonies, we did not have the expertise to manage the content adequately. Other British or American territories could be studied, but as more substantial projects have emerged in that area, it did not seem pertinent to duplicate other endeavors. One important slave colony remains understudied, Martinique. New financing would be required to incorporate what could be a substantial corpus of documents.

The time period varies from territory to territory. For Saint-Domingue, Lower Canada, Guadeloupe and French Guyana, we begin when newspapers appear in each colony and end with the last published advertisements or prison lists. The latter may be due to a revolution (Haiti), a *de facto* end to the legal enforcement of slavery (Lower Canada) or to the abolition of the institution (Guadeloupe and French Guyana). The temporal coverage for the three other territories (Jamaica, Louisiana, South Carolina) were defined as part of Prof. Le Glaunec's dissertation.

Implementation Strategies and Practices

Over a ten-year period, we have invested $50,000 (Canadian currency) in transcription, data entry, interface design, programming and translation. A specialist in the history of slavery and a historian experienced in digital humanities brought together their respective expertise to head the project. In the first phase, research assistants were hired to select and digitize advertisements and lists from the microfilm version of the *Affiches Américaines*. The available digitizer created pdf files which were then batch converted and resized into the jpg format using ImageMagick software.[37] We had to choose between optical character recognition (OCR) and human transcription. We settled on the latter because the quality of the images was too variable and the font used in this newspaper was not conducive to a successful OCR process.[38] Due to the limited funds available, we could not implement a double-blind transcription process, but according to sample corrections, the error level is below 3 percent. Given that the documents are transcribed as they appear in the original (except for characters which are no longer in use such as the long s), the errors generally result because the transcriber used a modern spelling instead of the original.[39] We have also verified if the research assistants had captured all the documents for one year and only one document out of a total of 359 had been missed.

Due to constraints in availability, the digitization and transcription work on the *Affiches Américaines* began before we could set up our database and interface, an inversion of process which is not recommended in such a project. While we could attribute the overused concept of "agility"[40] to our process, we must admit that in the early days, we were responding to constraints in funding and staffing. Given that we were ending up with directories full of digitized images and text documents with transcriptions, the file name of the image and the first line of each transcription were used to create a link between the two: the date, the type of issue (regular or supplement), the issue number, the page number and a sequential number for each advertisement or list in a given issue. This facilitated the creation of scripts to import images and text into the database. A side-effect of this decision is that the collection of images could be explored on their own without a database or easily imported into any other database system using the directory and file names to provide basic identification.[41]

The challenge of any digitization project is to define how much complementary data should be added for search and analytical purposes. Our importation scripts already defined the newspaper and its colony or state of origin, the date of publication and information regarding the issue it appeared in, the sequence in which they appeared in the issue, and the type of document (advertisement or prison list). Given that our objective was to provide access to the individual stories, our main effort was to create a record of each individual mentioned, with their name and gender when indicated. As a result, we even created a record for each unnamed person who escaped as part of a group.

While we worked with our three test years (1766, 1776, 1786), we also tested other types of data which could be entered for further analysis. Based upon Le Glaunec's previous work on the topic, a relational database (Figure 4.1) was created to accept data on individuals (age, occupations, language(s) spoken, body markings, ethnic origin, etc.) as well as mentions of slave owners and ship captains. Given the growing number of documents (358 advertisements and lists in 1766, 661 advertisements and lists in 1776, 856 advertisements and lists in 1786), it became obvious that the total number would exceed our expectations. For analytical purposes, the sample data from those three years would be sufficient to analyze different aspects of *marronnage*. Adding detailed data for other years would therefore not be of scientific use and would likely prevent us from digitizing and transcribing all the advertisements, which was our original goal. The importance of the prison lists raised another issue. While we were able to digitize and import the list with basic metadata into the database, it quickly became obvious that we could not transcribe them fully or extract the names of all individuals mentioned. Our analysis of 1776 data indicated that there were almost five times as many slaves mentioned in lists than appeared in advertisements (466 individuals in advertisements; 2,100 individuals mentioned in lists). Given the historiographical importance given to the advertisements, we chose to focus our identification efforts on these documents to provide the most basic coverage possible. Over time, we have been able to transcribe and enter data for approximately 10 percent of prison lists, which provides a usable sample for researchers who would wish to explore those documents.

Figure 4.1
Marronnage Database Model

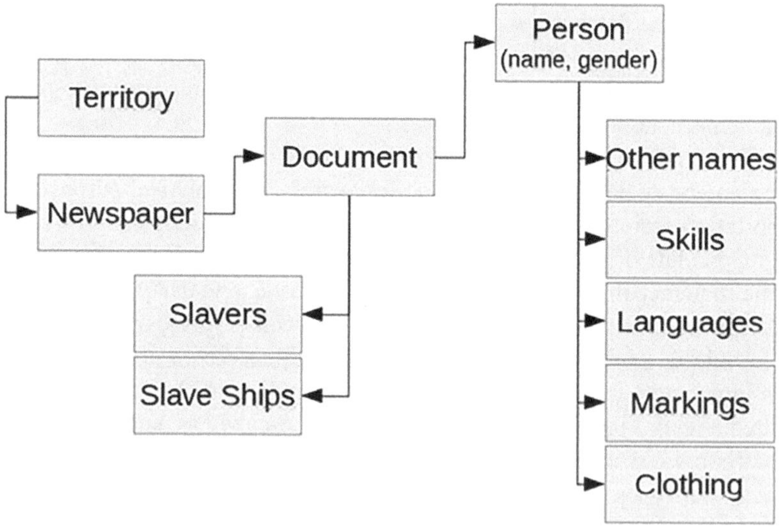

The extraction of names from prison lists from our sample raised another possibility: could we link individuals in both sources? If it were possible, it would open up new avenues to study escape routes, networks, and individual trajectories. Adapting procedures used in historical demography, we attempted to link individuals in both sources, based upon name, age, ethnic origin, height, and body markings. In the end, we could only reliably connect 32 people, which was less than 10 percent of the individuals identified in advertisements and 1.5 percent of those mentioned in prison lists. Our methodology was simple enough to be converted into an algorithm, but the limited results meant that it did not warrant further development to be applied to the full corpus.

The frequent association of people mentioned in the documents with various ethnonyms suggests that such a corpus can easily be used to study the origins of the captives who escape from slavery, possibly even of captives in general. On a practical level, there was an issue of standardizing the approximately 200 designations which appear in the documents so that our research assistants could manage the information efficiently. As we attempted to define a vocabulary, it became obvious that more research was required by specialists in the field before we could structure the information in a manner which could be used scientifically instead of reproducing slave trading categories.[42]

In parallel, we developed the database and its interface. We still maintained our policy of renaming files with clearly identifiable information, which meant that the importation script automatically added basic metadata for each document. The transcription could now be entered directly online (Figure 4.2), as well as the name(s) and gender of each individual mentioned. The database includes fields to identify individuals who participated in the transcription and in the data entry process.

The data for Guadeloupe and French Guyana was added using the same methodology except for the digitization stage which was done from the originals using a smart phone. In some cases, the image was corrected using the "Perspective" tool available in the GIMP image editor.[43] For Louisiana, Jamaica, and South Carolina, we did not have the images, but we had the transcriptions prepared by Le Glaunec for his thesis. The document structure made it difficult to import the data in bulk. As a result, we adapted the interface used to validate and correct existing transcriptions so that research assistants could create records for each document, add the basic metadata, copy, and paste the transcribed text and enter information about individuals mentioned. Given the size and somewhat diverse nature of the content, we needed a simple and effective interface for searching and browsing. Our original version attempted to provide access to as much information as possible, including to some of the attributes entered for the original three sample years of Saint-Domingue data. This provided unexpected results for users, given that few people consult methodological documentation. In the simplified current version, we chose to only offer access to the document images themselves and/or their transcriptions. Users first see a splash page with sample documents and a mention of our partners. The presentation page offers basic statistics on the content, a short text and a map showing the locations from which our documents originate. Users can find out more about our project under "À propos" and "Méthodologie," but the core is the "Corpus" tab.

Figure 4.2
Transcription Interface

Journal	Affiches américaines	
Repérage de l'annonce	Journal numéro 0, page 32, annonce #3 Cahier régulier paru le 1782-01-23 Type de document : annonce Intertexte	Remarques
Deux Negres étampés ſur le ſein droit THIBAUT & C, ſont partis marons le 15 décembre dernier : on ſoupçonne qu'ils ſe tiennent dans le quartier de l'Iſlet-à-Corne, ou aux environs de l'habitation des héritiers *Lalande*, à la Trouble. Ceux qui les reconnoîtront, ſont priés de les faire arrêter & d'en donner avis à M. *Thibaut*, Habitant audit lieu, à qui ces Negres appartiennent, ou à M. *Bertrand*, rue de Penthievre, au Cap : il y aura 66 liv. de récompenſe par tête.		Deux Negres étampés sur le sein droit THIBAUT & C, sont partis marons le 15 décembre dernier : on soupçonne qu'ils se tiennent dans le quartier de L'Islet-à-Corne, ou aux environs de l'habitation des héritiers Lalande, à la Trouble. Ceux qui les reconnoîtront, sont priés de les faire arrêter et d'en donner avis à M. Thibaut, Habitant audit lieu, à qui ces Negres appartiennent, ou à M. Bertrand, rue Penthievre, au Cap : il y aura 66 liv. de récompense par tête.

Source: *Marronnage* project.

In keeping with current practice, we offer a faceted search interface (Figure 4.3) with the facets on the left hand side of the screen, the transcription in the center and a miniature of the image on the right, when the image is available. When only the image is available, a notice appears to inform the user. A click on the miniature opens the full size version of the digitized image of the document, whether or not the transcription is available. A first page with 20 documents is loaded when the tab is first opened. Users have the option of browsing through the 1,125 pages of documents or use the facets to filter documents matching basic criteria.[44] The first three filters search the content of the documents: keywords, name, or sex. The word search tries to match the string of characters entered, searching for an exact match, including spaces. The names having been extracted from the documents, they have been indexed and the first letter type with bring up the list of corresponding names to facilitate search. The sex filter allows user to target their search to take into account gendered aspects of *marronnage*. The other four filters reflect metadata about the documents themselves: location (colony or state), newspaper title, document type and year of publication. The location and newspaper filters are linked so that once a location is selected, only the newspapers published in that colony or state are available. The document type is designed to focus a search on advertisements or on prison lists. We chose to offer a slider to define a time interval as opposed to typing in specific dates. This conforms to common interface design practices for academic projects and responds to the needs of most users who tend to generate a subset of data rather than search for individual documents. Finally, all filters can be reinitialized by clicking on a button which reloads the page.

The frontend of the system is currently only available in French, but the backend is designed to accommodate presenting the interface in many languages. Plans are underway to translate the interface into English and Haitian Creole, but the documents will remain in their original language of publication, whether French or English. Another upcoming modification, in line with open data standards, will be to allow users to download the metadata for their selection in text line with the third format.[45] Until now, data has been supplied to researchers when requested. The future of this data is another concern. University libraries are setting up data repositories, but our institution, the Université de Sherbrooke, at this date only offers a document repository. As a result, we will have to consider the Scholars' Portal to deposit our data.[46] While we have preferred developing our project independently for a decade so that we could focus on publishing using a light approach, we will need to consider depositing the data with a larger project on the history of slavery and resistance.

Conclusion

Over the course of a decade, the Marronnage project has succeeded in making more than 20,000 documents available online and in transcribing more than a million words. Our ambitions and our methodology have been defined by the resources available, keeping the site simple and efficient. This was furthermore achieved at a time when other research projects occupied most of the co-directors' attention. As the world of digital humanities moves towards big data projects requiring large infrastructures, there is still a place for small digitization and publication projects. These projects can follow basic guidelines to ensure their scientific quality and their medium-term existence. For the long term, project directors need to plan on depositing their data in a repository and/or partnering with larger projects to transfer their corpus. As we reflect upon this experience, we are the first to admit that we were not always able to follow the best practices in the field. Our exploratory approach has nevertheless brought to the fore documents which would otherwise likely remain hard to access. We believe that scholars who have digitized other such collections can also easily make them available online to increase knowledge about different local conditions. Sharing content will avoid duplication of effort and facilitate endeavors to connect and federate the many thousands of documents that have been digitized.

Figure 4.3
Searching and Browsing *Le marronnage dans le monde atlantique*

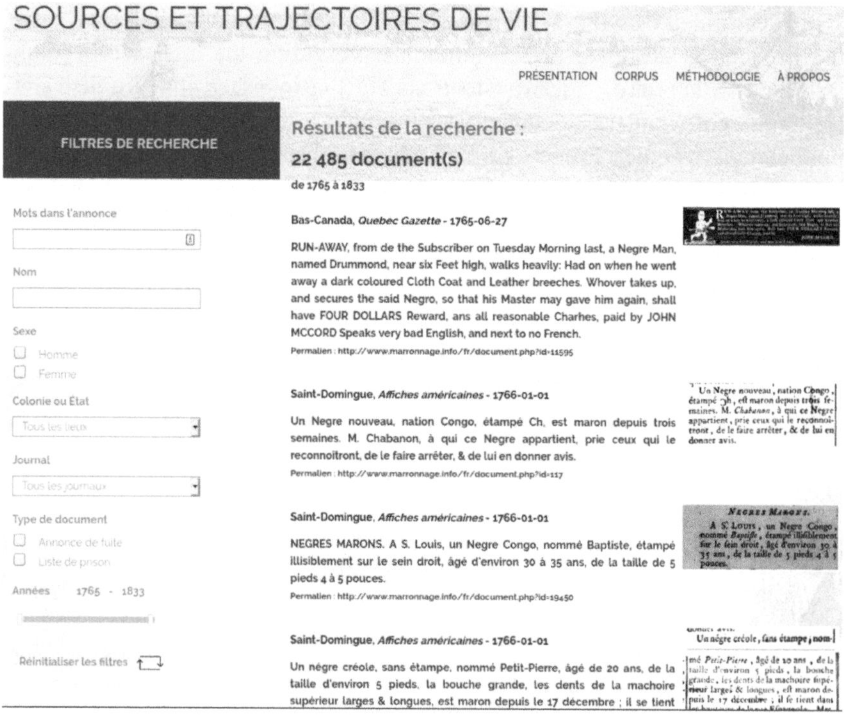

SOURCES ET TRAJECTOIRES DE VIE

PRÉSENTATION CORPUS MÉTHODOLOGIE À PROPOS

FILTRES DE RECHERCHE

Résultats de la recherche :
22 485 document(s)
de 1765 à 1833

Mots dans l'annonce

Nom

Sexe
Homme
Femme

Colonie ou État
Tous les lieux

Journal
Tous les journaux

Type de document
Annonce de fuite
Liste de prison

Années 1765 - 1833

Réinitialiser les filtres

Bas-Canada, *Quebec Gazette* - 1765-06-27

RUN-AWAY, from de the Subscriber on Tuesday Morning last, a Negre Man, named Drummond, near six Feet high, walks heavily: Had on when he went away a dark coloured Cloth Coat and Leather breeches. Whover takes up, and secures the said Negro, so that his Master may gave him again, shall have FOUR DOLLARS Reward, ans all reasonable Charhes, paid by JOHN MCCORD Speaks very bad English, and next to no French.

Permalien : http://www.marronnage.info/fr/document.php?id=11595

Saint-Domingue, *Affiches américaines* - 1766-01-01

Un Negre nouveau, nation Congo, étampé Ch, est maron depuis trois semaines. M. Chabanon, à qui ce Negre appartient, prie ceux qui le reconnoitront, de le faire arrêter, & de lui en donner avis.

Permalien : http://www.marronnage.info/fr/document.php?id=117

Saint-Domingue, *Affiches américaines* - 1766-01-01

NEGRES MARONS. A S. Louis, un Negre Congo, nommé Baptiste, étampé illisiblement sur le sein droit, âgé d'environ 30 à 35 ans, de la taille de 5 pieds 4 à 5 pouces.

Permalien : http://www.marronnage.info/fr/document.php?id=19450

Saint-Domingue, *Affiches américaines* - 1766-01-01

Un nègre créole, sans étampe, nommé Petit-Pierre, âgé de 20 ans, de la taille d'environ 5 pieds, la bouche grande, les dents de la machoire supérieur larges & longues, est maron depuis le 17 décembre ; il se tient

Source: *Marronnage* project.

EndNotes

1 This chapter was originally published in an extended version as "Behind the Marronnage Project. Balancing Resources, Methodology and Access in an Online Archive," *Esclavages & Post-esclavages* 3 (2020) www.doi.org/10.4000/slaveries.3112.

2 This article deals with archives created on paper which were then digitized. For an analysis of born-digital archives and their challenges for historians, see Ian Milligan, *History in the Age of Abundance? How the Web Is Transforming Historical Research* (Montreal and Kingston: McGill-Queen's University Press, 2019).

3 Melissa Dinsman, "The Digital in the Humanities: An Interview with Jessica Marie Johnson," *Los Angeles Review of Books* (2016) lareviewofbooks.org/article/digital-humanities-interview-jessica-marie-johnson/.

4 Walter Johnson, "On Agency," *Journal of Social History* 37:1 (2003), 113–24.

5 Federal Writers' Project. *Slave Narratives. A Folk History of Slavery in the United States from Interviews with Former Slaves* (Washington: United States Work Progress Administration, 1941).

6 Lathan Windley, *Runaway Slave Advertisements. A Documentary History from the 1730s to 1790*, 4 vol. (Westport, CN / London: Greenwood Press, 1983).

7 Shane White and Graham White, "Slave Hair and African American Culture in the Eighteenth and Nineteenth Centuries," *Journal of Southern History* 61:1 (1995), 45-76.

8 The pioneering work of *The Valley of the Shadows* and of *Who Killed William Robinson*, as well as initiatives by the Library of Congress, Library and Archives Canada (Archives Canada-France) to which we will refer below give only a small sample of the potential and scale of such projects.

9 Liam Hogan, "Debunking the imagery of the 'Irish slaves' meme," *Medium*, 14 September 2015 <https://medium.com/@Limerick1914/the-imagery-of-the-irish-slaves-myth-dissected-143e70aa6e74>; Natasha Varner, "The curious origins of the 'Irish slaves' myth," *Public Radio International*, 17 March 2017 <www.pri.org/stories/2017-03-17/curious-origins-irish-slaves-myth>.

10 Jean-Pierre Le Glaunec and Léon Robichaud, *Le marronnage dans le monde atlantique, 1760-1848. Sources et trajectoires de vie*, 2009-2019, www.marronnage.info. The project benefited from small-scale financing by the Université de Sherbrooke, the French Atlantic History Group, the Fonds de recherche du Québec – Société et Culture, the Social Science and Humanities Research Council of Canada, and the "Freedom Narratives" project, directed by Paul Lovejoy.

11 The *Affiches Américaines* have since been digitized as part of the Digital Library of the Caribbean project, <www.ufdc.ufl.edu/AA00000449/00027/allvolumes> (accessed 25 October 2019), a project which received its financing in July 2009 <www.ufdc.ufl.edu/cndl> at a time when we were preparing to launch the first version of our site.

12 *The NINCH Guide to Good Practice in the Digital Representation and Management of Cultural Heritage Materials*, released in 1998 and updated in 2002 <www.chnm.gmu.edu/digitalhistory/links/pdf/chapter1/1.17.pdf> (accessed 11 November 2019), is an example of efforts made to standardize practices. Large institutions have since developed guides adapted to local resources and practices. The "Resources" section of the *Our Digital World* website lists a number of such guides to cover various types of data and the different stages of the projects <www.ourdigitalworld.net/resources/digitization-projects/> (accessed 11 November 2019).

13 For example, a list of the "11 Best WordPress Themes for Museums" showcases a variety of visual templates to present virtual collections, *egrappler, Development Resources for Entrepreneurs* <www.egrappler.com/best-wordpress-themes-museums/> (accessed October 24 2019).

14 *Omeka*, open-source publishing platforms <www.omeka.org/> (accessed 11 November 2019).

15 *New France Archives* <www.nouvelle-france.org> (accessed October 24, 2019).

16 "Online Exhibits," *National Archives and Records Administration* <www.archives.gov/exhibits> (accessed 24 October 2019).

17 "Sites multimédias et expos virtuelles" *Bibliothèque nationale de France – Site institutionnel*, <www.bnf.fr/fr/sites-multimedias-et-expos-virtuelles> (Accessed 24 October 2019).

18 The "Urban Life through Two Lenses" virtual exhibit is an example of an award-winning project which is no longer available, "McCord Museum's Urban Life through Two Lenses wins award for on-line excellence," *McCord Museum*, 20 November 2003 <www.collections.musee-mccord.qc.ca/scripts/pagesXSL.php?file=119a_1.xml> (accessed 11 November 2019).

19 See for example the offerings by Gale and Proquest: *Gale | Primary Sources and Historical Documents* <www.gale.com/primary-sources> *Proquest – Six Centuries of Primary Sources.* <www.proquest.com/libraries/academic/primary-sources> (accessed 25 October 2019).

20 "MERLOT History," California State University System, *MERLOT*, 1997 www.info.merlot.org/merlothelp/topic.htm#t=Who_We_Are.htm

21 *The Martha Ballard Case Study: A Midwife's Tale* <www.dohistory.org> (accessed 25 November 2021).

22 *Great Unsolved Mysteries in Canadian History* <https://canadianmysteries.ca/>The author of this paper co-directed one of the mysteries in this series, "Torture and the Truth: Angélique and the Fire of Montreal."

23 *The Valley of the Shadow. Two Communities in the American Civil War* <www.valley.lib.virginia.edu> (accessed 25 November 2021).

24 *Seventeen Moments in Soviet History* <www.soviethistory.msu.edu> (accessed 25 November 2021).

25 *Les Patriotes de 1837@1838* <www.1837.qc.ca> (accessed 25 October 2019).

26 David Allington, Sarah Brouillette and David Golumbia, "Neoliberal Tools (and Archives): A Political History of Digital Humanities," *Los Angeles Review of Books*, 1 May 2016 <https://lareviewofbooks.org/article/neoliberal-tools-archives-political-history-digital-humanities/> (accessed 20 November 2021).

27 Melissa Dinsman, "The Digital in the Humanities. The Digital in the Humanities: A Special Interview Series," *Los Angeles Review of Books*, March-August 2016 < https://lareviewofbooks.org/feature/the-digital-in-the-humanities/> (accessed 20 November 2021).

28 *Louisiana Slave Conspiracies* <www.lsc.berkeley.edu/> (accessed 11 November 2019).

29 *Slave Revolt in Jamaica, 1760-1761. A Cartographic Narrative* <www.revolt.axismaps.com/> (accessed 11 November 2019).

30 *Digital Aponte* <www.aponte.hosting.nyu.edu/> (accessed 11 November 2019).

31 Jean-Pierre Le Glaunec, *Esclaves mais résistants. Dans le monde des annonces pour esclaves en fuite, Louisiane, Jamaïque, Caroline du Sud (1801-1815)* (Paris, Karthala, 2021).

32 *North Carolina Runaway Slave Advertisements, 1750-1865* <www.libcdm1.uncg.edu/cdm/landingpage/collection/RAS> (accessed 11 November 2019).

33 *Freedom on the Move* <www.freedomonthemove.org> (accessed 25 November 2021).

34 Previous versions of the site can be viewed on the Internet Archive's Wayback Machine, <www.web.archive.org/web/20160323142800/http://marronnage.info/fr/ressource.php> (Accessed 25 October 2019).

35 Jean-Pierre Le Glaunec, "Lire et écrire la fuite d'esclaves dans le Monde Atlantique: essai d'interprétation comparée et 'coopérante' à partir des annonces d'esclaves en

fuite, Louisiane, Jamaïque et Caroline du Sud, 1801-1815," Ph.D. Thesis, Anglophone Studies, université Paris 7 – Denis Diderot, Paris, 2007.

36 Frank Mackey, *Done with Slavery: The Black Fact in Montreal, 1760–1840* (Montréal / Kingston:McGill-Queen's University Press, 2010).

37 *ImageMagick - Convert, Edit, or Compose Bitmap Images*, <www.imagemagick.org> (Accessed 28 October 2019).

38 New tests would be required to verify if handwritten text recognition (HTR) would achieve better results as has been the case in some recent experiments made by the READ consortium, "Transkribus HTR competing in OCR-test of the Zurich University" <www.read.transkribus.eu/2019/07/30/transkribus-htr-competing-in-ocr-test-of-the-utrecht-university/> (Accessed 28 October 2019).

39 The most common error is for the transcriber to write "connaître" – the modern spelling – instead of "connoître," which was in use until the 1780s in the *Affiches Américaines*.

40 To understand the agile method of software development and its critique, the substantial Wikipedia entry provides an excellent summary, "Agile Software Development," *Wikipedia*, <www.en.wikipedia.org/wiki/Agile_software_development> (Accessed 30 October 2019).

41 The usual practice is for the file name to be attributed sequentially.

42 Such work is being accomplished by Paul E. Lovejoy, Érika Melek Delgado and Kartikay Chadha, see "Freedom Narratives of West Africans from the Era of Slavery" in this volume.

43 *GIMP. GNU Image Manipulation Program*, <www.gimp.org/> (Viewed 26 November 2019).

44 The facets use AJAX (Asynchronous Javascript and XML) technology, which makes it possible to reload a specific portion of a web page and make the interface more interactive. "Ajax (programming)," *Wikipedia*, <www.en.wikipedia.org/wiki/Ajax_(programming)> (Accessed 30 October 2019).

45 In the five level (or five star) rating system proposed by Tim Berners-Lee, founder of the World Wide Web, the third level is for data to be available in a non-proprietary file format. Open Knowledge Foundation, "Five Stars of Open Data," *Open Data Handbook*. <www.opendatahandbook.org/glossary/en/terms/five-stars-of-open-data/> Accessed 26 November 2019.

46 *Scholars' Portal Dataverse* <www.scholarsportal.info/> Accessed 26 November 2019.

5

Who Did What When? Acknowledging Collaborative Contributions in Digital History Projects[1]

Henry B. Lovejoy

As digital publications gain more traction, issues arise related to best practices of citing the contributors to major research initiatives. This project history explores *Liberated Africans* (www.liberatedafricans.org) to evaluate how to provide individual recognition within highly collaborative, database-driven archival repositories. The original website was built using HTML and first launched on 6 August 2015. It has since expanded into an interdisciplinary collaboration with support from different academic institutions and granting agencies. This article explains the second version relaunch of *Liberated Africans* on 15 March 2018, which involved improving the backend for searchability. The overarching aim of *Liberated Africans* is to retrace the lives of approximately 225,000 enslaved Africans taken off slave ships in British-led campaigns to abolish the slave trade between 1807 and 1896. As more and more scholars piece back together activities of some of the world's earliest international courts of humanitarian effort, crediting individual participation in a digital project has become an issue, especially as roles sometimes become defined, redefined, and refined over the natural evolution of website development.

The challenge of acknowledging credit within digital projects has implications for tenure and promotion, or indeed landing that highly competitive job. As Joseph Raben (2007) points out "the status of online publication as an inferior medium is probably the concern on the part of potential contributors... (and) not as highly regarded by the gatekeepers of tenure and promotion as the traditional hard-bound book and the article offprint." Unlike print publications, digital projects might never end because they continuously transform over time. Matthew G. Kirschenbaum (2009) raises the question: "What does it mean to 'finish' a piece of digital work?." The answer is not always obvious because the measure of academic success revolves around "the pressure of milestones, deadlines, deliverables and products (as opposed to projects)." Since most digital research is interdisciplinary, keeping track of contributions calls attention to varying levels of involvement at key benchmarks. As many digital collaborators realize, the role of any number of people in advancing a digital project can in essence be much more abstract and obscure (Posner 2016). After all, where does one give credit and who decides how to give it? As both a data repository and digital archive, *Liberated Africans* did not simply begin at its inaugural launch in 2015, but builds upon decades of digitally based research related to the history of Africa and the African diaspora dating back to the 1960s.

This paper aims to outline problems in acknowledging individual contributions and examines how digital projects in the field of Africa and the African diaspora history have been addressing best practices. It provides one example of how to credit the many participants in *Liberated Africans*, who either deliberately or inadvertently influenced its success. Recognizing all levels of involvement requires supplementary publications to strengthen its value as academic research and promote academic integrity.[2] Beyond decades of research published on paper, the creation of *Liberated Africans* would not be possible without well established, open access and crowdsourced websites. This type of research demands explanations of which participants contributed what materials and when. Project histories, such as the one embedded in the forthcoming discussion, provide a basis for assessing individual participation for tenure, promotion, and the job market.

Digital Historiography of the African diaspora

In 1969, Philip Curtin first raised fundamental questions about when and where people came from in Africa; and when and where they went in the transatlantic slave trade. His early research "brought together bits and pieces of incommensurate information" related to "the measurable number of people brought across the Atlantic." At a time when computers were emerging into the mainstream, Curtin argued that "the social sciences [were] becoming more quantitative." He also recognized how the historiography was "full of estimates that seem to agree to the range (of) fifteen to twenty-five million slaves landed in the Americas." Using statistical methods and his broad knowledge of the field, Curtin conservatively predicted that future research would reduce that range to 10.5 million departures and 8 million arrivals. He acknowledged that his inquiry was a starting point because "better data on the numbers carried by the trade at particular times should make it possible to project the annual flow of slaves from particular societies" (1969, xvi and 273). Meanwhile, Herbert S. Klein and "other [unidentified] scholars" collected data on slave-trading voyages and began coding them "into a machine-readable format" (Eltis 2018c). In the 1970s, David Eltis, inspired by Curtin and Klein, began compiling information more systematically into SPSS about illegal slaving voyages after British abolition in 1807. Eltis also created the "African Names Database," which amounts to a spreadsheet of over 68,000 Liberated Africans registered by Vice Admiralty Courts and Mixed Commissions in Sierra Leone, Cuba, and St. Helena (Eltis 1977; Eltis 1982; Eltis 1986; Eltis 1987).

By 1990, Eltis met Stephen Behrendt at the Public Record Office in Chancery Lane, which subsequently moved to Kew in 2003 and was renamed The National Archives. They quickly realized they were gathering complementary data about slaving voyages between 1785 and 1807 (Behrendt 1988; Behrendt 1993). In the spirit of collaboration, they decided to put "everything together on a CD-ROM," which was not a cheap technological proposition at the time. Two years later, Eltis and Behrendt approached Henry Louis Gates Jr. with their idea, he then gave them an office and support at Harvard University's W. E. B. Du Bois Institute for African and African American Research (now the Hutchins Center). The National Endowment for the Humanities (NEH) and the Andrew W. Mellon Foundation supported this pioneering effort. Over the next decade, Eltis and Behrendt brought David Richardson on board because he had amassed materials for British voyages leading up to 1785, especially for the port of Bristol. By 1999, *The Trans-Atlantic Slave Trade: A Database on CD-ROM* was released with data for over 27,000 voyages. It was highly acclaimed, but full of gaps, and more people began to contribute data from archives in Africa, Europe, and the Americas. With even more support from NEH and Harvard, a revised and expanded second edition of the database on CD-ROM came out in 2008. Soon after that, CD-ROM became obsolete, and the project migrated out of Harvard onto servers at Emory University where it was rebranded *Voyages: The Trans-Atlantic Slave Trade Database* (Williford 2010).

Since going online, *Voyages* has received more funding for various recoding updates, a Portuguese translation, pedagogical resources, samples of archival materials, data visualization tools (graphs, tables, charts, etc.) and an animated map illustrating some 36,000 voyages crossing the Atlantic to various destinations in the Americas, Africa and Europe (Kahn & Bouie 2015).[3] Statistically, *Voyages* revises Curtin's preliminary estimates upwards, so that now the data substantiate that approximately 12.5 million people were forced onto slave ships along the African coast, while only about 10.7 million reached the Americas due to mortality rates (Eltis et al. 2018b).[4] Meanwhile, the "African Names Database" has expanded to over 90,000 Liberated Africans and has formed the basis of *African Origins*, which is a platform that crowdsources interpretations of the languages of transliterated African names to assess the ethnolinguistic composition of the slave trade after 1807 (Nwokeji and Eltis 2002a; Nwokeji and Eltis 2002b; Eltis et al. 2018a). By 2009, I had transcribed registers compiled in Cuba and the Caribbean independently from Eltis and noticed inconsistencies with the transcription of the Havana registers. These changes have since been absorbed into *African Origin* (H. Lovejoy 2009). A year later, Suzanne Schwarz and Paul Lovejoy identified and began digitizing previously unincorporated materials from the Vice Admiralty Court in Freetown for 1808-1819 through support from the British Library Endangered Archives Programme. Since then, Schwarz, Paul Lovejoy, Eltis, Richard Anderson, Daniel Domingues da Silva, Philip Misevich, Olatunji Ojo, and Alex Boruki began taking stock of the various copies of the registers of Liberated Africans disembarked at Freetown held in archives in England and Sierra Leone (Anderson et al. 2013). Revisions to the total sample of registers have since occurred under the direction of Eltis and Misevich.

As *Voyages* and *African Origins* continue to evolve, with an upgrade of the former released in 2019, the issue about who contributed what and when remains fuzzy. As is standard practice on digital projects now, both websites list sponsoring organizations and institutions, as well as dozens of contributors grouped into categories. The pre and post 2019 version of *Voyages* included "Principal Investigators," "Project Team," "Steering Committee, and "Advisory Board." There is also an additional page called "Contributors of Data," which alphabetically listed nearly sixty people who had contributed data "since the publication of the 1999 CDROM" (Eltis et al. 2018a; Eltis et al. 2018b).[5] However, problems remain with this approach. How does this list based standard demarcate specific contributions? Why would a tenure or promotion committee seriously assess someone in an alphabetical list without knowing how, what and when they contributed under the direction of a prominent scholar? And how does this loose practice help younger generations receive tangible credit for their research donations to a larger collective? While these groupings certainly provide degrees of recognition, the ambiguity fails to recognize credit adequately, and might to some degree disincentivize others from making more contributions. Featuring in such lists is arguably akin to being mentioned in the acknowledgments of a published monograph or in the first footnote of a peer reviewed article – neither of which mentions would ever appear on a CV, let alone enter the discussion of tenure, promotion, or job interviews.

Eltis has recognized the problem of assigning credit within digital projects. On the 2018 *Voyages* "Acknowledgements" page, an anonymous author (most likely Eltis) included a sub-section called "Special Thanks," which states:

> Many people contributed to the successful completion of this project – enough that we fear in our attempts to acknowledge them, we may only call attention to having forgotten someone and their worthy assistance in our efforts. With apologies for any regrettable omissions and our sincerest thanks to everyone, named or anonymous, who graciously gave their time and expertise (Eltis 2018b).

Likewise, on the "About Project" page of *African Origins*, another anonymous author (probably Eltis) explained how "many individuals supported the work of the project and the project team, [but they are] too numerous to name here" (Eltis 2018a). My contribution to over 10,000 rows of data appears only as "Havana Register Research," which involved months of work required to transcribe the Havana registers, as well as working with Ojo, Abubakar Babajo Sani and Umar Hussein to interpret nearly 4,000 African names, which were then inputted one at a time into *African Origins* in 2013. The way in which these contributions are presented on Eltis' website would give little credence to support a case for tenure or promotion.

Eltis has not been the only scholar to encounter the issue of assigning credit to successful digital projects. In 2001, Jerome S. Handler and Michael Tuite launched *Atlantic Slave Trade and Slave Life in the Americas: A Visual Record* (Handler & Tuite 2018: www.slaveryimages.org). In the project's history, Handler explains how this website began as a collection of images for use in an undergraduate anthropology course at Southern Illinois University, Carbondale "in the late 1980s and early 1990s." This image archive was intended to show "everyday life of enslaved Africans and their descendants in the Americas." In attempts "to illustrate every lecture," Handler engaged staff at the university's Learning Resources Services to produce slides of well-known images of slavery. At a NEH Summer Institute for college teachers at the Virginia Foundation for the Humanities in 1998, Handler presented those slides whereby he recalls how "someone… probably [Joseph] Miller or a student… suggested that the whole slide collection should be scanned/digitized."

But who were the people who made those early slides and who really came up with the idea of putting the images online? Should they not receive recognition too? Handler seems to think so because he tries to assign credit to those specific ideas and contributions that were not his. Much like *Voyages*, the history of this image archive clearly has inconsistencies due to what Handler explains as "memory issues" (2018). The website, which used PHP, went live in September 2000 with only 150-200 images. Michael Tuite, the then director of the Multimedia Resource Center at the University of Virginia (now Robertson Media Center and Digital Lab), scanned and digitized the images and helped Handler develop a backend system. The project has since expanded to over 1,200 images. Despite the lack of specific names, Handler's project history has been maintained since I assumed the website's directorship in 2018, renaming the site *Slavery Images: A Visual Record of the African Slave Trade and Slave Life in the Early African Diaspora*. Brumfield Labs recoded and relaunched the website using Omeka-S and International Image Interoperability Framework (IIIF) on 15 January 2019.

Digitizing World Archives

In the 1990s, the digital camera became affordable, and hence data retrieval more accessible and processing much easier. Since then, numerous institutions, granting agencies and private funds have supported the mass digitization of primary source collections from archives around the world. The immeasurable amount of material currently available in digital format, with much more to follow, has rapidly and steadily been appearing online through different institutional websites, including the British National Archives and the British Library, as well as independent digital projects such as *Liberated Africans*. Arguably, the people doing the digitizing work do not always get the full credit they deserve. Generally, the task is perceived as non-analytical and "service" because it involves taking pictures of documents volume by volume, page by page. Truth be told, digitization efforts require much more recognition than simply being "service." The researcher must identify and justify what collection needs duplicating, assess if any digitization work has already been done, determine if the archive permits photography, apply, and wait for funding, hire and train research assistants, organize travel to the archive, take the time to photograph records, secure copyright, prepare the files for online publication, create inventories, develop metadata and ingest files into a content management system for public consumption. Jane Landers, a full professor, has received extensive credit for organizing research teams involved in digitizing over 700,000 images mostly from ecclesiastical and secular sources in slave societies related to approximately 6-8 million Africans and their descendants in the Americas. Her website conveys, quite clearly, who did what and when, including the numerous research assistants on numerous teams oftentimes, but not always, under her direction (Landers et al. 2018). Nevertheless, would this digital project be enough to get someone tenure or a promotion? Probably not at present in most history departments, despite the ramifications Landers' massive digital project will have throughout the field of Atlantic world history, as well as for the ancestry of Africans and their descendants, for generations to come.

Liberated Africans would not be possible if not for the Public Record Office and The National Archives which undertook the "Digital Microfilm Project" (2018). The current digital director explains how this initiative "became a 'first generation' digital archive: one that adopts a traditional, paper-based approach to selecting, preserving and providing access to records and replicates it as closely as possible using digital technology" (Sheridan 2017). Over several decades, dozens of collections were microfilmed, which were then converted into PDF formats around 2011 and 2012. *Liberated Africans* has been reorganizing on a document by document basis these digitized records from the Foreign Office 84 series called "Slave Trade Department and Successors: General Correspondence before 1906." This collection amounts to over 2,200 downloadable volumes containing thousands of individual documents (FO 84). At present, the National Archives does not provide much more explanation about the Digital Microfilm Project. A rather vague project history was obtained only after asking through email, chat rooms, telephone calls and by submitting a Freedom of Information request. *Liberated Africans* owes much to unidentified teams of people involved in this major digitization effort at the archive, which spanned several decades in two locations.

The British Library's "Endangered Archives Programme," established in 2004, preserves collections held in world archives that are at risk of being destroyed, and puts them in the public domain. *Liberated Africans* leverages digitized materials from the Sierra Leone Public Archives. Under the direction of Paul Lovejoy and Schwarz over the course of three grants, this preservation taskforce has duplicated over 270 volumes and 75,000 images (EAP 2009; EAP 2011; EAP 2015). The Chief Government Archivist in Sierra Leone, Albert Moore, oversaw the project on site, while digitization efforts involved Alfred Fornah, Abu Koroma, Aiah Yendeh. As best practice, Paul Lovejoy explains how "each digital file contains information about who digitized what and when."[6] Because of infrastructure difficulties in the archives, all images were checked, metadata prepared, and an inventory compiled, initially by Diane Lee, a librarian, at the Harriet Tubman Institute for Research on Africa and Its Diasporas at York University. In January 2017, Bruno Véras, a PhD student at York, took over this responsibility, but more project managers will likely follow.[7]

Liberated Africans hosts digital primary sources from personal archival collections, which oftentimes stem from years of research. For example, I digitized materials located in Barbados, Brazil, Cuba, Curaçao, France, the Netherlands, Spain, Suriname, and Great Britain between 2001 and 2014. Before, during and after my dissertation, I was employed as a research assistant on NEH and Endangered Archives Programme grants, as well as being awarded grants, fellowships and travel stipends through various institutes and departments at the University of California Los Angeles, Universities of California-Cuba Academic Initiative, Fulbright-Hays, Tabor Foundation, the Social Sciences and Humanities Research Council of Canada (SSHRC), Harvard, NEH and the Mellon Foundation. The material that was collected is openly shared with other scholars, and much of the relevant records now appears on *Liberated Africans*, most especially a complete copy of the registers of Liberated Africans from the FO313 series, "Archives of the Havana Slave Trade Commission." Beyond my own contributions, *Liberated Africans* also uses materials from the personal collections digitized by (in order of general importance): Richard Anderson, Suzanne Schwarz, Paul Lovejoy, Daniela Cavalheiro, Marial Iglesias Utset, Inés Roldán Montaud, Jorge Felipe and Sean Kelley.[8] As best practices, *Liberated Africans* compiles primary source inventories that attempt to reference who digitized what and when according to DublinCore standards.

Digital Project Creation and Development

Liberated Africans grew out of the environment of the highly competitive academic job market. Following a SSHRC postdoctoral fellowship, I enrolled in a certificate program, "Digital/Multimedia and Information Resource Design," at Seneca College in Toronto in the winter of 2015. The idea of *Liberated Africans* was born while learning how to code HTML, CSS and JavaScript and use Adobe Creative Cloud. Using a Bootstrap framework and hosted on GoDaddy, I put most of my dissertation research online. The initial website had over sixty individual HTML webpages, centered on 44 trials involving over 10,000 Africans liberated by the Havana Slave Trade Commission between 1824 and 1841 (Lovejoy 2009). A copyright license was obtained from the British National Archives to republish their digital records online, which were then rearranged into their respective cases involving over 750 documents, including: register copies, trial abstracts, captor declarations, expense reports, resettlement strategies, legislation, etc. Each case page had a summary, map, database, table, and graph. There were other data visualizations and analyses for the demographics of the total sample; and an "Image Gallery" with over 150 prints, paintings, photographs, and sketches of ships, barracoons, and Liberated Africans, which mainly derive from Handler's collection in *Slavery Images*. Other paintings, prints, sketches, and photographs were harvested from the British National Maritime Museum, British National Archives, and Brazil's Biblioteca Digital da Fundação Biblioteca Nacional. The original website also incorporated images digitized by me, Richard Anderson, Daniela Cavalheiro and Daryle Williams. Using Premier Pro, I also made a mini documentary about the Havana Slave Trade Commission, which is accessible through YouTube (Lovejoy 2015). Francis Otero consulted extensively on the short film and original website design.

The URL www.liberatedafricans.org circulated rapidly shortly after it was released in August 2015. Iglesias Utset invited me to present the digital project at a conference called "New Research on the Atlantic Slave Trade" at Harvard University on 2-3 October 2015. In preparation for the event, Anderson, Cavalheiro, Eltis, Schwarz and Williams were invited to join the initiative due to their expertise on the courts and cases in Sierra Leone and Brazil. Anderson and Williams submitted one case summary each to me for Freetown and Rio de Janeiro, including sample PDFs of case files. They also created preliminary case lists, which involved selections of data from *Voyages*. Test cases for Sierra Leone and Brazil were then hard coded into *Liberated Africans*, while a new homepage was being developed and the website's structural hierarchy expanded. To support this initiative, Henry Louis Gates, Jr., director of the Hutchins Center at Harvard, awarded me a $50,000 subvention grant publicly during the conference. After, Anderson and Williams were appointed co-principal investigators on this grant with support from Matrix: The Center for Digital Humanities & Social Sciences at Michigan State University.

Once *Liberated Africans* migrated to servers at Matrix, the next phase required that the website be re-coded for searches and prepared for the ingestion of more data related to the global abolition movement. Over the next two years, Anderson, Williams, Dean Rehberger, Alicia Sheill, oftentimes Catherine Foley, and occasionally Walter Hawthorne and Ethan Watrall assisted in the transformation of an HTML website into a more complex digital vehicle. To define the controlled vocabulary, Matrix hosted two in person meetings in East Lansing on 3-5 November 2015 and 26-29 July 2017. Between these two meetings, the project team met monthly to discuss the website's metadata structure for it to operate with the Matrix designed digital publishing platform, called KORA (Rehberger et al. 2018a). Other scholars were invited to join the meetings, and other experts were consulted, including (in a general order of importance): Matthew S. Hopper, Katrina Keefer, Andrew Pearson, Sharla Fett, Patrick Harries, Kyle Prochnow, Paul Lovejoy, Sean Kelley, Edward Alpers, among others.[9] Project participants from Matrix included: Seila Gonzalez Estrecha, Austin Truchan, Anthony D'Onofrio, among students listed on Matrix's website, although who specifically did what and when is not entirely clear despite efforts to discover. Matrix used Basecamp to keep a record of agendas, discussions, submitted data and other materials related to project development.

Originally, the hardcoded website operated around a structure relative to the location of courts and cases, which usually involved the capture of a slave ship in the *Voyages* database and the trial resulting in the emancipation of people on board. However, some cases did not involve slaving voyages, but rather coastal slave barracks or captured canoes transporting enslaved Africans along the coast or in the British Caribbean. On 20 July 2016, Lindsey Gish, who left Matrix shortly after, was consulted and she sketched a relational database scheme for *Liberated Africans* (Fig. 5.1).

Figure 5.1
***Liberated Africans* Relational Database Scheme**

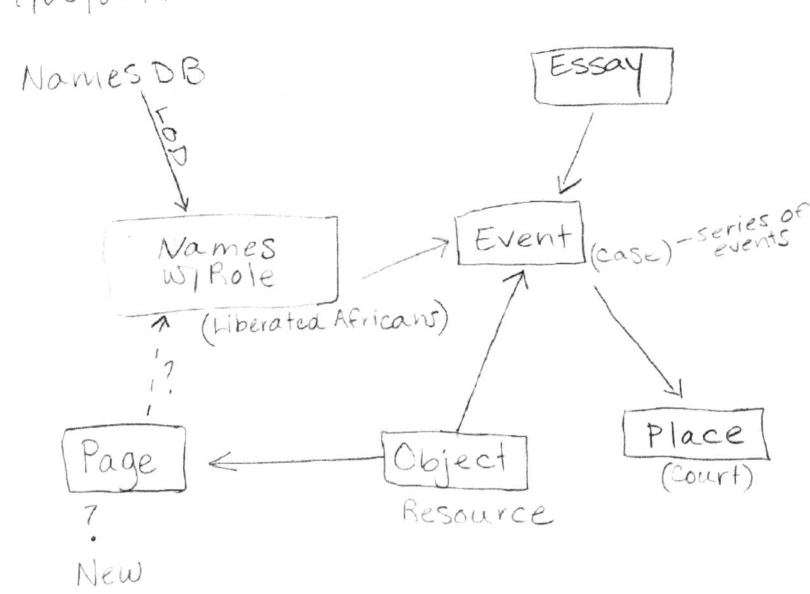

Initial Sketch (20 July 2016)

Each box in the above diagram represents a specific spreadsheet of available data obtained from my HTML coded design of *Liberated Africans*. The core team of historians initially had difficulty understanding and accepting this proposed concept, which deviated from the original website structure based on cases mostly involving voyages. It was clear that data scientists interpreted the available historical data differently than historians. Out of Gish's sketch, and during subsequent meetings, the relational database structure emerged into four key spreadsheets:

- **People**, which hosts definitive records for each person with a unique ID, whether registered or not. Content accommodates variations of data obtained from the Registers of Liberated Africans.
- **Events**, which includes pivotal information about the date an activity happened to an individual. At present, these data mostly revolve around slave voyages and trial proceedings, such as embarkation, capture, disembarkation, trial, registration, emancipation, etc. In the future, pre- and post-trial events can be added to link in evidence of baptisms, military service, post-trial resettlement, education, re-enslavement, second emancipation, marriage, birth of children, death, etc.
- **Places**, which involves geographic coordinates that are associated or connected with people and events. These data have implications for mapping, visualizations and analysis over space and time.
- **Sources**, which reflects the digital archive of primary source, multimedia objects, such as PDFs or JPGs. All source metadata adheres to DublinCore standards, and any published materials must abide by copyright law. Since all data derive from these digitized materials, each object links into the people, events, and places datasets; thus, access to the primary source provides users the capability to verify data accuracy.

This four-part design has implications for other digital projects because most humanities-based research revolves around the intersection of people, events, places, and multimedia – a typical format found in social media platforms, most especially Facebook. According to Rehberger, the four part *Liberated Africans* database scheme forms "the basis for *Enslaved: Peoples of the Historical Slave Trade*" (www.enslaved.org) – a complex Linked Open Data hub that aims to combine various databases for purposes of drawing on different datasets since January 2018.[10]

In terms of best practices, it has been next to impossible to record specific contributions to backend development. Many ideas and new directions transpired among different combinations of people during many Matrix meetings, and/or in individual communications via email, telephone or in person at conferences and workshops. By the fall of 2016, Sheill compiled a chart for the initial metadata values, which were discussed and altered over months of interactions. On 1 December 2016, I organized a panel, "The Liberated Africans Project: New Developments for the Study of the Abolition of the Atlantic and Indian Ocean Slave Trades," for the African Studies Association conference in Washington D.C.[11] On 10-12 June 2017, Paul Lovejoy hosted a conference at York University called "Liberated Africans and the Abolition of the Slave Trade" with over twenty participants, which was funded by a SSHRC Connections grant and supported via cost sharing from MSU, University of Colorado Boulder, Universidade do Estado do Rio de Janeiro, University of Worcester, Trent University and York University.[12] This conference resulted in an edited volume, which is a demonstrable contribution that *Liberated Africans* has had into a traditional print publication (Anderson & Lovejoy 2020).

A meeting at Matrix in July 2017 with Anderson, Foley, Sheill, and Williams culminated in a final decision on project metadata values. As specified by the World Wide Web Consortium for Linked Open Data interoperability, the project uses a Resource Description Framework, which incorporates Uniform Resource Identifiers in anticipation of its connectivity into Linked Open Data networks. At this meeting, the numbering system for the "people" dataset was finalized, which was generated as a combination of:

- **Case ID Number**, which derives from the ID numbers obtained from *Voyages* as indicated by a V in front of cases (hence V1266). If the case does not appear in *Voyages* an abbreviation of the location was assigned, as was a new number (hence SL1 or CU1 or BR1 – as in Sierra Leone, Cuba, and Brazil).
- **Individual Number**, which is a sequential number assigned to people/individuals as they were registered starting at 0001 for each new register/case.
- **Source**, which is a short reference to a source to resolve differences in variant copies of registers.

An individual's ID is expressed as: V1266-0001-FO313/58 or SL1-0001-SLPA16432-17002.

> By October 2017, the final metadata documentation, stemming from Sheill's initial charts and several months of discussion, resulted in a twenty page document reflective of how the backend of *Liberated Africans* operates. Determining metadata values is theoretical, collaborative, time consuming and often goes unnoticed. It is usually challenging to determine who has contributed what components over the course of two years of meetings and interactions with an interdisciplinary team. In the case of *Liberated Africans*, a core group of historians (myself, Anderson, and Williams) and a core group of data scientists (Sheill and Foley) defined project values for the four part relational database scheme (people, events, places, and sources). Much as in a monograph or peer reviewed article, the co-authors of the metadata document interpreted global collections of complex historical data into spreadsheets of rows and columns. Much as in the STEM disciplines, the twenty-page *Liberated Africans* metadata document might be best published as a standalone piece with a first,

second, third, fourth, fifth and sixth author with a footnote acknowledging a long list of experts who contributed their time and expertise. There does not yet exist a peer reviewed journal to publish metadata schemes, which is why the *Liberated Africans* metadata scheme is published online as a linked attachment in the original open-source article.

Published Datasets

Since individual scholarly recognition is not typically credited in contributions of data, especially spreadsheets provided by emerging scholars, *Liberated Africans* recognizes versions of the "Collaborators Bill of Rights" (Anon. 2011; Di Pressi et al. 2015; Boyles et al. 2018). Beyond the website's database, *Liberated Africans* cannot operate without different spreadsheets compiled by different people, which then must be modified and "cleaned" into the values outlined in the metadata scheme. At first glance, published datasets appear much more tangible in terms of assigning academic credit, but such data are constantly fluctuating and being modified by multiple people. Without doubt, *Liberated Africans* incorporates, builds upon, and expands Eltis' data from *Voyages* and *African Origins*, which has involved numerous contributors and revisions since the 1970s. The difference between *Liberated Africans* and Eltis' projects, however, is that *Liberated Africans* focuses on the human experiences of the people involved in the judicial process of the suppression of the slave trade, rather than the slaving voyage or interpretations of documented African names. *Liberated Africans* also goes one step further by linking digital copies of primary sources to the data so that users can verify accuracy of uncertain data for further analysis.

The Cuban dataset produced by the Havana Slave Trade Commission involves forty-four cases and over 10,000 rows (people) with 22 columns. Within these data, groups of people experienced similar events, which revolved around 44 slaving voyages and trials out of more than one hundred total cases in Cuba (Roldán de Montaud 2011). These data diverge from *Voyages* and *African Origins* by being based on a more complex numbering system for people, more biographical data, information about the capturing ship and crew and additional dates (capture, trial, sentence, registration, etc.). Drawing on the British National Archives and my own digitization efforts, over 750 PDFs were extracted from larger volumes and organized on a case by case basis. This process involved generating a document inventory according to DublinCore standards. The sources are connected to the relevant data for people, events, and places Sheill revised and cleaned project metadata for interoperability. Although *Voyages* and *African Origins* make references to primary sources, digitized copies are not available through either resource.

Improved Sierra Leone data derive from *Voyages* and *African Origins*, which have been cross-referenced with digital copies of primary sources from the FO 84 series. As Britain's primary base of operations for the abolition of the slave trade, these data are by far the most voluminous in terms of the overall scope of *Liberated Africans*. At different periods, five courts operated at Freetown, including a Vice Admiralty Court, and Anglo-Portuguese, Anglo-Spanish, Anglo-Dutch, and Anglo-Brazilian Mixed Commissions. Between 1808 and 1871, this judicial network adjudicated over 500 cases and emancipated over 100,000 individuals, 80,000 of whom were registered. Since August 2015, Anderson was also instrumental because he compiled the list of over 500 cases for Sierra Leone, including those cases which did not involve a slaving voyage. He also separated the person data from *African Origins*, reassigned numbers and added more data, specifically related to resettlements. Between 1 July 2017 and 30 June 2018, the project was awarded a joint NEH and Mellon Foundation fellowship for digital publication to build out Sierra Leone data. Leading up to the website relaunch in March 2018, Eltis' core data was improved by adding more dates and information to the events dataset, especially around the capture of slave ships. Anderson, Érika Melek Delgado and Thomas Garriss assisted in extracting and adding to the inventories of documents from the FO 84 and FO 315 series: and Sierra Leone Public Archives. With the website relaunch, these data and documents were added to *Liberated Africans* directly through Sheill.

Although most of the Brazilian data involve *Voyages*' data, *African Origins* does not include lists of enslaved Africans liberated by the Anglo-Portuguese and Anglo-Brazilian mixed commissions in Rio de Janeiro. The reason for this omission is that *African Origins* focuses on documented African names for interpretation and the Brazilian registers only recorded Christian names assigned to people in Brazil. In the fall of 2015, Williams compiled a case list of just under one hundred cases, while Cavalheiro transcribed twenty registers amounting to over 7,000 people. Cavalheiro also created an inventory of PDF copies of the registers she digitized from Brazil's Arquivo Nacional in Rio de Janeiro. Again, all data were cleaned before sending the data to Matrix for uploading into KORA.

New Website Design

Hosted and maintained on Matrix servers, *Liberated Africans* relied on the programming and design team based at Michigan State University (Matrix 2018). The website's underlying architecture used KORA3, which is a platform agnostic content management system based on Apache, MySQL and PHP7. Due to upgrading KORA2 to KORA3 (which occurred during the transition from PHP5.6 to PHP7), Matrix pushed back the relaunch date of *Liberated Africans* to 15 March 2018. Working closely with Sheill and Foley, Matrix's director of programming, Gonzalez Estrecha, and lead KORA developer,

D'Onofrio, reprogramed the search and browse pages for frontend access to data. Because Matrix is involved in hosting more than a dozen digital projects, project development and programming bleed in and out of one another. Hence acknowledgement of who did what when on the part of Matrix is complicated.

After less than a year, the initial version of the frontend user experience of *Liberated Africans* looked outdated. Despite attempts to preserve some elements, Truchan, Matrix's head designer at the time, redesigned the frontend with Sheill's assistance. The image of the website's logo is taken from the "Flag of an African Slaver" obtained in abolition efforts off the coast of East Africa (Anon. 1862). Using digital skills I obtained at Seneca college, the text, banners, flowcharts, maps and images for the overview, sources, copyright, contributors, and the acknowledgement pages were then created. Additional paragraphs of text and a selection of images related to court locations were submitted by Anderson (Sierra Leone), myself (Cuba), Williams (Brazil), Hopper (East Africa), Pearson (St. Helena), Caribbean (Kelley), United States (Fett), the Gambia (Prochnow), and Angola (Vanessa Oliveira); and then later revised for consistency in style.

Conclusion

Since digital humanities research is slowly gaining momentum, collaborative digital mediums should merit scholarly recognition as research at the same level as traditional, peer reviewed publications. Best practice in writing and publishing the history of a digital project is to assign credit and recognition to individuals in teams of people. This project history explores the creation of *Liberated Africans*, where the project data originated from, who produced it, how it was modified, and when that occurred between August 2015 and March 2018. Project histories should truthfully explain different levels of participation, the historiography, digitization efforts, the preparation of multimedia objects, the theorizing of metadata schemes, the compilation of metadata, as well as contributions to front and backend design. These necessary processes in digital projects, which are naturally collaborative and interdisciplinary, require more understanding, especially for purposes of tenure, promotion, and job search committees across all fields in the humanities. Christine L. Borgman explains how the disincentives to share are complex in both the sciences and the humanities but are being addressed. As the sciences learn how to share data and to share credit for their findings, the humanities can build upon their best practices. Intellectual property constraints remain a major stumbling block, and the considerations vary between the sciences and the humanities (Borgman 2009).

Each digital project differs through phases of development, especially as members join and leave the project for myriad reasons. Digital project directors have the responsibility of keeping track of individual contributions, as well as of the intangible theories and methods that went into consolidating a website's design and metadata schemes.

As a final note, this article was written to acknowledge and express my gratitude to the many people who have helped with *Liberated Africans*. I have, to the best of my ability, summarized and analyzed how *Liberated Africans* was developed as accurately as possible. Building a digital resource is interdisciplinary, collaborative, and full of abstract contributions. The difficulty of assigning credit in hindsight is that publishing digital project histories can easily overlook contributions no matter how big or how small.

Endnotes

1 Originally published in *Esclavages & Post-esclavages*, 3 (2020): https://journals.openedition.org/slaveries/2717.

2 The policies and procedures for tenure and promotion in the Department of History at the University of Colorado Boulder requires two peer-reviewed publications in addition to the digital project. One of these supplementary publications should be analytical and the other a project history.

3 David Eltis' conference presentation at Harvard University, "Slave Voyages and African-Origins since 2010: Problems, Retrospectives and Reassessments," "New Research on the Atlantic Slave Trade," 2 October 2015.

4 Based on the following search criteria from the "Estimates" page: 1501–1866 and embarked/disembarked.

5 It should be acknowledged that the descriptions of *Voyages* I quote herein have since changed and no longer exist online; hence I cite the version I accessed in February 2018.

6 Email with Paul Lovejoy, 19 February 2018.

7 Personal communication with Paul Lovejoy, 20 February 2018.

8 As is common practice, historians often share their digital collections, and I am pretty sure I have forgotten someone's name. My apologies. It is also worth noting that each scholar's trajectory to digitize records has involved similar trajectories to my own, which have involved different grants and research projects too numerous to list here.

9 It is also highly likely and plausible that other team members consulted with one another or elsewhere without my knowledge.

10 Email with Dean Rehberger, 21 February 2018.

11 African Studies Association annual conference. Washington DC (2016). Papers: Anderson, "Freetown's Anti-Slave Trade Courts and "Liberation" in the British Atlantic"; Hopper, "Freedom Without Equality: Liberated Africans in the Indian Ocean World"; Williams, "Africanos into Africanos Livres in Nineteenth Century Brazil." Panel chaired by Kristin Mann with Hawthorne serving as the discussant.

12 Conference participants included: Rosanne Adderley, Nielson Bezerra, Maciel Henrique Carneiro da Silva, Maria Clara Carneiro Sampaio, Daniella Cavalheiro, José C. Curto, Walter Hawthorne, Érika Delgado, Daniel Domingues da Silva, Aboubacar Fofana, Matthew S. Hopper, Allen Howard, Katrina Keefer, Sean Kelley, Martin A. Klein, Richard Anderson, Kyle Prochnow, Robert Murray, Sharla Fett, Vanes-

sa Oliveira, Jane Landers, Henry Lovejoy, Paul Lovejoy, Philip Misevich, Andrew Pearson, Dean Rehberger, Maeve Ryan, Inés Roldán de Montaud, Christopher Saunders, Suzanne Schwarz, Randy Sparks, Tim Soriano, David Trotman, Bruno Véras, Daryle Williams, Dan Yon, among other graduate students in attendance.

6

Freedom Narratives of West Africans from the Era of Slavery

Paul E. Lovejoy, Érika Melek Delgado, and Kartikay Chadha[1]

The project *Freedom Narratives: Testimonies of West Africans from the Era of Slavery* (www.freedomnarratives.org) centers on the enforced migration of enslaved Africans in the Atlantic world during the era of the slave trade. Through an examination of biographical accounts of individuals born in Africa who were enslaved from the sixteenth to the nineteenth century, the focus is on the organizing the testimonies of individuals who can be considered to have been "Atlantic Africans" by attempting to recover the voices of those who were involved in the slave trade. Initially a limited number of testimonies were collated and organized for comparative study to establish the proof of concept. Then a web portal was designed with the intention of developing an online digital repository for thousands of autobiographical testimonies and biographical digital identities of Atlantic Africans that will allow the analysis of patterns in the slave trade and life experiences of slavery and freedom, specifically in terms of where profiled individuals came from, why they were enslaved, and what happened to them.

Because *Freedom Narratives* focuses on those born in West Africa, in most cases people had been born free and therefore are to be distinguished from those who were born into slavery in the Americas or elsewhere. The important distinction between those born free from those born into conditions of slavery is highlighted by reference to their testimonies as "freedom narratives" rather than as "slave narratives," the term that is commonly used to categorize the personal accounts that have been recorded in the Americas. In the case of the surviving accounts of those born in Africa, at least, not only were most individuals born free but were subsequently able to regain their freedom. The experience of slavery was therefore only an aspect, even if important, of their personal experiences. By way of comparison, we postulate that the exposure to slavery was different for those born into slavery in the Americas and elsewhere who were socialized into slave societies from birth, even if individuals were able to acquire their freedom (P. Lovejoy 2011, 91-107).

The individuals in the *Freedom Narratives* repository include those who travelled within Africa as well as those who experienced the "Middle Passage," i.e., the Atlantic crossing, which is often considered a defining moment in the slavery experience. Even if individuals did not cross the Atlantic, they might experience similar lengthy journeys across the Sahara or within Africa via caravans, along rivers, and by sea to places such as Freetown, Sierra Leone, where international courts were established to justify the seizure of ships involved in the slave trade and where the people on board such vessels were formally "liberated" after a period of apprenticeship. These accounts recount the direct experience of natal alienation as opposed to subjugation through the memory of the Middle Passage and what had been retained about the homeland. As Atlantic Africans, anyone born in Africa and was enslaved faced the uncertain future of a Middle Passage, while those born in the Americas did not, even if individuals were sometimes transferred over considerable distances. Moreover, "freedom narratives" often recount the hope, sometimes realized, of being reunited with kin or members of natal societies that was more difficult and often impossible in the trans-Atlantic and trans-Saharan diasporas. Individuals who were never enslaved are also included because of the importance of identifying various kinds of relationships, not only those based on kinship and social interactions, but also relationships of dependency and subjugation.

Freedom Narratives enables an examination of biographical testimonies as the fundamental units of analysis in historical reconstruction, whether the primary texts arise from first person memory or survive via amanuensis. Whenever possible, original testimonies are supplemented with biographical details culled from legal, ecclesiastical, and other types of records. Personal profiles, or digital identities, are compiled from the surviving testimonies of individuals that are supplemented with biographical details culled from a variety of sources but also include cases for which there may not be testimony, only biographical fragments or shards of evidence extracted from different primary sources, such as from the Registers of Liberated Africans or newspaper accounts. Through its website, the *Freedom Narratives* project assembles, collates and displays biographical information on individuals who were born in Africa during the centuries of the slave trade as a means of understanding the episodes and trauma of the experience of slavery, whether the enslaved crossed the Atlantic to the Americas, remained in Africa or were taken across the Sahara.

Regenerating digital identities emerged out of several interrelated research agendas that began to collect biographical data from Africa. The initial inspiration was the collection of essays published by Philip D. Curtin in *Africa Remembered: Narratives of West Africans from the Era of Slave Trade* (1967). P. Lovejoy's Ph.D. thesis (1973), subsequently revised was based in part on biographical information on merchants engaged in the long-distance kola nut trade within Africa (P. Lovejoy 1980), and many of these merchants were of slave descent, although a focus on biography as a source for historical reconstruction in West Africa only attracted P. Lovejoy's attention in the mid 1990s (Lovejoy 1994: 151-180; Lovejoy 1997: 119-140). During this growing interest, Lovejoy began to collect biographical accounts, and with the assistance of Silke Strickrodt (2002), Francine Shields (1997), and Femi Kolapo (1999), an extensive amount of material was assembled, although in the era before digitization and databases, the information was arranged in a haphazard fashion. Subsequently, Lovejoy undertook several biography projects about enslaved Africans in the eighteenth and nineteenth centuries.[2] Recently, there has been a plethora of studies that examine other biographies, too many to enumerate here.[3]

The development of *Freedom Narratives*, therefore, is a major step forward in the organization of materials for open access and analysis of the personal lives of individuals caught in the nexus of slavery and the slave trade. The database and website include materials that relate to overlapping categories of sources: 1) published materials on individuals from travel accounts, missionary narratives, and other sources (Anderson 2017, 620-644). 2) Documentation on Liberated Africans, especially from the Sierra Leone Public Archives,[4] has also been shared with *Liberated Africans* (www.liberatedafricans.org) and *Languages of Marks* (www.languageofmarks.org). Both of these databases include "Registers of Liberated Africans" and much other documentation that is mined for incorporation. 3) Fugitive slave advertisements from Brazil, the French islands in the Caribbean, Jamaica, North America, which are housed on separate websites, initially focused on *Le Marronnage dans le Monde Atlantique* (www.marronnage.info). And, 4) baptismal, marriage records, memorials, military service documents, petitions, and other materials from the *Slave Societies Digital Archive* (www.slavesocieties.org) that can be used to reconstruct life stories in Spanish and Portuguese colonies in the Americas. Hence *Freedom Narratives* is not only a collaborative project that relies on internal feedback and criticism but is also designed to link with other websites through linked open data.

The purpose of this project history is to discuss best practices that have been adopted in the development of *Freedom Narratives*. This chapter provides explanations of how the history of digital humanities publications has developed, by whom, and according to what standards. The website acknowledges the project team, its direction, management, technical coordination, contributors, researchers, and financial assistance. The description of best practices explains the methodology, the use of controlled vocabularies, definitions, and the relevant citations. The fundamental building blocks are the controlled vocabularies, by which is meant the terms that are used to describe and present data that are carefully defined and applied in the organization of data, which in this case involve digital identities.

Best Practices in the Generation of the *Freedom Narratives* Database

The creation of a digital history database involves working with a team of researchers and computer programmers including website and database developers. All members of the team adopt best practices in processing clean data, that is, data that adhere to consistent application of clearly defined procedures and norms. Initially, biographical summaries and metadata are being written in English, although eventually the website will be available in at least English, French, Spanish, and Portuguese using online translation tools as they become more sophisticated. Primary materials will be processed in the original languages, depending upon the source of information. All materials and metadata entered in *Freedom Narratives* are examined by the two directors, and when necessary different opinions and interpretations are discussed more widely to reach consensus.

Since words and symbols have different meanings in spoken and written language than in a programming language particular attention is directed at defining terms clearly and using vocabularies that are exact and consistent, which are referred to as "Controlled Vocabularies," which are explained in more detail in the next sub-section. Otherwise data are not "clean" and cannot be processed by computer algorithms. *Freedom Narratives* initially used KORA, the backend system developed at Matrix: The Center for Digital Humanities and Social Sciences at Michigan State University. The data were curated using a combination of software including Google Drive, Google Documents, Microsoft Excel, and Adobe Acrobat Pro DC. Subsequently,

Kartikay Chadha developed *Decoding Origins Web Portal* (www.decodingorigins.org), initially for *Language of Marks* and then for *Freedom Narratives. Decoding Origins Web Portal* consists of a backend collaborative database using Structured Query Language (MySQL); and a user-friendly interactive platform employing novel algorithms to collect, analyze, and cross reference data.[5]

The *Freedom Narratives* database is designed to handle multiple types of documents from a variety of sources that often constitute different categories. This web portal employs user-sensitive inclusive design and iterative learning methodologies to improve data curation processes, which are not only for *Freedom Narratives* but compatible with other projects. *Decoding Origins Web Portal* provides a project-customized, collaborative environment to collect, organize, meta-tag, visualize and cross-reference data, and connect with external collections. The portal can also connect with public websites to enable real time publications of biographies and documents. *Decoding Origins Web Portal* allows historians to work in a team-based web-environment that reinforces rigorous analog best-practices developed by the *Freedom Narratives* research team. Instead of alteration between documents, *Decoding Origins Web Portal* allows researchers to link PDF documentation and corresponding work with "Controlled Vocabularies," simultaneously displayed on one screen. The "Source" tab of *Decoding Origins Web Portal* records metadata of digital files that are being processed. Through development, *Decoding Origins Web Portal* became the current platform, Regenerated Identities (RegID).

The basic structure of data management is based on four interrelated methods of identification, first establishing the "Person" as a unique individual, then examining the various known "Events" in that person's life, and the "Places" where such events occurred, and finally, the "Sources" from which digital identities are derived. These four categories are organized digitally as an open source relational database that forms the basis of a website www.freedomnarratives.org. This approach adopts Henry Lovejoy's initiative developed in the creation of www.liberatedafricans.org (H. Lovejoy 2020). A textual summary of what is known about an individual is posted on the website for easy reference. The template for summaries includes basic information, including the name of the individual, his/her sex, identification of ethnonym/language, an estimate of the year or range of years in which the person was born, and where the individual was born specifically as to place and geographic region. When, where, how and by whom an individual was enslaved is noted along with when and where the individual was taken and what happened later, such as emancipation, sale, escape, marriage and any unique details. Finally, the summary includes the year in which the information was recorded, who obtained the information, where this was done, and the final location of the individual if known.

The "Person ID" entry is a project-generated unique identifier for each digital identity entered in the *Freedom Narratives* database. Researchers are assigned a specific range of identifiers, which are called "FN Numbers." These identifiers follow the same format: "FN" followed by six digits (e.g., FN000001, FN000002, ...), which allow differentiating one individual from another who might have the same name. Each person working on the project can create a person file on *Decoding Origins Web Portal*. Once approved by the directors, "FN" ID number is automatically assigned to each case file for a new person; thus establishing a new digital identity with corresponding biographical data. Assigned cases are listed under "My Task" section of the web portal for purposes of workflow efficiency.

The biological sex of individuals as listed in the source document(s), often based on observations, is included as female, male, or unknown. All information about the physical appearance of an individual in primary documents are grouped according to characteristics under specific terms (e.g., wound; branding; height). Individual family relationships are considered part of an individual's identity, and hence parents, children, spouses, and other close family are identified. It is recognized that individuals virtually always understood more than one language, including languages of interrogation or interviews as well as those associated with ethnonyms, and in some cases literacy is indicated, such as when the primary documents state that the individual could write, or if it is possible to conclude that he/she could (e.g., if a document was written by this individual in a certain language).

Controlled vocabularies are used to enable the development of a database that allows analysis of patterns and facilitates interpretation. In some cases, such as in identifying gender, the controlled vocabulary is simple (male, female, unknown). In other cases, the controlled vocabulary is relatively straightforward, such as the controlled vocabulary for physical descriptions (scarification, tattooing, missing limbs, slave branding, yellowish complexion, dark complexion, Poro marks, partially blind, totally blind, smallpox marks, marks of illness). Other controlled vocabulary relating to ethnonyms, occupations and other details are more complicated and expand as new identifications are found.

Identification is further clarified with reference to the region in West Africa from which an individual came and the regions to which individuals subsequently went, both within West Africa and across the Atlantic or Sahara. Region of origin is determined with reference to the regionalization outlined in "Defining Regions of Pre-Colonial Africa: A Controlled Vocabulary for Linking Open-Source Data in Digital History Projects" (H. Lovejoy et al. 2021). The region of destination records the last location where an individual is noted in the sources, and ultimately, the location where he/she died, if known. For purposes of *Freedom Narratives*, regions of destination include the following designations: Caribbean, North America, Hispanic mainland, Brazil, western Europe, and Islamic North Africa and the Middle East. As an example: the "Region of Destination" for an individual found in the *Marronnage* documents would often be "Caribbean." If it is later discovered that a person travelled to, or died in, North America, this new information would replace "Caribbean," although full itinerary among regions would still be discernable. Thus, Baquaqua's itinerary identifies his origins in the Bight of Benin, his enslavement in Brazil, his liberation in North America, his sojourn in the Caribbean, his return to North America, his passage to Europe (England), and his final known destination in the Forest Region of West Africa because he was last reported in the American colony of Liberia. In cases where an individual was present at a place on the fuzzy border between regions, both regions are recognized on the assumption that it was highly probable that the individual could have traversed the border zone.

The events of each person's life entered into the dababase are recorded in a similar fashion, following best practices for content, data curation, Google Drive preparation, and programming, which are clearly articulated on the website for reference along with the Controlled Vocabularies that have been determined for the project. An "Event Type" is a category or class that captures an event's overarching impact or purpose, as noted in the primary sources. Some will be obvious since there is an "Information Recorded" event when the document is produced. Others require more reflection; for example, if a runaway African recorded in a *Les Affiches Américaines* newspaper is referred to by a French name, it can be assumed that there was a "Naming Ceremony" event, that could include baptism, at some point in the individual's personal history which had to have taken place before the "Information Recorded" event, and even before the "Resistance" event (when the person ran away from the master). Hence events may have an "Imputed date," but also there may be "imputed data," to recognize events during the person's life. Information is entered chronologically based on the Controlled Vocabulary for "Events."

The event description is a summary that captures a single event to clarify the purpose of the event or if something specific happened during an event. For example, a "resistance" event could mean the individual ran away from the master, started a rebellion, or refused to work, and hence might require further clarification. A "birth" event, by itself, is usually clear enough. However, if the primary document states that there were complications relating to the "birth", then details are noted. An event identifier provides a unique reference for each event to recognize connections among more than one person who participated in the same event, making it possible to search a specific event and everyone who is known to have been present. Events are connected to sources on the portal, as is all other data. The occupation of the person is noted for each event based on the Controlled Vocabulary. If other individuals, not including relatives, are involved in the event, reference is made to them based on the Controlled Vocabulary. For example, for an enslaved African the ship captain in the "Departure" and "Arrival" events can be determined through the *Trans-Atlantic Slave Trade* database. Ideally, the precise location where the event took place is noted, if known. If no precise location is given, a specific area (Street, City, District, Country, Region) is noted. The place where an event occurred is referred to according to the place type, ranging from streets to regions, with the exact coordinates of the location and wherever possible visualization of places.[6] Variant spellings of the names of places in primary sources and modern equivalents are noted.

The social position or status of the individual during each event is determined based on the Controlled Vocabulary (e.g., Free, Enslaved, Liberated, Fugitive). The age of the individual at the time of a particular event is recorded as found in the primary document or otherwise imputed to a specific year or range of years. Age categories, including child, adult, elder, are determined at the time of a specific event according to the Controlled Vocabulary. The start date and end date for an "Event" (year-month-day) is recorded according to documentation or imputed when the date is not cited in the original source but has been determined by calculation. An example of calculating an imputed date would be finding out the year when the "birth" event took place by subtracting the known or approximate age of an individual from the year the information was recorded or the event occurred. The circa period is clearly noted when the date is an approximation (a range of years). Religious affiliation at the time of the event is noted, including reference to a specific brotherhood, church, ritual society or other association if it can be determined.

If information links to a contributing digital humanities publication, such as *Voyages, Liberated Africans, Harvard Biographies*, *Language of Marks*, or *Le Marronnage dans le monde atlantique*, the ID number that identifies the document/information in that project's database is noted, which for the *Slave Voyages* database means the "Voyage ID" number; for *Le Marronnage* database the ID number for each slave advertisement (at the end of each document's URL), and for Liberated Africans, the registration number in the original documentation. Similarly, every person contributing to the project receives proper recognition for his/her work, which includes those who provided the data and those who entered the data in the database.

Naming for *Freedom Narratives*

One concern of a database that involves individuals relates to naming. *Freedom Narratives* confronts this problem in the following manner. First, each individual is assigned a unique identification number FN000000 that allows a potential database of a million people. The "Name" entry records the name of the individual as it is reported in the primary source document. For purposes of reference, a single name is taken as a primary name, which can be the name as reported in a source, a name that is the result of conversion to Christianity, or a nickname that was used for that person. Whenever possible, the African name of the individual is used. If this is not possible, the most common name is used, including every part of the name as it is written in the source: given/first name, surname/last name (e.g., André do Amaral). If the primary sources do not mention a name, the person is listed as "Unknown." Sometimes an individual is referred to by more than one name. "Alternative Names" can be name variations, nicknames, aliases, married/maiden names, assumed names, variant spellings of African and Christian names, alternative spellings with abbreviations or initials, among other identifiers. A semicolon differentiates multiple entries in various fields of the Web Portal, unless a multiple select HTML form type field is provided. All alternative names are recorded, so that the database can be searched for any variation. If a name is changed, such as through conversion to Christianity, the change is recorded as an event.

Freedom Narratives does not privilege the use of surnames. We consider an emphasis on surnames to be Eurocentric which reflects a Judeo-Christian tradition and not traditions that derive from the societies of the enslaved themselves. As noted in our distinction between "slave narratives" and "freedom narratives" makes clear, there were two categories of enslaved individuals, first those who were born in Africa and second those who were born in the Americas. Controlled Vocabularies that use a category of identification that is referred to as "surname," which is most often a Christian nomenclature, and occasionally Jewish, are irrelevant for the vast majority of cases involving enslaved individuals. The identification of surnames may be of use in some cases, admittedly, as in the fact that the enslaved who were able to gain their freedom in the Americas could take the surname of their master/mistress, and in cases of fugitive slaves such reference to individuals through the use of the owner's name was a means of identification. Ecclesiastical records in Portuguese and Spanish colonial settings usually did not record surnames, whose use was a practice among the free population of European descent. Spanish practice among the free population used the surnames of both the father and mother, with the father's surname usually coming first, while the opposite happened in Portuguese practice, where the mother's name could come first. Portuguese nomenclature could refer to other social relationships, not just the preferred surname of the master.

The enslaved who were born in Africa seldom if ever had surnames, at least not before conversion to Christianity. The use of surnames ignores the Muslim component of the enslaved population, wherein Muslims did not use surnames, and it conflates naming practices into an indistinguishable pattern. The insistence on surnames also mistakenly confuses African naming traditions and can incorrectly refer to someone like the individual whose birth name was Olaudah Equiano by the supposed surname, Equiano, when Equiano was not a surname. Therefore, for *Freedom Narratives*, the concept of surname is not used. Instead, individuals are identified by a unique identification number (FN000000) and the most common name used in the sources. As explained in the section on methodology on the website, individuals can be located through a search for any name or variation on the name that is found in the sources and further identified through other factors such as age and event. Variations of names, nicknames, Christian names, variations in spellings are all included under alternate names separated by a semi colon. If the only name that is known is a Christian name, then first and last names are included together, when known, separated by an underscore.

Names can provide clues to identity when they can be correlated with other factors, such as religion in the case of Muslim names, with days of the week, as in the case of Akan day names, and specific cultures when the meanings of names in a language can be discerned, as in the case of Olaudah Equiano. Attempts to equate names with specific ethnic groups are less certain, despite the attempt of to do so with reference to individuals taken off slave ships by the British Navy in the nineteenth century.[7] With respect to *Freedom Narratives*, this approach has very limited veracity. Names taken alone can be misleading because of possible similarities in the pronunciation of names that are not otherwise known to be identical in different societies and the uneven filtering of phonetic rendering of names by third parties who do not know the languages and cultural practices of those being attributed with specific origins. The difficulty of relying on names to establish identity is particularly pronounced when a correlation with ethnicity is claimed.

Ethnicity

The identification of individuals usually references an ethnonym or language, which for purposes of data entry and analysis is entered exactly as in the source. Variations in spellings and terminology are recorded with appropriate modern associations. The term "ethnonym" is used here rather than ethnicity which may not refer to anything more than a language that was a means of communication, whether the language was the first, second or even third language that allowed mutual understanding. The primary sources usually record identity in terms of what was perceived as ethnicity and usually use of a common language. Hence, the "ethnonyms" of an individual referred to ethnicity, tribe or nation and frequently language. The assumption that is made for *Freedom Narratives* is that such references are most likely related to the language(s) an individual spoke, usually not recognizing that most people spoke more than one language and often several. An "Ethnonym / Language in Original" entry is recorded exactly as in the primary documents (e.g., Poullar, Fula, etc.). These terms are then sifted through the controlled vocabulary, which is an ever-growing list containing terminology derived from Sources which includes variations of ethnonyms in primary sources, modern scholarship and common usage. Ethnonyms are linked to likely region of origin (e.g., Fulbe | Poullar; Pualard; | upper Guinea Coast or Senegambia), that is the broad area from where an individual originally came. If the primary document does not specify where the individual was born, the "Ethnonym / Language" Controlled Vocabulary can help approximate the location. As an example, if FN00XXXX is identified as Allada, the "Region of Origin" is the Bight of Benin.

The problem of identity is addressed in a parallel and derivative project, *Documenting Africans in Trans-Atlantic Slavery* (DATAS) (www.datasproject.org), which develops an innovative method to explore African ethnonyms from the era of trans-Atlantic slavery. Ethnonyms index African identities, places and historical events to reconstruct African culture that is linked to a history of slavery, colonialism and racism. The project centers on the need to understand the origins and trajectories of people of African descent who populated the trans-Atlantic world in the modern era. The development of a method for analysing demographic change and confronting social inequalities arising from racism constitutes a social innovation. The team's methodology implements a research tool for handling ethnonyms that can be applied in a trans-Atlantic context from western Africa to all parts of the Americas, Europe and the Islamic Mediterranean and Middle East. This innovation confronts methodological problems that researchers encounter in reconstructing the emergence of the African diaspora. A methodology for data justice that addresses issues that often exclude certain groups like "slaves," the dehumanizing implications of referring to people as "slaves," and the sensitivity of how Africans are perceived to have participated in world history is salient because ethnonym decision-making used in our digital platform requires a reconceptualization of the classification systems concerning West Africans.[8]

One difficulty of what is known when ethnicity is assumed or assigned relates to the meaning of ethnicity, which itself is contentious (Lovejoy 2003: 105-117; Lovejoy 2016: 195-218). We argue that references to ethnicity, tribe, etc. usually refer to language. Moreover, even when language is inferred from the reference, it is usually made in a manner that suggests that the individual knew only one language when in fact in most cases we know individuals spoke at least two and often several languages. Ali Eisami, who came from Borno, spoke Kanuri, but almost certainly spoke some Hausa, and he lived in the Oyo capital for at least five years and therefore had to have known Yoruba, while he learned English in Sierra Leone, which according to the linguist Sigismund Koelle was far from perfect (Lovejoy 2019). Hence, we prefer to talk about ethnonyms, not ethnicity. And we lump ethnonyms and language together because it is not usually possible to understand what a source is referring to when ethnicity is claimed. The related digital project, *Language of Marks*, described elsewhere in this volume, has adopted the designated ethnonyms as a means of analyzing African origins as represented in facial and body markings. In that context, ethnonyms are inscribed in an orthography upon the skin of those who are recorded (Keefer 2019; Keefer 2017: 1-26; Keefer 2013: 537-553).

The second problem is that the meaning of ethnicity in the diaspora in the Americas is not equivalent to ethnic designations in Africa. In the Americas, various terms are usually described as "nation," or "country," whether in Portuguese, Spanish, French or English, which are vague constructs that do not correspond with designations referred to as ethnicity in Africa and did not always correspond with a language, even in some broad sense of an original group of immigrants from Africa who might have understood the same language. Second, "ethnic" terms in the Americas, such as Lucumí in Cuba, Mandingo/Mandinga, Angola, Congo were broad categories that did not correspond to terms in Africa, despite fuzzy links. One attempt to deal with this problem is Gwendolyn Midlo Hall's study of ethnicity (Hall 2005),[9] despite debate and criticisms arising from the term "Mina" as examined by Robin Law (2005: 247-267), for example. Henry Lovejoy claims that the term "Lucumí" did not necessarily refer to Yoruba in Cuba, but as used in the sources was often hyphenated with some other ethnolinguistic term that complicates a simple correlation.[10] The possibility exists that individuals were interviewed or responded in Yoruba whether or not they actually also spoke another language and Yoruba was not their mother tongue. When the term is hyphenated with some other designation, such as Hausa, all that can be assumed is that the person so identified spoke at least two languages, Yoruba and Hausa.

Enslaved individuals and others in the database who were not necessarily enslaved at any point in their life are identified by the sub-region in Africa from whence the person came, when known. The increasing number of online archival databases of primary sources related to the history of the African diaspora and slavery have become freely and readily accessible for scholarly and public consumption. This proliferation of digital projects and databases presents a number of challenges related to aggregating data geographically according to the movement of people in and out of Africa across time and space. As a requirement to linking data of open-source digital projects, it has become necessary to delimit the entire continent of precolonial Africa during the era of the slave trade into broad regions and sub-regions that can allow the grouping of data effectively and meaningfully. The various sub-regions that have been identified apply a template that adheres to our Best Practices for the whole African continent which has been published in *History in Africa* for purposes of promoting scholarly reflection. *Freedom Narratives* focuses on West Africa, but other regions of Africa are relevant in some specific cases, such as that of Catherine Mulgrave Zimmermann, who was enslaved near Luanda in the region that has been named Kwanza North, taken to the Caribbean, and ultimately settled in the Voltaic region. Specific places are also identified; in this case Luanda, Spanish Town and Fairfield, Jamaica, and Accra on the Gold Coast. The identification of sub-regions is important when specific places are not included in the documentation, or origins are only identified by ethnonyms or language. When a person comes from a border area between two sub-regions, then both sub-regions are identified. In such cases it is usually impossible to determine which sub-region is the primary origin, and for purposes of searching the database, such exaction is not necessary. It should be noted that the Eurocentric designations of the Voyages database are specifically not used. Voyages divides Africa into coastal regions of departure that are seen from the bow of the slave ship and hence through the eyes of the slave traders and not from the perspective of the enslaved. From the perspective of West Africa, the sub-regional designations differ significantly from those adopted for the Slave Voyages database. First, no sub-region is identified by a term that can be confused with a modern country or a European colony, and no sub-region has a boundary that is identical to a modern or colonial boundary but to a great extent corresponds to geography and climate. Second, sub-regions have been determined according to historical patterns that characterized the period of the slave trade from the sixteenth to the nineteenth century and reflect political change during these four centuries.

The nine sub-regions that are most relevant to the *Freedom Narratives* project include the Sahara, the Senegambia basin that extends from the coast where the Senegal and Gambia Rivers enter the Atlantic inland to the source of these rivers in the Fuuta Jalon highlands; the upper Guinea Coast from Casamance to Cape Mount, bound inland by the Fuuta Jallon highlands and the interior of what is now the modern country of Sierra Leone and the headwaters of the Niger River; the Forests of West Africa include the territory inland from what could be called the Kru coast but stretching from Cape Mount to Grand Bassam and bound in the north by what is referred to as the western savannah, the sub-region that includes the savannah and sahel inland from the Senegambia basin to the middle Niger River basin southwestward from Timbuktu. The Voltaic sub-region incorporates the area east of Grand Bassam to the mouth of the Volta River and inland to the sources of the two branches of the Volta River. Continuing eastward, the Bight of Benin region includes the area from the Volta River to the eastern Niger River delta and northward to the confluence of the Niger and Benue Rivers and the area east of the Atakora Mountains. The Bight of Biafra hinterland includes the region to the east of the lower Niger River and south of the Benue River and extending to Cameroon as far as Gabon. Finally, the central savannah sub-region includes the region east of the Niger River below Timbuktu as far as the Lake Chad basin and southward to the Niger-Benue confluence. The fuzziness of some of the boundaries between these sub-regions is an important historical factor. Moreover, movement between and among sub-regions varied and is established in the database through several means, including identification of more specific places, the trade routes that crisscrossed West Africa, and other factors.

Conclusion

The *Freedom Narratives* website is an open source relational database comprised of original documentation in PDF format with metadata organized into data fields. The database facilitates access to all documentation through the public website. The intention is to enable the analysis of the important historical tragedy and crime against humanity that affected the history of Africa and was responsible for the demographic, cultural and social transformation of the Americas and elsewhere. The focus on biographical profiles of people in Africa during the era of the trans-Atlantic slave trade is an innovative approach to social history in relation to how the typical representation of enslaved Africans has been as numbers recorded in logs and accounts compiled by slave merchants and captains, as enumerated in *Voyages: The Trans-Atlantic Slave Trade Database* (www.slavevoyages.org). *Freedom Narratives* reveals the people who constitute the numbers.

Through its use of Controlled Vocabularies, the *Freedom Narrative* project provides a platform for the documentation and analysis of personal profiles of individuals who lived during the era of trans-Atlantic slavery and were identified with Africa. The collected data have required a reconceptualization of how Africa is perceived in terms of regionalization, the nature of ethnolinguistic data in historical context, and the interconnections between the various places within Africa and how these places were associated with trans-Saharan and trans-Atlantic migration. One of the problems with previous analysis is that patterns in the slave trade have been limited by uncertainties arising from a reliance on trans-Atlantic voyages and shipping data, which has resulted in the perception of Africa that was divided according to stretches of coast as seen from the decks of slave ships, not from the areas from where individuals came in Africa. Efforts to overcome this conceptual weakness have resulted in the analysis of the surviving names of individuals taken off slave ships, which in itself raises other conceptual problems in terms of deciphering the pronunciation of names and their identification with ethnolinguistic and religious factors that were internal to Africa.[11] *Freedom Narratives* carries the potential of resolving issues that are currently contentious, relying on information other than where ships took on their enslaved cargoes or the surviving names of those taken off slave ships as determined by scribes who could not have possibly distinguished where people came from on the basis of their names and did not attempt to do so.

Endnotes

1 We wish to thank Henry B. Lovejoy, Suzanne Schwarz, Sean Kelley, Jane Landers, Katrina Keefer, Bruno Véras, Leidy Alpízar, and Gwendolyn Midlo Hall for comments on the paper, as well as the editors of this volume. *Freedom Narratives* has been made possible because of financial support from the Social Sciences and Humanities Research Council of Canada and the Andrew W. Mellon Foundation.

2 An early effort to collect biographies of West Africans was Allan D. Austin, *African Muslims in Antebellum America: A Sourcebook* (New York: Garland, 1984). Also see studies of Venture Smith, Gustavus Vassa or Olaudah Equiano (P. Lovejoy 2006, 317-347), Muhammad Kaba Saghanughu (Daddi Addoun and P. Lovejoy 2007, 313-341), Ali Eisami (P. Lovejoy 2019), Catherine Mulgrave Zimmermann (P. Lovejoy 2011, 247-263), Mahommah Gardo Baquaqua (Law and P. Lovejoy 2001), and Nicholas Said (P. Lovejoy 2017, 219-232).

3 See, for example, seventeen contributions on testimonies included in the *UNESCO General History of Africa*, Vol. 10, Global Africa, General Editor, Augustin Holl.

4 See materials in the British Library Endangered Archives Programme, Preserving Nineteenth-Century Records in the Sierra Leone Public Archives (EAP782), Suzanne Schwarz, Director.

5 Kartikay Chadha, Katrina Keefer and Martha Ladly, "Decoding Origins Web Portal: Creating a Visual Database with Archival Sources from the Era of African Slavery," in this volume.

6 For example, www.epsg.io/map#srs=4326&x=-13.196640&y=8.430263&z=11&layer=streets.

7 See, for example, the "African Names Database" (www.african-origins.org) of David Eltis, Martin Halbert and Philip Misevich. Also see G. Ugo Nwokeji and David Eltis, "Characteristics of Captives Leaving the Cameroons for the Americas, 1822-37," *Journal of African History* 43:2 (2002), 191-210.

8 For a discussion of data justice, see Lina Dencik, Arne Hintz, Joanna Redden and Emiliano Treré, "Exploring Data Justice: Conceptions, Applications and Directions," *Information, Communication and Society* 22:7 (2019), 873-881.

9 Also see Lovejoy, "The African Diaspora: Revisionist Interpretations of Ethnicity, Culture and Religion under Slavery," *Studies in the World History of Slavery, Abolition and Emancipation*, II:1; Lovejoy and David V. Trotman, eds., *Trans-Atlantic Dimensions of Ethnicity in the African Diaspora* (London: Continuum, 2004); Lovejoy, "Transatlantic Transformations: The Origins and Identities of Africans in the Americas," in Boubacar Barry, Livio Sansone, and Elisée Soumonni, eds., *Africa, Brazil, and the Construction of Trans-Atlantic Black Identities* (Trenton, NJ: Africa

World Press), 81-112.

10 We wish to thank Henry Lovejoy for a discussion of the difficulty of Lucumí identification. Also see www.liberatedafricans.org.

11 For attempts to confront these problems, see Daniel B. Domingues da Silva, David Eltis, Nafees Khan, Philip Misevich and Olatunji Ojo, "The Transatlantic Muslim Diaspora to Latin America in the Nineteenth Century," *Colonial Latin American Review* 26:4 (2017), and Domingues, Eltis, Misevich and Ojo, "The Diaspora of Africans Liberated from Slave Ships in the Nineteenth Century," *Journal of African History* 55:3 (2014), 347-69.

7

Decoding Origins:

Creating a Visual Database from the Registers of Liberated Africans

Kartikay Chadha, Katrina Keefer, Martha Ladly

The trans-Atlantic slave trade was a centuries-long crime against humanity that saw over 12.5 million Africans forcibly taken from their homes and transported to work in the emerging plantation societies of the Americas. Those who survived the Middle Passage faced a pervasive effort to erase their African identities. The trauma of enslavement and sustained repression of language, culture, and beliefs, blurred enslaved individuals' memories and knowledge of their origins, their familial lineages, and their birthplaces. Attempts have been made to enable the descendants of former slaves to learn their histories by analyzing large datasets of names recorded in manumission records. These approaches are methodologically challenged by practices of slave renaming. The registers of Liberated Africans generated in the early nineteenth century in Sierra Leone contain thousands of entries that can be used to develop new methods to solve this problem with greater precision. This research project engages with this data to discover unique identifiers of African pre-slavery identities. Records of manumitted slaves include visual descriptions of body markings, including intricate tattoos and scarification that can be used to specifically identify societies and branches of a given family. The research question then is how to collect, analyze and present the considerable information within these datasets, in conjunction with culturally sensitive user design and ethno-linguistic and visual analysis, to extract meaningful information and reconstruct digital identities.

The foundational premise for the original project, which was entitled *Decoding Origins: Creating a Visual Language of Marks* was to address historical wrongs and the problems of lost identities created by the global slave trade and to ask how a visual approach to data collection could give rise to new discoveries and findings. The research and design team for this project and for the tool which arose from it is a culturally diverse group of including women researchers, people of color, and people of diverse sexual orientations. Cultural sensitivity is very important to our research process, and to our ongoing task of honoring the individuals whose lives and histories and bodies make up the information that we often hesitate to call "data." Our research objectives were to develop new paradigms through the collection, analysis, and visualization of information from nineteenth century slave manumission records and accounts, with specific reference to registers of Liberated Africans, which have been collected and digitized within the Sierra Leone Public Archives in Freetown, Sierra Leone. We employed historical and archival research in an interdisciplinary methodological approach adapted from art, history, design, and the digital humanities, with the application of accessible platforms and interfaces for lab and field work.

Incorporating user-sensitive design principles, we developed a collaborative database using Structured Query Language (SQL) and a user-friendly interactive platform employing novel algorithms to collect, analyze, and cross-reference data. With shared core principles including best practices for data collection, data descriptors, controlled vocabularies, meta-tagging, and analyses, our data "talks to" other open-source, online digital repositories, and databases of similar nature. We developed Deep Neural Network models to perform visual data analyses, semi-automating the transcription of the documents and cross-referencing information within the database(s). With these tools, we have reconstructed enslaved African digital identities, based on positive identification of their body markings recorded in the registers. We have sought to understand how this visual data collection, curation, visualization, and semi-automated analysis might help uncover new knowledge more quickly. Our visual database enables researchers and others to review, compare and decode visualized marks connoting individual identities, which may assist scholars and members of the public in better understanding critical questions of African identities and origins.

The main task of the *Language of Marks* project revolved around the accessible design and deployment of a visual database and an interface which could facilitate storage, access, and analysis of textual and visual information, by scholars and the public. To address these challenges, we developed a web-based platform and searchable visual database enabling body marks to be analyzed accurately, potentially revealing individual identities and origins. We are testing machine learning-based virtual mathematical models that are capable of cross-referencing marks from the registers – our pilot dataset – with all known patterns in the database, powering the likelihood of identifying kinship and birthplace. This approach sheds new light on demographic change, individual identities, and patterns of slave-taking. The new interfaces we have designed, the data visualizations, and the database, are tools to study familial history as we further refine them. The digital architecture is constructed to allow specialists to add and organize information for diverse analyses, and to ideate and perform research projects based on curated data. Our ultimate goals are to respect the provenance of important digital identities, and to use our design, data gathering, analytics and visualization skills to join with ongoing efforts to restore and recover African identities which the slave trade sought to erase.

Background and Motivation

Identity is complex at the best of times. We position ourselves in relation to our communities, our enemies, and our ancestors as we define ourselves. For Africans since antiquity, those relationships are codified and inscribed upon the skin in the forms of tattoos and scarification. Individuals are acculturated by their communities, with marks on faces and on bodies that signify systems of kinship, membership in initiation societies, personal accomplishments, and even illnesses which have been treated (Armitage 1924; Thévoz 1984; Schildkrout 2004; Keefer 2018). The skins of peoples who mark and are marked become texts which narrate the lives and relationships of individuals. And like a text, these narratives may be read if one is familiar with the orthography (Ojo 2008). Readings are personal; if one is an insider, the meanings which are conveyed may be nuanced and complex, while if one is an outsider, the meaning may simply be an association with a particular ethnolinguistic group. To a Gba-Mende, for example, facial and body marks may signify membership and individual rank in the regional Poro society along with kinship and community standing. To someone from a region that does not practice Poro, those marks simply indicate that a person is from the upper Guinea coast. The nuances are lost, but identification remains possible (Keefer 2013).

This work becomes particularly important in the context of the trans-Atlantic slave trade. A multi-century trauma, the trade systematically dehumanized and exploited those who survived the journey across the ocean and to survive in unstable communities, often in isolation. Renamed, far from home and without much hope of returning, the survivors of this forced migration endured incredible hardships in the slave societies of the Americas. Today, their descendants must struggle to trace their ancestry beyond the fracturing that was the Middle Passage. These are obscured identities, and while they are not lost entirely, reconstructing them is challenging. The importance of doing so is central to our research: those whose ancestors were commodified in this fashion have faced discrimination, ongoing marginalization, and violence. The effort to restore what has been taken historically is crucial to rebuilding identities and personal histories, and to addressing the crime against humanity which was the trans-Atlantic trade.

While those taken from the continent were often renamed multiple times, those who were marked in Africa did not lose those identifiers of their communities, their homes, and their lives. Their marked bodies have been recorded over time in a variety of locations – documents of sale, manumission papers, runaway slave ads, and volumes of liberation are some of the many sources which exist in archives throughout the Atlantic world. By developing a digital catalog of patterns – in effect, translating the language of marks we see written on skin – we can cross-reference historical documents describing these marks with an individual's identity prior to their transportation from Africa. This permits a new means of decoding identity and reading those embodied texts.

Design Thinking

The *Language of Marks* research team adopted "design thinking" methods to assist in our understanding of current methodologies followed by researchers of the trans-Atlantic trade and the difficulties and challenges for those working with related historical documents. Design thinking provides a framework for identifying and approaching complex problems and learning from experiences. This methodology was valuable in assisting us to formulate computational-based solutions, to address and surmount some of these challenges. Design thinking provides a productive, iterative approach used to engage divergent thinking (Greenwood et al. 2019), and to better understand the complexities faced by our researchers and eventually, members of the public, in handling this massive volume of analog and digitized information. Hence, Design Thinking offered an appropriate process to iterate our research approach in five successive stages: 1) Empathize, 2) Define, 3) Ideate, 4) Prototype, and 5) Test (Brodny and Kazmierczak 2017). The following sections elaborate on our motivations, and our efforts, to move this research from a mostly analog method to a mixed analog and digital approach, within these five iterations of the *Language of Marks* research.

Empathize

The empathize stage is used to discover and characterize the users of the data, and their requirements through various need-finding tools. The empathize stage is designed to better understand the needs of users – and not to find solutions. The need-finding tools may include interviews, detailed observations, diary studies, experience sampling, logging studies, user observations, etc. This step is one of the most important in the design process that enables the developer/designer to analyze the current methodological workflow to solve a particular research question and clearly define the design-based problem statements. Moreover, it also gives an opportunity for the developers/designers to understand the expectations of the users.

At this stage, we attempted to understand the current analog methodologies followed by other researchers working with historical documents, to contextualize these methods into steps, and to identify the challenges and steps that can be improved using digital technologies. One of our co-leads, Keefer, participated in the first iteration of our interdisciplinary approach, merging her analog research with digital technologies and ideation tools. Keefer had developed a method for tracing the origins of enslaved Africans through a close comparison of their facial and body scarification (Keefer 2013). Her work before this collaboration with Ladly was a slow and painstaking process of researching body markings through published works and her own archival research. While she was successful, the process was time consuming and inefficient. Keefer's early exploratory meetings with Ladly and researcher Chadha closely concerned the process of empathizing.

All team members were required to spend time learning about the broader context of the project, to understand the history of the slave trade, the cultural sensitivities of the information, and the magnitude of the proposed task. Working with African and diaspora collaborators, sharing expertise and absorbing information, the teams collectively learned from one another, refined processes and began to develop culturally sensitive research design approaches. Culturally sensitive design advocates that "the use of culturally sensitive research approaches to African and African American issues can use the cultural knowledge and experiences of researchers and their participants in the design of the research, as well as in the collection and interpretation of data" (Tillman 2002). We organized bi-weekly meetings with collaborators to train each member in the historical context of the trans-Atlantic trade, to explore available technologies, and to address problems of sensitive means of data-handling, identification, and codification of the enslaved individual's histories and recorded body markings.

Our *Language of Marks* design team members created an Empathetic Study, to analyze the analog method currently in use, to understand each step, and to identify those that could potentially be semi-automated, or automated. Over the course of this study, we worked closely with the *Freedom Narratives* research team (Chapter 6), to understand the complete process and best practices of creating biographies of liberated individuals. We organized multiple workshops with *Freedom Narratives* in 2019 and conducted one-on-one interviews and group interviews with five researchers from *Freedom Narratives*, to understand and identify the technical challenges faced in handling and recording enslaved individual's datasets using the current analog methodology. There follows a description of our study of the analog method, our findings, and suggested improvements, working towards the development and adoption of automated and semi-automated approaches to this important and sensitive data.

Analog Methods

As the research team applied Keefer's analog methodology to the development of a digital platform and interaction tools, we also adopted the analog processes of the *Freedom Narratives* team, with recommendations from Matrix at Michigan State University and other collaborators at that point who were working with similar historical documents. The following section describes the detailed study we undertook of the analog method developed by the *Freedom Narratives* team, which has since been refined, semi-automated, and adopted by our research team. We have divided the complete corpus into four major categories: people, events, places, and sources (Table 7.1), which was initially developed and applied in the construction of *Liberated Africans* (chapter 5). This four-part schema contains further data categories (henceforth named data fields) to capture information from the sources and build relationships between the four major categories.

The tools used for data reorganization and meta-tagging for a computer readable database were Google Drive, Google Docs, Microsoft Excel, and Adobe PDF Pro Reader. The people, events, places, and sources categories are represented both as four spreadsheets and documents (in Microsoft Excel document files and Google Doc files). The columns of spreadsheets represent data fields and rows containing reorganized information taken from historical documents, such as registers of Liberated Africans. The sources that are in spreadsheet format contain direct links to digitized archival files in PDF/JPG/JPEG/PNG formats that re uploaded to a shared Google Drive folder, which consist of multiple folders, whereby every folder was assigned to an individual in the database. The people folder contained a case file for unique digital identities created by the project directors with initial details on the person, helping researchers to search and locate the source documents. All processed digitized files, source documents, and images associated with a person, were also uploaded to these folders. A separate folder contained the raw versions of all files. The team followed standard file naming conventions, decided upon, documented, and described in their shared best practices documentation.

Table 7.1
The Four Categories and their Definitions

The Four Categories

1. ***Person*** : This category captures all the information or data about an individual that may be common among sources. Examples of these data fields include *Name, Alternative Names, Age, Gender, Offspring* etc. The *Person* category also captures the relationships between individuals within this dataset.

2. ***Event*** : This category contains all known life events of an individual, (such as enslavement, ship transport, manumission, apprenticeship, criminal charge, marriage, death) supported directly or imputed from various sources. FN defines eligible inclusion of a person into the dataset only if at least five directly or imputed events can be identified for that individual. Example data fields include: *Type of Event, Start Date, End Date* etc.

3. ***Place*** : This Category consists of a list of all places associated with *Persons* and *Events*, including all recorded details. Example data fields include: *Place Name, Region, Longitude, Latitude* etc.

4. ***Source*** : This Category consists of the actual raw data, or a part of an original source from a historical document, and captures all meta-information about that document. Example data fields include: *Title, Copyright Permissions* etc.

Initially, after the Person file entry was completed and reviewed at least twice, the folder along with all four spreadsheets was manually sent to the Matrix developers at Michigan State University, who then batch imported these files to the project server, updating the database and making files available on their public website, via KORA.[1] The Matrix team used programming languages including HTML supported by JavaScript and CSS styling, supported by MySQL databases and PHP and an Apache/2.4.33 (Unix) PHP/7.2.1 server hosted by Michigan State University. Subsequently, it was realized that new tools derived from implementation of the *Language of Marks* project and in collaboration with the Freedom Narratives project, that there was a structural difference contained within the *Language of Marks* project that divided the actual website with the backend of data entry. *Language of Marks* thereby spawned new tools, first *Decoding Origins*, and then following its transformation into *Regenerated Identities*, which allowed the *Freedom Narratives* team to enter data (one person at a time) directly, using a new platform, for real-time updates on the website. These digital identities and other data were then published on the *Freedom Narratives* website.

The data fields for each of the four categories adopted by *Liberated Africans*, *Language of Marks*, *Freedom Narratives*, and other websites are listed in Table 7.2. Some of the underlined data fields have predefined and evolving lists of controlled vocabularies that are saved in a separate Microsoft Excel/Google Doc spreadsheet tabs or text documents. Researchers use controlled vocabularies to enter cell values in the rows of the four main category spreadsheets and are constantly updated with each discovery of a new term in the data. All new entries in the controlled vocabularies are reviewed and discussed by project directors before being added.

Table 7.2
Data Fields for the Four Categories

PERSON	EVENT	PLACE	SOURCE
Person ID	Person ID	Place Identifier	Person ID
Name	Name	Place Name	FN Title
Alternative Names	Event Type*	Place Type*	Title
Ethnonym/ Language*	Status*	Latitude	Creator
Ethnonym/ Language in Original*	Age	Longitude -- city	Description
Region of Origin*	Age Category*	Variant Names	Publisher (Digital Source)
Region of Destination*	Start Date	Modern Equivalent	Contributor (Intellectual)
Gender*	End Date	City/Town	Date Original (YYYY-MM-DD)

Physical Characteristics*	Imputed Date	Province	Language*
Relationships (Kinship)[#]	Circa Period	Country / Colony	Date Digital (YYYY-MM-DD)
Literacy	Event Description	Country (Modern)	Resource Type*
Literacy - Language*	Event Identifier	Region*	Format
Summary	Occupation*		Source (Archival/ Collection)
Researcher's name	Relationship		Rights Management*
Source	Place*		Contributing Institution
Contributing Project IDs[&]	Place Identifier		Source Type*
Register ID	Religion*		Image
Data Entry	Brotherhood/ Church		Source PDF
	Sources		Document Pages
			Page Number
			Resource Identifier
			Notes
			Display
			Archive
			Event Associator
			Transcript
			Researcher Name
			Data Entry

[*]Data fields that have predefined and evolving lists of controlled vocabularies that are saved in a separate Microsoft Excel/Google Doc spreadsheet tabs or text documents.

[#]The Relationship record two variables: 1) Type of Relationship 2) Name or Unique ID of the person related

[&]Contributing projects include *Liberated Africans*, *Harvard Biographies*, *Freedom Narratives* and *Le Marronnage* project.

Analog Process

Based on detailed observations from our workshops and discussions with the *Freedom Narratives* team, the *Language of Marks* research team summarized the analog process into eight steps:

1. The project directors created shared Google Drive folders for each individual and assigned them a unique identifier (*Freedom Narratives* (FN) IDs). The folder was uploaded with at least one case file that contained brief information from one of the four categories, about each person. Researchers were assigned a range of FN IDs which were all listed on a shared Google Doc file for tracking progress. Subsequent developments overrode these initial details.
2. Researchers identified the folders for the *Freedom Narratives* IDs assigned to them. They reviewed the case file and searched original source documents for a limited period. If a source was not found, the missing data were added to the spreadsheet for the person ID, a step that was made unnecessary after further development.
3. Alternatively, if the source documents were found, they were to be downloaded and saved in a separate, shared folder of raw files on Google Drive. The relevant portions of the raw files were then to be cropped, highlighted, and uploaded to a person's folder. All files were to be passed through an Optical Character Recognition (OCR) computer program and then edited or cropped and highlighted, using the Adobe PDF Pro Reader.
4. A summary of people based on source documents was to be created and saved as a text file in the Person's folder.
5. The source spreadsheet was to be updated with the details of the documents and the information reorganized into data fields. Spreadsheets or text files containing controlled vocabularies were to be referred to, and all data for these inventories were to be entered to spreadsheets. This step has become redundant with the development of RegID.
6. Based on all sources, life events were to be identified for people, and the events spreadsheet was then supposed to be updated with each event. In case of a relationship event (for example a birth event relating a person with their parent/mother/father), the type of relationship was to be recorded in one of the events data fields along with either name or ID (if the related person exists in the database) of the related person. With RegID, the controlled vocabulary has been greatly expanded that has required many adjustments.
7. All events were thought to be linked to an object, a term that was later considered to be confusing and instead the term "source" was adopted. The primary documentation for the person and was to be recorded in the sources data field of the events spreadsheet, but in the development of RegID, the need for a spreadsheet has disappeared.
8. The people spreadsheet was to be updated with all shared information from sources. Any non-event relationships were to be recorded in the people spreadsheet following the same format including type of relationship and name or FN ID of the person. The development of

RegID has greatly simplified this process.

Improving the Analog Process

In addition to the workshops, the *Language of Marks* design team conducted one on one informal interviews with five *Freedom Narratives* team researchers in 2019, followed by an informal group interview with the same five participants. All participants were coded with a unique identifying number to maintain anonymity, avoiding any biases in the analysis. Four out of five had worked on the Freedom Narrative project for more than 18 months. One researcher started working four weeks prior to our interview sessions and was undergoing the training process. The interview sessions with the participants helped our team to understand their experiences with the current analog method of data curation and organization, and form in depth conclusions regarding the challenges they faced. The feedback from the fifth participant informed us on the difficulty, or ease of use of the current analog method, in terms of research learnings and how the training method could be improved. These observations in turn informed our design decisions on the development of automated and semi-automated data recording practices.

One of the common challenges mentioned by three out of five researchers concerned the rigorous process of looking up terms in the controlled vocabularies, while updating the Four Categories spreadsheets. Participants in our study related the following experiences:

> I have many spreadsheets tabs or text files open at the same time while updating just object data. I feel lost between switching applications and that distracts me from focusing on the real research work, like writing the person's summary!

> I am always very careful about copying terms from the controlled vocabulary to any of the main spreadsheets. They need to be exactly the same, so the overall data is clean.

Another participant added that any addition of a new term to the controlled vocabulary discovered while working with data needed to be discussed by the team and approved by project directors. They added that this process could take time and progress tracking could then become difficult. A researcher said that they created a local spreadsheet to keep track of new terms and another to keep a check on progress of work with every digital identity assigned to them i.e., recording what percentage of data fields were completed in any one record. During the group interview, this issue was one that all participants agreed was a challenge.

During another one-on-one interview, while navigating through the *Freedom Narratives* project Google Drive, another participant related: "I have no idea who made these changes on the drive and reorganized the files!

– This doesn't follow best practices and I have to fix this!" Clearly this was a tracking problem that had to be resolved through semi-automation. Under the "Activity" option within Google Drive applications, users can review a log of changes made to the drive. Recorded activities cannot be categorized separately by users, however, as data are organized across various files and folders. This realization led to a cross-referencing system between the Google Drive application and our data-entry systems.

Outcomes of the Empathetic Study of the Analog Process

During the group interview session, researchers discussed various questions and comments that arose, which could require further analysis, and potentially, technical intervention:

1. How can a new data field be introduced to any of the four-part schema; how will this effect, or be displayed on, the public website?
2. Some events may not have an exact start date. How can this be shown on a visual timeline? Can we manually decide the order of events?
3. How can we edit the design and layout of the public website? (Questions referred to various place holders on the website.)
4. Can the database provide feedback to users, in case the best practices are violated?

Participant ID 4 reported that he/she had about 473 folders for people on the Google Drive. About 125 sources had been located for 75 people, of whom only 56 digital identities were reorganized, reviewed, and entered on the spreadsheet over the previous 12 months. Accordingly, the overall progress rate on manual database production using the analog method was calculated to be very low over the twelve-month period.

Definition Process for *Problem Statements*

In this stage of development, we reviewed our detailed observations from the *Freedom Narratives* team during workshops and the interview sessions to reconsider our initial goals. At this stage in the formal process of Design Thinking, the Project team re-examined the stated challenges and needs of the users and reframed questions to seek best possible solutions. The *Freedom Narratives* data curation analog method was a combination of traditional research-based tasks (e.g., finding the relevant sources, entering data, writing summaries etc.) and technical tasks (organizing data in Google Drive folders, creating spreadsheets etc.). It was clear that *Freedom Narratives* the further codification, which is when Decoding Origins originated as a distinct backend for websites.

Although the computer tools being used at that point proved beneficial in data curation (Google Drive Applications, Microsoft Excel and Adobe PDF Reader), they came with various limitations and challenges, particularly when dealing with complex historical data. Moreover, we noted low uptake of features available within computer applications, among some researchers with minimal experience working with these tools, e.g., activity tracking, assignment of tasks within the document by linking a person's email address, using editing and suggestion modes on Google Docs.

Problem statements allow a research team using Design Thinking to form insights for the ideation process. The following problem statements and insights garnered from our empathetic study review were as follows:

1. The amount of data collected and reorganized requires computer programs that can easily access and process a high volume of data. The public database was developed using MySQL programming language which has proven to be an ideal choice of computer tool for the data. However, researcher access to the database was mediated by excel sheets and was limited.
2. The digitized documents were mostly in PDF, JPG, JPEG or PNG formats, and were organized on Google Drive, following standard naming conventions, and were linked to the Microsoft Excel sheets or Google Docs. Replacement and reorganization of Google Drive as a storage platform would lead to a discrepancy in the links attached to the Excel sheets, this then leading to incorrect linking between the Excel sheet records and actual source file. This was a reason that spreadsheets were eliminated.
3. Searching through spreadsheets and cross-referencing them with source files and other spreadsheets can only be done manually while the data is curated. Once uploaded to the *Freedom Narrative* server, the front-end website would have to be used to view all data, categorized using various filters.
4. It was envisioned that multiple technical tasks would be manually performed to enable future automatic cross-referencing within the database. This included entering unique identifiers in spreadsheets, without any visual aid representing these relationships. For example, FN IDs were assigned to every individual and were recorded in people, events, places, and sources spreadsheets, which were to be used to connect across

spreadsheets to search and display information on the public website. The actions of relationships between individuals on people or events spreadsheets was thereby recorded.

5. No computerized feedback or warning was available for researchers while working within the analog methodology, in case the best practices were violated.
6. The implementation of controlled vocabulary was based on standards described in detail in best practices. To manually cross-reference terms in the controlled vocabulary that exist in multiple spreadsheets or tabs or text files while entering or reorganizing data was a problem.

Challenges and Needs

Employing a Design Thinking protocol within an empathetic study, observations garnered during the need finding process allowed us to ideate the following challenges and needs:

1. The challenges revolved around the design and development of computer tools and a database portal, and a user-friendly visual interface that facilitates access, contributions, collection, identification, organization and re-organization, and analyses of historical documents, by scholars and eventually, by the public.
2. To do this, we needed to design new computer tools and protocols that provided a) real time visualization of the data during curation; b) feedback based on best practices; and c) offers team work based environment, customized to the terminologies defined by our users; which d) would improve the research progress rate of *Freedom Narratives*, and which e) we could also apply to *Language of Marks* as it developed.

At this stage, our design team brainstormed and ideated multiple approaches to overcome the challenges identified by the *Freedom Narratives* team in our Empathetic Study. This is pertinent to *Language of Marks*, as researchers were developing a similar type of Digital Humanities project, using similar materials, and with similar challenges. As we developed our project, we consulted with the *Freedom Narratives* team in the development process. They were able to use our tools and interfaces and provide feedback on multiple sections of the new computer tool while it was in its developmental stages, continuously refining the tool in iterative cycles. In addition to consultation with the five *Freedom Narratives* team participants, we also continuously reviewed our ideas within our own project team, and with collaborators from *Liberated Africans* at the University of Colorado, Boulder.

We proposed to create a user-friendly web-based portal, where collaborators, researchers and students could collect, re-organize, transcribe, and visualize data (including relationships amongst the data). Furthermore, the portal would provide a collaborative team environment, and a direct connection to the public website, giving researchers more control over real-time online publications and editing curated data. This portal would mitigate or address ongoing challenges with other Digital Humanities publications and develop new, efficient methodologies that could be shared across platforms. Based on our ideation and feedback processes, our design team mocked up speculative prototype interfaces for the database portal. We then organized a culturally-sensitive design workshop, working with our diasporic and African colleagues. *Freedom Narratives* researchers walked through the proposed prototypes alongside our *Language of Marks* design team, to gain valuable feedback.

In terms of organization, the information on the portal is organized into folders that are listed on the HTML home page of the portal (Fig.7.1-a). Each folder or list item has a consolidated editing page for people, events, places, and sources with re-organized data fields (Fig. 7.1-b). Events associated with a person's life were editable on another HTML page (Fig. 7.1-c). Controlled vocabularies were provided as dropdown menus. The portal provides different levels of access to users categorized as researchers, project managers, and administrators. Researchers have limitations to their access that restricts them from assigning tasks or creating a new Person entry within the folder. These tasks are allocated to users with project manager's access clearance. Administrators typically include those on the development team with technical expertise, who have full control over the portal and have access to all features. Only administrators may add new data fields or add new terms to controlled vocabularies. See the figures below for visuals of the prototype interfaces that evolved from our culturally sensitive design workshops.

Figure 7.1
Original Design of Front End User Interfaces

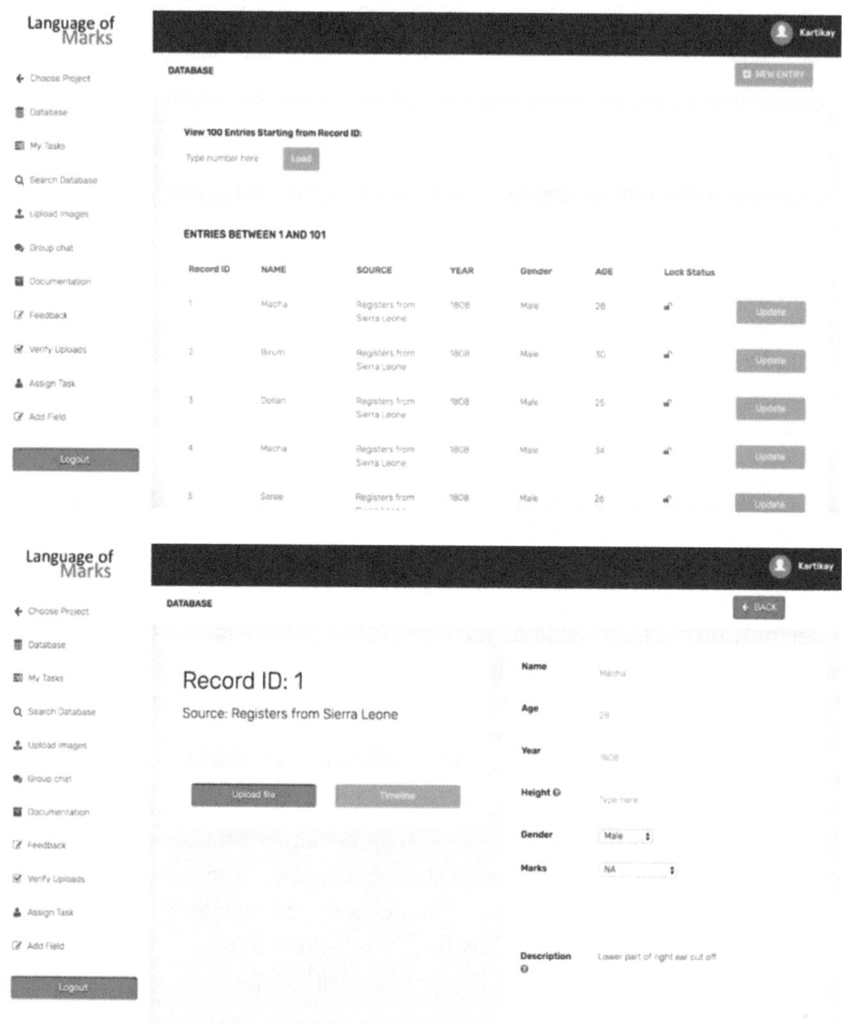

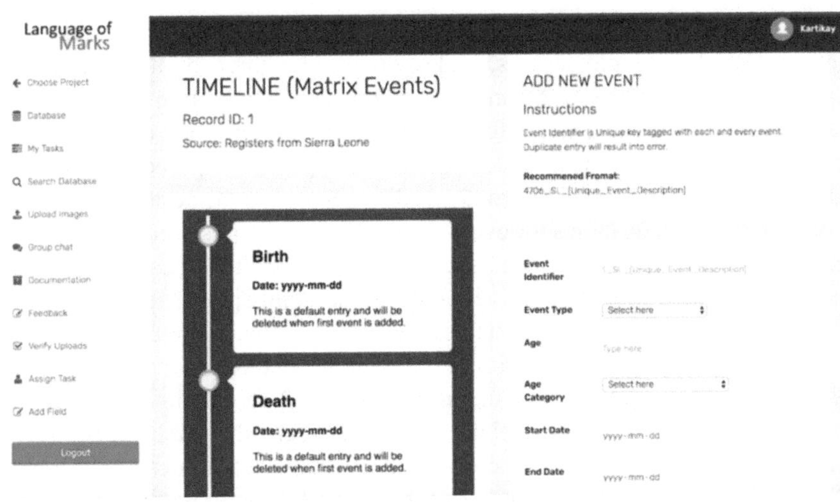
Language of Marks
Kartikay
Choose Project
Database
My Tasks
Search Database
Upload images
Group chat
Documentation
Feedback
Verify Uploads
Assign Task
Add Field
Logout
TIMELINE (Matrix Events)
Record ID: 1
Source: Registers from Sierra Leone
Birth
Date: yyyy-mm-dd
This is a default entry and will be deleted when first event is added.
Death
Date: yyyy-mm-dd
This is a default entry and will be deleted when first event is added.
ADD NEW EVENT
Instructions
Event Identifier is Unique key tagged with each and every event.
Duplicate entry will result into error.
Recommened Fromat:
4706_SL_[Unique_Event_Description]
Event Identifier
Event Type
Select here
Age
Age Category
Select here
Start Date
yyyy-mm-dd
End Date
yyyy-mm-dd

Language of Marks
Kartikay
Choose Project
Database
My Tasks
Search Database
Upload images
Group chat
Documentation
Feedback
Verify Uploads
Assign Task
Add Field
Logout
ENTRIES
Record ID
Name
Source
Marks
Creator
Assigned to
Re-Assign to
Registers from Sierra Leone
Kartikay
Select User
Assign

The data section in Fig. 7.2 includes MySQL tables recording re-organized information for people, events, and sources, like three of the four main categories as described in the analog method. The data section also contains tables with lists of data fields for each of the three data categories (people, events, and places). These tables are for all types of required documents, allowing customization of the frontend editing forms on the portal. Controlled vocabularies include tables for every data field that requires predefined terms, e.g., name, gender, religion etc. Every term in controlled vocabulary tables have unique identifiers that are recorded in the main spreadsheet (replacing the actual term). This method enables real-time editing of pre-existing terms within the controlled vocabularies, throughout the database.

The database architecture diagram in Fig. 7.2 represents the structure of the database, and the relationships between the tables and their connections. Places are now incorporated as a controlled vocabulary table. The relationship section in Fig. 7.2 consists of tables with mostly identifiers representing (n to n) relationships between the people, events, and sources entries. All rows in these three data categories now have their own identifiers (people, event, and source IDs) that build associations in relationships tables. In the analog method, sources spreadsheets contain associated people IDs as a data field, requiring duplication of rows to mark associations of a source with multiple people. This method is applied for source to person (table name: person, source); events to person (table name: person_event); and person to person (table name: person_kinship) relationships.

The frontend interface of the web portal is designed to provide a team based work environment. We have introduced new workflow features, e.g., forward and reply to assignments with direct messages, and group chats to promote better collaboration. In the newest version of the portal, we have been able to strictly implement the analog method and associated best practices. For example, the portal allows only users with project director or administrative access to create new Person entries; to assign tasks to researchers; to approve the addition of term to the Controlled Vocabularies; and to publish information to the online website. As all the data now exists on the same back-end architecture and server, manual transfer and organization is no longer required. The portal also allows users to upload multi-format files to the server directly; it automatically renames the file as per best practices, organizes it within the *Freedom Narratives* folders system, and creates an entry in the object table.

Figure 7.2
Database Architecture of the Portal

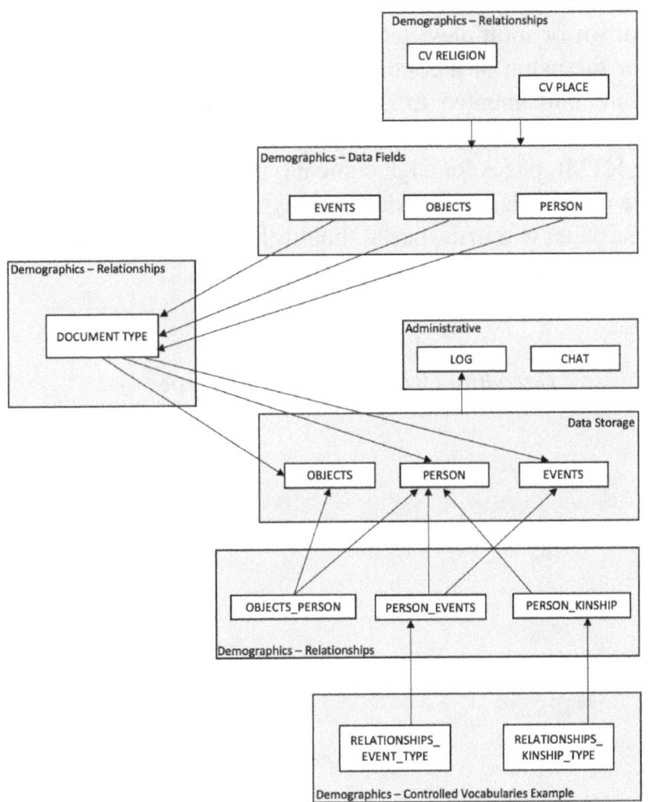

In contrast to our initial proposed design, the consolidated data editing page (7.3-b) of the portal is now split into three sections: people, events, and sources (Figure 7.3-a). All events for a person are listed in events data and each event has its own editing page, like the people data page. The attached objects (Figure 7.3-c) are listed with personalized editing forms. The grey boxes on the right-side bar (Figure 7.3-a) of the page represent person_person or person_events relationships, providing people and events data HTML editing pages, respectively. We introduced "document type" to categorize different types of documents and provide customized forms, e.g., Person, Event, Place, Source, case files etc. All document type data fields are pre-loaded for the project in the data section, as explained earlier. Data fields for all categories may have text, text area, date, time, dropdown, multiple-select or radio-type inputs, as appropriate.

The document type table also records data field type information. In the case of dropdown or multiple-select, either a list of values separated by a semi-colon, or the name of a controlled vocabulary table is required. Such algorithms were implemented to provide maximum administrative access to researchers with non-technical expertise. The intention for the portal is to create editing HTML pages for all document type tables, allowing researchers to add/remove data fields, change data field types, or create a new document type, etc. These pages within the portal should eliminate the major requirement of on-demand technical assistance for the research team.

Fig. 7.3 a-d

***Decoding Origins Portal* Prototype**

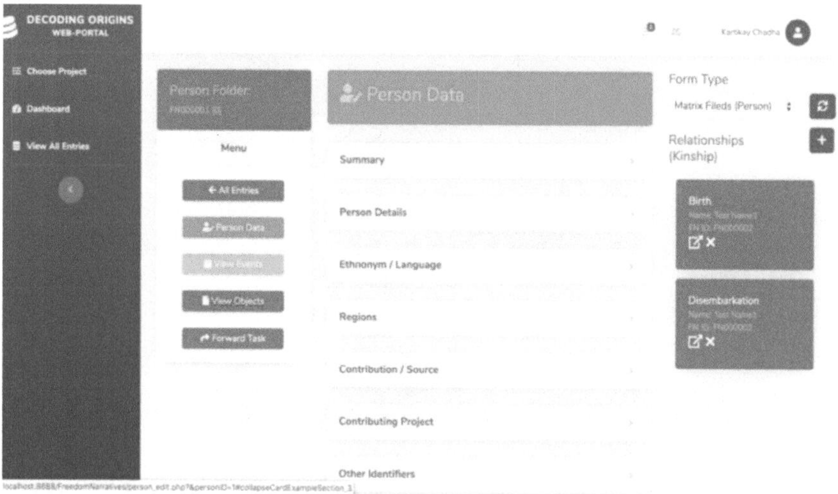

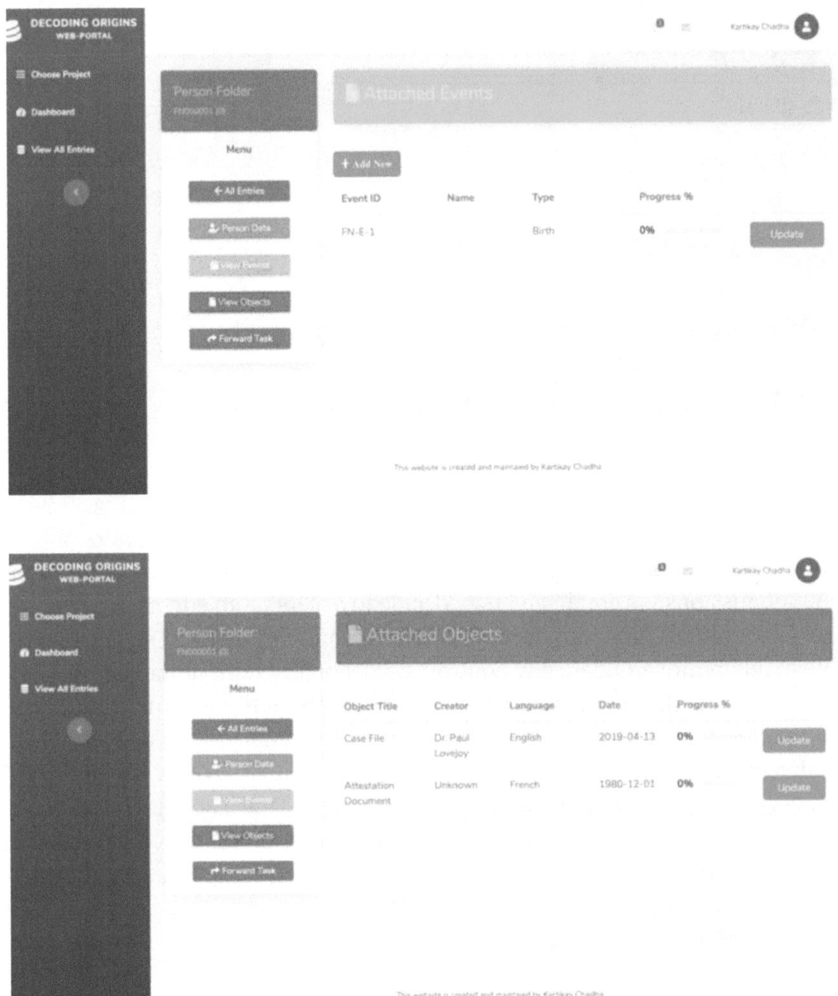
DECODING ORIGINS
WEB-PORTAL
Choose Project
Dashboard
View All Entries
Kartikay Chadha
Person Folder
Attached Events
Menu
Add New
All Entries
Person Data
View Events
View Objects
Forward Task
Event ID
Name
Type
Progress %
FN-E-1
Birth
0%
Update
This website is created and maintained by Kartikay Chadha
DECODING ORIGINS
WEB-PORTAL
Choose Project
Dashboard
View All Entries
Kartikay Chadha
Person Folder
Attached Objects
Menu
All Entries
Person Data
View Events
View Objects
Forward Task
Object Title
Creator
Language
Date
Progress %
Case File
Dr. Paul Lovejoy
English
2019-04-13
0%
Update
Attestation Document
Unknown
French
1980-12-01
0%
Update
This website is created and maintained by Kartikay Chadha

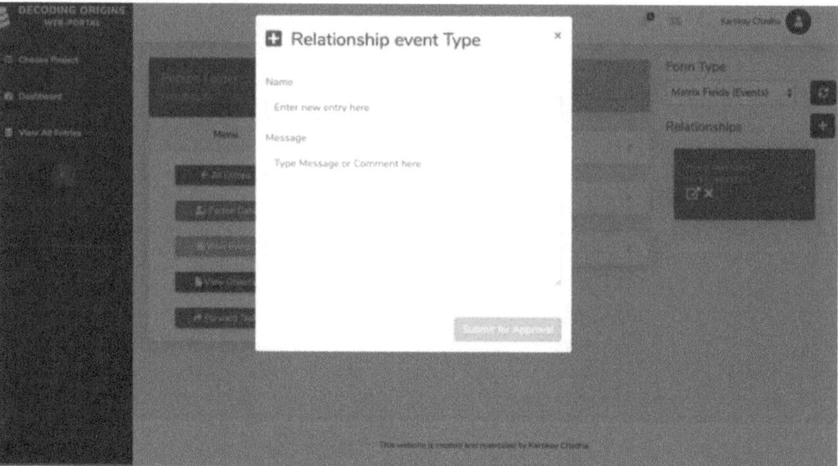

We also created controlled vocabularies submission forms (Fig. 7.3-d) that allowed researchers to submit new terms to the project directors, along with a personalized message or comments. Project directors were notified of new submissions via email, and they decide to accept or, to edit and accept the new terms for addition into the controlled vocabularies tables. They were also able to add/remove/update any controlled vocabulary term in the database.

Moreover, the portal was set up to log every activity on the interface. All updates were recorded in the log table that contained type of entry (edit or delete or add); data table information (people or events or sources); associated IDs; researchers names; and changes in data. The log HTML page filtered the table with entries for people, events, or sources; hence providing a complete documentation of all researcher workflows, including every update, along with a timestamp. A progress monitor was set up to track activities for every researcher, providing team contribution insights, for reference by the researchers and the project directors.

A preliminary testing protocol was designed for *Freedom Narratives* researchers/users to interact with the new *Language of Marks* portal prototype. Researchers tested both the functionality of the data portal, and the prototype Visual Interfaces for the portal, with reactions from the experienced users on the *Freedom Narratives* team positive and promising. These expert users walked through the functions of the portal with the design team and had an opportunity to interact with the new features and visual interfaces, completing tasks and queries, while researchers answered questions and made observations or notations.

Testing with the "Think Aloud" Method

For testing purposes, the *Language of Marks* design team implemented a "think-a-loud" testing and feedback methodology (Van Someren 1994). In this testing protocol, users continuously voice their questions and reactions to their experiences and interactions with the prototype, literally "thinking aloud" while using the prototype interfaces, testing new features, and performing both familiar and unfamiliar tasks.

The design team made detailed notes and user-observations during these sessions, without ever leading or directing the *Freedom Narratives* participants. After the "think-a-loud" sessions, the users and designers gathered for a debrief. They critiqued the new prototypes, and brainstormed together, offering user feedback and recommendations for improvements for the next iteration of the portal's functionality and interfaces. Designers asked questions such as: "Did you understand where and how you were navigating portal interfaces?" "Do you think this prototype could improve your efficiency?" "Would you use this tool for your work?" or "How might the portal's functions assist you to re-organize information from the historical documents?" as well as "What did you think wasn't working well?" and "What confuses you in this interface?" to "How could we improve our designs to make this portal and interface/ interaction/task more helpful, efficient or meaningful?" All this feedback was recorded for inclusion in the upcoming iterations of the *Language of Marks* portal, our visual interfaces, and data visualizations.

User Testing Responses

The overall responses from participant researchers in the ideation study to our prototypes was extremely encouraging, particularly regarding improved user experience with the portal's visual interfaces, better workflow, and the introduction of feedback loops (such as drop-down lists, direct input-to-publication, and immediate go-live) which increased user confidence in the completion of their research tasks. Some of the feedback statements and comments from a participant survey included:

> This is fantastic. I don't have to look for the original source file in different places. I can open it right there and transcribe it!
>
> The drop-down list is great. This will certainly eliminate any chance of typos.
>
> I can clearly see what assignments are for me and I can work on each of them without referring to shared Google Docs, as we used to.
>
> If the edits I make here, go on the public website directly…! That will be

wonderful and will speed up the research process.

Conclusions: Sustainability and Next Steps

The participants in our "think-a-loud" user testing critically reviewed various features of the *Language of Marks* portal and provided direct feedback based on their experiences and expectations. An important concern was raised about version controlling this tool and others were concerned about sustainability in long term use, and management of the data. A direct question related to this topic was: "What if we don't have a programmer working with us? Is it possible to make this tool self-sustaining so that I can add more data fields and controlled vocabularies myself?" Sustainability, without the requirement of constant expert technical intervention is a goal that we will strive to achieve.

Our observations concluded that the proposed design may assist the researchers tremendously, but some features are still slightly confusing and partially non-intuitive. The consolidation of the data fields from three main categories into one HTML page was overwhelming for most users. This indicates that more refinement of our interfaces had to be done, with further iterations, and user-testing, to make the portal interfaces more intuitive, easier to use, and more agile to accommodate the needs of different sorts of users, which will ultimately include the public.

Many of our questions and design adaptations focus on the challenges of designing data analysis tools intended for use by large and diverse international teams, often working remotely from each other. Simultaneously, the appropriate handling of sensitive historical data, intended for different projects and different analyses and outcomes, is challenging. The textual and visual records of historical African bodies and African lives provide a poignant historical legacy from legal documents and records including descriptions and visual iconography, to drawings, prints, publications, and photographs. These important records provide rich source materials for artists and designers and others working in the Digital Arts for culturally sensitive artworks, installations, performances, and curatorial opportunities, based on these important original historical materials.

We succeeded in designing a first successful iteration of the *Language of Marks* portal intended for researchers in the digital humanities, which was customized for our user workflow. The *Language of Marks* portal was specifically designed to support researchers working with highly detailed, complex, and sometimes difficult to decipher historical documents. Its features and functions were designed using Design Thinking methods, and culturally sensitive design principles. The new portal was adopted by the *Language of Marks* design team and further developed by the *Freedom Narratives* research team. The continued adaptation of the portal to the needs of the projects ultimately led to the development of an even more inclusive portal, which is named *Regenerated Identities*. We intended the *Language of Marks* portal to provide new means of addressing diverse challenges and opportunities. The continued digitization, handling, and recording multiple types of highly sensitive textual and visual information collected over the course of research on the trans-Atlantic slave trade can be extrapolated to serve similar Digital Humanities research projects, and in turn, offer our research and methods rich sources for diverse Digital Arts research creation projects. This research serves to inform the public at large, and especially people of African descent, in understanding their African past.

EndNote

1 KORA was developed by Matrix as an open-source, database-driven, online digital repository application for complex multimedia objects (text, images, audio, video). The application ingests, manages, and delivers digital objects with corresponding metadata, enhancing the research and educational value of the objects. KORA's platform is intended to provide researchers with direct access to the public website.

8

Equiano's World:

Databasing the Life and Times of Gustavus Vassa[1]

Paul E. Lovejoy and Kartikay Chadha[2]

Equiano's World: Gustavus Vassa and the Abolition of the British Slave Trade (www.equianosworld.org) chronicles the life and times of Gustavus Vassa (c. 1741-1797), who is known most frequently by his birth name, Olaudah Equiano. Vassa became well known in Britain after the publication of his autobiography in 1789 and his prominent role in the movement to abolish the British slave trade. The associated database includes all known documentation on Vassa and relevant information that informs a study of his biography. The research project is part of a broader initiative that explores the testimonies and personal profiles of Africans who were enslaved during the era of slavery, most of whom being taken to the Americas. This digital humanities publication is currently being developed at Walk With Web (WWW).

The study of individuals in great transformations places microhistory in a context that can shed light on larger events and processes. The biographic turn in the study of the African diaspora is one such example.[3] In the case of slavery, moreover, biography is significant because it reintroduces people into the study of history. Too often the study of slavery, abolition, and emancipation has dehumanized experience, reducing those who were enslaved or who were resisting oppression into faceless victims or nameless rebels. The term "slave" presents such problems of identity and recognition. Its use in scholarship has tended to project the legal status and burden of the property relationship that underlay the control of those who bought and sold people as if they were things or chattel, thereby disguising individuality behind a cloak of oppression. Likewise, we consider how use of the term "data" to refer to past lives is oppressive; hence, we apply the term "digital identity" to reflect upon how best to represent individuals in computational terms.

The representation of individuals in digital spaces, however, releases dignity and personality that counterbalance the exploitation that underlines slavery. This focus on individuals and their personal testimonies underlies the research that has been put into the study of digital identities, including *Liberated Africans*, *Freedom Narratives*, *Language of Marks*, among others discussed in this volume. In some cases, it has been possible to display the richness of individual life experiences, as is the case al-Hasan al-Wazzan, popularly known as Leo Africanus, for example (www.leoafricanus.com), or Mahommah Gardo Baquaqua (www.baquaqua.org), whose travels took him from West Africa to Brazil, the United States, Haiti, Canada, Britain, and perhaps back to a different part of Africa. The subject discussed here is the person who was born in what is now Nigeria as Olaudah Equiano and who became the famous abolitionist of the British slave trade, Gustavus Vassa.

This digital humanities publication on Gustavus Vassa, that is usually conceived today as the world of Olaudah Equiano, focuses on the movement to abolish the trans-Atlantic slave trade and ultimately to emancipate the Africans and their descendants who had been enslaved. The subject of the project is the life story of Olaudah Equiano, the enslaved Igbo boy who was later known by the name given to him as a slave, Gustavus Vassa. He identified himself as African, sometimes as Ethiopian and ethnically as "Egbo," that is Igbo. *The Interesting Narrative of Olaudah Equiano or Gustavus Vassa, the African, as Published by Himself*, first appeared in March 1789.[4] The release of nine editions in Britain and one in New York were influential in the abolition of the British slave trade, which was implemented in 1807.[5] Because of the book's literary merit and its political significance it has remained in print in several popular editions which are currently widely read in English Literature and Black Studies courses at universities in North America, Britain, and Africa. His contribution is highlighted in hundreds of articles and books devoted to an interpretation of his impact, which has been organized on the world wide web as his digital identity.

The story of this interesting African and black Briton has sometimes been labeled the classic slave narrative, written in the richness of eighteenth-century literature, which has subsequently shaped a whole genre of the literature identified as "slave narratives." Considering Olaudah Equiano did not know any English until he was eleven or twelve, whereupon he became known as Gustavus Vassa, this extraordinary recognition confirms his historical importance and moral influence. In the early 1790s, the heady days influenced by revolutionary France on those interested in parliamentary reform, the abolition of the slave trade, and the ending of slavery, Vassa was arguably the most influential African in London at a time when the Black community numbered perhaps 20,000, so that London had one of the largest "African" populations in the world at the time.[6]

There has been a considerable body of information collected, much of which is published in the various editions of *The Interesting Narrative*. Moreover, there is an extensive scholarly analysis of different aspects of Vassa/Equiano's significance and his place in the period in which he lived. *Equiano's World* builds on and consolidates this knowledge. Considerable historical work remains to be undertaken, particularly about the relationship of Vassa to the Black poor of London, his friendship with a radical leader, Thomas Hardy, who was tried for treason in 1794, his marriage to a white woman, Susannah Cullen, his commercial activities, his observations in the Caribbean, his involvement in the Mosquito Shore venture of Dr. Charles Irving, and his fascination with the Muslim world of the Ottoman Empire. The papers of the leading abolitionists, intellectuals, and political figures of the late eighteenth century and those who subscribed to the various editions of *The Interesting Narrative* reveal connections into British society that are astonishing in their range and depth. The research being conducted on places and individuals that were important in Vassa's life lends itself to the extraction of new meaning for information about him.

The development of the website dates to the first decade of the twenty-first century, although Paul E. Lovejoy has sustained a deep interest in the man since he was a graduate student at the time Curtin published *Africa Remembered: Narratives of West Africans in the Era of the Slave Trade* in 1967 and G.I. Jones (1967:60-98) explored the early years of the Igbo boy, Olaudah Equiano, in that volume. As discussed in the "Project History" on the website, Thomas Hodgkin published an excerpt of *The Interesting Narrative* in his pioneering collection of primary documents, *Nigerian Perspectives,* in 1960, which was subsequently followed by new editions of *The Interesting Narrative* by literary scholar, Paul Edwards, and Jones's annotated account of Equiano's boyhood life and enslavement in Curtin's edited collection of primary texts (1967).[7]

The explosion in publications on Vassa's literary production and his life dates from the end of the 1960s, therefore. It was from this period, influenced most especially by Paul Edwards that his name became popularized through his birth name, Olaudah Equiano, and not his legal name and the name he preferred in his lifetime, Gustavus Vassa. The Africanization of his name corresponded with the assertiveness of the Black Power movement of the late 1960s and 1970s. It is worth noting that he used both names on the cover of the nine editions which he published in his lifetime, so that neither name can be considered an alias, pen name or nom de plume. In his lifetime he never used the name Olaudah Equiano without also identifying as Gustavus Vassa, and he was not known by his birth name, as the extensive documentation on the website confirms. And most striking, he never used the name Equiano as if it were a surname, although much of modern scholarship refers to him as Equiano as if it was his surname. Igbo culture did not use surnames at the time unless someone converted to Christianity and took a Christian name. Hence, Vassa was his surname, while Equiano was not (P. Lovejoy 2012: 165-84).

By 2008, it became clear that the extensive documentation relating to Vassa's life and times could be assembled for purposes of constructing his digital identity in the form of a website that could reach a broad audience. By then, P. Lovejoy, with the assistance of M. B. Duffill was researching Vassa's life, and with the assistance of Rafael Carvalho Slobodian, Reneé Soulodre-La France, and Yacine Daddi Addoun, created the initial website which was launched in 2010. This initial website is now archived through the *Internet Archive WayBack Machine* (www.archive.org/web/) and locally saved in Portable Document Format (PDF), both of which can be found on the current website.[8] The project was associated with the Harriet Tubman Institute for Research on Africa and its Diasporas, originally the Harriet Tubman Institute for Research on the Global Migrations of Africa, with support from the Social Sciences and Humanities Research Council of Canada. In 2016, P. Lovejoy recruited a project coordinator, Bruno R. Véras, to develop a new website with updated information. Fernanda Sierra contributed to the design of the new website. Kartikay Chadha joined the team as the primary programmer and developer of the open-source website and associated databases in 2018, while Carly Downs supervised and assisted the production of new content in 2019-2020. The present *Equiano's World* website was officially launched on April 16, 2019, when Lovejoy presented the W.E B. Du Bois Lectures, "Equiano's World - Beyond Slavery and Abolition," at the Hutchins Center, Harvard University.[9]

As demonstrated in the site map (Fig. 8.1), the seven sections of the website are displayed in the global navigation menu bar located at the top of every page. The website is divided into different sections that establish the context in which Vassa lived, explore the places where he traveled, and the people whom he knew. There is also a section that raises questions surrounding Vassa's life, including where he was born to his views on race and slavery and hosts a forum for discussion and queries. Studying Equiano provides access to primary documents, published scholarly analysis, and web links relevant to the times and places of Vassa's life. Taken together, *Equiano's World* is an adventure into the history of abolition, accessible to scholars, students, and the interested public. The website's acknowledgments identify the intellectual and technical contributions of over forty individuals whose inputs during the past two decades underlie the website's content contributions.

Figure 8.1
***Equiano's World* Site Map**

- **Home Page**
  - Introducing Equiano's World
  - Project Direction
  - Acknowledgments
  - Project History
  - Best Practices
  - Copyright
  - Logo and Image
  - Platform
  - Credit and Support
  - Contact Us
- **Context**
  - The Bight of Biafra and the Atlantic
  - Slave Trade of Late 18th Century
  - Vassa's Middle Passage
  - The Seven Years War
  - London in the Late 18th Century
  - Britain in the Late 18th Century
- **Travels of Vassa**
  - Chronology
  - Maps
    - Map 1: Oliver and Ogborn Map
    - Map 2: Vassa's Middle Passage
    - Map 3: The Seven Years War
    - Map 4: Circum Caribbean World
    - Map 5: Travel in Mediterranean
    - Map 6: Arctic Expedition
    - Map 7: Mosquito Shore
    - Map 8: Vassa's London
    - Map 9: Vassa's Book Tour
- **Associates**
  - Family
  - Slavery
  - Abolition
  - Religion
  - Scientific
  - Military
  - Subscribers
- **Studying Equiano**
  - The Interesting Narrative of Olaudah Equiano, or Gustavus Vassa, the African
  - Editions of The Interesting Narrative
  - Vassa's Documents Database
    - Categories
      - Letters of Introduction
      - Letters written by Vassa
      - Letters written to Vassa
      - Letters written about Vassa
      - Letters written with Sons of Africa
      - Possible Attribution
      - Other Letters
      - Documents - Context
      - Baptism
      - Emancipation
      - Muster Lists
      - Marriage
      - Property
      - Loans
      - Advertisements
      - Reviews
      - Wills
      - Death Certificate
      - In Memoriam
      - Obituaries
    - Type of Sources
      - Newspaper
      - Archive
      - Private
      - Holding
      - Published
      - Source
      - Image/Photo
- **Questioning Equiano**
  - Where was Vassa born?
  - Significance of his Name
  - Igbo scarification
  - Portraits - Real or Not
  - Slavery and trade in Igboland
  - Views of Slavery
  - Attitudes towards Race and Culture
  - Vassa, Science, and the Industrial
  - Vassa and Abolition
  - The Mosquito Shore
  - Vassa and Sierra Leone
  - Equiano and Orientalism
  - Was Vassa an African, Igbo or what?
  - White and Black Abolitionists
  - Vassa's Legacy
  - Blumenbach and Vassa
  - PUBLIC FORUM
- **Resources**
  - Scholarly References
  - Audio and Video Resources
  - Websites on Vassa
  - Websites on Slavery and Diaspora

Equiano's World is organized in a manner that allows users to access specific information, including a list of the various editions of *The Interesting Narrative*, a bibliography of publications about Vassa and his work, materials that can be useful for teaching purposes, background information on his associates, and a list of those who subscribed to the different editions of his autobiography. The different sections of the website are labeled "Context," "Travels of Vassa," "Associates of Vassa," "Questioning Equiano," "Studying Equiano," and "Resources." A distinction is consciously made between references to the man from his teenage years until his death when he was known as Gustavus Vassa and to the popularized reference to him as Olaudah Equiano, or even Equiano, which is suggestive of an Igbo surname which he never had. Nonetheless, we cannot escape the fact that today he is known more generally by his birth name, and even the second part of his birth name, rather than by the name he preferred and indeed, upon which he insisted being called, viz., Gustavus Vassa, in which Vassa is indeed a surname.

Establishing context is important in understanding the significance of *Equiano's World* and the role that Gustavus Vassa played in the abolition movement. Vassa's autobiography does not always clearly establish context, and sometimes his misunderstandings cloud an appreciation of his evolution as an intellectual and political activist. Vassa's rendition of the notorious Middle Passage must be understood in context, for example. Similarly, Vassa's exploration of different religions is worthy of reflection, while his role in the abolition movement has spawned important scholarly literature. That Vassa's slavery overlapped with the Seven Years' War requires an understanding of where he was and when his risky adventures had an impact on him. His involvement in the first Sierra Leone colonization scheme in 1786-87 clarified his commitment to the abolition of the slave trade and subsequently resulted in his writing his autobiography in 1788. Its publication in the following year consciously coincided with the first parliamentary inquiry into the slave trade, while his book-selling tours of Britain over the next several years was instrumental in garnering public support for abolition. The outbreak of war with revolutionary France temporarily sidelined the abolition campaign, redirecting political action towards the expansion of the eligible base of British elections rather than the issue of slavery. Consequently, Vassa never lived to see abolition implemented in 1807 or emancipation in 1834, decades after his premature death. Nonetheless, the importance of his autobiography in the movement to abolish the slave trade and ultimately in ending slavery underlie the life and times identified on *Equiano's World*.

Included on the website is a section on historical context, which includes brief explanations of the Bight of Biafra and its interior where he was born and from where he was taken before his sale to a British ship. The discussion includes an account of the slave trade of the late eighteenth century, at a time when Britain was the most important slave-trading nation involved in transferring enslaved Africans to the Americas. British domination of the trade of the Bight of Biafra was particularly significant and virtually guaranteed that everyone left one of its two main ports, Bonny and Calabar, and would initially at least end up in a British colony in the Americas, as was Vassa's case. Vassa's discussion of the Middle Passage is particularly important because of his role in the abolition movement. His testimony and his public lectures were central to raising public awareness in Britain about the horrors of the slave trade. Vassa's stint in the Seven Years' War, even though he was a slave to a British naval officer, touched a patriotic nerve in Britain at the time he published *The Interesting Narrative* because, at that date in 1789, Britain was still smarting from its defeat in the American Revolutionary War. The discussion of British America is important because Vassa provided almost no commentary on the political history of British colonies in the Caribbean and North America, and he was virtually silent on the independence of the thirteen North American colonies that came to form the United States. The reconstruction of Vassa's London in the last half of the eighteenth century takes account of the period before urban renewal restructured much of the west end of greater London after 1800 when Trafalgar Square was laid out and many of the poorer parts of Soho and Haymarket were demolished. This was the setting for the abolition movement that figured so heavily in Vassa's life. The discussion of Britain in the late eighteenth century is intended to provide an overview of the industrializing areas that Vassa visited as well as those parts of Scotland and Ireland where Vassa travelled.

The section entitled "Travels of Vassa" takes the viewer through the chronology of Vassa's life and provides nine maps that show the main periods of his life, including an overview of his extensive travels from Africa to the Americas and onto Europe, the Arctic, and the Mediterranean. Other maps show his Middle Passage from the interior of the Bight of Biafra to Barbados and Virginia before re-crossing the Atlantic to England. The Seven Years' War displays the main battles he was in and other locations while the map of the circum-Caribbean indicates where he went in the Caribbean, and North America. Chronologically, his European and Mediterranean travels brought him back to places where he was stationed in the Seven Years' War but now as a seaman on commercial vessels that took him as far east as the Ottoman port of Smyrna, now Isna, on the Anatolian Peninsula. He then travelled to the Arctic beyond the Svalbard archipelago north of Norway, which stands in sharp contrast to his adventures to the Mosquito Shore of Central America. Except for voyages to Philadelphia and New York in the newly independent United States, he remained in Britain for the rest of his life, living mostly at various addresses in London and from 1789 traveling widely in England, Scotland, and Ireland over the course of his book tour to lecture and sell his autobiography.

Gustavus Vassa was acquainted with several prominent individuals, and he probably knew others for which there is no documentary evidence. *Equiano's World* features a section dedicated to his associates, which highlights the individuals he knew, or he possibly knew. It is divided into seven categories: First, his family, including his Igbo parents and siblings, as well as his wife and two daughters; second, his slavery associates identify many of the individuals whom he knew when he was enslaved; third, those people he associated with during the abolition campaign, which highlight the major figures who were prominent in the abolition movement in the late eighteenth century, as well as some of slave merchants and slave owners who opposed abolition; fourth, his religious affiliations focus on people he probably knew among Quakers, Anglicans, and the Huntingdonian Connexion; fifth, his involvement in the Seven Years' War associated him with various naval officers initially through his enslavement to Captain Michael Henry Pascal; sixth, his involvement in the activities of Dr. Charles Irving and his associates who brought him into contact with the scientific community; seventh, the lists of subscribers who purchased one or more copies of *The Interesting Narrative*, which uncovers a wide network of individuals associated with abolition and who undoubtedly made Vassa and his story very well known. *Equiano's* World also includes a section and database scheme for subscribers (Fig. 8.2), which captures three levels of data organization: the menu options (name and section_ID), the subheading (sub_heading and sub_heading_ID), and bucket sections based on alphabetical order (order). The interface allows users to navigate and search through a list of subscribers, which has curated and extracted data from over 75 pages of PDF documentation.

Numerous questions have arisen in terms of what Gustavus Vassa knew, what he did, and what he thought. The section called "Questioning Equiano" includes a discussion of where Vassa was born, the significance of his name, Igbo scarification and body markings, slavery, and trade in Igboland. It examines Vassa's views of slavery and his attitudes toward race and culture. There is also discussion of Vassa's relations with scientists and the industrial revolution, his recognized and unrecognized involvement in the abolition movement, and his connection with the Mosquito Shore of Central America and abolitionism in Sierra Leone. There are also discussions of Vassa's relationship with German anthropologist Johann Friedrich Blumenbach and Vassa's legacy. Finally, there is a "Forum" that allows public interaction via the website on issues that are not otherwise covered but which the website and the study of the topics related to Vassa and the abolition movement may have prompted.

Figure 8.2
Entity-Relationship (ER) Diagram for *Equiano's World*

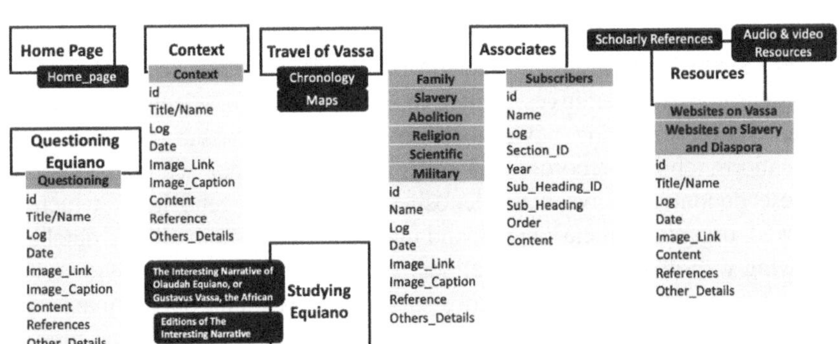

The section called "Studying Equiano" provides access to key documents and other primary source materials. This section features a full text of the first, ninth, and 1837 editions of *The Interesting Narrative*, as well as a list of other editions including those translated into German, Dutch, French, Russian, Italian, Spanish, and Hebrew, with anticipated translations into Igbo and Portuguese. The "Documentation Database" includes PDF copies of letters written by Vassa both published and unpublished, as well as important documents such as his baptismal record, marriage certificate, will, lease for Plaisterers Hall, and much more. Transcriptions of all documentation are provided for easy search. The Resources section includes a comprehensive bibliography of several hundred scholarly publications and unpublished theses used in the development of the *Equiano's World* project, as well as links to video and audio resources, and relevant websites. The literary merit of Vassa's autobiography has inspired scholarly critique that has continued to the present, which is highlighted on the website through an extensive list of scholarly references. Vassa's observations on his memories of Africa and his subsequent enslavement and role in the movement to abolish the slave trade have informed historical analysis and prompted a debate, sometimes heated, over how to interpret Vassa's account and his influence.

Equiano's World clearly articulates best practices that include recognition of those who have contributed to the research, the construction of a database, and the implementation of a website as a mechanism for dissemination of new knowledge. *Equiano's World* is an open-source, database-driven, online digital repository created at the Harriet Tubman Institute for Research on

Africa and its Diasporas at York University. *Equiano's World* respects best practices as developed while creating the website and generating data. In addition to the identification of the specific contributions of the research team and web development team, these best practices include a description of the methodology employed in the collection and production of web content. Since 2008, archival research has been conducted for the curation of content matters at archives located in Britain, Nigeria, Nicaragua, and the United States, including newspapers, parliamentary papers, contemporary publications, church records, and other sources. Digital scanned versions of these documents have been deposited into a local repository, which is reviewed, organized, meta-tagged, and uploaded to *Equiano's World* database following web-development guidelines. The intention is to permit viewers to access relevant documentation, however, not to create a digital archive.

All sources are referenced using Chicago reference style. Digital files on the website are optimized for easy access on lower bandwidth internet, which explicitly credits the artist and/or photographers, and the gallery, archive, or location where the content is housed. The image files are saved in a compressed image format standardized by the Joint Photographic Experts Group (JPEG) and every text or scanned document is uploaded in a Portable Document Format (PDF). Every image and file on the website are passed through an in-house developed Photoshop treatment protocol and are then tested to pass digital optimization requirements before moving to the production stage. Most historical images displayed on this website were created in the 18th and 19th centuries and are considered to be in the public domain under the "Fair Use" clause as recognized in most countries. The goal of *Equiano's World* is to disseminate knowledge based on scholarly analysis of primary sources related to the historical slave trade, and the struggle for freedom from slavery.

Equiano's World is a non-commercial and educational digital resource. The project does not own rights to materials held in this digital database and does not license or charge fees for the use of materials. The website relies on either in-house developed algorithms or open-source programming classes, and external plugins that are licensed under free, open-source software licenses such as the MIT license and the GNU General Public License series. As a permissive license, it puts very limited restrictions on reuse and has, therefore, high license compatibility. All elements of the project website are intended for open access in the public domain and acknowledgment should be clearly stated as described under the Copyright section of the Home page. Conditions of use of content from the website and its images, design, or texts should be provided with appropriate attribution providing bibliographic information. *Equiano's World* is the part of digital hub, *Studies in the History of the African Diaspora – Documents* (SHADD) (www.shadd.org).

The design of www.equianosworld.org aims to provide researchers and the general public with a clean, accessible, and fluid layout. The visual identity of the site highlights important moments in the life of Gustavus Vassa. In implementing this concept, we created a circular logo placing Vassa's silhouette at the center with the cover of his autobiography as the background. This silhouette was adapted from William Denton and Daniel Orme's portrait entitled Equiano made in 1789 for the frontispiece of his autobiography. The two letters on the side of the logo stand for *Equiano's World*. The font was developed using his original handwriting. The logo was designed by Fernanda Sierra Suarez, inspired by the logo used on the original website, developed in 2008.

Equiano's digital identity, in the form of this website, is a harmonized balance between multiple programming languages implementing various computer algorithms. The user front-end of this website is developed in HTML using the Bootstrap 4.0 framework, a front-end open-source toolkit, featuring Sass variables and mix-ins, responsive grid system, extensive pre-built components, and powerful JavaScript plugins. The backend database is developed in MySQL, an open-source relational database management system.[10] The website codes comprise a combination of both static HTML pages and/or PHP scripts allowing communication between the front end of the website and the MySQL database. Currently, the programming file system exists on SHADD managed server hosted by GoDaddy Inc. shared hosting services, running on a Linux operating system handled by cPanel version 78.0 (build 49), and operating PHP version 5.6.40 and MySQL version 5.6.47-cll-lve (as of 4 July 2020).

As part of the SHADD hub, *Equiano's World* relies on Walk With Web Inc, which provides development services, support, and preservation plans to digital humanities research projects. WWW has a digital content management service called Regenerated Identities, or RegID (www.regeneratedidentities.org), which supports the development, deployment, and long-term maintenance of digital research in North America, Europe, the Caribbean, Latin America, and Africa. RegID provides a custom graphical user interface that allows user-based management of *Equiano's World* website and database, handing over some control of the online publication to the researchers. RegID toolkit cover three technical aspects of the project: 1) digital curation, organization, and meta-tagging of documents, letters, and other types of manuscripts; 2) giving control to historians to self-publish information on the website; and 3) web security and management of on-going version updates of tools and software supporting the web presence of the project for long-term sustainability. *Equiano's World* on RegID is supported by similar or upgraded versions of programming languages and toolkits used to develop the front end website. The web-interface of RegID uses an open-source admin dashboard theme created by Blackrock Digital LLC. The codes of this theme were released under the MIT License on January 14, 2014.

As the Entity-Relationship (ER) diagram, Fig. 8.2, demonstrates, the website initially comprises static text that could be editing developers of this website and database. These sections are shown in the Rounded edge black color box. Subsequently, this structure was upgraded into database schemes through the implementation of the RegID toolkit, as shown in Fig. 8.3. The database on the SHADD server in real-time is managed and supported on Regenerated Identities and Walk With Web servers, respectively. The database is split into two sections, the first deals with the textual information on the website and is hosted on the SHADD server, and the second is a file and documents database, which is managed by Regenerated Identities and hosted by Walk With Web Inc. This combination of two supporting servers allows performance optimization by sharing incoming traffic from users. Moreover, the databases together are backed up on Walk With Web Inc. dedicated servers allowing long-term sustainability when SHADD hosting services are discontinued, after the completion of the project. The meta-field schemes in context to public visibility and database requirements, were created in-house by the developers in consultation with project director, researchers and collaborators. We implemented user-sensitive inclusive design to develop this website, associated databases schemes, and editing platforms (Newell, Gregor, Morgan, Pullin, and Macaulay 2011: 235-243). This method promotes narrowing the gap between developers and historians, allowing us to truly embrace the meaning of "Digital Humanities" and let the historians drive the development, supported by computer programming experts at every step.

Figure 8.3
Files on Equiano's World

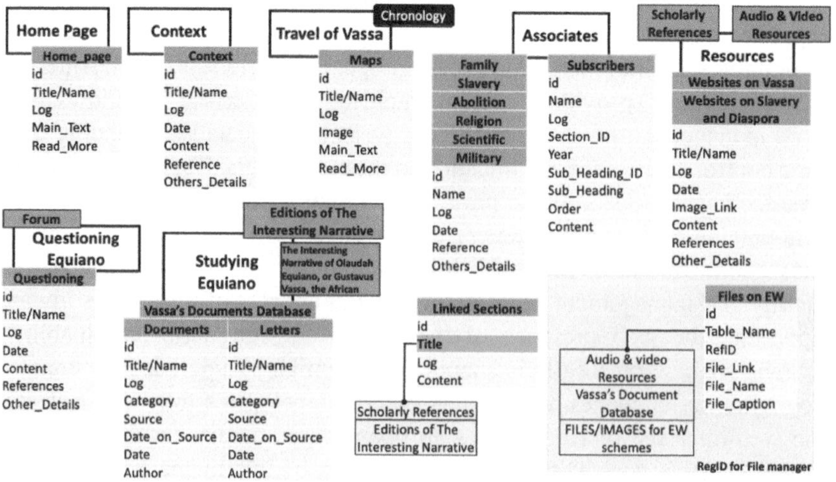

Secured file handling plugins installed across the website support the "Vassa's Documents Database" in the "Studying Equiano" section of the website. The file management algorithm allows researchers to self-publish multiple images or document type files, in various sections of the website. "Files on EW" scheme as displayed in Fig. 8.3 is managed and hosted by RegID which records uploads to the server by researchers and provides tags with the section name and entry ID. The frontend codes of *Equiano's World* are connected to the RegID plugin for file management that assists with hosting higher resolution images and large sized document type files through *Cloudshare,* another service provided by WWW. Internet-based access to *Equiano's World* is accessed through RegID via secure hypertext transfer protocol (HTTPS) protected by Secure Sockets Layer (SSL) certificates (Hirsch 2020). SSL Certificates are small data files that digitally bind a public cryptographic key of RegID's digital authentication identity, which is tested for all interacting between a server and client computers. The network also provides access to MySQL database for researchers that is secured using an in-house developed security gateway implementing the latest and most sophisticated one-way password hashing algorithms. All programming files are versionized using Git, stored on GitHub repository and versions are released for public access.[11] Git is a distributed version-control system for tracking changes in source code during software development. Access to any interface on RegID that allows public interaction with databases is protected by Google OAuth 2.0 authentication, which is the industry-standard protocol for authorization (Hardt 2012). OAuth 2.0 focuses on client developer simplicity while providing specific authorization flows for web applications, desktop applications, mobile phones, and living room devices. While most information stored on the databases is open source, RegID brings in a well-woven secured technical structure to allow long-term functionality of the *Equiano's World* website and protects it from unwanted or unauthorized digital treasons on the server.

The digital architecture (Fig. 8.4) for *Equiano's World* is compatible with the RegID environment that connects with the SHADD hub and is supported by Walk With Web. The system design is strategically divided into multiple access levels with security layers for developers, researchers, and the public at large to enable secure access to the backend MySQL database. The combination of shared and dedicated hosting for this project on the RegID network is managed by BlueHost services and Walk With Web Inc, respectively. The combination of these two types of hosting servers allows RegID to optimize incoming internet traffic, security gateways, and storage. RegID network is currently completely synchronized with SHADD shared server that is managed by GoDaddy web hosting services.

Figure 8.4
Digital Architecture of *Equiano's World*

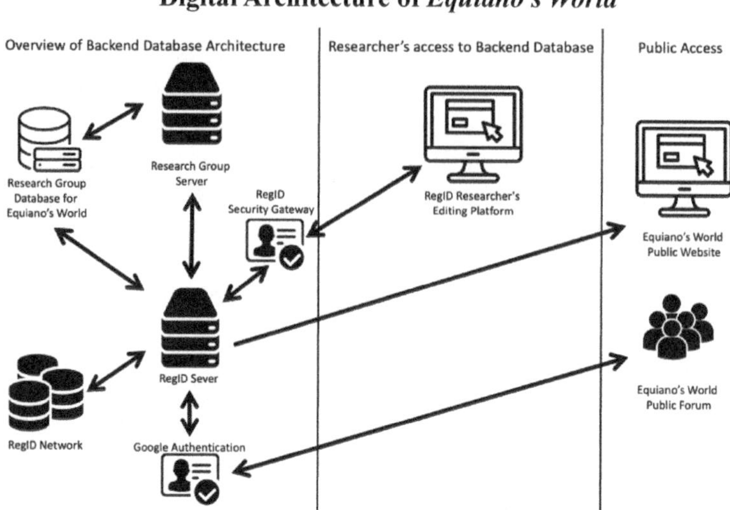

The public forum is a stand-alone web application integrated into the *Equiano's World* website that is managed by Walk With Web Inc. The interface allows public users to submit topics for discussion, which are then published by the project director (or assigned researcher(s) on the forum for open discussions. Responses from website users are recorded as publicly visible comments. User comments are non-editable and can only be deleted by the users themselves. The project director may discretionary request Walk With Web Inc. to remove a comment or topic of discussion from the website given a circumstance that may require such action. As this section of the website requires the interaction of public users with our databases, Walk With Web, Inc uses Google OAuth 2.0 authentication to verify the commenter's legitimacy. The Google API scope is restricted to email and profile information, which includes first name, last name, and Google profile image. Only the first and last name of the commenter is stored on our database to publish a comment. However, we also allow users to share their designation and affiliated institution optionally.

Equiano's World is intended to address the extensive interest in the man who today is often referred to by his birth name, Olaudah Equiano. The website attempts to include the numerous sources on Gustavus Vassa and those with whom he associated so that students, scholars and the public can participate in historical research and engage in the debate and discussion that arises from exposure to a wealth of documentation. The fascination with the life stories of the millions of people who were caught up in the nexus of slavery is promoting extensive research, as revealed in various websites, social media vignettes, and publications. As with *Freedom Narratives*, for example, biographical accounts are sufficiently numerous to offer the possibility of new levels of analysis into a history of slavery in the Atlantic world.[12] Rather than considering enslaved Africans as numbers without voice or agency, what is being learned is that scattered data can be assembled to establish digital identities for a large population that can reveal patterns in migration that previously have been thought impossible to disentangle. The *Equiano's World* website is a digital tool that allows open access to documentary materials and scholarly analysis that enables knowledge mobilization through a format that overcomes disparities in educational resources and access.

Endnotes

1 Originally published in *Esclavages & Post-esclavages*, 4 (2021): http://journals.openedition.org/slaveries/4140.

2 We wish to thank Carly Downs, Érika Melek Delgado, Bruno R. Véras, and Henry B. Lovejoy for their comments on this paper and Fahad Qayyum for technical support. The research for the development of the website was funded by the Social Sciences and Humanities Research Council of Canada, the Canada Research Chair in African Diaspora History, and the Mellon Foundation.

3 See, for example, Gwendolyn Midlo Hall, "Africa and Africans in the African Diaspora: The Uses of Relational Databases," *American Historical Review* 115 (2010), 136-150; Paul E. Lovejoy, "Freedom Narratives of Transatlantic Slavery," *Slavery and Abolition* 32:1 (2011), 91-107; Lovejoy, "Biography as Source Material: Towards a Biographical Archive of Enslaved Africans," in Robin Law, ed., *Source Material for Studying the Slave Trade and the African Diaspora* (Stirling: Centre of Commonwealth Studies, University of Stirling, 1997), 119-140; Richard Anderson, "Uncovering Testimonies of Slavery and the Slave Trade in Missionary Sources: the SHADD Biographies Project and the CMS and MMS Archives for Sierra Leone, Nigeria, and the Gambia," *Slavery and Abolition* 38:3 (2017), 620-644.

4 First edition: London, 2 vols.: Printed for and sold by the author, No. 10, Union-Street, Middlesex Hospital; sold also by Mr. Johnson, St. Paul's Church-Yard; Mr. Murray, Fleet-Street; Messrs. Robson and Clark, Bond-Street; Mr. Davis, opposite Gray's Inn, Holborn; Messrs. Shepperson and Reynolds. and Mr. Jackson, Oxford-Street; Mr. Lackington, Chiswell-Street; Mr. Mathews, Strand; Mr. Murray, Prince's-Street, Soho; Mess. Taylor and Co. South Arch, Royal Exchange; Mr. Button, Newington-Causeway; Mr. Parsons, Paternoster-Row; and may be had of all the booksellers in town and country, 1789.

5 Second edition, London: Printed for and sold by the author, 1789, 2 vols.; Third edition, London: Printed for and sold by the author, 1790; New York edition, Printed and sold by W. Durell, New York, 1791; Fourth edition, Dublin: Printed for and sold by the author, 1791; Fifth edition, Edinburgh: Printed for and sold by the author, 1792; Sixth edition, London: Printed for and sold by the author & G.G.J. & J. Robinson, Paternoster-Row and by Charles Stalker, Stationers-Court, Ludgate-Street, 1793 enlarged; Seventh edition, London: Printed for and sold by the author, 1793; Eighth edition, Norwich: Printed for and sold by the author, 1794; and Ninth edition, London: Printed for and sold by the Author, 1794. Subsequent editions were pub-

lished posthumously in 1809, 1813, 1814, 1815, 1819, 1837, and more recently in many editions since the 1960s. Translations have been published in Dutch (1790), German (1792), Russian (1794) and recently in Spanish, French, Italian, and Hebrew.

6 For a discussion of the size of the Black population in London, see Stephen J. Braidwood, *Black Poor and White Philanthropists: London's Blacks and the Foundation of the Sierra Leone Settlement, 1786-1791* (Liverpool: Liverpool University Press, 1994), Roy Porter, *London: A Social History* (London: Hamish Hamilton, 1994), Folarin O. Shyllon, *Black People in Britain1555-1833* (London: Oxford University Press, 1977), and James Walvin, *England, Slaves and Freedom, 1776-1838* (Basingstoke: Macmillan, 1986).

7 Thomas Hodgkin, ed., *Nigerian Perspectives: An Historical Anthropology* (London: Oxford University Press, 1960); Paul Edwards, ed., *Equiano's Travels* (London: Heinemann, 1967); Edwards, *The Life of Olaudah Equiano, or, Gustavus Vassa the African* (London: Dawson, 1969), and Jones, "Olaudah Equiano."

8 Available at <www.web.archive.org/web/20200218204140/http:/equianosworld.tubmaninstitute.ca/> (Accessed: 11 July 2020).

9 April 16-18, 2019; lectures posted on www.equianosworld.org.

10 "What is MySQL?". MySQL 8.0 Reference Manual. Oracle Corporation. Retrieved 3 April 2020. The official way to pronounce "MySQL" is "My Ess Que Ell" (not "my sequel"), but we do not mind if you pronounce it as "my sequel" or in some other localized way (www.dev.mysql.com/doc/refman/8.0/en/what-is-mysql.html).

11 "Releases - git/git," retrieved 1 June 2020, https://github.com/git/git.

12 Paul E. Lovejoy, Érika Melek Delgado and Kartikay Chadha, "Freedom Narratives of West Africans from the Era of Slavery," in this volume; and Érika Melek Delgado, "Freedom Narratives: The West African Person as the Central Focus for a Digital Humanities Database," *History in Africa* 47 (2021).

9

The *Spatial Historian*:

Building a Tool to Extract African Identities from the *Slave Societies Digital Archive*

Jane Landers, Jim Schindling, and Daniel Genkins

The *Slave Societies Digital Archive* (www.slavesocieties.org) preserves the most extensive serial records documenting the life histories of Africans and their descendants in the Atlantic World, as well as valuable information about the people of indigenous, European, and Asian descent with whom they interacted.[1] Archive holdings now include close to 1,000,000 digital images of manuscript originals dating from the sixteenth through twentieth centuries collected at local and regional archives in Angola, Brazil, Colombia, Cuba, and the United States. This study discusses the development of the *Spatial Historian* tool that captures and manages structured and unstructured data contained in archival sources and thereby facilitates subsequent data mining and geo-historical information exploration.

The largest and oldest collections in *Slave Societies Digital Archive* were generated by the Catholic Church. This is not surprising since Catholic priests in Iberia had been baptizing and incorporating Africans into their Christian brotherhood since the Middle Ages.[2] In the fifteenth century, the Church mandated the baptism of enslaved Africans throughout Iberian settlements, including those in West Africa and its offshore Atlantic Islands, and established a "mother Church" in Funchal, Madeira. The Church later extended the requirement to baptize the enslaved to the Iberian New World. The baptismal records preserved in *Slave Societies Digital Archive* are, thus, the oldest and most uniform serial data available for the history of Africans in the Atlantic World and they offer the most extensive information regarding African identities from the sixteenth through the nineteenth centuries.

In these records, Catholic priests across the Iberian Atlantic carefully recorded something they designated as an African's nation, meaning place of origin ("*nación*" in Spanish or "*nação*" in Portuguese). Scholars hotly debate the origins and meaning of these African ethnonyms (which we have used throughout as they appear in Spanish or Portuguese documents), and because the debate is not yet settled, we might think of these ethnonyms as ethnolinguistic identifiers of some importance, if not a fixed and permanent identity.[3] Africans and their descendants across colonial Latin America adopted these distinct "African identities" in a variety of associational fora and for a variety of purposes.[4] The preservation of these identifiers in a wide variety of documentary sources was, we argue, the result of both Iberian and African agency. While recognizing the tremendous changes wrought on cultural forms and ethnic identities over centuries of enslavement, dislocation, and repression, we find evidence in Iberian records that Africans themselves clung to something like a *nación* or *nação* well into the nineteenth century.[5] If Africans and their descendants made such an effort to preserve this "identity," however changed or changing, it behooves us as historians to continue our own efforts to explicate its meaning and significance.

Once baptized, Africans and their descendants were eligible for the sacraments of Christian marriage and burial, adding to their historical record. Through membership in the Catholic Church, families also generated a host of other religious documentation such as confirmations, petitions to wed, wills, and even annulments. In addition, Africans and their descendants joined church brotherhoods based on ties of shared ethnicity (*cofradías* in Spanish and *irmandades* in Portuguese), through which they recorded not only ceremonial and religious aspects of their lives but their social, political, and economic networks as well. Africans and their descendants left a documentary trail in municipal and provincial archives across the Atlantic World. These secular records, which are also preserved, include bills of sale, property registries, dowries, and letters of manumission, among many other types of records.

The goal of *Slave Societies Digital Archive* is to preserve as many of these rare and endangered documents from the ravages of time, tropical climates, and unfortunate neglect as possible and make them freely available in digital form so that current and future generations can continue to learn about the history of Africans and their descendants in the Atlantic World. The project is committed to training descendant communities in the countries in which we work. We train local students and archivists in international standards for digital preservation and provide our partners the latest digital equipment to enable them to preserve their own history while being paid stipends from our grants.

Developers Daniel Genkins and Jim Schindling have been working toward creating metadata describing the estimated four to six million individuals who appear in our records. This required designing a means of efficiently extracting detailed information about these individuals, such as their names, their African "identities," the historical contexts they inhabited, and the lives they lived from digital images of early modern texts.

The Challenge

On October 10, 1593, Alonso Castillo recorded the baptism of María Bran in a register in the Catedral de San Cristóbal in Havana, Cuba. Castillo, a Catholic priest, gave no surname for María, nor for her parents Domingo and María – only the descriptive Bran, indicating that they were from a region on the west coast of Africa. The clergyman also noted that they were *negros* owned by Sebastian Fernandez. Anton Çape, María's godfather, and Ysabel Biafara, her godmother, were also present at the baptism.[6]

The record of María's baptism (Fig. 9.1) is typical of many found in *Slave Societies Digital Archive* in that it contains a wealth of information beyond the names of participants in the ceremony. For example, it can be inferred that Domingo and the elder María were intimate partners, though it is unclear if they were married or whether their marriage would have been recognized by the church. Also, it is implicit that all of those mentioned in the entry were born prior to 10 October 1593 and (likely) died after that date. It can also be inferred that Sebastian Fernandez was a slaveholder who owned at least three slaves, including the newly baptized María. Anton Çape and Ysabel Biafara are listed as "*negros del rey*" indicating that they were slaves owned by the King of Spain. Alonso Castillo can be assumed to have been a member of the clergy, or at a minimum had an affiliation with the church where the ceremony was held. Because the Catedral de San Cristóbal still exists today, it is also possible to place the individuals mentioned (with the possible exceptions of Fernandez) at a specific location on a specific date.[7]

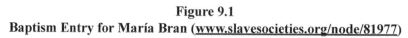

Figure 9.1
Baptism Entry for María Bran (www.slavesocieties.org/node/81977)

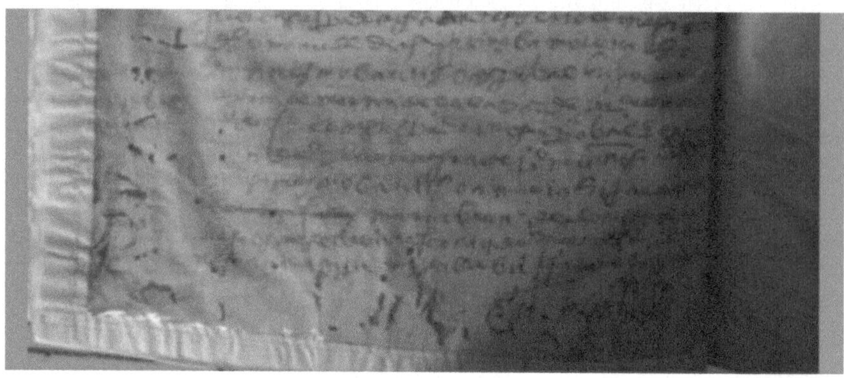

Taken in isolation, this baptismal entry offers valuable information but is not enough on its own to develop a deeper understanding of the individuals, let alone a larger narrative of the historical context in which they lived. Its true worth lies in assembling the contents of other materials and large continuous and longitudinal sets of baptismal, marriage, notarial, and other administrative records, adding movement and color to the picture by extracting and piecing together multiple references to people, places, and events over time. As an example, other entries in the records of the Catedral de San Cristóbal referring to Alonso Castillo might be used to frame his tenure. Other references to Sebastian Fernandez could offer more information about the extent of his slaveholding. Most importantly, examining the corpus of data in aggregate may offer a glimpse into the lives and extent of enslaved families and communities difficult to assess through other types of sources.

With close to 1,000,000 images containing references to millions of individuals, extracting and managing the information contained within these texts far exceeds the capabilities of spreadsheets and off-the-shelf GIS software. Historians are often faced with the task of organizing and analyzing unstructured materials such as these. In addition, there is the likely possibility that physical documents may have deteriorated, pages may be torn, or individual folios may be separated from their original bindings. Paleographic style, language, handwriting, and abbreviations of individual scribes must also be navigated to accurately interpret the author's intent. P. Bryan Heidorn suggests that in contrast to indexed data stored in formal data repositories and available online, these unacknowledged "dark data" are essentially invisible to researchers and the public.[8] Yet it is these data that promise to furnish the critical pieces of information necessary to advance historical research. Furthermore, while current research is often facilitated by computer-based technologies that streamline access to digital source data and documents, unstructured primary source materials are considerably more problematic and, arguably, require more sophisticated technological solutions.

For most social science researchers, neatly structured and spatially precise tabular data offers an ideal information source. Rows and columns of well labeled and consistently measured values are ready made for analysis. However, history is not always so accommodating in providing information in this way. Much of history is recorded as unstructured script in the form of ledgers and narratives. Names, numerical values, and relationships are embedded in narrative descriptions of events and places. In addition to extracting data from these sources, issues of interpretation are compounded by nuance, changing names, and even the use of obsolete units of measurement.

To address the challenge of information extraction, considerable effort has been applied toward developing methods for automating the parsing and interpretation of geographical content from unstructured texts.[9] Natural Language Processing techniques have been developed to extract information based on the syntax and semantics of written language, and gazetteers have been used to identify references to known locations and to assign geographic coordinates.[10]

But this process is far from simple. For example, in the sentence "She lived with her husband on a riverside plantation located thirteen miles south of the city that would later bear his name" there are references to two people, a river, and a city, along with an indication of distance. For a historian, knowledge of the name of any one of these features – Martha, George, the Potomac, and Washington, in this case – would help augment the record and provide a spatial context for the statement. For computer-based systems, this type of implicit, intuitive, and contextual understanding is difficult to replicate. Encouragingly, progress is being made in the development of technologies and techniques for automating the extraction, management, and analysis of data from historical texts.[11]

Historians commonly collect data and produce materials such as notes, transcriptions, translations, and metadata as they research. These materials are often stored informally by the individual scholar or even discarded upon completion of a research project and are therefore unavailable to their peers or publics – in essence, entering the domain of dark data. Beyond the publication of data, the preservation of collected and derivative materials is often an afterthought in humanities research.[12] Collaborative projects begin with specific research goals and, once satisfied, the long-term preservation of the artifacts of the process, digital or otherwise, may be of little concern to team members. In addition to the lack of prioritization, curation can appear to be a bewildering morass of standards and protocols, the mastery of which can challenge most researchers in terms of time, cost, or expertise.[13] Making the results of humanities research discoverable and accessible so that others can benefit from them is critical if they are to be of use for future study.

Our Technical Approach

Echoing the *Enslaved* framework, the work being done by the *Slave Societies Digital Archive* aims to understand the people, places, and events that appear in our records. Robust information management is required to not only record these individual components but allow them to be tightly linked within the underlying data structures and visually navigable from within the user interface. To this end, *Slave Societies Digital Archive* has developed an integrated customized system, called the *Spatial Historian*, capable of assisting historians in the collaborative real-time capture and management of structured and unstructured data contained in archival sources that facilitates subsequent data mining and geo-historical information exploration. The essential components of the system allow the researcher to manage libraries of source material, enter and normalize transcriptions, extract content, establish links between people, places, and events, and publish the results to external data services such as the *Enslaved* data hub.

The remainder of this essay provides a synopsis of the major functional components of the *Spatial Historian* user interface. It is important to note that this is not a complete summary of the capabilities of the system. For the sake of brevity, many of the features used to streamline data entry and facilitate navigation do not appear in this discussion, which refers only to the primary document management interface along with windows used to manage and link people, places, and events.

Document and Transcription Management

When working on a project in the *Spatial Historian*, the user initially views the document management interface (Fig. 9.2). The hierarchy tree on the left side of the screen is customizable based on the organizational preference of the researcher. In the example shown, documents are organized by the provinces, cities, and churches where the digitized volumes originated. The volumes themselves are then divided into individual folio sides. This organization mirrors the hierarchy of the document images in the *Slave Societies Digital Archive* collection and is an effective structure for mapping between the two.

Figure 9.2
Document Management Interface Customized for Specific Projects

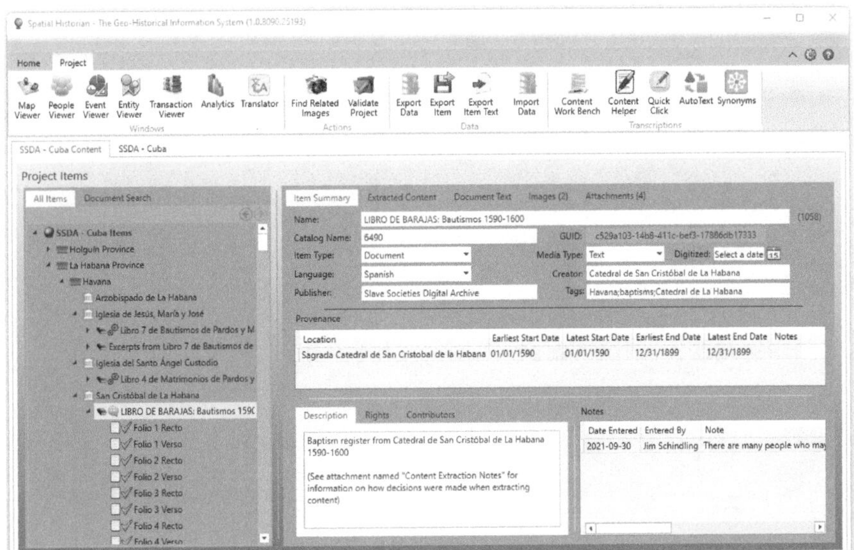

Researchers manage details about the individual items in the document hierarchy using the tabs located on the right side of the window, with the available maintenance options varying based on which type of item in the tree is currently selected. In the example in Figure 9.2, the baptism register named *Libro de Barajas: Bautismos 1590-1600* is selected in the hierarchy. On the *Item Summary* tab on the right the volume is defined as a *Document*, indicating that it is a single physical item, and its primary language is noted as being Spanish. The *Provenance* section shows the locations where the document has been archived and corresponding dates. The researcher can use this information to construct metadata for export and curation, and to help associate physical locations to the events recorded in the volume. The additional metadata fields on this tab can be used for export and curation as well.

Because neither documents nor other items in the hierarchy exist in isolation, the system allows the user to add attachments to items that may provide additional background and context. In Figure 9.3, an image of the cathedral where the document is located has been attached along with two supporting Word documents. The system supports the attachment of essentially any type of content and allows attachments to be ingested and stored internally or to be referenced by specifying a URL.

Figure 9.3
Attachments Linked to Selected Document

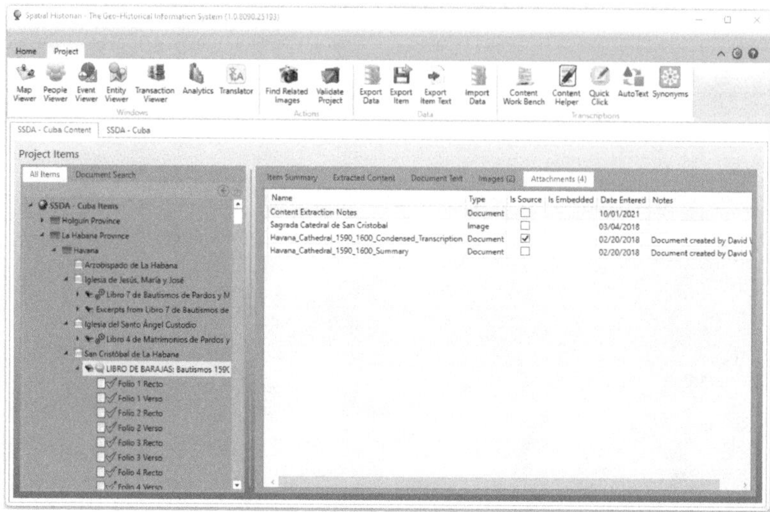

Figure 9.4
Folio Used for Curation of Transcription

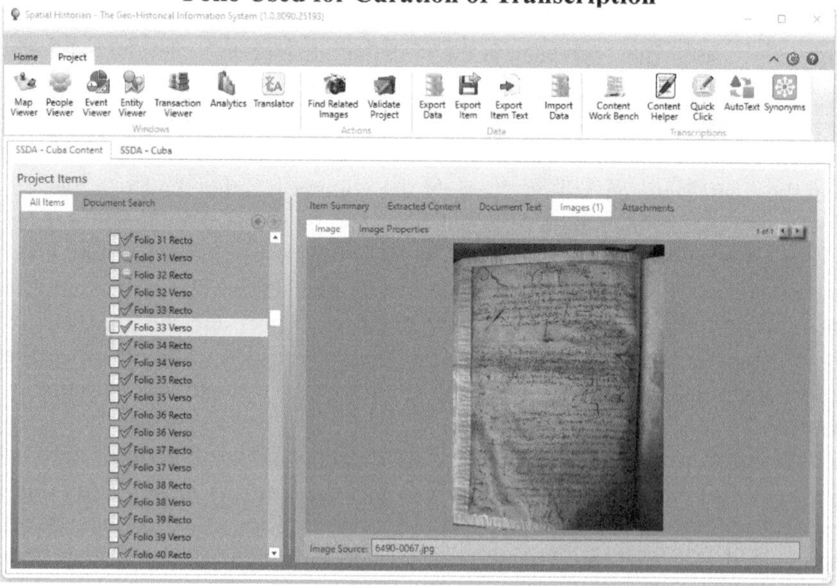

The system also allows the user to upload images of the selected item. The example in Figure 9.4 shows an image of the verso side of the first folio of Havana's *Libro de Barajas*. This image can be used as a visual reference when transcribing the corresponding page. To further aid transcription, the user can zoom and pan the image as well as open it for viewing in a separate popup window.

With a folio added to the hierarchy, the transcription itself can be entered and manipulated using the Document Text tab as shown in Figure 9.5. This tab supports a variety of functions including entry of the raw transcription, a "normalized" version in which spelling variants have been converted to standardized forms, and a translated version. These tools allow the user to enter a transcription directly and then instruct the system to generate normalized and translated versions.[14]

Figure 9.5
Transcribed Folio Text

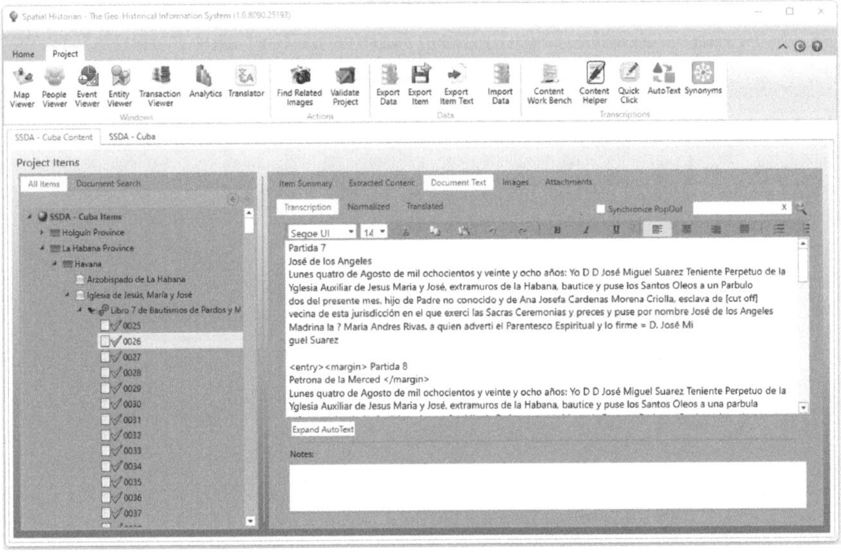

Content Extraction

Content extraction is the process of identifying and recording details about the people, places, events, and relationships recorded in the texts. Like transcription, content extraction is time-consuming and error-prone when performed manually. To mitigate the potential for errors and speed the process, several automated functions have been built into the *Spatial Historian.*

The first of these are text normalization and synonym matching. These processes support the detection of existing named entities (people and places) during content extraction. For example, in the entries recorded in the *Libro de Barajas*, Alonso Castillo is identified as the church official presiding over many of the ceremonies. It is therefore important to link him to these events and to the other participants while recording him as a single individual. By generating and matching against a normalized copy of the text, we can identify previously recorded entries and then give the user the option of referring to the existing entry rather than creating a new, and potentially duplicate, one.

The *Spatial Historian* also applies synonym matching while scanning transcribed or normalized texts for names. This process performs two functions: 1) highlighting any pieces of text that might be interpreted as a part of a name and 2) building a list of people already recorded in the system who are potentially referred to in the text. An example of such a scan appears in Fig. 6. In the example, all names found in the text are highlighted in blue and a list of twenty-one possible matches from other records is displayed.

Figure 9.6
Scanned Results Highlighting Names in Text and Potential Identifications

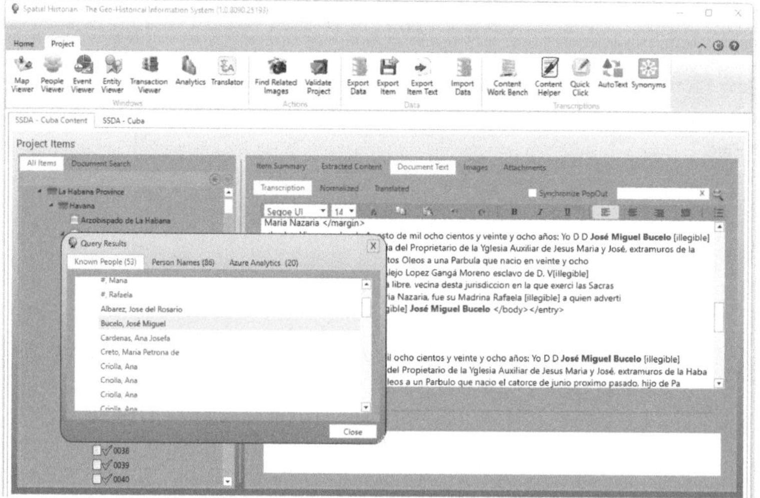

A second feature used to aid content extraction is a customizable window called the Content Helper. Rather than requiring the user to enter details for each person individually and then manually create event and relationship entries, this window performs all of these tasks in a single automated process. The Content Helper dynamically adjusts itself by modifying the number of people prompted for and the roles each might play based on the type of event recorded in the document section currently being processed. Figure 9.7 shows the Content Helper as it would be displayed when processing a baptism record. In this case, the window has an input field for the person being baptized (labeled "Self") along with blocks for up to two parents, two godparents, three slaveholders, the official presiding over the service, and a scribe. The bottom portion of the window allows the user to specify additional details about the event including its location and the date or range of dates when it occurred. Individuals can be added to the Content Helper in several ways: the names can be typed in directly, names can be dragged and dropped directly from the transcription text, or existing people can be dragged and dropped from the *people* window (discussed below).

Figure 9.7

Content Helper Configured to Extract Content from Baptism Record

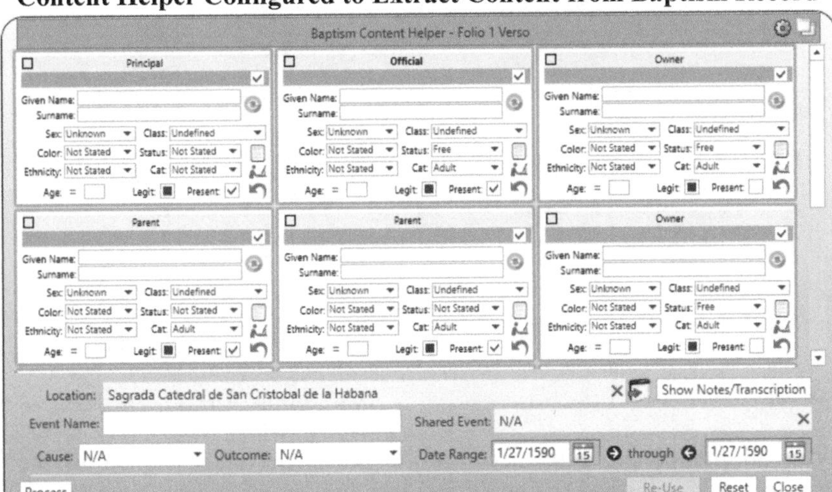

As the names of individuals are added to the Content Helper, the system adjusts the display to indicate whether linkages are expected. In the baptism example, when a person is entered in the Owner block the "Owner" label background color changes to green to indicate that one of the other individuals must be identified as a corresponding slave. For baptism entries this could be the person being baptized and/or any of the Parents or Godparents. Figure 9.8 shows an example with Owner/Slave relationships established between each of the Godparents and the Owner named Sebastian Fernandes. The green background on the role title of the Godparents indicates that their corresponding Godchild must still be identified. These linkages are established by dragging the related person's block onto the block of the person expecting a relationship. Note that as the user moved the mouse over a block, the border of the block turns blue. At the same time the borders of the blocks of any related people turn orange. In Figure 8, the user's mouse is over the block for Sebastian Fernandes and the borders of the related blocks for his slaves are orange.

Figure 9.8
Content Helper with Owner/Slave Relationship for Sebastian Fernandes

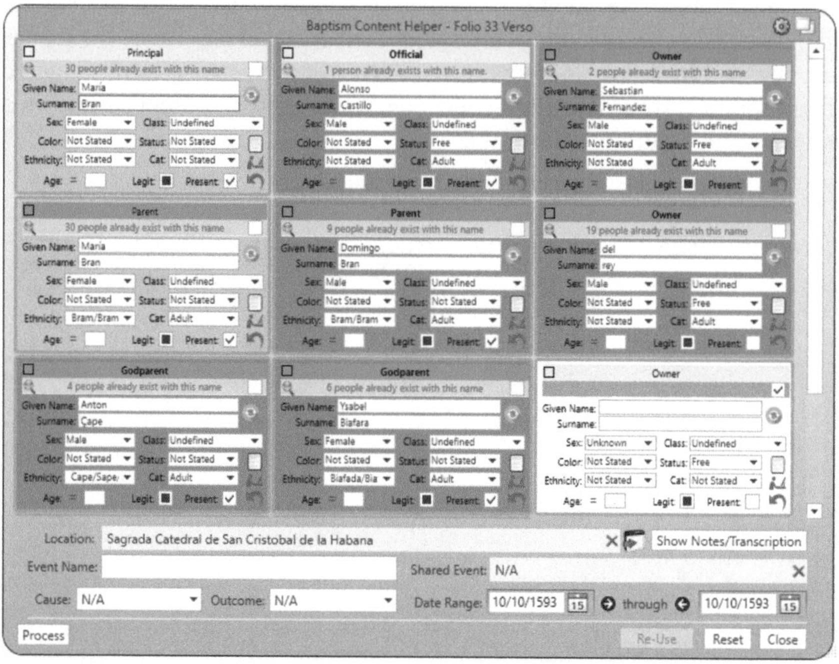

Once all the people referenced in the document are assigned to their corresponding roles and the additional location and date details are entered, the user can click the Process button to create a record for the event as well as records for the individuals present, their relationships, and their attendance at the event.

Managing People

The previous section discussed the management of documents in the *Spatial Historian* along with an expedited mechanism for extracting content related to the people, places, and events referenced therein. Once entered into the system, these data can be augmented with additional details such as for people: occupation information, physical characteristics, and property ownership. The following sections summarize how the people, events, and map viewer windows are used to manage and analyze these data.

The people window (Fig. 9.9) is the primary user interface for managing details related to individuals. This interface is used to create as well as update, merge, and delete entries. The left side of the window contains a hierarchical list of individuals with tabs that allow viewing by either paternal or maternal lineage. When a person is selected from within the hierarchy, their details are displayed in the set of tabs on the right. The Summary tab contains demographic information along with a list of individuals related to the selected person. Demographics can be updated by entering new details directly into the fields on the form while the references and other information are updated using content-specific pop-up forms.

In the example figure, María Bram is selected in the list of people and his information is shown in the detail section. As expected, the Summary tab indicates that she was born prior to October 10, 1593, she was described as a "negro," and since both of María's parents also appear in the record and she is not specifically described as illegitimate, the *Slave Societies Digital Archive* transcriber has marked her as legitimate. Also shown are María's relationships to her owner, parents, and godparents.

The *Spatial Historian* allows the user to navigate to any of the people, places or events listed in any interface element directly from the listing in question. To navigate to the details for Sebastian Fernandes in this example, the user can simply right-click on his name in the list of relationships and select the "Go to Person" option from the pop-up context menu. Similarly, to navigate to a reference document, the user can right-click on the reference and select "Go to Document."

Figure 9.9
People Window for María Bram including Hierarchical List of Attendees

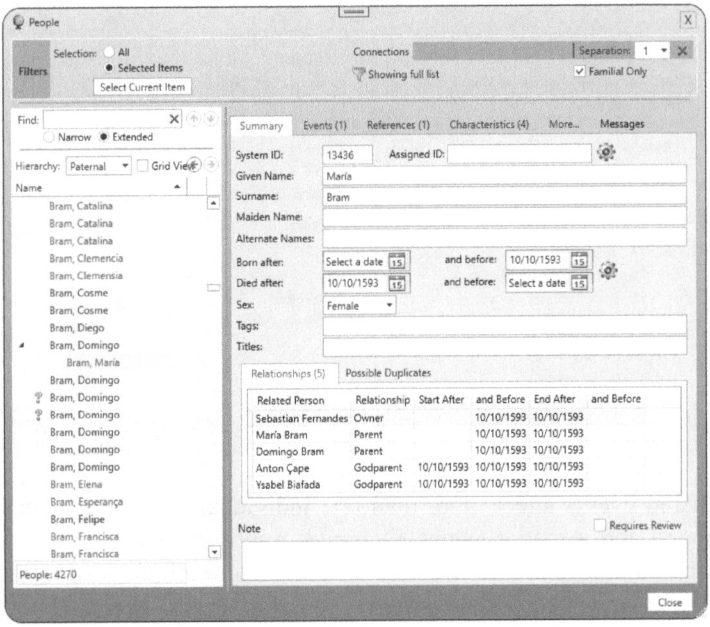

Managing Events

The events window is the primary interface for viewing and managing events centering on a single individual as well as shared events, defined as events that affect more than one person. Figure 9.10 shows the events window with the Baptism event for María Bram selected. The bottom left of the window lists the attendees at the baptism and the pane on the right shows details about the event. From this window the user can navigate from the list of events directly to the reference document or person, and from the Attendees list to the individual attendees' details. The *Spatial Historian* can also store location information for each event, allowing the user to navigate to the location of the event in the Map Viewer window (discussed below) by clicking on the globe icon in the Details section of the window.

Figure 9.10
Baptism of María Bram Listing Attendees and Details of Event

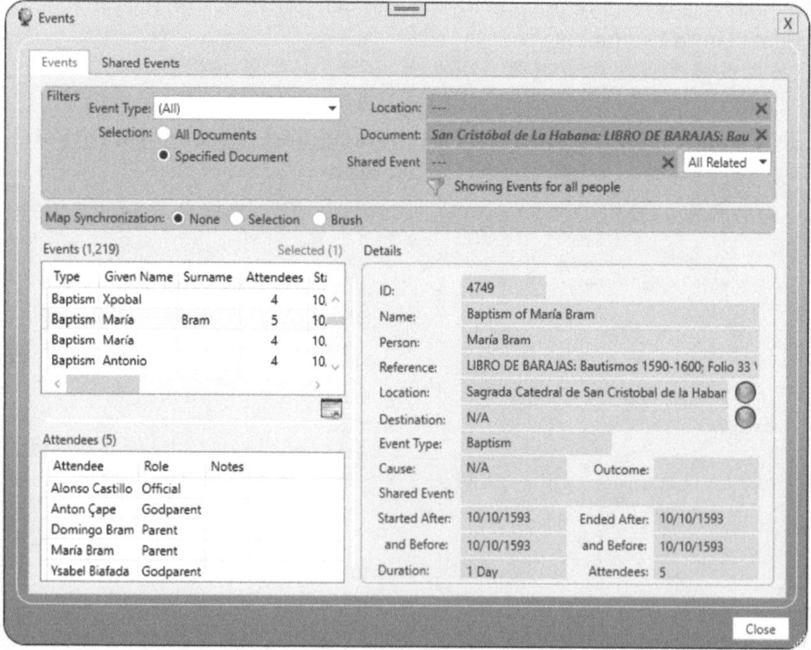

Shared events affect more than one individual. Such events have both a temporal and a spatial extent. Examples might include wars and treaties, slave rebellions, extreme weather phenomena, outbreaks of disease, or simply the arrival of a slave ship. In general, shared events result in life events for individuals. For example, a plague might result in a death and/

or burial event for a person, while the arrival of a slave ship at a port might result in a disembarkation event and likely a subsequent sale event for an enslaved individual. Shared events provide important linkages between those affected even if the individuals never met. They can also be used to supply implicit information about these individuals. For example, records of enslaved baptisms occurring within a short period of time after the arrival of a slave ship may indicate that the individuals being baptized arrived on the ship and therefore came from the region where the ship was loaded. Implicit connections can only be confirmed by large volumes of records, but even in the absence of ironclad evidence they exemplify previously unanswerable questions that can be explored using data collected by the *Spatial Historian*.

Managing Places

The Map Viewer window is the primary interface for displaying the places and spatio-temporal locations of events that appear in *Slave Societies Digital Archive* records. The interface consists of a project-specific hierarchy of places on the left and an interactive 3D map on the right (Fig. 9.11). The spatial extent or point location for each item in a project's geographic hierarchy can be defined if known or named placeholders can be created for toponyms with unknown locations. The underlying basemap can be either modern satellite imagery or a georeferenced historical map.

This simple display of the point location of churches can be enhanced by embedding 3D models. When the user zooms in to a specific location (as in Fig. 9.12) the symbology is updated to display a 3D representation. In this example, stock models are shown, however models of actual structures produced from photogrammetry, lidar, or other sources can be used when available.

Figure 9.11
Map Viewer of Churches in Havana

Figure 9.12
Map Symbology using 3D Models

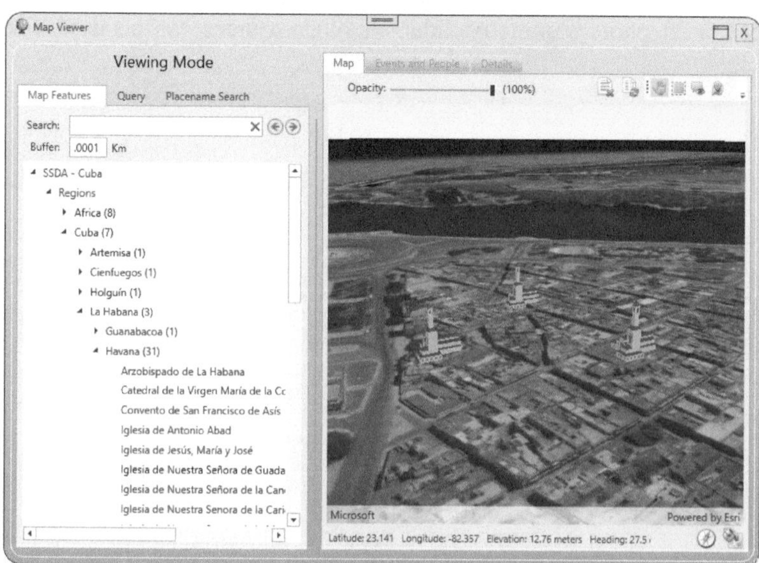

Event mapping differs from the normal mapping of locations in that events contain temporal extents as well as spatial coordinates. In the case of a baptismal register, for example, each baptism is located spatially at the coordinates of the church and temporally on the vertical axis of the map at a scaled height based on a user-defined date range. The height of each individual event marker is scaled to the duration of the event in days, and the width of each marker is scaled to the number of people attending the event (Figure 9.13).

Figure 9.13
Baptisms at Iglesia de Jesús, María y José, 20 June to 5 December 1828

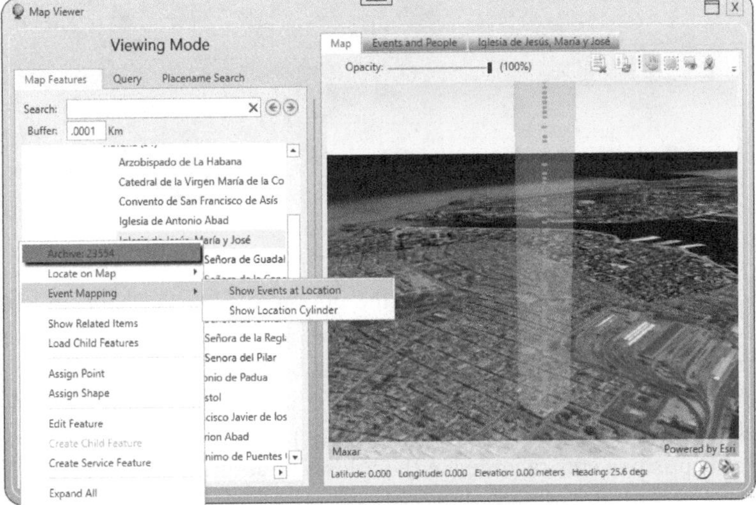

Figure 9.14
Arrival of Slave Ship (Gray Feature) and Baptisms at Iglesia de Jesús, María y José

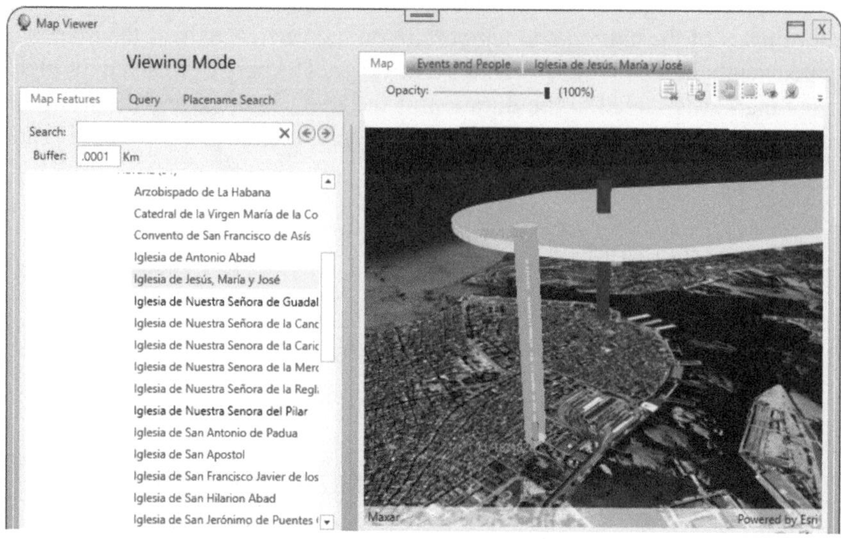

From this interface the user also has the option to filter the baptism events to show only those that coincide with the ship's arrival plus or minus a user-specified temporal buffer. Shared events can be mapped along with the life events of individuals to explore their possible interactions. In Figure 9.14 the arrival of a slave ship, represented by the gray plane, is shown along with the stack of baptism events recorded at the Iglesia de Jesús, María y José.

Concluding Thoughts

This has been a brief synopsis of the *Spatial Historian*'s user interface and information management features. Additional interfaces support functions such as project validation, speech-to-text, reporting, and data export, among others. The goal here has been to describe our approach to the challenge of extracting data to contribute to the *Enslaved* initiative and to offer a sense of the user interface components and information management required to support the project's goal of understanding the people, places, events, and sources recorded in primary sources describing the early modern Atlantic slave trade.

With the help of the *Spatial Historian*, *Slave Societies Digital Archive* has extracted and contributed to structured information related to hundreds of places and events and thousands of individuals. To this point, our work has been governed by the rule of thumb that 95 percent of the time spent on a given digital project is devoted to preparing systems and data, with only the remaining 5 percent allocated to producing results.[15] Transcription and content extraction are by far the most time-consuming operations in our workflow. With close to 750,000 digitized pages, each containing details about four or more events, even a crowd-sourced manual transcription process would take years to complete. As such, the pressing technical challenge for Slave Societies moving forward will be the development of paleographic optical character recognition to speed transcription and enhanced natural language processing to speed content extraction.

Endnotes

1 The Slave Societies Digital Archive was launched in 2004 with a National Endowment for the Humanities Collaborative Research Grant directed by Jane Landers and partners Mariza de Carvalho Soares, Universidade Federal Fluminense, Rio de Janeiro, and Paul Lovejoy, York University, Toronto. Major grants from the NEH, the American Council of Learned Societies, the Andrew W. Mellon Foundation, and the British Library Endangered Archives Programme have supported the project during the last decade and a half.

2 By the fourteenth century, African Christians had established two *cofradías* in Seville and by the fifteenth century, African *cofradías* had also been established in Cádiz, Jerez, Valencia, El Puerto de Santa María and Barcelona. Jane Landers, *Black Society in Spanish Florida* (Urbana: University of Illinois Press, 1999), ch. 1. Also see, Jane Landers, "African 'Nations' as Diasporic Institution-Building in the Iberian Atlantic," in "*Dimensions of African and Other Diasporas*, ed. Franklin W. Knight and Ruth Iyob (Kingston: University of the West Indies Press, 2014), 105-12 and "African Ethnic Groups in Florida," *Africa in Florida: Five Hundred Years of African Presence in the Sunshine State,"* ed. Amanda Carlson and Robin Poyner (Gainsville: University Press of Florida, 2013), 73-85.The Portuguese opened slave factories at Arguim (1448), Santiago de Cabo Verde (1458), San Jorge de Mina (1482) and São Tomé (1486). José Luis Cortes López, *Los origenes de la esclavitud negra en España* (Madrid: Mundo Negro, 1986), 80. On the baptism of Africans and African *irmandades* in early modern Portugal, see A.C. de C.M. Saunders, *A Social History of Black Slaves and Freedmen in Portugal, 1441-1555* (Cambridge: Cambridge University Press, 1982).

3 For a sample of these debates see for example, Paul E. Lovejoy, "Identifying Enslaved Africans in the African Diaspora," in Paul E. Lovejoy, ed. *Identity in the Shadow of Slavery* (London, 2000); Gwendolyn Midlo Hall, *Slavery and African Ethnicities in the Americas: Restoring the Links* (Chapel Hill, NC: University of North Carolina Press, 2005); Robin Law, "Ethnicities of Enslaved Africans in the Diaspora: On the Meanings of "Mina" (Again)," *History in Africa* 32 (2005), 247-267; Philip D. Morgan, "The Cultural Implications of the Atlantic Slave Trade: African Regional Origins, American Destinations and New World Developments," *Slavery and Abolition* 18:1 (1997), 122-145.

4 For the most detailed work on African ethnonyms in the Iberian Atlantic see David Wheat, *Atlantic Africa and the Spanish Caribbean, 1570-1640* (Chapel Hill: University of North Carolina Press, 2016). Also see Wheat, "Tangomãos en Tenerife y Sierra Leona a Mediados del Sigo XVI," *Cliocanarias* 2 (2020), 545-569 and "Bi-

afadas in Havana: West African Antecedents for Caribbean Social Interactions," in Ida Altman and David Wheat (eds.), *The Spanish Caribbean and the Atlantic World in the Long Sixteenth Century* (Lincoln, NE: University of Nebraska Press, 2019), 163-186, and "The First Great Waves: African Provenance Zones for the Transatlantic Slave Trade to Cartagena de Indias, 1570-1640," *Journal of African History* 52:1 (2011), 1-22.

5 In the nineteenth century, British Mixed Commissioners in Havana, Rio de Janeiro and Sierra Leone tried to record African names and ethnicities much as Spanish and Portuguese officials had being doing since the fifteenth century. See *Slavery, Abolition and the Transition to Colonialism in Sierra Leone*, Suzanne Schwarz and Paul E. Lovejoy (eds.), (Trenton, NJ: African World Press, 2015). For their digital preservation work in Sierra Leone see www.britishlibrary.typepad.co.uk/endangeredarchives/2016/01/transatlantic-slave-trade-sierra-leone-public-archives-freetown.html. On the British Mixed Commission records for Cuba see the website of Henry Lovejoy, Liberated Africans. Teams led by David Eltis created the vast SlaveVoyages database and are now trying to ascertain naming and ethnic patterns of Africans liberated by the British. See G. Ugo Nwokeji and David Eltis, "The Roots of the African Diaspora: Methodological Consideration in the Analysis of Names in the Liberated African Registers of Sierra Leone and Havana," *History in Africa* 29 (2002), 365-379.

6 Original transcription by David Wheat available online at www.drive.google.com/file/d/1Vskm3XvJNocjg-SWwK0do4FkEEypyzeQ/view.

7 María's parents were recorded as Bran and her godparents were Anton Çape and Ysabel Biafara. A substantial proportion of *Slave Societies Digital Archive* records contain similar information regarding the ethnicity of individual participants. Our collection offers serial, systematic evidence for the ascription of African ethnonyms over a period of two and a half centuries.

8 P. Bryan Heidorn, "Shedding Light on the dark data in the long tail of science," *Library Trends* 57:2 (2009), 280-299.

9 See, for example, Ian Gregory, David Cooper, Andrew Hardie, and Paul Rayson, "Spatializing and Analysing Digital Texts: Corpora, GIS, and Places" in David J. Bodenhamer, John Corrigan and Trevor M. Harris (eds.), *Deep Maps and Spatial Narratives* (Bloomington: Indiana University Press, 2015), 150-178 or Humphrey Southall, "Defining and Identifying the Roles of Geographic References within Text: Examples from the Great Britain Historical GIS Project," in *Proceedings of the HLT-NAACL 2003 Workshop on Analysis of Geographic References* (2003), 69-78.

10 Bruno Martins, Hugo Manguinhas, and Jose Borbinha, "Extracting and exploring the geo-temporal semantics of textual resources," in *2008 IEEE International Conference on Semantic Computing* (2008): 1-9.

11 Recent research in this vein includes Merrick Berman, "Modeling and Visualizing Historical GIS Data," in *Proceedings of the Spatio-Temporal Workshop* (2009) or Ian Gregory, Chirstopher Donaldson, Patricia Murrieta-Flores, and Paul Rayson, "Geoparsing, GIS, and Textual Analysis: Current Developments in Spatial Humanities Research," *International Journal of Humanities and Arts Computing* 9:1 (2015), 1-14.

12 Mary Anne Kennan and Lina Markauskaite, "Research Data Management Practices: A Snapshot in Time," *International Journal of Digital Curation* 10:2 (2015), 69-95; Phillip Lord, Alison Macdonald, Liz Lyon, and Davis Giaretta, "From Data Deluge to Data Curation," in *Proceedings of the UK e-science All Hands Meeting* (2004),

371-375.

13 Nor, of course, do efforts along these lines contribute meaningfully to professional advancement in most university settings. This barrier is particularly prohibitive to early career scholars who might otherwise be among the most engaged in interdisciplinary digital humanities projects such as those that comprise the *Enslaved* consortium. Although this discussion lies outside the scope of the present essay, count the *Slave Societies Digital Archive* project team among the many who hope to see the tenure system in the humanities adapt to take into account scholarly production beyond the analog monograph.

14 Graduate students from Vanderbilt or partner institutions in Latin America have transcribed many of our *Slave Societies Digital Archive* records. While this once again lies outside the scope of the present essay, we strongly believe that the paleographic and technical skills that graduate students build in doing this sort of work facilitate more advanced dissertation research and expand employment options in an increasingly difficult job market.

15 Anne Kelly Knowles, introduction to "Special Issue: Historical GIS: The Spatial Turn in Social Science History," *Social Science History* 24:3 (2000), 451-470.

Part II:

Digital Identities, Biographic Data and Lived Experiences

10

Documenting Africans in Trans-Atlantic Slavery

Paul E. Lovejoy

The problem with documenting Africans in trans-Atlantic slavery has generated an enormous amount of research and related publications that has prompted considerable innovation in the methods of research and analysis that are associated with the digital revolution in the social sciences and humanities. Africa was historically important in the peopling of the Americas after trans-Atlantic contact, inappropriately symbolized by Christopher Columbus's voyage in 1492. The subsequent migration was through slavery, now recognized as a crime against humanity. From the early sixteenth century through the 1860s, at least 12.7 million people were forcibly moved from Africa to the Americas, about half of whom came from West Africa. This migration was much larger than the movement of people from western Europe overseas in the same period or indeed any other migration before enforced trans-Atlantic migration ended in the middle of the nineteenth century. The arrival of Africans in the Americas was heightened even more because of the catastrophic collapse of the indigenous populations of the Americas. Given the United Nations International Decade for People of African Descent (2015-2024) and the objectives of the UNESCO "Slave Route Project: Resistance, Liberty, Heritage." Political authorities and the public are willingly or not grappling with issues concerning anti-Black racism and systemic inequalities that developed and have persisted for almost two hundred years since the enforced migration of enslaved Africans came under attack. It is no wonder, then, that slavery has attracted so much scholarly scrutiny considering the importance of slavery in the development of the modern world.

An international collaboration of scholars was formed as a contribution to the quest for social justice with respect to the racist legacy of slavery. A project that focuses on *Documenting Africans in Trans-Atlantic Slavery* (www.datasproject.org), with the acronym *DATAS*, was conceived in response to the call for proposals of the Trans-Atlantic Platform (T-AP) for Social Innovation, which involves collaboration between funders from several different countries. The *DATAS* platform aims to enhance the ability of funders, research organizations, and researchers to engage in transnational dialogue and collaboration. Multi-national and trans-Atlantic projects funded under this call are expected to both add to understandings of social innovation and deliver social innovation(s) through new research.

The trans-Atlantic collaboration in this research is intended to facilitate social challenges faced on both sides of the Atlantic. It proposes to address a world in which there is now a digital divide, not only between urban and rural developments and cohesion but also in access to public services and infrastructure. The social challenges include ethnic conflicts, human rights and legislation, the current state of democracy, equality, and social, political and human values. The focus on a theme that affects all sides of the Atlantic facilitates learning from the experiences of multi-sectoral collaboration for social innovation practiced on both sides of the Atlantic. This innovation affects forms of economic organization, new digital technologies and accessibility, and global and local environmental issues affecting sustainable development. The strategies for social cohesion require the integration of health and social care services, improvement of education and overcoming of linguistic barriers. The challenge is to apply and adapt approaches from one locale to another and generalizing and/or scaling-up of local experiences. In response to this initiative, the *DATAS* proposal received support from the Social Sciences and Humanities Research Council (SSHRC) in Canada, the Agence Nationale de la Recherche (ANR) in France, Fonds de recherche du Québec – Société et culture (FRQSC) in Québec, and the Economic and Social Research Council (ESRC) in the UK. The lead investigators for the coordinated but separate applications to the granting agencies included Lovejoy for SSHRC, Myriam Cottias for ANR, Jean-Pierre Le Glaunec for FRQSC, and Sean Kelley for ESRC, with Lovejoy designated as principal investigator overseeing the full collaboration. Approximately two dozen specialists are associated with *DATAS*.

DATAS initiates an innovative method to explore African ethnonyms from the era of the trans-Atlantic slave trade, circa 1500-1867, as a means of documenting Africans in trans-Atlantic slavery. The proposal centered on the need to understand the origins and trajectories of people of African descent who populated the trans-Atlantic world in the modern era. *DATAS* is intended to be a repository of biographical information on individuals who were forced into slavery and a forum for discussion of how people were identified and identified themselves during the period of slavery. As recognized in the award, the development of a method for analyzing demographic change and confronting social inequalities arising from racism constitutes a social innovation. The team's methodology implements a research tool developed in Canada for handling ethnonyms that can be applied in a trans-Atlantic context from France and the United Kingdom to Brazil, the Caribbean, and Africa. This approach confronts methodological problems that researchers encounter in reconstructing the emergence of the African diaspora. A methodology for data justice is salient because ethnonym decision-making and the types of queries used in the *DATAS* digital platform, requires a re-conceptualization of the classification systems concerning trans-Atlantic Africans.

This methodology depends on an open-source relational database that addresses important decisions that researchers face in the field about how to develop best practices and a controlled vocabulary for four important reasons. First, scholarly expertise on trans-Atlantic Africans is scattered globally. Second, the slave trade was rarely limited to one country or population and the transfer of people across borders has been part of the global relationship between colonial and colonized. Third, *DATAS* makes available a vast amount of information of immense value to marginalized communities deprived of information on their own history. Fourth, the trans-Atlantic and transnational nature of this project complements the aims of a platform predicated on global collaboration. The project treats ethnonyms as decision making tools as a method whose concepts require rethinking entrenched assumptions about data justice, research transparency, and demography. The database and ongoing analysis facilitate access to scholars, policy makers, students, and the general public.

Hence *DATAS* is an international collaboration that employs an innovative method to explore ethnonyms in global Africa during the era of the trans-Atlantic slave trade, circa 1500-1867. The plethora of terms that exist in source materials and are variously interpreted in the scholarly literature need to be examined in context, allowing for lack of precision in meaning. On the one hand, the observers who identified people often had marginal if any understanding of the African context. Terms like Mandingo/Mandinga, Mina, Congo, and Angola provide a vague connection with specific parts of Africa, the western Sudan in the case of Mandingo, which derives from Mandinke, the Voltaic region of the Gold Coast and the Bight of Benin for Mina, which derives from the major European trade castle at Elmina, or Congo and Angola that refer broadly to the Kingdom of Kongo and the Portuguese colony of Angola centered at Luanda. Such terms could easily be applied in a random way because terminology was often based on language. Hence someone could be labeled Carabali, a term often used to designate people who spoke Igbo, even if someone only understood a few words of Igbo. What is clear is that there was a complex and changing nomenclature that was used for purposes of identification. These were not "ethnodescriptors," as proposed in *Enslaved Peoples of the Historic Slave Trade*. Such a term obscures the context and allows for inadequate interpretation of the African background of individuals, such as the discussion in *Enslaved* of James Albert Ukawsaw Gronniosaw.

Databasing Ethnonyms

The concept of "ethnonym" is complicated because slave owners assigned ethnic designations to enslaved people without very much, if any, knowledge of the African backgrounds of people. The meanings of terms in the sources therefore require historians to provide best possible interpretations of what may have been intended. Sometimes ethnonyms referred to social constructions that might be thought to be ethnic but in fact referred to the language people were recorded as speaking, no matter what other means of identification may also have been used. By extension, ethnonym indicators sometimes became the basis of community formation even after initial languages of communication were discontinued but the origins of people continued to be associated with Africa. As the transformation of initial ethnic/language identities occurred, various distinctions became subsumed under more generalized identities that be thought of as super ethnicities where language became less and less important through the adoption of European languages of oppression. In turn these identities were racialized and account for the socialized injustices that persist to the present and often lose all memory of any specific African origins. The process of ethnonymic progression into racialized categories is the focus of the *DATAS* project.[1]

The issues surrounding ethnonyms relate to how ethnogenesis is conceived. There is an extensive literature dating back to at least the eighteenth century that attempts to address this problem, including such contemporary observers of slavery as Sandoval, Oldendorp, Clarke, Koelle, and Cust.[2] The focus of these early studies was often on language with an implicit or explicit recognition of what can be called ethnicity. These studies continued into the twentieth century, as reflected in Migeod and Rattray,[3] and more recently in the work of Westermann, Greenberg, Child and Keir Hansford, John Bendor-Samuel, and Ron Stanford.[4] Jesus Guanche has isolated over 1,200 terms in Cuban sources alone, although failure to provide references raises other questions about what that many distinctions might mean.[5] Specialist journals first appeared in the nineteenth century, such as *Zeitschrift für afrikanischen Sprachen*, and especially in the 1960s, which have continued the effort to identify the linguistic configuration of West Africa.[6] A focus specifically on ethnicity became increasingly a separate area of analysis, as in numerous unpublished colonial reports in archives such as Nigerian National Archives as Kaduna, Enugu, and Ibadan. Another strand of analysis has included efforts to identify ethnicity and "national" configurations among Africans and their descendants in diaspora. George Murdoch's Human Relations Area Files, started in 1949 at Yale University, and the Ethnographic Survey of Africa by the International African Institute under Daryll Forde between 1950 and 1977. The literature is now vast.[7] The registers of Liberated Africans taken off slave ships in Cuba reveals the extent of ethnic labeling.[8] Given the extent of scholarly interest in language and the social construction of ethnicity, there is considerable confusion in understanding how people identified and were identified, not only at any point in time but also as identification changed over time. The *DATAS* project is intended to examine the problem through a collaborative effort to compare and analyze materials in English, French, Portuguese and Spanish, in which languages African and people of African descent have most often been studied, although it is recognized that there is extensive data and studies in other European languages, especially Danish, Dutch and German.

Regenerated Identities through Ethnonyms

In response to the construction of databases that concern identity, Kartikay Chadha developed a research tool, "Regenerated Identities," which can be used to analyze ethnonyms which has the potential of examining fundamental dimensions of identity in a global context.[9] The app is intended for use in West Africa, the broader trans-Atlantic world and in large parts of the Islamic lands of North Africa and the Middle East. Ethnonyms index identities, places and historical events that can be used to reconstruct African cultures as they evolved and changed during the history of slavery, colonialism and racism. Such an approach amounts to a methodology for data justice, which is salient because decisions relating to social constructions of identification raises questions about what is meant in terms of identity formation and maintenance. The idea builds on a conception of "methodology through the ethnic lens" that was first proposed in 2003. The concept reverses the usual logic of research. Typically, the effort is to establish ethnic context and association, but the reversal asks what does reference to any terminology or designation mean? What purpose does the question serve? In short, a reference to ethnicity is the start of research into determination of what is meant and its context.

DATAS involves a digital platform that requires a re-conceptualization of the classification systems concerning Africans and people of African descent. By using this methodology, the project traces the origins and trajectories of an estimated 100,000-200,000 enslaved individuals through an open source, relational database that addresses important decisions that researchers face in developing best practices and controlling a vocabulary that affects analysis. The *DATAS* platform is intended to allow users to reconstruct demographic patterns of where individuals came from, why they were enslaved and what happened to them. An analysis of ethnonyms provides a methodological lens in doing so.

The innovation in the *DATAS* project is the creation of a new method for social sciences and humanities research that can enhance transnational research collaborations. This database project makes possible the application of a way to explore the meaning of African ethnonyms during the era of the trans-Atlantic slavery and after. The project centers on the need to understand the origins and trajectories of people of African descent who populated the trans-Atlantic world in the modern era by reconstructing biographical profiles drawing on a variety of documentation including marriage records, newspaper advertisements, Registers of Liberated Africans taken off slave ships by the British Navy in the nineteenth century, plantation inventories, sales, court records and other materials on individuals born in Africa, with the *DATAS* focus on West Africa. This platform is therefore for ethnographic and linguistic information on Africans who were forced into slavery, and its development enables a method for analyzing demographic change that can confront social inequalities arising from racism. *DATAS* therefore constitutes a social innovation.

The bodies of primary source material that are targeted for inclusion in the project are diverse. They include a considerable body of published primary texts, many of which are overlooked by those dealing with issues of identity. And they include an even larger body of primary sources that remain unpublished and have not been examined in relation to the issues at hand. These materials are to be found in the Nigerian National Archives in Kaduna and Ibadan, the Church Missionary Society Archives, the Methodist Missionary Archives, fugitive slave advertisements in Canada, the USA, the Caribbean, Brazil and West Africa, documentation on the West Indian Regiments, plantation inventories, plantation registers, and other materials in The National Archives, Kew, as well as archives in France, Brazil, Cuba and elsewhere. The Registers of Liberated Africans and "Disposals" in Sierra Leone, Cuba, Brazil and other sites of the Courts of Mixed Commission, Louisiana parish records; baptismal and marriage records from Brazil and various countries of Hispanic America, baptism registers in Italian cities and family archives/Notarial archives (Miniscalchi), workers registers in

Martinique and Guadeloupe, *matricules* registers, administrative councils for the French Antilles, slave freedom registers in Senegal, public and private plantation archives, and surviving *quilombo* communities in Mineas Gerais and other parts of Brazil, and registers of freedom for Guadeloupe, Guyane, and Martinique in 1828-1848.

Other relevant datasets and related websites include Liberated Africans (Henry Lovejoy), Slave Societies Digital Archive (Jane Landers), among other projects on Louisiana Parish Records (Gwendolyn Midlo Hall), Maranhão and Pará Archives (Walter Hawthorne), the Maroonage dataset (Jean-Pierre Le Glaunec) and Language of Marks (Katrina Keefer and Martha Ladly). The database of slave arrivals in Europe via the Atlantic Ocean, 1425-1787, created by Filipa Ribeiro da Silva and David Richardson (EURESCL, 7th PCRD) is another example. An indication of which team members are responsible for accessing collections and the time frame for processing materials for incorporation into the database are central to the structure of the project. The emphasis is compiling accurate information on people of African descent. The integration of vast quantities of primary source materials using an innovative methodology enables a reconstruction of a major theme in modern history – the role of slavery in a trans-national, trans-Atlantic and indeed global context. *DATAS* addresses how people identified and were subjected to social discrimination because of the impact of slavery in the development of the modern world and the legacy that continues to shape contemporary society through racism and discrimination and through resistance to social injustice. The *DATAS* website, social media formats, and related publications are intended to provide access to open source content for academic and nonacademic audiences that can assist in searching historical records of the slave trade and document the origins of people and the social constructions of identity. The deconstruction of patterns in the slave trade in relation to ethnonyms not only has implications for the study of the demographic and social history of slavery in Africa and in the diasporas of the Americas but also in the Muslim regions of North Africa, the Middle East and the Indian Ocean. *DATAS* is conceived as a project in which the research team will consolidate a platform for storing big data of primary sources and other materials which in combination can be used to reconstruct the life stories of individuals and can inform the ways in which communities have been formed and have survived with reduced methodological problems. The objectives are:

(1) to sustain a collaborative transnational research network to address social challenges faced on both sides of the Atlantic in terms of data collection on slavery in a global space;

(2) to consolidate a method for an online open source relational database that highlights ethnonyms;

(3) to use the database to confront social justice and ultimately help undermine racism by spreading knowledge.

The aim of this work is to utilize the scholarly expertise of collaborating scholars because transnational networks are important to social sciences and humanities research on the slave trade. Scholarly expertise on slavery is widely scattered, in part because slavery was a global phenomenon. The slave trade was rarely limited to one country and never targeted single populations. Instead, people were transferred across national borders establishing a global relationship between areas outside colonial boundaries that populated colonized nations. Recent achievements in database construction clearly prove that research on slavery is particularly amenable to collaborative engagement that is international in scope and that involves big data in complex formats and several languages.

The importance of accessibility to research in the social sciences and humanities is that digital management will enable new insights and increased access to knowledge that focuses on the testimonies of individual Africans who were not only sent to the Americas but who remained in West Africa or who were taken across the Sahara. Because the study of African diaspora formation has influenced the development of traditional disciplines in the social sciences and humanities, scholars in various disciplines will benefit from an original project based on a methodology that allows an analysis of large quantities of information collected in a digital database. The relational data that becomes available makes it possible to address questions about the meaning of ethnicity in historical context. We contend that a nuanced appreciation of information described through ethnonyms unlocks the historical context that shaped the experiences of people from Africa, and in the context of this initiative specifically West Africa. The results will enrich the study of demography and culture by demonstrating how complementary knowledge from different African contexts can be applied in transforming social science and humanities disciplines and practices. The use of digital spaces to inquire about the impact of the African diaspora on the global past opens resources to public access. Anyone may download, print and study previously inaccessible images and documents. The latest technology allows *DATAS* to expose bias and racism and to avoid discriminating against end-users. The overarching mission is to advance knowledge, combat racism and discrimination, and promote innovation for the benefit of humanity.

This digital humanities publication addresses three challenges: How do we create clean data? How can we move from one website to another and correlate information? How do we create an open source relational database in a trans-national context that follows best practices and uses a controlled vocabulary? To resolve these questions, a methodology will be applied in a trans-Atlantic context from France, Portugal, Italy, and the United Kingdom to Brazil, the Caribbean, Mexico, and the countries of West Africa. An innovation pertaining to ethnonyms highlights interactions between these countries and others. The participating scholars have access to considerable amounts of primary sources of various kinds, some of which has already been assembled in databases that will be incorporated into the *DATAS* Project. *DATAS* brings together a unique transnational collaboration of scholars that strengthens academic partnerships and addresses real world problems.

In terms of the methodology that is being developed, participants are divided into teams that include those with experience in creating the *Freedom Narratives* database and website (www.freedomnarratives.org) and several other relevant websites (see Walk With Web Inc, www.walkwithweb.org) being used in this project. In terms of methodology, we are employing what we have developed, and conceptually have proven, to a greatly expanded body of data which we intend to analyze in terms of the questions outlined above. With reference to biographies and contemporary personal testimonies, we will pursue the expansion of the "Freedom Narratives" database from 2,000 individuals to 200,000 (Melek Delgado 2022). Another focus will be the incorporation of records in French on the slave trade, including plantation records from the Caribbean and the many references to ethnicity and identity in West Africa (especially Senegal), the Caribbean and France. A third focus will be on materials in Spanish and Portuguese which will end the national silence on slavery on Portugal, Spain and Italy. Similarly, the United Kingdom has records on the Anglophone side concerning Africans in the slave trade and in other countries that will expand the data set and address issues of demography, political and economic history, ethnicity, gender, racism and the study of the enslaved migration. It can be expected that new data will also uncover information on the early migration of Africans to Europe. To this end, our methodology has four components:

1) Sourcing, i.e., the identification and processing of various bodies of primary documents;

2) Execution, i.e., the application of our technological experience in creating, expanding and combining databases for purposes of analysis;

3) Analysis, i.e., close reading of texts and comparison of texts to address the research questions concerning the origins of individuals, the mechanisms for enslavement, the contours of enforced migration, the demographic implications of migration, and the interrelationship among trans-Atlantic, Saharan and internal West African experiences, their status and ethnic/linguistic identification.

4) Interpretation, i.e., the reconsideration of the history of West Africa and the global context of migration that a re-evaluation of how slavery shaped the political, economic and social landscape of continental Africa

> and infused the receiving areas of migration with cultural influences, both within West Africa, across the Atlantic and in the Islamic world.

The collaborating teams use the methodology of data sorting to drive the questions that will be asked during analysis. The methodology that focuses on ethnonym as a tool for research, study and analysis employs a platform that shares the *Freedom Narratives* database and incorporates data from other websites. *DATAS* is an open-source, relational online database that is designed to be user friendly, is accessible, and enables access to all relevant documentation. As a sustainable platform, *DATAS* will function to preserve primary documentation and allow the mining of big data. The vast number of new and previously underused sources of primary materials on West Africans and those who trace their ancestry there contains biographical and other data on enough individuals to assess issues relating to ethnonyms. Information on individuals is being extracted and materials organized according to a unique identity for each person and within technical parameters described in the best practices for "Freedom Narratives."

The methodology involves working across websites and the incorporation of vast quantities of data, for which the development of *Regenerated Identities* (www.regeneratedidentities.org) has been crucial.[10] *Regenerated Identities* (RegID) supports a hub that transcends the limitations of isolated websites and databases that in effect constitute separate silos of knowledge. RegID is the backend of a digital hub, *Studies in the History of the African Diaspora Documents* (SHADD; see www.shadd.org), which demonstrates the concept of crossing websites. The relevant digital humanities projects involved in the development of SHADD have evolved from the *Freedom Narratives* website, whose continued expansion is ongoing. As demonstrated, databases and websites that have been developed as isolated silos are now interaction in ways that are searchable and facilitate the retrieval of knowledge for more sophisticated analysis. As a hub, SHADD enables the cross fertilization of new knowledge, which is a feature of data storage and retrieval that is central to the *DATAS* project. The success of the "Freedom Narratives" database, whose linked open data are being incorporated into the *DATAS* project, has prompted the development of the RegID tool that allows analysis and dissemination of data and research results.

To allow a search of these diverse materials, a controlled vocabulary has been established with clear definitions of all terms and procedures adopted for entering data directly into RegID. The controlled vocabularies are essential in creating metadata that accurately describe the contents and sources of documents and identify who exactly is responsible for every aspect of document discovery, retrieval, and management. The vocabulary is "controlled" because each term/name/place is clearly defined or located, so that spellings of the names of places, ethnicity/languages, means of enslavement, and all items listed in the metadata can be used consistently and uniformly. In the case of biographical information, each person who is recorded is assigned a unique number to establish an individual identity. Basic details of individuals are then recorded, including, gender, ethnonym and linguistic characteristics, physical markings, kinship relations that are known, religious affiliation, region of origin within West Africa, and destination. The known events in each individual life are then determined, from birth to the date on which the evidence on the person was recorded. The status of the person at the time of each event is registered, along with the age of the person if known or otherwise if the person was a child or adult at the time of the event, details on the event, whether it was enslavement, liberation, education, conversion, or some other activity relating to occupation or acquired skill, and relationships with other individuals at the time of the event, as well as the source for such data. Similarly, the place where each event occurred is recorded, including coordinates for mapping, region, name of modern country, and source. The purpose is to generate "clean" data that conforms to the definitions of the controlled vocabulary, so that metadata will enable the imposition of accurate standards of inventory, establish a search capability, and allow access to PDF versions of the actual primary documentation. RegID organizes materials for purposes of search and analysis, which technically assigns identification numbers to persons, places, and events in association so that researchers can search the database according to specific questions and parameters of applicability. The tool enables computer experts to upload data onto a robust platform that can serve as the backend of user-friendly websites yet to be contemplated.

DATAS focuses on the main period of enforced migration from West Africa to the Americas from the last part of the seventeenth century through the nineteenth century and includes a study of the significant enslaved movement across the Sahara and within West Africa itself. Ultimately these estimates should be situated in the political and social context of West Africa to inform our understanding of the numbers of people leaving or remaining in West Africa as slaves. Who were these people is a question that can encourage a supposedly understandable attempt to identify people according to ethnicity. By focusing on ethnonyms, *DATAS* engages the discussion over ethnicity as a concept, the problems of using the term, the social construction that belies stereotypes of primordial existence, fixed boundaries, and implicit genetic purity. While the concept of ethnicity tends to be timeless, ignoring or transcending change over time resulting from historical events, environmental factors, epidemiological shock, sociological factors determining marriage, child rearing, funerals, and responses to misfortune, our definition of ethnonym allows for historical factors that changed over time.

Such an analysis, based on the detailed compilation of biographical accounts and other data, can result in a clearer understanding of the direction and flow of the slave trade, the relative importance of trans-Atlantic, Saharan, and internal West African migration related to slavery. Until recently, the study of slavery and historical change as a result of enforced migration has focused heavily on the scale and direction of the trans-Atlantic migration only without much understanding of the origins of the enslaved population in Africa and with considerable debate over the resulting impact on social and cultural change in places where people came from and where they were destined. The shift to studying individuals has resulted in what can be labeled a biographical turn that is demonstrating how the study of slavery has to be more inclusive and not only trace the forced migration to receiving areas in the Americas but also situate that movement more globally. In the case of West Africa, this means weighing the relative scale of internal and external displacement. It is no longer possible to study the development of the African diaspora in the Americas without examining the impact of migration out of Africa to the Islamic lands of North Africa and the Middle East. The extensive domains of the Ottoman Empire in particular have to be placed alongside the Spanish, Portuguese, British, French and other European empires in the Americas. Similarly, a preoccupation with the migration of the slave trade narrowly defined as the "Middle Passage" across the Atlantic. The coastal points of embarkation on the African coast for Brazil, the Caribbean, North America, and the Spanish empire have to be understood in terms of the impact on the development of the political states and empires of West Africa, including Asante, Oyo, Dahomey, and the *jihad* states of Fuuta Jalon, Fuuta Toro, and the Sokoto Caliphate. Clearly far more slaves remained within West Africa than were sent across the Atlantic or the Sahara and hence must be taken into account in understanding the significance of ethnonyms.

The leap from biography to ethnonyms has methodological implications; ethnonyms refer to groups of people with common features, constructs, proximity in a homeland, and a shared language. Often it is difficult to separate language from what is referred to as ethnicity, especially when the same term is used for both. Biography studies the individuals who combined to a greater or lesser degree into groupings which are usually identified in ethnic terms even when all that is known is that individuals spoke a specific language. By focusing on the person and not the ethnic cohort, we assume that every individual story is unique, so that the group to which ethnonyms apply are comprised of cohorts of discrete individuals. Our assumption is that one can learn about the group by studying the individuals. There has been extensive research on the biographies of enslaved Africans over the past two decades, with the trend continuing unabated. Some full-length biographies of Africans who were enslaved in West Africa stand out because of the detail that situates individuals in historical context.[11] In addition, there are numerous relevant articles and collections, many of which are by members of the project team.[12] A section in the expanded *UNESCO General History of Africa, Vol. 10, Global Africa*, edited by Lovejoy, includes seventeen essays on life histories of Africans during the era of slavery. Theoretically, the study of biography and autobiography of people of African descent is a crucial sub-field in literary criticism and cultural history, as well as drawing increasing attention from historians. The genre of the "slave narrative" is recognized as constituting a distinct field in African and African-American studies.[13] Philip D. Curtin pioneered the study of West Africans in the era of the slave trade in the classic collection, *Africa Remembered* (1967), and since then there have been many additional studies both on individuals born in Africa and those born into slavery in the Americas. The problem that the *DATAS* project addresses is the correlation of the unique experiences of individuals into a database that enables broader historical analysis, i.e., that moves beyond the study of one person to situating several hundred thousand people in history.

Previously, analysis of demographic change has relied on the terminology and designations of *Slave Voyages* that attempt to trace the trans-Atlantic slave trade based on over 36,000 trans-Atlantic ship movements (www.slavevoyages.org). In the development of *Slave Voyages*, David Eltis and his associates unquestionably have shaped modern scholarship on the migration of enslaved Africans and the nature of slave society in the Americas. A weakness in their approach, however, is the reliance on the coastal schema that was presented in Curtin's seminal census of the slave trade in 1969 was adopted with only minor adjustments as the basis of analysis without a critique of the methodology and ignoring criticisms of that approach.[14] Recently, however, because of the turn of research to biography, a new schema has been developed that is closely associated with the *DATAS* project as well as *Freedom Narratives*.[15] In contrast with the Curtin-Eltis schema, the new division of sub-regions in Africa covers the whole continent, not just the coastal departure points for enslaved captives destined for the Americas, although the focus for *DATAS* is specifically on West Africa. The map highlights movement across the Sahara, Red Sea and Indian Ocean, as well as the Atlantic, and it portrays relocation within Africa, which often involves recognition of ethnonyms.

As the theoretical distinction between slave narrative and freedom narrative emphasizes, the focus on individuals born in West Africa allows a study of how people were enslaved, the conditions of where they lived when they were enslaved, the ways they were moved to markets, reached the Atlantic seaboard for transit to the Americas or taken into the desert for the journey to oases or North Africa, the Mediterranean and Ottoman Empire. The *DATAS* Project also allows a study of the individuals who were enslaved and remained in West Africa, which enables further comparative study. For analytical purposes, therefore, freedom narratives uncover patterns of historical action that are broader than a concentration on people born into slavery in the Americas. Many life stories can be gleaned from documentation in the Americas, which reveals what happened to West Africans after they crossed the Atlantic, and the inclusion of accounts that relate to the retention of people in West Africa and their deportation across the Sahara allows a much richer scenario for analysis. Examples of such analysis can be examined in the case of specific individuals, including Gustavus Vassa (aka Olaudah Equiano), who became one of the most prominent abolitionists in Britain after serving his slavery in the Seven Years' War and the Caribbean,[16] or Ali Eisami, who was enslaved in *jihad* in Borno in the early nineteenth century but lived most of his life as a Liberated African in Sierra Leone, publishing his autobiography, historical fragments, poetry and a dictionary and grammar of the Kanuri language in 1849-1854,[17] or Mahommah Gardo Baquaqua, who was taken from West Africa to Brazil in 1845, escaped from slavery in New York, lived in Haiti, and wrote his autobiography in Canada West in 1854.[18] Muhammad Ali Sa'id, who was kidnapped near Lake Chad and taken to the Ottoman Empire, eventually finding his way to Russia, subsequently enlisted in the all-Black 55th Regiment of Massachusetts and fought in the US Civil War.[19] The accounts in the UNESCO project and various publications of team members provide additional examples of what can be learned. In all these cases, an ethnic identity is implied and often explicitly stated.

A single biographical account is meaningful in terms of the reconstruction of the life history of one individual, and as such has value historically for a variety of purposes. Gustavus Vassa provides perspective on the Seven Years' War, the role of skilled slaves in the trade of the Caribbean in the 1760s, and the emergence of the abolition movement in Britain in the 1780s that ultimately led to the suppression of the trans-Atlantic slave trade after British abolition in 1807. But his account tells us little about the plight of African slaves who were Igbo in origin or the impact of slavery on females, although his account does demonstrate the emergence of Igbo as a recognized ethnic label and provides examples of the horrific treatment of females. His account nonetheless obscures much of what he experienced and what he thought. There is extensive first hand commentary on the Seven Years' War, but there is no mention of the war of independence of the thirteen North American colonies after 1776, although he was stationed at a major military base southeast of London that was meant to counter a French invasion should there be one. There are critical letters of the British engagement in North America published under his name but surely not written by him and without any reason to assume that the anti-government views in the newspapers were what he actually thought. Vassa clearly draws on a diary that he must have kept during the Seven Years' War and well into the 1770s, and he must have had papers relating to employment after his return from the Mosquito Shore in 1776 through the summer of 1788 when he was finishing his autobiography. None of these letters, notes, and documents have apparently survived, but given his propensity to write letters, as well as an autobiography, such materials most certainly have had to exist. No such materials are to be found in the papers that have survived, either in abolitionist circles or with his solicitors.

An examination of what can be known about the life of Baquaqua provides fleeting glimpses of slave life in Brazil and what freedom meant in Haiti and North America, and he was exceptional in traveling from West Africa to Brazil to North America, then the Caribbean, and perhaps even back to Africa. The fact that he resumed using his Muslim name after he achieved his freedom in New York is unusual. He was connected to the Free Will Baptist mission in Haiti and he attended New York Central College, being one of the first if not the first African to be enrolled in an educational institution of higher learning. During this period, he displayed his self identification as a person with a Muslim background, using the name Mahommah, and maintaining the nicknames that were used whenever a household had more than one male named for the Prophet Muhammad. He appears not to have had any contact with Muslims after his escape from slavery in New York City in 1847. Moreover, he came from Djougou, west of Borgu, in the interior of the Bight of Benin, north of Dahomey, but his name reflects his mother's Hausa background and her connection with family in Katsina, one of the principal cities and emirates within the Sokoto Caliphate, conquered during the jihad of 1804-1808. He had some knowledge of Arabic, as all boys in merchant families would have had. His father was of Dendi background who came from Borgu, which at the time meant that he was Muslim and associated with the network of Muslim merchants who predominated in the trade of Borgu. Baquaqua provides a list of words in Dendi, not Hausa, although it is not clear why he did this, since he clearly would have known the same terms in Hausa as he did in Dendi. His association with his mother's family is clear. He wanted to return to Katsina in Africa, not Borgu or Djougou, because that was where his mother was from. No matter the interpretation, Baquaqua had a Hausa name, was born in commercial center to the west of Borgu on the route to Asante, had a mother who was from a major city and emirate of the Sokoto Caliphate, and never renounced the names of his youth in Africa. He was named Muhammad because that was the name of his maternal grandfather. He could not be called Muhammad or a derivate like Mahommah out of respect for the grandfather and instead had two nicknames, Gardo and Baquaqua. He was sometimes called Gardo because he was born after twins, and this was a customary name. Moreover, the designation "gardo" rather than "gado" indicates that the Hausa dialect was associated with Katsina (and also Daura and other places), whereas "gado" was the pronunciation in Kano, Sokoto, Zaria and elsewhere. Finally, the reference to him as "baquaqua" or in Hausa as "ba kwakwa" or more accurately, "ba k'wak'wa," literally was the nickname given to a baby who was so attached to his or her mother to lack any interest in anything other than mother was considered not to be inquisitive, which is what *k'wak'wa* means. The Hausa language has two forms of "k", one that is explosive and relatively equivalent to the English "k" and the other, represented with a hook, "k'", that is implosive. A subtle distinction perhaps but nothing in language is subtle in terms of identification. The Hausa "ba" means "not." And hence the nickname Baquaqua, literally meant a baby who was not inquisitive but solely fixated on mother. It was a nickname of affection. This digression proves one important point: that ethnicity is a social construction that makes it difficult to understand the name of a person.

Similarly, the odyssey of Muhammad Ali Sa'id, later known as Nicholas Said, provides a personal account of the impact of *jihad* in Borno in the 1830s and 1840s and documents the trans-Saharan slave trade in the early 1850s, but Sa'id's unique experience in traveling from the Ottoman Porte to Russia and then widely in western Europe was someone who was Turkish, not Kanuri. Upon reaching North America and enlisting in the Union Army during the American Civil War, thereby complicating his identity even further, especially after he effectively renounced his Muslim background and switching his religious commitment to Swedenborgianism. He attained the rank of sergeant, while unusual, has significance because of his observations in analyzing the plight of African-Americans in the United States at that time. His ethnicity is again conjecture and situational. His mother was from Mandara, although there is a suggestion that he might have a Margi background. She became the wife of a leading military commander, Barca Gana, whose servile origins disguise where his family was from but he was brought up within a Kanembu family and associated with that connection. Muhammad Ali, aka Nicholas Said, grew up in Kukawa, the new capital of Borno established by Shehu al-Kanemi after the destruction of the historic capital at Birni Ngazargamu on the banks of the Komodogu Yo river that flows into Lake Chad from the west. Kukawa was established relatively close to Lake Chad in the midst of fertile pasture lands for livestock from the southern Sahara and from Kanem, to the northeast of Lake Chad. Said was in the Shehu's palace, the son of the leading general, and fully engaged in all the opportunities of inclusion in the royal household, including taking lessons in Arabic and Turkish. At this point, he was more aristocratic than ethnic, which had to do with servile status not with well being.

Later, after spending several years in Tripoli in the Mediterranean territories of the Ottoman Empire and then in the Ottoman Porte itself, he acquired the mannerisms of a royal Turkish servant. His sophistication was scarcely hidden beneath efforts to hide his unbelievable odyssey. By the time he wrote his autobiography, which was published in 1873, English was the eleven languages for which he claimed fluency. There is reason to believe that he also understood a twelfth, Hausa, which he never mentioned. However, in the 1830s and 1840s, Kukawa had become an economic satellite of Kano and other Hausa cities. Considering the number of prosperous Hausa merchants who visited the Kukawa court, it is difficult to imagine that Said did not learn at least some Hausa. For political reasons and the nature of class indoctrination in Borno, he never would have considered that he knew Hausa, but impossible to imagine that he didn't.

Biographies alone can be fascinating and informative, but how to relate biographies of broad patterns of change in a manner that allows analysis of deeper historical significance is the challenge that is being addressed in the *DATAS* project. The construction of the website www.datasproject.org demonstrates that the methodology of a biographical approach to studying the slave trade and slavery has merit by focusing on ethnonyms as a key detail. While one biography tells us little about broad patterns and historical change, the combination of thousands of biographical accounts allows analysis that has not been possible previously. In focusing on ethnonyms, it is necessary to extend the methodology to include references to specific instances to determine their relevance. Observers consciously or inadvertently provided observations on ethnicity, less so on language that was often stereotyped and often confused with ethnicity. Such commentary can be useful in assessing designations assigned to individuals as ethnic labels. At this point, materials are being searched for such references, following the best practices of "Freedom Narratives" and other web-based projects in searching materials. A sub-theme in the work flow allows for the processing of non-biographical data.

DATAS builds specifically on the "Freedom Narratives" project and the online digital repository of autobiographical accounts and biographical data of individual Africans assembled on the website www.freedomnarratives.org. By using the same methodology, it is possible to focus on ethnonyms and hence the meaning of ethnicity as associated with the individuals in the biographical database. At the outset of that project, it was not clear how many biographical accounts could be assembled and whether different types of data could be brought together in ways that would enable analysis of historical context and change. Through its team members, the project drew on a great variety of sources including advertisements for fugitive slaves, baptismal records, and the registers of enslaved people taken off slave ships by the Royal Navy after the British abolition of the slave trade in 1807.

DATAS has emerged as an online source that has primary historical material on people from West Africa in their global context. *DATAS* has a pedigree that connects with *SHADD: Studies in the History of the African Diaspora Documents*, *Freedom Narratives*, *Proyecto Baquaqua*, *Equiano's World*, and various workshops and seminars that highlight the value of biography in historical research and proposes a project that would apply the methodology of Freedom Narratives to a project that would focus on ethnonyms. Ethnonyms present a particular problem to researchers and represent confusion among students, the general and not a few scholars. The idea for the project emerged listening to scholars presenting papers on digital humanities, public history and African Diaspora. The scholarly discussions made it clear that collaboration was the operating level of discourse. The difficulties with meaning in trying to understand what ethnonyms are, how they changed or didn't, and the methodological problem of understanding how concepts change or do not over time can be addressed through the collation of massive quantities of data that have to be accessed in new ways. The team emerged in response to the call for papers. The existing collaborations provided the basis for developing a trans-Atlantic platform that focuses on ethnonyms.

Documenting Africans in Trans-Atlantic Slavery, DATAS (www.datasproject.org) is a digital platform on ethnonyms and is an open source relational database and website compatible with other web-based databases. It is visually pleasant and engaging, contains all known primary documentation, allows searches following a variety of topics, and encourages public interaction via social media and crowd sourcing (Hall 2010: 136-150). The model for a digital resource on ethnonyms evolved out of the successful development of the Liberated Africans project and the construction of Freedom Narratives. The *DATAS* initiative is compatible with the Linked Open Data hub, the *DATAS* project focuses on the people who were enslaved, owned slaves, or participated in slave trading. Our intention is to refine a hosting platform capable of managing and intersecting a growing collection of historical images and data; 2) expand the historical repository and metadata of biographical databases through active crowd-sourcing; 3) generate content for augmented, virtual, and/or mixed reality environments for K-12 and college audiences; 4) parse out metadata to operate with the SHADD Linked Open Data hub www.shadd.org.

Endnotes

1 For a discussion of the concept of ethnicity, see Gwendolyn Midlo Hall, *Slavery and African Ethnicities in the Americas: Restoring the Links* (Chapel Hill: University of North Carolina Press, 2005). Also see Paul E. Lovejoy, *Slavery in the Global Diaspora of Africa* (London: Routledge, 2019); Lovejoy "The African Diaspora: Revisionist Interpretations of Ethnicity, Culture and Religion under Slavery," *Studies in the World History of Slavery, Abolition and Emancipation*, II:1; Lovejoy and David V. Trotman, eds., *Trans-Atlantic Dimensions of Ethnicity in the African Diaspora* (London: Continuum, 2004); Lovejoy, "Transatlantic Transformations: The Origins and Identities of Africans in the Americas," in Boubacar Barry, Livio Sansone, and Elisée Soumonni, eds., *Africa, Brazil, and the Construction of Trans-Atlantic Black Identities* (Trenton, NJ: Africa World Press, 2008), 81-112.

2 Alonso de Sandoval, *Un tratado sobre la esclavitud* [De instauranda Æthiopum salute] (introdução, transcrição e tradução de Enriqueta Vila Vilar) Madrid: Alianza Editorial, 1987), G. C. A. Oldendorp, *Geschichte der Mission der Evangelischen Brider auf den Caraibischen Inseln S. Thomas, S. Croix and S. Jan* (Barby, 1777), John Clarke, *Specimens of Dialects: Short Vocabularies of Languages and Notes of Countries and Customs in Africa* (Berwick-upon-Tweed: Daniel Cameron, 1848), S.W. Koelle, *Polyglotta Africana*. Reprint, edited, with an introduction, by P. E. H. Hair (Graz, Austria: Akademische Druck- und Verlagsanstalt, 1963), Robert Needham Cust, *A Sketch of the Modern Languages of Africa* (London: Trubner & Company 1883), 2 vols.

3 Frederick William Hugh Migeod, *The Languages of West Africa* (London: Kegan Paul, Trench,Trubner & Co., 1913), 2 vols., R.S. Rattray, *The Tribes of the Ashanti Hinterland* (Oxford: Clarendon Press, 1932), 2 vols.

4 D. Westermann and M. A. Bryan, *Languages of West Africa: Handbook of African Languages*, Part II (London: International African Institute, 1952); Joseph H. Greenberg, *The Languages of Africa* (Bloomington: Indiana University Press, 1966).

5 Juan Guanche, *Africanía y ethncidad en Cuba* (Havana: Editorial de Ciencias Sociales, 2009), 199-227.

6 *African Language Studies* (1960); *Sierra Leone Language Review* (1962); *Africana Linguistica* (1962); *Journal of African Languages* (1962); *Journal of West African Languages* (1964); *African Language Review* (1967); and *Bulletin de la Société d'Etudes des Langues de l'Afrique* (1967).

7 See Onigu Otite, *Ethnic Pluralism and Ethnicity in Nigeria* (Ibadan: Shaneson C. I. Ltd., 1990); Stephan Bühnen, "Ethnic Origins of Peruvian Slaves (1548-1650): Figures for upper Guinea," *Paideuma: Mitteilungen zur Kulturkunde* 39 (1993), 57-110; Stephan Palmie, "Ethnogenetic Processes and Culture Transfer in AfroAmerican Slave Populations," in Wolfgang Bider, ed., *Slavery in the Americas* (Würzburg: Königshausen & Neumann, 1993), 337-363; P. E. H. Hair, "Ethnolinguistic Continuity on the Guinea Coast," *Journal of African History* 8: 2 (1967), 247-268; Hair, "An Ethnolinguistic Inventory of the Guinea Coast before 1700," *Sierra Leone Language Review* 6 (1967), 32-70; Colin Palmer, "From Africa to the Americas: Ethnicity in the Early Black Communities of the Americas," *Journal of World History* 6:2 (1995); Hall, *Slavery and African Ethnicities*; James Sidbury and Jorge Cañizares-Esguerra, "Mapping Ethnogenesis in the Early Modern Atlantic," *William and Mary Quarterly* 68:2 (2011), 181-208; David Wheat, "The First Great Waves: African Provenance Zones for the Transatlantic Slave Trade to Cartagena de Indias, 1570-1640," *Journal of African History* 52:1 (2011), 1-22.

8 Henry B. Lovejoy, "The Registers of Liberated Africans of the Havana Slave Trade Commission: Transcription Methodology and Statistical Analysis," *African Economic History* 38 (2010), 107-136.

9 Kartikay Chadha developed this app first as *Decoding Origins Web Portal*, which was used as the backend for "Creating a Visual Database with Archival Sources for the Era of African Slavery" and then applied to the "Freedom Narratives" project and further developed. See Kartikay Chadha, Katrina Keefer and Martha Ladly, "*The Decoding Origins Web Portal:* Creating a Visual Database with Archival Sources from the Era of African Slavery" and Paul E. Lovejoy, Érika Melek Delgado and Kartikay Chadha, "Freedom Narratives of West Africans from the Era of Slavery," both in this volume.

10 See Introduction and Kartikay Chadha, Appendix.

11 For Omar ibn Said, see Ala Alryyes, ed., *A Muslim American Slave: The Life of Omar Ibn Said* (Madison: Univ. of Wisconsin Press, 2011). For Gustavus Vassa, aka Olaudah Equiano, see Vincent Carretta, *Equiano, the African: Biography of a Self Made Man* (Athens, GA: Univ. of Georgia Press, 2005). For Yarrow Mamout, see James H. Johnston, *From Slave Ship to Harvard: Yarrow Mamout and the History of an African American Family* (New York: Fordham University Press, 2012). For Baquaqua, see Robin Law and Paul E. Lovejoy, eds., *The Biography of Mahommah Gardo Baquaqua: His Passage from Slavery to Freedom in Africa and America* (Princeton, NJ: Markus Wiener, 2nd ed., 2007) and Bruno Rafael Véras,."The Slavery and Freedom Narrative of Mahommah Gardo Baquaqua in the Nineteenth-Century Atlantic World," *UNESCO General History of Africa, Global Africa* (Paris: UNESCO, 2019), vol. 10. For Prieto, Henry B. Lovejoy, *Prieto: Yorùbá Kingship in Colonial Cuba during the Age of Revolutions* (Chapel Hill, University of North Carolina Press, 2018). For Domingos Sodré, see João José Reis, *Domingos Sodré, um sacerdote Africano: Escravidão, liberdade e candombl é na Bahia do século XIX* (São Paulo: Companhia das Letras, 2008). For Rosalie, see Rebecca Scott and Jean M. Hébard, *Freedom Papers. An Atlantic Odyssey in the Age of Emancipation* (Cambridge, MA: Harvard University Press, 2012). For the Robin Johns of Calabar, see Randy Sparks, *The Two Princes of Calibar* (Cambridge, MA: Harvard University Press, 2004). For Domingos Álvares, see James H. Sweet, *Domingos Álvares, African Healing, and the Intellectual History of the Atlantic World* (Chapel Hill: University of North Carolina Press, 2011). For Archibald Monteath, see Maureen Warner-Lewis, *Archibald Monteath, Igbo, Jamaican, Moravian* (Kingston: University of West Indies Press, 2006). Also see Dominique Rogers, ed., *Voix d'Esclaves: Antilles, Guyane et Louisiane Françaises, XVIIIe-XIXe Siècle* (Paris: Karthala, 2015).

12 Paul E. Lovejoy, ed., "Life Stories and Freedom Narratives of Global Africa," *UNESCO General History of Africa, vol. 10, Global Africa* (Paris: UNESCO, 2021).

13 Henry Louis Gates Jr., *The Signifying Monkey: A Theory of African-American Literary Criticism* (New York: Oxford University Press, 1988); Allen Austin, *African Muslims in Antebellum America: Transatlantic Stories and Spiritual Struggles* (New York: Routledge, 1997), William L. Andrews, *To Tell a Free Story: The First Century of Afro-American Autobiography, 1760-1865* (Urbana: University of Illinois Press, 1986), John W. Blassingame, *Slave Testimony: Two Centuries of Letters, Speeches, Interviews, and Autobiographies* (Baton Rouge, LA: Louisiana State University Press, 1977), Vincent Carretta, ed., *Unchained Voices: An Anthology of Black Authors in the English- Speaking World of the Eighteenth Century* (Lexington: U. of Kentucky Press, 1996); Audrey Fisch, ed., *The Cambridge Companion to the African American Slave Narrative* (Cambridge: Cambridge University Press, 2007).

14 Philip D. Curtin, *The Atlantic Slave Trade: A Census* (Madison, WI: University of Wisconsin Press, 1969) and a critique of the Curtin schema, see Henry B. Lovejoy, Walter Hawthorne, Paul E. Lovejoy, Edward A. Alpers, Mariana Candido, Matthew Hopper. "Redefining African Regions for Linking Open-Source Data," *History in Africa* 46 (2019), 5-36, and Paul E. Lovejoy, "The upper Guinea Coast and the Trans-Atlantic Slave Trade Database," *African Economic History* 38 (2010), 1-27.

15 Henry B. Lovejoy, Paul E. Lovejoy, Walter Hawthorne, Edward A. Alpers, Mariana Candido, Matthew S. Hopper, Ghislaine Lydon, Colleen E. Kriger, John Thornton, "Defining Regions of Pre-Colonial Africa: A Controlled Vocabulary for Linking Open-Source Data in Digital History Projects," *History in Africa* 48 (2021).

16 See the documentation on the website, "Equiano's World: Gustavus Vassa and the

Abolition of the British Slave Trade" <www.equianosworld.org>.

17 Paul E. Lovejoy, "Ali Eisami's Enslavement and Emancipation: The Trajectory of a Liberated African," in Richard Anderson and Henry B. Lovejoy, *Liberated Africans and the Abolition of the Slave Trade, 1807-1896* (Rochester: University of Rochester Press, 2019).

18 Robin Law and Paul E. Lovejoy, *The Biography of Mahommah Gardo Baquaqua: His Passage from Slavery to Freedom in Africa and America.* Princeton: Markus Wiener Publisher, 2nd rev ed., 2007; and Bruno Rafael Véras, "The Slavery and Freedom Narrative of Mahommah Gardo Baquaqua in the Nineteenth-Century Atlantic World," *UNESCO General History of Africa*, vol. 10.

19 Paul E. Lovejoy, "Mohammed Ali Nicholas Sa'id: From Enslavement to American Civil War Veteran," in Vicente Sanz Rozalén and Michael Zeuske, eds., special issue, Microhistorias de la esclavitud, *Millars. Espai i Història* 42 (2017) and Mohammed Bashir Salau, "Nicholas Sa'id of Borno: American Civil War Veteran," *UNESCO General History of Africa*. Dean Calbraith is completing a biography of Nicholas Said.

11

« Nations africaines » et esclavage en Louisiane :

Les enseignements de *Voyages* et de la *Louisiana Slave Database*

Ibrahima Seck

La Louisiane avait connu la domination successive des Français, de 1699 à 1766, et celle des Espagnols, de 1766 à 1803. C'est la période coloniale pour les Américains, qui prennent le relais à partir de 1803. Sous ces trois régimes successifs, près de 22.000 Africains avaient été introduits dans le pays dont certains étaient arrivés par le biais de la traite clandestine, après la décision prise par les autorités de mettre fin à l'importation de captifs dans le territoire américain à partir du 1er janvier 1808. Dans cette contribution, nous partons des enseignements des bases de données *Voyages: The Trans-Atlantic Slave Trade Database* (www.slavevoyages.org) de David Eltis et David Richardson et la *Louisiana Slave Database* (www.louisianaslavedatabase.org) de Gwendolyn Midlo Hall pour examiner la présence africaine en Louisiane avec un focus sur les représentants sénégambiens dont l'ethnonymie nous est plus familière. La Sénégambie dont il est question ici est la somme des anciennes provinces maritimes de l'empire du Mali que Boubacar Barry définit comme le Finistère de l'ouest africain s'étendant du sud de la Mauritanie aux confins de la Sierra Leone.[1] Les deux bases de données montrent une forte présence des Soudanais occidentaux (Maliens et Sénégambiens) au 18e siècle, quand la Louisiane était une colonie française puis espagnole. Parmi eux, nombreux étaient ceux qui portaient des identités nationales qui éclairent leurs origines.

Dans ce travail, nous défendons la validité de ces identités nationales affirmées par les déportés eux-mêmes par opposition aux identités qui leur étaient assignées par les maîtres et les marchands d'esclaves. Nous discutons ces identifiants pour démontrer leur validité contrairement aux thèses qui ne leur accordent aucun crédit car considérant ces ethnonymes comme de simples fabrications des marchands d'esclaves. Ces identités redonnent leur humanité aux captifs, qui cessent alors d'être de simples ombres perdues dans les méandres de l'histoire. Elles permettent aussi d'effectuer des recherches pointues sur les racines de la culture afro-créole de Louisiane qui a fini de donner à la culture américaine un rayonnement planétaire.

Les nations africaines de Louisiane, 1719-1820

La *Voyages* est une base de données sur le commerce transatlantique des esclaves. Elle contient des renseignements sur près de 36.000 expéditions négrières qui avaient transporté plus de 10 millions d'Africains aux Amériques entre le 16e et le 19e siècle. De l'avis même de ses initiateurs, cette base de données ne peut prétendre être complète. Les documents relatifs à de nombreux voyages ont en effet disparu et beaucoup de documents restent à trouver dans des archives publiques et privées. Il s'y ajoute l'équation de l'impact de la traite clandestine qui, par sa nature intrinsèque, ne sera jamais résolue. Sur un total de quarante-cinq cargaisons de captifs signalées à l'arrivée en Louisiane entre 1719 et 1830, dix-huit étaient originaires de la Sénégambie dont seize pour la période 1720-1743. L'Afrique centrale était l'origine pour douze cargaisons dont une seule était arrivée entre 1719 et 1743. C'était pendant cette même période que six des sept cargaisons originaires du golfe du Bénin étaient arrivées en Louisiane. Après 1743, la prochaine cargaison d'Africains n'était signalée qu'en 1784 avec l'arrivée du *Thétis* d'Afrique centrale. Trois navires étaient arrivés entre 1788 et 1790 mais les points de départ en Afrique restent inconnus. En 1792, *l'Aimable Victoire* clôturait la période espagnole avec une cargaison originaire d'Afrique centrale. À partir de 1803 se déroule la période américaine pendant laquelle dix-sept navires étaient signalés à l'arrivée à la Nouvelle Orléans, dont sept étaient originaires d'Afrique centrale, deux de la Sénégambie, deux du sud-est africain, un de la Gold Coast, un du golfe du Bénin, un du golfe de Biafra et trois autres aux origines inconnues.[2]

Ces données statistiques nous permettent donc de parler de la prépondérance sénégambienne au 18e siècle et de la prépondérance congolaise au 19e siècle sans négliger la présence remarquable des ressortissants du golfe du Bénin. Un simple calcul à partir de l'atlas qui accompagne la *Voyages* évalue à 64,5% la part de la Sénégambie (Sierra Leone incluse) parmi les 22.000 Africains débarqués le long du golfe du Mexique, principalement en Louisiane, entre 1719 et 1830.[3] On peut donc considérer que la Sénégambie avait joué un rôle crucial dans la genèse de la culture afro-créole de Louisiane dans la mesure où cette région détenait une place prépondérante dans la mise en place de la population africaine initiale. En outre, pendant environ quarante ans, entre 1743 et 1784, cette population originelle majoritairement sénégambienne était restée dans un vase pratiquement clos, avec très peu d'apports venant des Antilles. Toutefois, la banque de données consolidée par Gwendolyn Midlo Hall et une publication en cours de cette auteure informent de l'arrivée de captifs bantu en Louisiane en 1758. Le navire britannique Judith avait alors été capturé par les Français et amené à la Grenade où il fut condamné. Les deux tiers de sa cargaison avaient été vendus sur place et l'autre tiers avait été amené à bord de deux petits navires français à la Nouvelle-Orléans où ils avaient débarqué au total 124 captifs, dont 72 adultes et 52 enfants. Aucune autre documentation sur des expéditions négrières entre la Louisiane et les Caraïbes n'a été retrouvée pour la période française, mais des Africains originaires du golfe du Bénin apparaissent aussi dans les documents de la Louisiane et beaucoup d'entre eux étaient probablement arrivés via la Martinique à un moment où la traite atlantique des esclaves vers cette colonie française était concentrée sur le golfe du Bénin.[4]

Appelée plus couramment *Louisiana Slave Database*, cette banque de données a été construite principalement à partir d'archives judicaires ou notariées. Elle couvre une période d'un siècle entre 1719, date de l'arrivée en Louisiane du premier navire négrier des côtes africaines, à 1820, date à partir de laquelle la traite interne des êtres humains, depuis la Côte Est des États-Unis, était devenue la source principale des captifs importés en Louisiane. La lexicologie coloniale n'ayant pas encore inventé « l'ethnie », le concept de « nation » servait à identifier les origines africaines. Les inventaires des plantations, établis à la mort des propriétaires ou dans des cas de banqueroute, donnent des informations sur les origines des Africains plus précises et plus fiables que celles des manifestes des bateaux négriers et de la douane portuaire. L'esclave étant considéré comme de la marchandise que l'on portait à l'encan, l'origine pouvait être un critère essentiel dans la détermination de sa valeur marchande à côté de l'âge et du genre. On peut donc suspecter des identités assignées à des fins marchandes pour les captifs fraîchement débarqués des côtes africaines et vendus par des négriers. Une telle tentation pouvait aussi affecter des héritiers pour mieux vendre à l'encan les captifs inventoriés en leur présence dans des cas de succession. En réalité, il ne s'agit pas toujours d'identités assignées car, dans de nombreux cas, les concernés répondaient directement aux questions des officiels qui étaient très souvent des juges paroissiaux, lesquels faisaient aussi office de notaires. Certains individus étaient impliqués, en tant qu'accusés ou témoins, dans des affaires judiciaires ayant pour objet des crimes tels que le vol, le marronnage, le meurtre, la maltraitance par le maître, etc. On demandait au concerné de décliner son identité en indiquant son nom (selon les cas son nom africain), le nom du maître, sa nation, son âge, et sa religion. Les documents mentionnaient en outre les qualifications et les défauts des concernés. Il s'agit d'une tradition instaurée en Louisiane au temps des Français et qui s'était perpétuée sous les régimes espagnol et américain.

Hall considère à juste raison que les personnes que l'on retrouve dans les inventaires de plantations ou dans des procès criminels, avaient une claire conscience de leurs origines qu'ils pouvaient encore mieux exprimer d'autant plus que le captif devenu esclave retrouvait ses esprits après sa longue déportation, s'accommodait à sa nouvelle vie et n'était plus limité par des problèmes de communication.[5] Ceci est d'autant plus vrai qu'une langue commune avait vite émergé, à savoir le créole qui était parlé aussi bien par la population asservie que par les maîtres et leurs progénitures. Les captifs fraîchement débarqués en Amérique étaient décrits par des termes tels que « bruts » par les Français ou « bozales » par les Espagnols. Ils étaient aussi classés selon la provenance sur les côtes africaines. Très peu de captifs destinés à la Louisiane avaient été importés de la région allant du Cap des Palmes à la Côte de l'or. Le *Rambler*, le seul navire arrivé de la Côte de l'or, avait débarqué sa cargaison en 1807. Cependant, des captifs identifiés comme étant de nation Mina étaient nombreux en Louisiane. Le domaine traditionnel des Mina se situe sur les rives de la rivière Mono. Ils font partie des sept à huit sous-groupes du peuple Ewe, à cheval sur le sud-est du Ghana, le Togo et le Bénin occidental.[6] La fameuse Côte des Esclaves était surtout l'exutoire pour les personnes originaires de l'intérieur des terres comme les Kiamba (Tchamba), les Hawsa, les Nago (Yoruba) et les Fon/Arada. Ces peuples avaient aussi une présence remarquable en Louisiane. Le golfe du Biafra, centré sur le delta du Niger et la Cross River, s'étend à l'est jusqu'à la charnière camerounaise. Les esclaves provenant de cette région étaient identifiés en Louisiane comme étant de nations Edo, Ibo (Igbo), Ibibio et Calabar. « Igbo » est d'ailleurs devenu un nom de famille (Ebow) dans le sud-ouest de la Louisiane.

La grande côte de Loango, du Congo et de l'Angola était l'origine des esclaves dits de nation « Congo », nom générique sous lequel les captifs d'Afrique centrale étaient désignés en Louisiane où ils étaient arrivés en masse au 19e siècle. Pour Moreau de Saint-Méry, bien que la côte angolaise soit considérée comme la frontière de la traite destinée aux colonies françaises d'Amérique, des captifs avaient été importés de Monomotapa, du Mozambique et de Madagascar.[7] Des personnes originaires du sud-est de l'Afrique étaient appelés Makwa en Louisiane où ils figuraient parmi les dix-huit ethnies africaines les plus fréquentes dans les documents officiels. Ils étaient peut-être tous arrivés à bord de *l'Agent*, navire officiellement signalé deux fois à la Nouvelle Orléans en 1807 et 1808 en provenance de cette région éloignée. Également appelés Mirazi, les Makwa sont localisés essentiellement le long des rives du fleuve Ruvuma ou Rovuma, à la frontière entre le Mozambique et la Tanzanie. La Louisiane comptait aussi de nombreuses personnes identifiées comme « nègres de Guinée », une origine imprécise et sujette à controverse. Dans une large discussion de cet identifiant, Hall est persuadée que ces « nègres de Guinée » étaient en majorité des Sénégambiens.[8] Dans l'inventaire de la propriété de Jean Christophe Haydel, un riche planteur indigotier de la Côte des Allemands, figurait sept Africains, tous identifiés comme étant des « nègres de Guinée », dont un individu nommé Mass.[9] Près de vingt ans plus tard, trois d'entre eux étaient identifiés dans l'inventaire de la communauté de la fille de Jean Christophe, Magdelaine Haydel Becnel. À savoir Macré (sic), nègre sénégalais âgé de soixante-quinze ans ; Philipe, nègre de nation Aoussas, âgé de soixante ans et enfin Apollon, nègre Congo de trente-six ans. Six autres personnes étaient aussi identifiées dans cet inventaire comme étant des Africains, dont trois Bambara, deux Congo et Marie Joseph, âgée de soixante-dix ans, identifiée comme négresse de nation Mina et épouse du sénégalais Macré.[10] Mass étant le diminutif des noms sénégalais Maciré et Massamba, il est fort probable que le nom Macré soit le résultat d'une erreur commise par Alexandre Labranche, le juge et notaire de la paroisse Saint-Jean Baptiste à cette époque. A une date indéterminée, Magdelaine Haydel avait dû racheter Mass auprès de son frère Georges Haydel décédé en 1814. La plantation en question s'appelle maintenant Evergreen et est mitoyenne à Whitney Plantation, anciennement Habitation Haydel aussi, site du premier musée américain focalisé exclusivement sur l'esclavage.

L'Afrique centrale, la Sénégambie, le golfe du Bénin et le golfe du Biafra étaient bien représentés en Louisiane (Tableau 12.1). En ce qui concerne la Sénégambie, les Manding, les Bambara, les Wolof, les Fulɓe et les Nards figuraient parmi les « nations » africaines les plus fréquentes. La notion de « fréquence » se définit ici comme le nombre de fois des individus rattachés à une « nation » donnée apparaissent dans les archives. D'après les calculs effectués par Hall, sur 38.019 captifs dont l'origine est connue, 24.349 (64%) étaient nés en Afrique, dont 8.442 (22,2%) avec des indications précises sur leurs « nations » et 9.382 (38.5%) avec de vagues indications sur leur origine comme « côtes du Sénégal » ou « Guinée ». Pour quelques 5.973 cas (25.3%) il est simplement mentionné qu'ils étaient nés en Afrique.[11] On peut aussi parler d'identité vague pour les esclaves de « nation Congo » car nous avons affaire à un nom générique désignant tous les captifs originaires du bassin du Congo et de toute l'Afrique centrale. On pourrait aussi considérer « Sénégal » comme un nom générique même s'il est clairement établi que les « Nègres de nation Sénégal » étaient sans aucun doute des Wolof comme l'indique clairement Le Page du Pratz. Ce dernier avait vécu de 1718 à 1728 au poste des Natchez sur le Mississippi où il y avait une forte concentration d'Africains esclaves. Il quitta ce lieu peu avant le massacre de la colonie française par les Indiens habitant cette région pour s'établir à la Nouvelle Orléans où il servit, de 1729 à 1731, comme intendant de la plantation du roi de France, située sur la rive droite du Mississippi, à l'opposé de la Nouvelle Orléans. Il avait donc une connaissance intime des Africains de Louisiane à un moment où, à la suite de la Compagnie d'Occident, la Compagnie des Indes occidentales déployait des efforts immenses pour faire venir la main-d'œuvre servile, surtout de la toute proche concession du Sénégal. Dans le volume 3 des mémoires de Le Page du Pratz, l'identité des Wolof ne fait aucun doute. Il leur prêtait des qualités exceptionnelles et recommandait aux planteurs de les affecter à des tâches domestiques ou d'en faire des commandeurs et des ouvriers qualifiés :

> Je dirai seulement que pour tel service que ce puisse être, à la maison, je ne conseille de prendre d'autres Nègres & Négresses, jeunes & vieux, que des Sénégal qui se nomment entre eux Djolaufs, parce que de tous les Nègres que j'ai connus, ceux-ci ont le sang le plus pur ; ils ont plus de fidélité & l'esprit le plus pénétrant que les autres, & sont par conséquent plus propres à apprendre un métier ou à servir. Il est vrai qu'ils ne sont pas si robustes que les autres pour les travaux de la terre, & pour résister à la grande chaleur.... Ils sont bons commandeurs des autres Nègres, tant à cause de leur fidélité & leur reconnoissance, que parce qu'ils semblent être nés pour commander. Comme ils sont orgueilleux, on peut aisément les encourager à apprendre un métier ou à servir dans la maison, par la distinction qu'ils acquereront sur les autres Nègres, & la propreté que cet état leur procurera dans leurs habillemens.[12]

Tout en reconnaissant la complexité de l'histoire des formations sociales en Afrique, notamment la création artificielle de catégories ethniques dans le contexte colonial et celui antérieur de la traite des esclaves, Michael Gomez s'appuie sur les sources arabo-musulmanes pour constater que le fait ethnique est ancien en Afrique aussi bien à l'échelle des grandes formations politiques avec un État centralisé qu'au niveau des petites communautés dont l'identité ne dépasse pas le village ou la contrée. En ce qui concerne la Sénégambie, les témoignages des Européens de la première heure lèvent toute ambiguïté quant à l'identité des peuples rencontrés notamment les Wolof, les Manding et les Fulɓe.[13] La Sénégambie que les Européens découvrirent au 15e siècle, avait été façonnée pendant plusieurs siècles par ses relations transsahariennes notamment en ce qui concerne la toponymie et la nomenclature des peuples, la configuration du commerce et l'évolution politique, la religion et les mœurs de ses habitants, voire la musique et ses instruments. Les chroniqueurs arabo-berbères nous renseignent amplement sur les peuples et les entités politiques de la vallée du fleuve Sénégal comme Takrûr, Senghâna et Ghâna. Ces toponymes apparaissent dans le *Kitāb al-Masālik wal-Mamālik* (*Livre des Itinéraires et des Royaumes*) du géographe andalou Al Bakrī, publié à Cordoue en 1068. Senghâna y est décrit comme étant la région des *Sûdan* (Noirs) la plus proche des Berbères occidentaux (Banu Djudäla), une ville « composée de deux cités sur les deux rives du Nîl » et, détail édifiant, « ses terres habitées s'étendent sans discontinuité jusqu'à l'océan ».[14] Il est clair qu'il s'agit bien ici du Waalo, composante amphibie du Jolof [le pays des Wolof], d'où ils essaimèrent par la suite le long de l'océan pour créer les royaumes de Kajoor et Bawol.

Selon Jean Boulègue, le Grand Jolof, dont l'hégémonie s'étendait aussi aux pays sereer, avait débuté sur les bords du fleuve Sénégal. La légende de l'ancêtre fondateur Njajaan Njaay, à travers le mythe d'une ascendance almoravide, rend compte d'une réelle influence musulmane.[15] Le nom Sénégal a été donc forgé à partir de *Senghâna*, toponyme que les géographes arabes du Moyen Age utilisaient pour désigner un royaume situé sur le delta du fleuve Sénégal. Le toponyme Senghâna avait donné Sénégal car, à la suite des Arabes, les sources portugaises évoquaient le royaume de Senega, nom que l'on retrouve aussi dans les sources françaises au moins jusqu'à la fin du 17e siècle.[16] À son arrivée sur les lieux en juin 1686, le père Jean-Baptiste Gaby avait constaté que « l'endroit où habitent les François, avant sa découverte appartenait au Roy Brak, dont le païs ne s'appelle pas Senega, mais Ouhalle (Waalo) ».[17] Il est donc assez symptomatique que dans les colonies françaises de l'Amérique, notamment en Louisiane, les esclaves wolof étaient tous désignés dans les documents officiels comme étant de « *nation Sénégal* » et sans confusion avec leurs voisins méridionaux appelés « *nègres de nation Sérer* ».

Al Bakri situe *Takrûr*, immédiatement à l'est de *Senghâna*, plus précisément sur le fleuve. Il décrit ses habitants comme étant des *Sûdan* (Noirs) qui suivaient autrefois la *madjusiyya* (paganisme) et adoraient les *dakakir* (idoles) jusqu'au moment où un de leurs souverains devint musulman et fit de l'Islam la religion du pays. Ce souverain, qui s'appelait Wâr Dyabi, mourut en 1040-1041.[18] Les traditions locales rattachent le peuple sereer aux *Jaa-oogo*, des métallurgistes et excellents agriculteurs qui donnèrent au *Takrûr* sa première royauté avant leur chute face aux *Manna*, dynastie à laquelle appartenait War Dyabi. C'était alors l'avènement de l'État marchand et l'apogée du royaume qui sera plus tard confondu avec l'empire du Mali, tant sa notoriété était grande en Orient. Un pont était jeté entre le fleuve Sénégal et les pays de la Méditerranée et les souverains razziaient les populations réfractaires à l'Islam pour les vendre dans le commerce transsaharien.[19] Sous la pression des forces nouvelles portées par l'Islam, les *Sereer* étaient contraints d'abandonner leurs villages de la vallée du fleuve Sénégal pour essaimer autour du Siin et du Saalum, cours d'eau éponymes des royaumes qu'ils fondèrent en symbiose avec les Gelwaar, guerriers *malinke* qui étaient aussi à l'origine des principautés établies le long du fleuve Gambie.[20] *Takrûr* n'est rien d'autre que le *Fuuta Tooro* des *Fulɓe*, un pays à cheval sur la moyenne vallée du fleuve Sénégal. Les termes *Toucouleurs* et Tocchoroes, respectivement issus de la littérature coloniale française et portugaise, ne sont que la corruption de *Takrûrî* (habitant du Takrûr en arabe). Les habitants du pays, les *Fulɓe* (sing. Pullo), avaient depuis longtemps choisi de s'auto-désigner sous le terme fédérateur de *Haal Pulaar* (les locuteurs du *pulaar*) incluant les nombreux étrangers qui vivaient parmi eux. Les *Fulɓe* déportés comme esclaves dans les colonies françaises de l'Amérique étaient désignés comme étant de « nation Poulard ». *Sénégal* et *Poulard* sont encore aujourd'hui les noms de famille pour des milliers de Noirs de la Louisiane, surtout dans les régions du sud-ouest où ils cohabitent avec les descendants des Acadiens, colons de souche française, expulsés de la Nouvelle Ecosse par les Anglais dans le contexte de la Guerre de sept ans.

En Louisiane, l'identifiant « Poulard » était moins fréquent dans les archives, comparé aux Bambara, Manding et même Wolof. Par rapport à la traite atlantique, le Fuuta-Tooro était davantage une zone de passage qu'une terre pourvoyeuse d'esclaves. Selon Saugnier, « les Poules (Fulɓe) ne viennent jamais ou rarement vendre leurs captifs ». Ils viennent dans la colonie pour vendre leur mil, leurs peaux, leur morfil, etc., contre du fer et de la laine. Toutefois, « en cas de guerre de nation à nation, on y trouve d'excellens et superbes esclaves ».[21] Tel était le cas après le triomphe de la Révolution des Marabouts *Toorobbe (*sing*: Tooroodo)* en 1776. Les partisans de la dynastie déchue des Satigi s'était installés sur les marges du royaume, multipliant les pillages.[22] À partir de cette période, la population pulaarophone de Louisiane acquiert une visibilité remarquable, d'autant plus qu'elle était fort probablement renforcée par les Fulɓe du Fuuta-Jalon où le parti maraboutique avait couronné Karamoko Alfa comme *Almaami* après le triomphe de la révolution musulmane en 1725. À la mort de ce dernier vers 1751, le pouvoir revenait à Ibrahima Sori Mawdo, commandant en chef de l'armée. Sous prétexte de guerre sainte, le nouveau *Almaami* avait engagé le Fuuta Jalon dans une politique agressive contre les pays voisins afin de se procurer des captifs dont l'aristocratie locale et les négriers de la côte avaient besoin.[23] Il reste évident que de nombreux Fulɓe engagés dans cette chasse à l'homme en faisaient aussi les frais. C'était le cas de Abdul-Rahmaan Bari, fils d'Almaami Ibrahima Sori, qui fut capturé dans une guerre contre les Manding du Gaabu vers 1788 et vendu sur le marché des esclaves de la Nouvelle Orléans à Thomas Foster, un planteur du Mississippi.[24] Aux Fulɓe du Fuuta Tooro et du Fuuta Jalon, la Louisiane avait aussi fort probablement reçu des Fulɓe du Fuuta Masina dans la Boucle du Niger et des Fulɓe du Fuuta Adamawa au nord du Nigeria et du Cameroun.

De *Takrûr*, Al Bakri nous transporte dans les pays *Soninke*, plus précisément à *Silla*, toponyme désignant, comme *Takrûr* et *Senghâna*, une ville à cheval sur les deux rives du fleuve et un royaume puissant au point de rivaliser avec *Ghâna* et qui aurait été islamisé au temps de War Dyabi. Immédiatement après Silla, Al Bakri évoque la ville de *Kalambü* que les historiens ont fini aujourd'hui d'identifier avec le Galam, épine dorsale du commerce du fleuve Sénégal pendant le 18e siècle.[25] Les informateurs d'Al Idrisi, auteur du 12e siècle, fréquentaient certainement la route commerciale transsaharienne qui longeait l'océan, à partir du Maroc, et aboutissait aux salines d'Awlil (Waalo) dans le sud-ouest de la Mauritanie actuelle où commençait le pays wolof. Ces salines étaient dès cette époque le principal support d'un commerce intérieur très actif qui préfigurait le commerce de Galam sur le fleuve Sénégal. À la suite d'Al Bakri, Al Idrisi confirme le fait que le sel d'Awlil était transporté dans des embarcations et vendu en amont à Takrûr, Silla, Ghâna et dans tout le Soudan.[26] Ghâna est reconnu comme le premier empire qui prospéra au Soudan Occidental. Cette entité politique, que ses fondateurs *Soninke* appelaient *Wagadu,* fut détruite sous les effets combinés de l'avancée du front islamique et celle du désert. On prête aux Almoravides (*Al-Murabitûn*), les Marabouts de la littérature coloniale, le fait d'avoir détruit Kumbi-Saleh (Kumbi-la-Sainte), la capitale de l'empire. Le toponyme Ghâna serait-il dérivé du pays que les Wolof appellent *Gannaar*, le pays des Naar, immense territoire désertique, inexploré par les Européens jusqu'au 19e siècle ? Les Français appelaient ce territoire *Barbarie*, domaine des nomades berbères ou arabo-berbères qu'ils désignaient sous le terme générique *Maures*. En Louisiane, les esclaves Maures étaient identifiés comme étant de « *nation Nard* », nom par lequel les Wolof les désignent encore aujourd'hui. Les Maures, appelés Safalɓe (sing. *Capaato*) par les Fulɓe, étaient sans doute ceux qui avaient le plus contribué à la vente des habitants du Fuuta-Tooro comme esclaves. Selon Saugnier, ils conduisaient des captifs toute l'année au Sénégal, excepté pendant les trois à quatre mois que dure la mauvaise saison, les débordements du fleuve les obligeant alors à se réfugier dans l'intérieur des terres.[27] En entreprenant une thèse sur le Fuuta Toro aux 18e et 19e siècles, Oumar Kane était guidé par l'idée que la chute du régime des Satigi (1512-1776) et son remplacement par le régime maraboutique étaient le résultat d'une évolution interne marquée par les progrès constants des marabouts qui consolidaient leur influence en élargissant leur clientèle. En compulsant les documents d'archives, l'évidence sautait aux yeux : la chute des Satigi était le résultat de la mainmise maure sur les affaires du pays. La chasse à l'homme était une activité très ancienne qui permettait aux Maures de satisfaire leurs propres besoins pour le travail domestique, la garde des troupeaux, la mise en valeur des forêts de gommiers et de palmiers dattiers, de même que l'exploitation des salines du Waalo et du

Cap Blanc.

Le commerce atlantique avait donné aux Maures le goût du pillage à caractère mercantile. Ils gardaient les enfants et vendaient les adultes aux négriers de la côte. Aussi les Maures appelaient-ils le fleuve Sénégal Adyak (la rivière aux esclaves). La Révolution musulmane consacrait l'affranchissement du Fuuta du péril maure et le prestige d'Abdul Qadiri Kan, premier *Almaami* du Fuuta Tooro, s'était considérablement renforcé dans son pays et dans toute la Sénégambie, particulièrement dans les pays qui avaient souffert des pillages maures. Thierno Sileymani Baal, le principal chef de guerre, mourut au front après avoir refusé les fonctions d'Almami pour continuer la bataille contre les Maures.[28] Il n'est pas alors étonnant que la présence des Maures en Louisiane fût à son niveau le plus élevé autour de l'année 1780. La fréquence des *Nards* dans les archives locales était encore relativement élevée entre 1790 et 1810 nous renseigne la *Louisiana Slave Database* de Hall. Fulɓe et Safalɓe sont des peuples voisins qui partagent un certain nombre de traits culturels. Ils ont toujours en commun le pastoralisme nomade, une activité très ancienne dans les immensités devenues arides de Barbarie. L'un est spécialiste de la vache et excellent agriculteur s'il est sédentaire. L'autre est le maître du dromadaire et propriétaire de palmiers dattiers dans les oasis du désert. Sur le plan de la production musicale, leur présence dans la vallée du Mississippi avait sans doute contribué à donner au blues rural sa base mélodique la plus caractéristique.

Boubacar Barry considère que l'influence du commerce atlantique était limitée dans le royaume Sereer du Siin qui s'était d'ailleurs replié sur lui-même pour assurer sa cohésion devant le contexte global de violence. Le Saalum, autre royaume Sereer, jouait un rôle plus important dans le commerce atlantique mais la chasse aux esclaves affectait surtout les faibles États voisins.[29] D'après les estimations de Philip Curtin, toute la Petite Côte, entre le Cap Vert et le fleuve Gambie, exportait moins de 150 esclaves par an dans les années 1740 et tout au plus 200 esclaves en 1762. Le principal port était celui de Joal dans le Siin qui avait cependant exporté à lui seul 90 à 100 esclaves en 1779.[30] Dans la banque de données de Hall, quatorze entrées sont relatives à douze personnes de nation *Cérer* ou *Sérer,* dont quatre à la Nouvelle Orléans et un nombre égal pour la Côte des Allemands et pour la Côte des Acadiens. Parmi eux, Louis Jupiter dit Gamelle, condamné à mort le 21 mars 1744 pour vol en réunion et exécuté sur la place publique à la Nouvelle Orléans. Alexandre, de nation Sénégal (Wolof), avait été aussi condamné pour complicité dans cette affaire de vols avec effraction, commis dans le magasin du roi à la Nouvelle Orléans, parmi les témoins à charge, Marianne de nation Mandinga.[31] Il y avait aussi ceux que Jean Boulègue appelle Sereer du Nord-Ouest ou *Sereer Cangin* et différents des Sereer du Siin et du Saalum. La région qu'ils habitent jusqu'à nos jours est relativement accidentée et naguère très boisée. C'était une zone-refuge enclavée entre les royaumes wolof du Kajoor et du Bawol. Leurs traditions orales rendent compte d'une hostilité constante à l'égard du pouvoir central wolof. Comme l'avait constaté Ca da Mosto, ils n'étaient pas soumis au roi de Senega. Ils n'avaient pas de roi ni de seigneur en particulier et n'en voulaient pas parmi eux, afin que leurs épouses et enfants ne leur fussent pas retirés pour être vendus comme esclaves.[32] Moreau de Saint-Mery faisait probablement allusion à ce peuple en parlant des « Nègres du Cap Verd (...) qui bordent le pays de Yoloffes, et qu'on nomme fort improprement aux Antilles des Calvaires. Leur couleur noire est encore plus foncée que celle des Sénégalais ; leur taille est avantageuse, leurs traits sont heureux ».[33] Dans la Louisiana Slave Database, deux groupes classés dans la rubrique « unidentified nations », sous les noms « *Djobass* » et « *Diass* », étaient probablement des Sereer du Nord-Ouest car deux toponymes similaires désignent respectivement une contrée et un village dans le pays *Cangin* au Sénégal.[34] Toutefois, la Note du Docteur Corre sur les peuplades du Rio Nunez, reproduite par Bérenger-Féraud, signale un groupe nommé Diobas ou Yola mélangé aux Landuma et aux Nalu depuis la conquête du Gabou par les Fulɓe.[35] À l'exception des Kisi et des Kanga dans le sud de la Sénégambie, la Louisiana Slave Database répertorie moins fréquemment des personnes de nations Diola (Joola), Papel, Beafada, Soso (Susu), Temne, etc. Boubacar Barry considère que les rivières du sud favorisaient la traite clandestine mais elles servaient plus à acheminer des esclaves de l'intérieur que les populations locales elles-mêmes.

Il est important de signaler une grosse difficulté soulevée par Paul Lovejoy en ce sens que les catégories ethniques actuelles ne peuvent toujours pas être plaquées sur le passé sans risque d'erreurs grossières car l'ethnie est une réalité en perpétuelle redéfinition. Par exemple, la nation Kiamba (Tchamba) de la littérature esclavagiste désigne plutôt les Konkomba et les Gurma de la région de la Haute Volta et non les Tchamba du bassin de la rivière Bénoué au Nigeria dont le domaine se prolonge au Cameroun.[36] À travers la nation Makwa, il faudrait peut-être voir des personnes aux origines diverses venant de tout le sud-est africain voire d'Afrique centrale car on trouve des Makoua au Congo. Les Kanga ou Canga ne doivent pas être confondus avec les Congo. Ils étaient fort probablement ceux que Moreau de Saint-Mery appelle les Mesurades, issus de la région de Sierra Leone-Liberia. Selon Douglas Chambers, les esclaves de l'arrière-pays du Cap Mesurade étaient souvent appelés « Canga » dans les Amériques, terme qui signifiait « étranger barbare » chez les Akan et qui avait dû leur être appliqué par ces groupes voisins à l'est.[37] Avant Paul Lovejoy, Jean-Loup Amselle et Elikia M'Bokolo s'appuyaient sur les trouvailles d'un ouvrage collectif pour constater aussi que l'ethnie est une réalité mouvante. Amselle considère qu'un ethnonyme peut recevoir une multitude de sens en fonction des époques, des lieux et des situations sociales. À ce propos, il évoque l'ancêtre des Jakite Sabashi, à l'origine Soninke ou Bamana et portant le nom Jara ou Konaté, qui avait pris le patronyme Jakité pour s'assimiler au groupe dominant des Fulɓe au Wasolon. L'un de ses fils avait repris le patronyme Konaté pour s'assimiler à un autre milieu dominé par les Manding où il avait créé une chefferie.[38] Cela est vrai pour la Sénégambie où des communautés entières avaient connu des changements d'identité dans des mouvements qui avaient transformé des Fulɓe, des Maures et des Bamana en Wolof, des Wolof en Fulɓe, des Manding en Sereer, des Sereer en Joola, etc.

Dans un contexte de servitude en Louisiane, cette tradition avait certainement contribué à rapprocher les exilés plutôt que de les disperser. Jeroen Dewulf considère que le concept de « nation » dans un contexte d'esclavage regroupe des personnes originaires de vastes régions d'Afrique, obligées de construire une identité commune dans la diaspora, car l'identification à un groupe se produit pour des raisons opportunistes dans les dures conditions de l'esclavage. Ainsi des esclaves, qui ne formeraient qu'une petite minorité, pouvaient tisser des réseaux de solidarité au sein d'une nation très bien représentée.[39] Aussi Paul E. Lovejoy parle-t-il à juste raison de « pan-ethnicities » ou « super ethnic groups » dont la genèse avait commencé en Afrique avant de se poursuivre sur la route de l'esclave et en diaspora. Il distingue ainsi six grands groupes dont la formation était déterminée à la fois par l'ethnie et la religion : Akan, Ewe/Fon, Yoruba (Lukumi-Aku-Nago), Igbo/Calabari, Kongo et le groupe des Musulmans plus souvent désignés sous le nom Mandingo.[40] Le modèle défini par P.E. Lovejoy et les affinités géographiques et historiques nous incitent à distinguer le groupe des Soudanais que nous appelons aussi « gens du Mande » dont la présence en Louisiane demande une attention particulière.

La prépondérance Mande et la controverse autour de la nation Bambara

Nous appelons « gens du Mande », ou « gens du Komo », les membres de la grande famille des Mande dont le domaine traditionnel s'étendait le long du Joliba (Niger), depuis le lac Debo au nord du Mali jusqu'aux rives du Tinkiso en Haute Guinée. Dans le groupe, Maurice Delafosse distinguait les Mande du nord (Bozo, Somono, Soninke, Jula), les Mande du centre (Kagoro, Bambara, Xaasonke, Foulanke, Malinke ou Manding) et les Mande du sud (Jallonke, Samo, Samorho, Sia, etc).[41] Cette liste est loin d'être exhaustive car elle n'inclut pas des peuples qui avaient essaimé dans la région dite des Rivières du Sud, notamment les Kissi, Toma, Susu, Temne, Mende, etc. Bambara est une corruption de l'ethnonyme Bamana. Cette appellation n'est utilisée ci-après que dans le cadre de citations d'autres auteurs. Bamana et Manding portent les mêmes patronymes (Coulibaly, Diarra, Traoré, Doumbia,

Keïta, Koné, Konaté, etc.) et parlent aussi des langues mutuellement intelligibles.[42] Le Komo est leur plus grande société initiatique par laquelle les adolescents entrent dans la case des hommes.[43] Bamana et Senufo parlent aussi des langues apparentées, partagent un certain nombre de patronymes et ont en commun le culte du Komo. L'habitat primitif des Bamana se situerait à l'extrême sud-est du Mande sur la rive droite du Niger, à hauteur de Siguiri en Haute Guinée. Ils auraient quitté cette région dès le début du 13e siècle pour échapper à la domination des empereurs du Mali. Ainsi, l'arrivée des Bamana dans la moyenne vallée du Niger aurait-elle affecté les Senufo dont certains furent absorbés et d'autres migrèrent vers le sud, notamment dans la région de Sikasso et le nord de la Côte d'Ivoire.[44] Les Bamana avaient fondé le royaume de Segu, qui s'affirma, à la fin du 17e siècle, après la chute de l'empire Songhay. Des Bamana dissidents furent à l'origine du royaume du Kaarta, plus à l'est, à proximité du comptoir français de Galam par où transitèrent des milliers de captifs réputés être des Bambara. Ces derniers étaient acheminés à Saint-Louis du Sénégal d'où ils étaient déportés, directement ou via l'île de Gorée, vers les colonies françaises d'Amérique. D'autres avaient transité par d'autres ports négriers, de la Gambie à la Sierra Leone. Les gens du Mande, surtout des Bamana et des Manding, avaient une visibilité remarquable parmi la population servile de Louisiane, surtout au moment où cette colonie était sous le contrôle de la Compagnie des Indes occidentales en même temps que la Concession du Sénégal. Les données consolidées dans la banque de données de Gwendolyn Midlo Hall, placent les Bambara et les Manding parmi les « nations » africaines les plus fréquentes dans les archives de la Louisiane. Certainement les autres composantes du groupe Mande étaient amalgamées sous les noms génériques Bambara et Mandinga ou Maniga. Autrement dit, une fois en Louisiane, les esclaves qui s'identifiaient comme Bamana ou Manding appartenaient bien à ces « nations » ou à des groupes apparentés.[45] Il était plus probable pour un Senufo, un Somono ou un Bozo de s'identifier comme Bamana ou Manding plutôt que comme un Yoruba ou un Mina. Il est aussi fort probable que d'autres groupes du Mande comme les Soninke, les Xaasonke, les Jaxanke s'étaient retranchés dans le groupe Manding/Bambara car ces ethnonymes n'apparaissent pas dans les archives. L'empire Songhoy qui s'était affirmé à partir du milieu du 15e siècle à la place du Mali, était entré en déclin à la fin du 16e siècle suite à l'agression marocaine. Les Songhoy n'apparaissent nulle part dans les documents d'archives car, ils étaient peut-être amalgamés avec les Bambara et les Manding ou, plus probablement, avec les Hawsa.

Dans son livre *Africans in Colonial Louisiana*, Hall consacre tout un chapitre exclusivement aux Bambara sur une période qui s'étale des années 1720 au début des années 1750.[46] L'auteure a été guidée vers cette option par deux facteurs. D'une part, cette période correspond à l'apogée du royaume de

Segu sous le règne de Mamari Coulibaly Biton (1712-1755). Ce dernier s'était distingué par les persécutions perpétrées contre ceux de ses compatriotes qui n'appartenaient pas à la même famille que lui, notamment les Traoré et les Diarra, de même que les Coulibaly de la branche aînée (les Massassi) qui furent à l'origine du royaume bambara du Kaarta.[47] Les nombreuses guerres étrangères, notamment contre les Fulbe du Maasina, de même que les incessantes luttes intestines avaient, de toute évidence, fait beaucoup de captifs parmi les Bamana. D'autre part, il s'agit aussi de la période la plus faste de la traite française au Galam sous le contrôle de la Compagnie de Indes Occidentales et celle de la mise en place de l'essentiel de la population servile de Louisiane sous le régime français. Des captifs réputés être des Bambara auraient contribué à côté des Indiens, au massacre de 237 Français autour de l'établissement de Fort Rosalie dans le pays des Natchez. La Compagnie des Indes avait abandonné la Louisiane deux ans après cet évènement qui remonte à l'année 1729. En juin 1731, alors qu'ils attendaient des renforts de France pour punir les Natchez, les officiels découvraient une « conspiration » qui devait se traduire par le massacre de tous les Français et par la prise de contrôle de la capitale de la colonie par les insurgés. Selon les estimations du gouverneur Périer, environ 400 esclaves Bambara étaient impliqués. Le cerveau de cette conspiration était un certain Samba Bambara, un maître de langues (interprète) qui faisait la navette entre le Galam et Saint-Louis du Sénégal avant sa déportation en Louisiane dans des conditions qui restent à élucider. Il aurait d'ailleurs continué à servir comme interprète auprès du Conseil Supérieur de la Louisiane. Samba et sept de ses complices furent exécutés sans jamais avouer un quelconque crime malgré la torture aux mèches ardentes qu'on leur fit subir pendant leur interrogatoire.[48] Les pages consacrées par Hall à Samba Bambara ont été essentiellement construites à partir du rapprochement d'incidents qui se sont produits à la même époque, au Sénégal et en Louisiane, lesquels incidents sont relatés par Le Page du Pratz. Selon l'auteur de l'histoire de la Louisiane, Samba avait été dans son pays le chef de la révolte qui avait enlevé le Fort d'Arguin aux Français. Samba fut en conséquence déporté en Louisiane sur l'Annibal, où il avait encore projeté d'égorger l'équipage du vaisseau pour s'en rendre maître. Mais les Officiers du Navire en étaient avertis. Ils le firent mettre aux fers ainsi que tous les autres hommes jusqu'à la Louisiane.[49]

Ce qui précède n'était qu'un amalgame destiné à enfoncer Samba car la prise d'Arguin, le 11 janvier 1722, était orchestrée par le chef maure Ali Shandora au profit de ses alliés hollandais.[50] La détention de Samba Bambara pendant cinq ans avant sa déportation était très peu probable, ce d'autant plus que l'Annibal n'arrive à La Nouvelle Orléans qu'en 1727. La documentation dépouillée par Delcourt faisant foi, un certain Samba Bambara vivait encore au Galam en 1722. Le 12 octobre, il avait fait écrire une lettre par Charpentier, directeur du fort, à St. Robert, directeur général de la Concession du Sénégal, pour demander à ce dernier d'empêcher le mariage de sa femme, Yéram Galé, avec les marchands de la grande terre (île de Sor). Si elle persévérait dans son infidélité, Samba voulait que St. Robert la fît chasser de l'île de St. Louis.[51] S'il est probable que sa présumée déportation était liée à un crime passionnel, par contre il n'est pas évident que le Samba Bambara évoqué par Delcourt et le Samba évoqué par Le Page du Pratz désignaient le même personnage.

C'est d'ailleurs l'une des nombreuses observations formulées par Peter Caron par rapport à ce qu'il convient d'appeler désormais la « controverse bambara ».[52] Cet auteur avait publié un article cinq ans après la parution de *Africans in Colonial Louisiana* de Hall, un livre qui avait alors fini d'engranger des distinctions des plus prestigieuses. Caron n'attaque pas de façon frontale le traitement de la question bambara par Hall mais il est clair que l'essentiel des critiques formulées lui sont destinées. Il considère, entre autres, que l'auteure ne discute pas suffisamment la question de l'assignation commode, parfois à des fins marchandes, de l'identité bambara, à des gens venant d'horizons très divers. Cependant, Caron pousse la critique trop loin, au point de sous-estimer l'apport de l'élément bambara dans la traite destinée à la Louisiane, notamment quand il affirme que la phase d'expansion du royaume de Ségou, à partir de 1712, aurait moins exposé les guerriers de ce pays à une éventuelle mise en captivité. Cette tendance à la sous-estimation de l'apport bambara est aussi bâtie sur une hypothèse contestable qu'il attribue à Curtin et selon laquelle le flot de captifs venant de l'intérieur des terres avait tari entre 1721 et 1733 quand les différentes factions bambara s'étaient coalisées pour combattre un ennemi commun, les Ormankoobe du royaume du Maroc. Or, poursuit-il, comme cette période correspond avec la mise en place de l'essentiel de la population servile de la Louisiane sous la Compagnie des Indes, il est plus probable que les captifs déportés dans ce pays sous le label « Bambara » seraient plutôt des non-musulmans provenant de la côte plutôt que de l'intérieur des terres.[53] Caron écarte ainsi le fait que dans une guerre tout est possible et que de nombreux guerriers avaient pu être capturés et vendus comme esclaves par leurs ennemis. D'autre part, Caron n'apporte aucune précision sur l'identité de ces non-musulmans originaires des côtes sénégambiennes.

Nous concédons cependant à Caron que fort probablement le Samba Bambara de Saint-Louis n'avait jamais mis les pieds en Louisiane car son nom n'apparait nulle part dans les archives du Conseil Supérieur de la Louisiane en tant qu'interprète. Par exemple le 5 septembre 1729, Changereau, un esclave de nation bambara, âgé d'environ vingt ans, était attrait devant le tribunal du Conseil supérieur de la Louisiane pour délit de marronnage et vol d'une génisse. Le défendant ne parlait pas français, encore moins le créole qui était encore une langue en gestation. Le procureur avait fait appel aux services d'un interprète, qui n'était pas Samba Bambara mais l'armurier Jean Pinet. Ce français était aussi l'interprète de Pierrot, David et Sabany, les compagnons de marronnage de Changereau, également identifiés comme des nègres de nation bambara.[54] Jean Pinet était un armurier originaire de Rochefort et employé de la Compagnie des Indes. Il était établi à Gorée puis à Saint-Louis où il fut jugé et condamné en 1724 pour avoir battu à mort un matelot mulâtre nommé Pierre LeGrain pendant une soirée bien arrosée à son domicile. Il fut transféré et incarcéré à Nantes où sa peine de prison fut commuée en déportation en Louisiane à la requête de la Compagnie des Indes qui avait grandement besoin de ses services. Quelques années plus tard, sa femme Marie Baude, une Sereer originaire de Joal, l'avait rejoint à La Nouvelle Orléans.[55] Pinet était donc un locuteur du *bamanakan*, une langue qu'il avait apprise à Gorée et Saint-Louis, deux cités qui avaient chacune son quartier bambara dans les années 1720 déjà. La présence *bamana* en Louisiane n'est donc pas un mythe. Ce qui rend parfaitement opératoire le concept de nation dans le contexte louisianais.

À l'arrivée des Européens sur les côtes africaines, l'Afrique de l'Ouest était déjà sous l'influence de l'empire du Mali pendant plus de deux siècles durant lesquels les Jula Malinke avaient réussi à tisser des réseaux commerciaux reliant les régions forestières aux régions de savane et du Sahel jusqu'aux marchés nord-africains, européens et orientaux à travers le Sahara.[56] Au nord, toute la vallée du fleuve Sénégal était sous la domination du Mali. Selon Al-Umari, les Égyptiens avaient provoqué le courroux de l'empereur Mansa Moussa, en l'appelant roi du *Takrûr.* Le souverain malien, alors en route pour la Mecque, tenait à préciser que ce n'était là qu'une des nombreuses dépendances de son immense empire.[57] De nombreuses dynasties qui avaient régné en Sénégambie étaient d'origine malinke. Le Mandinka était devenu une lingua franca et l'Islam un dénominateur commun pour la majorité des habitants malgré la résistance de certains peuples. L'islamisation du Soudan occidental était avant tout l'œuvre des commerçants Jula, un nom qui a donné au pulaar le verbe juulde (prier) et les mots njuulu (la prière), njulaagu (commerce) et julanke (commerçant).[58] En plus d'être l'ancêtre du banjo américain, le ngoni ou konting des gens du Joliba (fleuve Niger), appelé xalam par les Wolof, hoddu par les Fulɓe et tidinit par les Nards, avait largement contribué à la naissance de la culture du blues au point que beaucoup de spécialistes considèrent le Mali comme l'origine de cette culture musicale. Sous le vernis islamique, l'institution du masque dit « Komo » avait essaimé sous différents noms partout le long des cours d'eau, du Sénégal à la Sierra Leone. La fameuse tradition des Black Masking Indians de la Nouvelle Orléans et le Komo ont certainement des liens qui méritent d'être mieux explorés. De nos jours, ces « Indiens Noirs » constituent encore un des aspects les plus pittoresques de la communauté afro-américaine de la Nouvelle Orléans. Le jour du Mardi gras, ils organisent des parades, musique et danse à l'appui. Les principaux membres, avec à leur tête le Big Chief, revêtent de somptueux costumes cousus de rubans, de plumes et de perles, le tout dans une profusion de couleurs très vives, allant du blanc éclatant à l'écarlate. Après le Mardi Gras, le jour le plus important pour les Black Indians est le Super Sunday, le troisième dimanche de mars jouxtant la Saint Joseph. Des études pointues permettront certainement de retracer l'itinéraire des « gens du Komo », principalement des Manding et des Bamana, des rives du Joliba à celles du Mississippi. Il est absolument erroné de penser que les gens du Mande avaient oublié le *Komo* dans un contexte de servitude, d'autant plus qu'ils devaient faire face à un système extrêmement violent et dont l'une des stratégies consistait à éradiquer les liens que les personnes esclaves tenaient à maintenir avec leurs racines africaines. Les Black Masking Indians sont les héritiers d'une tradition de refus et de résilience dont la genèse est à chercher dans les espaces de marronnage.

La prépondérance malinké au 18ᵉ siècle est clairement indiquée par la *Louisiana Slave Database* mais elle est occultée par la littérature coloniale qui met plutôt en exergue les « Nègres sénégalais » (Wolof) dans la construction de la culture afro-créole de Louisiane. Les chroniqueurs européens, comme Le Page du Pratz, avaient produit une littérature révélatrice des représentations qu'ils se faisaient des habitants du Sénégal et qui décrivaient les « nègres de nation Sénégal » comme les Africains les mieux cotés dans les colonies françaises parce qu'étant les plus intelligents, les plus propres, les plus beaux et plus aptes au commandement et à l'apprentissage des métiers. Ces perceptions avaient fini par générer ce qu'il convient d'appeler le « syndrome sénégalais », c'est-à-dire cette sorte de « sénégalomania » qui met en exergue l'agentivité supérieure des esclaves d'origine sénégalaise. James F. Broussard était tombé dans ce piège dans son étude sur le créole louisianais. D'emblée il considérait que les planteurs de Louisiane possédaient un grand nombre d'esclaves dont l'origine était à dominante sénégalaise, une affirmation qui ne correspond pas à la réalité des statistiques de la traite des esclaves. Par ailleurs, il affirmait que ces mêmes nègres sénégalais étaient préférés à ceux venant du Congo à cause de leur caractère traitable et leur intelligence supérieure, et qu'ils avaient créé le créole à partir de la langue de leurs maîtres, dans une communauté où le français était exclusivement parlé.[59] Le mythe du Sénégalais à l'intelligence supérieure a été malheureusement utilisé pendant toute l'aventure coloniale française pour en servir les desseins.[60] Toutefois, Les influences wolof sont parfaitement lisibles notamment dans les contes animaliers (Bouki et Lapin) et les traditions culinaires. Jeroen Dewulf a choisi de faire une lecture de la culture afro-créole de Louisiane en relation avec le bassin du Congo. Dans son livre, *From the Kingdom of Kongo to Congo Square,* il a cherché à identifier les origines des Black Masking Indians de la Nouvelle Orléans, en particulier dans une danse de guerre congolaise appelée *sangamento*. Cette lecture d'auteur d'origine belge a été probablement déterminé par les liens historiques de son pays avec le bassin du Congo. D'emblée, il convoque dans son argumentaire son compatriote Robert Goffin, auteur d'une étude pionnière sur le jazz qui considère l'Afrique centrale comme l'origine de ce genre musical.[61] Jeroen Dewulf a reconnu les limites de sa démarche tant elle exclut dans une large mesure les influences toutes aussi importantes venues d'autres régions d'Afrique.[62] C'est le lieu de reconnaître que, très souvent, nous interprétons la diaspora à partir de nos propres affinités avec l'Afrique. Chambers est devenu le spécialiste des Igbo en diaspora grâce à ses relations suivies avec Igboland au Nigeria.[63] Il est l'un des principaux contributeurs à l'ouvrage *Igbo in the Atlantic World* édité par Toyin Falola et Raphael Chijioke Njoku.

Auparavant, Toyin Falola était coéditeur d'un ouvrage sur les Yoruba en diaspora alors que Kwasi Konadu avait choisi de mettre en miroir la diaspora noire en Amérique avec le monde Akan.[64] L'Angolais Simão Souindoula, initiateur du réseau Bantulink et expert de l'Unesco, s'était aussi beaucoup intéressé aux Bantu en diaspora.[65] Il en de même pour Linda Heywood et d'autres éminents historiens de la traite des esclaves en Afrique centrale comme Joseph C. Miller et John K. Thornton.[66]

La contribution des gens du Soudan Occidental ou « Sénigambiens » (Manding, Bambara, Wolof, Poulard, Nard, Sereer, Jola, Susu, etc.) à l'édification de la culture afro-créole de Louisiane est immense. Mieux que Sénégambie, appellation coloniale héritée des Anglais, « Sénigambie » est un concept qui fédère mieux les habitants de la Sénégambie proprement dite, du nord au sud, et tous les peuples organisés autour du Joliba, c'est-à-dire autour du fleuve Niger depuis sa source jusqu'à sa boucle et son delta intérieur. Cette Sénigambie correspond aussi à la région dite Western Savanna dans un nouveau découpage de l'Afrique selon les régions de traites esclavagistes proposée par l'équipe de Henry B. Lovejoy dans le cadre d'un projet destiné à faciliter l'interconnexion des nombreuses banques de données relatives à l'esclavage. Cette nouvelle toponymie divorce d'avec la toponymie coloniale, lève les ambigüités sur les lieux de traite et permet d'harmoniser les nombreuses banques de données achevées ou en gestation afin de permettre leur interconnexion.[67]

Nous terminons ce papier avec la relation d'évènements à la fois anecdotiques et tragiques impliquant un groupe d'esclaves appartenant en grande majorité au groupe Mande. Le 21 juillet 1764, un fugitif nommé Louis avait été jugé par contumace par le tribunal du Conseil Supérieur de Louisiane et condamné à avoir les oreilles coupées et l'épaule droite marquée d'une fleur de lis. Au cours de cette même audience, son compagnon César, un esclave créole et marron récidiviste, avait été condamné à mort. Quelques jours plus tard, il était sur la Place d'Armes, devant l'église paroissiale (site de la future cathédrale Saint-Louis), portant tout juste une chemise longue, la tête nue, à genoux et la corde au cou. Il tenait dans ses mains une torche ardente et clamait tout haut, sous l'injonction de ses bourreaux, qu'il avait méchamment commis les crimes dont il se repend et en demande pardon à Dieu, au roi de France et à la justice. Séance tenante, sa main droite fut coupée sur un poteau planté exprès devant l'entrée principale de l'église, puisqu'il était accusé d'avoir utilisé ce membre pour tirer sur une patrouille nocturne. Ensuite, sur le même tombereau à immondices qui avait servi à son transfert à l'église, César fut transporté de l'autre côté de la ville, sur la place publique, pour, disait-on, être brisé sur la roue. Il fut solidement attaché à un échafaud dressé spécialement pour son exécution, en fait une grande roue, axe enfoncé dans le sol. Ses bras, jambes, cuisses et reins furent rompus vifs par « l'exécuteur de la haute justice » qui ensuite laissa son corps sur la roue pour une longue agonie, la face tournée vers le ciel. La dépouille de César fut par la suite jetée à la décharge publique, sur le chemin du bayou Saint-Jean, où elle resta exposée jusqu'à consommation totale. Louis n'avait pas porté très longtemps le deuil de son compagnon. A quelques détails près, il avait subi le même sort que César après son arrestation et sa condamnation à mort le 10 septembre 1764. A cette même audience, Marie Jeanne, une esclave de nation Arada (Fon), avait été condamnée à être marquée de la lettre V sur l'épaule pour recel de biens subtilisés par Louis. Le film de l'exécution de ce dernier relève aussi d'une pédagogie de la terreur qui rappelle le chemin de croix. Louison et Julie, toutes deux de nation Mandinga, avaient été condamnées à assister à l'exécution de Louis pour lui avoir accordé leur *jatigiya* (hospitalité en bamanakan). Elles devaient faire partie de cette procession macabre qui commençait à l'église paroissiale, traversait la ville en direction de la place publique, où avait lieu l'exécution, et aboutissait au chemin du bayou Saint-Jean, à la décharge municipale, où le corps de Louis resta aussi exposé jusqu'à consommation totale.[68]

Louis était arrivé des côtes africaines en Louisiane via le Cap François à Saint-Domingue. Il avait été vendu au sieur Blevin du pays des Illinois d'où il s'était échappé pour rallier la capitale à bord d'une pirogue. Il était marron pendant dix mois au moment de son arrestation et de sa présentation devant le tribunal du Conseil Supérieur de la Louisiane. Accusé de vols multiples avec effraction et marronnage long, son interrogatoire avait été accompagné de torture. Julie, connue sous le nom Comba ou Mama Comba, demeurait alors à l'Hôpital des Pauvres, une propriété des religieux de l'ordre des Capucins. Elle avait été arrêtée et présentée devant le tribunal pour témoigner sur les agissements de Louis et ses relations avec le fugitif dont elle était la *jatigi* (hôte en bamanakan). Elle le connaissait depuis son arrivée à la Nouvelle Orléans mais ignorait qu'il était marron. Julie Mama Comba avait l'habitude d'aller voir son amie Louison dans le jardin de l'habitation Cantrelle. Un jour elle y trouva plusieurs personnes de nation bambara autour d'un repas. Une autre fois qu'elle était invitée chez Louison, elle y trouva encore Louis. Ils soupèrent ensemble au gombo filé préparé par Fatema[69], une esclave au sieur de Lafrenière, procureur pour le roi auprès du Conseil Supérieur de Louisiane. Elle avait demandé à Louis s'il était marron. Il répondit non et ajouta qu'il était descendu des Illinois avec sa maîtresse qui le laissait libre parce qu'il avait mal à une jambe et ce jusqu'à ce qu'il fût guéri. Selon Louison, la bande avait soupé plusieurs fois au jardin Cantrelle. César apportait toujours le tafia. Louis et César apportaient régulièrement à la compagnie de la viande de volailles, notamment des dindes et des poules, braconnées sur différentes plantations. Une fois ils tuèrent un porc sur la plantation des Jésuites mais la carcasse était si lourde qu'ils étaient obligés de couper l'animal en deux, chacun se chargeant de faire passer sa part au-dessus de la palissade. Louis avait vendu une partie de sa moitié de porc près du bayou Saint-Jean aux esclaves du sieur Brazilier mais il n'avait jamais été payé. Il avait apporté le reste de la viande à l'Hôpital des Pauvres. Sa générosité en bandoulière, Louis était comme un polygame passant alternativement ses nuits dans la cabane de Louison ou dans celle de Julie Mama Comba. Doté d'un sang-froid sans égal, Louis ne se cachait point. Selon Louison, il marchait sans crainte dans toute la ville. Il avait un fusil qu'il avait apporté des Illinois, avec lequel il aurait tiré sur une patrouille nocturne. Pendant le temps de son marronnage à la Nouvelle Orléans, Louis avait organisé un réseau pour l'écoulement de biens volés dont beaucoup d'effets vestimentaires. Ses intermédiaires étaient des femmes dont Marie Jeanne qui habitait aussi à l'Hôpital des Pauvres. Louis s'était aussi distingué par son industrie. Selon le témoignage de Mama Comba, il avait subtilisé dix carottes de tabac à une pirogue qui était descendue du poste des Natchitoches. Il avait tout vendu à des Noirs pour acheter de la toile dont il avait fait des chemises et des culottes qu'il vendait à travers son réseau qui s'étendait jusqu'à Barataria. Il avait pignon sur rue, devant la porte de l'hôpital, où il confectionnait tranquillement les habits avec des aiguilles fournies par Mama Comba.[70] D'après les procès-verbaux, « en langage et idiome de son pays », c'est-à-dire dans la langue bamana ou bamanakan, le nom de Louis était Foy. Foua et Doua sont des prénoms que l'on trouve au Fouta Tooro mais leur fréquence y est faible et leur origine très certainement malienne.

À l'exception de la dahoméenne Marie Jeanne et du créole César, voilà donc un groupe de personnes qui se réclamaient sans ambages du groupe Mande, à savoir des Bamana et des Manding, qui parlaient des langues mutuellement intelligibles, et dont certains portaient des noms africains. Le temps d'une longue fugue, Foy était le liant de cette communauté qui nous permet d'imaginer toutes les possibilités alors ouvertes aux personnes esclaves pour organiser leurs récurrents « bals de Nègres », réinventer leur gastronomie et former des congrégations vouées à des choses beaucoup plus sérieuses comme les rituels religieux. La mythique Place du Congo, à la Nouvelle Orléans, était le lieu de cristallisation des cultures africaines dans un contexte de servitude, et le berceau d'une culture musicale qui a essaimé dans le monde entier. Les fameuses danses dominicales performées par les Noirs (esclaves comme libres) étaient certainement et en partie animées avec la musique malienne. Une discussion approfondie de l'appellation Place du Congo, à la lumière d'une tradition que l'on retrouve dans toutes les anciennes villes de l'empire colonial français, nous mène aussi sur la piste malienne. L'île de Saint-Louis au Sénégal avait son marché sur un lieu-dit « la savane », situé du côté du petit bras du fleuve, sur une esplanade jouxtant le fort français et sa place d'armes. Ce lieu servait aussi de rencontre pour toutes les festivités des indigènes, notamment la danse et les séances de lutte.[71]

C'était sur la « savane », place publique à Gorée, que des centaines de captifs wolof en transit avaient assisté à l'exécution de leurs chefs pour donner suite à une révolte dans les années 1740.[72] Aux Antilles françaises, en Guyane, au Québec et à la Réunion aussi, plusieurs villes coloniales conservent encore chacune sa « place de la savane ». Fort-de-France a toujours sa Place de la Savane, appelée aussi Savane des Esclaves, au pied du Fort Saint-Louis, face à la baie. L'actuelle Place des Palmistes à Cayenne, en Guyane française, était appelée Place de la savane, un espace créé au 18e siècle et qui abritait le premier marché de la ville. Au Québec, Montréal a aussi gardé sa Place de la Savane. En Guadeloupe, plusieurs lieux sont appelés « savane », le nom oublié de la Place de la Victoire à Pointe-à-Pitre. Sur l'île de la Réunion, au moins Saint-Denis et Saint-Benoît ont gardé leurs places de la Savane.[73] La Nouvelle Orléans ne pouvait pas être en reste. Il y a lieu de penser que la Place du Congo était en réalité la Place du *kungo* ou Place de la savane, *kungo* signifiant « savane/brousse » en bamanakan. La place du Congo était donc une contribution éloquente des Africains à la définition et à la configuration de l'espace public colonial, inspirée d'une tradition dans l'espace soudanais où chaque ville et village a traditionnellement sa place publique appelée *dingiral* par les Fulɓe, *penc* par les Wolof et *fɛrɛ* en bamanakan. C'est la place où se tiennent le marché hebdomadaire, les festivités nocturnes des jeunes filles et garçons, les séances de lutte et les prestations des troubadours accompagnés de tambours et de cordophones. Il y a donc lieu de croire que le nom Place du Congo (Congo Square) vient fort probablement de ce que les Bamana de la Nouvelle Orléans appelleraient *Kungo Fɛrɛ* au 18e siècle. La prépondérance congolaise en Louisiane au 19e siècle a probablement contribué à déterminer le choix d'auteurs comme Jeroen Dewulf mais nous considérons que toute recherche sur les racines de la culture afro-créole de Louisiane qui ignore la piste malienne risque d'être sérieusement tronquée.

Conclusion

Dans un contexte de servitude et de ségrégation raciale, les Africains et leurs descendants avaient toujours fait preuve d'une agentivité remarquable dans la construction économique et culturelle de la vallée du Mississippi où avaient éclos les éléments de cette culture afro-créole qui a donné à la culture américaine son rayonnement planétaire. Au-delà de la construction des fondations originelles des économies, les Africains mis en esclavage et leurs descendants ont contribué à façonner et à définir les cultures et les identités des Amériques. La déportation depuis les côtes africaines était certainement une histoire de nudité car les captifs africains entraient dans les cales des bateaux pratiquement nus et complètement démunis de leurs identités. Mais comme nul n'a besoin de valises pour transporter sa culture, ils pouvaient reproduire leurs cultures matérielles et immatérielles pour s'accommoder à leur nouvelle vie par le biais d'une créativité permanente qui prend en compte toute l'expérience nouvelle acquise sur les lieux d'exil.

La question de l'identité a été certainement utilisée pour effacer les liens entre les populations réduites en esclavage et leurs patries. Nous pensons avoir prouvé que cette odieuse posture n'a pas totalement réussi en Louisiane. Les archives de l'esclavage de ce pays sont très précieuses en ce sens qu'elles permettent de rétablir les identités de milliers de personnes, facilitant l'exploration des racines africaines de sa culture afro-créole. C'est là que réside toute l'importance de la *Voyages* d'Eltis et de Richardson et de la *Louisiana Slave Database* de Hall, de même que les nombreuses bases de données en gestation. Le mémorial dit « Allées Gwendolyn Midlo Hall » est certainement le plus saisissant des quatre mémoriaux de Whitney Plantation Museum of Slavery, en ce sens qu'il figure plus d'une centaine de milliers de noms extraits de la *Louisiana Slave Database* et gravés sur 216 plaques de granit montées sur dix-huit murs enchevêtrés. C'est un hommage mérité rendu à Hall certes, mais le plus important est que son travail permet aujourd'hui aux nombreux Afro-Américains qui visitent le musée, d'avoir un cimetière virtuel où se recueillir, attendu que leurs ancêtres étaient enterrées dans les bois, dans des tombes anonymes dévorées depuis longtemps par une nature luxuriante. On peut lire sur ces plaques de granit les noms de personnes comme Samba Bambara, Foy Bambara, Julie Mama Comba, Fatema, pour ne citer que quelques noms évoqués dans ce texte. D'emblée, des personnes qui disposent d'inventaires de plantations où leurs ancêtres étaient retenus en esclavage, ont pu retrouver ces derniers avec beaucoup d'émotion. Avec un peu de patience, beaucoup d'autres y parviendront.

Tableau 11.1
Navires négriers arrivant en Louisiane, 1719-1830

Nom de bateau	Année d'arrivée	Principale région africaine d'embarquement	Total embarqués en Afrique	Total des Africains debarqués
Aurore	1719	Bight of Benin	201	200
Duc du Maine	1719	Bight of Benin	250	250
Ruby	1720	Senegambia	130	127
Néréide	1721	West Central Africa	323	294
Duc du Maine	1721	Bight of Benin	391	349
Fortuné	1721	Bight of Benin	340	303
Afriquain	1721	Bight of Benin	214	182
Maréchal d'Estrées	1721	Senegambia	200	196
Courrier de Bourbon	1723	Senegambia	105	90
Expédition	1723	Senegambia	100	95
Mutine	1725	Senegambia	235	222
Aurore	1726	Senegambia	350	290
Annibal	1726	Senegambia	372	326
Prince de Conty	1727	Senegambia	300	296

Duc de Noailles	1727	Senegambia	356	273
Diane	1728	Bight of Benin	516	464
Vénus	1728	Senegambia	348	341
Flore	1728	Senegambia	400	356
Galathée	1728	Senegambia	400	313
Vénus	1729	Senegambia	450	363
Duc de Bourbon	1729	Senegambia	400	383
Saint Louis	1730	Senegambia	361	325
Saint Ursin	1743	Senegambia	220	190
Thétis	1784	West Central Africa	203	185
Feliz	1788		274	228
Catherine (a) Santa Catalina	1788		216	204
Guipuscano	1790		236	197
Aimable Victoire	1792	West Central Africa	337	307
Sally	1803	West Central Africa	211	174
Africain	1803		325	247
Confiance	1803	Senegambia	223	204

Margaret (a) Sally	1804	West Central Africa	222	200
Sarah	1804	West Central Africa	244	219
Alexander	1805	West Central Africa	199	179
Miriam	1807	West Central Africa	114	100
Armed Neutrality	1807	West Central Africa	239	200
George Clinton	1807	Senegambia	120	100
Rambler	1807	Gold Coast	233	208
Agent	1807	Southeast Africa	267	201
Ethiopian	1807	West Central Africa	167	140
Agent	1808	Southeast Africa	180	135
Empresa	1810	Other Africa	170	140
Alerta	1810	Bight of Benin	197	170
Josefa Segunda	1818	Bight of Biafra	314	250
Fenix (a) Phoenix	1830		95	82
Total			**26,000**	**22,000**

Source : *Voyages* (www.slavevoyages.org). Accessed and calculated by Erin Greenwald, 29 November 2015.

Tableau 11.2
Les 18 « nations » les plus fréquentes en Louisiane (1719-1820)

Régions/Nations	Genre		Total
	Hommes	Femmes	
Sénégambie			**2,756**
Bamana/Bambara	413	53	466
Mandinga	617	305	922
Nards/Maures	101	35	136
Poulard/Fulɓe	160	50	210
Senegal/Wolof	363	234	597
Kisi	51	35	86
Kanga	210	129	339
Golfe du Bénin			**1,777**
Tchamba	276	139	415
Mina	430	198	628
Fon/Arada	126	117	243
Hausa	122	11	133
Nago/Yoruba	247	111	358
Golfe du Biafra			**819**
Edo	38	28	66
Igbo	287	237	524
Ibibio/Moko	61	21	82
Calabar	88	59	147
Afrique Centrale			**2,988**
Congo	2,064	924	2,988
Côte Est			102
Makwa	67	35	102
Total	**5,721**	**2,721**	**8,442**

Source : les calculs effectués par Gwendolyn Midlo Hall, *Afro-Louisiana History and Genealogy*

Endnotes

1 Boubacar Barry, *La Sénégambie du XV*[e] *au XIX*[e] *siècle, traite négrière, Islam, conquête coloniale* (Paris : L'Harmattan, 1984), 7.

2 En tenant compte de la banque de données de Gwendolyn Midlo Hall, dix-neuf des quarante-cinq cargaisons de captifs signalées à l'arrivée en Louisiane entre 1719 et 1830, étaient originaires de la Sénégambie dont seize pour la période 1720-1743 (Tableau 12.1). L'Afrique centrale était en fait l'origine pour treize cargaisons dont deux étaient arrivées entre 1719 et 1743. Sur les dix-sept navires signalés à l'arrivée à la Nouvelle Orléans pendant la période américaine, sept étaient originaires d'Af-

rique centrale, trois de Sénégambie, deux du sud-est africain, un de la Gold Coast, un du golfe du Bénin, un du golfe de Biafra et deux dont l'origine est inconnue.

3 David Eltis et David Richardson. *Atlas of the Atlantic Slave Trade* (New Haven and London: Yale University Press, 2010), 220.

4 Gwendolyn Midlo Hall, *Slavery, Race Mixture, and Diversity in Louisiana* (Baton Rouge, Louisiana State University Press, 1992). Gwendolyn Midlo Hall, *Afro-Louisiana History and Genealogy, 1719-1820*, https://www.ibiblio.org/laslave/, (accessed 2022).

5 Gwendolyn Midlo Hall, *Slavery and African Ethnicities in the Americas: Restoring the Links* (Chapel Hill, NC: University of North Carolina Press, 2005), 42-45.

6 Kofi Awoonor, *Guardians of the Sacred Word-Ewe Poetry* (New York: Nok Publishers, 1974), 13.

7 Moreau de Saint-Mery, *Description de la Partie française de l'Isle de Saint-Domingue*, tome 1, B. Maurel et E. Taillemite (ed.) (Paris : Sté de l'Histoire des colonies françaises et Larose, 1958), 54.

8 Hall, *Slavery and African Ethnicities in the Americas,* 80-100.

9 Actes originaux la paroisse Saint-Jean Baptiste (SJB) ci-après, suivi du numéro du dossier et l'année. SJB-3-1801/*Acte de Partage des biens du défunt Christophe Haydel entre ses héritiers et qui sert à constater la propriété de ce qu'ils ont eu* (15 janvier 1801).

10 SJB-33-1830/Inventaire des biens de la feue dame veuve Pierre Becnel (18 février 1830).

11 Hall, *Afro-Louisiana History and Genealogy* (consultée le 26 septembre 2010).

12 Le Page du Pratz 1758, *Histoire de la Louisiane* (Paris : De Bure, 1758), tome 1, 344-345.

13 Michael Gomez, *Exchanging Our Country Marks: The Transformation of African Identities in the Colonial and Antebellum South* (Chapel Hill, NC: University of North Carolina Press, 1998), 6-7 et 45.

14 Al Bakrî, *Kitâb al-Masâlikwal-Mamâlik.* In Joseph Cuoq, *Recueil des sources arabes concernant l'Afrique Occidentale, VIII*[e] *-XVI*[e] *siècle-Bilâd al-Sudân* (Paris: CNRS, 1975), 96.

15 J. Boulègue, *Les royaumes wolof dans l'espace sénégambien (XIII*[e]*-XVIII*[e] *siècle)* (Paris : Karthala, 2013), 40-41.

16 Saliou Kandji, *Sénégal n'est pas Sunugal ou de l'étymologie du toponyme Sénégal* (Dakar: Presses Universitaires de Dakar, 2006).

17 J.B. Gaby, *Relation de la Nigritie* (Paris : Edme Couterot, 1689), 83.

18 Cuoq, *Recueil des sources arabes,* 96.

19 Abdourahmane Ba, *Le Takrur, des origines à la conquête par le Mali (VI*[e]*-XIII*[e] *siècles)* (Dakar : CRIAA-Département d'Histoire, Université de Nouakchott-IFAN/UCAD, 2002), 145.

20 Boulègue, *Les royaumes wolof dans l'espace sénégambien*, 37-39 et 55-57. Bruno Chavane, *Villages de l'Ancien Tekrour, Recherches archéologiques dans la moyenne vallée du fleuve Sénégal* (Paris : Karthala-CRA, 1985).

21 Saugnier, *Relations de plusieurs voyages à la côte d'Afrique, à Maroc, au Sénégal, à Gorée, à Galam, et.* (Paris : Roux et Compagnie, 1792), 182 et 193.

22 Saugnier, *Relations de plusieurs voyages*, 183.

23 Barry, *La Sénégambie du XV*[e] *au XIX*[e] *siècle*, 150-152.

24 Terry Alford, *Prince Among Slaves* (New York : Oxford University Press, 1977).

25 Omar Kane, *La première hégémonie peule. Le Fuuta Tooro de Koli Teŋella à Almaa-*

mi Abdul (Paris/Dakar : Karthala et Presses Universitaire de Dakar, 2004), 65-66 et glossaire (p. 655).

26 Al Idrissi, *Description de l'Afrique et de l'Espagne* (Leyde: E.J. Brill, 1866, R. Dozy et M. M. de Goeje, eds.), 2.

27 Saugnier, *Relations de plusieurs voyages à la côte d'Afrique*, 183.

28 Oumar Kane, « Les Maures et le Futa-Toro au XVIIIe siècle », *Cahiers d'études africaines* 14 :54 (1974), 237-252 ; Kane, *La première hégémonie peule,* 308.

29 Barry, *La Sénégambie du XVe au XIXe siècle,* 135-136.

30 Philip D. Curtin, *Economic Change in Precolonial Africa. Senegambia in the Era of the Slave Trade* (Madison: University of Wisconsin Press, 1975), 184.

31 Archives du Conseil Supérieur de la Louisiane, Louisiana State Museum Historical Center, New Orleans (ACSL ci-après). *Interrogatoires et jugement relatifs au cas Louis Jupiter dit Gamelle,* 21 mars 1744, RG # 1744-03-21-01 à 05.

32 Ca Da Mosto, *Relation des voyages de la côte occidentale d'Afrique (1455-1457)* (Paris: Leroux, 1895, Charles Schefer, éd.), 103.

33 Moreau de Saint-Mery, *Description de la Partie française de l'Isle de Saint-Domingue*, 48.

34 Diass est devenu le site du tout nouvel aéroport international Blaise Diagne, au sud de Dakar.

35 L. J. B. Bérenger-Féraud, *Les Peuplades de la Sénégambie* (Paris : E. Leroux, 1879), 337.

36 Paul E. Lovejoy, « Transatlantic Transformations: The Origins and Identities of Africans in the Americas », in Boubacar Barry, Elisee Soumoni, Livio Sansone (eds.), *Africa, Brazil and the Construction of Trans-Atlantic Black Identities*. (Trenton, NJ: Africa World Press, 2008), 87.

37 Douglas B. Chambers, « Ethnicity in the Diaspora: The Slave-Trade and the Creation of African 'Nations' in the Americas », *Slavery and Abolition* 22 :3 (2001), 29.

38 Jean-Loup Amselle et Elikia M'Bokolo (éd.), *Au cœur de l'ethnie. Ethnies, tribalisme et État en Afrique* (Paris : La Découverte, 1985), 10, 36-38.

39 Jeroen Dewulf, *From the Kingdom of Kongo to Congo Square : Kongo Dances and the Origins of the Mardi Gras Indians* (Lafayette, LA: University of Louisiana at Lafayette Press, 2017), XVI-XVII.

40 Lovejoy, « Transatlantic transformations », 81-112.

41 Maurice Delafosse, *Haut-Sénégal-Niger* (Paris : Maisonneuve et Larose, 1972), tome 1, 252-300.

42 Sékéné M. Cissoko, *Histoire de l'Afrique occidentale. Moyen Âge et Temps modernes, VIIe siècle-1850* (Paris : Présence Africaine, 1971), 234.

43 Delafosse, *Haut-Sénégal-Niger*, 410-411.

44 Père Sauvant, *Grammaire Bambara* (Alger : Maison Carrée: Imprimerie des Missionnaires d'Afrique, 1913), VI.

45 Voir à ce propos une discussion additionnelle du terme Bamana par Hall dans *Slavery and African Ethnicities in the Americas,* 96-100.

46 Gwendolyn Midlo Hall. *Africans in Colonial Louisiana - The Development of Afro-Creole Culture in the Eighteenth Century* (Baton Rouge & London : Louisiana State University Press, 1992), chapitre 4 (*The Bambara in Louisiana : From the Natchez uprising to the Samba Bambara conspiracy*, 96-118.

47 Delafosse, *Haut-Sénégal-Niger*, tome 2, 287.

48 Hall. *Africans in Colonial Louisiana*, chapitre 4 (*The Bambara in Louisiana : From the Natchez uprising to the Samba Bambara conspiracy*, p. 96-118.

49 Le Page du Pratz, *Histoire de la Louisiane* (Paris : De Bure, 1758), vol. 3, 304-317.

50 Jean-Baptiste Labat, *Nouvelle relation de l'Afrique occidentale* (Paris : Cavelier, tome 1er, 1728). Voir le chapitre X (État du Fort d'Arguin jusqu'à sa prise), 116-132.

51 André Delcourt, *La France et les Etablissements Français au Sénégal entre 1713 et 1763* (Dakar : Mémoires IFAN, 1952), 129.

52 Peter Caron, « Of a Nation which the Others Don't Understand: Bambara Slaves and African Ethnicity in Louisiana, 1718-60 » in David Eltis and David Richardson (eds), *Routes to Slavery. Direction, Ethnicity and Mortality in the Transatlantic Slave Trade* (London : Frank Cass, 1997), 98-121. Les travaux cités en références par l'auteur sont : Philip D. Curtin, *Economic change in Precolonial Africa. Senegambia in the era of the slave trade* (Madison, Wisconsin, 1975) ; Daniel H. Usner, « From African Captivity to American Slavery. The Introduction of Black Llaborers in Colonial Louisiana », *Louisiana History* 20 (1979), 25-48.

53 Caron, « Of a nation…, » 98-121.

54 ACSL. *Interrogatoire des nommés Changereau, Pierrot et Sabany,* 5 septembre 1729, RG # 1729-09-05-03, 05 et 06. *Interrogatoire du nègre David,*16 novembre 1729, RG # 1729-11-16-01.

55 Jessica M. Johnson, *Practicing Freedom : Black Women, Intimacy and Freedom in the Atlantic World.* Philadelphia: University of Pennsylvania Press, 2020. L'histoire de ce couple constitue la trame du livre.

56 Walter Hawthorne, *Planting Rice and Harvesting Slaves: Transformations along the Guinea-Bissau Coast, 1400*-1900. Portsmouth, NH: Heinemann, 2003), 30-31.

57 Al-Umari, *Masalik al-absar fi mamalik al-amsar* (achevé vers 1340), in Cuoq, *Recueil des sources arabes concernant l'Afrique occidentale,* 263.

58 Kane, *La première hégémonie peule,* 70 et 344-8.

59 James F. Broussard, *Louisiana Creole Dialect* (Baton Rouge : Louisiana State University Press, 1942), IX-X.

60 Cette approche a été déterminante dans la sélection sur les côtes sénégalaises, à Saint-Louis, Rufisque, Gorée et Dakar, des premiers citoyens français qui, dès 1848, pouvaient élire un député au parlement français. Cette politique d'assimilation sélective devait créer des auxiliaires de l'administration coloniale française formés dans un esprit favorable à la France. Voir Ibrahima Seck, « Les Français à la rencontre du Sénégal : Prémices d'une politique d'assimilation sélective » in Mélanges offerts au Professeur Iba Der Thiam, *Revue Sénégalaise d'Histoire*, Nouvelle série, n° 9, décembre 2019, 483-505.

61 Robert Goffin, *Aux Frontières du Jazz* (Paris : Éditions du Sagittaire, 1932).

62 Dewulf, *From the Kingdom of Kongo to Congo Square*.

63 Chambers, *Murder at Montpelier: Igbo Africans in Virginia* (Jackson, MI: University Press of Mississippi, 2005). Douglas B. Chambers, *Igbo Diaspora in the Era of the Slave Trade. An Introductory History* (Glassboro, NJ: Goldline & Jacobs Publishing, 2014).

64 Toyin Falola et Raphael Chijioke Njoku (éd.), *Igbo in the Alantic World. African origins and Diasporic destinations*. Bloomington & Indianapolis: Indiana University Press, 2016. Toyin Falola & Matt Childs (éd.), *The Yoruba Diaspora in the Atlantic World*. Bloomington: Indiana University Press, 2004. Kwasi Konadu, *The Akan diaspora in the Americas*. Oxford: Oxford University Press, 2010.

65 Feu Simão Souindoula était un historien et anthropologue angolais, expert de la civilisation bantoue et de l'histoire de l'esclavage, membre du comité scientifique du projet de l'UNESCO "La Route de l'esclave". Il est l'auteur de nombreux articles

et ouvrages sur l'influence des cultures africaines en Amérique, dans les Caraïbes et en Asie. Site de l'UNESCO : https://en.unesco.org/womeninafrica/experts [1er mai 2019].

66 Linda M. Heywood and John Thornton, *Central Africans and Cultural Transformations in the American Diaspora* (Cambridge: Cambridge University Press, 2002).

67 Voir Henry B. Lovejoy, Paul E. Lovejoy, Walter Hawthorne, Edward A. Alpers, Mariana Candido, Matthew S. Hopper, Ghislaine Lydon, Colleen E. Kriger, John Thornton. African Regions for Linking Open-Source Data from the Era of Slavery, *History in Africa* 48 (2021), 1-25. Toutefois la région dénommée Western Savanna n'inclue pas les Rivières du Sud, upper Guinea Coast pour les anglophones, qui devient une entité à part désormais appelée Rivers. Certainement, le professeur Boubacar Barry n'acceptera jamais que sa vision de la Sénégambie, qu'il a tant peiné à construire, soit amputée des Rivières du Sud. Le concept de « Sénigambie » permet tant soi peu de rectifier cette anomalie parce que les peuples des Rivières du Sud sont originaires du Soudan occidental.

68 ACSL, *Jugement et condamnation des nègres César et Louis,* 21 juillet 1764, procès-verbal N° 1822, RG # 1764-07-21-05. *Condamnation du nègre Louis,* 10 septembre 1764, procès-verbal N° 1843, RG # 1764-09-10-02.

69 Son nom indique origine soudanaise mais l'archive ou sa nation est mentionnée est endommagée.

70 ACSL, *Interrogatoire de la négresse au sieur Cantrelle nommée Louison,* 14 juillet 1764, procès-verbal N° 1813, RG # 1764-07-14-01. *Interrogatoire de la négresse Comba,* 4 septembre 1764, procès-verbal N° 1835, RG # 1764-09-04-01. *Interrogatoire du nègre Louis,* 4 septembre 1764, procès-verbal N° 1838, RG # 1764-09-04-02. *Interrogatoire de Marie Jeanne,* 5 septembre 1764, RG # 1764-09-05-01. *Confrontation du nègre Louis,* 5 septembre 1764, procès-verbal N° 1836, RG # 1764-09-05-02. Interrogatoire du nègre Kebbe, 7 septembre 1764, procès-verbal N° 1839, RG # 1764-09-07-01. *Mise à la question du nègre Louis,* 10 septembre 1764, procès-verbal N° 1842, RG # 1764-09-10-01.

71 F. Deroure, « La vie quotidienne à Saint-Louis par ses Archives (1779-1809) », *BIFAN*, série B, 26:3-4 (1964), 401 et 423.

72 Pruneau de Pommegorge, *Description de la Nigritie* (Amsterdam-Paris : Maradan, 1789), 110.

73 Nous avons retrouvé ces places grâce au recoupement d'informations postées sur plusieurs sites internet qu'il serait fastidieux de reproduire ici. Le lecteur peut y parvenir en utilisant la machine de recherche Google.

12

The Resistance of West African Women in the Antioquia Mines of New Granada

Paola Vargas Arana

This study is based on judicial processes and inquisition trials that concern West African women in the gold mines of Antioquia, New Granada, during the late sixteenth and early seventeenth centuries. African women constituted around half of those enslaved in the mines, and their participation was structural both to the operation of the mines and in the revolts, escapes and formation of maroon communities that began in 1597. The ethnic origins suggested in their names allows a discussion of the influence of the African context surrounding their background. The women examined here reveal responses that were used in opposing the oppressive conditions of the mines and how they formulated strategies to obtain freedom. Their biographies are part of the collection of personal testimonies included in *Freedom Narratives* (www.freedomnarratives.org), whose aim is to chronicle the life trajectories of those enslaved in West Africa during the era of trans-

Atlantic slavery. Through the application of a controlled vocabulary and best practices in creating digital identities of individuals, it has been possible to connect life histories to African ethnic origins. The online project will enable comparison with how women responded from various backgrounds in different parts of the Americas.

As the historiography has shown, the colonial economy of New Granada was based on gold production, and it was the work of enslaved women and men that enabled production. From the sixteenth to the eighteenth century, the New Granada economy depended on gold, although the mining areas lacked agricultural foodstuffs and cotton to make textiles (West 1952, 112). According to Germán Colmenares (1999), slaveholders had no interest in improving extraction technology nor agricultural production, but instead continually looked for new frontiers where gold might be found. Once a gold vein was exhausted, they sent miners to another site. Moreover, they did not maintain minimum living conditions for the enslaved, furnishing them with little food and providing unhealthy living conditions, but instead imported foodstuffs and replaced the enslaved who got sick or died by buying other workers. This mode of production benefited a market-based economy, in which the merchants speculated on the prices of the enslaved and luxury goods shipped from the Caribbean, and on the food, clothing, and mining tools produced in other parts of New Granada, buying goods on credit at high interest rates.

From the middle of the sixteenth century, the search for gold pushed Spanish prospectors further inland from the Caribbean and Pacific coasts. The largest deposits were discovered 400 kms south of Cartagena, the main port on the Caribbean, in the transition zone between the humid Caribbean savanna and the foothills of the Andes Mountains between the Cauca and Magdalena rivers (Map 12.1). This location required the Spanish colonizers to build roads to transport the gold that was produced and to establish cities where administrations could document production and keep track of the enslaved indigenous and African workers.

The exploitation of Buriticá, the first mine in the far interior, began around 1540. In 1560, the city of Remedios was founded, which thereafter was relocated on at least three occasions due to strong indigenous opposition. Remedios was within the jurisdiction of the province of Mariquita, although the gold that was extracted there was smelted and registered in Antioquia. Hence Remedios has been considered part of the Antioquia mining district (Navarrete 2005, 152). In 1576 the Spanish founded Cáceres, and, in 1581, Zaragoza was established in the alluvial plains of the Nechí and Porce rivers, which are tributaries of the Cauca River. In 1611, despite opposition from the local indigenous population, Guamocó was located near Zaragoza. Although the "Leyes Nuevas"[1] promulgated in 1542 prohibited the enslavement of the indigenous people, the decline in population caused by the violence of the

Spanish occupation, the continued enslavement against the law, and epidemics that followed conquest resulted in a steady population decline. As a result of the enforcement of the Leyes Nuevas, the Spanish began to introduce enslaved Africans in Antioquia after 1580 (Colmenares 1999, 272).

Map 12.1
Mining District of Antioquia

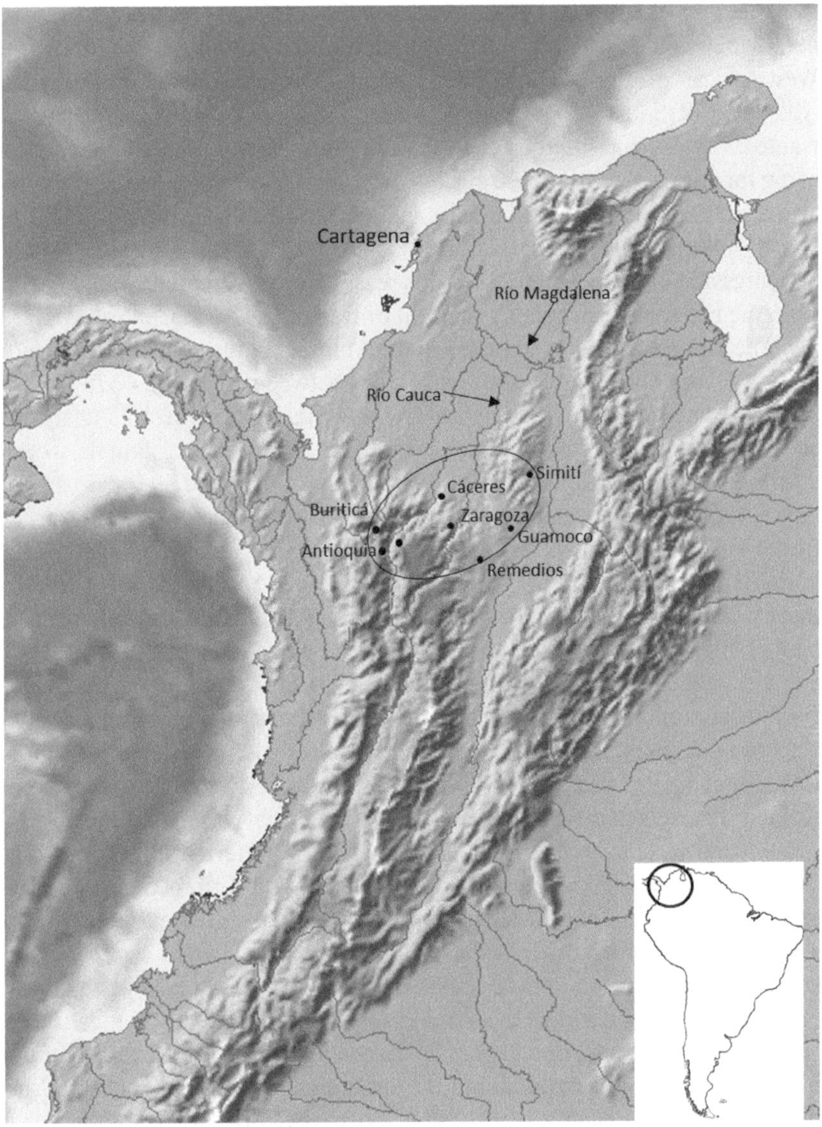

Source: Germán Colmenares, "Mining District of Antioquia" (1972, 24).

From the beginning African women were involved in mining. As a petition dating from the late sixteenth century makes clear, the Spanish miners in New Granada wanted a substantial number of women among the arrivals from Africa. The petition requested 2,000 Africans and so that they "do not become maroons [i.e., run away] your highness must send a third women of the said two thousand blacks so that their affection will keep all of them safe and quiet."[2] What the petition failed to recognize is that African women were not docile caretakers of men because they also opposed slavery, too, and fled if they could. Although the exact date of the petition is not known, the West African origins of the enslaved immigrants is clear.[3] In 1622, the Real Audiencia of Santa Fe de Bogotá, where the royal court was located, also wanted a significant number of women brought from Africa, the instructions being for one third of the 1,500 enslaved Africans to be women. The authorities also tried to minimize relationships among those being brought from Africa, and it was thought that a mixture of backgrounds was desirable to avoid uprisings and other resistance. For this reason, the government wanted people from the upper Guinea coast, the Bight of Benin, and West Central Africa.[4]

The ratios of females to males in the Antioquia mining district was much closer to equal, however. Based on sources between 1656 and 1676 from the Archivo Histórico de Antioquia (AHA), Ivonne Suárez Pinzón's analysis of eleven properties reveals that there were 185 male and 125 female workers during those two decades, that is, 40.3 percent female and 59.7 percent male (1993, 188). Moreover, she concluded that such proportions were not constant. In the case of eight lists of lawsuits between 1587 and 1634 that I found during Ph.D. research in the Archivo General de la Nación in Bogotá (AGN), there were almost identical numbers of women and men, 134 women and 133 men (Table 12.1 in Appendix). It is difficult to say with exactness if there were any differences between the ratio of females and males among arrivals in the Caribbean ports and those found in the mines during the period under study, since no documentation has been studied from which a reliable, continuous estimate can be extracted. Nevertheless, from these two studies, we see that women represented a sizable proportion of the enslaved population.

Several reasons explain this phenomenon of preferred import ratios and the actual numbers of people by gender in the mining regions. The main factor relates to the diversity of activities necessary to make gold extraction viable. The operation of the mines was as follows: A Spanish owner sent a *cuadrilla* (team) of enslaved workers to areas suspected to have gold. Each team was under the command either of a "miner," who was generally a mestizo who administered the mine, or a *capitán de cuadrilla*, an enslaved overseer trained in the callous task of maintaining the strenuous work regime and punishing those who failed to comply, resisted or otherwise rebelled. The miner or the *capitán de cuadrilla* would have the enslaved clear the area being prospected and dig eight to ten feet deep; then supervise the washing of the soil with abundant water to determine if there was gold. Where traces of gold were found, the workers settled and were divided into those clearing the vegetation with axes and machetes and those in charge of washing the earth and separating the gold. Men were employed more to do the heavy work of clearing the forest and constructing basins for washing the soil, while women undertook the actual task of panning for gold.

From the beginning African women were involved in mining. As a petition dating from the late sixteenth century makes clear, the Spanish miners in New Granada wanted a substantial number of women among the arrivals from Africa. The petition requested 2,000 Africans and so that they "do not become maroons [i.e., run away] your highness must send a third women of the said two thousand blacks so that their affection will keep all of them safe and quiet."[5] What the petition failed to recognize is that African women were not docile caretakers of men because they also opposed slavery, too, and fled if they could. Although the exact date of the petition is not known, the West African origins of the enslaved immigrants is clear.[6] In 1622, the Real Audiencia of Santa Fe de Bogotá, where the royal court was located, also wanted a significant number of women brought from Africa, the instructions being for one third of the 1,500 enslaved Africans to be women. The authorities also tried to minimize relationships among those being brought from Africa, and it was thought that a mixture of backgrounds was desirable to avoid uprisings and other resistance. For this reason, the government wanted people from the upper Guinea coast, the Bight of Benin, and West Central Africa.[7]

The ratios of females to males in the Antioquia mining district was much closer to equal, however. Based on sources between 1656 and 1676 from the Archivo Histórico de Antioquia (AHA), Ivonne Suárez Pinzón's analysis of eleven properties reveals that there were 185 male and 125 female workers during those two decades, that is, 40.3 percent female and 59.7 percent male (1993, 188). Moreover, she concluded that such proportions were not constant. In the case of eight lists of lawsuits between 1587 and 1634 that I found during Ph.D. research in the Archivo General de la Nación in Bogotá (AGN), there were almost identical numbers of women and men, 134 women and 133 men (Table 12.1 in Appendix). It is difficult to say with exactness if there were any differences between the ratio of females and males among arrivals in the Caribbean ports and those found in the mines during the period under study, since no documentation has been studied from which a reliable, continuous estimate can be extracted. Nevertheless, from these two studies, we see that women represented a sizable proportion of the enslaved population.

Several reasons explain this phenomenon of preferred import ratios and the actual numbers of people by gender in the mining regions. The main factor relates to the diversity of activities necessary to make gold extraction viable. The operation of the mines was as follows: A Spanish owner sent a *cuadrilla*(team) of enslaved workers to areas suspected to have gold. Each team was under the command either of a "miner," who was generally a mestizo who administered the mine, or a *capitán de cuadrilla*, an enslaved overseer trained in the callous task

Map 12.2
Map of a Zaragoza Mine, 1601

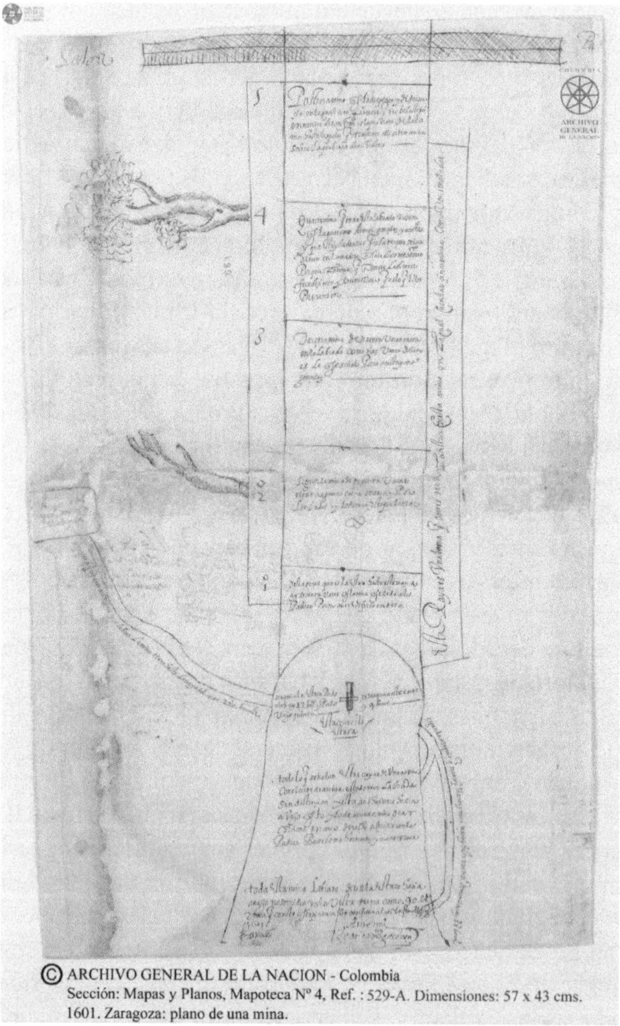

© ARCHIVO GENERAL DE LA NACION - Colombia
Sección: Mapas y Planos, Mapoteca Nº 4, Ref. : 529-A. Dimensiones: 57 x 43 cms.
1601. Zaragoza: plano de una mina.

Source: AGN, Mapas y Planos, Mapoteca, N. 4, 529-A

The proximity of a stream was essential, and the enslaved men, mostly, needed to dig a water canal, construct a bank where water could be retained to wash the gold, and build a water pumping facility to make the water flow. They also constructed a system where the gold that was filtered could be dried. For the extraction of gold, it was necessary to move the soil to the washing site or open a sinkhole, according to the type of deposit (alluvial or vein) and finally grind, beat, dry, and weigh the gold. Therefore, for the slaveholders, establishing limits of jurisdiction over a current of water was essential and mapping was used to resolve disputes. Map 12.2 depicts how a site in 1601 was divided into sections for five slaveholders operating in the area based on use of a common irrigation channel, which shows the kind of water facilities the enslaved had to construct and maintain.

The enslaved population also had to build *rancherías*, that is, the temporary huts where they slept and cooked, close to the extraction site. And their work did not end there since the slaveholders barely provided them with food. Therefore, they also had to cultivate the land to provide themselves with provisions. This implied planting, harvesting, building storage facilities, and fighting corn pests. They also tended and milked livestock. Thus, the enslaved had to survive practically on their own while they produced gold for the slaveholders. The expectation of the latter was to maximize gold production by constantly increasing the number of enslaved to extract surface gold, although finding gold deposits was irregular, as also was the supply of enslaved Africans who were brought from Cartagena, which was the main port on the Spanish Caribbean.

As productive units, the *cuadrillas* increased in size over time, as the diversification of activities increased. According to West (1952, 98-99), there were large *cuadrillas* by the 1630s.

> A *señor de cuadrilla* of Remedios in 1632 possessed a total of 94 slaves; another had a gang of 109. In the first, 50 Negroes were engaged in mining and washing gold, 22 in farming; 22 were old people and children who performed household duties. Of the miners 18 were men, 32 were women; the farmers were composed of 16 men and 6 women. The second *cuadrilla* had about the same proportions of men and women.

West's analysis is another demonstration that there were as many women as men working at the extraction sites, and sometimes more women than men because, for instance, women were particularly proficient in panning the gold to separate it from the soil (*bateadoras*). In 1547, Gonzalo Fernández de Oviedo provided an early description of the stirring work of women in the alluvial mines of Española (today the Dominican Republic and Haiti), which was like their role in Antioquia.

> The ones that wash are mostly indian or black women. ... These women or washers sit in the water's edge, and put their legs into the water up to the

> knees or almost, depending on the water course; and, by two handles, in their hands hold big wooden pans, and after they have the soil brought to their wooden pans, they stir it rhythmically, taking water from the current water with a particular dexterity and wiggle that it does not enter any more water than the amount they want; and with the same dexterity and artistry, take water from one side and drain it from the other at once.[8]

Gonzalo Fernández de Oviedo provides one of the first visual representations of the work regime. The version published in 1547 depicts Santo Domingo (Fig. 12.1). The image shows an individual, probably a woman, panning gold, while another person carries a new wooden pan to the work site, and a man digging a hole in the riverside.

Figure 12.1
Gold Mining in Santo Domingo

Source: Fernández de Oviedo, Gonzalo. Crónica de las Indias: la hystoria general de las Indias agora nueuamente impressa corregida y emendada, Libro VI, Cap. VIII, (Salamanca, Casa de Juan de Junta) 1547, 141, disponible en Biblioteca Nacional de Madrid online: http://bdh-rd.bne.es/viewer.vm?id=0000134786&page=1h

In addition to panning for gold, women were essential in preparing and taking the gold to the *cuadrilla*. According to Fernández de Oviedo, in the so-called farmstead and houses there are women who continuously prepare the food and make bread and wine (they do it of maize or of casava), and others bring the food to the ones that are working in the field or in the mine.[9]

In Antioquia, women also served as midwifes. According to Ivonne Suárez Pinzón,

> Medical assistance was also conceived as a mechanism to protect the investment made in slaves. As it seems, this led to the mastery of some slave women as midwives, to assist the black women from their *cuadrilla*. Sometimes such a midwife was leased by the slaveholder to assist women from other *cuadrillas*. For instance, among the debts that Pedro Gutiérrez

> Colmenero had in 1685, he included: "…Margarita, Captain Martínez's slave, $8 for the assistance in slave births."[10]

In general, men oversaw tasks that required more physical strength. Still, we find cases of mines worked only by women, who had to carry out even the harshest tasks. The Ordinances of 1587 that aimed to regulate Antioquia mine labor and account for the gold that was extracted required owners to keep "mining books" that detailed the daily work at each deposit (Rodas 1888 [1587], 249-262). Juan de Espinosa's book recorded a mine that was worked for at least one year almost exclusively by two women, Clara, and Juana, between 1626 and 1632.[11] The work was so exhausting that, at various periods during the year, Clara fell ill and was absent from the mine; hence Juana had to work alone. In January 1628, both women were sick, and the mine stopped producing. To resume work, Espinosa brought in four other enslaved individuals whose gender is not reported. In February, Clara and Juana returned to work with the other four, but in May the two women fell ill again and stopped working. Although the document does not describe their symptoms, we can infer that the exhausting work at the mine was probably a factor, which suggests the extreme exploitation experienced by the enslaved at these mines, including the impact on women.

In addition to severe working conditions, there is evidence that African women were subjected to violent punishment. In February 1597, Pedro de Aguirre, a slaveholder from Zaragoza, was accused of brutality against various enslaved workers. The case was so complex that it passed through several New Granada judicial districts, including Zaragoza, Remedios, Santa Fe de Bogotá, Tocaima, and Mariquita. Pedro de Aguirre was accused of cutting off the nose and ears of María Terranova, mutilating the virile member of an enslaved man, and slaughtering Francisca Biafara, in addition to mistreating the enslaved of other slaveholders.[12] In October 1597, the Zaragoza council wrote alarmed to Cartagena governor, Pedro de Acuña, informing him that Zaragoza village

> is in danger of being lost due to the great force of maroon blacks who have retreated to a fort they have made from where they go out to do a lot of damage and to summon and induce the blacks who are at peace to take them with them as they do every day and are with so much force of people that there will be 8 days they defeated a captain with 40 soldiers and killed some of them.[13]

The fugitives established a fort, from where they planned the destruction of slaveholder property and persuaded other enslaved workers to escape and join them. As the Zaragoza council reported, the rebels became so strong they defeated a troop of 40 soldiers and even killed some of them. Slaveholder brutality, as exemplified by Aguirre, most probably triggered the escapes and the revolt, and therefore the colonial government had to prosecute Aguirre;

the trial of "his majesty's prosecutor against Pedro de Aguirre" taking place in 1600 before the Real Audiencia of Bogotá.[14] Aguirre's lawyer claimed his client was not guilty because he had not raised his hand against anyone but had commissioned the *capitán negro de su cuadrilla* ("black captain of his gang") to assassinate Francisca Biafara, murder an enslaved named Pedro, castrate another one, and whip "a black called Simon, master of the black musicians."[15] As stated above, the position of the *capitán de cuadrilla* was one of the most cruel, since it required an individual trained in maintaining the work regime using the whip. As the case of Pedro de Aguirre demonstrates, the actions of a *capitán de cuadrilla* also expiated the guilt of the slave-owners who were the source of the brutality, punishments, and murders, so that the masters remained with their hands clean of blood.

In this case Aguirre was unable to keep his hands completely clean as the judge immediately called to testify "María black who heard was originally from Terranova and was in Diego Morgado's service."[16] María said she knew Aguirre for six years, which indicates she was probably in Antioquia at least since 1595. Her testimony sought justice before the Real Audiencia, as she asserted that it was Aguirre who cut off her nose and ears. This information is significant since there are very few occasions in which the voices of African women are heard in colonial documentation, especially in taking positions against a slave owner. María's statement shows that enslaved women in Antioquia were not always passive subjects; on the contrary, when they had the opportunity, they denounced oppression and demanded justice through the legal system.

The Real Audiencia's judgement was disappointing, however, because it only stipulated that Aguirre pay the equivalent of wages for thirty days "for the death of the slave Francisca and for cutting off the nose and ears of the slave María and other complaints."[17] Such a lenient sentence was certainly related to the little weight given to crimes against enslaved workers when slavery was in force. It is likely that the abuses committed by Aguirre in 1596 exceeded the patience of the enslaved, nonetheless. Aguirre was convicted in court in February 1597, and as noted, in October of that same year, hundreds of enslaved revolted, attacked colonial towns and the river trade, and fled to the mountains around the mines (Vargas Arana, 2019).

African Origins of Women in the Antioquia Mines

Before interpreting how African women participated in the revolts that began in 1597, I will analyze their African origins, since this is fundamental to understanding both their connection with their African background and their influence on the socio-political processes at the Antioquia mines, especially with the type of resistance they instituted. This objective connects the research with the *Freedom Narratives* project by gathering biographical information of West Africans. Accordingly, the digital identities of West Africans found in civil and inquisition lawsuits are being introduced to this repository, using the controlled vocabularies designed to enable future comparison that associate their stories with other West Africans, and to African history. The Antioquia mines constitute an interesting case as they allow isolating an identifiable cohort of Africans to highlight the importance of specific connections with the Atlantic and with African history (P. Lovejoy 2019, 198).

This is precisely the case of María Terranova. In the most detailed study of this ethnonym, Olatunji Ojo and Henry B. Lovejoy (2015) argue that Terranova, a name that was used by the Portuguese, identified Yoruba speakers from the Bight of Benin. Ojo and Lovejoy discuss references to the Terranova ethnonym found in documentation between 1540 and 1640 from Cuba, Hispaniola, Mexico, Cartagena, Panama, Venezuela, and Peru. As such, the case of María Terranova demonstrates that Yoruba speakers also arrived in the Antioquia mines. Moreover, their methodology shows how biographic data of Africans in the Americas can be used as a source to retrieve African history and there lies the importance of disclosing this particularity in the *Freedom Narratives* repository. According to the authors, "'Terranova' emerged to describe people taken from a 'new' region of commercial activity to the west of [the Kingdom of] Benin control, which would later be known as the 'Slave Coast' or indeed the broadest usages of the eastern 'Costa da Mina'" (H. Lovejoy and Ojo 2015, 356).

While the ethnic name Terranova is not common among the enslaved workers in the mines, María's statement against Aguirre establishes that people from the Bight of Benin were present in Antioquia since the sixteenth century. The use of the ethnonym Terranova from 1540 to 1640 points out that slave traffic moved west of Benin control, which could had happened because of an embargo the Portuguese imposed on Benin trade in 1550. The embargo related to Benin's rejection of Christianity. Portugal sent missionaries in 1539, but the Oba, the title of the main authority of the kingdom, impeded religious instruction in preparation for baptism and confirmation. Besides refusing catechesis, the Oba refused to see the missionaries for a year and mistreated them so badly that they requested authorization to depart from the region.[18] It may be that Benin's dispute with the Portuguese was associated with the Oba's prohibition on the export of enslaved males (Green 2019, 158-159,180). Willem Bosman reported this prohibition two centuries later at the end of the seventeenth century, "All male slaves here are foreigners; for the natives cannot be sold for slaves, but are all free, and alone bear the name of the king's slaves. Nor it is allow'd to export any male slaves that are sold in this country, for they must stay there" (Bosman 1721, 462).

Eight lists of enslaved workers have been identified at the Antioquia mines between 1587 and 1634 (Table 12.1 in Appendix). Of 267 individuals, 46 percent were from the upper Guinea coast and Senegambia, with ethnic names such as Biafara, Bran, Mandinga, Bañol, Zape, and Casangue. Another 24 percent came from west central Africa, especially Congo and Angola, while there were only two Arara individuals from the Bight of Benin region where María Terranova was from, which corresponds to less than 3 percent of those individuals in the lists. This pattern relates to the fact that the Antioquia mines reached maximum gold production between 1580 and 1620, a period which coincided with the peak of human trafficking from upper Guinea and the shift to west central Africa as the center of trade (Mendes 2008 and Green 2012).

The upper Guinea coast was a tumultuous region which supplied many captives, as is clear in the names of the major part of the Africans in these lists, who actively participated in the 1597 resistance. Biafara (37) and Bran (31) accounted for almost half of the population arriving from the upper Guinea coast. They came from the area near Cacheu (Buhnen 1993), which was related to the concentration of the Portuguese traffic around this port. Cacheu became important after 1558 as an outpost for Cabo Verde (Torrão, 1991). Some men, including a Jewish contingent relocated to Cacheu after a disastrous drought hit Cabo Verde. Upon settle in Cacheu, these men married African women who were connected into local kinship and commercial networks, thus creating a mixed-race merchant elite which promoted the slave traffic in the surrounding area (Horta, 2000).

The population coming from west central Africa increased during the seventeenth century. Of the 25 individuals identified as Congo, 22 were recorded in the lists for the years 1630 to 1634. According to Wheat (2011: 4), this sudden and specific concentration coincided with "a second surge in the transatlantic slave trade to Cartagena [which] took place from 1617 to 1625, with Angola and upper Guinea essentially reversing roles. For the first time, Angola supplied approximately half of all voyages disembarking captives in Cartagena, while upper Guinea provided just under one-third."

Among the enslaved population from upper Guinea were four African women who worked in the Zaragoza mines and who were tried before the Inquisition in Cartagena, where officials accused them of being "witches," an accusation that accorded with the European imagination of the period. According to Diana Luz Ceballos (1995), the Inquisition proceedings at Cartagena charged the accused with preconceived conceptions of witchcraft as, in fact, all included a script with night flights, pacts with the demon, open rejections of the Christian faith and "akelarres" which meant a "diabolic assembly" called "junta diabólica" or just "junta" in the Spanish Inquisition records. However, if we read these accounts between the lines and contextualize them in the socio-political and economic processes happening on both the American and the African sides of the Atlantic, we see more than just a simple metaphor of European occult ideas. According to James Sweet (2003), Daniela Calainho (2004), Francisco Bethencourt and Philip Havik (2004) and Didier Lahon (2004), these biased sources highlight cultural expressions and personal memories that are almost the only colonial sources where Africans were allowed to talk directly about their lives. These Inquisition accounts can inform cultural and personal elements, beyond the prejudices of the officials who were responsible for recording details. In the case of New Granada, Adriana Maya (2005) has analyzed the trials of Africans and Afro-descendant people before the Cartagena Inquisition Court, arguing that Africans in New Granada maintained their own matrix of knowledge, to which they added European and indigenous knowledge acquired during their various travels across the Atlantic.

For the *Freedom Narratives* repository, Inquisition trials are therefore a rich source of biographical data that enables detailing ritual, musical, medical, and gastronomical practices which are omitted in most other documentation. Included in the dataset in relation to discrete events, each piece of information referred to in the trials has been dissected and then introduced into a common database through interconnected controlled vocabularies. Among details in the database, an individual who arrived at Antioquia with an "ethnonym" referring to the upper Guinea coast would be classified following the controlled vocabulary designed to link open-source data in African history projects (H. Lovejoy et.al., 2021). Once having the person's life connected with their African past, we add the deeds described in the trial using another set of controlled vocabularies regarding "religion" and "events." There it is specified, for example, that an individual practiced "spirit possession," although "baptized" by the Jesuits upon arrival in Cartagena. Inputting data extracted from the source using controlled vocabularies generates a unique combination for each life history, which subsequently allows comparison with other life histories employing precisely the same discrete categories that constitute these vocabularies.

West African Resistance in the Antioquia Mines

Adriana Maya (2005) addressed the four "relaciones de causa" against African women from the Zaragoza mines but did not explore links between insurgencies occurring in the region.[19] The links are revealed starting in 1619, when the Inquisition court at Zaragoza began five simultaneous proceedings against enslaved miners (Table 12.2 in Appendix). The proceedings began when Francisco de Santiago, the master of Leonor Zape and Guiomar Bran, accused the women of being witches. The women were brought before the Cartagena court in 1620 where their cases were examined for the next two years, until a sentence was reached in 1622. What made this slaveholder so angry to the point of dispatching five of his enslaved to the costly Inquisition tribunal that would prevent them from working in his mines for such a long time? In this regard, historian Jorge Enrique Sánchez suggests that

> The excesses that witchcraft practices generated in this area forced Francisco de Santiago to request the rapid intervention of the Inquisition officers in 1618. The event was associated with the dangerous situation that some slave witches set off in his properties located near the mining district of Zaragoza (Sánchez 1997, 226).[20]

In this way, according to Sánchez, Francisco de Santiago brought these Africans before the Inquisition because their witchcraft practices posed a danger to his property. Sánchez suggests that these women acted in open resistance to the slaveholder. They appear to have met together in what the Inquisitors described as "diabolic assemblies" (*juntas*), which included the denial of the Catholic faith, charges of wanton sexual intercourse, and night flights. Whether or not these charges were accurate or just reflected European obsessions of the period, we do not know. The testimonies still reveal motivations, events of personal history, and the cultural knowledge of the African population. The accused Africans from the Antioquia mines described the preparations for ritual assemblies. One of the accused, Guiomar Bran, confessed that she had been initiated into a *junta* in the savanna two days distant from the mines around 20 years before the trial. Her description of a *junta* suggests that there was spirit possession, drumming, and a commitment to destruction:

> they had ready the tables with tablecloths and they had brought a lot of meat of savage pork, couscous, *chicha* and that the women were by their own and the young men too, and both, the elders and the women, became chicken and the men cats, and the most important demon into a male goat, and in such a way they ate and when the food was finished they played a drum with one of the demons as a servant and men and women danced [and] from such juntas the accused and other witches went flying along with the demon to the different locations in Zaragoza and its mines to make a lot of damages in the creatures and in the fruits of the land (Archivo Histórico Nacional de Madrid (AHNM), Inquisición, Libro 1020, transcribed in Splendiani 1997, tomo 2, 219-220).[21]

Food was clearly a main feature of the *juntas*. The assemblies included preparation of couscous (probably made of maize where wheat was not grown), plantains, pork, and cooked tubers (*bollos*), which were served with *chicha* (an alcoholic maize drink). There was also dancing, which in some testimonies are described as being performed in a circle, accompanied by drums around an altar or a spiritual leader, which also may express African style ceremonies. The ceremonies involved possession by animals and plans for the destruction of slaveholder property.

During the seventeenth century, these assemblies not only occurred at the Antioquia mines but also in Cartagena and its surroundings and were associated with funerals that included drumming and dancing, spirit possession, and transmutation into animals, as well as a ritualized cycle of crying in which designated individuals were authorized to cry, called *lloros* (crying), during certain parts of important funerals. This is the case of the *lloro* of Juan Bran, a great spiritual leader (*gran brujo*) who lived in the village of Getsemaní, near Cartagena, whose transition to the afterlife was described by numerous of the accused, including the African-descendant Paula de Eguiluz. Eguiluz claimed that during this *lloro*, they heard a loud noise of the approaching military, so they quickly transformed themselves into pigs to avoid being seen performing their rituals (AHNM, Inquisición, 1620, Exp. 10, segunda causa). In this case, the alleged transmutation into animals provided protection from authorities representing the Inquisition who were attempting to prevent these practices. Maya (2005) suggests this was a reinvention of African memories but did not engage in other African cultural practices that may have been remembered in the *lloros,* while Kathryn Joy McKnight (2016, 166) has found an association between these ritual assemblies and "marronage." According to Paula de Eguiluz, people fled to the Montes de María to join the fugitives during the ceremonies, and after finishing they returned to Cartagena. Hence what was being done at Antioquia was common among the enslaved population in Cartagena and probably elsewhere.

To prove the hypothesis that the meetings were intended to combat the power of the slave owner, we will analyze the acts described by these women to determine if a motivating factor was resistance against the oppression of slavery they were experiencing. The intention is neither to debate the effectiveness of the practices narrated nor to demonstrate that acts of witchcraft as such existed but rather to examine the ideological reasons that would had moved them to sustain those claims and the arguments they raised in their defence.

The first of the accused was Leonor Zape, originally from the upper Guinea coast, more specifically from the Sierra Leone River, where the Zape lived (Table 12.2 in Appendix). In the sixteenth century, internal wars and political change related to the Mane invasion from the interior upset political stability in the region. According to Walter Rodney, between 1545 and 1560 the Mane effectively subjugated the Sape (1970, 46), precisely when the Portuguese networks, including many Jewish merchants who married locally, became active in the trade (Horta, 2000). David Wheat notes that Zape/Sape arrived at Cartagena de Indias after 1560, at the time that Cartagena became a principal arrival point for Africans in the Americas (Wheat, 2020). It was in this context that Leonor Zape was forcibly transported to Cartagena and then sent to the Zaragoza mines.

At the hearing in Cartagena, Leonor Zape informed the court that she was around 50 years old and had first arrived in Santa Marta port of New Granada, "before she could give birth," that must have been when she was 12 or 13 years old. This means Leonor was captured when she was still a child, dismembering her family and community of origin. This also implies that, at the time of the trial, Leonor had lived in America for more than 35 years. While in Santa Marta, Leonor recounted that she had given birth four times, although omitting any information about the fate of her children. Thus, we can assume that they were taken away from her to be enslaved. After giving birth to her children, she was sent to Zaragoza to work in Francisco de Santiago's mines. Leonor was accused before the Inquisition in 1618 of participating in assemblies from the end of the sixteenth century that had resulted in the uprising of 1597 at the Zaragoza mines.

At the Zaragoza Inquisition, Francisco de Santiago denounced Leonor for witchcraft, which she apparently admitted:

> Around the said month and year [of November 1618], a black slave of him, by name Lorenza, came to him and told him that there was a great deal of damage in the ranchería [enslaved huts] that he had in Las Zabaletas, because there were witches and that he had them at home and that she had been mistreated in such a way by them, that from the waist down she was like dead (Archivo Histórico Nacional de Madrid (AHNM), Inquisición, Libro 1020, transcribed in Splendiani 1997, tomo 2, 211).[22]

Lorenza blamed two women for her paralysis: Leonor Zape and Guiomar Bran. When Santiago told his brother what was happening, Leonor Zape was seized and whipped until she told the truth. While being whipping, she declared that it was "because the said Lorenza served in the [slaveholder's] house, she and another black woman named Guiomar, also a slave of the witness, disliked her so much."[23] Maya has interpreted this episode as an indication that domestic slaves had less harsh lives than those who worked in the mines, which led to quarrels between them (2005, 574). However, further examination indicates that Leonor may have had additional reasons beyond bitterness for Lorenza's domestic role. The episode nonetheless reveals how enslaved Africans were treated and explains their willingness to react.

Francisco de Santiago asked Leonor how she paralyzed Lorenza and who helped her, and she replied that she had done it with Guiomar Bran. Both had found Lorenza leaving Las Zabaletas towards Porce and, when they said goodbye, they gave her a hug and with the hug "they stole her soul, tying it to a cloth."[24] Then, Leonor assured him that this restraint could only be released with Guiomar's cooperation. Accordingly, Francisco called Guiomar and told him "to undo the damage he had done to the said black Lorenza and she, intimidated by her master, who is the witness, replied that it was finished."[25] When Francisco asked Leonor "how he was sick and crippled in his legs, for four years, without having any pain, and she told him that the said Guiomar had them tied."[26] As for Francisco's untying, he said that

> this witness who, feeling his legs impeded and telling the said Leonor how bad he was still, replied that the said Guiomar had not completely untied

> him and one night, around eight or nine, while the witness was in his bed, the said Leonor reached out to him and rubbed his legs and knees and he felt as if fire was coming from his right leg, from the inside ankle.[27]

The condition which both Francisco de Santiago and Lorenza, his enslaved domestic, suffered was paralysis in the lower part of their bodies which was called by Leonor "*amarre*" ("tie-up"), allegedly caused by her and Guiomar Bran. At the time, *amarre* was defined as erotic enchanting, aimed at stimulating sexual desire between two people. There are narratives about tying up individuals from New Spain or Cuba (García 2009). However, in this case, the so-called *amarre*, apparently was meant to prevent Francisco and Lorenza from having sexual intercourse. This brings us back to Spain where accusations of "*ligaduras*" ("bindings") that led to a person's sexual impotence were common. According to Anna María Splendiani, in the case of Cartagena, both the binding and the tie-up "define the power that will join a man to a woman or define any type of sorcery that would weaken an individual's will" (Splendiani 1997, Tomo 2, 317).[28] Under any circumstances, among the obsessions of the Spanish Inquisition, were the procedures to induce the will to love, to cause male frigidity, to provoke impotence, or to separate two lovers (Moral de Calatrava 2012; Miranda Ojeda 2018). In that sense, it is possible to think that Francisco de Santiago sent these African women before the Inquisition due to the physical condition that afflicted him and Lorenza, which had no other explanation, and which made it impossible to bring them to the justice in any other way.

Slaveholders often had children with enslaved domestic women and usually did not recognize their children nor grant them freedom (Davis, 2005; Blumenthal 2009; Burnard 2004). These circumstances enabled the colonial elite to "use" the enslaved woman's body, with the resulting children being the fruit from rape and systematic sexual violence. In addition, the slaveholder could remove these children from their mother at his own will (Davis 2005). Consequently, the children of an enslaved domestic women maintained the same status as their mother. In the Atlantic slavery period, the child inherited the mother's status, which in turn engendered the perpetuity of slavery. By inheriting the condition of being a slave, the system guaranteed that the descendants of African people would continue being captives until abolition, except for the small number of individuals who managed to buy their freedom, were manumitted or who fled. Yet, women did not necessarily accept that role, as was the case of Leonor Zape and Guiomar Bran who accepted responsibility for paralyzing Lorenza and Santiago.

The next witness in the Zaragoza inquisition court, who appears without a name, was a black accomplice whom we assume was African as she testified through an interpreter. The accomplice said that she and Leonor were witches and went flying from the slaveholder's Zabaletas site to Cana, where they were responsible for murdering the *capitán de cuadrilla*. One night, they flew out of the *junta* where they had both been participating,

> and the said Leonor Zape, in the presence of this and the other witness, killed Isabel Biafara, her slave companion of the said her master, drowning her by the nose, ... the demon asked why they had killed her and she said that because so often she flogged them.... [Later] the said Leonor and the other companion, finding a black captain of his master sleeping in the gold washing site, drowned him in the gorge water because he whipped them (AHNM, Inquisición, Libro 1020 transcribed in Splendiani 1997, Tomo 2, 212).

In effect, Leonor killed the *capitán de cuadrilla* who, as we have explained, was the figure in charge of punishing the enslaved. We assume that Isabel Biafara was also a *capitán*, since Leonor maintained she whipped her, and only the *capitán de cuadrilla* had that power. In this way, the second set of crimes for which Leonor was accused were acts that confronted the oppression lived under Francisco de Santiago's rule. It is important to bear in mind that murdering the *capitán de cuadrilla* certainly was a considerable economic loss for the slaveholder.

Based on both accusations: on the one hand Lorenza and Francisco's paralysis; on the other, the murder of Isabel Biafara and the *capitán de cuadrilla*, on February 8 of 1620 Leonor was taken to the jail of the Inquisition of Cartagena. On February 20 she testified that she participated in some *junta* held between Las Zabaletas and Porce. There, after eating and the drumming ceremony, around 150 workers of the mines,

> divided into troops according to each ranchería, and they were sent to do all the damage they could, and that the little children them killed, she and the others, sucking their blood through their navels and the big ones through their noses (AHNM, Inquisición, Libro 1020 transcribed in Splendiani 1997, Tomo 2, 215).

As explained, the *rancherías* were the temporary camps where a group of enslaved exploiting a site lived which were built next to the vein or river where there was gold. This means that the third set of criminal acts to which Leonor confessed was the murder of enslaved children who lived in the *rancherías*. This was undoubtedly a dramatic act that, seen from the slaveholder's view, would mean a reduction of his capital.

Although we do not find other cases of infanticide for the seventeenth century than those reported by the Inquisition trials, it is noteworthy that infanticide as a resistance strategy to avoid the enslavement of children was frequent on the part of the enslaved women in Antioquia and, in general, among those enslaved in the mines of New Granada. In this regard, the historiographical research has concentrated on the eighteenth and nineteenth centuries, which reveals that enslaved women committed infanticide for different reasons, among them, when there was an intention to separate them from their children when the slaveholder intended to sell them; or when they hoped that the murder of their new-born would prevent the children from becoming slaves. The murder of a new-born baby resulting from rape by the slaveholder could also occur or the assassination of children who were sexually or physically abused by the slaveholder (Buenaventura Gómez 2015; Betancur and Nieto 1990; Gutiérrez Urquijo 2009; Spicker, 1998).

Renée Soulodre-La France analyses a case of infanticide in Tolima, a province south of Antioquia, where the mother argued that she killed her daughter out of love, to which Soulodre-La France (2002, 94) adds that "they chose the only independent action open to them, the killing of the child, an act that reaffirmed their sovereignty over the child's body and their own reproduction." Thus, according to Soulodre-La France the most painful act that infanticide certainly implied was the empowerment on the part of enslaved women, with which they demonstrated they could use their margin of freedom to show they preferred their children dead to seeing them become slaves. Enslaved men also committed infanticide during the eighteenth century as Marcela Echeverri reveals for the Barbacoas mines, in Cauca province, south of Nueva Granada, where a group of enslaved individuals assassinated several children with the aim of drawing attention to the justice system about the abuse that they were experiencing at the hands of a tyrannical mine owner. Echeverri (2006, 387) concludes that

> The slaves argued that if justice did not intercede on their behalf, murderous practices could resurface in the mine. That is to say, the slaves used infanticides and violent actions as a strategy to negotiate their rights.

The moral prejudices of the Inquisition do not allow us to determine whether, in effect, the infanticides that Leonor claimed to have committed expressed opposition to the enslavement she was experiencing. Nonetheless, Leonor undermined the expansion of the slaveholder's property and prevented the following generations from enduring the suffering Leonor and her companions were forced to live. Leonor was also charged with another crime that confirms this interpretation. She was charged with destruction of crops. As she admitted, the leader of the *juntas* sent them to do this "in order to harm the produce, [and] sent locusts to damage the corn and chop it down as in fact they did, as they stand in front of the sun obstructing its light and thus, dispatched in the air, they darken the sun since the dawn" (AHNM, Inquisición, Libro 1020 transcribed in Splendiani 1997, Tomo 2, 214).[29]

We reiterate our intention is not to debate the existence or not of techniques to send pests to destroy harvests, far less that such a technique could result from a spell. The objective here is to record how the people at the time interpreted events and what they claimed was their responsibility. We suggest that their interpretation arose from the ways they were being treated and hence indicate resistance to oppression. In fact, there was a locust plague in 1616, two years before Leonor appeared before the Inquisition. According to West (1952, 99) "a plague of locusts destroyed the maize crop around Remedios. Rations per slave were reduced to four yucas (sweet manioc roots) and two maize cakes per week."[30] In a 1619 petition the residents of Tocaima, south of Remedios, reported another locust invasion that "during a lapse of three years in all warm lands, in particular where the said *vecinos* [Spaniard settlers who paid tribute] inhabit, have been such a great plague of multitude of locusts that they have not allowed to enjoy the fruits of the land nor have they been able to cultivate the seeds that they produced to pay their taxes."[31] If we assume that human acts are not able to cause plagues of locusts, then we see here an African woman who claimed responsibility for a locust invasion, with the aim of exhibiting a position of power against a colonial slave-owning elite based on fear and superstition. Leonor's alleged crimes suggest that the acts classified as witchcraft by the Inquisition were rather narratives and/or initiatives that expressed dissatisfaction with mistreatment and with the obligation to reproduce perpetual slavery through children born to be enslaved.

Depicting Life Histories of West African Women in the Antioquia Mines

Apropos trans-Atlantic slavery, Paul Lovejoy (2019, 195) argues that Africans were displaced immigrants who despite the use of force retained links to their original background, which was often revealed through identities constructed in the Americas that involved strategies designed to survive slavery. This approach allows depicting the life histories of women in the *Freedom Narratives* repository, which includes disclosure of the degree of oppression that enslaved women experienced in the Antioquia mines. This oppression explains the fierce responses that were designed, as well as the associations or hostile relations they established in America with other African ethnicities.

In November 1618, after Leonor Zape testified, the Inquisition called Guiomar Bran to Zaragoza court, and on 8 February 1620 she was sent to Cartagena. Guiomar was also from the upper Guinea coast, where the Bran were located around Cacheu, where Portuguese traffic became important during the second half of the sixteenth century. Guiomar confessed to a series of murders and claimed that she crippled various enslaved individuals from the mines (AHNM, Inquisición, Libro 1020 transcribed in Splendiani 1997, Tomo 2, 220). Among the victims were a number of Biafara individuals whom she assassinated (Table 12.2 in Appendix). Returning to P. Lovejoy's proposition that African life histories in America relate to the internal history of Africa (2019, 199), it is necessary to ask why a Bran woman killed other Africans who were classified as Biafara. In my research for my Ph.D., I found four cases in which Biafara individuals were the *capitanes de cuadrilla* who oversaw the enslaved miners and punished their disobedience, especially the escapees.[32] Bowser (1974, 63-64) suggests that "Perhaps in part to prevent such escapes, the associates selected one black to be the 'captain' of the slave gang during the trip. This man was probably also responsible for the general welfare of the slaves and may have acted as interpreter." This would mean these *capitán de cuadrilla* were selected among Africans who could speak various languages and thus served as interpreters to transmit slaveholder commands. This could be the case of the Biafara, although animosities around Cacheu where Bran and Biafara were neighbors may have been transferred to America by individuals such as Guiomar.

Like Leonor, Guiomar was also around 50 years old and although she did not say when or how she arrived in Antioquia, she did affirm that she had been attending the *juntas* for about 20 years (Table 12.2 in Appendix). Consequently, Guiomar lived in Antioquia at least since she was 30 years old and was also a participant in the ceremonies in the period in which the 1597 uprising began. In the middle of her declaration, Guiomar affirmed that the *juntas* took place on Juan de León hill. Polonia Bran, the next of the accused to testify before the Inquisition, introduced herself as a woman of about 40 years, original from the upper Guinea coast and enslaved precisely to Juan de León del Castillo (AHNM, Inquisición, Libro 1020 transcribed in Splendiani 1997, Tomo 2, 217). In 1596, Juan León del Castillo was the first to expose the presence of maroons near Guamocó, a rich gold deposit located near the Porce and Nechí rivers, which was also part of Zaragoza jurisdiction.[33] Consequently, de León did an entry trying to recapture them and, in 1598, even with maroons inhabiting the area and performing ceremonies, the crown conceded him the lands around Guamocó.[34]

The next African taken to Cartagena for participating in the *juntas* was Cosme Nalu Biafara, also from the upper Guinea coast, who declared also being enslaved to Juan de León del Castillo (AHNM, Inquisición, Libro 1020, transcribed in Splendiani 1997, Tomo 2, 232-233). Cosme did not make any declaration during the trial and consequently was released by the Inquisition tribunal, as was the norm. Cosme was barely 30 years old when he was brought before the Inquisition and said that, for more than 20 years he had worked for de León. Apparently, Cosme had been forcibly taken from Africa when he was a child of about 10 years old.

This was the same fate for "María Linda, black, known as Mandinga, of the Terranova nation"[35] the last African tried before the Cartagena inquisition. María Linda was originally from the same region as María Terranova who testified in Aguirre's trial and was an enslaved to Mateo Carreto at the Cana mine. She had Mandinga as a nickname. She was between 30 and 40 years old and, like the others, claimed to have been a participant in the *juntas*. She added that she had sent to Zaragoza "before she could give birth." Therefore, she was also arrived when she was a child and was in Antioquia in 1597 when the insurgency developed (AHNM, Inquisición, Libro 1020, transcribed in Splendiani 1997, Tomo 2, 222-223).

Of the five Africans accused at the Zaragoza Inquisition, three of them: Leonor Zape, Cosme Biafara and María Linda Terranova, were enslaved when they were children, forcibly transported to Antioquia, which reveals the underlying violence suffered by the African population introduced to the Antioquia mines. Besides, for women the violence was harder, as they were sexually abused as well. Therefore, it should not be surprising they sought ways, sometimes extreme, such as infanticide, to express their resistance and to demonstrate that, even under extreme conditions of oppression, they could exercise some power of self-determination. The association between the Guamocó gold site where the maroon community was located and the place where the *juntas* took place reinforces what McKnight (2016) found for Cartagena, that these ritual ceremonies were linked to rebellious escapees and to the shaping of communities against the oppression of slavery.

Conclusion

Enslaved African women expressed their opposition to the oppression they were subjected in the Antioquia mines during the sixteenth and seventeenth centuries. When possible, they used the secular justice system as a channel to denounce slaveholder brutality, as in the case of María Terranova. They also organized themselves to exercise ritual practices such as the *juntas*," and they would have used inquisitors' superstitions in their favor, to establish narratives that showed a clear intention of diminishing slave-owner capital, as assassinating the *capitanes de cuadrilla*, or claiming to be architects of plagues that left the mining sites without food. Thus, ultimately, in the case of the African women accused of witchcraft by the Inquisition, although Francisco de Santiago does not touch on the matter, it is worth asking if the decrease in capital and the damage to slave property, would have been reasons to send them before the costly and lengthy Inquisition tribunal. Although we will never be certain that Santiago acted for this reason, from the point of view of the African women, we consider that all that web of sins, witchcraft, demons, and heresies obsessively sought by the inquisitors were used by the former to express their radical opposition to the oppression of slavery. Finally, for contemporary historiography, the *Freedom Narratives* online repository allows disclosing these life histories as important examples of how, in America, West Africans created identities connected to their African past, which simultaneously influenced the American historical processes.

APPENDIX

Table 12.1

Origins of Enslaved Mine Workers of Antioquia, 1587-1634

Ethnonym	Number of individuals			Total per region
	F	M	Total	
Biafara	19	18	37	upper Guinea Coast and Senegambia 124
Bran	14	17	31	
Caramandinga Mandinga	8	4	12	
Bañol	2	9	11	
Sape Zape	5	3	8	
Casangue Casanga Sanga	2	4	6	
Bioho Biojo	3	3	6	
Nalu	2	2	4	
Cocoli		3	3	
Balanta	1	1	2	
Soso	2		2	
Fulupa Folupa	2		2	
Arara	2		2	Bight of Benin 2
Congo Conga	13	12	25	Central Africa 63
Angola	11	8	19	
Cabanga Bango Ango Cango Cambangala Cambangaba	3	2	5	
Lemba Malemba Limba		3	3	
Gandumba Gandumbe Grandumbo	2	1	3	
Ñenguela		2	2	
Quisama		2	2	
Loango		1	1	
Jagalon		1	1	
Gualungo Galumbo Galumbero		2	2	

Criolla(o)	20	11	31	African Descent 34
Criolla(o) de Cabo Verde	1	1	2	
Mulata	1		1	
European surnames or occupations	21	23	44	Not clear 44
Total	134	133	267	

Source: AGN, Negros y Esclavos, Antioquia, 1, D.27; AGN, Negros y Esclavos Antioquia, 1, D. 32; AGN, Negros y Esclavos, Antioquia, 4, D.11; AGN, Negros y Esclavos, Antioquia, 2, D.11; AGN, Negros y Esclavos, Bolívar, 12, D. 11; AGN, Minas, Antioquia, 5, D.1; María Cristina Navarrete (2005, 152-153).

Table 12.2
Zaragoza Africans Tried by the Inquisition of Cartagena, 1620-1621

Leonor Zape	Age c. 50 years
	Enslaved before she was able to give birth, that is about 40 years before the trial
	Participated in *juntas* since she was 24 years of age, for more than 20 years.
	Declared first in Zaragoza in January 1619 and was sent to Cartagena prison on 8 February 1620
	Arrived in Santa Marta before she was able to give birth. There she gave birth four times. She gave no information about her children. Afterwards she was sent to Zaragoza.
	Alleged crimes
	1. Denial of Catholic faith.
	2. Paralysis from the waist down of Lorenza, Santiago's enslaved domestic servant.
	3. Paralysis of Santiago's legs.
	4. Killing of Isabel Biafara because she beat her.
	5. Killing of a gang captain because he whipped them.
	6. Practicing anal sex during *juntas*.
	7. Murder of five babies in the *racherías*
	Punishment: Flogging. One year in jail and wearing the *hábito de reconciliada* in public.

Guiomar Bran	Age: c. 50 years
	Enslaved to another slaveholder before Francisco de Santiago
	Participated in the *juntas* for more than 20 years
	Brought to the Inquisition court on 8 February 1620
	Alleged crimes:
	1. Denial of the Catholic faith.
	2. Paralysis from the waist down of Lorenza, Santiago's enslaved domestic servant
	3. Paralysis of Santiago's legs.
	4. Paralysis from the waist down of another enslaved person.
	5. Killing of the gang captain because he whipped them.
	6. Made a free black woman (*horra*) sick. Then she untied and liberated her.
	7. Murdering of slaves from the Biafara nation.
	8. Threatened an enslaved person who denounced her.
	9. Killed an enslaved person belonging to Santiago, still an infant, of the Terranova nation.
	10. Attempted murder an enslaved person because he was ill.
	11. Killed a freed "black" baby (*horro*).
	12. Murder of six or seven children and adults.
	13. Practicing anal sex at meetings.
	14. Murder of babies in the mining huts.
	Punishment: Permanent incarceration and wearing the *hábito de reconciliada* in public.
Maria Linda Mandinga	Age: 30 to 40 years old
	She was already in Zaragoza before she was able to give birth. That is about 30 years before the trial.
	Participated in the *juntas* for more than 16 years.
	Brought to the Inquisition court on 21 March 1621.
	Alleged crimes
	1. Denial of the Catholic faith
	2. Killing of a "Black" individual by drowning him by the nose.
	Punishment: Permanent incarceration and wearing the *hábito de reconciliada* in public.

	Age: 40 years
	Participated in the *juntas* for four years
	Brought to the inquisition on 25 March 1621
	Alleged crimes
	1. Denial of the Catholic faith
	2. Killing of children by sucking them
	3. Killing an 8-year-old enslaved boy by sucking his navel
	4. Practicing anal sex
	Punishment: Subjected to three turns of the *potro* (rack). At the third she fainted. Permanent incarceration and wearing the *hábito de reconciliada* in public.
Cosme Biafara Nalu	Age: 30 years
	Enslaved since 9 or 10 years of age
	Brought to the Inquisition court on 25 March 1621
	Punishment: Subjected to three turns of the *potro* (rack). He was released because he did not confess.

Source: AHNM, Inquisición, Libro 1020.

Endnotes

1 The Leyes Nuevas are laws that prohibited the enslavement of the indigenous population which the Spanish crown promulgated in November 1542 following complaints made by the Dominican friar Bartolomé de las Casas and others denouncing mistreatment and exploitation that were leading to their decimation.

2 In Spanish: "no se hagan cimarrones ha de mandar vuestra merced que la tercia parte de los dichos dos mil negros sean mujeres para que con el cariño de ellas estén seguros y quietos todos." Archivo General de Indias (AGI), Patronato, 238, N.4, R.1, f. 2r.

3 By the seventeenth century petitions included those who had been enslaved in west central Africa, while the indigenous decline was no longer mentioned as justification for their arrival.

4 AGI, Santa Fe, 52, N. 172.

5 In Spanish: "no se hagan cimarrones ha de mandar vuestra merced que la tercia parte de los dichos dos mil negros sean mujeres para que con el cariño de ellas estén seguros y quietos todos." Archivo General de Indias (AGI), Patronato, 238, N.4, R.1, f. 2r.

6 By the seventeenth century petitions included those who had been enslaved in west central Africa, while the indigenous decline was no longer mentioned as justification for their arrival.

7 AGI, Santa Fe, 52, N. 172.

8 In Spanish: "Estos que lavan por la mayor parte son mugeres indias ó negras. ... Estas mugeres ó lavadores están assentadas orilla del agua, é tienen las piernas metidas en el agua hasta las rodillas ó quassi, segun la dispussicion del assiento é del agua;

é tienen en las manos sendas bateas assidas por dos assas ó puntas que tienen por assideros, y después que en la batea tienen la tierra que se les trae de la mina para lavarla, mueven la batea á balances, tomando agua de la corriente con cierta maña é agilidad é vaivén que no entra más cantidad de agua de la que el lavador quiere é con la misma maña é arte, y encontinente que toma el agua, la vacían por otro lado é la echan fuera" (Fernández de Oviedo, 1851 [1535], Primera parte, Tomo 1, 185).

9 In Spanish: "en aquellas tales estancias é moradas hay mugeres continuamente que les guisan de comer y hacen el pan, y el vino (donde lo hacen de maíz ó del caçabi), y otras que llevan la comida á los que andan en la labor del campo ó en la mina" (Fernández de Oviedo, 1851 [1535], Primera parte, Tomo 1, 185).

10 In Spanish: "La asistencia médica fue concebida igualmente como un mecanismo de protección de la inversión en esclavos. Al parecer, el proceso condujo a la especialización de algunas esclavas como parteras, para asistir a las negras en su cuadrilla. En ocasiones, la partera era alquilada por el amo para asistir mujeres de otras cuadrillas. Así, entre las deudas que tenía Pedro Gutiérrez Colmenero en el año de 1685, figuraban: "a Margarita, esclava del capitán Martínez, $8 por la asistencia de los partos de los esclavos, AHA Mortuorias, 206, 4982" (Suárez 1993, 176).

11 AHA, Mortuorias 224, 5216, f. 319 – 324.

12 AGN, Abastos, 12, D.28, f. 1002-1007.

13 In Spanish: "está en peligro de perderse por la mucha fuerza de negros cimarrones que se han retirado a un fuerte que tienen hecho de donde salen a hacer muchos daños y a convocar e inducir los negros que están de paz para los llevar consigo como lo hacen cada día y están con tanta fuerza de gente que habrá 8 días desbarataron un capitán con 40 soldados y le mataron algunos de ellos" (AGI, Indiferente General, 745, N. 80, f. 88B r).

14 AGN, Negros y Esclavos, Antioquia, 5, D.6, f. 936-1025.

15 AGN, Negros y Esclavos, Antioquia, 5, D.6, f. 1001.

16 In Spanish "María negra natural que oyó ser de Terranova y del servicio de Diego Morgado." AGN, Negros y Esclavos, Antioquia, 5, D.6, f. 996 v.

17 AGN, Negros y Esclavos, Antioquia, 5, D.6, f. 1010.

18 Monumenta Missionária Africana, serie 1, vol. 2, 79-80.

19 The "relaciones de causa" were extended summaries of the Inquisition trials in progress in the Cartagena tribunal, which the Inquisition officers had to send periodically to the Supreme Court in Spain (Maya 2005, 506-507). A major part of the proceedings from the Cartagena Inquisition tribunal have disappeared, Approximately ninety are available at the Archivo Histórico de Madrid.

20 In Spanish, "Los excesos que propició el uso de la brujería en estos términos, obligaron a Francisco de Santiago a pedir la rápida intervención de los funcionarios inquisitoriales el año de 1618. El hecho lo originó la peligrosa situación que algunos esclavos brujos desencadenaron entre sus propiedades ubicadas en inmediaciones del distrito minero de Zaragoza."

21 In Spanish " Y luego habían puesto las mesas con sus manteles y habían traído mucha carne de puerco del monte al cuzcuz y chicha y que las mujeres estaban de por sí y los muchachos también y de la misma suerte los viejos y que las mujeres se volvían figura de gallina y los hombres de gatos y el demonio mayor [léase el líder de la junta] en la de cabrón y en esta manera comían y acabada la comida les tocaba un tamboril uno de los demonios sirvientes [léase un miembro del culto] y ellos y ellas bailaban. […] Y de las dichas juntas salían esta rea y otras brujas en compañía del demonio volando e iban a diferentes partes de los términos de Zaragoza y sus minas

a hacer muchos daños en las criaturas y frutos de la tierra."

22 In Spanish: "Por el dicho mes y año [de noviembre de 1618], que se llegó a él una negra esclava suya, por nombre Lorenza, y le dijo que había mucho daño en la ranchería que el dicho testigo tenía en Las Zabaletas, porque había brujas y las tenía en casa el testigo y que a ella la habían maltratado de tal manera que de la cintura para abajo estaba como muerta" (AHNM, Inquisición, Libro 1020 transcribed in Splendiani 1997, Tomo 2, 211).

23 In Spanish: "declaró fue qué, porque la dicha Lorenza servía en casa, la querían mal ella y otra negra llamada Guiomar, esclava también del testigo" (AHNM, Inquisición, Libro 1020, transcribed in Splendiani 1997, Tomo 2, 211-212).

24 In Spanish: "le había robado el alma, amarrándola en un trapo" (AHNM, Inquisición, Libro 1020, transcribed in Splendiani 1997, Tomo 2: 212).

25 In Spanish: "que deshiciese el daño que había hecho a la dicha Lorenza negra, y ella, amedrentada de su amo, que es el testigo, respondió que ya estaba acabado" (AHNM, Inquisición, Libro 1020 transcribed in Splendiani 1997, Tomo 2, 212).

26 In Spanish: "que deshiciese el daño que había hecho a la dicha Lorenza negra, y ella, amedrentada de su amo, que es el testigo, respondió que ya estaba acabado" (AHNM, Inquisición, Libro 1020 transcribed in Splendiani 1997, Tomo 2, 212).

27 In Spanish "este testigo que sintiéndose impedido de las piernas y diciendo a la dicha Leonor cómo estaba malo todavía, le respondió que la dicha Guiomar no lo había desamarrado del todo y una noche, como a las ocho o nueve, estando en su cama el testigo, se llegó a él la dicha Leonor y le sobó las piernas y rodillas y sintió que de la pierna derecha, por el tobillo de la parte de adentro, le salía fuego" (AHNM, Inquisición, Libro 1020 transcribed in Splendiani 1997, Tomo 2, 212).

28 In Spanish: "para definir la unión forzada de un hombre y una mujer o para definir cualquier tipo de hechicería que doblegara la voluntad" (Splendiani 1997, Tomo 2, 317).

29 In Spanish: "para hacer mal a los frutos de la tierra, mandaba langostas que fuesen a hacer daño en los maíces y los talasen como lo hacían y que todos se pusiesen delante del sol y le estorbasen la claridad y así, puestos al aire, obscurecían el sol al amanecer."

30 AGN, Minas de Antioquia 7, f. 72r (1635); AGI, Santa Fé 65, as cited in West 1952, 99.

31 In Spanish: "de tiempo de 3 años que en toda tierra caliente en particular donde los dichos vecinos están ha habido tan grande plaga multitud de langosta que no les ha dejado gozar de los frutos de la tierra ni han podido labrar sus sementeras della y las que se hacían para pagar sus tributos." AGN, Tributos, 7, D.4 f. 159-191.

32 Francisco Goli Biafara AGN, Minas Antioquia 1, D. 9, f. 69r – f. 70r; Elvira Biafara, AGN, Minas Antioquia, 5, D. 1, f. 93r; Diego Biafara AGN, Minas de Antioquia 7, D.1, f. 74r; and Isabel Biafara in Splendiani 1997, Tomo 2, 212).

33 AGN, Miscellaneous, 40, D. 4, f. 149.

34 AGI, Santa Fe, 128, N.32.

35 In Spanish "María Linda, negra, alias Mandinga, de nación Terranova."

13

Enslaved Africans in Santo Amaro de Ipitanga Parish, Bahia

Telma Gonçalves Santos and Nina Maria de Meira Borba

Baptismal records serve as an excellent source of research in the present time for scholars who study African slavery in the Americas since they allow researchers to access relevant information about portions of lives from those who had their existence marked by the tragic experience of the slave traffic.[1] From the brief lines dedicated to the baptismal register of a particular African – which consists of the names of the enslaver, the godmother, the godfather, the clergyman, the Christian name given to the African, age or age group, nation or ethnolinguistic classification, and status (enslaved/freed person) – it is possible to go beyond the quantitative history of the trans-Atlantic traffic that for decades disregarded the individuality of those who were enslaved. While in the province of Rio de Janeiro, specific baptismal registers (*Livro de batismo dos brancos*) kept track of the free population, in which captive Blacks and freed people were not included. In Bahia, everyone had their baptism registered in the same book, regardless of their origin, color, social, or civil status. The registers were organized chronologically and by parish (Soares 1998: 74-75).

The baptism of Africans was part of the rite of constructing the enslaved person. Sometimes it happened in the ports in Africa during the embarkation process, such as in Angola, where Portugal occupied Luanda since 1549 (Boxer 1969:7, Boxer 1975:231), or upon arrival in the ports of Brazil. The display of cruelty was masked with a Christian justification, the salvation of souls, that marked the transition from a pagan life into Christianity.[2] The Catholic Church gave to the slavery society of the period a theological argument that consisted of the salvation of souls through redemption by the conversion of human beings into captives (Santos 2014: 53). Lived stories like the ones that will be presented in this work can be extracted from the baptismal books recorded by the Catholic Church during the colonial and imperial period of Brazil.

Fig. 13.1
Santo Amaro de Ipitanga

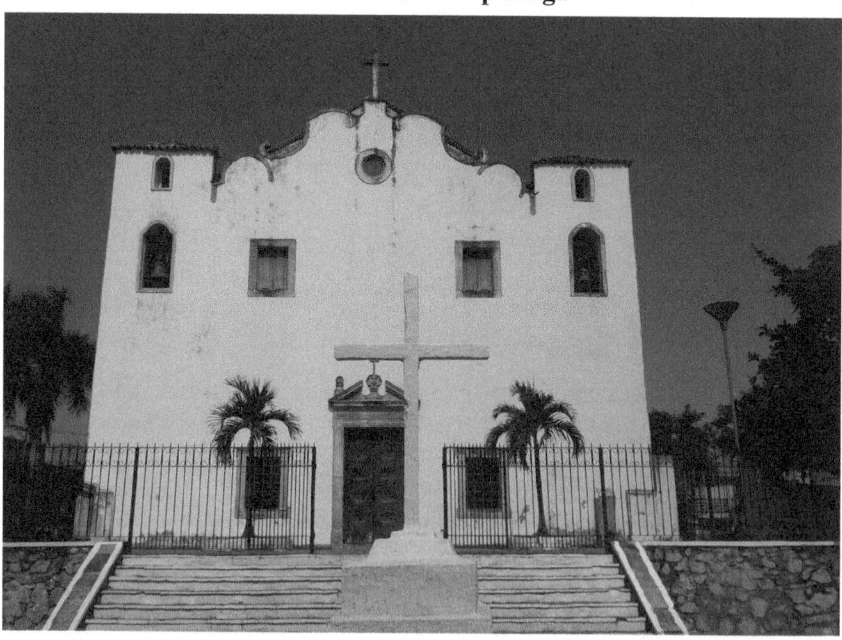

Source: Damasio de Queiroz Ferreira, Paróquia de Santo Amaro de Ipitanga, Wikimedia Commons (29 September 2017, Lauro de Freitas, Bahia).

The ecclesiastical records in Santo Amaro de Ipitanga reveal a society with a profoundly complex social background. This was not only characteristic of Bahia but throughout Brazil. The baptismal records designate the following distinctions : *brancos* (white people), *pardos,*[3] *cabras,*[4] *crioulos,*[5] *caiçaras,*[6] *indígenas* (indigenous people). This phenotypical classification obviously relied on the perception of the person who was classifying individuals and could reflect their place in society (Teles dos Santos 2005: 128). 6,314 individuals were mentioned in the records.[7] Nonetheless, the research focus was on individuals born in Africa, specifically West Africa. looked at a particular group of people within a broader context since this paper is based on participation in the *Freedom Narratives* project. As a result, the paper is concerned solely with the presence of Africans in the baptismal records. The *Freedom Narratives* project (https://freedomnarratives.org) is a database-driven website focused on testimonies of West Africans during the era of the slave traffic between the sixteenth and nineteenth centuries, as described in Chapter 6 in this volume. *Freedom Narratives* allows an analysis of life stories which can be reconstructed from surviving documentation, which is also on the website in PDF format along with summaries of known events in each person's life. These resources enable users to examine the individual stories of Africans by giving names, context, location, and events to their stories. *Freedom Narratives* allows users to trace information from a large-scale perspective, while also examining cohorts of the documented life stories. This paper will analyze patterns in ethnolinguistic identification of Africans, by contextualizing the primary sources as documented in the records of one parish in Bahia, Santo Amaro de Ipitanga. We discuss the methodology applied in gathering, recording, and analyzing the primary source material, including the context, period, place and physical aspects of the data. The baptismal records allow an analysis of how part of society in the slavery period dealt with the modernization of laws, attempted to maintain the slave traffic, and tried to preserve the slavery system in Brazil.

Our focus is on the information in five baptismal registers from the Matriz Santo Amaro de Ipitanga, a church located in Lauro de Freitas, a municipality within the metropolitan region of Salvador, Bahia. The registers contain information on 352 individuals, including those being baptized, parents of children and godparents, who were also born in West Africa. The documents cover one century from 1770 to 1871. The five registers consist of a total of 796 folios. The first book has 145 folios from October 1770 to December 1783; the second 134 folios from January

Table 13.1
People Born in Africa

Status	Being Baptized	Godparents	Parents	Total
Enslaved	225	32	61	318
Free	0	6	13	19
Unknown	7	5	3	15
Total	232	43	77	352

Source: Registros Batismais Paroquiais, 1770-1890, Lauro de Freitas, Bahia.

1784 to December 1794; the third 209 folios from October 1815 to January 1830; the fourth 202 folios from December 1830 to June 1844; and the last volume106 folios from December 1857 to February 1871. It can be noted in Table 13.1 that even though 232 individuals appear as being baptized (66 percent), Africans were also recorded in those registers as parents (22 percent) and as godparents (12 percent). Another significant aspect noted in Table 13.1 is that there is no record of an African person being baptized as a free person in those registers, while 225 are clearly stated as enslaved people (97 percent). The number of enslaved Africans as godparents, parents or being baptized is extensive, with 318 individuals (90 percent) from the total number of 352 people, while only 19 individuals are identified as free (5 percent). The number of individuals who do not have their status classified in the baptismal records is 15 (4 percent).

From the data presented in Table 13.2, it can be seen that 352 individuals were identified as being born in Africa. The generic term "African" was used to classify 137 individuals (39 percent of total), including 115 registered as enslaved and 15 persons designated as freed, while seven were not registered as enslaved or as freed. Of the 215 whose origins are identified further (61 percent), 149 came from West Africa (69.3 percent), 56 came from West Central Africa (26 percent), and ten came from southeast Africa (4.7 percent). For West Africa, 85 of the 149 individuals were women (57 percent) and 64 were men (36.8 percent), while the known gender division among those from West Central Africa included 37 women (66.1 percent) and 19 men(33.9 percent). From southeastern Africa were eight women and two men. Overall 60 percent of those at the baptisms who came from Africa were female. In addition, 138 of the 149 West Africans in the registers were classified as being enslaved with their owner's names attached, although two names are illegible. Thereza Franca, identified as Gege, is the only West African person who was explicitly identified as freed. Thereza, together with Vicente, who also was identified as Gege, were godparents of Jacinto, a freed Brazilian boy baptized on 18 July 1840. While Thereza was a freed woman, Vicente was an enslaved man owned by Rodrigo Jorge dos Santos.

Table 13.2
Africans in the Baptismal Registers Classified by Region of Origin

Book Number	West Africans	West Central Africans	East Africans	Africans	Total
Book 1 – 1770-1783	34	2	0	0	36
Book 2 – 1784-1794	18	10	0	0	28
Book 3 – 1815-1830	59	27	10	8	104
Book 4 – 1830-1844	37	17	0	98	152
Book 5 – 1857-1871	1	0	0	31	32
Total – 1770-1871	149	56	10	137	352

Source: Registros Batismais Paroquiais, 1770-1890, Lauro de Freitas, Bahia.

Ten West Africans are not registered as being either enslaved or as being freed. Only two of these ten had been baptized, the other eight being registered as parents or godparents. Of the 56 West Central Africans, 54 were classified as enslaved and the names of their enslavers were also recorded, although three names are illegible. Two people from West Central Africans are not registered as enslaved or as freed people; both were Angola women baptizing their children. Their names were Francisca and Joana. The former, Francisca, baptized her son on 30 March 1823, a baby of one month, born in Brasil, named Eloi. Even though Francisca's status is not mentioned, her son is depicted as one of the enslaved persons of João Ladislau de Figueiredo Mello, and hence she must have been, too. The latter, named Joana, baptized her twin sons, Cosme and Damião, on the same day as Francisca. Both children were also identified as being enslaved to João Ladislau de Figueiredo Mello.

All ten East Africans were classified as enslaved with the names of their owners being registered. Seven of them were owned by João Ladislau de Figueiredo Mello. One of the Seven East Africans owned by João Ladislau de Figueiredo Mello was a woman from Mozambique, named Romana. She was identified as being twenty-six years old on the day she was baptized, 30 March 1823. Her godparents were a white man named João Pereira Martins and the saint Nossa Senhora da Conceição.

In organizing these records, we maintained the chronological order of their compilation. A log was created to specify the origins of the enslaved Africans. From this point, we followed two separate courses simultaneously. With respect to Africans of West Africa origin (Table 13.3), we categorized the digital identities of individuals following the controlled vocabulary of *Freedom Narratives*, which was entered into the relational database following best practices as determined for the project. The relevant excerpts from the sources were transcribed and uploaded into the database along with a PDF of the original text. Each unique individual uploaded into *Freedom Narratives* received an identification number, thereby providing an individual's digital identity. Since Freedom Narratives focuses on West Africa, a second approach was used to identify individuals from East Africa and West Central Africa, as well as individuals designated by the generic term *African*. Their inclusion in the present study allows a comparison of baptismal patterns.

The number of West, West Central and East Africans that appear in the records as parents or godparent is 66 (31 percent) among the 215 individuals from West, West Central and East Africa who are identified in the baptismal records. 48 individuals (32 percent) in the total number of West Africans participated in the baptisms as parents or godparents. Individuals from West Central Africa who partook in the baptisms as parents or godparents numbered 18 (30 percent) of the total number of West Central Africans; of the ten Africans from Mozambique, three were registered as parents of the individuals being baptized and seven were recorded as being baptized. 57 women, including the woman who was also baptized herself, appear in the registers as parents or godparents which was 86 percent of the total number Africans recorded as parents or godparents. It should be noted that Africans did not often serve as godparents for the baptism of Africans.

Table 13.3
Region of Origin of Africans in the Baptismal Registers

Status	West Africa	West Central Africa	East Africa	Generic Africa	Total
Freed	1	0	0	15	16
Not stated	10	2	0	7	19
Enslaved	138	54	10	115	317
Total	149	56	10	137	352

Source: Registros Batismais Paroquiais, 1770-1890, Lauro de Freitas, Bahia.

Table 13.4
People Born in West Africa

Book Number	Baptized	Godparents	Parents*	Total
Book 1 – 1770-1783	20	0	14	34
Book 2 – 1784-1794	13	1	4	18
Book 3 – 1815-1830	44	6	9	59
Book 4 – 1830-1844	25	7	6	38
Book 5 – 1857-1871	0	1	0	1
Total – 1770-1871	102	15	33	150*

* Brasida, a woman from West Africa classified as Nago, appears in the baptismal records twice, first being baptized on 21 May 1839 and then while baptizing her daughter on 31 December 1839, thereby affecting the total here because of the double counting.

Source: Registros Batismais Paroquiais, 1770-1890, Lauro de Freitas, Bahia.

Table 13.5
People Born in West Central Africa

Book Number	Baptized	Godparents	Parents	Total
Book 1 – 1770-1783	2	0	0	2
Book 2 – 1784-1794	7	0	3	10
Book 3 – 1815-1830	15	1	11	27
Book 4 – 1830-1844	14	0	3	17
Book 5 – 1857-1871	0	0	0	0
Total – 1770-1871	38	1	17	56

Source: Registros Batismais Paroquiais, 1770-1890, Lauro de Freitas, Bahia.

Only three individuals from West and West Central Africa are registered in the baptismal records as godparents for other Africans. Maria, an enslaved African woman identified as Gege, was the godmother of an enslaved African man named Lino, classified as Nago, on 9 September 1833. Lino's master was Basilio Jorge dos Santos. Faustino and Raquel were other two Africans who appear in the records as godparents of another African. The baptism took place on 21 February 1840. Faustino was identified as Nago and Raquel was categorized as Congo. They were godparents of Josefa, an African woman identified as Nago. All three were enslaved to Antonio Vaz de Carvalho.

The Terms *Nação* and *Gentio*

Until the seventeenth century Africans were described in generic terms, such as *gentio da Guiné* or *negro da Guiné* (Parés 2006: 24). In the baptismal records of Santo Amaro do Ipitanga, Africans were called by these two terms. The term *gentio* (gentile) designated individuals who were neither Christian, Jewish nor Muslim, while *nação* (nation) attempted to reflect directly ethnicity. *Gentios* were the ones perceived by the Christian Church as pagans. Parés argues that in the eighteenth century the generic reference gradually changed to *nações*, reflecting the diversification of origins of people in Africa and on the necessity to classify individuals, seeking one more way to control the enslaved population. According to Parés, the term *nações*, which the colonial elite used when classifying enslaved Africans, was not related to African ethnolinguistic self-determination. Instead, the classification corresponded to "a distinction elaborated by dominant classes in mind of the slavery system's interest" (Parés 2006: 24-25). Hence what were perceived as the *nações* of Angola, Mina, Cabo Verde, and Saint Thomas began to appear in the records produced by administrative agents in the seventeenth century seeking to keep tabs on the departure ports of captives. However, exceptions to the pattern existed, for example, the terms Gege[8] and Nago did not have specific meanings associated with departure points but distinguished differences of people from the Bight of Benin. All terms and their variations are important in conveying meanings perceived by the enslaved and by their masters. In the context of *Freedom Narratives*, all distinctions in terminology are entered into the controlled vocabulary of the website and the focus of the DATAS project.

The concept of ethnicity is confusing in the context of trans-Atlantic patterns of identification. As noted in the controlled vocabulary of *Freedom Narratives*, "it is not usually possible to understand what a source is referring to when ethnicity is claimed." The term "ethnonym" was adopted by *Freedom Narratives* to allow an appropriate identification of the digital identities assessed in the database. The *Freedom Narratives* scholars argue that the terms ethnicity, origin, and in the case of the baptismal records of Santo Amaro do Ipitanga *nação* and *gentio* are related to geographic locations and often were based on the language that enslaved Africans spoke, without taking into consideration that those individuals could speak more than one language.

African Ethnonyms in the Baptismal Registers

In the six baptismal registers assessed in this study, 215 individuals were identified by ethnonyms, while 137 were solely classified as Africans. In total 352 Africans can be identified as Jeje/Gege, Mina, Costa, Nago, Hausa/Uçá, Calabar, Bornu, Boraus [Bororo, i.e., nomadic Fulbe], Cabo Verde, Gentio da Costa, Congo, Angola, Cabinda, Benguela, Bantu, or solely as Africans. The analysis of *Paroquia de Santo Amaro de Ipitanga* parish between the years of 1770 and 1871 not only indicates African backgrounds in a significant number of cases from West Africa but also reveals a change in the classification of Africans, as can be seen in Tables 13.6 and 13.7.

The data gathered through the analysis of the digital identities of Africans suggest important information regarding the slavery system in Santo Amaro de Ipitanga. Through those records it can be seen that 15 different terms were used to classify Africans. The Gege was the most prominent ethnonym of enslaved Africans with 46 people, followed by those identified as Nago with 44 people. It can be also noted that while the number of Africans in the baptismal records who were classified as Gege decreased 74 percent in the baptismal records from 1830 to 1844, the number of Africans classified as Nago increased 142 percent in the same period.

Table 13.6 shows the number of Africans associated with Angola accounted for 66 percent of the total of West Central Africans in the Baptismal records, being the third most prominent ethnonym in the records and the largest identifiable group of West Central Africans. Of the 56 individuals, 37 enslaved people were identified as Angola, ten were Congo, seven were Cabinda, followed by the generic term Bantu and Benguela, each with just one person. As can be seen from these designations, the references were to geographical location, with the exception of Bantu, which like African, is a non-specific indication of African born and nothing more, although Bantu only referred to people who spoke one of the closely related Bantu languages that prevailed in the southern third of the continent.

The data support the argument that the number of West Central Africans was smaller in comparison with West Africans. Since the great majority of enslaved Africans who embarked in Luanda were baptized before crossing the Atlantic, due to the laws that enforced the baptism of Africans in the embarkation ports in Angola. Unfortunately, it is unknown why 20 of those classified as Angola were baptized in Brazil. In areas north of Angola beyond Portuguese control Africans were baptized in Brazil, as can be seen, 16 Cabinda and Congo individuals listed are being baptized in Santo Amaro de Ipitanga, only one Cabinda woman named Domingas is identified as not being baptized, but baptizing her child, Maria.

Table 13.6
Geographic Classification of West Central Africans in the Baptismal Registers

Geographic classification						
Book Number	Angola	Congo	Cabinda	Benguela	Bantu	Total
Book 1 – 1770-1784	2	0	0	0	0	2
Book 2 – 1784-1794	10	0	0	0	0	10
Book 3 – 1815-1830	15	6	4	1	1	27
Book 4 – 1830-1844	10	4	3	0	0	17
Book 5 – 1857-1871	0	0	0	0	0	0
Total – 1770-1871	37	10	7	1	1	56

Source: Registros Batismais Paroquiais, 1770-1890, Lauro de Freitas, Bahia.

The Tables 14.6 and 14.7, also reveal a changing pattern regarding the classification of Africans. On 26 December 1827, the baptism of the African woman named Rosa was the first time an individual was classified solely with the generic term *African*.[9] Rosa was baptized by Pedro Vieira, and her godparents were an enslaved woman named Rufina and a man named José Alhanasio. The name of her master is not stated. Because the slave traffic of Africans was outlawed in Brazil in 1831 the terms of identification began to shift. Generic terms became common in the baptismal records, both in the register from 1830 to 1844 and 1857-1871, when virtually all enslaved Africans present in the records of Santo Amaro de Ipitanga were only called Africans. Of the 32 Africans registered in the baptismal book of 1857-1871, only one person was identified as Nago, and there was no mention of West Central Africans or East Africans in this register.[10]

There is a significant variation in ethnonym identification between West Africa, at least for the Bight of Benin, and west central and southeast Africa. An analysis of Tables 13.6 and 13.7 reveals a different pattern in terminology used to identify individuals. The terms for west central Africa (Table 13.6) consist of geographic divisions representing portions of its coastal area, Cabinda north of the Congo River, Congo designating the area dominated by the Kingdom of Kongo, Angola, representing the Portuguese colony and most important port of the trans-Atlantic slave trade, Luanda, and finally Benguela, the Portuguese outpost in southern Angola. The single reference to one Bantu is revealing, because this whole area, along with southeastern Africa was "Bantu" in that the languages of the southern third of the continent were closely related Bantu languages, while the many languages of West Africa were not closely related at all, with the exception the Gege designation to refer to various Gbe languages.

Table 13.7
Ethnolinguistic Classification of West Africans in the Baptismal Registers

Book	Jeje	Mina	Costa	Nago	Hauçá	Calabar	Bornu	Boraus*	Cabo Verde	Total
Book 1 1770-1784	19	2	12	1	0	0	0	0	0	34
Book 2 1784-1794	3	13	1	1	0	0	0	0	0	18
Book 1815-1830	19	12	5	12	5	3	2	1	0	59
Book 4 1830-1844	5	0	0	29	2	0	0	0	1	37
Book 5 1857-1871	0	0	0	1	0	0	0	0	0	1
Total 1770-1871	46	27	18	44	7	3	2	1	1	148

* Bororo, i.e., nomadic Fulbe. The Bororo category consists of a sub-culture of Fulfulde-speaking individuals who were highly nomadic and who lived as pastoralists off herds of cattle. See C. Edward Hopen, *The Pastoral Fulbe Family in Gwandu* (London: Oxford University Press, 1958), 1-2; A. G. Adebayo, "Of Man and Cattle: A Reconsideration of the Traditions of Origin of Pastoral Fulani of Nigeria," *History in Africa* 18 (1991), 2.

Source: Registros Batismais Paroquiais, 1770-1890, Lauro de Freitas, Bahia.

It can be inferred that geographic terms for West Central Africans were needed since ethnolinguistic terms might have been perceived as confusing due to the similarity among the Bantu languages. The term Bantu is the only exception for the geographic terms, since it is a generic term for West Central Africans based on a linguistic classification (H. Lovejoy et al. 2021: 16). Francisco, was the individual identified as Bantu. He was baptized while enslaved to Domingos Gomes da Costa on 7 April 1817, his godparents were José and Joanna Maria. The terms of classification for West Africa (Table 13.7), on the other hand consisted of ethnonyms. By contrast the ethnonyms for West Africans appear to be based on language clusters, with Gege representing people who spoke a Gbe language, as already indicated, Nago representing those who spoke Yoruba, Mina indicating people who spoke the Akan language, Twi, and so forth. Moreover, the records that 97 percent of the individuals from West Africa were actually from the Bight of Benin, with overlap into the Gold Coast region. The exceptions were individuals identified as Calabar and Cabo Verde. Calabar was one of the most important slave ports in the Bight of Biafra, and those who are now considered to speak Igbo were often identified as Kalabari or Calabari, while Cabo Verde islands identified the coast of Senegambia and especially Cacheu and Bissau (H. Lovejoy et al. 2021: 16). With these exceptions, virtually all of Africans identified as coming from West Africa came from the Bight of Benin.

Individual Identities of *Freedom Narratives*

Various cases from the registers demonstrate what can be learned about individuals in the baptism records.The *Freedom Narratives* project through its methodology allows researchers to combine digital identities in a larger structure and look for patterns without losing the significance of each individual that comprises the larger scope. One of the 352 Africans who are in the registers of Santo Amaro de Ipitanga is Luiza. She was the youngest African found in the records of Santo Amaro do Ipitanga being only seven years old. She also had another unique aspect which is the name of her master is not known, an odd aspect, since in all five books analyzed for 1770 to 1871, all enslaved people baptized had the names of their owners identified, since the baptismal records also constituted evidence of property. In 1776, she was taken to the church of Nossa Senhora de Ipitanga to be baptized, receiving at the same time her Christian name, Luiza.[11] The little girl, probably still terrified after passing through a lengthy maritime crossing that had started a couple of months earlier. She was accompanied by her godfather, Leandro de Araújo, described as a married man. Her godmother, Marianna de Figueiredo, could not attend the ceremony due to reasons unspecified in the baptismal record. She was represented by Matheus Rodrigues de Fernandes, through a power of attorney. On 4 July, the Father Vicente Ferreira took a leave of absence. Therefore, Luiza's baptism was conducted by the priest Antônio Dias Figueiredo. Luiza, besides being given a Christian name was also identified as belonging to the *nação* Mina. This designation indicates that she came from the Bight of Benin, according to the terminology of the time, although she could have come from anywhere east of Elmina on the Gold Coast, where Twi was the language of the Fante population along the coast. It is possible that she came from east of the Volta River and could have spoken one of the Gbe languages, however. (Lovejoy et al. 2021: 15). It is unclear which port she might have embarked from in the Bight of Benin, for in the eighteenth century, the designation Costa da Mina extended from the city of Elmina to as far as the western Niger River delta.

The date of baptism and Luiza's age allow us to know the approximate year she was born, 1769, to infer the year she embarked on the slave ship 1775, and when she disembarked in Bahia in 1776. It was in the slave trader's interest to sell the enslaved person as soon as possible, for the less time an enslaved person stayed on the slave ships in the Cidade da Bahia, the lower were the maintenance costs. Taking into account the inferred date of disembarkation in Bahia, the *Transatlantic Slave Trade Database* (Eltis et al., *Voyages: The Trans-Atlantic Slave Trade Database*) shows that slave ships that arrived in Bahia between January and July of 1776 were twelve. Among those ships, seven departed from West Central Africa, more specifically, from Benguela and Luanda, five departed from the Bight of Benin, two from the Mina Coast, one from Badagary/Apa, one from Epe, and one from Ouidah.[12] Therefore, it can be inferred that Luiza must have embarked on a ship from the Mina Coast or Ouidah. In the same baptismal book that Luiza was registered, another 19 West Africans were baptized in Santo Amaro de Ipitanga, but any possible connections are not certain.

Patterns of African lives revealed in the *Freedom Narratives* project enables researchers and scholars to explore methods that part of society in the slavery period employed as an attempt to maintain the slave traffic and preserve the structure of slavery in Brazil when laws regarding those topics start to be advanced in the judicial and legislative spheres. As the baptismal registers enter the second quarter of the nineteenth century, the identification of individuals from Africa passes through a generalization process, and the generic term *African* becomes regularly utilized in the baptismal registers.

The legislation issued in 1831 imposed penalties on anyone who was involved in the trans-Atlantic trade in enslaved Africans. The legislation applied to everyone from the financers of ships to the crew of the slave ships. There were also penalties for any individual who purchased newly arrived Africans. Despite these measures, however, the slave traffic continued and hundreds of Africans continued to be trafficked to Bahia every year.[13] Among them, there were 17 Africans whom were named in their baptism as Pompeo, Angélica, Juvêncio, Manoel, Maria, Tubalcaim, Sinfronio, Cyro, Melania, Bonifacia, Ambrosio, Job, Limcão and Enoch.[14] They must have been disembarked in a port in Bahia where slave traders would be able to circumvent the laws against the traffic of Africans that had been issued in Brazil three years before their arrival. Once on land, their traffickers sold them to João Ladislau Figueiredo, a wealthy man and owner of Engenho de Campina Grande. In Brazil, these men and women were lawfully free. However, due to the violation against the slave trade proclamation committed by Ladislau de Figueiredo, they were treated as his property and registered in the baptism records as enslaved.

Their baptism was performed by the priest José Pereira Martins on 25 December 1834 in Capela de Campina Grande, in the Freguesia de Brotas municipality. Pompeo, Angélica, Juvêncio, Manoel and Maria had Manoel da Conceição as their godfather of consecration.[15] Tubalcaim, Sinfronio and Cyro had Joanna Rita as their godmother, who was also belonged to the same master.[16] Melania and Bonifacia's godmother was Joana, a woman enslaved to a relation of João Ladislau Figueiredo, named D. Rosa Ladislau de Figueiredo.[17] Enoch was baptized by another enslaved woman named. She was owned by another family member of João Ladislau, named D. Vigencia Ladislau de Figueiredo.[18] Ambrosio, Job, Limcão were had as their godmother the saint, Nossa Senhora da Conceição.[19] All of the individuals baptized had as their godfather a man called José da Conceição.

João Ladislau Figueiredo at various times held prominent positions within the political system of Bahia (Gomes de Oliveira 2016: 1032). In 1824 he was elected to the Government Council. Four years later, he was a member of the General Council of the Province, and in 1830, he appointed *provedor* (protector) of the Santa Casa de Misericórdia, one of the most influential brotherhoods in Bahia. The name João Ladislau Figueiredo is mentioned 46 times as a master of enslaved Africans in the registers of Santo Amaro do Ipitanga. Thirteen are in the baptismal records of 1815-1830 and 33 in the baptismal records of 1830-1844. In 1835, another 16 Africans were illegally bought by João Ladislau. When they arrived in the Engenho de Campina Grande, those Africans must have encountered the ones who had arrived in 1834 and on the years before. The names given to them in their baptism on 24 June 1835 were Felipe, Simião, Benjamim, Cadmo, Elisio, Faustino, Gonçalo, Jorge, José, Labão, Livito, Moyses, Pitágoras, Nuno, Vicente and Thenceu.[20] They were all baptized in Capela de Campina Grande and had the same godfather, the lieutenant Marcelino de Jesus.

A current pattern that can be perceived in the baptisms of those thirty-three individuals enslaved to Ladislau Figueiredo that took place in 1834 and 1835 is the generic term *African*. The baptismal records do not refer to their ethnonym or a geographic region of origin but instead, use the generic term *African* without revealing a more specific region of origin or embarkation. Nonetheless, such a pattern is not present in the baptism registers of Africans enslaved to the same master and performed by the same priest in the years before 1831. On 30 March 1823, the clergyman, José Pereira Martins, baptized two Calabari women, Raquel aged 24 years and Matilda aged 22,[21] one man, identified as Mina, Antonio, aged 28 years,[22] and three women from Mozambique, Eva, aged 23, Esperança, 30, and Perpetua, also aged 30.[23] On the same day, José Pereira Martins baptized the eleven months old infant, Olimpio, whose mother, Ritta, was a Calabari woman.[24] Ernestina, Bernardo and Hipolito, whose mothers were three Mozambique women, Romana, Joliana and Esperança.[25] He also baptized the children of two Angola women, the twin sons of Joana, Cosme and Damião and Francisca's son Eloi.[26] All of those individuals had the same godparents, João Pereira Martins and the saint Nossa Senhora da Conceição. The Africans being baptized and baptizing their children had the same owner, João Ladislau Figueiredo. It can be noted a clear shift in the pattern of classification of Africans in the baptismal records from Books 1-3 to Books 4-5. A pattern that is also present in the baptism of individuals enslaved to João Ladislau, which exemplifies the different maneuvers utilized by the elite of the slavery system to conceal more apparent evidence of crimes in slave trading from 1831 onwards and as an attempt to preserve the slave system in Brazil by perpetuating the traffic and use of enslaved Africans on their property. Chalhoub argues that the measures taken in the legislative and judicial spheres reverberated "towards the relations between the enslavers and enslaved persons" (Chalhoub 2012: 30).

Freedom Narratives allows researchers to search into the micro history of enslaved Africans, through its unique methodology, focused on the digital identities of Africans who are usually overlooked in history. Surviving documentation made available by *Freedom Narratives* enables scholars and researchers to analyze the life stories of Luiza, Lino Josefa, Rosa, Francisco, and other newly arrived Africans who arrived in Brazil and underwent the process of adjusting as constructed enslaved people. Their stories contributed to the maintenance and expansion of slavery within Brazil, as enslaved people, as did Joana, Francisca, Domingas, Faustino, Vicente, Maria and Úrsula, and even the exceptions such as Thereza Franca, who were able to obtain their freedom after the horrors of slavery. The details and access to the primary sources enable users to examine the individual stories of Africans and compare their experiences with thousands of others, by giving names, context, location, and events to their stories.

When united in a larger perspective, the fragments of life histories give researchers a unique perspective on the societies those individuals were living in. This paper reveals the significant variation in the identification between west Africa, at least for the Bight of Benin, and west central and southeast Africa, the shift of patterns in the classification of Africans from 1831 onwards, and the considerable presence of distinguished groups from different regions and ethnonyms in Santo Amaro do Ipitanga. Through Luiza's story, important patterns on the enslavement of Africans in the Bight of Benin and the utilization of the term *nação* to classify African groups are exemplified. As exemplified by the shift in the pattern of baptisms of people enslaved to João Ladislau, it is possible to analyze how part of society in the slavery period dealt with the modernization of laws and their attempts to maintain the slave traffic and to preserve the slavery system in Brazil. Nonetheless, the patterns and shifts enabled through the larger perspective of the African lives regard their existence and life stories as a priority. The slave traffic united their stories in many aspects, but each life present in the *Freedom Narratives* project carries its singularity and importance as unique experiences and stories of African lives in the period of slavery.

Endnotes

1 The registers of baptisms, together with death and marriage records, are part of the parochial registers required by the Council of Trent in 1563, institutionalized by the Coimbra Constitution. According to Maria L. Marcilio, in 1590 this regulation applied to all Portuguese colonies. See José C. Curto and Raymond R. Gervais, "A Dinâmica Demográfica De Luanda No Contexto Do Tráfico De Escravos Do Atlântico Sul, 1781-1844," *Topoi* (Rio De Janeiro) 3:4 (2002), 85-138. Also see Maria Luiza Marcílio, "Dos Registos Paroquiais À Demografia Histórica No Brasil," *Anais De História* 2 (1971), 85-86.

2 See Silvia Hunold Lara, *"Legislação Sobre escravos africanos na América Portuguesa"* in Nuevas aportaciones a la historia jurídica de Iberoamérica. Madrid: Fundación Histórica Tavera, 2000 (CD-Room). Lara examines the judicial system towards enslaved Africans in Brazil, the shifts, transformations, the development of laws , and the relationship between the Catholic church and the judicial and legislative system in Portugal and Brazil. See Silvia Hunold Lara, "Legislação sobre escravos africanos na América Portuguesa," in *Nuevas aportaciones a la historia jurídica de Iberoamérica* (Madrid: Fundación Histórica Tavera, 2000), 75, 163, 248, 252, 341, 436.

3 The term, *pardo,* classified individuals who were perceived of mixed white/black background. According to Jocélio Teles dos Santos, this identifying term could reveal nuances related to the social context in which the categorized individual lived. See: Jocélio Teles dos Santos, "De Pardos Disfarçados a Brancos Pouco Claros: Classificações Raciais No Brasil Dos Séculos XVIII-XIX," *Afro-Ásia* 32 (2005), 132.

4 Teles dos Santos (2005: 119) states that the term, *cabra,* identified the children of Black people.

5 Crioulo distinguished African descendants born into slavery in the Americas from the Africans who were enslaved and transported to the Americas. See Charles Stewart(ed.), *Creolization: History, Ethnography, Theory* (Walnut Creek, CA: Left Coast Press, 2016), 7.

6 The term, *caiçara,* has its roots in the Tupi-Guarani term *"caá-içara,"* which was utilized to classify indigenous groups which inhabited the coastal area of Brazil. People so designated were considered to have been the produce of miscegenation of Natives, Europeans and Africans. The research on *caiçaras* focuses mainly in the south and southeastern areas of Brazil. However, as can be seen in the ecclesiastical records, these groups were also present in Bahia. See Cristina Adams, "As Populações Caiçaras e o Mito Do Bom Selvagem: a Necessidade De Uma Nova Abordagem Interdisciplinar," *Revista De Antropologia* 43:1 (2000), 146.

7 Paróquia de Santo Amaro do Ipitanga, Registros Batismais Paroquiais, 1770-1890, Lauro de Freitas, Bahia. Digitized by FamilySearch International, 2013. Relevant portions also accessible on *Freedom Narratives*, www.freedomnarratives.org.

8 The term "Gege" is often thought to be a phonetic variation of an African ethnonym, although which one is not clear. See Rodrigues 2010: 103, 105; Verger 2000: 23; Lima 2003: 22-23; Oliveira 2003: 70-71. But see Matory 1999: 62-63 who rejects a possible phonetic variation.

9 Registros Batismais Paroquiais, 1815-1830, Lauro de Freitas, Bahia.

10 Registros Batismais Paroquiais, 1857-1871, Lauro de Freitas, Bahia.

11 Registros Batismais Paroquiais, 1770-1794, Lauro de Freitas, Bahia.

12 "Trans-Atlantic Slave Trade - Database." *Slave Voyages*, https://www.slavevoyages.org/voyage/database, accessed 24 July 24 2021.

13 Chalhoub estimates that more than 750,000 thousand Africans arrived in Brazil in 1831. See, Sidney Chalhoub, A Força Da Escravidão: Ilegalidade e Costume No Brasil Oitocentista (São Paulo, SP: Companhia das Letras, 2012), 30.

14 Registros Batismais Paroquiais, 1830-1844, f. 82r-84v.

15 Ibid, f. 82v; 83v; 83v; 83v; 84r.

16 Ibid, f. 82r; 82v.

17 Ibid, f. 84r.

18 Ibid, f. 82v.

19 Ibid, f. 83r.

20 Registros Batismais Paroquiais, 1830-1844, f. 90r; 88v; 89r; 89r; 87v; 88v; 88r; 89v; 89r; 88r; 88v;87r; 88r.

21 Registros Batismais Paroquiais, 1815-1830, f. 115v; 116v.

22 Ibid, f. 116v.

23 Ibid, f. 116v; 116r; 115v.

24 Ibid, f. 114r.

25 Ibid, f. 114r; 114v; 115r.

26 Ibid, f. 115r; 115v.

14

Microhistory and "Prize Negroes":

Reconstructing the Origins and Fates of African Captives in the Indian Ocean World through Serial Data

Sue Peabody

Microhistory methods can animate social science methodologies that analyze data serially as evidence of longer-term cycles. Records generated by the British government in Mauritius in the early nineteenth century resulting from the naval seizure of a particular French slaver, the *Succès*, allow the reconstruction of the "apprenticeship" system for captives trafficked from Zanzibar after the slave trade was banned by British and French governments. Placing individual slaves as the protagonists of this story forces the historian to ask new questions of the serial data generated for the administration of empire, including the conditions that led particular

Africans to be vulnerable to enslavement and their possible places and communities of origin on the continent.

This chapter explores how historians may use serial sources to navigate between historical scales, individual and contextual, by exploring the fates of one group of "prize negroes:" 324 men, women, and children confiscated by the British navy in 1821 on board the French brig *Le Succès* in violation of both countries' slave trade bans. This small population is a microcosm of the larger Indian Ocean slave trade, which transported between 1.6 and 2.1 million captives away from the African continent between 1500 and 1873 (Allen 2015: 23). Other historians have studied the *Succès*' two maiden voyages in 1820-1821 with regard to the legal and political suppression of the Indian Ocean slave trade and its profitability, but these conventional social science approaches have tended to replicate the concerns of the British and French authorities who generated the records, rather than the experiences of the captives themselves (Scarr 1998: 112-126; Allen 2001: 102). Here, I propose to use the same archives to reconstruct the lives of individual captives in order to consider the conditions that led to their enslavement and their fates within the "free" labor in the context of abolition and emancipation.

The "wide angle lens" of social science history, often shaped by national/imperial area studies, and peppered with anecdotal "evidence" from ships or cases, sometimes makes it hard to appreciate the lived experience of people transiting these boundaries on the ground (or, in this case, at sea). Re-situating the narrative to foreground the perspectives of the trafficked captives forces the historian to ask new questions of the same archives, yielding both glimpses of their humanity and, using genealogical and text databases, their life trajectories within the wider stream of history. Their specific histories prompt the historian to ask new research questions, which may be investigated using traditional social science methods, or occasionally necessitating the invention of new methodologies.

Microhistory

Historians of early modern Europe first proposed the microhistory to investigate the culture and subjectivities of peasants, who – largely illiterate – left few written records in their own hand or voices. The method, often based in legal testimony (petitions, depositions, confessions), allows historians to draw upon the voices of subordinate, under-documented populations (e.g., women, slaves, colonized people) who, through exceptional circumstances, leave (albeit mediated) records of their voices in the archives (Peltonen 2001; Trivellata 2011). The goal is to shed light not only upon the protagonists of the stories, but to generate new understandings of their social and cultural domains.

While the term "microhistory" is familiar, I propose a specific definition: an intensive investigation of a particular event, community, or individual within its wider historical context, foregrounding the perspectives of people in subaltern social positions, explicitly addressing the contingent relationships of archival evidence and historical narration. In emphasizing "the contingent relationships of archival evidence and historical narration," I mean that true microhistories do not merely take evidence found in the archives at face value; they (should) explicitly consider the historical forces that produced the archives, and read the documents both "with" and "against the grain," considering the purposes for which they were created and investigating them at cross-purposes to the aims of the institutions that generated the archive in the first place. In all microhistories, there is a tension between the fact that a handful of subaltern individuals were unusually well documented (and thus exceptional) and the degree to which these people can be considered "representative" of the wider experiences of a general population. Before we can focus on unique individuals, let's examine the wider context that generated the documents in which they were inscribed and how microhistories impact regenerating digital identities.

The Failures of the *Succès*

In 1820, a Nantes ship owner, François Michaud, paid for the construction of a new ship, the *Succès*, for the purpose of slave trafficking. On its maiden voyage, the *Succès* was arrested and prosecuted twice, first by the French authorities of Isle Bourbon in 1820 and then by the British of Mauritius in 1821.[1] The British had extended the 1807 Atlantic ban of the slave trade to the Indian Ocean in 1811, during their occupation of both Mascarene Islands in the Napoleonic Wars. When the Treaty of Paris restored Isle Bourbon to French control in 1814 and awarded Ile de France (Mauritius) to England, both countries maintained the slave trade ban, with (Gerbeau 1980: 275-276; Scarr 1998: 113). An 1817 treaty concluded between Britain and King Radama I of Madagascar had officially abolished the slave trade from that island, cutting off what had been an important supply for the Mascarene Islands. This ban pushed most European smugglers north along the East African coastline, including the island port of Zanzibar (Carter and Gerbeau 1988: 198-199; Campbell 1988: 169; Allen 2015: 168). There they were welcomed by authorities reporting to Seyyid Sa`id ibn Sultan al-Bu Sa`idi (r. 1804-1856), who did much to expand the slave trade, as well as plantation agriculture, on both Zanzibar and the neighboring island of Pemba in the first half of the nineteenth century (Alpers 1975: 234-38).

On its first run, the *Succès* arrived in Bourbon, trading manufactured goods from Nantes (brandy, wine, hats, shoes, umbrellas, crockery) for credit and provisions (fruit, vegetables, beef), before continuing to Zanzibar. There the captain and supercargo purchased 248 slaves in July and August 1820 with two barrels of gold coins worth 33,000 francs.[2] Arriving back in Bourbon in October, the crew unloaded the surviving slaves (13 percent died during the crossing of smallpox or dysentery) at an obscure cove during the night and sold them to many of the island's most prominent planters.[3] Gendarmes reported the illegal transfer to authorities, but the governor advised the ship's officers that they would not be convicted, and, after a quick trial and appeal, the *Succès* was acquitted (Peabody 2021: 288). On 4 January 1821, the ship weighed anchor again, bound for Zanzibar.[4]

On this second run, the *Succès* purchased at least 324 slaves during the four weeks anchored at Zanzibar.[5] However, during the crossing past the Amirantes Islands, the British naval cruiser, H.M.S. *Menai* intercepted the slower French ship, gave chase, and boarded the *Succès* "without opposition or resistance."[6] Captain Fairfax Moresby forced Captain Vincent Bertrand and the French crew to sail to Port Louis, Mauritius, where the Vice Admiralty Court pronounced Captain Bertrand guilty of slave trading on 8 May 1821. The British Crown seized the "Vessel, her guns, boats, tackle, apparel, and Furniture, and the goods, Wares, Merchandises, and the Persons in number 324" in accordance with the 1807 Act for the Abolition of the Slave Trade.[7]

The Captives in Serial: Quantitative Analysis

The *Succès* was by no means the first ship to be prosecuted for slave trading in Mauritius. Between 1813 and 1825, the English admiralty and colonial courts condemned thirty ships for trafficking slaves in the Indian Ocean.[8] However, the *Succès*' cargo of 324 persons was the second largest of these, carrying almost four times the average number of captives confiscated on other ships.[9] These types of data are easily quantifiable in digital formats.

The Vice Admiralty Court produced a detailed inventory of the nine females and 315 males confiscated aboard the *Succès* in conformity with practices already developed throughout the British empire.[10] In addition to sex and origin, a customs clerk recorded the captives' names, heights, ages, and an elaborate catalogue of "marks," consisting of tattoos and scars (the latter mainly ornamental, but occasionally resulting from smallpox or injury) for future identification in the event that they might escape. It was common practice to employ first-generation slaves from a particular region to translate during the collection of these details. The ages were estimates (since it was uncommon for Africans to know their date or year of birth), but the fact that the heights were calculated down to the quarter inch suggests that these measurements took place. What can the heights and ages suggest about the people vulnerable to trafficking in East Africa more generally?

The youngest slaves were catalogued as thirteen years old and the oldest was forty-four, but the great majority of the slaves were in their mid-teens and twenties, with a mean age of 21.7 years (Fig. 14.1); the greatest number (44) were estimated as sixteen.[11] The preference for male slaves in their teens or twenties reflected the planters' demand for laborers with strength and stamina in harvesting sugar cane, the islands' most lucrative export.

Figure 14.1
Distribution of Ages, 324 Slaves Inventoried Aboard the *Succès*, 1821

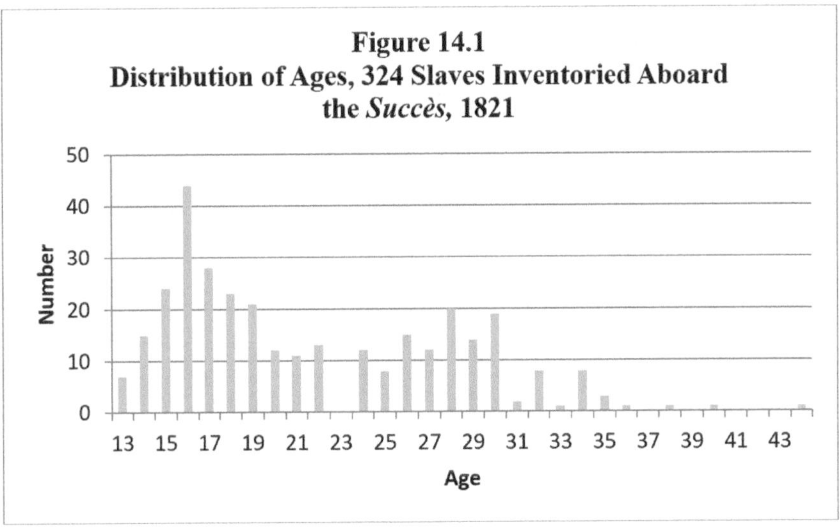

The captives' heights (Fig. 14.2) may be their most surprising feature, at least by modern expectations, and mitigates against a stereotype of burly young men. The mean height of the 204 adult male captives was just under five feet tall (59.58" or about 151.3 cm.).[12] While it may be tempting to explain their diminutive stature through a genetic predisposition to shortness, anthropometric studies suggest that shortness usually reflects inadequate access to protein, perhaps even famine conditions, in the communities where they spent their growing years, as well as social systems of inequality that denied them adequate nutrition and made them vulnerable to enslavement. On one hand, the captives' average adult male height of 151 cm is considerably shorter than early nineteenth-century averages in other parts of the world. For example, Mexican men in the 1820s (160.6 cm), African American men born 1775-1810 (170 cm), Norwegian peasants born 1809-1815 (170 cm), all averaged ten to twenty cm. (4-8 inches) taller (Challú 2010: 38; Steckel 1979: 377; Margo and Steckel 1982: 523; Tanner 1981: 159-60). On the other hand, the average height of Frenchmen who survived the deprivations of the Revolutionary and Napoleonic era was not much taller: 155 cm, or 5' 1" (Tanner 1981: 162).[13] The *Succès*'s captives were a good five inches shorter than the average height of male slaves in Trinidad in the early nineteenth century – 65 inches (5' 5" or 165 cm) – which were "among the shortest populations for whom there are recorded heights" (Friedman 1982: 486-87). Today, the average height of urban men in Malawi is 166 cm (5' 5 ½"); for men raised in rural regions of eastern Africa it is likely somewhat shorter (Msamati and Igbigbi 2000: 364).[14] Again, these probably reflect a combination of genetic and environmental/social factors.

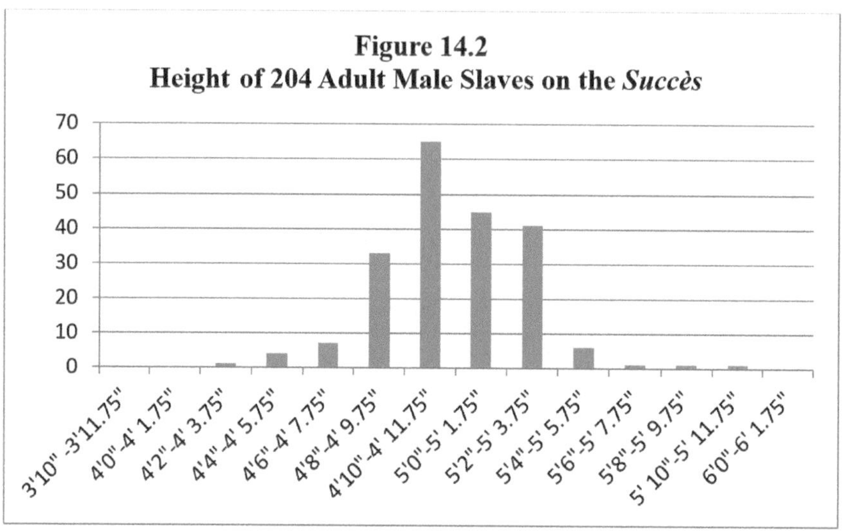

The Fate of the *Succès* Captives

After the vice admiralty court pronounced sentence on 8 May 1821, the collector of customs distributed the *Succès* captives as soldiers, sailors or apprentices in service of state officials or private colonists who had applied to receive them. Seven months later, the government took stock of their whereabouts (Table 14.1). Mortality was high within the first few months of the captives' arrival in Mauritius; most survivors were conscripted into colonial military forces.

By any measure, the mortality rate of slaves who arrived via the *Succès* was very high. We do not know how many captives died at sea, before the initial inventory of 21 April 1821, but 79 of the 324 who landed in Mauritius died before 1 January1822 (a mortality rate of 24.4 percent). This rate cannot be easily compared with mortality rates for other slaving ships, which are usually computed solely based on slaves who died at sea.[15] Nevertheless, it points to the fragile health of the captives when they boarded the *Succès* in Zanzibar, their poor treatment on board the ship, and/or an epidemic that weakened a large portion of those trafficked.

Over half of the *Succès* captives were conscripted into military service. The largest portion (25 percent of 324) joined the British army. The army selected older men as soldiers – the mean age of the conscripts from the Succès was 24.6 years; their heights were not exceptional within this group (avg. 4'11" in.). Once turned over to the army, they were no longer tracked carefully by the collector of customs, so we can't be sure how long any of them survived as trainees or soldiers.[16]

Table 14.1
Fate of 324 Captives aboard the *Succès*, 1 January 1822

			Mortality	
	No. of Captives	% of Total	Died by 1/1/1822	% of Category
Died (by 11 May)	15	4.6		
Unapprenticed	49	15.1	44	90
British Army				
Conscripts	54	16.7		
Ceylon Reserves	60	18.5	6	10
Servants to Army Officers		8.0		11.5
56th regiment	15		2	
82nd regiment	11		1	
Navy	5	1.5		
Mariners	51	15.7	5	9.8
Civil Engineering Artificer	13	4.0	3	23.1
Civil Apprenticeship				
Servant to civilians	46	14.2	3	6.5
To Royal College	2	0.6		
Cook	2	0.6		
Carpenter	1	0.3		

Source: "Detailed Statement of Blacks Seized Since the last Return," 1 January 1822 (NAUK CO 167/71).

While most of the *Succès* captives who entered the army did so as soldiers, twenty-six would become servants to officers of the 56th and 82nd regiments stationed in Mauritius (their mortality rate was relatively high:

11.5 percent).[17] We can glean a little bit about their lives through regimental histories. An attachment of the First Battalion of the 56th West Essex Regiment of Foot had participated in the conquest of Isle Bourbon and Mauritius in 1810 under Lieutenant-Colonel Keating but was subsequently relocated to various stations during the Napoleonic Wars (Anon. 1844, 30-31). In July 1819, the 56th returned to Port Louis, where Major-General Darling declared upon inspection:

> A finer body of men than compose this regiment is perhaps nowhere to be seen; they are clean and soldierlike in appearance, well appointed, and in no respect deficient: in short, the care and attention of Lieut.-Colonel Barclay, and of the officers, and the good disposition of the men, are evident, and could alone have led to the state in which the Fifty-Sixth Regiment now is (Anon. 1844: 47-48).

Lieutenant-Colonel Fletcher Barclay was among the officers to receive two captives from the *Succès* as his servants: Sipandé, age 25, 5' ½", and Materora, age 30, 4' 10½", but the latter soon died.[18] The 56th Regiment remained in the capital city of Port Louis until moving to Mahébourg, in southeastern Mauritius, until called back to England in 1826 (Anon. 1844, 48). The 82nd Regiment of Foot (Prince of Wales's Volunteers) was originally raised to combat the French in 1793. It arrived in Mauritius in 1819 and would remain there until 1831 (Jarvis 1866: xi).[19] The commanding officer, Lieutenant-Colonel Charles Edward Conyers, received one of the *Succès*'s oldest and tallest captives, Vomon (age 30, 5' 3½) as his personal servant.[20] In October 1823, he returned to England on leave of absence (Jarvis 1866: 68).[21]

The next largest group of conscripts (18.5 percent) was assigned to "the Ceylon military service."[22] Governor Farquhar told the minister that one hundred (an exaggeration, in fact only sixty according to the customs collector's inventory[23]) were reserved "for the augmentation of the Caffre Corps, at Ceylon." The governor of Ceylon had stated that "that he did not want a great many, & that he would take only those who were young."[24] By "Caffre Corps,"[25] Farquhar was probably referencing the 1st Ceylon Regiment, "composed principally of Malays, nearly 2,000 strong," and, according to one observer:

> … one of the finest regiments in His Majesty's service. I have never seen any native troops on the continent of India to equal the 1st Ceylon light infantry, either in appearance or manoeuvring, and their conduct during the Kandyan war [1815-1818] proved them to be inferior to no light infantry in the world. Their dress is dark green, and their arms a compact rifle, with a short strong sword attachable instead of a bayonet. They are native officered, as in the E. I. C.'s sepoy regiments, with European officers to each of the 16 companies, and their fidelity to their leaders has been evinced in every possible manner whenever an opportunity presented itself. I have seen many regiments of different nations under

> arms, but none ever offered to my view such a striking *coup d'œil* as H. M.'s 1st Ceylon rifle regiment (Martin 1835: 545).

Indeed, this corps of non-European troops was so elite that eighteen of the sixty that the customs collector initially assigned to the Ceylon Reserve were rejected in October 1821 (of these, six died in October and November, so ill health was likely the grounds). Most of these became "artificers" – unskilled or semi-skilled manual laborers – in the civil corps of engineers, which was responsible for canals, roads, and other infrastructure in Mauritius. Another thirteen (4 percent) joined this work crew directly (without being "reserved" for Ceylon), where their mortality rate (23.1 percent) was disproportionally high.

After the Army, the next most important employment for the *Succès* male captives (fifty-one of them or 15.7 percent) was as mariners; these averaged about twenty years of age and 4' 7¾" tall, not as robust as the army recruits. Their mortality rate (9.8 percent) was comparable to those set aside for the Ceylon Reserves. It is not (yet) clear to which ships these sailors were assigned, but an additional five captives (1.5 percent), all teenaged boys, were set aside for Captain Moresby of the *Menai*, the ship that had captured the *Succès*.[26] Makoutchirenga (age 13, 4' ½"), Akoïsira (13, 3' 11¼"), Nohihaye (15, 4' 1¾"), Matandika (15, 4' 3¾"), and Songore (16, 4' 6½") joined the crew of the *Menai* on 2 June 1821 in the harbor of Port Louis.[27] I will return to two of these, Akoïsira and Songore, in a moment.

Civilian Apprenticeships

In the last category, servants and skilled laborers apprenticed to civilians, we begin to get a clearer picture of life for the Succès's "Prize Negroes," thanks to supporting narratives describing their masters' residency in Mauritius. Only five captives obtained skilled positions: two cooks, a carpenter, and two servants in the Royal College; the rest became the "servants" of private individuals, many of whom were government employees. The great majority of their masters had British, not French, last names. These included eight women and girls who survived long enough to become the servants of married women in Port Louis (Table 14.2), whose average age was 15.6 years and average height was just under 4'6".

Their mistresses belonged to a tight-knit set of families in Mauritius who had either married British colonial officers or arrived since with the transfer of the island from France to Britain in 1814. Maria Hassard (23 November 1799-17 May 1832) was the new wife of the widower John Finniss, captain in the 56th Regiment, and the future chief of police of Mauritius; they were married on 25 February 1821, just a few months before the distribution of the *Succès*' captives.[28] Mrs. "C. LeBrun" was almost certainly Coralie Mabille (1799-

1859), the wife of the missionary, Jean Lebrun, who founded several schools in Mauritius for "religious instruction of the lower classes," i.e. free people of color (Telfair 1830, 60). Kawianao's mistress, Mrs. E. Bathfield, was very likely Elisabeth Bathfield, née Adam, the wife of William Henry Bathfield.[29] In 1819, two years before the arrival of the *Succès*, Mr. Bathfield had owned two creole "brownish-black [*brune noire*]" slaves, Zélie, age 20, and her sister, Lisa, age 10, surnamed Cupidon.[30] By 1822, Zélie was no longer part of the household; her 13-year-old sister, Lisa, now a creole seamstress, remained with her new "yellowish [*jaunâtre*]" niece, Eliza Cupidon, 6 months old.[31] The color designations reflect the awareness of miscegenation in successive generations of this family; it seems likely that Bathfield or another white man had impregnated Zélie, and she had either died or been sold prior to his marriage to Elizabeth.[32] Several years later, Bathfield took another apprenticed "prize negro" (not of the *Succès*) with him to Madagascar, where the young man tried to escape.[33]

Table 14.2
Fate of the Nine Female Slaves aboard the *Succès*

Captive	Age	Height	Mistress	Husband's Position	Husband's *Succès* Captives
Namakeika	13	4' 4¼"	Mrs. C. Bates	H. Bates, Major, Royal Artillery	1
Antideye	13	4' 3¾"	Mrs. M[aria] Finniss	J[ohn] Finniss, Paymaster 56 Reg.	1
Fehiamana	14	4' 1"	Mrs. T. Carey	T. Carey, Asst. Dep. Com. General	1
Marenguy	14	4' 4¾"	Died before apprenticed		
Kawianao	16	4' 3½"	Mrs. E. Bathfield	?	0
Achiagonguy	16	4' 5½"	Mrs. M. Bartram	A[lfred] Bartram: Purveyor Civil Hosp.	1
Amirangue	17	4' 7"	Mrs. C[oralie Mabille] LeBrun	[Jean Lebrun, missionary]	0
Anbonburie	18	4' 9"	Mrs. J. Hassard	Lt.-Col. J[ohn] Hassard, Royal Engineer	2
	18	4' 9½"	Mrs. A. Shaw	[Major General George Shaw?]	0

Source: "Detailed Statement of Blacks Seized Since the last Return," 1 January 1822 (NAUK CO 167/71); *The Royal Kalendar, and Court and City Register for England, Scotland, Ireland, and the Colonies for the Year 1820* (London: T.C. Hansard, [1820]), 223.

Mrs. Bartram, wife of Alfred Bartram, the purveyor of the civil hospital, had arrived only a year before the *Succès*, in February 1820, with her husband and daughter; she bore a second daughter in 1821 ([Bartram] 1930: 34). Presumably, the sixteen-year-old Achiagonguy helped her mistress with the household and the girls. Mrs. Bartram was good enough to leave a memoir of her seven years in Mauritius, and she describes the apprentices' lives, though she did not hold them in high esteem:

> Two or three captures were made of French slave ships by our men-of-war on the coast of Africa, and the negroes, on being landed at the Mauritius, were placed in a large building called the Bagne, where they were fed and clothed at the expense of government, until they were apprenticed, to any individuals who chose to apply for them, as domestic servants:—the term of apprenticeship was fourteen years, after which they were to be considered at liberty to work for themselves; such, however, is the natural indolence of Africans, that I fear very many will not find freedom a blessing; for, to be thrown on their own exertions will be, to the greater part, to be deprived of the means of subsistence :—with creole blacks the case would be very different; they are an active, intelligent set of people, participating largely in the vivacity, shrewdness, and liveliness of fancy of their French owners; they, if obliged to support themselves by their own labour, would, no doubt, be very industrious; but Africans have so great an aversion to all active employment, that they will beg, steal, or suffer want, rather than work ([Bartram] 1830: 153-154).

Nevertheless, her memoir also hints at the servants' labors, here performed by enslaved people:

> The floor of their [drawing] rooms is of a dark wood which takes a fine polish, and by being rubbed every morning with wax and a brush, rivals in brilliancy a mahogany table; this process is performed at an early hour, and the slaves are extremely expert at it; they fix one foot on the brush, which is a large flat one, and jumping alternately on the other foot, with a bend of the body each time, pass the brush rapidly up and down the floor, with a motion not unlike that of skating ([Bartram] 1830: 58-59).

Also within this English social circle were the brothers, Charles Edward Telfair (1778-1833) and William Telfair (1786-1837), both originally of Belfast. The *Succès*' Simambi, age 17, became a servant to William on his plantation, Bon Espoir. Charles was an eccentric and pious planter who initiated a series of progressive reforms on his Mauritius plantation, Belombre, which his brother emulated at Bon Espoir (Telfair 1830: 223). He aimed to prepare his slaves for eventual freedom with jury trials for petty infractions, wages for the enslaved commanders, and a savings bank that allowed slaves to amass savings to spend on small creature comforts (clothing, furniture), or to save toward the purchase one's own freedom or that of relatives.[34] When Charles was attacked in the pages of the *Anti-Slavery Reporter* for an excessively high mortality rate among his slaves (12 percent), the missionary Le Brun (husband of Mrs. C. Le Brun, recipient of one of the *Succès*'s female captives), publicly defended him.[35]

The elder Telfair brother's social experiment included the reception of 92 captive apprentices from a variety of trafficking ships (though not the *Succès*); he was by far the largest private recipient of their labor.[36] (William, by contrast, received only four.) Charles's self-exculpatory account describes the poor condition of the apprentices upon their arrival as being worse than creole slaves, born and raised in the colony:

> [A]midst the abundance and comfort enjoyed by the Slaves, the most squalid forms of human wretchedness were at times to be seen wandering over the grounds of Belombre, in a state of apparent starvation. They were Government Negro apprentices, who had been captured, and who had been distributed, from time to time, by the collector of the customs at Port-Louis. On such occasions a portion of sickly and emaciated Blacks were generally left on hand, whose feeding, clothing, and general treatment entailed a heavy expense on the captors, or on the Government. To shut them up within the Government hospital would have aggravated their misery, instead of contributing to their cure. Belombre was a charitable refuge for them.... Soon as they were able to crawl, their wish was to saunter about the grounds. This practice was, in some cases, found prejudicial: many suddenly sickened, without apparent cause; their diseased appetites led them, during their wanderings, to eat indigenous wild fruits and seeds, of which several are poisonous. In one day fifteen were brought to the hospital, under the narcotic influence of the Dolichos Amara, and of the Jatropha Curcas, the fruit of which is tempting to the eye and pleasant to the taste. Afterwards, these apprentices were accompanied in their walks by a Slave, and thus were prevented from eating anything but what was prepared by the hospital cook. Notwithstanding all our care and expense, numbers died; and, as a compensation, after the lapse of ten years, our humanity to free Blacks is misconstrued, by ignorant malevolence, into barbarity to the Slave (Telfair 1830: 38).

Indeed, a delegation sent to Mauritius to report on the conditions of slaves and free people of color, stated that thirty-three (almost 36 percent) of Charles Telfair's apprentices had died in his care over a period of about fifteen years.[37] Whether or not we accept Telfair's defensive explanation, his assertion that the apprentices began their lives in Mauritius more sickly than creole slaves seems accurate, given the mortality rates observed among the survivors of the *Succès*' middle passage.

In fact, the mortality rate for the *Succès*'s captives far exceeded that of any of the ships prosecuted by the British in Mauritius between 1808 and 1827. With only one exception, other ships' mortality rates ranged from 0-8 percent, but 28 percent of the men, women, and children on the *Succès* died before they were even assigned to apprenticeships.[38] The *Succès*'s voyages coincided with a cholera epidemic that spanned the full Indian Ocean world in 1817-1821 and may have been one of the purveyors of the bacteria (Gauzere and Aubry 2012: 131-136).

Microhistory: Akoïsira and Songore

The serial data generated by British colonial government in Mauritius have allowed us to reconstruct the experiences and fates of the captives apprenticed in general terms, but certain documents make it possible to glimpse the personal destinies of individuals. In this section, I explore the histories of two young men discovered on board the *Succès.* Documentation from 1830 that allows us to trace their lives forward and backward longitudinally over more than a decade. New questions arising from these narratives suggests future avenues for further research and how to capture so many details about well-documented microhistories in digital formats.

Songore and Akoïsira were born around 1805 and 1808 somewhere in East Central Africa, and, like all the other captives aboard the *Succès*, were designated "Mozambique."[39] The first puzzle is to try to locate their place and community of birth. Historians note that Europeans applied the label "Mozambique" generically to encompass "the entire deep hinterland of Mozambique north of the Zambezi River right into northeastern Zambia..., southern Tanzania, [and] ... the country laying inland from the southern Mozamibican port of Inhambane" (Teelock and Alpers 2001: 111).

Songore's name hints that the catchment area for slaves labeled "Mozambique," may have reached as far as a thousand miles further north.[40] Since 2005, Songore is the name of a U.N. refugee transit center in northern Berundi, on the border of Rwanda (U.N. High Commissioner for Refugees, 2005). Today, Songore is a family name in Rwanda.[41] Given the upland proximity of this borderlands region between Rwanda and Burundi west of Lake Victoria to Zanzibar, it is plausible that the *Succès*' Songore (in fact, two young men with the same name) originated in this region. In fact, there were five men and boys aboard the *Succès* for whom the clerk recorded this name.[42] Perhaps they all originated in a slave raid from the same area and were transported to Zanzibar for sale.[43]

As for Akoïsira, Stephen Paas, a Dutch linguist and missionary who authored the *Oxford Chichewa-English Dictionary*, thinks that his name might tie him to the Chipeta or Chewa people, residing in today's Malawi and Zambia. In modern Chichewa, *a-ku-i-sira* could be translated as "when he is being merciful towards."[44] Perhaps "Akoïsira," was the name given to him by a previous Chewa-speaking master, meaning roughly: "the beneficiary of my mercy." Or, alternatively, when the English customs clerk asked this man his name through the translator, perhaps the translator responded: "one worthy of mercy." Or perhaps Akoïsira, sensing the gravity, if not the specifics of the interrogation, begged, "Have mercy," which became garbled in translation. This example suggests the possibilities – but also some of the difficulties – in using transliterated African names, or anthronyms, to trace African places and communities of origin (Nwokeji and Eltis 2002; Anderson, et al. 2013).[45] While neither name appears in the *African Names* database,[46] which consists primarily of West African anthronyms, a similar compilation of personal names might yield more insight into the geographical origins of captives circulating in the Indian Ocean.

Upon their arrival in Mauritius, the collector of customs recorded all the *Succès'* captives' tattoos and scars, presumably for later identification.[47] The small drawings seem to represent ornamental scars, rather than tattoos (the latter of which are frequently mentioned but never depicted). Tattoos and ornamental scarification were ubiquitous amongst the *Succès'* captives; only thirteen bore no marks whatsoever.[48] Can we use those of Akoïsira and Songore (Fig 14.3) to clarify their places of birth or ethnicities?

Figure 14.3
Marks: Akoïsira (a) and Songore (b)

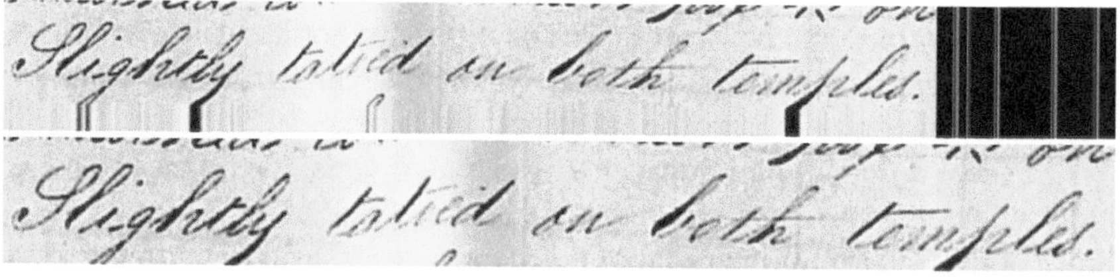
Slightly tatted on both temples.
Slightly tatted on both temples.

Source: "Schedule A. Three hundred and twenty-four persons, natives of Africa, that were found on board the brig Succès," 21 April 1821 (NAUK CO 167/92).

From the late eighteenth to the mid-twentieth centuries, European travelers to east central Africa observed widespread body markings and concluded that the patterns reflected kinship ties. For example, the British merchant William White, who visited southern Mozambique in 1798, wrote:

> They are all tattooed, some down the middle of the forehead, and point of the chin . . .; and of their temples, of this shape X: their bodies are so likewise, particularly on the chest, but none of them are exactly alike; those, however, of the same family, are tattooed very nearly in the same manner (White 1800: 27).

Historians of Africa, however, have noted that this assumption that tattoo patterns reflected kinship ties is problematic, since it embodies the overarching colonialist trope that "Africans were divided along 'tribal' lines, with ethnicity

Table 14.3
Stacked Chevron Marks

Customs ID No.	Name	Age	Marks
152	Akoïsira	13	 on forehead, tattooed on temples
125	Hatipo	13	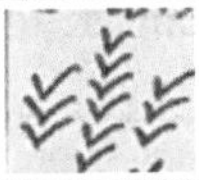 on forehead, tattooed on temples & cheeks
145	Kapingua/ Kapingue	15	 on forehead, tattooed on temples
166	Namaly	16	 on forehead, tattooed on temples & belly
181	Kiowololio	16	 on forehead, tattooed on temples; 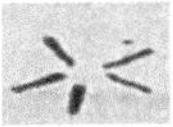 on cheeks
199	Sagola	16	 on forehead  on cheeks, tattooed on temples
213	Malombé	16	 on forehead  on cheeks & temples
284	Songolo	19	on belly on forehead, tattooed on temples
24	Ketengue	25	 tattooed on forehead, stomach, temples; scar on belly
281	Nampinga	29	Tattooed on belly  tattooed on forehead, temples
282	Serikosa	29	 on belly  on forehead  on cheeks, tattooed all over
118	Makatsy	30	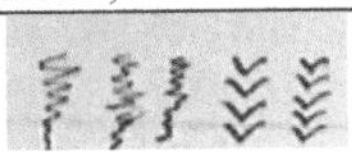 on left side of belly;  tattooed on forehead
119	Mavira	30	 on forehead; tattooed on belly and cheeks
272	Atomba	30	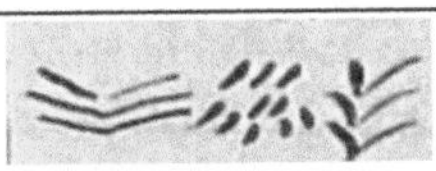 on forehead;  on both cheeks;  on both temples

Source: These fourteen captives bore a version of the stacked chevron. They are organized here by age in 1821, with Akoïsira first. "Schedule of (324) … persons, Natives of Africa, found on board the Brig Succès, and seized by His Majesty's Ship Menai," 21 April 1821 (NAUK HCA 35/4, no. 284).

and its subcategories (for example clan or lineage) determining how people decorated their bodies – even when decorative marks did not follow such divisions perfectly." Bodily styles of adornment have fluctuated historically, even within a generation, and were more likely tied to political or geographic than ethnic affiliations (Gengenbach 2003: 111-14, 120-121). Therefore, we need to push against the assumption that meanings or fashions recorded in later periods can be easily read backward to an earlier historical period, or that Europeans' imputations of kinship were accurate.[49]

The customs clerk transcribed Akoïsira's ornamental scars as a column of four chevrons on his forehead and temples. Analysis of the *Succès* captives reveals that fourteen (4.3 percent) bore some version of the stacked chevron pattern, alone or in combination with other symbols (Table 14.3).[50] These fourteen men also reflect a pattern noted throughout the collection: younger people had simpler patterns, with fewer strokes, in their ornamental scars. Evidently, they accumulated body art with age.

Strong diagonals are rare in the patterns illustrated by nineteenth century European explorers. David Livingstone drew several examples of a pronounced "V" shape, often combined in elaborate patterns, in his field journals from 1865, associating them with an ethnic group, the Chipeta (Livingstone 1866, images 0095 and 0106). He noted that the Chipeta "live … on the plains" (Livingstone 1867). The word "Chipeta," means "1) unused land covered by grass; 2) dancing by bending down" in the Chichewa dialect of the Nyanja language (Paas 2018a and 2018b: 309). Today they are considered a subset of the Chewa-speaking Moravi.

Forty years after the capture of the *Succès*, Livingstone identified what he believed were Chipeta for sale at Zanzibar:

> On visiting the slave market, I found about 300 slaves exposed for sale - The greater part of them come from Lake Nyassa & the Shire - I am so familiar with the peculiar faces and markings or tattooings that I expect them to recognize me - One woman said that she had heard of our passing up Lake Nyassa in a boat but she did not see me - Others came from Chipeta S W of the Lake (Livingstone 1866-1872, image 0037).

The region southwest of Lake Nyasa (Lake Malawi) remains the home of many Chipeta today, including people with this surname.[51] Livingstone likewise drew an inverted chevron pattern that he labeled "Chawa," also located in this region along the modern borderland between Malawi and Zambia (Fig. 14.4).

While neither Akoïsira's name nor his chevron marks alone are sufficient to prove his Chipeta origins, the cross-correlation of linguistic and ornamental marks are suggestive. Further analysis of the names borne by other men with similar marks may help to confirm or reject this hypothesis. As of now, none of the names of the other captives with similar patterns have been identified by the linguist Stephen Paas as likely Chipeta-Chewa.

Figure 14.4

Livingtone's Drawings of the "Chawa" and "Chipeta" Tattoos

Source: David Livingstone, "Field Diary VI, 24 October-23 December 1866." Livingstone Online. Adrian S. Wisnicki and Megan Ward, dirs. 2020. Web. https://livingstoneonline.org/in-his-own-words/catalogue?query=liv_000006&view_pid=liv%3A000006, accessed 16 April 2020, Image 95.

We have no testimony by Akoïsira or Songore of their subjection to slavery, the duration of their lives in slavery on the African mainland, their overland transport to the coast, their transportation by dhow to Zanzibar, their retention there prior to purchase by the officers of the *Succès*, or even their transportation across the sea until the *Menai* redirected their ship to Port Louis, Mauritius. Akoïsira was about thirteen years old when he landed in Mauritius in 1821, and, by modern standards, tiny: only 3' 11¼" tall. His companion, Songore, estimated age sixteen, had achieved some growth, but still only stood 4' 6½" tall.[52] Like the rest of the captives aboard the Succès, both had likely been subjected to poor nutrition in their early years.

The Fate of Akoïsira and Songore in Mauritius

Following Vice Admiralty Court's decision of 9 May 1821,[53] the customs collector assigned them, along with three other captives from the *Succès*, to "Naval Service on board His Majesty's ship Menai," the very ship that had captured the *Succès*.[54] Did Captain Moresby personally select them, and if so, by what criteria? It was not unusual to employ youths of various nations onboard ships.[55]

Service in the royal navy apparently did not suit these young men, for in May 1823, Captain Moresby found them "totally inadequate to and incapable of the performance of [the] Duties of Seamen,"[56] and discharged them as "being unfit for Service."[57] Moresby looked for someone to direct Songore and Aloïsira's apprenticeships in "some useful and profitable Trade whereby they may be made, at the expiration of their Apprenticeship to obtain an honest and sufficient livelihood for themselves." He found a "Mr. Jean Joseph Maurice

Joly, … a Tradesman of Port Louis," who agreed to instruct the young men, now fifteen and eighteen, "in the trade business or Employment of Taylor and Matrasse maker." The act of the indenture stated that Joly would teach them all the necessary skills, provide for the washing, mending, and repairing of their clothes, "sufficient meat, Drink and Lodging, according to the custom of the Colony, … heal [them] … with humanity and kindness" for a period of fourteen years. Neither Joly nor his heirs would be permitted to "sell them … or permit or cause them … to be sold as … slaves." However, in the case of Joly's death, the contract permitted the executors of his estate to assign Songore and Akoïsira over to new masters in the same trade for the duration of the term of apprenticeship. Any violation of the contract could be penalized with a fine of $1,000.[58]

As in so many microhistories, a conflict brought subalterns to the attention of authorities, whose investigated generated pages of documentation for the archives. Seven years into their apprenticeship, Songore and Akoïsira lodged a formal complaint with the Protector of Slaves, asserting that Songore had been "loaded with an iron ring weighing 7¼ lbs., being 4¼ more than the weight which the law permits to be placed on the leg of a Slave." Joly admitted having done so, but excused himself, "that it was affixed merely for one night, from the want of a Block, and to prevent the apprentice Songore, at that time in a state of intoxication, from running away." Mr. Joly was found guilty and penalized.[59]

E.A. Draper, the acting collector of customs, brought Songore and Akoïsira's indenture to the attention of Judge Edward B. Blackburn of the Vice Admiralty Court. According to Draper, Moresby's act of indenture, which transferred the captives' apprenticeship to Mr. Joly, was invalid; "a more illegal instrument, in my humble opinion, was never penned." By its language, their fourteen-year term, which should expire in 1835, would be extended two additional years, until 1837. The legal question at stake was "[w]hether the Negroes, since their discharge from the Naval Service, ought to be considered in the light of free men, or as apprentices, under the protection of the Government, for such unexpired term as would remain from the date of their condemnation."[60] Judge Blackburn determined that they were not slaves, and thus remanded them to the custody of the collector of customs,[61] who determined that "they should be re-apprenticed to the Local Government, for a period of twelve months," while waiting for final instructions from London.[62]

The net result was that their complaint allowed one year to be reduced from their original fourteen-year contract, but their living conditions as they waited for freedom would depend upon the labor to which the government assigned them, which, as we have seen with the artificers' road crew, could be dangerous. Moreover, once "free," they would no longer have guaranteed employment, food or shelter, and would have to fend for themselves as wage laborers in a society still dependent on slavery. Abolition would not arrive in Mauritius until 1835.

Conclusion: Conditions of "Prize Negroes" in Mauritius

Between 1813 and 1828, the Admiralty Court seized 2,990 "Prize Negroes." Of these, only 1,703 remained apprentices when the commissioners on Inquiry arrived in Mauritius to investigate in 1828. Five captives (3 males and 2 females) had been liberated and thirty had "gone missing," but another 592 (24.4 percent) had died during their period of apprenticeship.[63] Roughly one-fifth (569 individuals) fell off the records of the customs office through death (prior to apprenticeship), or conscription into military or naval service, at which point they were no longer the charge of the customs office. (It is unfortunate that the commissioners did not itemize these categories since they probably mask an exceptionally high mortality rate.) Some of the women had gone on to bear 315 children, now also wards of the state.[64]

Were these apprentices treated any better than slaves? The commissioners noted many abuses in a program whose aim had been to protect the trafficked Africans from enslavement and to prepare them to support themselves in the wage economy. They commented that:

> The food and clothing of the Prize Negroes are the same as are given to Slaves.... And Lawful marriages have not been introduced amongst them in any instances.... [A] few individuals appear to have had a larger number of Negroes Apprenticed to them, than it was likely from their own occupations, that they could possibly have instructed in any art or trade.[65]

In other words, many "apprentices" were functioning as unskilled plantation laborers, no different from slaves.[66] Even the small proportion assigned to learn skilled trades or crafts (e.g., carpentry, sewing, cooking, gardening, cabinetry, smithing, masonry, bookbinding[67]) were subject to exploitation. The commissioners found that:

> Masters have not in all instances fulfilled this engagement nor have they been careful to give the Apprentices instruction in some other art equally useful to them with that which was named in the Indenture.[68]

In fact, "[a] practice has ... prevailed unchecked of hiring out Apprentices" as field hands at a profit, allowing these "employers" to collect wages on labor that, under law, belonged to the state.[69] Based upon testimony by the collector of customs, the commissioners determined that "we have never heard of an instance in which any one of them had made an improper use of his power over the Services of the Negroes,"[70] but this is certainly belied by Songore's experience (reported two years later), when he was chained for drunkenness with a weight greater than that permitted for the punishment of slaves.

The commissioners recommended a series of interventions, based in part on William Telfair's innovations, that would prepare the apprentices for their eventual freedom: wages comparable to those of free laborers (to be paid by the masters), the establishment of savings accounts, government support for the sick and invalid, selection of masters from non-slaveholders, regular assessment of the apprentices' training and capacity to support themselves, and reduction of the term of apprenticeship when a wage position has been achieved.[71] These liberalizing reforms contributed to London's policies as it prepared for abolition. The 1833 Act re-designated all slaves as "apprentices," but it did not address the post-emancipation labor problem for sugar cultivation. Planters' profits demanded cheap labor during the expansion of the "Second Slavery" of the mid-nineteenth century, which forced indentured laborers into agricultural regimes not unlike slavery (Tomich and Zeuske 2008).

The reconstruction of the maiden voyages of the *Succès*, with its unusually large number of captives, allows some statistical analysis of the makeup and destinies of the Africans "rescued" from slavery through the British government's conscription and apprenticeship program. The quantifiable data shows that the mortality rates are very high and that the survivors were placed in a range of menial laboring positions, from servants to soldiers to manual labor in public works. Some of these "servants" worked and lived alongside slaves in the cane fields, their daily lives indistinguishable.

The microhistories of Akoïsira and Songore – placing subaltern people as the protagonists of a historical narrative – confirm these general trends, while generating new questions for wider historical research, especially in terms of digital research. It may be able to use the captives' names and ornamental "marks" to locate the geographies of their prior enslavement in east central Africa through the development of more comprehensive databases devoted to captives recorded in the Indian Ocean basin, including the codification of "markings" and their correlation with anthronyms and ethnonyms. A study of the historical climate fluctuations in this region might yield some of the "push" factors that made the captives of the *Succès* vulnerable to enslavement in this period. A more nuanced analysis of the cholera epidemic of 1817-1824 can reveal the role of slave smuggling in its far reach, from India to East Africa. Working "downstream" – identifying the genealogical descendants of the participants in these dramas (smugglers, captives, masters, trafficking crusaders) will allow us to understand the impact of these events over subsequent generations.

Endnotes

1 These two trials and their aftermaths generated thousands of pages of documentation held today in archives in London, Paris, Aix-en-Provence, La Réunion, and Mauritius.

2 "Extrait du Compte d'Armement et Cargaison du Brick Le Succès" (The National Archives, Kew, hereafter TNA, CO 167/92); "Compte de vente et net produit de la cargaison du brick *Le Succès,* Cap[ne] Bertrand, vendu à Bourbon pour compte des intéressées à l'armement dudit navire" (*ibid.*), hereafter, "Compte de vente et net produit."

3 "Tableau de 220 Nègres & Negresses de la Cargaison du Brick le Succès de Nantes…" (*ibid.*) ; "Compte de vente et net produit,"; [Letorzec] to Michaud, 27 October 1820 (*ibid.*); "Interrogatoire des gens de l'équipage du Succès," 18 October 1820 (Archives départementales de La Réunion, hereafter ADR, U1495).

4 "Compte de dépenses faites par le Succès … jusqu'au 29 8bre jour de son départ de St. Paul" (TNA CO 167/92) ; [Letorzec] to Gamin, 4 January 1821 (*ibid.*).

5 "Schedule of (324) Three Hundred Twenty-Four Persons, Natives of Africa, found on board the Brig Succès," 21 April 1821 (TNA CO 167/92), hereafter "Schedule of (324) … Persons."

6 "Sentence of Vice Admiralty Court at the Mauritius," 8 May 1821, attachment no. 1 to Farquhar to Bathurst, 11 June 1821, (TNA CO 167/57, n° 46).

7 *Ibid.*

8 "Return of Vessels & Slaves condemned from 1808 to 1827." Commission on Eastern Enquiry, Appendix B, no. 21 (TNA CO 415/11). Five ships were condemned at the Cape of Good Hope in 1813-1815, but the rest were condemned in Mauritius.

9 *Ibid.* Thirty ships carried 2,497 captives for an average of 83.2 captives per ship. *La Parisienne* was convicted of carrying 356 slaves to Mauritius in 1815. Another 488 captives were discovered to have been illegally imported within the island, for a total of 2,985 individuals seized by the Crown between 1813 and 1826.

10 There are two copies of this Table: "Schedule of (324) … Persons," 21 April 1821 (TNA CO 167/92) and (TNA High Court of Admiralty 35/4, no. 284).

11 The fact that no slaves were listed as "23" is odd, and underscores the likelihood that ages were estimated by the English customs officials.

12 While statistically most boys stop adding height at age sixteen, I have been more conservative, designating adults over the age of eighteen; there were 204 men and 2 women in this category.

13 Tanner is summarizing the work of nineteenth century French doctor and economist Louis-René Villermé and I am selecting the data Chiavari, in the Apennine mountains, which may well be an outlier even in his data. According to Tanner, "In all France, Villermé found that conscripts taller than 165 cm. (5 feet, 1 inch) constituted 45 per cent of the total in 1816-17 and 50 percent in 1826-1827, with a regular increase in between" (Tanner 1981: 162-63), which suggests a taller national average, though it is difficult to compare.

14 For a sophisticated meta-study of inequality in modern Africa, based on height but using a coefficient variant rather than raw mean heights (which makes it difficult to compare their conclusions to those discussed above), see Moradi and Baten 2005.

15 Of the 34 Atlantic voyages begun in 1821, the average mortality rate was 5.7 percent. *Slave Voyages*, www.slavevoyages.org/, accessed 30 January 2020.

16 As a point of comparison, the mortality rate for British soldiers serving in the 82nd regiment of Mauritius between 1820 and 1831 was 3.7 percent (Martin 1835: 513).

17 "Detailed Statement of Blacks Seized Since the last Return," 1 January 1822 (TNA CO 167/71).

18 The officers of the 56th regiment to receive apprenticed servants were: Lieutenant Colonel J.F. Barclay (2), Major J. Gualy (2), Captain F. W. Foreman, Captain R.

Barrington, Captain T.W. Foreman, Lieutenant W.H. Arthure, Lieutenant H.E. Hill, Lieutenant J. Kinny, Ensign L. Butt, Ensign William H. Husetson [sp?], Surgeon H. W. Markham, Surgeon W. Bell, and Paymaster J. Finniss. "Detailed Statement of Blacks Seized Since the last Return," 1 January 1822 (TNA CO 167/71).

19 According to the regimental history, "Nothing worthy of record occurred during the years of 1820, 1821, and 1822" (Jarvis 1866: xi, 67).

20 The officers of the 82nd regiment to receive apprenticed servants were Lieutenant Colonel J.E. Conyers, Major B. Firman, Lieutenant J. L. Hewetson, Lieutenant R. J. Latham, Lieutenant J. Delancey, Lieutenant Thomas J. Slater, Lieutenant Adjutant R. Elliott, Ensign E. M. Wigley, Ensign J. Harford, Ensign J. Walmsley, Surgeon J.B. Kell. "Detailed Statement of Blacks Seized Since the last Return," 1 January 1822 (TNA CO 167/71).

21 I have not yet determined whether any of these servants accompanied their masters to the U.K., though given the prestige that black servants conferred in Europe, it seems likely that some did. Myers (1993: 48) notes that, since 1731, London Corporations had banned the apprenticeship of black men, which limited their economic opportunities.

22 "Detailed Statement of Blacks Seized Since the last Return," 1 January 1822 (TNA CO 167/71).

23 "Detailed Statement of Blacks Seized Since the last Return," 1 January 1822 (TNA CO 167/71).

24 Farquhar to Bathurst, 11 June 1821 (TNA CO 167/57, no. 46).

25 The term "Caffre" (from the Arabic *kaffir*, meaning non-Muslim Africans) was a generic label applied to slaves from mainland East Africa.

26 "Detailed Statement of Blacks Seized Since the last Return," 1 January 1822 (TNA CO 167/71).

27 Fairfax Moresby, Indenture for "Five Male Negroes," 19 May 1823, (TNA CO 167/150); hereafter "1823 Indenture."

28 For marriage date and John Finniss's profile, see *Geneanet*, www.gw.geneanet.org/amf?n=finnis&oc=24&p=john, accessed 25 May 2020.

29 Elisabeth Adam, Geneanet, www.gw.geneanet.org/hmaurel?lang=en&p=elisabeth&n=adam, accessed 25 May 2020.

30 Office of Registry of Colonial Slaves and Slave Compensation Commission, Mauritius Slave Registers, 1819, Personal Slaves, 2 (TNA T71/580) accessed via the database "Former British Colonial Dependencies, Slave Registers, 1813–1834" (www.ancestry.co.uk), 7 February 2020.

31 Office of Registry of Colonial Slaves and Slave Compensation Commission, Mauritius Slave Registers, 1822, Personal Slaves (TNA T71/583) accessed via the database "Former British Colonial Dependencies, Slave Registers, 1813–1834" (www.ancestry.co.uk), 7 February 2020.

32 As of January 1829, Kawianao remained with Mrs. Bathfield. Report of the Commissioners of Inquiry at Mauritius upon the state of the Prize Negroes Apprenticed in that Colony, Appendix No. 3 (TNA CO 167/143).

33 *Ibid.*

34 Report of the Commissioners of Inquiry at Mauritius, Appendix A (TNA CO 143).

35 "A Picture of the Negro Slavery Existing in the Mauritius," *Anti-Slavery Monthly Reporter*, 2:19 (January 1829), 376-381, and "Extract from a Letter to Mr. Telfaire from Mr. Le Brun, Missionary, dated Port-Louis, October 15, 1829" in Telfair 1830: 184-186.

36 Report of the Commissioners of Inquiry at Mauritius upon the state of the Prize Negroes Apprenticed in that Colony, Appendix No. 3 (TNA CO 167/143).

37 Report of the Commissioners of Inquiry at Mauritius upon the state of the Prize Negroes Apprenticed in that Colony, 15 July 1828, Appendix No. 3 (TNA CO 167/143).

38 "Return of Vessels & Slaves condemned from 1808 to 1827." Commission on Eastern Enquiry, Appendix B, no. 21 (NAUK CO 415/11). I calculated mortality rates based on the number of captives who died before they could be assigned to apprenticeships divided by the total number of captives in that ship's cargo. The other exception is *L'Industrie*, captured later the same year, with 19 percent of the captives dying.

39 "Schedule of (324) … Persons."

40 "Detailed Statement of Blacks Seized Since the last Return," 1 January 1822 (TNA CO 167/71).

41 For example, Abdulaye Songore, born in Kigali, Rwanda, in 1986, migrated to France, where he died in 2010. *Geneanet.org*, accessed 5 February 2020.

42 "Schedule of (324) … Persons."

43 Livingstone would travel inland to this region via the Ruvuma River during his final voyage in 1871, though he does not mention the hamlet by name. Thanks to the digitization project, *Livingstone Online*, I can conclude that the term "Songore" does not appear with that spelling in the database of his field diaries, although there is a gap between Field Diary XIII (concluding 25 February 1871) and Field Diary XIV (beginning 14 November 1871).

44 Steven Paas offered this derivation in private correspondence, 27 May 2020: "Perhaps the word '*ako*' is spelled in modern Chichewa: *aku* or *aka*….Then the word '*akuisira*' could consist of the following elements: *a-ku-i-sira,* or: *a-ka-i-sira*. *a* (3rd person sg and pl) = he, she, they; ku (infix denoting present continuous tense); *ka* (infix denoting: when); *i* (infix referring to an object of i/z class sg. or of the m/mi class pl.); *sira* (stem of verb) = is pitiful, merciful, compassionate. If this applies, the word could mean: 1. He or she is/ They are being pitiful with … (an object denoted by the infix: i); 2.When he or she is/ When they are being pitiful with … (an object denoted by the infix: i)."

45 For example, Klara Boyer-Rossol (2015: 81-82) emphasizes that masters often renamed their slaves upon acquisition, and therefore slaves' names are more likely to reflect the ethnolinguistic origins of the master than their own.

46 *African Names – Slave Voyages,* www.slavevoyages.org/resources/names-database, accessed 2 January 2021.

47 "Schedule of (324) … Persons." For example, Moresby also included these in his indenture of the five men to his ship, *Menai*; "1823 Indenture."

48 "Detailed Statement of Blacks Seized Since the last Return," 1 January 1822 (TNA CO 167/71).

49 Klara Boyer-Rossol (2015: 193-199) notes that African conceptions of kinship could diverge widely from Europeans' and that fictive kinship was an important lens by which captives understood their relationships in slavery.

50 I am much indebted to my research assistant, Lana Guetterman, for the painstaking work of coding and cataloguing the tattoos, as well as Klara Boyer-Rossol and Stephen Paas for their review of this data in light of their ethnographic knowledge.

51 Steven Paas, private correspondence, 26 May 2020. I am very much indebted to Mr. Paas for sharing his knowledge of the Chewa language with me.

52 "Schedule of (324) … Persons."

53 E.A. Draper, Acting Collector of Customs, to G.A. Barry, Chief Secretary to Government, 8 October 1830 (TNA CO 167/150).

54 "1823 Indenture." When the collector of customs filled out his annual report on on January 1, 1822, both youths were listed as "taken by Senior Naval Officer for H. M. Sea Service." "Detailed Statement of Blacks...," 1 January 1822 (TNA CO 167/71).

55 The *Succès* itself had two French ship's boys (*mousses*), ages 14 and 16, among its crew. Interrogatoire des gens de l'équipage du Succès, 18 October 1820 (ADR U1495).

56 "1823 Indenture."

57 E. A. Draper, Acting Collector of Customs, to His Honor E.B. Blackburn, Judge in Admiralty, 4 September 1830, copy (TNA CO 167/150, no. 190).

58 "1823 Indenture."

59 E.A. Draper, Acting Collector of Customs, to E. B. Blackburn, Judge in Admiralty, 8 October 1830 (TNA CO 167/150, no. 189).

60 E. A. Draper, Acting Collector of Customs, to His Honor E.B. Blackburn, Judge in Admiralty, 4 September 1830, copy, (TNA CO 167/150, no. 190).

61 Edward B. Blackburn, Chief Judge and Commissary of Justice, to E. A. Draper, Acting Collector of Customs, 5 October 1830, copy, (TNA CO 167/150).

62 Charles Coleville, Governor of Mauritius, to George Murray, Secretary of State for War and the Colonies, 29 October 1830, duplicate, (TNA CO 167/150, no. 75).

63 W. M. P. Colebrook and W. Blair to George Murray, 27 January 1829 (TNA CO 167/143), 4-5.

64 Report of the Commissioners of Inquiry, 15 July 1828, Appendix 2 (TNA CO 167/143).

65 W. M. P. Colebrook and W. Blair to George Murray, 27 January 1829 (TNA CO 167/143), 8, 13.

66 *Ibid.*, 8-9. Some 215 had been designated as "farm servants…, classed and associated with the description of Slaves submitted to the severest drudgery."

67 Report of the Commissioners of Inquiry, "No. 4: Return of the Trades & Occupations for which the Several Prize Negroes have been apprenticed at Mauritius, from 1813 to 1827," 31 August 1827 (TNA CO 167/143).

68 W. M. P. Colebrook and W. Blair to George Murray, 27 January 1829 (TNA CO 167/143), 10.

69 *Ibid.*, 16-21.

70 *Ibid.*, 7.

71 *Ibid.*.

15

Du Mozambique à l'île Maurice, trajectoires de vie d'Africains « Libérés » :

L'exemple des « Libérés » du *Lily* interrogés en 1846 par Eugène de Froberville à Port-Louis[1]

Klara Boyer-Rossol

Issu d'une famille aristocratique française établie depuis la fin du XVIIIe siècle à l'île Maurice (alors Ile de France), Eugène Huet de Froberville (1815-1904) avait hérité de son père une grande fortune, bâtie sur le commerce des denrées coloniales (et en particulier le sucre). La famille quitta l'île Maurice à la fin des années 1820 pour s'installer en France. À Paris, Eugène de Froberville évoluait dans les cercles intellectuels et mondains les plus prestigieux. Membre de diverses sociétés savantes (Société d'Ethnologie de Paris, Société de Géographie), il comptait parmi ses relations des ministres (Guizot), des explorateurs-scientifiques (Jomard) ou encore des artistes

(Offenbach) de renom. Eugène de Froberville consacra sa vie et sa fortune aux sciences et aux arts. Musicien, amateur de peinture, il fut aussi considéré comme un des premiers ethnographes français de l'Afrique. Au milieu des années 1840, au pic de la période abolitionniste française, Froberville proposa à la Société de Géographie de mener une étude sure « les races et les langues de l'Afrique de l'Est au sud de l'équateur ».[2] Froberville ne se rendit jamais lui-même sur le continent africain, mais il fit son enquête ethnographique aux îles Mascareignes.

À la Réunion et surtout à Maurice[3], Eugène de Froberville interrogea, entre 1845 et 1847, plus de 300 anciens captifs est-africains. Selon les îles où ils ont été introduits, ces migrants forcés africains, catégorisés comme « Mozambiques »[4] ou « Makoua [Macoua/Makua] »,[5] ont connu des statuts juridiques et des conditions sociales variés. Tandis que les « Makua » à la Réunion étaient encore en situation d'esclavage, à l'île Maurice, l'institution servile avait été abolie une dizaine d'années plus tôt (1835). Eugène de Froberville avait lui-même passé son enfance à Maurice entouré d'esclaves domestiques. À Paris, il avait embrassé les idées abolitionnistes et libérales qui se diffusaient dans certains cercles intellectuels des années 1830-1840. Dans ses écrits, Eugène de Froberville dénonçait l'esclavage -notamment tel qu'il était pratiqué à Bourbon, tout en défendant « l'immigration africaine » pour valoriser les colonies et « régénérer » l'Afrique.[6]

À Maurice, les natifs du continent africain interrogés au milieu des années 1840 par Froberville avaient le statut d'affranchis, d'apprentis ou de « Libérés ».[7] En 1846, à Port-Louis, Eugène de Froberville interrogea environ 50 des 265 Africains Libérés arrivés six ans plus tôt à bord du navire britannique le *Lily*.[8] Esclaves, Engagés ou Libérés Africains avaient fait l'expérience commune de la traversée forcée depuis les côtes de l'Afrique orientale jusqu'aux Mascareignes. Dans ces îles, Froberville recueillit auprès d'eux une somme considérable de savoirs (géographiques, linguistiques, ethnologiques, etc.) sur l'Afrique orientale. Les quelques articles publiés à l'époque par Froberville laissaient entrevoir la richesse des matériaux collectés : cartes, vocabulaires, portraits mettant en exergue les tatouages caractéristiques des divers peuples d'Afrique orientale, notes sur « les mœurs, coutumes et traditions » ainsi qu'une collection de 62 bustes moulés en plâtre.[9] Or, ni les notes manuscrites d'Eugène de Froberville ni les bustes originaux, n'avaient été jusqu'à présent accessibles ou connus des chercheurs.[10]

Il faut souligner l'intérêt qu'a suscité à l'époque la collection Froberville dans les cercles savants en France, en particulier pour ceux qui s'intéressaient à l'ethnologie.[11] La série de 62 bustes humains moulés par Froberville était peut-être, avec celle réunie par Dumoutier, la plus importante collection « extra-européenne » de bustes anthropologiques en France au milieu du XIXe siècle.[12] Or, contrairement à la collection de Dumoutier,[13] celle de Froberville est restée mal connue, et donc inexplorée. En croisant archives muséales et archives privées Froberville, j'ai pu retracer la circulation des bustes en plâtre originaux, des Mascareignes en France, où j'ai finalement localisé leur lieu de conservation (château de Blois).[14]

En accédant en 2018-2019 aux archives privées Froberville (en France et à l'île Maurice), j'ai pu consulter les fameux carnets manuscrits d'Eugène de Froberville. Dans ses carnets de « terrain »,[15] Eugène de Froberville a consigné : des vocabulaires, des récits, des itinéraires, des dessins (portraits avec tatouages et dents limées), des chants et partitions de musique etc. Les 11 carnets représentent à eux-seuls plus de 1000 pages de notes manuscrites. Il faut souligner l'importance du volume de ces archives privées Froberville.[16] Y sont conservés, entre autres, deux livres manuscrits d'Eugène de Froberville sur son enquête ethnologique sur l'Afrique orientale (*Notes ethnologiques sur l'Afrique orientale 1846-1847* et *Ostro-Nègres 1846-1848*)[17], qui totalisent plus de 500 pages. On relève en outre plusieurs dossiers rassemblant diverses notes manuscrites et des dessins (1845-1848) ainsi qu'une abondante correspondance tenue par Froberville lors de son séjour aux Mascareignes entre 1845 et 1847.[18] Je me réfère ici à un ensemble archivistique d'environ 2000 pages.

En m'appuyant sur les notes manuscrites d'Eugène de Froberville, j'ai répertorié pour le moment 173 Est-Africains sur les 300 qu'il interrogea entre 1845 et 1847 aux Mascareignes. Pour chacun de ces informateurs, j'ai pu associer le lieu et la date des entretiens, leurs noms, origines, itinéraires, récits de vie, types de savoirs transmis, portraits, et éventuellement leurs moulages faciaux en plâtre. Parmi ces 173 informateurs, j'ai identifié au moins 23 Libérés Africains du *Lily* interrogés par Froberville en 1846 à Maurice.[19]

Les archives mauriciennes (Archives Nationales de Maurice ou MNA, Mahatma Ghandi Institute ou MGI) nous renseignent sur le devenir des Libérés du *Lily* à Maurice (recrutements et rémunérations, alliances matrimoniales, etc.). En revanche, elles ne révèlent que très peu d'informations sur leurs origines et leurs trajectoires de vie avant leur introduction dans l'île.[20] Selon Marina Carter et Mark Hall, les voix et les visages des Africains Libérés disparaissent du récit victorien. Leur identité africaine paraît « s'effacer » dans les archives coloniales.[21] Or, ce sont précisément les origines des Africains Libérés du *Lily* qui intéressaient Eugène de Froberville. À travers ses notes manuscrites nous parviennent des voix de Libérés.

En croisant archives privées Froberville et archives mauriciennes, je propose de retracer les origines et les trajectoires de vie de 23 Libérés du *Lily* interrogés par Eugène de Froberville en 1846 à Port-Louis. Ma démarche consiste à associer leurs voix à des visages (dessinés et moulés).[22] J'ambitionne enfin d'analyser les dynamiques socio-culturelles de ces Africains Libérés du *Lily* durant les premières années qui suivirent leur introduction à l'île Maurice.

L'enquête ethnographique de Froberville auprès d'Africains du Lily

Au milieu des années 1840, en pleine période abolitionniste française, Eugène de Froberville proposa à la Société de Géographie de mener une étude sur « les races et les langues de l'Afrique de l'Est au sud de l'équateur ».[23] À Bourbon et à Maurice, entre 1845 et 1847, il interrogea plus de 300 anciens captifs déportés de l'Afrique orientale, parmi lesquels « une cinquantaine avaient quitté récemment leur pays ».[24] Ces derniers faisaient partie des 265 Africains Libérés du *Lily* introduits à l'île Maurice en 1840. Ces « Recaptifs » avaient été embarqués en 1840 depuis le port de Quelimane à bord du navire négrier le *José*, à destination du Brésil. Peu après avoir quitté la côte du Mozambique, le *José* fut intercepté par un croiseur britannique et s'échoua près du littoral. Une partie des naufragés du *José*, environ 340 captifs, fut transportée à bord du navire de guerre le *Lily* vers la colonie anglaise de Maurice. Environ 265 survécurent à cette traversée. À Maurice, Froberville interrogea une cinquantaine d'Africains « saisis à bord du négrier le *José* par la corvette anglaise le Lily », auprès de qui il collecta une « mine d'informations » sur l'Afrique orientale.[25]

Leur arrivée récente représentait un atout pour Froberville, qui accordait de la valeur aux savoirs empiriques, basés sur l'expérience des informateurs, et/ou leur témoignage oculaire. Eugène de Froberville précise ainsi avoir toujours eu soin de ne questionner ses informateurs africains que sur « les sujets dont ils avaient une connaissance personnelle ».[26] Leurs témoignages étaient d'autant plus précieux que leur départ du continent africain était proche dans le temps et donc leurs mémoires du pays d'origine potentiellement peu altérées.

Parmi la cinquantaine de Libérés du *Lily* interrogés par Froberville, j'ai identifié 23 individus dont les entretiens ont été retranscrits dans ses notes manuscrites. Pour chacun de ces individus il a été possible d'associer : les lieux et dates d'interviews, leurs noms, âges, sexes, tailles, origines, récits et trajectoires de vie, types de savoirs transmis, portraits, tatouages et dents limées, et enfin, pour une dizaine d'entre eux, leurs visages moulés en plâtre.[27] Il faut souligner la diversité des connaissances transmises par ces informateurs africains. On relève, entre autres ; des récits (parfois retranscrits à la première personne) sur le pays d'origine, des itinéraires, des chants et partitions de musique, ou encore des vocabulaires.

Les entretiens se sont déroulés entre mai et décembre 1846 à Port-Louis. Tous les Africains du *Lily* interrogés par Froberville étaient des hommes assez jeunes (entre 17 et 35 ans environ), dont près de la moitié étaient des enfants lorsqu'ils ont été transportés de force à travers les mers. Cet « échantillon » reflète les caractéristiques générales de ce groupe d'Africains Libérés du *Lily*, dont la majorité était des hommes et des jeunes garçons.[28]

En général, les individus de sexe masculin, qu'ils soient adultes ou jeunes adolescents, étaient les plus nombreux dans les populations « Mozambiques » des îles de plantation des Mascareignes. L'historienne Vijayalakshmi Teelock a montré la sur-représentation des hommes chez les « Mozambiques » à Maurice.[29] Il semble que la nette prévalence des hommes parmi les informateurs africains de Froberville était aussi en partie due à un choix de l'enquêteur. Parmi les 173 informateurs africains que j'ai pu identifier, un seul était de sexe féminin. Il est possible que Froberville préférait éviter de passer de longs et fréquents entretiens en compagnie de femmes africaines, ce qui aurait pu être interprété comme une forme de libertinage et entraîner des rumeurs graveleuses au sein de la haute société coloniale, dont faisaient partie les Froberville. Issu d'une famille influente,[30] Eugène de Froberville comptait de nombreuses relations dans la colonie mauricienne. Il semble que ce soit le collecteur des douanes Cunningham lui-même qui ait facilité l'accès à Froberville aux travailleurs du *Lily*.

> Parmi les personnes dont les encouragements m'ont accompagné et soutenu durant mes recherches, je n'aurais garde d'omettre (...) l'honorable Cunningham Directeur des douanes », notait Froberville.[31]

On peut rattacher les Libérés interrogés par Froberville en 1846 à Port-Louis avec les 50 Africains du *Lily* remis en 1841 par le collecteur des douanes à des officiers du gouvernement, en particulier des officiers britanniques.[32]

Les Africains du *Lily* avaient contracté des engagements de durée différentes en fonction de l'âge qu'ils avaient à leur introduction dans la colonie. En 1846,ceux qui avaient été déportés très jeune (en dessous de 11 ans) devaient être encore des apprentis, d'autres (arrivés vers 11-12 ans) achevaient leur apprentissage. La majorité des informateurs de Froberville(arrivés à Maurice à plus de 13 ans ou 14 ans) avait en principe terminé leur apprentissage (de cinq, quatre ou trois ans).[33] Ils n'avaient pas encore reçu la totalité de leurs salaires, qui représentaient parfois des sommes importantes.[34] Leur statut était encore hybride.[35] Certains avaient déjà reçu leur acte de liberté quand d'autres étaient sur le point de l'obtenir. En raison du grand besoin de domestiques dans la colonie, Cunningham négocia des termes d'engagement avantageux, plaçant les apprentis dans une position favorable.[36] Froberville ne mentionne pas dans ses carnets les noms des employeurs des Libérés du *Lily* qu'il interrogea à Port-Louis, mais on peut penser que la majorité d'entre eux, et en particulier les plus jeunes, avaient été recrutés comme domestiques.[37]

L'identification des Libérés du Lily

On retrouve dans les archives mauriciennes l'enregistrement en octobre 1840 de plusieurs engagements de Libérés du *Lily*, dont les noms correspondent pour certains à ceux d'informateurs de Froberville, tels que : « Dick », « Victor » ou encore Lafleur ».[38] L'identification des Africains du Lily interrogés par Froberville exige toutefois de la prudence. Dans les archives mauriciennes, les noms d'origine (ou « noms africains ») des « Libérés » du

Lily semblent disparaitre,[39] au profit des noms assignés à Maurice (un nom individuel français ou anglo-saxon, accompagné du nom du navire le *Lily*, utilisé comme un patronyme.

Dans les carnets manuscrits de Froberville, les « Libérés » du *Lily* portent souvent plusieurs noms individuels composés d'le nom d'origine ou « nom africain » (comme « Joao » ; « Kalēngo »), le nom donné à Maurice (à l'instar de « Dick » ; « Victor ») et le nom du navire le *Lily*.[40] Des Africains du *Lily* se sont vu parfois assigner les mêmes noms à Maurice : ainsi on retrouve par exemple plusieurs « John Lily ». Parmi les 23 Africains du *Lily* interrogés en 1846 par Froberville, quatre ont été surnommés « John » : Mulōtuia dit John Lily (20 à 25 ans), Mavēa dit John Lily (18 ans), Rants'io dit John Lily (âgé de 25 ans) et Kāska dit John Lily (25 à 30 ans). En l'absence du nom d'origine dans les archives mauriciennes, il est difficile de repérer quels John Lily correspondent à ceux interrogés par Froberville. Un des principaux informateurs africains de Froberville était un certain João dit Djek [Dhiek/Dieko/Dick/Jack] du *Lily*. On retrouve dans les archives mauriciennes un « Dick Lily Quanasarah »,[41] mais ce dernier nom « africain » ne semble pas concorder avec l'informateur de Froberville. Enfin, dans certains cas, Froberville ne mentionne pas le nom du navire ; il en est ainsi d'un nommé Lafleur, interrogé en 1846 à Port-Louis et qui semble être un des « Libérés » du *Lily*. Toutefois, en l'absence du nom du navire, je ne peux inclure ce Lafleur parmi les informateurs du *Lily* interrogés par Froberville.

L'agentivité des informateurs africains

Froberville a mené des entretiens plus ou moins nombreux et longs avec ses informateurs africains. La plupart ont été interrogés plusieurs fois entre les mois de mai et décembre 1846. Je n'ai pas encore pu clarifier la question de la rémunération des informateurs et des modèles africains, qui passaient parfois de longues heures à répondre aux questions de Froberville sur leur pays et langues d'origine, ou à se prêter aux opérations de moulage. Froberville livre toutefois des indications précieuses sur l'agentivité de ses informateurs africains. Le riche héritier et aristocrate français devait user de la flatterie pour convaincre ces anciens captifs africains à se laisser interviewer.

> Quel dommage que ces mauricauds là soient libres, ou comme ils le disent, soient Blancs. Ils font les renchéris et il faut flatter leur Seigneurerie pour obtenir d'elles quelques heures de conversation », se plaignait Eugène de Froberville.[42]

La(es) langue(s) de l'enquête

La question de la langue de l'enquête paraît centrale. En parlant des Africains du *Lily*, Eugène de Froberville notait : « Ces hommes jeunes et intelligents avaient déjà passé dans la colonie un temps suffisant pour entendre et parler couramment le jargon créole ».[43] Les entretiens se seraient principalement déroulés en créole mauricien (basé sur le français) qu'Eugène de Froberville, natif de l'île, parlait couramment. « Les Africains que j'avais à interroger s'exprimaient tous avec suffisamment de clarté dans le jargon français ou anglais des colonies », écrivait Froberville.[44] On peut émettre l'hypothèse qu'au moins une partie des Africains parlant la langue anglaise était employée par des Britanniques. Eugène de Froberville parlait lui-même couramment l'anglais, ainsi que quelques rudiments de portugais. Au moins une partie des Africains du *Lily* avait des connaissances linguistiques en portugais, ce qui n'est pas étonnant puisqu'ils étaient en majorité issus de territoires sous juridiction portugaise au Mozambique.

Passage de l'oral à l'écrit : retranscription des entretiens dans les carnets manuscrits

Les informations collectées par Froberville en créole français et en anglais ont été consignées par écrit en français dans ses carnets manuscrits. Ci-dessus, un exemple d'un entretien retranscrit par Froberville dans ses carnets.[45] On peut lire sur cette page l'indication « à Port-Louis, le 27 septembre 1846 », ainsi que les noms, âge et origines de l'informateur :

Fig. 15.1
Une page d'un des cahiers manuscrits d'Eugène de Froberville

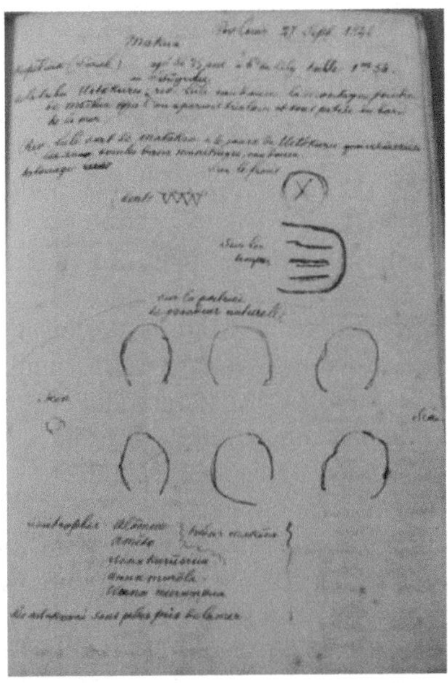

Source: Entretien avec Kupēlina (Sarah) dit aussi Charles Lily. Archives privées Froberville. Cahier Makua II. @K.Boyer-Rossol, 2019.

« Kupēlina (Sarah) [dit aussi Charles Lily], 25 ans, est venu à bord du *Lily*, taille 1m56, de la tribu des Uitūgulu [Makua] ».[46] En bas de la page, sont mentionnés les noms des « tribus » makua limitrophes des Uitūgulu [que l'on peut situer dans l'arrière-pays de Moçambique].[47] Sur cette même page, on peut observer des dessins à la plume de dents limées et de tatouages : sur le front un signe de croix, sur les tempes des traits horizontaux et, sur la poitrine, en grandeur nature, la forme d'un fer à cheval, « signe de nationalité » des *Amakoua*.[48] Des mots de vocabulaire makua transmis oralement par Kupēlina dit Charles Lily ont été consignés par écrits dans ce même carnet (Makua II).

Froberville a retranscrit divers vocabulaires est-africains (collectés oralement) en se basant sur la phonétique et en utilisant des caractères latins.[49] Par soucis de rigueur scientifique, Froberville vérifiait les données linguistiques collectées auprès de divers informateurs, qui en confirmaient ou non le sens et la prononciation. Concernant l'orthographe et la grammaire, Froberville suivait en général assez fidèlement « les formes employées par les indigènes ».[50] De fait, on retrouve dans ses notes manuscrites les préfixes du pluriel (Va, Ua, A ou Ma) précédant les noms de groupes ; Froberville écrit les « Va-Dhiàoa », les « A-Makua », les « Ma-Kuzi » etc. On retrouve également le préfixe du singulier (Mu), tel que, un « Mu-Dhiao », un « Mu-Niungue » etc ; ou encore la syllabe U ou Ku qui précède les noms de territoires. Ainsi, « Ku-Dhiàoa » signifie « le pays des Va-Dhiàoa » ; « U-Makua » signifie le pays des « Amakua ».[51]

Origines des Africains du *Lily* interrogés par Froberville

Les Libérés du *Lily* interrogés par Froberville se sont réclamés de divers groupes sociolinguistiques de l'Afrique centrale de l'Est (Mozambique, Malawi, Zambie) : Makua, Mangāndzia, Manika, Maravi, Musēnga, Niungue, Tsoambo, Makuzi, ou encore Mutōnga.[52] Ces migrants forcés est-africains ont transmis des connaissances parfois très détaillées sur la géographie de leur pays d'origine. Froberville recueillit auprès d'eux des itinéraires qu'il consigna par écrit et cartographia en partie.[53] Il collecta en outre des récits sur l'organisation politique, sociale ou religieuse de leurs sociétés d'origine ou des sociétés voisines des leurs.[54]

D'après les ethnonymes et toponymes rapportés par les Africains du *Lily*, ceux-ci étaient en majorité originaires de la vallée du Zambèze, notamment de régions sous autorité portugaise.[55] Certains étaient nés dans l'arrière-pays de Quelimane, d'autres dans des régions plus reculées à l'intérieur de la vallée du Zambèze. Les informateurs nyungwe du *Lily* ont décrit leur pays d'origine tel qu'ils l'avaient connu autour des années 1820-1830, avant leur départ forcé à la fin des années 1830.Les captifs du Zambèze étaient issus de sociétés patrilinéaires (en général, les groupes de la basse vallée du Zambèze, tels que les Sena) ou matrilinéaires (en général, les groupes de la haute vallée du Zambèze, tels que les Nsenga, Manganja, ou Chewa établis au sud des actuels Malawi et Zambie).

La diversité des groupes linguistiques

Si on considère seulement les 23 Africains du *Lily* pour lesquels Froberville a transcrit leurs noms et leurs interviews, il apparaît une dizaine de groupes linguistiques d'origine. Parmi les savoirs linguistiques transmis par des informateurs du *Lily*, on relève des vocabulaires muniungue [munyungwe], mangāndzia, makua [emakhuwa], ou encore maravi. Dans leur pays d'origine à l'intérieur du continent africain, les Libérés du *Lily* se trouvaient déjà dans des situations de multilinguisme. Ils parlaient souvent plusieurs langues ; leur langue maternelle, une ou plusieurs langues de groupes voisins, et/ou plusieurs langues apprises au cours de leurs trajectoires de vie à l'intérieur de l'Afrique centrale du Sud-Est.

Mts'īsanga dit Alexandre Lily, était un jeune homme Makhuwa né dans l'actuel nord Mozambique, dans une région proche du littoral (située à quatre jours de la mer). Mts'īsanga avait vécu une année dans le pays des Mangāndzia (au Nord de la vallée du Zambèze, correspondant au sud de l'actuel Malawi). Auprès de Mts'īsanga, Froberville recueillit des vocabulaires makua et mangāndzia [manganja]. Mts'īsanga dessina lui-même un tatouage caractéristique des Mangāndzia.[56] Mts'īsanga parlait également probablement le portugais. Il est probable qu'une large partie des Libérés du *Lily* parlait des rudiments de portugais, en particulier ceux issus des groupes « Niungue » [Nyungwe] établis autour de Tèete dans l'intérieur des terres, ainsi que des « Tso'ambo » et des « Makūzi » établis dans le delta du Zambèze ; tous étaient dans des territoires sous juridiction portugaise.[57]

Selon Froberville, une certaine proximité culturelle et linguistique apparaissait entre des groupes voisins du centre et du nord de l'actuel Mozambique. D'après les informations recueillies auprès de Mtètiua dit Boncoeur Lily, les A-Tukùani, qui occupaient « le pays situé à l'Ouest du canton makua Omuàpe », semblaient avoir beaucoup de rapports avec les A-Makua. Comme ces derniers, les garçons A-Takùani faisaient une retraite dans les bois lors de la cérémonie de la circoncision. Froberville décrivait la langue tukùani comme un « dialecte maravi, mêlé de mots makua ».[58] En s'appuyant sur le vocabulaire niungue [nyungwe] transmis par João, « un des Noirs saisis sur le *José* »,[59] Froberville affirmait que la langue des Maravi était elle-même proche de celle des Niungue [Nyungwe].

Eugène de Froberville établissait une analogie entre les différents groupes linguistiques de l'Afrique orientale au sud de l'équateur.[60] Il englobait les populations de cette vaste partie du continent sous le terme générique d'« Ostro-Nègres ».[61] Pour en donner une description, il réalisades portraits dessinés et des moulages en plâtre de ses informateurs africains, parmi lesquels des « Libérés » du *Lily*.

La description des diverses « races » de l'Afrique orientale au sud de l'équateur

La plupart des portraits réalisés par Froberville ne mentionnent pas les noms des individus dessinés, mais seulement les noms de « types » ou de « races » que les modèles étaient censés représenter. Ci-contre, des portraits dessinés par Froberville au crayon de divers groupes de l'Afrique orientale dont étaient issus les informateurs africains : Mudhiaoa [Yao], Mutongi, Tsiambo, Makua, avec leurs tatouages caractéristiques, ainsi que des dessins de leurs dents limées.[62] Ainsi, le tatouage facial d'un « Niambane » dessiné par Froberville est en tout point similaire à celui des « Inhambanes » [captifs déportés depuis le port d'Inhambane au sud Mozambique], décrit par Rugendas comme « une ligne de perles qui court le long du visage sur le nez et le menton » (portrait en haut à gauche de Rugendas).

Fig. 15.2
Portraits de divers groupes de l'Afrique orientale (Mudhiaoa [Yao], Mutongi [Tonga], Tsiambo, Makua), avec leurs tatouages caractéristiques

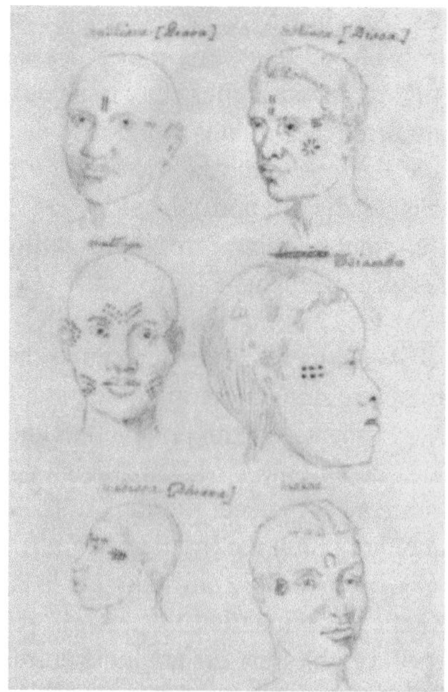

Source : Eugène de Froberville aux îles Mascareignes (1845-1847). Archives privées Froberville @K. Boyer-Rossol, 2019.

Fig. 15.3
Dessins (au crayon) de dents limées d'un Muniungue

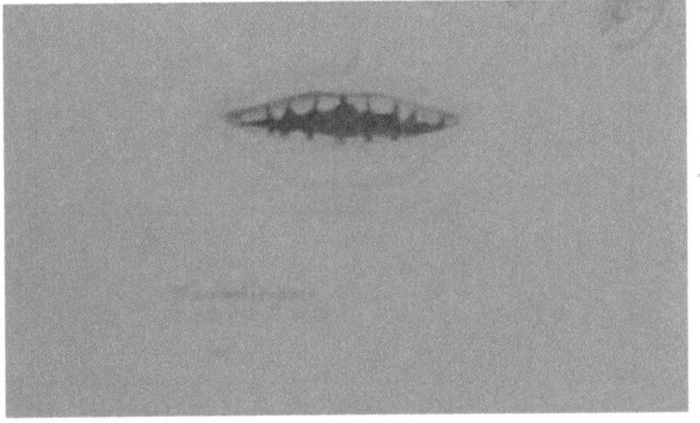

Source : Archives privées Froberville @K. Boyer-Rossol, 2019.

Les tatouages comme indices pour déterminer les identités de groupes d'origine

En mettant en perspective les portraits d'Est-Africains dessinés par Froberville en 1845-1847 aux Mascareignes, avec les portraits de « Mozambiques » réalisés par Rugendas au Brésil en 1822-1825, on retrouve parfois la description de tatouages similaires.[63]

Fig. 15.4
Dessins (au crayon) de dents limées d'un Maravi

Source : Archives privées Froberville @K. Boyer-Rossol, 2019.

Fig. 15.5
« Niambane » avec ses tatouages caractéristiques

Source : Eugène de Froberville aux îles Mascareignes (1845-1847). Archives privées Froberville. @K. Boyer-Rossol, 2019.

Le tatouage des « Matibani » [Makua Matibane], caractérisé par « une demi-lune au-dessus du nez »[64] (portrait en bas à droite de Rugendas), peut correspondre à la « forme d'un fer à cheval » tatouée sur le front de tous les « Amakoua » rencontrés par Froberville aux îles Mascareignes.[65]

Les tatouages peuvent apporter des indices sur les origines des captifs africains, mais non pas de manière précise ou systématique. Par exemple, le tatouage en forme de croix sur le front (portrait du milieu des « Mozambiques » par Rugendas) peut renvoyer à des descriptions de divers groupes socioculturels du Mozambique, tels que les « Tsoambo » [Cuabo] du littoral autour de Quelimane ou des Maravi de l'intérieur des terres. Toutefois, confronter les tatouages avec d'autres données (linguistiques ou géographiques), permet parfois de dessiner des grandes aires culturelles d'origine. Au cours de la première moitié du XIXe siècle, le classement des langues d'Afrique orientale était considéré comme essentiel pour élaborer une ethnographie de cette partie du continent.[66] Eugène de Froberville considérait ainsi la linguistique et la géographie comme les deux branches fondamentales de son étude ethnographique sur l'Afrique orientale au sud de l'équateur.

Les Libérés du Lily dans la collection de bustes anthropologiques

Froberville considérait sa collection de bustes anthropologiques comme le matériau le plus précieux pour la description physique des diverses « races » de l'Afrique orientale au sud de l'équateur. Tout comme les portraits dessinés, les moulages en plâtre devaient illustrer des « types » ou groupes de population, et non pas des individualités (comme c'était le cas pour le moulage d'hommes célèbres). Ainsi, sur le socle des bustes en plâtre, on peut lire gravés en gros caractère des noms de groupes d'Afrique centrale de l'Est, tels que les « Mu-Tsoambo », « Makua » ou encore « Mu-Niungue ».

Fig. 15.6
Portraits de « Mozambiques », avec leurs tatouages, réalisés par Rugendas au Brésil dans les années 1820

Source : Rugendas, 1835, *Voyage pittoresque dans le Brésil*, Paris, Engelmann & Cie.

Fig. 15.7
« Makua » avec leurs tatouages caractéristiques. Portraits dessinés par Eugène de Froberville aux îles Mascareignes (1845-1847).

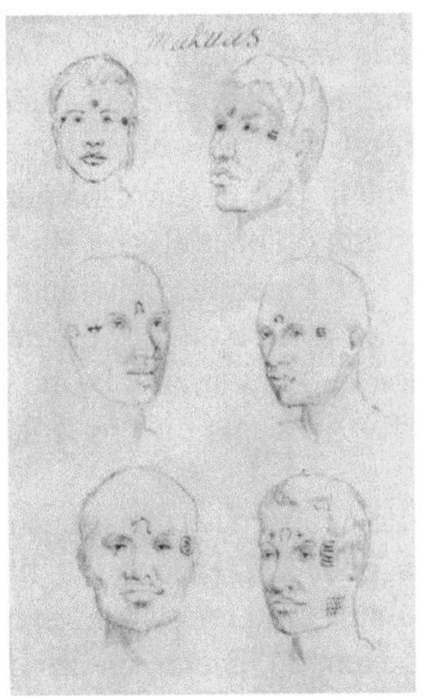

Source : Archives privées Froberville. @K. Boyer-Rossol, 2019.

Fig. 15.8
Buste en plâtre de Padekhio dit Coco du Lily

Source : Collection Froberville (originale). Numéro d'inventaire 34.2.22. @ChâteaudeBlois, 2020. Tous droits réservés.

Toutefois, des noms individuels ont été inscrits en caractères plus petits sur le socle (à l'avant ou sur le côté) ou bien à l'arrière des visages moulés, à l'intérieur de la cavité.

Tel est le cas par exemple du moulage de Padekhio, dit Coco du Lily. Âgé d'environ 25 ans en 1846, Padekhio dit Coco du Lily, était né vers 1820 à « Sososõmbue », dans le pays des Mu-Niungue, dans la vallée du Zambèze (actuel Mozambique).[67] Sur la photographie ci-contre, on peut lire sur le socle l'inscription « Mu-Niungue », laquelle fait référence au groupe socio-culturel d'origine du modèle africain (les Nyungwe étaient établis près du fleuve Zambèze, à proximité de la ville de garnison portugaise de Tete). Sur la photographie ci-après, à l'arrière, on peut lire : « Mu Niungue. Coco ». Cette dernière référence renseigne sur l'identité individuelle du modèle. Grâce à ces inscriptions secondaires, à l'arrière ou sur le côté des moulages, j'ai pu identifier dans cette collection de bustes une dizaine d'individus Libérés du *Lily*. Les moulages de ces dix Africains du *Lily* ont été réalisés en 1846 à Port-Louis.

La collection originale de Froberville consistait en 62 bustes en plâtre. Les rares modèles africains pour qui Froberville fit faire des doubles de bustes étaient des informateurs de premier plan, avec qui Froberville passa de longs entretiens, comme par exemple, Diekh, un des Libérés du *Lily*, dont on retrouve un buste et une copie originaux.[68]

Le pays niungwe

Padekhio dit Coco et son demi-frère Dhiek (Djeck, João), ont été présentés par Froberville comme les « deux Va-Niùngue les plus intelligents » qu'il avait interrogés.[69] Froberville recueillit auprès d'eux une somme considérable de connaissances sur le pays des « Niungue » [Nyungwe] (vocabulaires, récits, itinéraires, chants et partitions de musique, description de tatouages etc).[70]

Fig. 15.9
Buste en plâtre de Padekhio dit Coco du Lily

Source : Collection Froberville (originale). Numéro d'inventaire 34.2.22. @ChâteaudeBlois, 2020. Tous droits réservés.

« Niungue » [Nyungwe] (vocabulaires, récits, itinéraires, chants et partitions de musique, description de tatouages etc).[70]

À partir des récits recueillis auprès d'informateurs africains, Froberville note à propos du pays niungue [nyungwe] :

> Les Va-Niùngue habitent sur la rive droite du Zembèdzi, vis-à-vis des ilots nommés Matsirùmba et Kanìmbi (…). Leur territoire, appelé Ku-Niùngue, est sous la domination des Portugais qui y ont une ville, dont la position parait concorder avec celle de Tete (…), la plus reculée des villes portugaises situées sur le Zembedzi.[71]

Fig. 15.10
Portrait dessiné avec tatouages d'un « Muniungue » [Nyungwe].

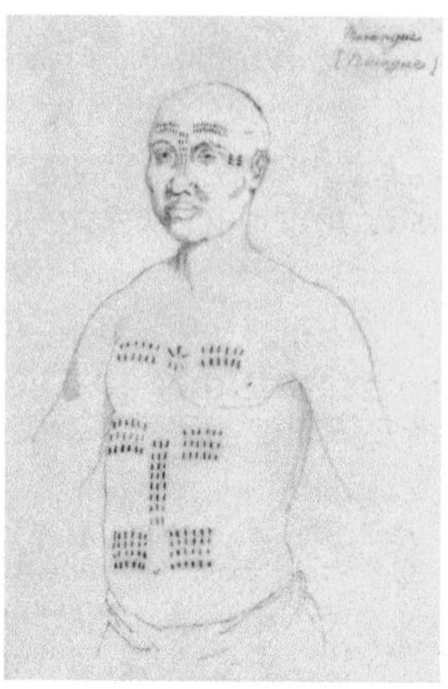

Source : Archives privées Froberville @K. Boyer-Rossol, 2019.

Cette description géographique semble mettre en évidence l'ouverture des sociétés de la vallée du Zambèze vers la façade maritime. En effet, si l'on se tourne pour faire face à la mer, les Nyungwe étaient en effet établis « à droite » (ou à l'Est) du fleuve Zambèze, mais si au contraire on fait dos à la mer, leur territoire s'étendait à gauche (ou à l'Ouest) du Zambèze. On peut aussi dire que les Niungue [Nyungwe] habitaient dans la région autour de Tète, au sud du fleuve Zambèze. Dans les années 1830, la circulation des hommes et des marchandises était intense dans la vallée du Zambèze, comme le suggèrent les témoignages des informateurs niungue [nyungwe] de Froberville. Un des principaux informateurs parmi les Libérés du *Lily*, Dhiek (Dick, Djeck, Jack et João) se rattachait à la « nation » Niungue [Nyungwe]. Il était né vers 1810 à « Ku-Niùngüe », c'est-à-dire dans le territoire des Niungue, autour de la ville de Tète, dans une région qui était sous autorité portugaise.[72] Diekh était âgé d'environ 30 ans lorsqu'il fut déporté en 1840 à l'extérieur du continent et transporté jusqu'à Maurice. À Port-Louis, durant les mois de juin, juillet et octobre 1846, Dhiek a passé en tout 14 jours d'entretien avec Eugène de Froberville. Cet homme niungue servit aussi de modèle à Froberville pour sa collection de bustes anthropologiques sur l'Afrique orientale. Ci-contre, on peut observer son buste original. Sur la photographie de face, on peut lire l'inscription « Mu-Niungue » gravée sur le socle. Sur la photographie ci après, le moulage de profil.

Diekh a transmis une somme importe de savoirs (géographiques, linguistiques, ethnologiques etc) sur le pays niungue, ainsi que sur la région de la vallée inférieure du Zambèze en général ; entre autres, divers itinéraires entre Ku-Niùngüe (ou province de Tete) et Msèna (ou Sena) par voie de terre ou par voie fluviale.[73] Il fait la description d'une société niungue [nyungwe] décentralisée, reposant sur un système patrilinéaire, et organisée en classe d'âges. Les assemblées de vieillards et de chefs de famille conservaient le pouvoir politique et l'exercice de la justice. Une classe spécifique était constituée de jeunes guerriers (Va-Uaniài) engagés auprès d'un petit chef (Màmbua) à faire la guerre sous ses ordres et à travailler la terre pour son compte.

> En temps de paix, ils [les guerriers Va- Uaniài] s'occupent de travaux agricoles, de la construction des huttes, de la fabrication d'objets mobiliers, d'armes, d'ustensiles, s'exercent au maniement des armes ou vont commercer au loin pour leur chef. Les Uaniài habitent tous le hameau du Muàna-Màmbua. C'est au milieu de ses camarades qu'il [le Uaniài] se fait tatouer, qu'il apprend à se servir du fusil que lui donne leur chef et qu'il s'instruit dans les coutumes et les traditions nationales. L'engagé ne peut rompre le pacte qui le lie au Muàna-Màmbua jusqu'au jour de son mariage, qu'en payant à celui-ci une indemnité de quatre bœufs.[74]

Ce récit détaillé sur les jeunes guerriers Va-Uaniài laisse penser que l'informateur (Diekh), qui était adulte et marié lorsqu'il fut arraché à son pays d'origine, avait peut-être lui-même expérimenté ce temps et ces pratiques sociales, dans le cadre desquels il fut tatoué. Diekh a rapporté des récits d'origine,[75] des descriptions de rites funéraires,[76] des cérémonies de circoncision, ou encore des chants nyungwe. Selon Froberville, la littérature orale niungue [nyungwe] se distinguait par son raffinement : « Les poètes Va-Niùngue sont bien supérieurs à leurs confrères du nord [du Zambèze »], affirmait-il.[77] Cette remarque laisse suggérer que Froberville aurait entendu et/ ou recueilli des poésies chantées d'autres groupes du Zambèze.[78]

Fig. 15.11
Buste en plâtre de Diekh (Dieko, Djeck, João)

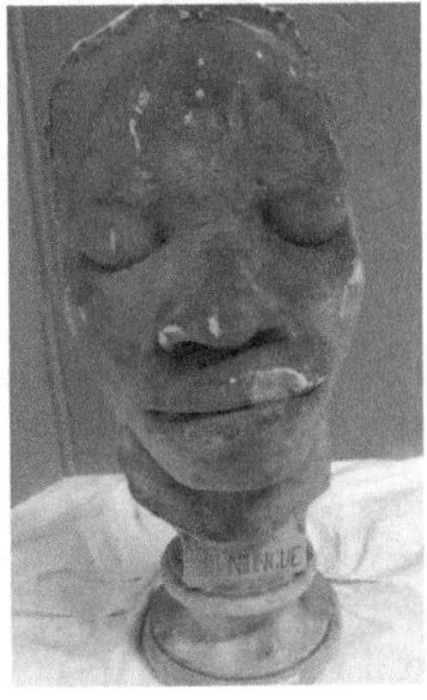

Source : Collection Froberville (originale). Numéro d'inventaire 34.2.19. @ChâteaudeBlois, 2020. Tous droits réservés.

Fig. 15.12
Buste en plâtre de Diekh (Dieko, Djeck, João)

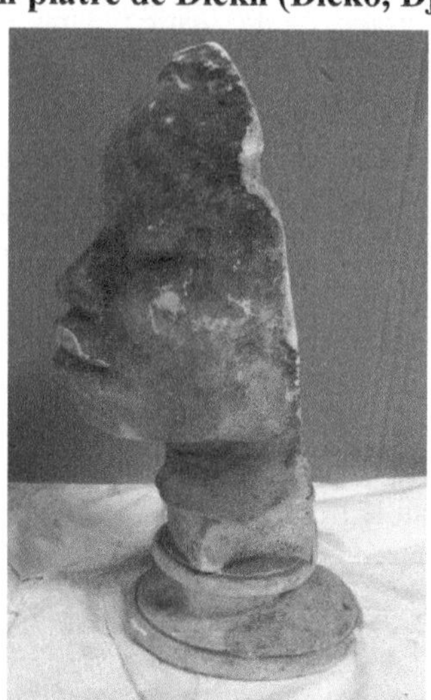

Source : Collection Froberville (originale). Numéro d'inventaire 34.2.19. @ChâteaudeBlois, 2020. Tous droits réservés.

Dans la province de Tète, on cultivait « des grains, du coton et du tabac qu'on exporte à Sena, d'où l'on tire des toiles, du sel et divers objets de fabrication européenne ».[79] La ville de garnison portugaise de Tète apparaissait comme un important marché où convergeaient des réseaux de traite de longue et moyenne distance. Le « niungue » (nyungwe) était utilisé comme une langue commerciale. Diverses populations (Les A-Vìza, les A-Gòa, les Va-Mbo, les Ua-Bàrua, Va-T'ànda, les A-Khipèta) de la vallée du Zambèze et d'au-delà, y venaient échanger leurs produits : dents d'éléphant, toiles, tabac, outils en fer, bœuf, coton, sel, or.[80] L'or provenait essentiellement de la province du Mañīka et/ou du royaume de Barue. Apparus dès le XVe et XVIe siècles, ces États étaient dirigés par des dynasties Karanga héritières du Grand Zimbabwe. Leur prospérité dépendait de l'extraction et du commerce de l'or.[81]

La traite de l'or depuis les royaumes Manica et Barue

Un informateur de Froberville nommé Mutadzo dit Victor Lily, était né autour des années 1810 dans le royaume Mañīka [Manica].[82] « Le village du roi de Mañīka était situé près d'une montagne appelée « Nats'is'upue » », se souvenait-il. Adulte lorsqu'il fut arraché à son pays d'origine, Mutadzo manifeste une connaissance solide sur sa géographie, les pratiques sociales et culturelles et les activités économiques qui y avaient cours entre le milieu des années 1810 et le milieu des années 1830.[83] On retrouve dans les notes de

Froberville un récit de Mutadzo sur son pays d'origine qui a été retranscrit à la première personne :

> La rivière de Luãngua [Luenha] traverse mon pays, elle reçoit le Mangūru dont un des affluents charrie en abondance des parcelles d'or. Les peuplades riveraines recueillent et lavent le limon de cette rivière et en retirent l'or qu'ils vendent aux Portugais.[84]

Comme l'atteste l'exemple de la rivière Luenha [juste au-dessus de l'inscription « Manica » et à l'Ouest de « Barue » sur la carte ci-contre], qui traverse en effet le Manica, des Africains du *Lily* ont gardé en mémoire des toponymes (et des ethnonymes), qui apportent des indications précieuses pour situer leurs régions d'origine. En outre, des éléments de périodisation apparaissent dans des récits sur le pays d'origine. « À Masekesa, on voit des maisons en briques habitées par des Portugais »,[85] rapporte Mutadzo. Masekesa était la principale foire (*feira*) des Portugais dans le Manica. À partir du début des années 1830, marquées par le pic de la sécheresse et les raids Ngoni [Nguni],[86] l'extraction et le commerce de l'or déclinèrent. Entre 1830 et 1835, les *feira* des Portugais dans le Manica n'ont cessé d'être attaquées[87]. Ces marchés furent finalement abandonnés en 1835.[88] Ainsi, Mutadzo décrit une situation du Manica antérieure au milieu des années 1830. La traite de l'or se maintenait par l'intermédiaire du royaume de Barué, qui contrôlait les routes commerciales entre le Manica et les Portugais de Sena.[89]

Un certain Gafume dit Joseph du Lily, était né aussi autour des années 1810 dans le royaume Barue, aussi appelé le « pays des Barge ». Son pays était traversé par la rivière de Kaverēsa, où l'on trouvait des hippopotames, des caïmans, et de l'or. Parmi les mots de vocabulaire barue transmis par Gafume, on relève entre autres, le roi : « Makombe » ou encore les Portugais : « Purtigezi ». Dans les années 1830, le Barue apparaissait comme un royaume autonome, allié des Portugais, mais divisé par des luttes intestines de succession au trône.[90] Le Makombe et ses principaux subordonnés prélevaient des taxes sur les marchandises (en particulier l'or) qui transitaient à travers leur territoire. Gafume Joseph Lily a rapporté les noms des groupes voisins des « U-Barge » : « les Uniāma à l'Ouest, les Untōnga à l'Est, les Utēne au Sud, les Tsungu à l'Est, les Oz'erāma au Sud et les Uēsa au Nord ».[91]

Les enfants captifs parmi les « Libérés » du Lily

L'étendue des savoirs transmis par des informateurs tels que Diekh sur la société niungue [nyungwe], s'explique en partie par la durée de leur trajectoire de vie dans leur pays d'origine (dont ils furent arrachés alors qu'ils étaient déjà des hommes adultes, mariés et initiés). Toutefois, il ne faudrait pas se hâter de conclure que les captifs plus jeunes, et surtout les enfants, ne détenaient que peu ou pas de savoirs locaux sur leur pays de naissance en Afrique ; une acception communément partagée, qui justifierait notamment l'impossibilité du retour au pays d'origine. L'apprentissage, la mémorisation et la transmission de connaissances sur le pays d'origine se révèlent aussi dans les parcours de vie de très jeunes captifs africains. Ainsi, des Libérés du *Lily* qui avaient été capturés enfants, ont transmis des toponymes et des ethnonymes qui permettent de situer leurs sociétés d'origine dans l'actuel Mozambique, et en particulier dans l'hinterland de Quelimane. Ci-contre, l'image du buste en plâtre de Dionokea dit Snap Lily (Fig. 15.13). Sur le socle du buste, on peut lire l'inscription en gros caractères « Mu-Kuzi », du nom du groupe d'appartenance d'origine. Tout en bas du socle, en caractères plus petits, on peut lire le nom individuel du modèle : « Dionokea ».

Carte 15.1
Les populations apparentées aux Shonga

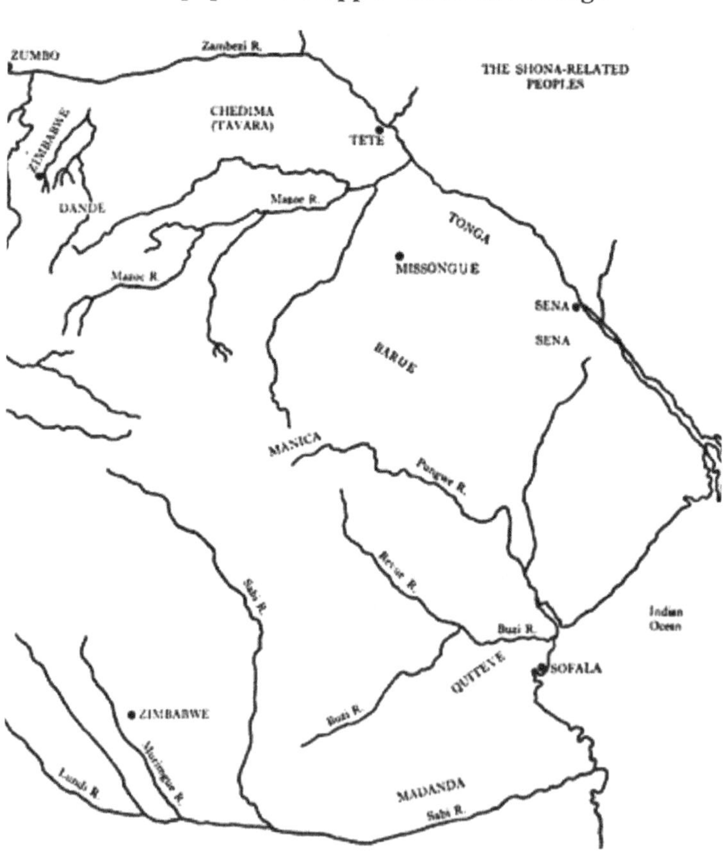

Source : Allen Isaacman, « Madzi-Manga, Mhondoro and the use of oral traditions – A chapter in Barue religious and political history », *Journal of African History*, XIV, 3, 1973, p. 397.

Alors qu'il n'était âgé que de dix ans environ lorsqu'il fut embarqué à bord du *José*, Dionokea dit Snap Lily a transmis des données géographiques, linguistiques et ethnologiques sur le pays des Makuzi. Lui-même se rattachait aux identités de groupe Makuzi et Tso'ambo[Tsoambo, Cuabo], qui étaient établis dans le delta du Zambèze. Dionokea était né près de Quelimane, au poste portugais d'« Oluàna », dans un territoire donc sous juridiction portugaise. On va ordinairement en deux jours du pays makùži à Quilimane .[92] Les Makūzi vivent au bord de la mer. Ils habitent le littoral à environ 20 miles [soit 32 kms] à l'Est de Quilimane [Ts'ilimàna, Khilimàne].[93]

Fig. 15.13
Buste en plâtre de Dionokea dit Snap Lily

Source : Collection Froberville (originale). Numéro d'inventaire 34.2.13. @ChâteaudeBlois, 2020. Tous droits réservés.

Dionokea portait sur la poitrine des tatouages caractéristiques des Makuzi.[94] Froberville a noté :

> Les A-Makùži ne se font ordinairement pas de marques au visage, mais ils se tatouent la poitrine comme simple ornement et se rasent les cheveux de diverses manières. (…) Ils enterrent leurs morts la tête [tournée] vers le couchant, et enfouissent avec le corps un grand nombre d'objets précieux qui ont appartenu au défunt .[95]

Ainsi, à l'âge d'environ 10 ans, Dionokea était déjà tatoué et instruit sur l'identité sociale de son groupe d'origine. Son lieu de naissance était assez proche du lieu de baraquement et de déportation. Après une marche forcée de deux ou trois jours environ, Dionokea fut vendu à Quelimane.

À la fin des années 1830, Quelimane apparaissait comme le principal port de traite des esclaves pour la vallée du Zambèze. Issus de régions parfois très éloignées dans l'intérieur ou de régions proches du littoral, des captifs étaient détenus sur la côte en attente de leur déportation à travers les mers. Parmi eux, Diekh João Lily, Padekhio dit Coco Lily, Gafume dit Joseph Lily, Mutadzo dit Victor Lily, ou encore Dionokea dit Snap Lily, ont été embarqués sur le *José*. À bord du navire brésilien, ils rejoignirent plusieurs centaines d'autres survivants de la traversée forcée à l'intérieur de l'Afrique.

De l'intérieur du Mozambique à Maurice : la traversée forcée des Africains du Lily

Au XIXe siècle, esclaves, engagés ou Libérés africains avaient fait l'expérience de la traversée forcée depuis le continent, jusqu'aux îles Mascareignes. À Maurice, des Libérés du *Lily* ont transmis des récits sur leur traversée forcée, dont on peut distinguer trois grandes étapes : les trajectoires forcées à l'intérieur de l'Afrique centrale du Sud-Est, celles entre l'intérieur du continent et la côte, et enfin celles à travers les mers. Comme le rappelle l'historien Alpers, le « passage du milieu » commençait à l'intérieur même de l'Afrique.[96] Certains des Africains du *Lily*, comme Joachim, avaient déjà connu une première forme d'esclavage en Afrique.

L'expérience servile en Afrique : le récit de Joachim.

Joachim Manuel était né autour des années 1810 à Quelimane. Son père était Makuzi et sa mère Ts'oāmbo (Tchōambo) [Cuabo, Cwabo], des groupes qui, d'après son témoignage, étaient établis respectivement dans l'arrière-pays et à proximité directe de Quelimane.[97] Joachim se définissait lui-même comme un Tso'āmbo, dont il parlait la langue.[98] Le tso'āmbo, parfois confondu avec le « tchidirame », était une langue véhiculaire à Quelimane. Joachim y était né esclave. Il vécut une longue expérience servile en Afrique, puisqu'il avait déjà une trentaine d'années lorsqu'il fut embarqué à bord du navire le *José*.

Fig. 15.14
Buste en plâtre de Joachim-Manuel

Source : Collection Froberville (originale). Numéro d'inventaire 34.2.31. @ChâteaudeBlois, 2020. Tous droits réservés.

Bien avant sa déportation à travers les mers, Joachim avait connu diverses trajectoires serviles à l'intérieur même du continent. Vers 1834, son maître l'envoya sur l'îlot d'Uregoni, situé à quatre jours de « Tchirimane » [Quelimane]. Durant trois jours, Joachim fit le trajet par voie de terre ; « Il passa d'abord, me dit-il, par l'endroit appelé Maìndo, puis successivement Kalùngu, Musèlo, et Msangàni », rapporte Froberville. Au quatrième jour, Joachim atteignit Ap'òzo, où il embarqua sur une pirogue pour finalement arriver à l'îlot d'Uregoni. Les Portugais y possédaient des plantations de cocos, de cannes à sucre et de coton. Joachim y resta six années comme cultivateur pour le compte de son maître, qui était resté à Quelimane. Le récit de Joachim livre de précieuses informations sur l'esclavage au sein de sociétés zambéziennes sous juridiction portugaise. Il montre qu'un esclave « domestique », né et ayant grandi en ville, pouvait être utilisé à certaines périodes de sa vie, en particulier lorsqu'il était au pic de sa capacité de production, pour accomplir des tâches agricoles. Il explique enfin et surtout qu'un esclave né chez le maître pouvait être vendu et exporté par ce dernier plusieurs décennies après l'avoir servi. « Il [Joachim] n'en fut tiré [des plantations d'Uregoni] que pour être embarqué [à Quelimane en 1840] sur le *José*, bâtiment négrier dont la corvette anglaise le *Lily* s'empara seulement quelques jours après [son départ] ».[99]

Ci-contre, le buste en plâtre de Joachim. Sur le socle on peut lire l'inscription gravée en gros caractères : « Mu-Ts'oabo » [Tso'ambo/Chuambo], en référence au nom d'un groupe socioculturel établi à l'embouchure du Zambèze, dans la zone du littoral autour de Quelimane, dans l'actuel

Mozambique. En bas du socle, en caractères plus petits, apparaissent les noms individuels du modèle : Joachim Manuel.

L'essor de la traite des esclaves et des esclavages internes au sein des sociétés du Zambèze

Dans les années 1830-1840, les grandes sécheresses, les famines, l'avancée des Nguni et l'essor de la traite externe des esclaves, ont entrainé des bouleversements profonds pour les populations du Mozambique. L'espace zambézien fut particulièrement impacté par ces mutations. La traite des esclaves et l'esclavage internes s'y sont développés significativement au cours de cette période. Les récits et témoignages des Libérés du *Lily* dépeignent des sociétés du Zambèze en crise, déchirées par des guerres intestines et bouleversées par une marchandisation accrue des êtres humains. D'après les vocabulaires est-africains collectés par Froberville à l'île Maurice, le terme « kōndo » était utilisé par divers groupes linguistiques des actuels Mozambique et Malawi (Nyungwe, Khipēta ou Chichewa, Maravi etc) pour parler de la guerre. Froberville notait :

> Les Va-Sēnga [Nsenga ?] se font sans cesse la guerre ; le grand chef Kahīmbua est lui-même le premier à susciter des querelles aux chefs subalternes et à s'emparer de leurs gens pour les vendre aux A-Viza qui viennent faire le commerce dans le pays. C'est ainsi que mes informateurs Kalēngo dit Verd bois et Khiasōva dit Lafleur ont été réduits en esclavage.[100]

Kalēngo Victor dit Verd bois avait environ 19 ans lorsqu'il fut amené à Maurice par la corvette anglaise le *Lily*.[101] Kalēngo a transmis des vocabulaires « msēnga », que l'on peut rapprocher du « nsenga » parlé dans les actuels Zambie et Mozambique. La présence des Nsenga était particulièrement importante dans la région de la basse vallée du Luangwa, un des affluents principaux du Zambèze. Tandis que les Nsenga étaient établis à l'Ouest du cours principal du Zambèze, les « A-Viza » occupaient des territoires à l'Est de celui-ci. Froberville rapporte que la langue des A-Viza n'était pas comprise par les Msenga (ou Va-Senga). Ainsi les Va-Sēnga vendus aux A-Viza ont fait l'expérience d'une altérité exacerbée. Kalēngo Victor dit Verd bois aurait ainsi connu un premier processus d'acculturation au sein de la société des A-Viza. Selon le récit de Kalēngo, le commerce d'êtres humains était pleinement intégré à la traite à courte et moyenne distance entre les différents groupes sociolinguistiques du complexe zambézien.

Ci-contre, le buste de Kalengo dit Verd-Bois du Lily. Sur le socle a été gravé le nom de « Mu-Sena », en référence à un groupe sociolinguistique que l'on retrouve dans les actuels Mozambique et Zambie. En bas du socle, a été écrit en petits caractères le nom de Kalengo.

Parmi les principaux moyens pour acquérir des captifs, on relevait le commerce, la guerre et l'enlèvement.[102] Un chant de guerre niungue [niungwe] fait référence à l'enlèvement de femmes dans le camp ennemi :

Kùza kua ts'èkulu mambo	Pour venir avec le grand chef
Kupàra mafùmo	Polissez vos sagaies
Nguète didahòna	Nous avons eu des revers
Pa Nia-Utàle.	À Utàle (pays vassal du royaume Barue)
Tòla, kuòna mkàzi !	Enlevez les femmes que vous trouverez
Ndògonātso !	mportez-les !
Unilìra Khièro	Demain vous pleurerez (Ô Ennemis !)[103]

Les femmes (et les enfants) étaient particulièrement exposées au rapt. L'essor de la traite interne des esclaves a sans doute participé à affaiblir la position des femmes au sein de la société (patrilinéaire et polygame) nyungwe. « Dans les cas ordinaires d'infidélité conjugale, le mari se défait de sa femme en la vendant comme esclave aux Portugais », a rapporté un informateur niungue [nyungwe].[104] Les coupables de crimes tels que l'adultère, le vol ou le meurtre, pouvaient être condamnés à être vendus comme esclaves.

De telles pratiques judiciaires suggèrent que l'esclavage était, en cours de la première moitié du XIXe siècle, en voie d'être institutionnalisé au sein de certaines sociétés zambéziennes telle que la société niungue [nyungwe]. Chez les Nyungwe, une telle condamnation pouvait être décrétée pour donner suite à des crimes mineurs. « Le soupçon de petits vols amène quelquefois l'accusé devant le chef Muana-Màmbua ou l'assemblée des anciens ; s'il est convaincu du crime après l'avoir nié, il est vendu comme esclave au profit du chef », poursuivait Diekh.[105]

Contrairement aux sociétés afro-portugaises des *prazos* où les femmes étaient aussi propriétaires de terres et d'esclaves, dans des sociétés africaines du Zambèze, telles que les sociétés nyungwe ou barue, il semble que les personnes qui bénéficiaient de la vente des esclaves ou qui en étaient eux-mêmes propriétaires étaient en majorité des hommes,[106] en particulier des hommes puissants (chefs, rois). Ceux-ci exerçaient en général leur autorité sur des hommes et des femmes de différents statuts (libres, dépendants, esclaves etc).

Fig. 15.16
Buste de Kalengo dit Verd-Bois du Lily

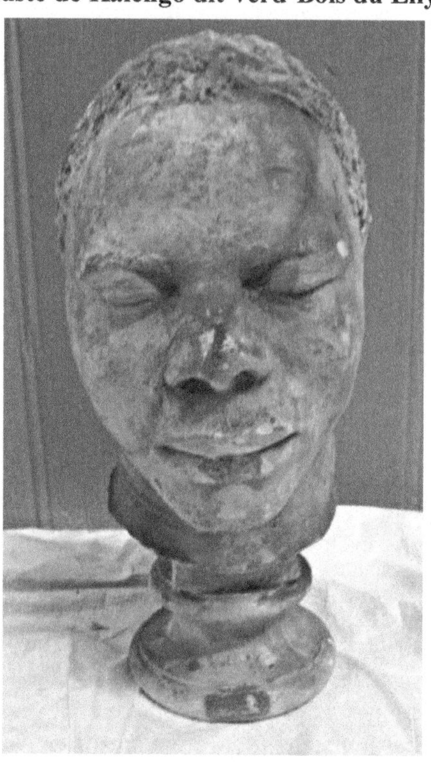

Source : Numéro d'inventaire 34.2.17. @ChâteaudeBlois, 2020. Tous droits réservés.

Un informateur Niungue [Nyungwe] a transmis le récit de funérailles royales dans le Barue, auxquelles il avait lui-même assisté au milieu des années 1830. « Lorsque Kapànga, Makombe ou roi de Barue, mourut il y a une dizaine d'années, on tînt sa mort secrète durant un an ». Après une année de rites funéraires, la mort du roi fut annoncée, et son corps transporté à la montagne de Hùmbue, où les rois défunts du Barue reposaient dans une caverne. À l'occasion de ces funérailles royales, auxquelles assistait une foule de gens et qui étaient dirigées par des responsables religieux et des chefs du Barue, on procéda à des sacrifices humains : la première épouse du roi défunt et « le chef de ses domestiques » ou « son premier serviteur » furent enfermés vivants dans la caverne ; « victimes dévouées au service posthume du monarque ».[107] Le sacrifice d'esclaves dans le cadre de rituels funéraires royaux était une pratique répandue dans certaines sociétés est-africaines et malgaches du XIXe siècle.[108] Dans ce récit sur des funérailles royales barue, il est intéressant de relever qu'il est fait mention parmi les victimes sacrificielles de « domestique » ou « serviteur », et non pas d'« esclave » [en français].

Dans les récits de Libérés du *Lily*, le terme « esclave » est employé pour parler autant de personnes capturées, vendues et/ou asservies à l'intérieur de l'Afrique centrale de l'Est, que de personnes exportées au-delà des mers. Aux îles Mascareignes, Froberville a recueilli auprès d'anciens captifs africains des séries de vocabulaires, Et a répertorié 31 langues est-africaines. Dans son *Vocabulaire comparé de l'Afrique orientale au Sud de l'Equateur*, classé par ordre alphabétique, le mot « esclave » est traduit par « mutùmua » ou « mtùmua » (pl Uatùma) par les Swahili, Makonde, et Yao, et par bien d'autres groupes sociolinguistiques situés dans la vaste zone d'influence swahili, sur la côte et à l'intérieur des terres des actuels Tanzanie et Nord Mozambique. Au Sud de la Tanzanie, dans le Nord Mozambique et dans la vallée du Zambèze, les Makonde, les Yao, et les Makua utilisaient les termes « mutùmua » ou « akapòro » pour désigner un esclave alors que les groupes de la vallée du Zambèze (Khipeta ou Chewa, Nyungwe, Manganja, Makuzi, Tsiambo ou Cuabo etc) employaient quant à eux, les termes « akapòro » et/ ou « mudzakàzi » (pl. Adzakàzi).[109] En langue niungue [nyungwe], le terme « mudzakàzi » ou Mdzagàzi était employé pour parler d'un esclave ou d'un captif.[110] Si des vocabulaires de l'esclavage, tels que les termes « mutùmua » ou « akaporo », étaient parfois diffusés dans de très larges zones du continent africain, cela ne veut pas dire que les systèmes serviles étaient similaires. Derrière les dénominations, les pratiques serviles ont sans doute sensiblement varié et évolué au cours du XIXe siècle,[111] une période marquée par un essor de l'esclavage interne en Afrique.[112]

Selon Isaacman, « l'esclavage domestique » au sein des sociétés africaines du Zambèze[113], aurait été très différent de l'institution servile au sein des *prazos* portugais.[114] Comme on peut le voir sur cette carte de Newitt, ces domaines de la couronne portugaise étaient principalement concentrés dans la basse vallée du Zambèze.[115] À l'intérieur de la société des *prazos*, les *colonos* (habitants autochtones) possédaient aussi des esclaves, qu'ils avaient la réputation de mieux traiter que ne le faisaient les *prazeros* ou grands propriétaires Afro-Portugais.[116] Alors que les seigneurs de terre Afro-Portugais pouvaient posséder des centaines d'esclaves (sur le modèle de l'esclavage colonial de plantation), un homme riche africain possédait rarement plus qu'une dizaine d'*akaporo*.[117] Tandis que le statut servile au sein des *prazos* se transmettait à travers les générations, les *akaporo* était rapidement intégrés au sein des sociétés autochtones du Zambèze par la voie des alliances matrimoniales. Isaacman définit ainsi les *akaporo* comme des « dépendants-adoptés » qui étaient « traités comme des membres de la famille ».[118] Cette manière de présenter l'esclavage endogène en Afrique comme une extension de la parenté est à relativiser. [119]

Carte 15.2
La zone de concentration des *prazos* portugais dans la basse vallée du Zambèze [en hachuré], et les états africains au sud du Zambèze

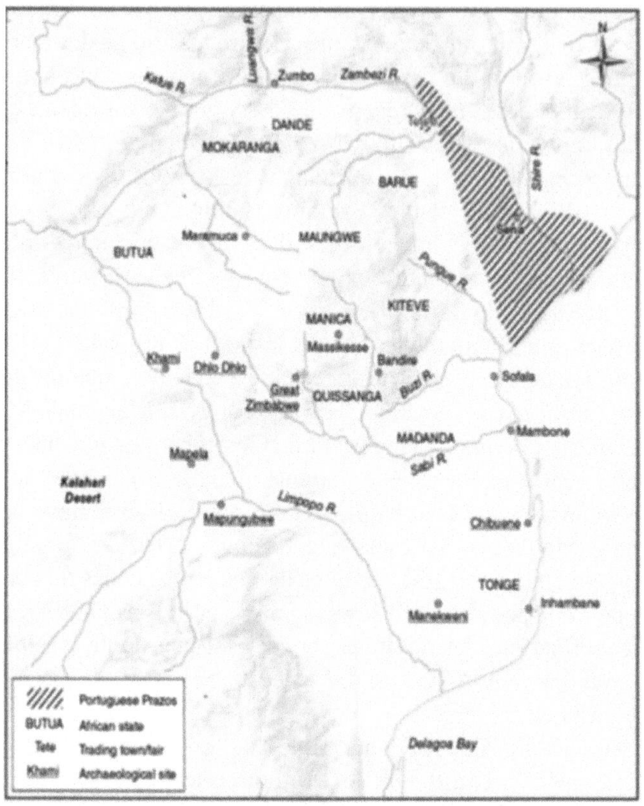

Source : Carte de M. Newitt (2018).

Par ailleurs, dans un contexte de crise, comme celui des années 1830 dans la vallée du Zambèze caractérisé par la sécheresse, les famines, les raids nguni, et l'essor de la traite des esclaves), l'acquisition de dépendants ne répondait pas seulement à l'objectif d'étendre et de renforcer le lignage, mais représentait un moyen de sauvegarder le lignage, et d'éviter ainsi de vendre les membres de sa propre famille. Après la saison sèche, quand le manque de nourriture se faisait davantage ressentir, les Manganja vendaient à des traitants de Sena leurs esclaves ou les membres de leurs familles. Les esclaves s'achetaient avec des pièces de tissu en coton et des grains alimentaires.[120] Les *akaporo* étaient acquis principalement dans le cadre de relations commerciales entre des groupes de populations voisines.[121]

Kāska dit John du *Lily*, était issu de la « nation » Khipēta [Chewa].[122] Son pays d'origine était situé sur la rive droite du Zambèze. Kāska évoque les relations commerciales entretenues avec les Unūmbue (Niungue) [Nyungwe], établis sur la rive gauche du Zambèze. Il rapporte que les Khipēta achetaient du sel aux Nyungwe, qui se livraient à un grand trafic d'esclaves.[123]

Établis autour de la ville de garnison portugaise de Tète, les Niungue [Nyungwe] auraient joué un rôle d'intermédiaires dans le commerce inter-régional des esclaves dans la vallée du Zambèze. Très schématiquement les groupes du Nord (Chewa, Manganja, Nsenga etc) fournissaient en esclaves les marchés du Sud (Sena, Quelimane).

D'après des informateurs nyungwe du *Lily*, les Portugais marquaient leurs esclaves avec un fer chaud.[124] De telles pratiques serviles étaient aussi un moyen de contrôler la mobilité des esclaves. D'après Livingstone, « les maîtres portugais de Tète étaient rarement cruels avec leurs esclaves, comme ils craignaient que ceux-ci ne s'enfuient ».[125] Les fugitifs étaient appelés « mundu kutàua » en Va-Niùngue, et « mutu tàua » dans la langue des Makuzi et Tsoambo.[126] Tous les fugitifs n'étaient pas nécessairement des captifs ou des esclaves. Dans les années 1820-1830, les déplacements contraints de population étaient en général très importants dans cette région de l'Afrique centrale de l'Est, profondément bouleversée par les invasions des Ngunis.

Les raids nguni et l'essor des traites internes des esclaves dans la vallée du Zambèze

Les raids des Maviti [Nguni] provoquèrent un désordre considérable et une augmentation de la traite interne des esclaves en Afrique centrale de l'Est (Mozambique, Malawi, Zambie). En se référant à des témoignages d'informateurs tonga et niungwe, Froberville notait :

> Ces tribus nomades et guerrières se donnent à elles-mêmes le nom de Va-Ngùnu. (…) Ils sortirent, il y a une dizaine d'années [années 1830], du pays de Mahangàle, en bandes nombreuses armées de lances et de boucliers, et marchèrent vers le nord, amassant sur leur passage d'innombrables troupeaux de bœufs.[127] (…) Ils ravagèrent successivement le pays des Va-Tònga et des Sifàla (Sofàla), puis ils se dirigèrent vers la province de Manika (…) et firent des ravages terribles dans l'intérieur du Barue, dont le roi s'était enfui à la nouvelle de leur approche. On les voit ensuite (…) se diriger vers la ville de Ku-Niùngue [Tete], dont ils ne purent s'emparer. Ils traversèrent le Zembédzi, et se répandirent sur les terres des Maràvi, d'où on les perd de vue.[128]

Fig. 15.17
Portrait d'un « Mu-Khipēta », avec ses tatouages caractéristiques

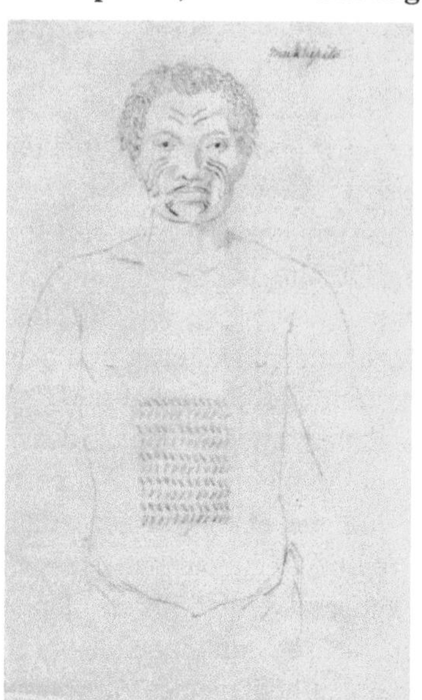

Source : Archives privées Froberville. Dessins réalisés par Eugène de Froberville aux îles Mascareignes (1845-1847) @K. Boyer-Rossol, 2019.

Des informateurs du *Lily* issus de divers groupes sociolinguistiques d'Afrique centrale de l'Est ont transmis des vocabulaires ngunis. Ils avaient appris la langue des envahisseurs Nguni au cours de leurs trajectoires forcées en Afrique. L'un de ces témoins, un Tonga (Mutōnga) nommé Malavira, était né sur la côte de « Mambane », à une semaine de la mer, une région du littoral proche d'Inhambane, au sud du Mozambique. Après avoir été pendant deux années prisonnier des « Mabsìti », Malavira s'échappa « des mains de ses maîtres cruels » et se réfugia « chez une tribu voisine, dont le chef le voyant sans défense le vendit aux Portugais ».[129] Les itinéraires forcés de plusieurs années de Malavira l'ont ainsi conduit d'une région voisinant Inhambane jusqu'à Quelimane, d'où il fut embarqué à bord du *José*.[130]

D'autres Libérés du *Lily* ont rapporté avoir été capturés et vendus alors qu'ils tentaient d'échapper aux invasions des Nguni.

Récits de Diekh et Padekhio

Diekh et son demi-frère Padekhioont transmis le récit de leur traversée depuis l'intérieur de l'Afrique centrale de l'Est jusqu'à l'île Maurice. Une version originale de ce récit a été retranscrit par Froberville dans ses carnets manuscrits :[131] [132]

> Il y a environ sept ans [vers 1838-1839], les nations qui vivent au Sud du Zembedzi se virent assaillir par les hordes nombreuses d'un peuple appelé Mabsiti [Maviti]. Détruisant tout sur leur passage, ces sauvages pénétrèrent (…) jusqu'à Ku-Niùngue, dont ils massacrèrent en partie les habitants. Un petit nombre d'entre eux se réfugièrent dans la ville près des Portugais [Tete] (…). D'autres, parmi lesquels João [Diekh] et Padèkhio, poursuivis de près par les Mabsìti, réussirent à passer le Zembèdzi et se sauvèrent chez les Va-Zìmba, qui les firent prisonniers et les vendirent aux marchands d'esclaves de Quilimane, où ils furent embarqués sur le négrier le *Jòse*.[133]

Le récit de Diekh et Padekhio semble concorder avec les sources portugaises,[134] qui situent le franchissement du Zambèze par un des groupes armés nguni (Maseko) en 1839.[135] Les « Va-Zìmba », chez qui Diekh et son frère Padekhio se sont réfugiés, étaient un groupe maravi établi au nord-est du Ku-Niùngue [territoire occupé par les Niungue], sur la rive droite du Zambezi, dans une région qui échappait au contrôle des Portugais. Ces derniers se rendaient à certaines saisons vers ces régions du Nord-Est (en direction de l'actuel Malawi), pour commercer avec les groupes locaux, tels que les Zimba. C'est ainsi que Diekh et Padekhio, qui étaient des hommes adultes, ont été vendus à des marchands portugais de Quelimane (« Khi'ilimàna » ou « Ts'ilimàna »), où ils furent transférés à bord du *José*, en provenance du Brésil.[136]

Nombreux parmi les captifs africains embarqués sur le *José* étaient des enfants qui avaient été kidnappés et/ou vendus. Uāntuavzīnu (dit Alfred du *Lily*) était âgé d'une dizaine d'années lorsqu'il fut enlevé par des courtier portugais et vendu pour une pièce de toile bleue. Les esclaves de 30 ans se payaient bien plus chers car leur valeur pouvait atteindre cinq à six pièces de tissu soit l'équivalent de plusieurs fusils.[137] Le commerce des esclaves générait de grands profits pour les traitants de Quelimane, où les esclaves se vendaient dans les années 1820-1830 jusqu'à dix fois plus cher qu'à l'intérieur des terres.[138] Dans les marchés d'esclaves à Quelimane, les esclaves étaient lavés, huilés et divisés en groupes selon leur âge et leur santé physique (à fortiori leurs prix).[139]

Certains enfants captifs venaient de régions éloignées, comme c'est le cas de Kanvāntu dit Jambon Lily. Kanvāntu était un Mangāndzia (Manganja, de l'actuel sud Malawi) âgé d'une dizaine d'années lorsqu'il fut emmené de force par des voleurs d'enfants vers le sud, en direction de Khirimane [Quelimane]. Ses kidnappeurs lui mirent une chaîne au bras gauche, « c'est de ce que côté qu'il voyait chaque matin le soleil se lever durant le voyage [de l'intérieur à la côte] ».[140] On peut se demander si la traversée forcée à l'intérieur de l'Afrique centrale de l'Est se déroulait uniquement par voie de terre, ou si une partie des itinéraires serviles empruntait la voie fluviale, notamment au moyen de petites embarcations remontant ou descendant le Zambèze.

D'autres enfants captifs embarqués à bord du *José*, étaient originaires de régions du littoral voisines de Quelimane ou de son arrière-pays immédiat (des territoires donc sous juridiction portugaise). Deux informateurs du *Lily*, Dionōkea (dit Snap Lily) et Mulòtiua (dit John Lily), étaient nés au bord de la mer, près du poste portugais de « Oluàna », à une journée de « Tchirimane » [Quelimane]. Dionōkea et Mulòtiua se rattachaient tous deux à une identité de groupe d'origine Makuzi.[141] Les Makuzi étaient tributaires des Portugais, à qui ils fournissaient un grand nombre d'esclaves. En l'absence du tribut annuel (une balle de riz), les Portugais leur « déclaraient la guerre », en enlevant des hommes et en les vendant. En cas de pénurie de nourriture, des Makuzi pouvaient être contraints de vendre leurs propres affiliés. Dionōkea (dit Snap) et Mulòtiua (dit John) respectivement âgés d'une dizaine etd'une quinzaine d'années, furent vendus par leurs propres familles à des marchands d'esclaves de Quelimane.[142]

Ainsi, la traversée forcée à l'intérieur de l'Afrique des Makuzi Dionōkea dit Snap Lily et de Mulòtiua dit John Lily, était bien plus courte que celle d'autres enfants comme le Manganja Kanvāntu ou d'hommes adultes tels que le Tonga Malavira. Dionōkea et Mulòtiua, et en général les captifs enfants du *Lily* qui étaient nés dans les environs de Quelimane, parlaient tous le « tsoambo » (tchōambo) ou « tsirīmāne » (tchidīma) [langue parlée à Quelimane].[143] Usité à Quelimane et dans ses environs immédiats, le « tsoambo » [echuwabo, cuabo, cuwabo][144] a probablement été utilisé comme langue de communication par les captifs en attente de leur déportation à travers les mers.[145]

Fig. 15.18
Portrait d'un « Makuzi », avec ses tatouages caractéristiques

Source : Archives privées Froberville. Dessins réalisés par Eugène de Froberville aux îles Mascareignes (1845-1847) @K. Boyer-Rossol, 2019.

Ainsi, des Libérés du *Lily*, qui se rattachaient à diverses identités de groupes (Manganzia, Makua etc) ont transmis, en plus de leurs langues de naissance, des vocabulaires en « tsoambo » [echuwabo, cuabo].[146] Ils avaient sans doute appris des rudiments de « tsoambo » lors de la période de baraquement à Quelimane, qui pouvait durer parfois plusieurs semaines. On retrouve également le « tsoambo » (« tzchoambo ») parmi des langues collectées par Rugendas au Brésil, dans les années 1820, auprès d'esclaves Mozambiques.[147]

Au début du XIXe siècle, l'essor de la traite des esclaves du Zambèze était fortement lié à la demande brésilienne.[148] À la fin des années 1830, dans un contexte de mise en illégalité progressive de la traite des esclaves,[149] nombreux étaient les traitants brésiliens à s'approvisionner au marché de Quelimane, expédiant leurs cargaisons humaines à Rio de Janeiro.[150] Quelimane concurrençait alors l'île de Moçambique comme le principal marché d'esclaves en Afrique de l'Est portugaise.[151] En 1839, le gouvernement britannique autorisa ses vaisseaux à chercher et arrêter les vaisseaux portugais impliqués dans la traite des esclaves.[152] C'est ainsi que le navire le *José*, en provenance et à destination du Brésil, et circulant sous pavillon portugais, fut intercepté en 1840 par un croiseur britannique dans le canal du Mozambique. Des Libérés du *Lily* ont rapporté le récit de la capture du *José*, sur lequel ils avaient été embarqués à Quelimane.

La capture du José par le croiseur britannique le Lily

Kalengo (dit Victor Lily) et Mts'īsanga (dit Alexandre Lily) étaient des jeunes hommes dont la tranche d'âge se situait entre 14 et 19 ans, lorsqu'ils furent embarqués à bord du *José*. Froberville a mis en perspective les témoignages recueillis auprès d'informateurs africains du *Lily* avec des documents émanant des autorités britanniques de Maurice, avec qui il entretenait des accointances en particulier avec le collecteur des douanes Cunningham. Ainsi, Froberville fait un récit détaillé de la capture du *José* et de la traversée des mers des « recaptifs » à bord du *Lily* :

> Peu après [sa sortie du port de Quelimane] le navire négrier fut intercepté par la corvette anglaise le *Lily*. Commandé par le capitaine Seymour, le *Lily* croisait à l'embouchure du Zambèze. Le 17 mai 1840, il aperçut un brick d'apparence suspecte qui sortait du port de Quelimane.[153] On se mit à sa poursuite et au moment de l'atteindre, le navire se jeta volontairement à la côte et fut bientôt mis en pièces. C'était le *José*, négrier portugais chargé de 550 esclaves. Le capitaine et l'équipage avaient gagné la terre, et lorsque les embarcations accostèrent la carcasse du bâtiment, elles ne trouvèrent à bord que 324 Noirs ; le plus grand nombre ayant péri en s'efforçant d'attendre le rivage. Le *Lily* embarqua les esclaves et se dirigea vers l'île Maurice après avoir touché à la baie de St Augustin. Durant la

> traversé, 59 Noirs moururent de la petite vérole et l'épidémie sévissait encore lorsque le navire mouilla au Port-Louis.[154]

La capture du *José* est à replacer dans la campagne britannique contre la traite des esclaves dans l'océan Indien, qui était dirigée au cours de la première moitié du XIXe siècle vers l'Afrique du Sud-Est et les îles Mascareignes. Entre 1808 et 1848, environ 9.100 captifs africains ont été ainsi « libérés », dont 4.000 ont été dirigés à la colonie de Maurice. Durant cette première phase de campagne anti-traite, la mortalité était haute parmi les captifs transférés à bord des navires britanniques.[155] Entre 18% et 25% de l'ensemble des captifs transférés à bord du *Lily* auraient péri au cours de la traversée des mers de la côte du Mozambique jusqu'à l'île Maurice et qui durait environ trois semaines ;[156] un taux de mortalité à peu près équivalent à celui de 21 % enregistré pour la traite des esclaves entre l'Afrique orientale et l'île Maurice à la fin du XVIIIe siècle et début du XIXe siècle.[157] Comme dans le cas du *Lily*, les épidémies (de dysenterie, petite vérole etc) à bord des navires ont parfois entrainé de véritables hécatombes parmi les captifs africains déportés aux îles Mascareignes.[158]

À Port-Louis, l'arrivée de survivants

Au mois de juin 1840, le navire de sa Majesté le *Lily* arriva devant le port de Port Louis, à l'île Maurice, avec à son bord entre deux et trois cents captifs africains. Déjà affaiblis par leur traversée forcée à l'intérieur de l'Afrique et le naufrage du *José*, les captifs africains transférés à bord du *Lily* souffrirent de privation (carence d'eau et de nourriture) au cours de la traversée des mers. En outre, la promiscuité et la chaleur ont sans doute favorisé la propagation de l'épidémie de variole à bord du voilier. À leur arrivée à Maurice, la majorité des Libérés du *Lily* se trouvaient dans un grave état d'émaciation. Selon le médecin-chirurgien Gardner,[159] sur les 340 captifs africains du *José* transférés à bord du *Lily*, 90 étaient morts durant la traversée jusqu'à Maurice ; « beaucoup de variole, d'autres d'atrophie ».[160] D'après Gardner, 250 Libérés du *Lily* auraient survécu à la traversée forcée des mers. D'autres sources évoquent le chiffre de 265 survivants.[161] Comme l'épidémie de variole sévissait à bord du *Lily*,[162] le gouvernement décida de mobiliser deux navires pour recevoir les malades. Le chirurgien Gardner fut chargé de surveiller et soigner les individus à bord de ces deux navires, placés en quarantaine pendant treize semaines.[163] Il fut dénombré un total de huit morts causés par la variole au cours de cette période. L'épidémie fut contenue avec succès. Après plus de trois mois en quarantaine dans le port de Port-Louis, 242 à 257 « Libérés » du *Lily* furent autorisés à débarquer sur la terre.

À l'île Maurice, des « Libérés » Africains en situation de multilinguisme et de multiculturalisme

À Maurice, les « Libérés » du *Lily* ont été catégorisés comme des « Mozambiques ».[164] Ce terme générique a été employé aux XVIIIe et XIXe siècles pour désigner des captifs est-africains déportés à travers le Sud-Ouest de l'océan Indien.[165] Selon les périodes et les endroits où ils ont été introduits, ils ont connu des statuts et des conditions diverses : esclaves, « engagés » ou encore « libérés » africains ont formé des groupes « Mozambiques » dispersés dans les îles de l'océan Indien occidental. La notion de groupe paraît importante car elle a déterminé au moins en partie les stratégies (identitaires, sociales, économiques etc) conduites par d'anciens captifs africains ayant fait l'expérience commune du « passage du milieu ». Au cours de la traversée forcée des mers, les captifs africains ont résisté en tissant entre eux des liens, qui ont été éventuellement interprétés sur le registre de la parenté.[166] Cas assez exceptionnels, certains captifs déportés sur le même navire, comme Padekhio et Diekh du *Lily* (qui étaient demi-frères et se réclamaient du même père), partageaient des liens de parenté qui préexistaient à leur départ forcé du continent africain. Dans leur cas, la perte de parenté n'a pas été totale.

Issus de divers groupes (Nyungwe, Manganja, Makua, Nsenga, Tsiambo etc) d'Afrique centrale du Sud-est (actuels Mozambique, Malawi et Zambie), les « Libérés » introduits à Maurice à bord du *Lily* ont été englobés dans la « caste » « Mozambique ».[167] Ils ont pu aussi être désignés de « Quelimanes »[168], du nom du port de départ. Apparu dans le cadre de la traite des esclaves, le terme « Mozambiques » a continué d'être utilisé bien après l'abolition, pour désigner et se réclamer d'une identité africaine. Ainsi, au milieu des années 1840, Froberville notait :

> Ce terme de Mozambique est fort impropre, attendu que tous les Noirs tirés de la côte orientale d'Afrique se disent Mozambiques (...). Ce n'est qu'en les pressant de questions qu'on obtient d'eux le véritable nom de leur nation.[169]

Cette remarque suggère une réappropriation de l'identité « Mozambique » par les anciens captifs africains qui, à l'intérieur du groupe élargi, se distinguaient entre eux en se référant à diverses identités de groupes d'origine. On peut ainsi considérer différents degrés de sentiment d'appartenance. Le facteur linguistique a sans doute joué un rôle déterminant dans l'élaboration de liens entre les captifs « Mozambiques », en majorité déportés de la côte de l'actuel Mozambique. Selon les zones de baraquement et les ports de traite de départ (Moçambique, Quelimane, Inhambane etc), les captifs ont utilisé pour communiquer entre eux diverses langues diffusées sur le littoral est-africain (emakhuwa, cuabo, tonga etc), dont ils ont parfois maintenu la pratique dans les îles où ils ont été déportés (Madagascar, Comores, Mascareignes etc).[170] On peut émettre l'hypothèse que les captifs est-africains catégorisés comme « Yambane » [déportés depuis le port d'Inhambane »] et « Makua », ne parlant pas les mêmes langues est-africaines, ont pu employer aux Mascareignes le créole pour communiquer entre eux et mener éventuellement des logiques de groupes, y compris des stratégies de résistances collectives. Selon l'historienne V. Teelock, les « Mozambiques » étaient prédominants parmi les « Grands Marrons » à Maurice.[171]

L'essor de la traite des esclaves au Mozambique, à la fin du XVIII e et au début du XIXe siècles, a entrainé une hausse de la population servile « Mozambique » aux îles Mascareignes. Au début du XIXe siècle, les esclaves « Mozambiques » représentaient à l'île Maurice près de la moitié de la population servile dans plusieurs districts, y compris la capitale de Port-Louis. Sur 60.646 esclaves (Malgaches, Créoles, Indiens etc), les « Mozambiques » s'élevaient au nombre de 26.670.[172] En 1830, d'Unienville présentait les « Mozambiques » comme la « quatrième classe » des esclaves à Maurice, formant « les deux cinquièmes environ de la population esclave »,[173] qui s'élevait au total à 67.619 individus. En 1835, au moins 40% de la population d'esclaves était composée d'hommes « Mozambiques ».[174] Ils ont été pour la plupart assignés au travail de la terre. Suite à l'abolition de 1835, beaucoup d'anciens esclaves quittèrent les plantations. En 1846, Eugène de Froberville décrit les « Mozambiques » comme une population déclinante à l'île Maurice.

« Quant aux Noirs, on n'en voit plus ; je me demande où sont passés ces 80 mille affranchis qui peuplaient l'île il y a dix ans.[175] Rien de plus rare à Maurice qu'un Makondé, qu'un Mjaua, qu'un Makoua. Je crains si fort que leurs langues ne deviennent comme le grec et le latin des langues mortes, que j'en ai fait un vocabulaire, le premier, le seul, que l'on connaîtra en Europe », écrivait Eugène de Froberville, à Port-Louis, le 1er janvier 1846.[176]

C'est ainsi en pensant que les langues est-africaines allaient bientôt disparaitre à Maurice qu'Eugène de Froberville s'employa à recueillir systématiquement des vocabulaires auprès de natifs de l'Afrique orientale[177]. Comme évoqué précédemment, la principale langue de l'enquête ethnographique menée par Eugène de Froberville était le créole mauricien. À Maurice, « les Libérés Africains ont été renommés, vêtus, acculturés, notamment à travers l'apprentissage de nouvelles langues ».[178] L'arrivée de migrants forcés africains à Maurice a souvent été présentée comme une coupure radicale sur le plan identitaire. Comme le soulignait Alpers, on ne sait pas bien comment les « Mozambiques » sont devenus des Créoles à Maurice.[179] Toutefois, on peut penser que le processus de créolisation a sans doute été plus long et moins abrupte qu'il n'a été dépeint jusqu'alors. Dans le cadre de la traite des esclaves, le processus de créolisation a été interprété comme une forme de « dé-culturation » des captifs nés sur le continent, ayant entrainé « la disparition des identités africaines ».[180] Le cas des Libérés du *Lily* invitent à nuancer une telle interprétation.

Introduits à la colonie de Maurice au début des années 1840, dans un contexte de forte demande de main-d'œuvre, les Libérés du *Lily* ont pu tirer profit d'une politique avantageuse (salaires hauts etc) pour mener des logiques de groupe (accumulation d'un capital, stratégie de retour en Afrique) et bénéficié d'une certaine autonomie de groupe (notamment sur le plan culturel). Les divers identités, langues, cultures et croyances, accumulés au cours de leurs trajectoires de vie, ont coexisté et se sont maintenus au moins durant la première décennie qui a suivi leur arrivée à Maurice. Les Africains du *Lily* y ont connu des situations de multilinguisme et de multiculturalité. Dans leur cas, l'apprentissage du créole mauricien (basé sur le français)et de l'anglais n'a pas entrainé l'abandon des langues est-africaines (cuabo, nyungwe, manganja, emakhuwa etc). Au moins une partie des Africains du *Lily* – y compris les plus jeunes-avaient conservé la connaissance de langues usitées dans les actuels Mozambique, Malawi et Zambie. Une décennie après leur arrivée dans l'île, ils ont transmis d'abondants vocabulaires à l'enquêteur Froberville se prêtant à des exercices de grammaires et traduisant spontanément des phrases.

Pier Larson avait déjà mis en évidence le maintien de la langue malgache par des esclaves importés aux îles des Mascareignes.[181] Ce multiculturalisme aurait perduré plusieurs décennies après l'abolition, en particulier dans des villes portuaires comme Port-Louis.

Le 20 juin 1846 à Port-Louis, Eugène de Froberville interrogea cinq hommes Makua. Âgé entre 25 et 50 ans, ils étaient issus de diverses régions du Nord Mozambique, et étaient arrivés à l'île Maurice à différentes périodes.[182] Parmi eux, Niamakaniua dit Jean Hector était âgé d'environ 45 ans en 1846. Ce dernier avait quitté son pays lorsqu'il avait approximativement 17 ou 18 ans, autour donc des années 1820, à une époque où la traite des esclaves aux Mascareignes était considérée comme illégale. Un autre informateur, Rantsio dit John Lily, avait environ 25 ou 26 ans au moment de l'enquête de Froberville. Tandis que Niamakaniua Jean Hector était établi depuis près de trois décennies dans l'île, Rantsio John Lily avait été introduit seulement six années auparavant, en 1840, à une époque post-abolitionniste. Auprès d'eux, Froberville recueillit des vocabulaires makua. L'un et l'autre portait les mêmes tatouages sur le corps. Le partage de la langue et de culture de naissance transcendait ainsi la diversité des statuts et des conditions expérimentés par ces anciens captifs africains à l'île Maurice.

Par ailleurs, le processus de créolisation n'a pas démarré à leur arrivée à l'île Maurice, mais plutôt à l'intérieur du continent africain. Comme le rappelait Edward Alpers, en examinant la formation identitaire de « Mozambiques » à l'île Maurice et au Brésil au début du XIXe siècle, le processus de créolisation commençait dès l'arrachement des personnes à leurs sociétés d'origine et leur déportation de l'intérieur du continent vers la côte.[183] Ce processus se prolongeait à travers la « traversée du milieu » et atteignait sa maturité au sein des sociétés esclavagistes.[184] Dans le cas de Libérés du *Lily*, le processus de créolisation s'est déroulé tout au long de leurs trajectoires de vie, de l'intérieur de la vallée du Zambèze à l'île Maurice, et s'est poursuivi bien après l'abolition de l'esclavage.[185]

L'expérience d'une hybridation culturelle pouvait même être antérieure au moment de la capture (ou de la vente). Les Africains du *Lily* nés dans des territoires sous juridiction portugaise dans la vallée du Zambèze, comme les Niungue [Nyungwe] des environs de Tète, ou les Makuzi et « Tsoambo » [Cuabo, Cwabo] des environs de Quelimane, avaient évolué dans des sociétés en partie influencées par une culture chrétienne et lusophone.

Comme évoqué précédemment, les Niungue [Nyungwe] entretenaient des relations commerciales avec les Portugais de Tète.[186] Insérés dans des réseaux de traite de longue et moyenne distance, les Niungue échangeaient des produits acquis de groupes voisins (corne d'éléphants, captifs etc) contre des manufactures importées d'outre-mer (pièces de tissu, armes à feux etc). Ainsi, des personnes issues de l'intérieur de la vallée du Zambèze avaient fait l'expérience d'horizons lointains bien avant leur départ forcé du continent. Deikh mentionne entre autres la présence d'une église à Tète. Tète, Sena, et Quelimane étaient des villes africaines importantes, en étant à la fois des centres administratifs, scolaires, commerciaux et ecclésiastiques, et nantis des bâtiments gouvernementaux, des boutiques d'artisans et des églises.[187]

L'influence chrétienne en Afrique de l'Est portugaise est mise en évidence par certains noms d'origine de Libérés du *Lily* à l'instar de Joachim dit Manuel Lily. Son nom, « Joachim », d'origine biblique, était sans doute un nom servile qui lui avait été assigné par son maître. Né esclave à Quelimane, Joachim avait grandi dans une société de langue portugaise et de langue tsoambo (cuabo).

Carter et Hall soutiennent qu'à Maurice, « le catholicisme est devenu la religion dominante des Africains Libérés et de leurs descendants, de sorte que l'héritage africain a finalement été remplacé par une identité chrétienne afro-créole ».[188] Les notes manuscrites de Froberville sur les Africains du *Lily* remettent en question l'hypothèse d'un « remplacement » ou d'une disparition rapide d'identités africaines au profit d'une « identité (chrétienne) afro-créole ». Pour une large partie des Libérés du *Lily* originaires de la vallée du Zambèze, l'influence du catholicisme à Maurice n'était en rien quelque chose de nouveau. Plutôt que de précipiter la disparition d'identités et de cultures africaines d'origine, le partage de référents religieux chrétiens a pu au contraire participer à renforcer les liens entre des communautés d'Africains du *Lily* (en particulier celles établies à Port-Louis). En outre, des Libérés du *Lily* issus de diverses sociétés est-africaines ont pu utiliser la langue créole, apprise à Maurice, pour communiquer entre eux ainsi qu'avec d'autres communautés d'ex-captifs africains.

Selon Marina Carter, le remplacement d'un héritage africain par une « identité chrétienne afro-créole » aurait été d'autant plus rapide dans le cas des apprentis du *Lily* qu'ils étaient pour la plupart d'entre eux des enfants.[189] Ceci devrait conduire à réviser le présupposé selon lequel les enfants captifs n'avaient que peu de mémoires et/ou de connaissances sur leur pays d'origine en Afrique, et donc qu'ils étaient mieux« assimilables » constituant pour ainsi dire des meilleurs candidats à l'acculturation. On peut rappeler que les récits de vie d'ex-captifs est-africains qui nous sont parvenus, ont été rapportés par des individus qui étaient pour la plupart des enfants au moment de leur déportation forcée.[190]

D'après les notes de Froberville, des informateurs du *Lily* qui étaient des enfants lorsqu'ils furent embarqués à bord du *José*, ont transmis des savoirs linguistiques, géographiques et même ethnologiques sur leur pays d'origine. Plusieurs situaient leur pays de naissance dans l'arrière-pays direct de Quelimane, d'autres en pays nyungwe et en pays makhuwa. Mavēa dit John Lily avait environ 12 ans lorsqu'il fut transféré à bord du *Lily*. Il portait sur le front et les tempes les tatouages caractéristiques des Makua, dont il réclamait d'ailleurs l'identité de groupe. Malgré son jeune âge, Mavēa avait peut-être déjà été initié au sein de sa société d'origine.[191] Comme Mavēa, tous les informateurs du *Lily* qui avaient été embarqués à bord du *José* lorsqu'ils étaient enfants, ont transmis leurs « noms d'origine » ou les noms qu'ils portaient avant leur départ forcé du continent africain.

Les registres d'état civil dans lesquels apparaissent les Libérés du *Lily* ne retiennent le plus souvent que les noms individuels donnés à la colonie de Maurice (« John », « Alfred », « Victor »), accompagnés du nom du navire le *Lily*, utilisé comme un patronyme. L'absence dans les registres des « noms d'origine » ou des « noms africains » (tels que Mulōtuia, João, Mutadzo ; des noms issus de langues et cultures est-africaines, mais aussi des noms portugais et chrétiens) ne signifie pas que les Africains du *Lily* ne les utilisaient plus pour se définir eux-mêmes. Carter et Hall citent l'exemple d'une source d'archives coloniales mentionnant une dispute survenue en 1847 entre un certain « Hugon Lily » et un certain « Boncoeur Lily », révélant l'usage de prénoms français et la disparition du « nom de famille africain ».[192] Or, à peine une année avant cette dispute, Eugène de Froberville interrogea en 1846 Mtētiua dit Boncoeur Lily, âgé de 30 à 35 ans, « de la tribu des A-Takuāni ». Ceux-ci vivaient près de la côte, là où se jetait la rivière Luli, à l'Ouest « d'Omuàpe », un « canton makua ». Mtētiua avait les dents limées.[193] Comme la quasi-totalité des informateurs du *Lily* interrogés par Froberville, Mtētiua Boncoeur Lily a transmis les différents noms qu'il a portés au cours de sa trajectoire de vie. Au lieu d'une coupure avec leurs identités africaines, l'attribution de nouveaux noms à Maurice a plutôt élargi l'éventail des identités mobilisables. La coexistence de ces divers noms met en évidence l'agentivité des captifs est-africains à modeler leurs identités à travers le temps.[194]

Des stratégies de retour en Afrique

Selon Froberville, aucun des Africains du *Lily* « n'avait profité de la liberté qu'on leur avait donné de retourner dans leur pays à l'expiration de leur engagement ».[195] En fait, ils avaient été probablement dissuadés par les autorités coloniales de retourner au Mozambique. Certains Libérés du *Lily* ont mené des stratégies collectives de retour au Mozambique, manifestant le maintien de liens (symboliques ou réels) avec le pays d'origine en Afrique.[196]

Ainsi, en novembre 1851, une décennie après leur arrivée à Maurice, un petit groupe de « Mozambiques », composé de plusieurs Libérés du *Lily*, adressa aux autorités coloniales de l'île Maurice la demande de retourner à Quelimane [Thelman], sur la côte du Mozambique, d'où ils avaient été déportés. Parmi les 17 pétitionnaires, on retrouve des informateurs de Froberville, tels que Coco [Padēkhio dit Coco Lily] et « Joua Jack » [Diekh, Djek, Dik, João], deux hommes Niungue [Nyungwe] qui partageaient des liens de parenté. Diekh ou « João Jack » apparaît comme un des deux représentants des pétitionnaires du *Lily*, chez qui la réponse des autorités coloniales devait être envoyée. On apprend ainsi qu'il résidait au faubourg de l'Ouest, rue de la Côte d'or, à Port-Louis.[197] Diekh semble avoir joué un rôle de leader au sein de la communauté des Libérés du *Lily* de Port-Louis. En 1847, Boncoeur Lily se disait être « au service du Sieur Dik ».[198] Diekh, qui était un homme adulte lorsqu'il fut vendu à des marchands d'esclaves de Quelimane, connaissait très bien sa société et sa région d'origine, qu'il situait aux environs de la ville de Tète, dans la vallée du Zambèze. On comprend qu'en raison de la diversité de leurs origines, il était plus fédérateur pour les Libérés du *Lily* de choisir comme destination le port de départ de Quelimane, où leur destin de groupe s'était forgé. Le Collecteur des douanes à Maurice déclara qu'il n'était pas capable de les aider, et les mettait en garde sur les dangers de retourner en Afrique, où ils risquaient d'être revendus en esclavage.[199]

Fig. 15.19
« Mtakuàni [Nom de groupe] Mtétiua dit Bon Cœur »

Source : Archives privées Froberville. Portrait dessiné de Mtētiua Boncoeur Lily, avec ses tatouages, par Eugène de Froberville, île Maurice 1846-1847. @K. Boyer-Rossol, 2019.

Les moulages d'Est-Africains à Maurice, y compris des Libérés du Lily

Pour rendre compte de la description physique des diverses « races de l'Afrique orientale au sud de l'équateur », Eugène de Froberville a produit divers « documents anthropologiques » : 62 moulages en plâtre, 52 dessins avec tatouages, des spécimens de chevelures, ainsi que des mesures corporelles.[200] On peut ainsi mettre en perspective des bustes en plâtre avec des portraits dessinés de certains modèles, comme Munliūa dit Nigaud Lily, un homme Makua d'environ 35 ans, mesurant 1m 65.[201]

Le moulage et la mesure de ces anciens captifs africains posent la question de l'exploitation des corps de dépendants,[202] dans le contexte d'essor de la science des races.[203] Admettant une hiérarchie des races au sommet de laquelle dominaient les Européens, Froberville était monogéniste, et se disait vouloir réhabiliter les « races nègres » au sein des « races » humaines.[204]

Ci-contre, le buste en plâtre de Munliūa. Sur le socle est gravé en gros caractère : Makua, du nom d'un important groupe sociolinguistique du Nord Mozambique. Le portrait dessiné par Froberville de Munliūa dit Nigaud Lily, met en évidence les tatouages qu'il portait sur le visage. Froberville réalisa une grande partie de sa collection de 62 bustes anthropologiques en plâtre à Port-Louis, durant les mois de juillet, août et septembre 1846. Pour amadouer les Africains récalcitrants à se laisser mouler, Eugène de Froberville leur aurait donné du rhum à boire.[205] L'enivrement peut expliquer que certains modèles s'endormaient pendant les longues opérations de moulage. Celles-ci étaient inconfortables car les modèles respiraient à travers des plumes mises dans le nez, et douloureuses dans la mesure où le plâtre arrachait leurs cheveux.

Fig. 15.20
Buste en plâtre de Munliũa dit Nigaud Lily

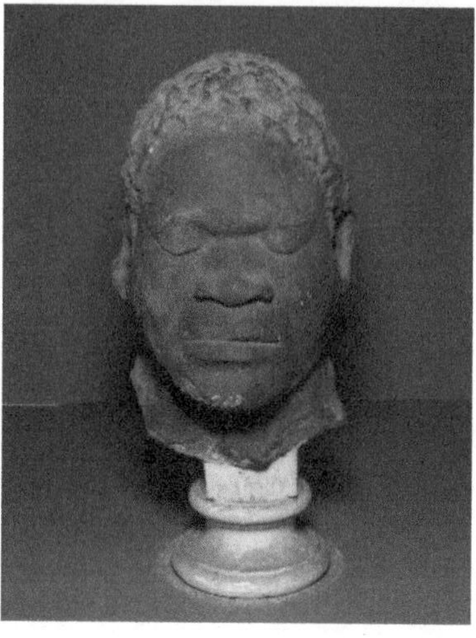

Source : Collection Froberville (originale). Numéro d'inventaire 34.2.41. @ ChâteaudeBlois, 2020. Tous droits réservés.

Fig. 15.21
« Munliũa dit Nigaud Lily » avec tatouages faciaux

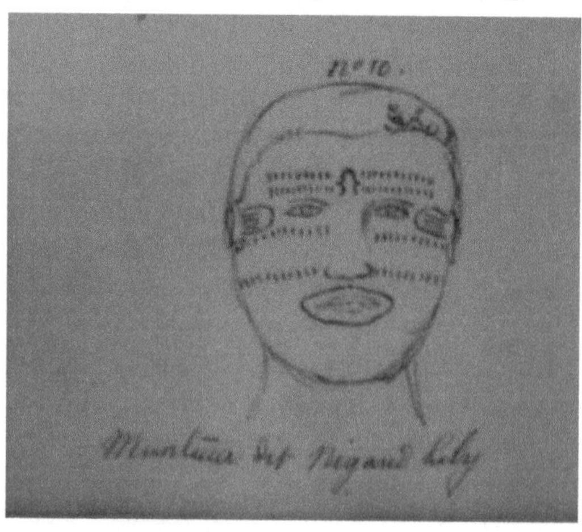

Source : Portrait dessiné par Eugène de Froberville, Archives privées Froberville. @K. Boyer-Rossol, 2019.

L'influence du Père-Laval auprès des natifs du continent africain établis à Port-Louis

Pour convaincre les modèles de se laisser recouvrir de plâtre, Froberville joua sur l'influence qu'exerçait le père Laval (1803-1864) auprès de la population noire de Port-Louis. Eugène de Froberville écrivait :

> J'eusse néanmoins échoué devant les craintes superstitieuses de mes modèles, devant leur répugnance à se laisser couvrir le visage d'une substance qu'ils croyaient être de la chaux, si je n'avais trouvé une assistance influente en Mr l'abbé Laval, qui depuis deux ans s'est voué à l'instruction morale et religieuse de la population africaine de la colonie, population pervertie par un long esclavage et puérilement défiante vers les Blancs. C'est en invoquant le nom vénéré du respectable missionnaire que j'ai décidé la plupart de mes nègres à se laisser mouler.[206]

Chargé de la Mission des Noirs à Port-Louis en septembre 1841, le père Laval a en seulement quelques années réalisé une œuvre importante d'évangélisation auprès des « Créoles », « Malgaches » et « Mozambiques ». Laval plaçait beaucoup d'espoir dans ces deux derniers groupes de population, qui étaient perçus comme des païens coupés de toute connaissances du christianisme. Rapidement, le nombre des baptêmes augmenta et le mouvement de conversion s'amplifia. Alors qu'en 1844, 250 personnes ont été instruites et baptisées, parmi lesquelles des « Malgaches » et « Mozambiques », au cours des années 1847 et 1848, Laval et ses confrères ont baptisé plus de 600 adultes, dont 300 « Malgaches » et 170 « Mozambiques ».[207] Les Libérés du *Lily* étaient englobés dans cette dernière catégorie. On peut penser que certains des Africains du *Lily* ont assisté à des prêches à la Cathédrale de Saint-Louis à Port-Louis, unique église de la Mission des Noirs jusqu'en 1849. Le Père Laval prêchait en langue créole,[208] que les Libérés du *Lily* comprenait très bien. Caroline de Froberville, l'épouse d'Eugène, écrivait en 1846 :

> Depuis quelque temps, il est venu à Maurice un missionnaire français spécialement occupé de la conversion des Noirs ; il prêche en créole, il leur explique familièrement les préceptes de la foi et il a réussi en ce sens que toute cette population ne quitte plus l'église.[209]

Pour les évangélisateurs chrétiens, les Africains nouvellement arrivés, comme les Libérés du *Lily*, représentaient des groupes de populations marginalisés à convertir.

Pour les Africains Libérés, l'adhésion à une communauté religieuse élargie à la colonie de Maurice pouvait participer à renforcer entre eux des liens de réciprocité, et à en créer en dehors de leur groupe. On sait que certains groupes d'Africains Libérés ont mené des stratégies de conversion à Maurice. Ainsi, une quarantaine d'individus parmi les Libérés du navire *Mascareignes*, introduits dans l'île en 1856[210] et résidant à Port-Louis, ont suivi les cours de préparation au baptême en la chapelle de Notre-Dame de Bon-Secours ; leur baptême eut lieu en juillet 1859 à Sainte-Croix. L'influence grandissante du christianisme chez des Libérés du *Lily* à Port-Louis a sans doute participé à accélérer le processus de créolisation. Toutefois, langue et culture créole ont coexisté avec des langues et cultures est-africaines, que des anciens captifs nés sur le continent ont maintenu à l'île Maurice en période post-esclavagiste.

Fig. 15.22
« Grand Buste » sculpté en 1863 (du vivant du Père Laval) par Prosper d'Epinay à Port-Louis, Maurice

Source : Hym Bernard Père, 2016, *Cœur à cœur avec le Père Laval à travers ses écrits*, Diocèse de Port-Louis, Ile Maurice, p. 331.

Le maintien de cultures est-africaines : musiques et danses (makua, nyungwe, nghindo, inhambane etc)

Au cours de son séjour aux îles Mascareignes en 1845-1847, Eugène de Froberville a assisté à des danses (notamment inhambane)[211] et écouté des musiques est-africaines (notamment makua). Il a recueilli auprès d'informateurs africains, y compris des Libérés du *Lily*, des chants et des mélodies dont il a retranscrit les partitions de musique dans ses carnets manuscrits. Eugène de Froberville, qui était aussi musicien, a même accompagné au violon des chants est-africains (notamment nghindo) entonnés par d'anciens captifs nés sur le continent et déportés à l'île Maurice.[212] Un des Libérés du *Lily*, Diekh, a transmis une des « mélodies favorites des Va-Niungue » ; cette chanson relate « l'histoire d'une mère qui, ne pouvant endormir son enfant, l'avait confié à un lièvre pendant qu'elle travaillait aux champs ». Froberville en a retranscrit la partition de musique et les paroles (traduit en français) : [213]

> La mère : « Lièvre, Lièvre, apportes mon enfant, je m'en vais »
>
> Le lièvre : « Je le garde, je le garde »
>
> L'enfant, criant : « Ehen ! Ehen ! »
>
> Le lièvre, berçant l'enfant : « Trr', trr' – Travaillez donc, je vous l'apporterai tantôt ».

Ci-après, on peut observer des dessins de musiciens et danseurs makua, réalisés par Eugène de Froberville aux îles Mascareignes (1845-1847). Froberville a fait le portrait de scènes auxquelles il avait assisté. En l'absence de noms individuels, on ne peut identifier des Africains du *Lily* parmi ces portraits dessinés de musiciens et danseurs africains. Toutefois, on peut soutenir que ces Africains Libérés évoluaient dans une société où des savoirs, des techniques et des pratiques culturels est-africains circulaient encore dans les années 1840 à Maurice.

Froberville fit même envoyer des instruments de musique est-africains (makua et nghindo), de l'île Maurice en France.[214] Il avait commandité auprès de certains informateurs africains la confection de tels objets culturels, qui furent intégrés au sein de ses collections privées au château familial de Villeouet (en France). Eugène de Froberville y fit également expédier ses carnets et livres manuscrits qu'il tînt durant son enquête ethnographique aux Mascareignes en 1845-1847. La constitution des archives et des collections Froberville au XIXe siècle en France était ainsi étroitement liée à la circulation de savoirs et d'objets produits par d'anciens captifs déportés de l'Afrique orientale aux îles de l'océan Indien occidental.

L'historien Alpers a rappelé que la transformation culturelle des « Mozambiques » en situation de diaspora à l'île Maurice était un processus continu.[215] Après l'abolition de 1835 à Maurice, l'introduction ponctuelle de Libérés Africains jusque dans les années 1860, a sans doute participé à réinsuffler des apports culturels et linguistiques est-africains de l'apport culturel et linguistique est-africain au sein de ces communautés diasporiques.[216] Il est probable que des cultures et des langues est-africaines se soient maintenues (même de façon isolées et modestes) à Maurice, et plus généralement aux Mascareignes, jusqu'à la disparition des derniers ancêtres nés au Mozambique, à la fin du XIXe siècle.

Fig. 15.23
Chant nyungwe et partition de musique avec ses paroles en nyungwe, traduites en français

Source : Archives privées Froberville. Carnets manuscrits d'Eugène de Froberville (Mascareignes, 1845-1847). Cahier Vaniungue. Tsi'iambo. Tsidima.. @K. Boyer-Rossol, 2019.

Fig. 15.24
Musiciens et danseurs Makua : Un joueur de tàngara, instrument de musique makua à cordes

Source : Archives privées Froberville. Dessins d'Eugène de Froberville réalisés lors de son voyage aux Mascareignes (1845-1847). @K. Boyer-Rossol, 2019.

Fig. 15.25
Musiciens et danseurs Makua : Un danseur et ses apparats, portant des masheves aux chevilles, et tenant dans les mains des instruments de musique à grelots

Source : Archives privées Froberville. Dessins d'Eugène de Froberville réalisés lors de son voyage aux Mascareignes (1845-1847). @K. Boyer-Rossol, 2019.

Endnotes

1 En mémoire à Pier Larson (1961-2020).

2 Eyriès, Malte-Brun, 1847, « Analyse d'un Mémoire de M. Eugène de Froberville sur les langues et les races de l'Afrique orientale au sud de l'équateur », *Nouvelles Annales des voyages, de la géographie et de l'histoire…*, Paris, Arthus Bertrand, ser.5, t.9, p. 219.

3 En novembre 1845, Eugène de Froberville passa une quinzaine de jours à la Réunion, où il collecta des vocabulaires et des récits auprès d'esclaves makua. Tout le reste de son séjour (de décembre 1845 à février 1847) se déroula à l'île Maurice.

4 Les « Mozambiques » ou « Makua » ont formé une diaspora africaine issue de la traite des esclaves dans l'océan Indien (et dans l'espace atlantique). Les noms qui leur ont été assignés, en référence à des critères ethniques ou géographiques, les rattachaient au Mozambique, principal pays exportateur d'esclaves est-africains pour les îles du Sud-Ouest de l'océan Indien au XIXe siècle. Voir E. A. Alpers, 2005, « Mozambique and "Mozambiques": Slave Trade and Diaspora on a Global Scale », in B. Zimba, E. Alpers, A. Isaacman, *Slaves Routes and oral Tradition in Southeastern Africa*, p. 39-62.

5 Plusieurs graphies ont été utilisées pour désigner des Est-Africains locuteurs de l'emakhuwa : Makhuwa [du Mozambique], Makoa [en malgache], Makoua/Macoua [en français], Makua [en anglais].

6 Eugène de Froberville, 1847, « Notes sur les mœurs, coutumes et traditions des Amakoua. Sur le commerce et la traite des esclaves dans l'Afrique orientale », *Bulletin de la Société de Géographie*, p. 328-329.

7 Le terme de « Recaptifs » paraît plus approprié pour parler des captifs africains interceptés lors de leur déportation à travers les mers et transférés à bord des croiseurs de la *Navy*, puis envoyés vers les colonies anglaises les plus proches. Pour faciliter toutefois la lecture de ce papier, je mentionnerai par la suite le terme de Libérés sans y ajouter de guillemets. Sur l'emploi du terme de Libérés, voir Marina Carter, Mark Hall, 2008 (May), *The "Last Slaves" of Mauritius*. Sur l'histoire économique du travail à Maurice, voir Allen Richard B., 1999, *Slaves, Freedmen and Indentured Laborers in Colonial Mauritius*, Cambridge University Press

8 J'écris le nom du Lily en italique pour parler du navire, et sans italique quand il est utilisé comme un patronyme.

9 Eugène de Froberville, « Notes sur les mœurs, coutumes et traditions des Amakoua… », p. 312.

10 Déjà en 1999, l'historien Edward Alpers avait souligné la richesse des matériaux recueillis par Froberville et soulevait l'intérêt de retrouver ses notes manuscrites. Edward A. Alpers, 1999, « Becoming « Mozambique » : Diaspora and Identity in Mauritius », papier présenté dans le cadre du séminaire Harriet Tubman, Université de York, Toronto, 19 p.

11 P. Flourens, E. Serres, 1850, « Rapport sur les races nègres de l'Afrique orientale au Sud de l'équateur, observées par M. de Froberville », *Comptes rendus hebdomadaires des séances de l'Académie des sciences,* t. XXX, p. 679-690.

12 Hamy a mis en perspective les bustes de « Makoua » moulés et peints par Dumoutier en 1840 à Bourbon et par Froberville en 1846 à Maurice. E. T. Hamy, « La collection de Froberville au Muséum », *La Nature*, 1879, p. 237.

13 La collection de Dumoutier était constituée de 51 bustes moulés entre 1837 et 1840 dans l'océan Pacifique et dans l'océan Indien. En 1840 à Bourbon, Dumoutier fit quelques moulages de « Mozambiques » et de Malgaches. Des photographies de ces moulages sont conservées dans les fonds de la Société d'Anthropologie de Paris (SAP) aux archives du Muséum National d'Histoire Naturelle à Paris.

14 Les copies (58) de cette collection Froberville se trouvent au Musée de l'Homme, alors que les originaux (55) sont conservés dans les combles du château de Blois. Ainsi, il existe aujourd'hui davantage de copies (58) que d'originaux (58). Je tiens à remercier la responsable des collections du château de Blois, Morgane Lecareux, qui m'a autorisée à utiliser des images des bustes en plâtre originaux. Leurs droits de diffusion sont strictement réservés.

15 L'émergence de la notion de terrain est relativement récente en histoire des sciences. Voir Isabelle Surun, « Du texte au terrain : reconstituer les pratiques des voyageurs (Afrique occidentale, 1790-1880) », in *Sociétés & Représentations*, 2006, 1, n°2, p. 213-223.

16 Depuis 2018-2019, je mène avec le principal propriétaire des archives privées Froberville en France, un inventaire et une numérisation de ces archives.

17 Ces volumes reliés ont été écrits (à l'encre) de la main d'Eugène de Froberville. Ils n'ont jamais été publiés.

18 Archives privées Froberville (France). Eugène de Froberville, *Tribus africaines* ; *Notes géographiques et ethnographiques sur l'Afrique orientale au sud de l'équateur* ; *Notes ethnographiques sur l'Afrique orientale au sud de l'Equateur ; avec planches et cartes géographiques 1848*.

19 Au moins trois autres informateurs africains mentionnés dans les notes manuscrites d'Eugène de Froberville seraient également des Libérés du *Lily*. En l'absence du nom de navire associé à leurs noms individuels, je préfère rester prudente et ne pas

les comptabiliser pour le moment dans les Libérés du Lily interrogés par Froberville.

20 Je tiens à remercier Satyendra Peerthum, qui a beaucoup travaillé sur la question des Libérés à Maurice en général, et des Libérés du Lily en particulier. Satyendra a été d'une aide précieuse pour me familiariser avec les archives mauriciennes relativement à ce sujet de recherche.

21 Marina Carter, Mark Hall, 2008 (May), *The "Last Slaves"...*

22 Je considère ainsi les bustes en plâtre eux-mêmes comme des objets et des sources pour l'histoire. Voir Dominique Juhé-Beaulaton, Vincent Leblan, « Introduction », in Dominique Juhé-Beaulaton, Vincent Leblan (coord.), *Le spécimen et le collecteur. Savoirs naturalistes, pouvoirs et altérités (XVIIIe-XXe siècles)*, Paris, Muséum National d'Histoire Naturelle, Publications Scientifiques, collection archives, 2018, p. 7.

23 Eyriès, « Analyse d'un Mémoire », p. 219.

24 Eugène de Froberville, 1847, « Notes sur les mœurs...», p. 311.

25 Archives privées Froberville. Eugène de Froberville, *Notes ethnographiques sur l'Afrique orientale....*

26 Archives privées Froberville. Eugène de Froberville, *Notes ethnologiques sur l'Afrique orientale (1846-1847).*

27 On peut identifier parmi les 55 bustes sauvegardés de la collection originale, 12 moulages d'Africains du *Lily*, dont deux copies (c'est-à-dire 10 individus moulés).

28 Parmi les 255 survivants de la traversée du *Lily*, ont été relevés 63 hommes, 8 femmes, 123 garçons et 61 filles. W. H. Gardner, 1852, « History of an Epidemic of Small-Pox in the Mauritius : With Remarks on the Protective Power of Vaccination », *London Journal of Medicine*, Vol. 4, N°37, Janv., p. 39.

29 Teelock Vijayalakshmi, 2005, « From Mozambique to Le Morne Brabant Mountain : Being Young, Male and Mozambican in Colonial Mauritius », in B. Zimba, E. Alpers, A. Isaacman, *Slaves Routes and Oral Tradition in Southeastern Africa*, Maputo, Filsom Entertainment Lda, p. 279-294.

30 Le nom des Huet de Froberville jouissait à Maurice d'une certaine renommée. Entre autres, le grand-père d'Eugène, Barthélémy Huet de Froberville (1761-1835), était une figure importante de la société coloniale mauricienne du début du XIXe siècle.

31 Archives privées Froberville. Eugène de Froberville, *Notes ethnographiques sur l'Afrique orientale...).*

32 M. Carter, M. Hall, 2008, *The "Last Slaves"...* ; M. Carter, V. Govinden, S. Peerthum, 2003, *The Last Slaves. Liberated Africans in the 19th Century Mauritius*, CRIOS, p. 42 ; 56.

33 Voir Marina Carter, Mark Hall, 2008, *The "Last Slaves"...*

34 M. Carter, V. Govinden, S. Peerthum, 2003, *The Last Slaves...*, p. 63.

35 Ce n'est que quelques années plus tard, entre 1848 et 1850, que les Libérés Africains sont devenus des sujets britanniques libres à la colonie de Maurice. Satyendra Peerthum, 2005, *« Voices From the Edge » : The Life Histories and Experiences of the Liberated Africans in British Mauritius during the Age of Indenture with Comparative Perspectives (1808-1943)*, MA thesis University of Mauritius, p. 42.

36 M. Carter, V. Govinden, S. Peerthum, 2003, *The Last Slaves...*, p. 41.

37 En général, la vaste majorité des Africains Libérés dans l'océan Indien ont été placés comme travailleurs domestiques ou travailleurs agricoles. Hopper Matthew S., 2019, « Liberated Africans in the Indian Ocean World », in Anderson Richard & Lovejoy Henry B, *Liberated African and the Abolition of the Slave Trade, 1807-1896*, University of Rochester Press, p. 276.

38 MNA. I– Z7E3 Letters concerning the Liberated Africans from 1835 to 1850. Indentures (october 1840). Custom House, Port Louis 28 september 1843.

39 Marina Carter, Mark Hall, *The "Last Slaves... "*.

40 J'écris dans cet article les noms des informateurs africains tels qu'ils apparaissent dans les carnets et notes manuscrites d'Eugène de Froberville.

41 Marina Carter, Mark Hall, *The "Last Slaves... "*

42 Archives privées Froberville. Lettre d'Eugène de Froberville à sa mère Eugénie de Froberville. Port-Louis, le 5 mai 1846.

43 Archives privées Froberville. Eugène de Froberville, *Notes ethnographiques sur l'Afrique orientale....*

44 MNHN. BIB Centrale. Ms 165 I. Eugène de Froberville, *Notes sur les races de l'Afrique orientale au sud de l'Equateur*, février 1849.

45 Archives privées Froberville. Cahier Makua II. Entretien de Kupēlina (Sarah) du Lily, 25 ans. Port-Louis, le 27 septembre 1846.

46 Archives privées Froberville. Eugène de Froberville, *Notes ethnologiques sur l'Afrique orientale....*

47 Voir la carte d'Edward Alpers, « Mozambique and Macuana ». E. A. Alpers, 1975, *Ivory & Slaves in East Central Africa*, London, Heinemann, p. 154

48 E. de Froberville, 1847, p. 314.

49 « L'orthographe adoptée pour les vocabulaires est le résultat d'une audition attentive. Sauf quelques exceptions inévitables, j'ai donné aux lettres la valeur qu'elles ont dans la plupart des langues néolatines », notait Froberville. Archives privées Froberville. Eugène de Froberville, *Notes ethnographiques sur l'Afrique orientale...*

50 Archives privées Froberville. Eugène de Froberville, *Notes ethnographiques sur l'Afrique orientale...*

51 Archives privées Froberville. Eugène de Froberville, *Notes ethnographiques sur l'Afrique orientale...*

52 Pour les noms de groupes, d'individus, ou de lieux, je me réfère dans cet article à l'orthographe utilisé par Froberville dans ses notes manuscrites. Cette graphie n'était pas fixe puisque Froberville utilise fréquemment diverses orthographes pour un même nom (d'individu, de groupe ou de lieu). Par exemple, il écrit tantôt Niungue, tantôt Niumbue, pour parler d'un même groupe de la haute vallée du Zambèze [Nyungwe]. J'insère entre parenthèses (...) les variantes utilisées par Froberville et entre crochets [....] les orthographes plus communément admises aujourd'hui.

53 Certains itinéraires ont été dessinés au crayon à papier dans ses carnets, parfois de la main des informateurs africains eux-mêmes. À partir des données recueillies auprès d'anciens captifs à Maurice (y compris des Libérés du Lily), Froberville établit des cartes de l'Afrique orientale. Entre autres, on peut mentionner une carte remarquable d'une partie du Nord Mozambique et du Sud de la Tanzanie. Archives privées Froberville. Eugène de Froberville, *Esquisse des pays situés entre les fleuves Luvûma et de Lufidźi (Afrique orientale). D'après les relations des indigènes*, Ile Maurice, 1847.

54 On retrouve fréquemment dans les entretiens retranscrits, les noms de groupes ethniques voisins. Il est probable que les informateurs africains répondaient à des questions préparées en amont par Froberville, en vue d'établir une géographie de cette vaste région de l'Afrique centrale de l'Est.

55 Archives privées Froberville. Eugène de Froberville, *Ostro-Nègres*, p. 299. ; Archives privées Froberville. Eugène de Froberville, *Notes ethnographiques sur l'Afrique orientale....*

56 Archives privées Froberville. Carnets manuscrits d'Eugène de Froberville. Cahier Makua II. Entretiens avec Mts'īsanga dit Alexandre Lily, âgé d'environ 25 ans. Port-Louis, 26 et 28 mai 1846.

57 Archives privées Froberville. Eugène de Froberville, *Ostro-Nègres*, p. 295.

58 Archives privées Froberville. Eugène de Froberville, *Notes ethnologiques sur l'Afrique orientale 1846-1847*.

59 Archives privées Froberville. Cahier Vaniungue. Tsi'iambo. Tsidima.

60 Froberville a réalisé une carte ethnolinguistique de l'Afrique orientale au sud de l'équateur, qui reste tout à fait originale pour l'époque. Archives privées Froberville. Eugène de Froberville, *Tableau Synoptique indiquant la parenté analogique des langues de l'Afrique méridionale*, 1851.

61 Muséum National d'Histoire Naturelle (MNHN). Bibliothèque Centrale (BIB). Ms 165 I. Eugène de Froberville, *Notes sur les races de l'Afrique orientale au sud de l'Equateur*, février 1849.

62 Il est probable que des « Libérés » du *Lily* aient servi de modèles pour ces dessins.

63 Johann Moritz Rugendas, 1835, *Voyage pittoresque dans le Brésil*, Paris, Engelmann & Cie, p. 26.

64 Adrien Balbi, 1826, *Introduction à l'atlas ethnographique du globe*, Paris, Chez Rey et Gravier, tome I, p. 225.

65 Eugène de Froberville, 1847, « Notes sur les Moeurs, Coutumes et Traditions des Amakoua, sur le commerce et la traite des esclaves dans l'Afrique orientale », *Bulletin de la Société de Géographie*, Paris, p. 314.

66 Adrien Balbi, *Introduction à l'atlas*..., p. 224.

67 Archives privées Froberville. Cahier Vaniungue. Tsi'iambo. Tsidima.

68 Archives privées Froberville. Dossier sur la collection de moulages. Listes des bustes moulés.

69 Eugène de Froberville, août 1848, « Notes sur les Va-Niungue et les Mabsiti, peuples de l'Afrique Orientale », *Bulletin de la Société de Géographie*, p. 66.

70 Eugène de Froberville, « Notes sur les Va-Niungue... », p. 65-81.

71 En réalité, Zumbo était la ville portugaise du Zambèze la plus occidentale. Créé en 1720, Zumbo était toutefois abandonnée par les Portugais à l'époque de ces raids Nguni. Gerhard Liesegang. "Nguni Migrations between Delagoa Bay and the Zambezi, 1821-1839." *African Historical Studies*, vol. 3, no. 2, 1970, p. 29 ; Archives privées Froberville. Eugène de Froberville, *Notes ethnologiques sur l'Afrique orientale... ;*« Notes sur les Va-Niungue...», p. 66 ;*Notes ethnographiques sur l'Afrique orientale*...

72 Eugène de Froberville, « Notes sur les Va-Niungue...», p. 67.

73 Archives privées Froberville. Eugène de Froberville, *Ostro-Nègres*, p. 300-303 ; Eugène de Froberville, « Notes sur les Va-Niungue...», p. 69.

74 Archives privées Froberville. Eugène de Froberville, *Tribus africaines*.

75 On retrouve notamment un récit de tradition niungue [nyungwe] relatif à la création de l'homme. Dans cette version du péché originel, la pomme est remplacée par une marmite. La femme persuade l'homme de soulever le couvercle de marmite ; un rat s'en échappe, grimpe sur l'arbre de la connaissance, et emporte le fruit défendu. Dieu en colère punît la désobéissance de l'homme et de la femme, les chassant du beau jardin. Eugène de Froberville, « Notes sur les Va-Niungue...», p. 70-71 ; Eugène de Froberville, *Ostro-Nègres*, p. 307.

76 Le décès d'un Mu-Niüngue donne lieu à une véritable fête (Khàua) qui dure cinq jours. Le corps, soigneusement lié avec une liane, reste pendant ce temps dans la

hutte. Lorsque la fête est terminée, on brûle la hutte et l'on procède à l'enterrement du mort que l'on place dans une fosse profonde la tête tournée vers le couchant. Eugène de Froberville, *Notes ethnologiques sur l'Afrique orientale*….

77 Archives privées Froberville. Eugène de Froberville, *Notes ethnologiques sur l'Afrique orientale*…

78 Froberville a en effet retranscrit dans ses carnets manuscrits des chants et partitions de musique maravi, qu'il avait collectés à Maurice et à Bourbon.

79 Archives privées Froberville. Eugène de Froberville, *Ostro-Nègres*, p. 317 ; Eugène de Froberville, « Notes sur les Va-Niungue…» ,p. 77.

80 Archives privées Froberville. Eugène de Froberville, *Notes ethnologiques sur l'Afrique orientale*… ; *Ostro-Nègres*, p. 318

81 Allen Isaacman, 1973, « Madzi-Manga, Mhondoro and the use of oral traditions – A chapter in Barue religious and political history », *Journal of African History*, XIV, 3, p. 395 ; Malyn Newitt, 2018, « Southern Zambezia States and Indian Ocean Trade, 1450–1900 », *Oxford Research Encyclopedia of African History*

82 Archives privées Froberville. Cahier Manika. Barge. Vatonga. Makossi. Niambane. Unguanati. Tzibin. Entretien avec Mutadzo (dit Victor Lily) âgé de 30 ans, taille de 1m68, venu sur le Lily. Port-Louis, le 12 juillet 1846.

83 Mutadzo décrit entre autres des rites funéraires : « Les Manika enterrent leurs morts en terre dans la position d'un homme assis, les mains placées sur leurs épaules. (…) Suivant le rang et les richesses du défunt, on garde son cadavre de huit jours à un mois avant de l'enterrer ». Archives privées Froberville. Cahier Manika. Barge. Vatonga. Makossi. Niambane. Unguanati. Tzibin. Entretien avec Mutadzo (dit Victor Lily) âgé de 30 ans, taille de 1m68, venu sur le Lily. Port-Louis, le 12 juillet 1846.

84 Eugène de Froberville, *Notes géographiques et ethnographiques sur l'Afrique orientale*….

85 Archives privées Froberville. Cahier Manika. Barge. Vatonga. Makossi. Niambane. Unguanati. Tzibin. Entretien avec Mutadzo (dit Victor Lily) âgé de 30 ans, taille de 1m68, venu sur le Lily. Port-Louis, le 12 juillet 1846.

86 Les Nguni établirent le royaume de Gaza, qui couvrait à son apogée toute la vaste région au sud du Zambèze jusqu'à la rivière du Limpopo. Les anciens états Karanga du Manica et du Barue survécurent comme des tributaires du Gaza. Voir Malyn Newitt, « Southern Zambezia…».

87 Newitt, *A History of Mozambique*, Indiana University Press, 1995, p. 216.

88 *Ibidem*, p. 286.

89 Allen Isaacman, « Madzi-Manga…», p. 405.

90 *Ibidem*, p. 400.

91 Archives privées Froberville. Cahier Manika. Barge. Vatonga. Makossi. Niambane. Unguanati. Tzibin. Entretien avec Gafume (dit Joseph Lily) âgé de 30 ans, 1m64, venu du Lily. Port-Louis, le 14 juillet 1846.

92 Archives privées Froberville. Eugène de Froberville, *Notes ethnologiques sur l'Afrique orientale*…

93 Froberville utilise différentes graphies pour retranscrire le nom des Makuzi ; il écrit tantôt « Makūzi », tantôt « Makǜzi » ou encore « Màkuzi ».

94 Archives privées Froberville. Carnets manuscrits d'Eugène de Froberville. Cahier Va-Niungue. Entretien avec Dionokea dit Snap, venu sur le Lily, âgé de 17 ans, 1m56. Port-Louis, 15 juillet et 20 décembre 1846.

95 Archives privées Froberville. Eugène de Froberville, *Notes ethnologiques sur l'Afrique orientale*…

96 E. A. Alpers, 2007, « The Other Middle Passage. The African Slave Trade in the Indian Ocean », in ed. Emma Christopher, Cassandra Pybus and Marcus Rediker, *Many Middle Passages. Forced Migration and the Making of the Modern World*, Berkeley, University of California Press, p. 21.

97 Les Makuzi étaient en effet établis plus en arrière que les Tsoambo [Chuabo]. Ces derniers occupaient des territoires autour de l'embouchure du Zambèze et du voisinage immédiat de Quelimane. R. C. F. Maugham, 1910, *Zambezia. A general description of the valley of the Zambezi river, from its delta to the river Aroangwa, with its history, agriculture, flora, fauna, and ethnography*, London, John Murray, p. 326.

98 Archives privées Froberville. Cahier Makua II. Entretien de Joachim dit Manuel du Lily, âgé de 35 ans, 1m55. Port-Louis 2, 4, 5 août 1846. Froberville recueillit auprès de Joachim du vocabulaire tso'ambo -aussi retranscrit tchōambo.

99 Archives privées Froberville. Eugène de Froberville, *Ostro-Nègres*, p. 295-296.

100 Archives privées Froberville, Eugène de Froberville, *Tribus africaines.*

101 Archives privées Froberville. Cahier Mudhiaua. Entretien avec Kalēngo Victor dit Verd bois du Lily, 20 à 25 ans. Port-Louis, 4 mai 1846.

102 Allen Isaacman, 1972, p. 48.

103 Archives privées Froberville. Carnet Vaniungue Ts'iambo. Tsidima. (1845-1847) ; Eugène de Froberville, *Notes ethnologiques sur l'Afrique orientale…*

104 Archives privées Froberville. Eugène de Froberville, *Ostro-Nègres*, p. 314.

105 *Ibidem*, p. 316.

106 L'essor de la traite des esclaves et l'esclavage internes en Afrique centrale de l'Est au XIXe siècle, aurait peut-être favorisé (à court terme) les sociétés patrilinéraires, au détriment des sociétés matrilinéraires.

107 Archives privées Froberville. Eugène de Froberville, *Notes ethnologiques sur les principales tribus de l'Afrique orientale au sud de l'équateur (1845-1848)*, p. 326-327.

108 Voir Klara Boyer-Rossol, *Histoire et Mémoires des Makoa à l'Ouest de Madagascar. XIXe-XXe siècles*, thèse de doctorat, 2015, p. 592-593.

109 Archives privées Froberville. Eugène de Froberville, *Vocabulaire comparé des langues de l'Afrique orientale au Sud de l'Equateur*, Bourbon et Maurice, 1845, 1846 et 1847, tome II, p. 263.

110 *Ibidem*, tome I, p. 129 ; tome II, p. 263.

111 Voir Henri Médard, 2013, « Introduction », in Médard Henri, Derat Marie-Laure, Vernet Thomas, Ballarin Marie-Pierre (dir.), *Traites et esclavages en Afrique orientale et dans l'océan Indien*, Paris, Karthala, p. 9-28.

112 Voir Paul E. Lovejoy, 1983 (2000, 2012, 2017), *Transformations in Slavery : A History of Slavery in Africa* Cambridge University Press.

113 Isaacman présente « l'esclavage domestique » au sein des sociétés africaines zambéziennes comme un système de dépendance endogène ayant préexisté à l'installation des Portugais au Mozambique. Allen Isaacman, 1972, *Mozambique : The Africanization of a European Institution, the Zambesi Prazos 1750-1902*, Madison, p. 48-51.

114 Le *prazo* était une terre appartenant à la couronne portugaise, louée à un colon ou un marchand en échange d'une redevance annuelle. Ce système existait dans la vallée du Zambèze de la fin du XVIe siècle au XXe siècle. Voir Malyn Newitt, 1969, « The Portuguese on the Zambezi : An Historical Interpretation of the Prazo System », *The Journal of African History*, vol. 10, n° 1, p. 67–85.

115 M. Newitt, « Carte d'états africains et de ports de traite indiens » in Malyn Newitt, 2018, « Southern Zambezia…».

116 Le récit de Livingstone a sans doute alimenté la réputation des seigneurs de la terre Afro-Portugais d'être des maîtres cruels. David Livingstone, 1865, *Narrative of an expedition to the Zambesi and its tributaties and of the discovery of the lakes Shirwa and Nyassa*, 1858-1864, London, Murray, p. 50.

117 Barbara Isaacman and Allen Isaacman, « Slavery and Social Stratification among the Sena of Mozambique. A study of the kaporo system », in Suzanne Meirs and Igor Kopitoff, *Slavery in Africa*, Madison, University of Wisconsin Press,1977, p. 110.

118 Barbara Isaacman and Allen Isaacman, « Slavery and Social Stratification…», p. 119.

119 Allen Isaacman, *Zambesi Prazos*, p. 49.

120 Le prix moyen par esclave s'élevait entre trois et six mètres de tissu et divers volumes de grain. Allen Isaacman, *Zambesi Prazos,* p. 48.

121 Allen Isaacman, *Zambesi Prazos*, p. 50. Barbara Isaacman and Allen Isaacman, « Slavery and Social Stratification…», p. 107.

122 Population d'Afrique australe, les Chewa vivent principalement au Malawi où ils forment le groupe sociolinguistique le plus nombreux. Ils sont également présents en Zambie, au Mozambique et à un moindre degré au Zimbabwe.

123 Archives privées Froberville. Cahier Mudhiàua. Entretien avec Kāska (John), de la nation Nakhipēta, venu sur le Lily. 25 à 30 ans, taille 1m65. Port-Louis, le 11 juillet 1846.

124 Archives privées Froberville. Cahier Vaniungue.

125 David Livingstone, *Narrative of an expedition…*, p. 48.

126 Archives privées Froberville. Eugène de Froberville, *Vocabulaire comparé…*, p. 302.

127 Les Nguni ont formé des monarchies militaires puissantes basées sur la propriété du bétail. M. D. Newitt, *A History of Mozambique*, Bloomington : Indiana University Press, 1995, p. 263.

128 Froberville, *Ostro-Nègres*, p. 337. Froberville a publié une version de ce récit dans ses « Notes sur les Va-Niungue… »

129 Froberville, *Ostro-Nègres*, p. 333.

130 Archives privées Froberville. Cahier Manika. Entretien avec Malavira dit John, venu à bord du Lily. 30 ans, 1m72. Port-Louis, 13 juillet 1846.

131 Diekh était l'aîné de Padekhio. Tous deux avaient le même père. Ils ont fui les raids nguni, puis ont été vendus à des marchands de Quelimane et depuis ce port, embarqués à bord du *José*, puis transférés sur le *Lily* et conduits jusqu'à l'île Maurice.

132 Il apparait plusieurs versions du récit de vie de Diekh, qui ont été retranscrites par Froberville dans ses carnets et livres manuscrits, ainsi que dans un article publié dans *les Bulletins de la Société de Géographie* (1848).

133 Archives privées Froberville. Cahier Vaniungue. Entretien avec Diekh (Djeck, João), entre 30 et 35 ans, venu sur le Lily. Port-Louis, le 27 octobre 1846.

134 Liesegang. « Nguni Migrations… », p. 332 ; Leonard D. Ngcongco, « Le Mfecane et l'émergence de nouveaux états africains » in J. F. Ade Ajayi (dir), *L'Afrique au XIXe siècle jusque vers les années 1880*, Histoire Générale de l'Afrique, vol 6., Paris, Unesco, 1996, p. 147.

135 Deux décennies plus tard, à la fin des années 1850, Livingstone présente les Maviti (« Landins » ou « Zulu ») comme les « seigneurs de la rive droite du Zambèze », à qui les Portugais payaient un tribut annuel. David Livingstone, *Narrative of an*

expedition…, p. 30.

136 Froberville, *Ostro-Nègres*, p. 298-299.

137 Archives privées Froberville. Cahier Vaniungue. Entretien avec Uāntuavzīnu, dit Alfred du Lily, âgé de 16 à 17 ans, 1m 67. Port-Louis, le 20 décembre 1846.

138 Allen Isaacman, *Zambesi Prazos*, p. 89.

139 Allen Isaacman, *Zambesi Prazos,* p. 88.

140 Archives privées Froberville. Eugène de Froberville, *Dossier Tribus africaines.*

141 Dionōkea avait un père Makuzi et une mère Tsoambo. Mulòtiua un père Makuzi et une mère Makua.

142 Archives privées Froberville. Cahier Makua II. Entretien avec Dionōkea dit Snap, âgé de 17 ans, 1m56, venu sur le Lily. Port-Louis, 15 juillet et 20 décembre 1846 ; Entretien avec Mulōtuia dit John du Lily. Entre 20 et 25 ans. Entre 1m60 et 1m65. Port-Louis, 27 août 1846.

143 Archives privées Froberville. Cahier Vaniungue. Entretien avec João dit Alfred du Lily, âgé de 17 ans, 1m62. Né à Uani, près de Quelimane, de mère et de père Mangāndzia. Port-Louis, 2, 4 et 5 août 1846 ; Entretien avec Kiendiēndi dit Joseph du Lily, âgé de 20 à 25 ans, 1m63. Port-Louis, 11 juillet 1846 ; Entretien avec Thongōra dit César du Lily, âgé de 18 ans, taille de 1m52. Port-Louis, le 4 juillet 1846.

144 Voir Rozenn Guérois, 2015, *A grammar of Cuwabo (Mozambique, Bantu P34)*, thèse de doctorat en science du langage, Université Lumière Lyon 2.

145 Selon Alpers, le sena [langue parlée par les Sena de la basse vallée du Zambèze] aurait également été utilisé comme langue véhiculaire par les captifs détenus à Quelimane. Edward A. Alpers, 2003, p. 33.

146 Archives privées Froberville. Cahier Makua II. Entretien avec Namōta dit Georges, Makua du Lily. 22 ans, 1m59. Namōta a transmis des vocabulaires en makua et tchoambo ou tchirimane. Port-Louis, 3 août 1846.

147 Parmi eux, « Les Tzcoambo [Tsoambo, Cuabo] et les Matibani [Makua Matibane ?] vivent sur la côte de Mozambique » Rugendas, *Voyage pittoresque…*, p. 26 ; Adrien Balbi, *Introduction…*, p. 224-225.

148 Allen Isaacman, *Zambesi Prazos*, p. 86.

149 Sous la pression britannique, le Portugal promulgua un décret en 1836 qui abolissait totalement la traite des esclaves. Le trafic se poursuivit notamment en direction du Brésil, qui avait pourtant officiellement interdit l'importation des esclaves depuis 1830. Newitt, *History of Mozambique*, p. 268-269.

150 Texugo, *A Letter on the Slave Trade Still Being Carried on along the Eastern Coast of Africa*, London, 1839, p. 34

151 Allen Isaacman, *Zambesi Prazos*, p. 87.

152 Peu après, en 1842, le Portugal signa avec l'Angleterre un traité, qui reconnaissait la traite des esclaves comme de la piraterie et légalisait le droit de recherche. Entre les années 1840 et 1890, la traite illégale des esclaves s'est maintenue au Mozambique, en particulier pour alimenter les marchés d'esclaves de Madagascar, ainsi que les marchés en « engagés » des îles françaises de Nosy-Be, Mayotte et la Réunion. Voir Klara Boyer-Rossol, *Entre les deux rives…*.

153 Après 1840, le trafic se déplaça un peu au nord et au sud du port de Quelimane, vers les petites criques et embouchures de rivières plus discrets où les esclaves étaient parqués et embarqués durant la nuit dans des navires à destination du Brésil ou de Cuba. Allen Isaacman, *Zambesi Prazos*, p. 94.

154 Archives privées Froberville. Eugène de Froberville, *Tribus africaines*.

155 Hopper, « Liberated Africans…», p. 273 ; 277.

156 Archives privées Froberville. Eugène de Froberville, *Tribus africaines* ; W. H. Gardner, 1852, « History of an Epidemic of Small-Pox in the Mauritius : With Remarks on the Protective Power of Vaccination », *London Journal of Medicine*, Vol. 4, N°37, Janv., p. 38.

157 J. M. Filliot, « La Traite vers l'Ile de France. Les contraintes maritimes », in *Slavery in South West Indian Ocean*, 1989, p. 91. Cité par Huber Gerbeau, 2002, « L'océan Indien n'est pas l'atlantique. La traite illégale à Bourbon au XIXe siècle », in *Outre-mers*, tome 89, n°336-337, p. 103 ; Auguste Toussaint, *La Route des Iles*, 1967, Paris, p. 451, Annexe I, Tableau 3. Cité par Edward A. Alpers, 2003, « Creolization and Identity among « Mozambiques » in Mauritius and Brazil », *Revi Kiltir Kreol*, Nelson Mandela Centre for African Culture, p. 34, note de bas de page 13.

158 Selon Colin, la quasi-totalité des morts à bord des bateaux faisant la traite des esclaves entre Moçambique et l'Île de France au début du XIXe siècle, était à attribuer à la dysenterie. En 1832, environ un tiers de captifs déportés de façon clandestine à Bourbon aurait succombé à la dysenterie. E. Colin, « Notice sur le Mozambique », p. 328 ; Hubert Gerbeau, *L'esclavage et son ombre*, chapitre VI, p. 534.

159 William Henry Gardner (1814-1889) avait obtenu une formation médicale aux hôpitaux de Londres. Diplômé, il se rendit à la colonie de Maurice, où il exerça en qualité de chirurgien à l'hôpital et à l'établissement de quarantaine (notamment pour les malades de la variole).

160 Gardner, « History of an Epidemic… », p. 38.

161 Voir Marina Carter, Mark Hall, 2008, *The « Last Slaves….* »

162 The *Anti-Slavery Reporter* Nov 4, 1840 p. 285-286

163 Gardner, « History of an Epidemic… », p. 40.

164 Ce processus d'ethnogenèse des « Mozambiques » à l'île Maurice a été bien décrit par Alpers. E. A. Alpers, 2001, « Becoming « Mozambique » : Diaspora and Identity in Mauritius », in V. Teelock & E. A. Alpers, History, *Memory and Identity*, p. 117-155 ; Alpers,« Mozambique and « Mozambiques »… »», p. 39-61.

165 Les « Mozambiques » ont formé une diaspora africaine issue de la traite des esclaves, que l'on retrouvait aussi bien dans l'océan Indien que dans l'espace atlantique. Alpers, « Mozambique and « Mozambiques »… »p. 39-62.

166 À l'Ouest de Madagascar, des Makoa se sont rattachés à des ancêtres venus de « Morima » [de l'Afrique] sur le même bateau. Comme ces ancêtres étaient considérés comme des « frères » et « sœurs », l'union entre leurs descendants a été frappée du sceau de l'inceste, et était toujours proscrite dans les années 2000 dans certaines régions de l'Ouest de Madagascar. Voir Boyer-Rossol, *Entre les deux rives…*, p. 193-199.

167 Archives Nationale de Maurice (ANM) – Z7E3 Letters concerning the Liberated Africans from 1835 to 1850 ; Gardner, « History of an Epidemic…», p. 39.

168 Alpers,« Creolization and Identity… », p. 35.

169 Eyriès, « Analyse d'un Mémoire…», p. 219 note 3

170 Sur le maintien au XXe siècle de la langue makoa à l'Ouest de Madagascar, voir K. Boyer-Rossol, *Entre les deux rives….*

171 Teelock, « From Mozambique to Le Morne », p. 280.

172 *Ibidem*, p. 283-284.

173 D'Unienville (baron de), 1838, *Statistique de l'ile Maurice et ses dépendances, suivi d'une notice historique sur cette colonie et d'un essai sur l'île de Madagascar*, Paris, G. Barba, vol. 1., p. 279.

174 Teelock, « From Mozambique to Le Morne », p. 286.

175 En 1842, le père Laval mentionne tantôt 80.000, tantôt 70.000 Noirs émancipés à Maurice. On estime généralement entre 60.000 et 70.000 le nombre de personnes affranchies par l'abolition de 1835 à Maurice. Lettre du père Laval à Mr Nicolas Laval, son oncle, curé de Tourville-la-Campagne. Port-Louis, 1842 ; Lettre du père Laval à M. l'Abbé Nicolas-Philippe Letard, curé d'Epieds. Port-Louis, 23 juillet 1842. Hym Bernard Père, 2016, *Cœur à cœur avec le Père Laval à travers ses écrits*, Diocèse de Port-Louis, Ile Maurice, p. 61 ; p. 63-64.

176 Archives privées Froberville. Lettre d'Eugène de Froberville à sa mère Eugénie de Froberville. Port-Louis le 1er janvier 1846.

177 Aux Mascareignes, entre 1845 et 1847, Froberville recueillit des vocabulaires de 31 langues est-africaines (usitées dans une zone très étendue, du Sud de la Tanzanie aux actuels Malawi et Mozambique). Il en dressa divers lexiques comparés tout à fait originaux pour l'époque. Ces manuscrits ne furent jamais publiés. Archives privées Froberville. Eugène de Froberville, *Vocabulaire comparé*....

178 Hopper, « Liberated Africans... », p. 275.

179 Alpers, « Creolization and Identity », p. 37.

180 Carter, Govinden, Peerthum, "The Last Slaves", p. 100.

181 Voir Pier Larson, *Ocean of Letters : Language and Creolization in an Indian Ocean Diaspora.* Cambridge, Cambridge University Press, 2009.

182 Archives privées Froberville. Cahier Makua II ; Eugène de Froberville, *Tribus africaines.*

183 On retrouvait ce phénomène dans l'espace atlantique. Comme le rappelle Catherine Coquery-Vidrovitch, le processus de créolisation s'est déroulé en Afrique même, tout au long de la traite atlantique. Catherine Coquery-Vidrovitch & Eric Mesnard, 2013, *Être Esclave. Afrique-Amériques, XVe-XIXe siècle*, Paris, La Découverte, p. 187-208.

184 Alpers, « Creolization and Identity... », p. 31.

185 Concernant la créolisation en contexte d'esclavage à Maurice, voir l'ouvrage de Megan Vaughan, *Creating the Creole Island : Slavery in Eighteenth-Century Mauritius*, Duke University Press. 2005.

186 Archives privées Froberville. Cahier VaNiungue ; Froberville, *Ostro-Nègres*.

187 Newitt, *History of Mozambique*, p. 145.

188 Carter and Hall, 2008 (May), *The « Last Slaves » of Mauritius.*

189 *Ibidem.*

190 Voir Edward E. Alpers, « The Story of Swema : Female Vulnerability in Nineteenth-Century East Africa, » in Claire G. Robertson and Martin A. Klein (eds.), *Women and Slavery in Africa*, Madison, 1983, p. 185 ; A.C. Madan, *Kiungani or Story and History from Central Africa written by Boys in the Schools of the Universities' Mission to Central Africa*, London, George Bell and Sons, 1887 ; Petro Kilekwa, *Slave Boy to Priest : The Autobiography of Padre Petro Kilekwa*, trans. From Chinyanja by K.H. Nixon Smith, London, Universities' Mission to Central Africa, 1937. Cités par E.A. Alpers, « The Other Middle Passage », p. 24 ; 29.

191 Archives privées Froberville. Cahier Makua II. Entretien avec Mavēa dit John Lily, 18 ans, taille 1m60cms, Makua, tatoué sur le front et sur les tempes. Port-Louis, 28 août 1846.

192 Marina Carter, Mark Hall, 2008 (May), *The « Last Slaves »*....

193 Archives privées Froberville. Eugène de Froberville, *Notes ethnologiques sur l'Afrique orientale.*

194 Edward A. Alpers, « Creolization and Identity… », p. 31.
195 Archives privées Froberville. Eugène de Froberville, *Tribus africaines*.
196 Ces stratégies de retour en Afrique peuvent être qualifiées de stratégies diasporiques. Selon J. Harris, pour être opératoire, le concept de « diaspora africaine » suppose que soient réunies les trois conditions suivantes ; la dispersion globale à partir de l'Afrique, l'identité culturelle fondée à l'étranger sur l'origine et la condition sociale, et le retour psychologique ou physique à la terre natale en Afrique. J. Harris (ed.), 1993, *Global Dimensions of the African Diaspora*, Washington, DC, Howard University Press.
197 M. Carter, V. Govinden, S. Peerthum, 2003, *The Last Slaves*, p. 87.
198 *Ibidem*, p. 75.
199 *Ibidem*, p. 88.
200 MNHN. BIB Centrale. Ms 165 I. Eugène de Froberville, Notes sur les races de l'Afrique orientale au sud de l'Equateur, février 1849.
201 Archives privées Froberville. Cahier Makua II. Entretien avec Munliũa dit Nigaud Lily. Port-Louis, 2 août 1846.
202 Voir Nélia Dias, 2004, *La mesure des sens. Les anthropologues et le corps humain au XIX*[e] *siècle*, Paris, Aubier.
203 Voir Claude Blanckaert, « Les conditions d'émergence de la science des races au début du XIXe siècle », in S. Moussa (dir.), *L'Idée de « race » dans les sciences humaines et la littérature (XVIII*[e] *et XIX*[e] *siècle)*, Paris, L'Harmattan, 2003, p. 133-149.
204 L'ethnologie ou la « science des races » était encore dans sa phase naturaliste et s'inspirait de la zoologie pour construire des classifications raciales
205 Traditions orales familiales recueillies auprès de descendants de Huet de Froberville, en France, 2021.
206 Archives privées Froberville. Eugène de Froberville, *Notes ethnographiques sur l'Afrique orientale au sud de l'équateur ; avec planches et cartes géographiques (1848)*.
207 Père Bernard Hym, 2016, *Cœur à cœur avec le Père Laval à travers ses écrits*, Diocèse de Port-Louis, Ile Maurice, p. 62 ; 71 ; 217.
208 Joseph Michel, 1988, *De l'Esclavage à l'apostolat. Les auxiliaires laïcs du Bienheureux Jacques Laval apôtre de l'île Maurice*, Paris, Beauchesne, p. 86-87.
209 Archives privées Froberville. Lettre de Caroline de Froberville à sa belle-mère Eugénie de Froberville. Port-Louis, 29 décembre 1845.
210 325 Africains avaient été transportés en 1856 à bord du navire le *Mascareignes*. Ils avaient été embarqués à Ibo, au nord du Mozambique. Beaucoup était des jeunes garçons asservis à Ibo par des maîtres arabes et portugais. M. Carter, V. Govinden, S. Peerthum, *The Last Slaves*, p. 4.
211 Il est probable qu'Eugène de Froberville ait assisté à ces danses Inhambanes à Bourbon. Il en a fait des dessins (au crayon) qu'il a conservés au sein de ses collections privées en France.
212 Eugène de Froberville a ainsi notamment de la musique avec un vieil homme Nghindo, qui était un de ses principaux informateurs africains à Maurice et un « employé » à l'usine sucrière de la Baraque [Savannah] dans le sud de l'île. Archives privées Froberville. Correspondances d'Eugène de Froberville avec sa mère Eugénie née Bon (1845-1847).
213 On retrouve le lièvre comme une figure emblématique dans les contes makhuwa. N.J. Gueunier, « Documents sur la langue makhuwa », p. 315.
214 Archives privées Froberville. Lettre de Caroline de Froberville à sa belle-mère Eu-

génie de Froberville. Ile Maurice, le 19 mai 1846 ; Liste de caisses expédiées de Maurice en France.

215 Alpers, « Creolization and Identity », p. 32.

216 Alpers, « Creolization and Identity », p. 37 note de bas de page 29.

16

Documenting and Digitizing with Dignity:

Ethical Considerations and the West African Frontier Force Personnel Records

Katrina Keefer, Eric Lehman, Michael McGill, and Gabriela Mattia[1]

It was 1944, and Musa Fula[2] was in the process of being sentenced to three years of hard labor for his part in a series of thefts which took place at the place where his battery was stationed. A year earlier, he had been punished for being insufficiently alert while on duty and fined for his offense. Twice that year, Fula had been away without leave, and each time he was given a fine. After his sentence was completed, he was discharged from service with dishonor for his crime. He had been in the Frontier Force for only three years. Prior to his enlistment in 1941, Fula was an eighteen-year-old student, and was a practicing Muslim, like his father, the paramount chief Bunting Williams of

Mattru in Jong Chiefdom.[3] The crime he was accused of committing took place in India, far from his homeland of Sierra Leone, where British colonial battalions like the Frontier Force were to fight against the Japanese. Both in India and in Burma, African soldiers fought valiantly, meriting medals, and losing their lives as World War II raged. While broad-strokes narratives of these conflicts are known, and some details exist concerning the decorations which were earned, there have been few sources to understand what life was like for colonial soldiers like Musa Fula. In his file, which is held in a rice bag in the Sierra Leone Public Archives with approximately 6,000 others, the full transcripts may be found of his court martial, and the evidence heard against him. In his attestation papers, his vaccination scars are described, along with his height of 5'7", his skin tone, his religion, his home village, and his medical history during his brief time in the Frontier Force. Signatures as well as carefully inked and pressed thumbprints adorn the documents which present a snapshot of a young man finding himself in India, in the army, and before long, in trouble.

For soldiers who spent decades enlisted, the files which exist, in this case within the Sierra Leone Public Archives, represent lengthy narratives of their lives. They detail family visits, spouse's, parents', and children's names, vaccination records, accomplishments, offenses, and more. They often include photographs of individual soldiers, hand- and fingerprints, and dental records as well as identification tags in some cases. Regimental conduct sheets present detailed, year-by-year accounts, each one dated, signed, and documented. Attestation papers required each recruit to identify their home village, district, previous occupation, father's name, and ethnonym. They describe and typically include drawn versions of all identifying facial and body marks, differentiating between so-called "tribal" marks—including tattoos, secret society initiation marks, and ethno-linguistic scarification identifiers—and marks from medical interventions or past injuries. The value to modern scholars of this rich dataset is extraordinary, and applicable to a wide range of fields of study. Preserving, protecting, digitizing, and organizing these documents so that scholars can analyze and explore them is a clear need, and unquestionably, the information within this remarkable trove of material demands attention. In a broader context, this largely untouched dataset can be used as an exemplar for other, comparable datasets. Records of enslavement and manumission may present the same sets of challenges in terms of their important cultural heritage and need for preservation; the Frontier Force data poses a different challenge which pertains specifically to best practices. Because the information within these files is deeply personal, and in many cases comparatively recent, questions of anonymity, identity, and privacy arise which impose a reconsideration of best practices in these types of data. Scholars of slavery may wonder why this additional ramification is important, particularly with respect to centuries-old data, but it is our contention that when handling any individual and biographical data which could be connected to a living person, consideration should always be given to applying an ethical standard of practice. This approach rehumanizes the individuals and respects the fundamental dignity which belongs to every person, alive or dead.

From another perspective, the Frontier Force material is also well positioned to be an example of a dataset that requires technology and digital analysis due to its varied content. The richness of detail in each soldier's file necessitates the use of databases, and the condition of the documents demands that they be preserved. These data are clear, informative, and each file holds information which would be of interest to a variety of disciplines. There are significant challenges, however, which have caused our team to develop a standard of practice around each of them as we have engaged with them. We have identified the central challenges within this source as ethical, geographic, and organizational. In our haste to digitize, preserve, and examine the West African Frontier Force collections held throughout the former British West African colonies, it would be easy to forget that these men whose lives are so clearly recorded may well be the fathers and grandfathers of people alive today. The archives in Freetown hold extraordinarily rich material, and in quantities which are staggering in comparison to the usual dearth of accounts concerning the rank-and-file Frontier Force troops. Our first challenge is that within these files are many personal details of these men; their medical records often record venereal diseases, and court martial records can reveal behavior that would be embarrassing were the men in question alive today. There are ethical considerations which we as researchers must bring to bear as we begin the crucial process of preservation and digitization. Without question, these documents hold extraordinary potential—but it is potential which must be tempered by conscious efforts to protect the individual privacy of the people whose lives we are studying. Further, these documents represent the cultural heritage of a nation—as we work to preserve it, the issues of ownership and agency arise. We argue that in complex circumstances such as we find in Sierra Leone, new approaches must be employed to respect the archive itself as well as the lives it holds. In organizing the dataset, we have developed a method which permits us to efficiently catalog individual soldiers' lives and documents. A rich set of documents like the Frontier Force records represents a situation where we have individual soldier's files within which are multiple official forms, each one comprising multiple pages (Fig. 1).

As we digitize these files, we generate many files which must be arranged so that their contents can easily be sorted and analyzed. Our solutions are drawn from museological practices, and the theories of cataloging which have been developed for artifact acquisition. From the outset of our analysis, we realized that given the detail concerning individual soldier's home villages, we could plot demographics and patterns of recruitment. But this rapidly became a clear challenge as well. With respect to geography, we must carefully consider any effort to map these individual soldiers, as mapping itself poses methodological considerations. A deliberate from within this rich dataset. Overall, our team has explored each challenge in turn and collaboratively developed solutions which we propose as best practices in approaching any such dataset. Our proposals encompass scholarly applications, archival necessities, and ethical considerations which we argue should govern all digital humanities projects where a historical approach is required for the complex task of reconstructing trajectories, origins, and narratives from lives.

Figure 16.1
Court Martial of Musa Fula

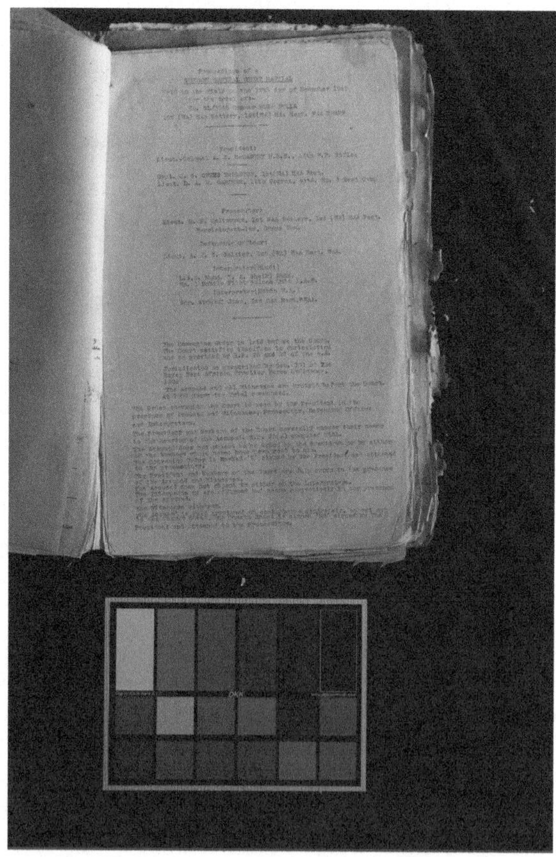

Source: West African Frontier Force Collection, Sierra Leone Public Archives

The Sierra Leone Public Archives

When considering the ethical elements of digitization and preservation of data sources such as this one, it is important to recognize the unique circumstances facing the archive itself. Established in 1895, the Sierra Leone Public Archive was formed to house British colonial government documents. During the Second World War, as the archival space was being used for the war effort, the documents from the archive were transferred to military buildings where they remained until after the war. In the 1950s, Christopher Fyfe was hired as Government Archivist to catalog, restore and preserve the collection of archives which had been left in disarray and was deteriorating from neglect. In 1965, under the Sierra Leone Public Archives Act, the Public Archives Office was founded and, under the direction of the Minister of Education, was designated to act as custodian of the national archives. Many of the documents in the archive are of vital interest and importance in understanding the trans-Atlantic Slave Trade and are made more remarkable by their survival in the face of social unrest and conflict. Today, the archives are located on the fourth floor of the Kennedy Building at Fourah Bay College atop of Mount Aureol in Freetown, the first westernized university established in West Africa.

Due to location changes during the war, previously well cataloged and indexed collections have become fragmented, leading to a chaotic situation within the archive which is aggravated by chronic understaffing and underfunding. When our team visited in February 2019, the Frontier Force records, in particular, were without an index and were held in approximately 60 rice bags kept on the floor around the perimeter of the archive. Each bag held at least one hundred personnel files. Clearly, this is not an ideal method of physical preservation, given the exposure to temperature and humidity in the space where the archives are housed. While the situation seems dire, understanding the underlying causes is important in working toward solutions. The problems faced by the archive are not due to lack of initiative or effort on the part of the team working within it but rather are due to a lack of resources and funds flowing to the archives. These make it difficult on an institutional level to properly catalog and preserve this otherwise rich collection, and the Frontier Force records especially.

The archivists outlined five distinct challenges to the archives when interviewed, all of which derive from a lack of annual capital to sustain the organization. The first issue is staffing deficiencies and fair wages for the university-trained archivists who earn very little each month. The second issue is personal safety and lack of protective equipment to handle deteriorating documents which have insect infestations and mold, and lack of access to equipment that would prevent dust and chemical exposure. Archivists noted that if they are exposed to illness-inducing levels of toxicity, they are responsible for their own medical bills. The third difficulty concerns education and being isolated and not part of an international community. There is no institutional budget to pay national or international membership fees, so archivists cannot regularly participate in seminars and training initiatives beyond those provided by generous international scholars on an individual basis. The fourth obstacle is at the level of technology. With ongoing advances in digital technology, cameras able to capture the highest resolution images of degrading documents are essential to preserve materials for future use. Regular and stable internet access is vital to allow cloud storage of digitized data, but this problem arises from ongoing difficulties around power generation in the country. Here again, cost restrictions militate against the proper preservation of archival materials. The fifth restriction has to do with the physical archive reaching capacity and the inability to receive new acquisitions. A lack of physical space means that the archive could potentially be turning down new collections that come to them. In addition to the five problems outlined by the archivists, there is another. The condition of the building in which the archives are held does not lend itself to effective conservation. During our 2019 visit there was a broken window by the tables where the team was working to digitize documents, exposing them to dust and other environmental elements from outside and aiding in the deterioration of the archive's holdings. These issues are systemic, pervasive, and governed by limitations within the country which cannot be easily met by securing periodical external grants or through personal funds raised by researchers.

In recent years, the British Library's Endangered Archives Programme (EAP) has been actively involved in funding preservation efforts at the Sierra Leone Public Archives. Five grants totalling just over £110,000 have been awarded to digitize records at the archives.[4] Complex research networks funded in part by these grants have been developed by leading international scholars including Paul E. Lovejoy and Suzanne Schwarz, and these scholars have actively worked to secure ongoing funding to support the archive and seek training for the archivists, including forthcoming grants both from the British Library and Canada's Social Sciences and Humanities Research Council. A further CDN $25,000 has been dedicated to the preservation of the archive from Lovejoy's research funds, and a further CDN $23,000 from Katrina Keefer's projects concerning the digitization of the WAFF records. Lovejoy and Schwarz's projects in particular have systematically digitized materials beginning with the earliest documents and moving forward chronologically in an ongoing effort. Under the EAP funding initiative, many historical documents including registers of Liberated Africans, registers of birth, John Clarkson's letter book and journal, important treaties and agreements, census, military, school and police records, and railway and communication documents have been digitized and shared online to assist research into the histories of Sierra Leone and the trans-Atlantic Slave Trade. Without question their work has been transformative for the archive, with a total of 264 volumes digitized to date, amounting to 74,000 images, and with funds dedicated to the individual training and support of archivists overseas. While the EAP is a valuable granting approach and the work of international teams has been extraordinary, the Endangered Archives Programme does not go nearly far enough and cannot be expected to fill the existing funding gap—these problems are deeply rooted, and solutions must ultimately come from within the nation. No matter how monumental the ongoing work to digitally preserve these documents has been, the hurdles are greater by several orders of magnitude than can be met by any international team or granting agency no matter how generous. The underlying problems of chronic underfunding at the national level, an inventory in disarray and a building in disrepair, are compounded by the fundamental disruption of the civil war, and many documents were left in very bad condition, which has necessitated a triage approach for the teams working in the archive over the past ten years. This is a matter of developing capacity in-country and working toward a self-sustaining system which is less reliant upon international granting agencies and which funds the archive adequately on a regular yearly basis from within the country, permitting the reorganization and inventory of holdings, and the preservation of the physical documents. The mandate of the EAP is not to conserve the actual physical documents but to preserve digitally the information contained in the archives for future generations and provide access (Case 2015, xliv). As Barry Supple observes:

> it was not envisaged that the EAP would support focused work on the physical preservation of material. . . it was not always easy to maintain the distinction between preserving by sustaining and copying and preserving by protecting archives through the acquisition of storage materials and other means of physical maintenance of archives (Supple 2015: xii).

Ongoing efforts by international scholars such as Lovejoy and Schwarz to obtain funding to support the archives in Freetown are testament to their individual commitment to the incredible collection there alongside fulfilling the EAP's overall purpose. In effect, they have modelled a standard of practice in their extraordinary efforts in Freetown. Their teams posted rules in the reading room to ensure that visiting researchers respected the archives, and collaboratively developed a mandate that all digitization which takes place should result in a copy being left with the archive also. While the archive is in disrepair, it is proof of intense work both by the archivists themselves and by scholars such as Lovejoy and Schwarz that matters are improving, and ceaseless work by the chief archivist, Mr. Albert Moore, is ongoing to address the need to include archive preservation into the national budget. Collaborators are working with engaged Afro-descendants to secure additional funding to preserve the physical space of the archive and improve the conditions of the collection.

To see these archives as neglected or to assume that their present condition is due to disinterest misrepresents the efforts of the archivists themselves as well as committed international collaborators. These archives are underfunded. The archivists who work there do so out of a pride and affection for the material not necessarily held by the researchers who step through the doors. It is *their* history, or as one archivist, Aiah Yendeh, stated in 2019, it is their "beloved archives." He elaborated in an interview with our team that "The motivation, I think, is just passion. For me, I see these records as my baby. You know, I love it so much. It's not always about money. Preservation of our history, you know, to me, is key. That is why I am here, and I have no intention of leaving." Similarly, archivist Joannes Caulker stated that

> [T]hese documents have [great] importance, they have vital records.... The money wasn't my focus, actually. I was thinking about how best I could promote the institution in my own little way and giving out what I can. So that is what has been keeping me and because of the nature, like I said, of the [archive] I grew a love for it and it's because of the love that has kept me in the profession up to this time.

Unfortunately for too many researchers, digitization of images without consideration of the ongoing benefit of the archive or its physical holdings remains a serious problem. This is the crux of the ethical considerations we have developed: although we respect the incredible importance of digitally preserving these materials through programs like the EAP, and the work done by teams of researchers to this point, our team also believes that the best practices that should be developed in this case and others in equally challenging circumstances must also be respect for the dignity of the archive itself, and the continued preservation of original documents in addition to any digitization effort. As such, our project follows established standards of practice developed by Lovejoy and Schwarz, and is dedicated to developing a clear process and method as we engage with these records, as well as with the physical building and the people who work with them.

While still abiding by the British Library standard procedure for digitization to ensure the highest possible quality of image, we believe that researchers must find ways to support the physical preservation of these materials as well as their digitization. Digital researchers must not only be engaged in the process of preserving the historical documents that are housed within the archive, but also in making relationships with the archivist teams who have worked to preserve them. Lovejoy and Schwarz's efforts over the past decade are exemplars of this approach, and we believe that all teams should similarly develop close connections and assist in building local capacity to their best of their abilities. For these archivists, the archives are like home. As Jacques Derrida noted, the word "archive" is derived from the Greek word *arkheion* meaning house, and the *archons* are the guardians of the documents which reside in the archive (Derrida 1996, 2). Archives are sites of power. What archivists do is "literally creat[e] archives, deciding what is remembered and what is forgotten, who in society is visible and who remains invisible, who has a voice and who does not" (Kenosi 2000, 67). These theoretical considerations and ideas are not abstract in our example. Archives can preserve colonial legacies and maintain histories of unequal access, privileging outside researchers over the people whose histories are preserved there. This is not to say that this is inevitably the case, but the power imbalance is one which we believe must be considered as research teams approach archives which are already facing challenging circumstances. We argue here that the most effective approach in these post-colonial nations must explicitly be to return the power to African control, and to work in harmony with those who are preserving their own cultural heritage. Just as we are working to consider issues concerning individual privacy for the lives recorded within these archives, we believe that the guiding principle in digital humanities projects include explicit consideration and respect for the physical space of the archive and those who work within it.

Approaching the Data: Cataloging Concerns and Access Possibilities

As we develop guidelines on a theoretical level engaging with the ethics of the archive, we also have been developing a meticulous approach to the intake and digitization of the personnel files themselves. The variety of types of information held within an individual soldier's folders is remarkable, both in the sense of types of record generated by the military itself and in variations we have documented of these records. This poses a series of unique challenges as we organize and transcribe the information within each document. During three years of cataloging and the digitization of raw data, we have identified over a hundred types of military record. A systematized intake process is necessary not only for this dataset but for other rich sources of data which offer complex problems in terms of their diversity or organizational structure.

> The process of digitizing the original documents happens *in situ*, following the British Library guidelines given the unique environment of the archive itself. Not every building in which the documents are housed has regularly available electricity, and in particular, the Student Centre in which the Frontier Force materials are held was without power during our trips. The digitization is done with a black fabric laid out on the archive's floor, with a color reference to ensure accuracy in reproduction, a digital SLR camera, remote tethering software and controls, and a tripod. Our research teams were trained in digitization at the Harriett Tubman Institute at York

> University, and all such digitization adheres to digitization standards of practice as closely as is possible. Documents are photographed and checked for focus using a remote shooting application on a tablet and are saved in both RAW and .jpg format to permit the highest resolution as well as quick reference. Over three years of trips collecting this data with a limited team, we have accumulated over four thousand photographs using this process. The team is now developing ways of organizing and presenting the documents so that scholars and others interested in conducting primary research can access the information in organized files. A central aspect of our methodology hinges on our team's theories of identity, ethics, and the meanings behind data. Not only do we want people to read the transcripts and the original documents, but we also want to organize what is collected in such a way that people will understand a fundamental theme of our work: before the image, before the paper, even before the moment something happened and that someone decided to write it down—there were people. People living their lives, within a society, with complex relations and organization. The document will never fully explain that unique life, but considered in the context of other documents, oral history, and visualization, scholars and the general public can potentially understand more of the connection between past peoples and modern cultures.

To achieve this goal, it is fundamental to know the content of the files and to catalog the information. The cataloging process itself requires a strategy to match the users' needs (Rodrigues 2006). Faced with thousands of digitized files divided by the year they were created; we have identified the main hurdles: how to approach the files ethically given the intensely private details held within each personnel file? How can we keep the information interlaced and connected without dismembering the folders and files? How can we keep all the files together if we have medical records within other documents and need to apply an anonymizing filter?

We decided to approach each person's personnel file as one object for the purposes of organization. This means that all the individual documents of one person are seen as subdivisions of the object, each file receiving a sequenced number, the first one being "0001" and the others following. Each such entry is in effect a digital folder, identified by the army identification number and the person's last name. Within it, we input the files, replicating the original sequence within the physical folder, and so respect any meaning that the original sequence may have had. A problem we are still discussing is the number of the whole object and collection in our catalog. We understand that for privacy reasons, the last name and army number cannot be the main information provided to the general public. We further recognize that those who have personal, familial connections to a given soldier whose documents we have digitized would reasonably expect access to their family member's documents. We are therefore working to implement procedures relating to concerns about access and privacy which respect family connections while preserving the dignity of the person behind the data. One possibility is to create an alphanumeric number for each such object. This would mean that by looking at the inventory of alphanumeric Frontier Force data, researchers would immediately ascertain which collection the file is from and its origin—this has the potential to allow further research into West African Frontier Force documents in different archives beyond the Sierra Leone dataset. It would also show us how many objects we have and how many subdivisions each one has. The alphanumeric number would start with the collection, "WAFF" for West African Frontier Forces, followed by its origin, "SLPA" for Sierra Leone Public Archives. The object receives a number (according to the order of appearance), and its files have the sequenced number (beginning with "0001"). So, as an example, the first file of the first object, the alphanumeric number would be "WAFF_SLPA_I_0001". If the team finds some West African Frontier Force folders in the National Archives of Nigeria, for example, the first object with its first file would be "WAFF_NAN_I_0001".

Each object, meaning each personnel file, has a form created as it is digitized to provide metainformation and allow for data management. This can be accessed by the team manager of this project, with some sections available to the public. Metainformation around data management begins with a section of identification with a catalog number, army number and last name, and original (physical) source. There would be also the year the data was recorded; the researcher responsible for the digitization; date of last edition in the form; how many subdivisions the form has. Then a table showing the file's alphanumeric number in the first column, the title of the military record in the second column, and the third column showing which documents within the personnel file are confidential. The last column to be filled would be completed if a personnel file includes additional data pertaining to research projects—in our case, body-marking information. We are proposing that the section would end with a contextualization that would explain in a less formal way what the files contain about that person, and that would be available in the platform for general users.

Following the identification section, we are developing an object history element. Based on Peter Van Mensch's dimensional matrices and his approach to the incorporation of artifacts into museums (1987), we are organizing our structure with one designated space for physical properties (information on the material that supports the information), a second for meanings and roles (primary, second and metaphysical) and a third for the object's history (where it was produced, who filled it; its first uses and how it ended in the archive (object path/track) (Mensch 1987). In addition, we are developing a management of the object section. Ideally, we would have automatically updated data on the use of the object and, specifically, its subdivisions. As an example, if there were a video that appears in one file, it would appear in the object's documentation form and would track access and views by the general public in the platform. This would permit real-time harvesting of meta-data around the uses of harvested and curated information by researchers and the public. In this section there is also information on current study-projects that are using the object, references to studies published, uses in web exhibitions, blog posts, educational activities, and any other purpose.

It is important to keep in mind that the catalog and the information about each document will keep growing. Not only will the team continue collecting raw digitized files, but we intend to harvest metrics around how many people open the files, which files, and who the people are who are accessing the documents. One way of achieving this is for users to access our platform through a social media, such as Google or Facebook, sharing demographic information (gender, age, and country). They could have a simple profile enabling them to have easy access to what they have found and "saved", the reports they have created through the advanced searching tool.

But how can we make the data more approachable and accessible? We aim to provide a relevant and useful platform for scholars and researchers which at the same time engages students, the public, and all of those interested in non-formal ways of learning. We must also continue to respect the dignity of the people whose data this is, which means working to anonymize certain information to preserve privacy. We are still studying ways of achieving this, through patrimonial education, museology approaches, public history, and web design combined in an interdisciplinary approach (Saye 2015). Our team is also collaboratively developing protocols to manage the often-sensitive information which these personnel files include. The medical records specifically would not be entirely accessible to researchers nor to the public, but they would be cataloged. While we fully recognize the importance of studying medical history—particularly military medical history—the team is developing a different approach to the data. We intend to have all information transcribed and organized in metadata, which will allow researchers to access reports which would be anonymized and cleaned of identifying individual information. Those reports would be created based on the advanced search tool, with the term searched for each period, resulting in quantified information. This might be exclusively applied to medical information or even expanded to other types of documentation. Our purpose here is to preserve the dignity of individual soldiers while ensuring access to importance data points for statistical analysis.

Challenges of Mapping Colonial Sources

The West African Frontier Force material offers scholars and researchers an extraordinary glimpse into the careers and lives of enlisted Africans. Files also permit possible demographic analyses, as every attestation includes information which locates the recruit in time and space. It would seem simple enough to develop a map of these clearly indicated origins and homes, and determine distribution of recruits from different provinces, districts, and villages. But in practice it proved to be considerably harder than we had anticipated.

African geography drawn from colonial sources has been a consistent problem for cartographic scholars.[5] Mapping even in the supposedly rational nineteenth century was ultimately propositional in nature (Bassett and Porter 1991, 370). Maps are at their core visualizations which serve to shape our collective idea of geography. As a medium, cartography is represented as authoritative and accurate, but until the age of satellite mapping, cartography was often not as objective nor as true as viewers might imagine.[6] The debate over the ultimately imaginary "Kong Mountain range" is one example of a case where cartographers and geographers' efforts to define and reify the land they saw was filtered through theories, inherent biases, and debate (Bassett and Porter 1991, 381). It was assumed that there had to be a mountain range to explain the transition between the Sahara Desert and the forest belt, and European cartographers ultimately decided that the "Kong Mountains" stretched across the continent to explain this phenomenon; of course, they do not actually exist! They were first created in 1798 on a map of the continent which relied on accounts by Mungo Park and were replicated on all subsequent maps. These fictional mountains existed purely in the realms of imagination from the early 19th century until eventually dispelled after the late 1880's expedition of Louis-Gustave Binger (Fig. 16.2).

More often than not, in fact, explorers' and geographers' mapping relied heavily on local knowledge of the regions being mapped. African scholars have described many of the challenges which European explorers faced when attempting to grasp spatial relationships in Africa (Jones and Voigt 2012, 12). Mapping served to articulate a European-dominated perspective of the continent as a largely empty land in such narratives. Traveller accounts, which included African accounts of geography and regions, had to be compared carefully to European accounts for veracity, but all such accounts were relying upon accessibility of terrain, and the so-called reliability of African informants (Fritsch 2009). Maps are perceived as unbiased and neutral but, particularly during the colonial era, they served to reinforce biases. If a map published by a reputable press did not indicate that a place existed, then it did not exist. All maps distort reality to some degree, as they are ultimately abstractions which attempt to reduce a complex reality into analog clarity (Stickler 1990, 329).[7] Few maps prior to the present day allowed enough space to accurately reproduce smaller settlements, which often led to the erroneous conclusion that regions of a given map were uninhabited.

Figure 16.2
The Fictional Kong Mountain Range

Source: John Cary, *A New Map of Africa, From the Latest Authorities*, London, J. Cary, Engraver & Map-seller, 1805.

West Africa is one of the densest geographic regions on the continent with respect to the variation of ethnic groups, language, religion, and heritage. Attempts to map this region, especially historically, have proven extremely difficult, as the density and turbulence of West Africa makes tracing groups and states challenging. The sheer amount of variation in the area has historically led to immense changes over short periods of time, quickly making previously up-to-date maps obsolete, and as Henry B. Lovejoy (2019) has noted, historical maps of the region depended on misguided ideas of the geography, inaccurate accounts, and incomplete data. Once Europeans began to map the region in pursuit of colonial goals, they did so with little sensitivity to accuracy. European records were sloppy, inaccurate, and often filled with misinformation. Moreover, European cartographers were reliant not only on

African informants, but also on well-trodden African trade paths and networks (Fritsch 2009, 89). Colonial European explorers were stepping into a region with its own spatial understandings already at work, intent on making names for themselves back in Europe as discoverers, relying on African narratives and assistance. Some European travelers recorded the ways in which local knowledge and approaches to mapping differed from their own, anticipating further complications that we would encounter in our own effort to accurately place Frontier Force birthplaces reliably onto a map of Sierra Leone. Maps of the colonial era represent a shift in the way that Europeans approached Africa on a conceptual level. They reflect the establishment of administrations on the ground which demanded the identification of local populations but were otherwise often wildly inaccurate (Stone 1988, 59). This lack of accuracy becomes more serious when dealing with identities and origins during the slave period. Our team approached the colonial period with care, initially assuming that as more maps were being produced at that time for purposes of expansion and exploitation, we might have more material to work with. Instead, as we rapidly discovered, the issues cartographic scholars have raised with mapping and colonialism made achieving accuracy extremely difficult.

One of the central requirements of our project is to trace and map the trajectories of the individuals who served in the Frontier Force. This is a fundamental prerequisite for the visualization of demography and analysis of enlisted Africans. The data within each soldier's attestation is helpful information, but once again, the colonial officers who recorded this information were prone to misidentification characterized by misspellings. This has presented specific and unique problems as we attempted to trace the geographic origins and destinations of these individuals. It is of the utmost importance to outline and approach these challenges carefully, to be aware of cultural sensitivities and change, and to work towards finding the best possible outcomes. Some complexities in mapping have already been laid out, but it is important to explore them in more detail. Even use of current best practices in QGIS presents problems, as "within this scope of an immeasurable amount of missing data, the maps… must always be treated as approximations because of inexact and missing data, limitations in software functionality and any errors of interpretation of the sources" (Lovejoy 2019, 129). Accurate historical mapping even with the best possible tools is no small challenge. Regional conflicts during the precolonial period, as well as during the era of the slave trade, saw kingdoms and smaller states rise and fall on a regular basis. Of course, the invasion and formal colonization of much of West Africa in the 19th century saw borders redrawn, states abolished, and ethnic groups either obliterated or forced into common larger groupings. The cartographic face of West Africa was in regular flux and not merely in the context of uncertain maps and inadequate data.

The source material itself for developing a clear and accurate map of Sierra Leone from the appropriate period is problematic. When the Europeans arrived, there was little care taken to preserve the history of the region, which was largely handed down by local traditions and oral communication. With the division, separation, and exploitation of many groups, the oral source material was lost, making rebuilding the exact geography difficult. There were certainly attempts at mapping the region, but many of the European efforts, without the contextualization of local traditions, were inaccurate. This, again, is because earlier Europeans largely remained along the coast to trade slaves and other goods and took extreme liberties in mapping the interior. Moreover, later cartographers would work with these older maps and base their new renditions on that misinformation. In effect, errors were reified and often magnified as maps were drawn from previous maps rather than from personal experience. The Kong Mountains provide the best example of mistakes becoming normalized.

In specific terms, as we tried to reconcile the Frontier Force data with existing maps of Sierra Leone, the largest immediate problem we faced was the mislabelling and misspelling of toponyms. If information is not accurate, it can very quickly make a map obsolete. The notes of the colonial officers and cartographers used to produce many presumably authoritative nineteenth century maps were regularly inconsistent and were often based on phonetic representations of an original word. Moreover, colonial-era maps were often generated in comparative haste, necessitating colonial surveys which relied on District Officers, themselves amateur cartographers. At their best, these mapmakers required professional expertise they often lacked, the maps themselves necessitating cadastral surveys intended to define alienated land, townships and building plots, roads, and railways to administer and establish control (Stone 1988, 60-61). Such surveys took time and care, and resulting from the fragmented expertise available, the colonial period represents an often disjointed approach to mapping in Africa caused by the pressures of administration and the exertion of colonial authority. Colonial maps for Sierra Leone offer numerous examples of this disjunction, not the least of which is the irregularity of ethnonyms applied to specific regions and the inconsistent naming of settlements and villages. For instance, the Temne ethnic group would often be labelled as "Timmannee" or "Timene," or the Vai as "Foy" or even "Gallina." Given the complex tapestry of ethnic groups in the region, this often blurred the lines for colonial officials, who had very little prior knowledge of these groupings. These are some of the clearer examples of misunderstanding to be found in European notes and writings. Despite the descriptions of home villages in the Frontier Force attestations, when we tried to locate the villages in questions, some proved entirely untraceable.

Map 16.1
Sierra Leone, 1898

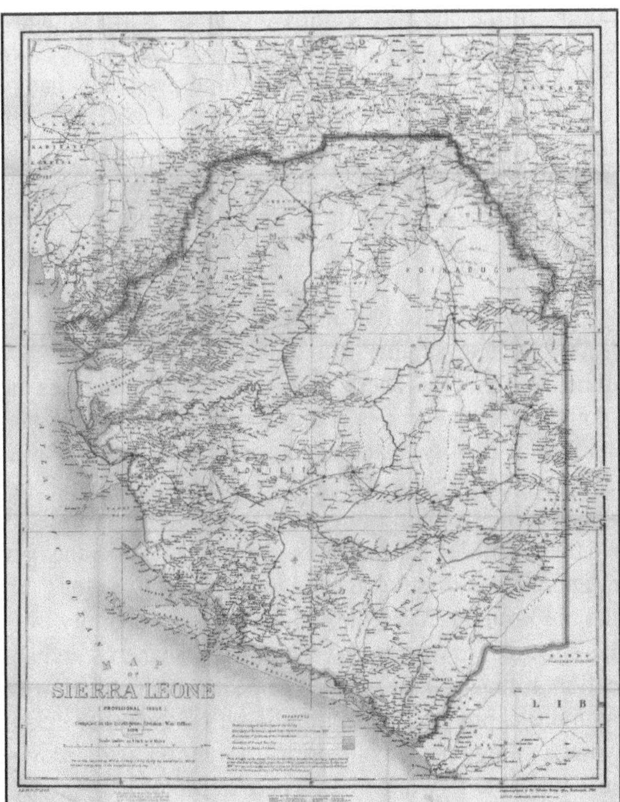

Source: Provisional Issue, Intelligence Division, War Office, London, from survey by E. de P. O'Kelly, 1897-1898.

For our project, we began with a map (Map 16.1) that we selected primarily because of the relative time- period in which it had been drawn, and the considerable number of small villages that we found named on it. It is a typical example of a colonial-era map and includes a remarkable number of small settlements and villages, primarily situated along the waterways which colonial officials could readily navigate. This map also represents a combination of the multiple issues we have identified. The survey was prepared by E. de P. O'Kelly in 1897–1898 and was published in 1898, which makes it one of the earlier extant maps of Sierra Leone's interior. Previous maps focused on the coast and largely neglected the kingdoms inland. This one was important because it was published only a short time after the Paris Treaty of 1895, which formally established the colony's boundaries. Even more significantly, the map was created at the outset of the Hut Tax War of 1898, fought between Sierra Leoneans and the British over severe taxation of local populations. In the end, that conflict decimated the population, and quite literally wiped entire villages off the map (Abraham 1974). Because of the results of the 1898 war, as well as other colonial pressures that we have outlined, subsequent maps do not provide the same level of detail as the 1898 version, and many villages can no longer be found. This is only one part of the issue, however. The 1898 map, while much more useful in its detail, falls victim to the mislabelling and misspelling typical of similar colonial maps. Many of the village and town names are entirely misspelt or placed in the wrong location altogether. The shifting borders, which were being negotiated at that time and only settled into their modern configuration in 1912, make it nearly impossible to map smaller settlements in the present-day border regions with Guinea and Liberia. These are just some of the hurdles facing us when it comes to mapping the origins of the Frontier Force individuals. The intricate combination of density, colonialism, and cartographic biases in the region have greatly impeded scholars' ability to accurately map this period of Sierra Leone's history. It is difficult to retrace and follow the trajectories of individuals when there is little chance of locating their origin in the first place.

Our project approaches these challenges in a variety of ways. First, we are fortunate that the Frontier Force files contain a large quantity of detailed information. This allows us to work with various factors when searching for an individual's location. If their village or town name is misidentified, we are still able to deduce a more approximate location based on the other information. For example, when a village name is incorrect, the individual's province and chiefdom are still available to work from. The chiefdoms still largely reflect those established at the end of the 19th century, which is beneficial to us. Once we have located the areas in question, we are able to search more closely on present-day maps to try and determine an approximate location for a village. Best practices would therefore require us to analysis derived from many maps spanning many years, prioritizing the earliest and most detailed, and using more recent maps to cross-reference. This is in line with H. Lovejoy's methodology to defragment multiple primary and secondary source-maps (H. Lovejoy 2013, 444). While this does not always succeed, we are able at least to deduce what region or chiefdom of the country these individuals originated from, which is still entirely useful data. Modern mapping technology, particularly satellite-based examples like Google Maps, is useful in many cases when it comes to mapping smaller villages. However, it is still necessary to conduct research into possible alternate names and spelling, so that searches will prove fruitful. This project is about tracing origins with the tools we have, and thanks to newer technologies we are drawing steadily closer to our goals. For the time being, however, the methods we are developing require this careful cross-referencing system and are time-consuming and inefficient.

A major element to our approach to the mapping of individuals onto geography is the importance our project places on awareness of potentially neocolonial processes. Our efforts require ongoing collaborative discussion with those whose countries and histories we are mapping. Their experience within the regions, and their access to traditions which may clarify the ways that place names have changed, are crucial parts of reconstructing Frontier Force soldiers' lives. Working to share ideas with scholars and archivists on the continent also ensures that there is ongoing African input concerning the cultural histories which after all originate in and belong to Africans.

Mapping West African history, especially with respect to ethnicity, religion, and language, is difficult. Descriptions of locations, groupings of people, or other ethnic signifiers were largely written and produced by Europeans, many of whom were colonial officials. The sources are often misleading, inaccurate, misspelt, or incorrectly labelled, with the result that reliable sources became ever more difficult to find. Colonialism and subsequent postcolonial conflict in West Africa have led to the loss of much useful source-material as well as to the production of problematic, frequently inaccurate, and sometimes biased maps.

We have explored our specific project and how it relates to the visualization of West African geographic history, and in particular the complexity of situating enlisted Africans in relation to their birthplaces. With a close reading of the Frontier Force records, we are beginning to piece together information and to map the locations of soldiers. But this is only a small contribution. We have taken steps to work with connections in Sierra Leone itself, which is a vital methodological approach to mapping history. Without the assistance of local West Africans, and their valuable input as members of the communities whose geography we are trying to rebuild, all efforts would be in vain. The people know their own societies and cultural traditions better than anyone; their involvement is therefore of paramount importance. It is not that we *should* work with West Africans in attempting to map the historical geography of the region, but that we *must* work with them to retrace successfully and honestly what has been lost. It has been written that "history is both a discourse of knowledge and a discourse of power" (Mudimbe 1988, 188). Rebuilding the past is no different. We must share that power equally and avoid straying once again down a colonial road.

Even as maps have served to define colonial power, so too have archives served to preserve selective evidence. Just as the blank space on an inaccurate map can neglect or obscure African power in a framing of narrative, so too have archives held the potential to frame national narratives in how they preserve and what they preserve. Our team is therefore considering these elements as we develop a process which may be applied to similarly complex collections.

We are working to develop a best practice which recognizes the two forces at play here: Without question, it is important to preserve important documents such as the Frontier Force collection for future generations, but at the archival level we must move beyond mere preservation and towards empowering the archivists and giving them agency to act as guardians of their own records, keepers of their own house. In this way, the project will continue to engage in discussion with the archival team to develop initiatives and partnerships which address the needs they have expressed to us. The eventual ideal outcome would be that even in the absence of privileged scholars arriving with significant grant monies, the archive can preserve and conserve the histories of their nation on an ongoing basis. More training and dialogue are planned for when the team returns, and projects are being developed which would fuel capacity-building and autonomy. While researchers may have received grants for their own research, there is often little to spare for conservation efforts. As regards raising salaries, hiring more archivists, and designating more space and adequate conditions for documents, this an evolving process. Helping the archivists in their mission to validate the importance of this national treasure is a step in the right direction. Individual project teams can only do so much, but as we collectively develop a method which not only emphasizes the importance of data, but prioritizes people, we believe that we can do much more than salvage history.

This development extends to efforts to map history and origins; as with the archive, it is crucial for scholars to consider all sources of information including oral histories and local knowledge. This is integral to the practice of restoring control to the descendants of those whose lives these documents describe and integral to our methodological practice as we continue our own project and research. Our central contention with respect to best practices is this: that all work being done on the continent must begin with a theoretical consideration of ways of developing and facilitating agency in a way that is not just non-colonial but actively anti-colonial in its approach. The data which we digitize belongs to the nations within which it is found, and the stories we work to tell as historians demand that we dignify the people whose stories they are. Otherwise, they vanish into obscurity, like Musa Fula, whose brief experience captured within data from the Frontier Force represents the only glimpse at a life. As the son of a chief who was wrongfully accused and convicted of cannibalism in 1912, but who clearly returned to father him, Musa Fula's story deserves more remembrance than a trial for petty theft in 1944 and then dust-choked silence.

EndNotes

1 Originally published in *Esclavages & Post-esclavages* 3 (2020): https://journals.openedition.org/slaveries/3498.

2 Fula's name is spelled throughout his personnel file variously as Mussa Fula, Musa Fula, or Musa Fulla.

3 Fula's paternity is of interest because his father was one of the main suspects in the 1913 Special Commission Court cases which were heard in Gbangbama, Sierra Leone. They concerned claims of cannibalism and a society of men in the region called the Human Leopards, and as a group the cases display competing interests and ongoing tensions in the Protectorate there. For more, see Keefer, Katrina, *Under the Leopard Skin*, forthcoming.

4 British Library, "Endangered Archives Programme," www.eap.bl.uk/ (last accessed, October 2020).

5 Recent scholarship, such as Henry B. Lovejoy's contributions to the methodology of mapping, have been of considerable help for our own project. In the next phase of our project, we will be applying his QGIS methods to address the issues raised in this article. See H. Lovejoy 2019.

6 Beyond honest inaccuracies, there are considerable issues with maps which consistently under-represent African settlement sizes, reinforcing colonial biases and perceptions. See Stickler 1990.

7 As Stickler explains, however, often this pragmatic need to reduce the complexity of towns in settler societies such as South Africa led to the excision of African towns, while settler towns remained, producing a false and biased view of reality.

Appendix

"Walk With Web Inc: Technical Description of Digital Humanities"

Kartikay Chadha

The WWW technical architecture (Fig. 1) was designed to support research projects by ensuring on-going addition of data and sustainability. The dedicated servers provided by WWW hold physical backup of the research data creating new "digital best practices" in versioning the development process by using professional services, such as Github, to allow possible roll backs and reports on development timelines. The RegID web-application was intended to act as an interface between users, including researchers and/or the general public, and the backend servers. This architecture also relied on a combination of multiple hosting server computers, which allowed sharing of large volume resources among projects and promoting inter-connection between datasets.

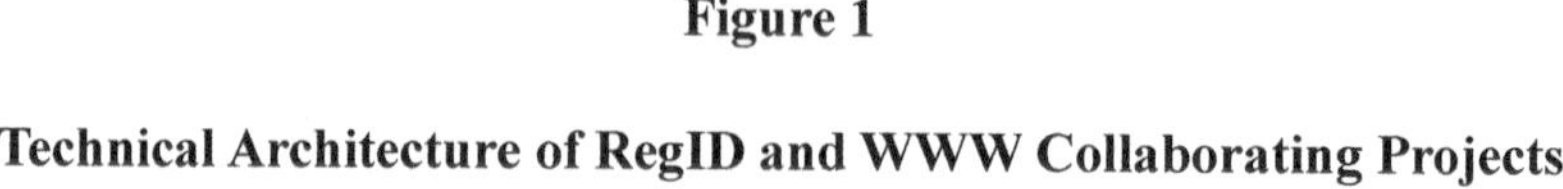

Figure 1

Technical Architecture of RegID and WWW Collaborating Projects

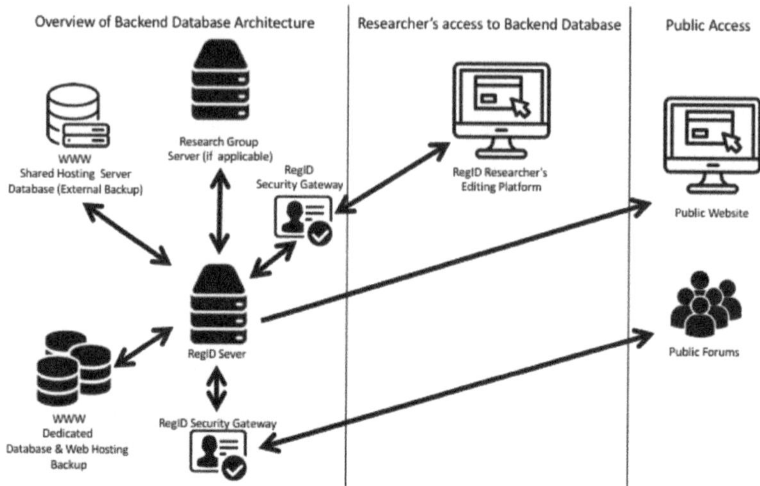

The research data, although open source, was to be secured using a novel RegID security gateway to allow different access levels to developers, project directors, researchers and members of the public at large (Fig. 2). WWW methodology was designed with four primary components:

1. Sourcing, i.e., the identification and processing of various bodies of primary documents such as historical manuscripts.
2. Execution, i.e., the application of WWW technological experience in creating, expanding, and combining databases for purposes of analysis.
3. Analysis, i.e., automation of research analytical methodologies to address research questions concerning the origins of individuals, the mechanisms for enslavement, the contours of enforced migration, the demographic implications of migration, individual status and ethnic/linguistic identification.
4. Interpretation, i.e., reconsideration of African content in the form of digital identities and in the global context of migration allowing re-evaluation of how slavery shaped the political, economic, and social landscape of continental Africa and infused the receiving areas of migration with cultural influences, both within West Africa, and across the Atlantic in Americas and the Sahara to the Mediterranean.
5. Sustain, i.e., preserve the digital outcomes of research projects in a secured virtual space for long-term access, ensuring accommodation

of new discoveries and interpretations.

Figure 2
Five principles of Design Thinking process in User-centered Design

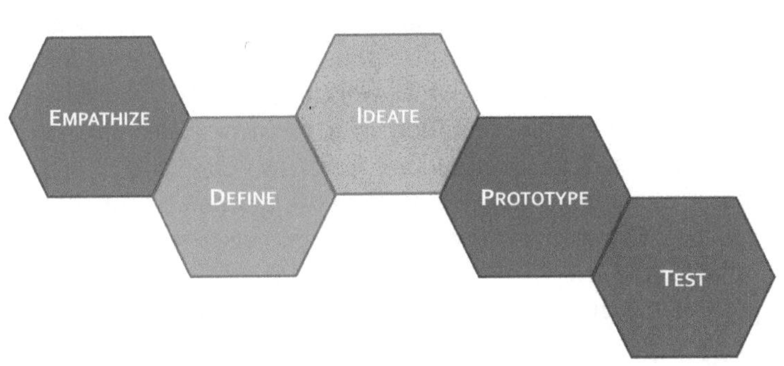

These components were derived by employing research methodologies like *Design Thinking* in UCD. The theoretical concept of UCD is defined as interaction of human and machine to improve usability of digital platforms, software, websites, and mobile applications (Newell et al. 2011). *Design Thinking* methods provide a productive, iterative approach to engage divergent thinking by offering an appropriate process to iterate the research approach in five successive stages (Greenwood et al. 2019): Empathize, Define, Ideate, Prototype, and Test (Fig. 2). This method has allowed computer developers to understand user needs and develop solutions by involving user input at every step of the development process.

WWW has divided the technical end of digital humanities into two components: the front-end interfaces and the back-end databases. The *design thinking* process directly assists in development of the front-end interface, while supporting the backend database framework. According to Abras, Maloney-Krichmar & Preece (2004), UCD methods that are implemented in development of digital interfaces include a design process that improves information dissemination. They explain how involving users in the development process improves the performance of the overall system. Their analysis tells "designers that products should be intuitive" but that "design principles are needed to guide the design" (p.2). Furthermore, they explain the process of *design thinking* in relation to the five principles of UCD, which are the core principles of WWW as previously stated.

The goal of "Empathize" is to allow computer experts to understand user needs and expectations by carrying out different tasks to build empathy. These tasks involve field visits with implementation of various research methods, such as interviews, focus groups and participant observation, to understand the challenges on the ground. This step also involves studying analog best practices used by scholars working with historical manuscripts, learning about the history of the slave trade, and understanding cultural sensitives that could arise. This step takes a substantial amount of time of the complete *Design Thinking* process and allows interdisciplinary developers to understand the challenges faced by researchers while working towards research goals. The "Define" step concerns the definition of a problem statement, challenges, and user needs based on observations from the "Empathize" stage. Clear understanding of the gap in information flow is important to propose solutions. This step in the UCD process allows computer experts to reflect on the problem statement from the user perspective, which then in-turn aids formulation of prospective design solutions. The "Ideate" step involves research and ideation of prospective solutions. For example, the *Decoding Origins Web Portal* is a solution to the problem explained by Melek-Delgado (2021) about working with multiple text and excel documents to curate meta-data for historical manuscripts. By streamlining the process of meta-tagging and allowing features like drop-down selection menus on-screen instead of typing controlled vocabulary terms, the *Decoding Origins Web Portal* has improved the efficiency of researchers to curate information. Next, the "Prototype" step of the design process, involves creation of interactive models as proof of concept of the prospective solution. An iterative process of creation, based on the ideation and feedback from users helps improve the usability of the front-end interfaces. The final step, "Test," involved the testing of the prototypes by the end-user, in this case researchers and sometimes members of the general public. The tests are carried out on the visual interfaces of these computational tools to understand shortcomes and evaluate usability. "Think-a-Loud" testing and feedback methodology (Van Someren, 1994), self-administer questionnaires combined with detailed notes and user observations are some methods to conduct the final step of the design process.

In African digital humanities, most computer experts play the role of service providers instead of researchers who implement such design processes. This is problematic because without design thinking processes the developed product may not meet user expectations or resolve their needs. WWW on the contrary attempts to break this usual convention and allow more interaction between computer experts and researchers in African digital humanities. This also follows the recommendation by Abras, Maloney-Krichmar & Preece (2004) that developers should identify different types of potential users and their needs, even before starting the development process. Implementing research methods such as focus groups, interviews and usability testing allowed the formation of a clear understanding of user needs, which is a crucial step in defining research problems and developing solutions and guides. Failure to incorporate UCD in the design process can lead to "ill-thought-out designs" (Abras, Maloney-Krichmar & Preece 2004, p.11) and not meet user expectations, resulting in unsatisfactory outcomes. Clear definition of user requirements, creation of multiple prototypes and testing are as important as an acknowledgment of the digital component of research and its documentation in African digital humanities. The links that tie computer science and African studies are computational algorithms that require human-computer interaction and UCD implementation. Website and database development depend upon algorithms that support the dissemination of research outcomes and data curation and research.

The concept of UCD and its potential benefits can be further understood by a comparative evaluation of two websites as research tools in African digital humanities, namely the *Afro-Louisiana History and Genealogy* database by Gwendolyn Midlo Hall (inaugurated in 1984) and the *Slave Voyages database* (formally called *Trans-Atlantic Slave Trade* and first published in 1999) by David Eltis, Stephen D. Behrendt, David Richardson, and Herbert S Klein (Littlefield, 2002; Eltis, 2007). These databases were first created on CD-ROM and in 2000 were published as websites on the world wide web. Hall curated information on over 100,000 Africans and people of African descent from historical manuscripts in Louisiana beginning with the courthouse in Pointe Coupee Parish. The *Slave Voyages* website is a quantitative database that documents the number of slaving voyages (approximately 36,000) that allow an estimate of the number of enslaved (approximately 12.5M) based on multiple historical sources. Both projects involved the creation of relational databases using Microsoft Excel and IBM SPSS datasheets to perform manual quantitative calculations, which were converted into a searchable website. The databases revolutionized African digital humanities by providing accessible platforms for scholars to search research data.

However, these two projects demonstrate a need for an interdisciplinary approach involving UCD paradigms in African studies. Microsoft excel sheets and SPSS datasheets on CD-ROM brought a structure to the data of these two research databases, but the computer file formats and sizes were difficult to access on machines with lower processing speed such as personal computers. This is an example where failure to incorporate end users in the design process directly affects the usability and outreach of research outcomes, not that either pioneering venture could have had the insight of UCD in constructing something that had never been done before. Moreover, the computer files were specifically designed for Microsoft Windows operating systems, which has now become obsolete with the evolution of technology as newer versions of operating systems, mobile and interactive devices have developed. The pioneering websites provided a wider and easier outreach because they were accessible on most internet browsers. However, these websites were less intuitive and user friendly partly due to the limitation of technology in late 90s but the lack of UCD paradigms to incorporate end user perspectives was also a factor.

According to Sheehan-Dean (2004) the documentation on Hall's online search engine (https://www.ibiblio.org/laslave/introduction.php) is user-friendly, although its multiple search options along with a complicated instructional manual make it less intuitive. Although Sheehan-Dean claims that the website has "many search options," the critique relates to the relevance of the search options from the perspective of UCD. Similarly, the *Slave Voyages* database includes information on an estimated 36,000 voyages involving more than 12.5 individuals, which makes the search functionality extremely complicated. Researchers using the website who are new to the field and the great number of students of slavery studies find the website very difficult to use. Williams (2018) reviews these two databases and points out how technology has evolved over time, but the question is: Is technology evolving in the right direction?

Considering the current scope of technology, Hall's original website underachieves in usability performance because it requires prerequisite knowledge of data organization before searching. Instead, and as incorporated in Hall's revised website, the search functionalities have to relate to "tasks." As defined by Abras, Maloney-Krichmar & Preece (2004), these tasks should address three different types of users: primary, secondary, and tertiary. The primary users of both these websites have been scholars studying African slavery and genealogists, who are expected to use these websites more frequently compared to secondary and tertiary users. The secondary users are researchers including students who benefit from these websites more on an intermediate basis compared to primary users. The tertiary users are the general public who may approach this website with an intention to learn about African history.

According to best practices in UCD, the digital organization of the data on these websites should follow data optimization strategies for information retrieval from a user perspective. There is a need for implementation of UCD which has been missing data gathering strategies as indicated by Hall (Rowell 2006). This directly affects the efficiency and accuracy of the research based on information retrieved from the website. An important step for computer programmers should be to analyze the existing datasheets and implement data transformation to optimize technical architecture. UCD helps define the primary user needs. Usability testing with the target audience should be conducted and documented, which is important in re-organizing the structure of databases to allow intuitive searching abilities for all types of users. The two research websites discussed in this article and associated databases are important examples to understand the scholarly expectation from digital platforms due to its outreach and current usage within the field. UCD methods which are not yet well implemented (and not just in African studies) may allow developers to capture a broader range of user needs to improve web design and accessibility (Mao 2005).

Taking the concept of user need-finding further into the content side of African digital humanities is also important. It's not just about creating intuitive websites but also to portray correct research information on the websites and in a format that is familiar to targeted users. The digital presence of African studies directly connects with the personal history of individuals who were enslaved and experienced a traumatizing life during the era of slavery. Empathy with this historical trauma can be defined by involving tertiary users in the design process who may represent Africans and the African diaspora. It's important to involve, acknowledge and respect community values as the content of these digital platforms can be sensitive for individuals who may directly or indirectly connected with the African slave trade.

In collaboration with digital humanities researchers at the Michigan State University as part of a new project called *Enslaved* (Shimizu 2020), *Slave Voyages* has recently entered the era of linked open data. The Enslaved project aims to link multiple digital humanities research output using the "link open data" (Liu et al. 2017) concept that allows navigation through multiple large volumes of datasets. The technological algorithm of connecting the *Slave Voyages* database with multiple other projects in African digital humanities is admirable. This opens digital collaboration and system assisted cross-referencing between big databases which can be useful in the field of African studies. However, the user-end websites of the project are likely to be benefited by usability evaluation. The website provides easy access to different file formats that capture the relationship between various project data. Although helpful from a computer programmer view, this might not be the optimal output for African scholars with minimal knowledge of these file formats or resources to access them. No doubt, this step is an advancement in the field of African digital humanities, however lack of usability evaluation with target users may have led this new website towards complex functions for its end-users. Again, this example emphasizes the need and requirement for a UCD based research trajectory to allow incorporation of end users in the development process. The *Enslaved* project's computational ontology, which is a detailed documentation of relationships between various "data points" (meta-data or meta-fields across multiple digital humanities projects) is an outstanding example of how contemporary technologies can serve historical studies. However, the bridge between the researchers and usability of such advanced technologies is yet to build in order to have meaningful output.

Before implementing contemporary technology in the field of African studies, the understanding of what is actually required is important. The users of these websites are around the globe that brings in more technical challenges such as low internet bandwidth that may not support high-resolution images on these websites. As technology has evolved from desktop computers to mobile devices, these websites should be upgraded to be responsive to match the speed of evolving technology. Moreover, creation and following research practices such as UCD can contribute to the long-term sustainable use of African research websites around the globe.

Bibliography

Digital Publications:

Abras, Chadia, Diane Maloney-Krichmar, Jenny Preece, "User-Centrered Design," in W. Bainbridge, *Encyclopedia of Human-Computer Interaction* "Thousand Oaks: Sage Publications. 2004"

Allington, Daniel., Sarah Brouillette. and David Golumbia. "Neoliberal Tools (and Archives): A Political History of Digital Humanities," *Los Angeles Review of Books* (1 May 2016) www.lareviewofbooks.org/article/neoliberal-tools-archives-political-history-digital-humanities/

Anon. "Collaborators' Bill of Rights," *Off the Tracks: Laying New Lines for Digital Humanities Scholars* (2011)

Anon. "From Dust to Digital: Millions of Images from the World's Endangered Archives Made Available" (London: British Library, 17 February 2015) www.bl.uk/press-releases/2015/february/endangered-archives-programme-10-years

Boyer-Rossol, Klara. "Slavery Digital Humanities – Websites, Databases, Digital Archives and Collections: An Inventory (October 2021) https://www.dependency.uni-bonn.de/en/research/slavery-digital-humanities

Di Pressi, H., S. Gorman, M. Posner, R. Sasayama, and T. Schmitt. "'A Student Collaborators' Bill of Rights," *The CDH Blog* (Los Angeles: Center for Digital Humanities, 8 June 2015) www.cdh.ucla.edu/news/a-student-collaborators-bill-of-rights/

Digital Microfilm Project, www.nationalarchives.gov.uk/help-with-your-research/research-guides/free-online-records-digital-microfilm/ London: British National Archives (Accessed February 2018)

Dinsman, Melissa. "The Digital in the Humanities: An Interview with Jessica Marie Johnson," *LA Review of Books* (23 July 2016) www.

lareviewofbooks.org/article/digital-humanities-interview-jessica-marie-johnson/

Hedges, Blair. *Caribmap: A Cartographic History of Caribbean Islands* www.caribmap.org (Accessed 2019)

Hogan, Liam. "Debunking the Imagery of the 'Irish Slaves' Meme," *Medium* (14 September 2015) www.limerick1914.medium.com/the-imagery-of-the-irish-slaves-myth-dissected-143e70aa6e74

Kahn, A., and J. Bouie. "The Atlantic Slave Trade in Two Minutes," *Slate Magazine* (25 June 2015) www.slate.com/articles/life/the_history_of_american_slavery/2015/06/animated_interactive_of_the_history_of_the_atlantic_slave_trade.html

Lovejoy, Paul E. "Before the War, After the War: Preserving History in Sierra Leone," Endangered Archives Programme. Award #284 (London: British Library, 2009) www.eap.bl.uk/project/EAP284

Lovejoy, Paul E. and Suzanne Schwarz, dir. "Nineteenth Century Documents of the Sierra Leone Public Archives," Endangered Archives Programme. Award #443 (London: British Library, 2011) www.eap.bl.uk/project/EAP443

Rizzo, Gerald J. *Afriterra: The Cartographic Free Library,* www.afriterra.org (Accessed 2019)

Schwarz, Suzanne, "Preserving Nineteenth-Century Records in the Sierra Leone Public Archives," Endangered Archives Programme. Award #782. (London: British Library, 2015) www.eap.bl.uk/project/EAP782

Sheridan, J. "The Generation Game: Evolving with the Digital Record," *The National Archives Blog* (London: British National Archives, 21 Sepember 2017) www.blog.nationalarchives.gov.uk/blog/generation-game-evolving-cope-digital-record/

Varner, Natasha. "The Curious Origins of the 'Irish Slaves' Myth," *Public Radio International* (17 March 2017) www.pri.org/stories/2017-03-17/curious-origins-irish-slaves-myth

Websites:

African Origins, David Eltis, et al., dir. www.african-origins.org (accessed 2021).

Enslaved: People of the Historic Slave Trade, Dean Rehberger, Walter Hawthorne, and D. Watrall, dirs. www.enslaved.org/ (accessed February 2018).

Equiano's World: Gustavus Vassa and the Abolition of the British Slave Trade, Paul E. Lovejoy, dir. www.equianosworld.org (accessed 2021)

Freedom Narratives: Testimonies of West Africans from the Era of Slavery, Paul E. Lovejoy and Érika Melek Delgado, dir. www.freedomnarratives.org (accessed 2021)

Le marronnage dans le Monde Atlantique, 1760-1848, Sources et trajectoires de vie (2009-2019), Jean-Pierre Le Glaunec and Léon Robichaud, dir. www.marronnage.info/fr/index.html (accessed 2021).

Liberated Africans, Henry B. Lovejoy, dir. www.liberatedafricans.org (Accessed August 2021).

Louisiana Slave Database Gwendolyn Midlo Hall, dir. www.louisianaslavedatabase.org (accessed 2021).

Slave Societies Digital Archive, Jane L. Landers, dir. www.vanderbilt.edu/esss/index.php (accessed 2021)

Walk With Web Inc., Kartikay Chadha, dir. www.walkwithweb.org (accessed 2021).

Publications:

Anon. "Albion's Seed: Four British Folkways in America—A Symposium," *William and Mary Quarterly* 48:2 (1991), 224-308

Anon. *Historical Record of the Fifty-Sixth or the West Essex Regiment of Foot* (London, Parker, Furnivall, and Parker, 1844)

Abraham, Arthur. "Bai Bureh, the British, and the Hut Tax War," *The International Journal of African Historical Studies* 7:1 (1974), 99-106

Adams, Chrstina. "As Populações Caiçaras e o Mito Do Bom Selvagem: a Necessidade De Uma Nova Abordagem Interdisciplinar," *Revista De Antropologia* 43:1 (2000), 145-182

Adepegba, Cornelius Oyeleke. *A Survey of Nigerian Body Markings and their Relationship to other Nigerian Arts*. Ph.D. thesis, Indiana University (1976)

Aguet, Isabelle. *A Pictorial History of the Slave Trade* (Geneva: Editions Minerva, 1971)

Al Bakrī, "Kitāb al-Masālikwal-Mamālik," in Joseph Cuoq (ed.), *Recueil des Sources Arabes Concernant l'Afrique Occidentale, VIIIe -XVIe siècle-Bilād al-Sudān* (Paris: CNRS, 1975)

Al-Idrisi, Muhammad b. Muhammad al-Sarif. "Description de l'Afrique et de l'Espagne par al-Idrisi," in M. J. de Goeje, Reinhart Pieter Anne Dozy (eds.), (Leyde: E.J. Brill, 1866)

Al-Umari. "Masalik al-absar fi mamalik al-amsar (achevé vers 1340)," in Joseph Cuoq (ed.), *l'Afrique Occidentale du VIIIe au XVIe siècle* (Paris: Éditions du Centre National de la Recherche Scientifique, 1975)

Alford, Terry. *Prince Among Slaves* (New York: Oxford University Press, 1977)

Allen, Colin and the InPhO Group. "Cross-Cutting Categorization Schemes in the Digital Humanities" *Isis* 104:3 (2013), 573-583

Allen, Richard B. *Slaves, Freedmen and Indentured Laborers in Colonial Mauritius* (Cambridge: Cambridge University Press, 1999)

Allen, Richard B. "Licentious and Unbridled Proceedings. The Illegal Slave Trade to Mauritius and the Seychelles during the Early Nineteenth Century," *Journal of African History* 42:1 (2001), 91-116

Allen, Richard B. *European Slave Trading in the Indian Ocean, 1500-1850* (Athens: Ohio University Press, 2015)

Alpers, Edward A. *Ivory & Slaves in East Central Africa* (London: Heinemann, 1975)

Alpers, Edward A. "The Story of Swema: Female Vulnerability in Nineteenth-Century East Africa," in Claire G. Robertson and Martin A. Klein (eds.), *Women and Slavery in Africa* (Madison: University of Wisconsin Press, 1983), 185-201

Alpers, Edward A. "Becoming 'Mozambique': Diaspora and Identity in Mauritius," in Vijayalakshmi Teelock and Edward A. Alpers (eds.), *History, Memory and Identity* (Port-Louis: Nelson Mandela Centre for African Culture and University of Mauritius, 2001), 117-155

Alpers, Edward A. "Creolization and Identity among 'Mozambiques' in Mauritius and Brazil," *Revi Kiltr Kreol* 3 (October 2003), 31-38

Alpers, Edward A. "Mozambique and 'Mozambiques': Slave Trade and Diaspora on a Global Scale," in Benigna Zimba, Edward A Alpers and Allen F Isaacman (eds.), *Slaves Routes and Oral Tradition in Southeastern Africa* (Maputo: Filsom Entertainment, Lda., 2005), 39-62

Alpers, Edward A. "The Other Middle Passage. The African Slave Trade in the Indian Ocean," in Emma Christopher, Cassandra Pybus and Marcus Rediker (eds.), *Many Middle Passages. Forced Migration and the Making of the Modern World* (Berkeley: University of California Press, 2007), 20-38

Ala Alryyes, Ala (ed.). *A Muslim American Slave: The Life of Omar Ibn Said* (Madison: Univ. of Wisconsin Press, 2011)

Amselle, Jean-Loup and Elikia M'Bokolo (eds.). *Au cœur de l'ethnie. Ethnies, tribalisme et État en Afrique* (Paris: La Découverte, 1985)

Anderson, Richard. "Uncovering Testimonies of Slavery and the Slave Trade in Missionary Sources: The SHADD Biographies Project and the CMS and MMS Archives for Sierra Leone, Nigeria, and the Gambia," *Slavery and Abolition* 38:3 (2017), 620-644

Anderson, Richard, "Liberated Africans," *Oxford Research Encyclopedias* (Oxford: Oxford University Press, 2021)

Anderson, Richard, A. Boruki, D. Domingues da Silva, D. Eltis, P. Lachance, P. Misevich, and O. Ojo. "Using African Names to Identify the Origins of Captives in the Transatlantic Slave Trade: Crowd-Sourcing and the Registers of Liberated Africans, 1808-1862," *History in Africa* 40 (2013), 165-91

Anderson, Richard. and Henry Lovejoy (eds.). *Liberated Africans and the Abolition of the Slave Trade* (Rochester: Rochester University Press, 2000)

Andrews, William L. *To Tell a Free Story: The First Century of Afro-American Autobiography, 1760-1865* (Urbana: University of Illinois Press, 1986)

Armitage, C.H. *The Tribal Markings and Marks of Adornment of the Natives of the Northern Territories of the Gold Coast Colony* (London: Royal Anthropological Institute of Great Britain and Ireland, 1924)

Austin, Allan D. *African Muslims in Antebellum America: A Sourcebook* (New York: Garland, 1984)

Awoonor, Kofi. *Guardians of the Sacred Word-Ewe Poetry* (New York: Nok Publishers Ltd., 1974)

Ba, Abdourahmane. *Le Takrur, des origines à la conquête par le Mali, VIe-XIIIe siècles* (Dakar: CRIAA-Département d'Histoire, Université de Nouakchott-IFAN/UCAD, 2002)

Balbi, Adrien. *Introduction A L'Atlas Ethnographique Du Globe, 1826* (Paris: Kessinger Publishing, 2010)

Ball, M.S. and G.W.H. Smith. *Analysing Visual Data* (London: Sage, 1992)

Barry, Boubacar. *La Sénégambie du XVe au XIXe siècle, traite négrière, Islam, conquête coloniale* (Paris: L'Harmattan, 1984)

Bartram, M. *Recollections Seven Years Residence at the Mauritius, Isle of France By A Lady,* (London, James Cawthorn, 1830)

Bassett, Thomas J. and Philip W. Porter. "'From the Best Authorities': The Mountains of Kong in the Cartography of West Africa," *Journal of African History* 32:3 (1991), 367-413

Behrendt, S. D. "A Commercial History of the British Slave Trade, 1785-1806: A Preliminary Study," M.A. Thesis, University of Wisconsin-Madison (1988)

Behrendt, S. D. "The British Slave Trade, 1785-1807: Volume, Profitability and Mortality," Ph.D. Thesis, University of Wisconsin-Madison (1993)

Bérenger-Féraud, L-J-B. Les peuplades de la Sénégambie; Histoire, Ethnographie, Mœurs et Coutumes, Légendes, etc (Paris: E. Leroux, 1879)

Berman, Merrick. "Modeling and Visualizing Historical GIS Data," in *Proceedings of the Spatio-Temporal Workshop* (2009)

Betancur Gómez, J. M. and G.P. Nieto. "Infanticidio en la provincia de Antioquia entre los años 1756 y 1807," *Medicina: Academia de medicina en Colombia* 23:1 (2001), 80-87

Bethencourt, F. and Peter Havik. "A África e a Inquisição portuguesa: novas perspectivas," *Revista Lusófona de Ciência das Religiões* 3:5/6 (2004), 20-27

Blanckaert, Claude. "Les conditions d'émergence de la science des races au début du XIXe siècle," in S. Moussa (ed.), *L'Idée de "race" dans les sciences humaines et la littérature XVIIIe et XIXe siècle* (Paris: L'Harmattan, 2003), 133-149

Blassingame, John W. *Slave Testimony: Two Centuries of Letters, Speeches, Interviews, and Autobiographies* (Baton Rouge, LA: Louisiana State University Press, 1977)

Blassingame, John W. *The Slave Community: Plantation Life in the Antebellum South* (New York: Oxford University Press, 1981)

Blumenthal, D. *Enemies and Familiars: Slavery and Mastery in Fifteenth Century Valencia* (Ithaca: Cornell University Press, 2009)

Borgman, C. L. "The Digital Future is Now: A Call to Action for the Humanities," *Digital Humanities Quarterly* 3: 4 (2009)

Bosman, Willem. *A New and Accurate Description of the Coast of Guinea, divided into the Gold, the Slave, and the Ivory Coasts* (London: Sir Alfred Jones, 1721)

Boubacar Barry. *La Sénégambie du XVe au XIXe siècle, Traite Négrière, Islam, Conquête Colonial* (Paris: L'Harmattan, 1984)

Boulègue, J. *Les Royaumes Wolof dans l'Espace Sénégambien XIIIe-XVIIIe siècle* (Paris: Karthala, 2013)

Bowser, Frederick P. *The African Slave in Colonial Peru, 1524-1650* (Stanford: Stanford University Press, 1974)

Boxer, C. R. *Salvador De Sa and the Struggle for Brazil and Angola, 1602-1686* (Westport: Greenwood Press, 1975)

Boxer, Charles R. *The Golden Age of Brazil: Growing Pains of a Colonial Society* (Berkeley: University of California Press, 1969)

Boyer-Rossol, Klara. "Entre les deux rives du canal du Mozambique. Histoire et Mémoires des Makoa à l'Ouest de Madagascar. XIXe-XXe siècles," Ph.D. Thesis: Université Paris 7 (2015)

Boyles, C., Cong-Huyen, A., Johnston, C., McGrath, J., and Phillips, A. "Precarious Labor and the Digital Humanities," *American Quarterly* 70:3 (2018), 693-700

Brathwaite, Edward Kamau. *The Development of Creole Society in Jamaica, 1770-1820* (Oxford: Oxford University Press, 1971)

Brazilian Institute of Museums (Instituto Brasileiro de Museus – IBRAM). *Caderno da Política Nacional de Educação Museal* (Brasília, DF: IBRAM, 2018)

Brazilian National Institute of Artistic and Historical Patrimony (IPHAN). PINHEIRO, A. R. S. (ed.), *Cadernos do patrimônio cultural: educação patrimonial* (Fortaleza: Secultfor: Iphan, 2015)

Brindley, Lynne. "The International Dimensions of Digital Science and Scholarship: Aspirations of the British Library in Serving the International Scientific and Scholarly Communities," in Rae Earnshaw and John Vince (eds.), *Digital Convergence—Libraries of the Future* (London: Springer, 2008), 65-73

Brodny, J., J. Kazmierczak. "The Design Thinking Method and Its Stages," *Systemy Wspomagania W. Inzynierii Produkcji, Inzynieria Systemow Technicznych* 6:6 (2017), 247-254

Broussard, James F. *Louisiana Creole Dialect* (Baton Rouge: Louisiana State University Press, 1942)

Brügger, Niels and Ian Milligan. (eds.), *The SAGE Handbook of Web History* (Los Angeles: SAGE, 2019)

Buenaventura Gómez, L.A. "Tentativas del 'enemigo malo'. Relaciones Ilícitas e Infanticidios en la Provincia de Antioquia (Nueva Granada) 1765-1803," Undergraduate Monograph: Universidad del Rosario (2015)

Bühnen, Stephan. "Ethnic Origins of Peruvian Slaves (1548-1650): Figures for upper Guinea," *Paideuma: Mitteilungen zur Kulturkunde* 39 (1993), 57-110

Burnard, Trevor. *Mastery, Tyranny, and Desire: Thomas Thistlewood and his Slaves in the Anglo-Jamaican World* (Chapel Hill: University of North Carolina Press, 2004)

Ca Da Mosto. *Relation des Voyages de la Côte Occidentale d'Afrique (1455-1457),* in Charles Schefer (ed.), (Paris: Leroux, 1895)

Calainho Buono, Daniela. "Africanos penitenciados pela Inquisição portuguesa," *Revista Lusófona de Ciência das Religiões* 3:5/6 (2004), 37-63

Campbell, Gwyn. "Madagascar and Mozambique in the Slave Trade of the Western Indian Ocean, 1800–1861," *Slavery and Abolition* 9:3 (1988), 166-193

Candido, Mariana. "Os Agentes Não-Europeus Na Comunidade Mercantil De Benguela, c. 1760-1820," *Saeculum Revista de História* 29 (2013), 97-124

Candido, Mariana. "Trans-Atlantic Links: The Benguela-Bahian Connections, 1700-1850," in Ana Lucia Araujo (ed.), *Paths of the Atlantic Slave Trade. Interactions, Identities, and Images* Amherst: Cambria Press, 2011), 239-272

Candido, Mariana. "Negociantes Baianos no Porto de Benguela: Redes Comerciais Unindo o Atlântico No Setencentos," in Roberto Guedes (ed.), *Brasileiros e Portugueses na África, Séculos XVI-XIX* (Rio de Janeiro: MAUAD, 2013), 67-91

Caron, Peter. "Of a Nation which the Others Don't Understand: Bambara Slaves and African Ethnicity in Louisiana, 1718-60," in David Eltis and David Richardson (eds.), *Routes to Slavery. Direction, Ethnicity and Mortality in the Transatlantic Slave Trade* (London: Frank Cass, 1997)

Carretta, Vincent (ed.). *Unchained Voices: An Anthology of Black Authors in the English- Speaking World of the Eighteenth Century* (Lexington: University of Kentucky Press, 1996)

Carretta, Vincent. *Equiano, the African: Biography of a Self Made Man* (Athens, GA: University of Georgia Press, 2005)

Carter, Marina, and Hubert Gerbeau. "Covert Slaves and Coveted Coolies in the Early 19th Century Mascareignes," *Slavery and Abolition* 9:3 (1988), 194-208

Carter, M., Govinden, V., Peerthum, S. (eds.), *The Last Slaves. Liberated Africans in the 19th Century Mauritius* (Port Luis: Centre for Research on Indian Ocean Societies, 2003)

Carter, Hall Mark. "The 'Last Slaves' of Mauritius: Retracing the History of the Forgotten Liberated Africans," paper presented to the *International Workshop*, University of California, Liberated Africans as Human Legacy of Abolition (2008)

Carvalho Soares, Mariza de. "Mina, Angola e Guiné: Nomes d'África no Rio de Janeiro Setecentista," *Tempo* 3:6 (1998), 74-75

Case, Anthea, "The Endangered Archives Programme after ten years," in Maja Kominko (ed.), *From Dust to Digital: Ten Years of the Endangered Archives Programme* (Cambridge: Open Book Publishers, 2005), xliii-xlvi

Cassia Gomes de Oliveira, Nora de. "Elites Políticas no Império: Bahia, 1828-1834," in *Anais do XVII Encontro Estadual de História*," (João Pessoa: Associação Nacional de História, 2016), 1032-1045

Ceballos Gómez, Diana Luz, *Hechicería, Brujería, y Inquisición en el Nuevo Reino de Granada: un Duelo de Imaginarios* (Medellín: Universidad Nacional de Colombia, 1995)

Chalhoub, Sidney. A Força da Escravidão: Ilegalidade e Costume no Brasil Oitocentista (São Paulo: Companhia das Letras, 2012)

Challú, Amílcar E. "The Great Decline: Biological Well-Being and Living Standards in Mexico, 1730-1840," in *Living Standards in Latin American History: Height, Welfare and Development, 1750-2000* (Cambridge and London: Harvard University David Rockefeller Center for Latin American Studies/Harvard University Press, 2010), 23-68

Chambers, Douglas B. "Ethnicity in the Diaspora: The Slave-Trade and the Creation of African 'Nations' in the Americas," *Slavery and Abolition* 22:3 (2001), 25-39

Chambers, Douglas B. *Murder at Montpelier: Igbo Africans in Virginia* (Jackson: University Press of Mississippi, 2005)

Chambers, Douglas B. "Slave Trade Merchants of Spanish New Orleans, 1763–1803: Clarifying the Colonial Slave Trade to Louisiana in Atlantic Perspective," *Atlantic Studies* 5:3 (2008), 335-346

Chambers, Douglas B. *Igbo Diaspora in the Era of the Slave Trade. An Introductory History* (Glassboro: Goldline & Jacobs Publishing, 2014)

Chavane, Bruno. *Villages de l'Ancien Tekrour, Recherches Archéologiques dans la Moyenne Vallée du Fleuve Sénégal* (Paris: Karthala-CRA,1985)

Cissoko, Sékéné M. *Histoire de l'Afrique Occidentale. Moyen Âge et Temps Modernes, VIIe Siècle-1850* (Paris: Présence Africaine, 1971)

Clarke, John. *Specimens of Dialects: Short Vocabularies of Languages and Notes of Countries and Customs in Africa* (Berwick-upon-Tweed: Daniel Cameron, 1848)

Clement, Tanya; Wendy Hagenmaier; and Jennie Levine Knies. "Toward a Notion of the Archive of the Future: Impressions of Practice by Librarians, Archivists, and Digital Humanities Scholars" *The Library Quarterly: Information, Community, Policy* 83:2 (2013), 112-130

Colmenares, Germán. "Problemas de la Estructura Minera en el Nuevo Reino de Granada (1550-1700)," *Anuario Colombiano de Historia Social y de la Cultura* 6:7 (1972), 5-55

Colmenares, Germán. *Historia Económica y Social de Colombia 1537-1719* (Bogotá: Tercer Mundo, 1999), Tomo I

Colin, Epidariste. "Notice sur Mozambique," in Victor Adolphe Malte-Brun (ed.), *Annales des Voyages, de la Géographie et de l'Histoire* 9 (1809), 312-315

Coquery-Vidrovitch, Catherine and Mesnard Eric. *Être Esclave. Afrique-Amériques, XVe-XIXe siècle* (Paris: La Découverte, 2013)

Côrtes de Oliveira, Maria Inês. "Quem Eram Os 'Negros Da Guiné'? A Origem Dos Africanos Na Bahia," *Afro-Ásia* 19/20 (1997), 37-73

Cortes López, José Luis. *Los origenes de la esclavitud negra en España* (Madrid: Mundo Negro, 1986)

Costa Lima, Vivaldo da. *A Família de Santo nos Candomblés Jeje-Nagôs da Bahia: Um Estudo das Relações Intragrupais* (Salvador: Corrupio, 2003)

Crouser, R. Jordan and Lyndsey Franklin, Kris Cook. "Rethinking Visual Analytics for Streaming Data Applications" *IEEE Internet Computing* (2017), 72-76

Cuoq, Joseph. (ed.), *Recueil des Sources Arabes Concernant l'Afrique Occidentale du VIIIe au XVIe Siècle, Bilad al-Sudan* (Paris: Institut de Rechercher et d'Histoire des Textes, 1975)

Curtin, Philip D. *The Atlantic Slave Trade: A Census* (Madison: University of Wisconsin Press, 1969)

Curtin, Philip D. *Africa Remembered: Narratives of West Africans from the Era of Slave Trade* (Madison: University of Wisconsin Press, 1967)

Curtin, Philip D. *Economic Change in Precolonial Africa. Senegambia in the Era of the Slave Trade* (Madison: University of Wisconsin Press, 1975)

Curto, José C., and Raymond R. Gervais. "A Dinâmica Demográfica de Luanda no Contexto do Tráfico de Escravos do Atlântico Sul, 1781-1844," *Topoi* 3:4 (2002), 85-138

Cust, Robert Needham. *A Sketch of the Modern Languages of Africa* (London: Trubner & Company, 1883), 2 vols.

Daddi Addoun, Yacine and Paul E Lovejoy. "The Arabic Manuscript of Muhammad Kaba Saghanughu of Jamaica, c. 1820," in Annie Paul (ed.), *Creole Concerns: Essays in Honour of Kamau Brathwaite* (Kingston: University of the West Indies Press, 2007), 313-41

Davidson, Basil. *Black Mother. Africa: The Years of Trial* (London: Victor Gollancz, 1961)

Davis, Angela. *Mujer, raza y clase* (Madrid: Alcal, 2005)

Delafosse, Maurice. *Haut-Sénégal-Niger* (Paris: Maisonneuve et Larose, 1972)

Delcourt, André. *La France et les Etablissements Français au Sénégal entre 1713 et 1763* (Dakar: Mémoires IFAN, 1952)

Dencik, Lina, Arne Hintz, Joanna Redden, and Emiliano Treré. "Exploring Data Justice: Conceptions, Applications and Directions," *Information, Communication and Society* 22:7 (2019), 873-881

Deroure, F. "La Vie Quotidienne à Saint-Louis par ses Archives (1779-1809)," *BIFAN*, Série B, 26:3/4 (1964), 401-423.

Derrida, Jacques. *Archive Fever: A Freudian Impression* (Chicago: University of Chicago Press, 1996)

D'Unienville (baron de). *Statistique de l'ile Maurice et ses dépendances, suivi d'une notice historique sur cette colonie et d'un essai sur l'île de Madagascar*, vol. 1 (Paris: G. Barba, 1838)

Dewulf, Jeroen. *From the Kingdom of Kongo to Congo Square: Kongo Dances and the Origins of the Mardi Gras Indians* (Lafayette: University of Louisiana at Lafayette Press, 2017)

Dias, Nélia. *La Mesure des Sens. Les Anthropologues et le Corps Humain au XIXe siècle* (Paris: Aubier, 2004)

Diouf, Sylviane (ed.). *Fighting the Slave Trade: West African Strategies* (Athens: Ohio University Press, 2003)

Domingues da Silva, Daniel B. "The Atlantic Slave Trade from Angola: A Port-by-Port Estimate of Slaves Embarked, 1701–1867" *International Journal of African Historical Studies* 46:1 (2013), 105-122

Domingues da Silva; Daniel B., David Eltis, Philip Misevich and Olatunji Ojo. "The Diaspora of Africans Liberated from Slave Ships in the Nineteenth Century," *Journal of African History* 55:3 (2014), 347-69

Dusinberre, William. *Them Dark Days: Slavery in the American Rice Swamps* (New York: Oxford University Press, 1996)

Echeverri, Marcela. "Conflicto y Hegemonía en el Suroccidente de la Nueva Granada, 1780-1800," *Fronteras de la Historia* 11 (2006), 355-387

Earnshaw, Rae. and John Vince (eds.). *Digital Convergence—Libraries of the Future* (London: Springer, 2008)

Eltis, David. "Nutritional Trends in Africa and the Americas: Heights of Africans, 1819-1839," *Journal of Interdisciplinary History* 22 (1982), 453-475

Eltis, David. "Slave Departures from Africa, 1811-1867: An Annual Time Series," *African Economic History* 15 (1986), 143-171

Eltis, David. "Slave Voyages and African-Origins since 2010: Problems, Retrospectives and Reassessments," Conference presentation, New Research on the Atlantic Slave Trade, Harvard University (2 October 2015)

Eltis, David. "The Export of Slaves from Africa, 1821-1843," *Journal of Economic History* 37:2 (1977), 409-433

Eltis, David. *Economic Growth and the Ending of the Transatlantic Slave Trade* (New York: Oxford University Press, 1987)

Eltis, David et al. *The Trans-Atlantic Slave Trade: A Database on CD-ROM* (Cambridge: Cambridge University Press, 1999)

Eltis, David and David Richardson. *Atlas of the Atlantic Slave Trade* (New Haven and London: Yale University Press, 2010)

Eltis, David, Philip Morgan, and David Richardson. "Agency and Diaspora in Atlantic History: Reassessing the African Contribution to Rice Cultivation in the Americas," *American Historical Review* 112:5 (2007), 1329-1358

Eltis, David, and G. Ugo Nwokeji. "Characteristics of Captives Leaving the Cameroons for the Americas, 1822-37," *Journal of African History* 43:2 (2002), 191-210

Eltis, David, and G. Ugo Nwokeji. "The Roots of the African Diaspora: Methodological Considerations in the Analysis of Names in the Liberated African Registers of Sierra Leone and Havana" *History in Africa* 29 (2002), 365-379

Eyriès, Malte-Brun. "Analyse d'un Mémoire de M. Eugène de Froberville sur les Langues et les Races de l'Afrique Orientale au Sud de l'Équateur,"

Nouvelles Annales des Voyages, de la Géographie et de l'Histoire, Serie 5 (Paris: Arthus Bertrand, 1847), Tome 9, 216-226.

Falola, Toyin and Matt Childs (eds.). *The Yoruba Diaspora in the Atlantic World* (Bloomington: Indiana University Press, 2004)

Falola, Toyin and Raphael Chijioke Njoku (eds.). *Igbo in the Alantic World. African origins and Diasporic destinations* (Bloomington & Indianapolis: Indiana University Press, 2016)

Federal Writers' Project. *Slave Narratives. A Folk History of Slavery in the United States from Interviews with Former Slaves* (Washington: United States Work Progress Administration, 1941)

Fernández de Oviedo, Gonzalo. *Historia General y Natural de las Indias, Islas y Tierra firme del mar Océano*, Parte 1, Tomo 1 (Madrid: Imp. de la Real Academia de la Historia, 1851 [1535])

Fields-Black, Edda L. *Deep Roots: Rice Farmers in West Africa and the African Diaspora* (Bloomington: Indiana University Press, 2008)

Fisch, Audrey (ed.). *The Cambridge Companion to the African American Slave Narrative* (Cambridge: Cambridge University Press, 2007)

Fisher, David Hackett. *Albion's Seed* (Oxford University Press, 1989)

Flourens, Duperrey, Serres (commissaires rapporteur). "Rapport sur les Races Nègres de l'Afrique Orientale au Sud de l'Équateur, Observées par M. de Froberville," *Comptes Rendus Hebdomadaires des Séances de l'Académie des Sciences* (Paris, 1850), Tome 30, 679-690

Freyre, Gilberto. *The Masters and the Slaves (Casa-Grande and Senzala): A Study in the Development of Brazilian Civilization*, Trans. Samuel Putnam (New York: Alfred A Knopf, 1946; Portuguese ed., 1935)

Friedman, Gerald C. "The Heights of Slaves in Trinidad," *Social Science History*, Trends in Nutrition, Labor, Welfare, and Labor Productivity 6:4 (1982), 482-515

Fritsch, Kathrin. "'You Have Everything Confused and Mixed Up...!' Georg Schweinfurth, Knowledge and Cartography of Africa in the 19th Century," *History in Africa* 36 (2009), 87-101

Froberville, Eugène de. "Notes sur les Mœurs, Coutumes et Traditions des Amakoua, sur le Commerce et la Traite des Esclaves dans l'Afrique Orientale," *Bulletin de la Société de Géographie* (Paris, 1847), 311-329

Froberville, Eugène de. "Notes sur les Va-Niungue et les Mabsiti. Peuples de l'Afrique Orientale," *Bulletin de la Société de Géographie* (Paris, 1848), 65-81

Froberville, Eugène de. *Notes sur les Races de l'Afrique Orientale au Sud de l'Equateur* (Paris, 1849)

Gaby, J.B. *Relation de la Nigritie* (Paris: Edme Couterot, 1689)

García Ávila, Celene. "Amuletos, conjuros y pócimas de amor: Un caso de hechicería juzgado por el Santo Oficio (Puebla de los Ángeles, 1652)," *Contribuciones desde Coatepec* 17:2 (2009), 45-63

Gardner, W. H. "History of an Epidemic of Small-Pox in the Mauritius: With Remarks on the Protective Power of Vaccination," *London Journal of Medicine* 4:37 (1852), 38-44

Gates Jr., Henry Louis. *The Signifying Monkey: A Theory of African-American Literary Criticism* (New York: Oxford University Press, 1988)

Gauzere, B.-A. and P. Aubry. "Les épidémies de cholera a La Réunion au XIXe siècle," *Médecine et santé tropicales* 22:2 (2012), 131-136

Gengenbach, Heidi. "Boundaries of Beauty: Tattooed Secrets of Women's History in Southern Mozambique," *Journal of Women's History* 14:4 (2003), 106-141

Gerbeau, Hubert. "L'océan Indien n'est pas l'atlantique. La traite illégale à Bourbon au XIXe siècle," *Outre-mers* 89:336-337 (2002), 79-108

Gerbeau, Hubert. "L'esclavage et son ombre," Ph.D. Thesis: Université de Provence Aix-Marseille (2005)

Goffin, Robert. *Aux Frontières du Jazz* (Paris: Éditions du Sagittaire, 1932)

Gomes, Flávio. "'Atlantic Nations' and the Origins of Africans in Late-colonial Rio de Janeiro: New Evidence," *Colonial Latin American Review* 20:2 (2011), 213-231

Gomez, Michael. *Exchanging Our Country Marks: The Transformation of African Identities in the Colonial and Antebellum South* (Chapel Hill: University of North Carolina Press, 1998)

Gonçalves Santos, Telma. "Comércio de Tecidos Europeus e Asiáticos na África Centro-Ocidental: Fraudes e Contrabando no Terceiro Quartel do Século XVIII," M.A. Thesis: Universidade de Letras de Lisboa (2014)

González-Molina, O. J. "Inquisición y Hechicería Novohispana: Ideología y Discurso en el Proceso a Catalina de Miranda," *Revista de la Inquisición:(Intolerancia y Derechos Humanos)* 17 (2013), 65-84

Green, Toby. *A Fistful of Shells: West Africa from the Rise of the Slave Trade to the Age of Revolution* (London: Penguin, 2019)

Green, Toby. *The Rise of the Trans-Atlantic Slave Trade in Western Africa, 1300-1589* (New York: Cambridge University Press, 2012)

Greenberg, Joseph H. *The Languages of Africa* (Bloomington: Indiana University Press, 1966)

Greenwood, April; Benjamin Lauren, Jessica Knott, Dànielle Nicole DeVoss. "Dissensus, Resistance, and Ideology: Design Thinking as a Rhetorical Methodology," *Journal of Business and Technical Communication* 33:4 (2019), 400-424

Gregory, Ian, David Cooper, Andrew Hardie, and Paul Rayson, "Spatializing and Analysing Digital Texts: Corpora, GIS, and Places" in David J.

Bodenhamer, John Corrigan and Trevor M. Harris (eds.), *Deep Maps and Spatial Narratives* (Bloomington: Indiana University Press, 2015), 150-178

Gregory, Ian, Christopher Donaldson, Patricia Murrieta-Flores, and Paul Rayson, "Geoparsing, GIS, and Textual Analysis: Current Developments in Spatial Humanities Research," *International Journal of Humanities and Arts Computing* 9:1 (2015), 1-14

Guanche, Jesus. *Africanía y ethncidad en Cuba* (Havana: Editorial de Ciencias Sociales, 2009)

Gudeman, Stephen, and Stuart B. Schwartz. "Cleansing Original Sin: Godparenthood and the Baptism of Slaves in Eighteenth-Century Bahia," in Raymond T. Smith (ed.), *Kinship Ideology and Practice in Latin America* (Chapel Hill: University of North Carolina Press, 1984), 35-56

Guerlac, Suzanne. "Humanities 2.0: E-Learning in the Digital World" *Representations: The Humanities and the Crisis of The Public University* 116:1 (2011), 102-127

Guérois, Rozenn. "A Grammar of Cuwabo (Mozambique, Bantu P34)," Ph.D. Thesis: Université Lumière Lyon 2 (2015)

Gueunier N. J. "Documents sur la Langue Makhuwa à Madagascar et aux Comores (fin XIXe - début XXe siècles). Avec un Lexique du Makhuwa de Madagascar," *Etudes Océan Indien* 35-36 (2005), 149-223

Gutiérrez, Urquijo and Natalia María. "Los Delitos de Aborto e Infanticidio en Antioquia, 1890-1930," *Historia y Sociedad* 17 (2009), 159-177

Hair, P.E.H. "Ethnolinguistic Continuity on the Guinea Coast," *Journal of African History* 8:2 (1967), 247-268; Hair,

Hair, P.E.H. "An Ethnolinguistic Inventory of the Guinea Coast before 1700," *Sierra Leone Language Review* 6 (1967), 32-70

Hall, Gwendolyn Midlo. *Africans in Colonial Louisiana - The Development of Afro-Creole Culture in the Eighteenth Century* (Baton Rouge: Louisiana State University Press, 1992)

Hall, Gwendolyn Midlo. *Afro-Louisiana History and Genealogy 1699-1860* (Baton Rouge: Louisiana State University Press, 2000)

Hall, Gwendolyn Midlo. *Slavery and African Ethnicities in the Americas: Restoring the Links* (Chapel Hill: University of North Carolina Press, 2005)

Hall, Gwendolyn Midlo. "Africa and Africans in the African Diaspora: The Uses of Relational Databases," *American Historical Review* 115 (2010), 136-150

Hall, Gwendolyn Midlo and Charles Henry Rowell, "Gwendolyn Midlo Hall with Charles Henry Rowell," *Callaloo* 29:4 (2006), 1049-55

Hamy, E. T. "La collection de Froberville au Muséum," *La Nature* (1879), 237-238

Handler, Jerome S. "Survivors of the Middle Passage: Life Histories of Enslaved Africans in British America," *Slavery and Abolition* 23:1 (2002), 25-56

Handler, Jerome S. and A. Steiner. "Identifying Pictorial Images of Atlantic Slavery: Three Case Studies," *Slavery and Abolition* 27:1 (2006), 49-69

Hanger, Kimberly. *Bounded Lives, Bounded Places: Free Black Society in Colonial New Orleans, 1769-1803* (Durham: Duke University Press, 1997)

Harris, Joseph E. (ed.). *Global Dimensions of the African Diaspora* (Washington: Howard University Press, 1993)

Hawthorne, Walter. *Planting Rice and Harvesting Slaves: Transformations along the Guinea-Bissau Coast, 1400*-1900 (Portsmouth: Heinemann, 2003)

Heidorn, P. Bryan. "Shedding Light on the Dark Data in the Long Tail of Science," *Library Trends* 57:2 (2009), 280-299

Heywood, Linda M., and John K. Thornton. *Central Africans and Cultural Transformations in the American Diaspora* (Cambridge: Cambridge University Press, 2002)

Heywood, Linda M., and John K. Thornton. *Central Africans, Atlantic Creoles, and the Foundation of the Americas,* 1585-1660 (Cambridge: Cambridge University Press, 2007)

Hindley, Meredeth. "The Office of Digital Humanities Turns Ten," *Humanities: The Magazine of the National Endowment of the Humanities* 39:2 (2018)

Hopper, Matthew S. "Liberated Africans in the Indian Ocean World" in Richard Anderson and Henry B. Lovejoy (eds.), *Liberated African and the Abolition of the Slave Trade, 1807-1896*, (Rochester: University of Rochester Press, 2020), 271-293

Horta, José. "Evidence for a Luso-African Identity in 'Portuguese' Accounts on 'Guinea of Cape Verde (Sixteenth-Seventeenth Centuries)," *History in Africa* 27 (2000), 99-130

Hym, Bernard Père. *Cœur à cœur avec le Père Laval à travers ses écrits* (Ile Maurice: Diocèse de Port-Louis, 2016)

Ingersoll, Thomas. *Mammon and Manon in Early New Orleans: The First Slave Society in the Deep South, 1718-1819* (Knoxville: University of Tennessee Press, 1999)

Inikori, Joseph E. "The Known, the Unknown, the Knowable and the Unknowable: Evidence and the Evaluation of Evidence in the Measurement of the Trans-Atlantic Slave Trade," unpublished paper presented at the Conference on the Trans-Atlantic Slave Trade Database (Williamsburg, Virginia, September 1998).

Isaacman, Barbara and Allen Isaacman. "Slavery and Social Stratification among the Sena of Mozambique. A Study of the Kaporo System" in

Suzanne Meirs and Igor Kopytoff (eds.), *Slavery in Africa* (Madison: University of Wisconsin Press, 1977), 105-120

Isaacman, Allen. *Mozambique: The Africanization of a European Institution, the Zambesi Prazos 1750-1902* (Madison: University of Wisconsin Press, 1972)

Isaacman, Allen. "Madzi-Manga, Mhondoro and the Use of Oral Traditions – A Chapter in Barue Religious and Political History," *Journal of African History* 14:3 (1973), 395-409

Jarvis, Samuel Peters. *Historical Record of the Eighty-Second Regiment or Prince of Wales's Volunteers* (London: W.O. Mitchell, 1866)

Johnson, Jessica M. *Practicing Freedom: Black Women, Intimacy and Freedom in the Atlantic World* (Philadelphia: University of Pennsylvania Press, 2020)

Johnson, Walter. "On Agency," *Journal of Social History* 37:1 (2003), 113–24

Johnston, James H. *From Slave Ship to Harvard: Yarrow Mamout and the History of an African American Family* (New York: Fordham University Press, 2012)

Jones, Adam and Isabel Voigt. "'Just a First Sketchy Makeshift': German Travellers and Their Cartographic Encounters in Africa, 1850–1914," *History in Africa* 39 (2012), 9-39

Joseph, R. "Tenure, Promotion and Digital Publication," *Digital Humanities Quarterly*, 1:1 (2007)

Juhé-Beaulaton, Dominique and Vincent Leblan. (eds.), *Le Spécimen et le Collecteur. Savoirs Naturalistes, Pouvoirs et Altérités (XVIII*[e]*-XX*[e] *siècles),* Publications Scientifiques, Collection Archives (Paris: Muséum National d'Histoire Naturelle, 2018)

Kandji, Saliou. *Sénégal n'est pas Sunugal ou de l'étymologie du toponyme Sénégal* (Dakar: Presses Universitaires de Dakar, 2006)

Kane, Omar. *La Première Hégémonie Peule. Le Fuuta Tooro de Koli Teŋella à Almaami Abdul* (Dakar: Karthala et Presses Universitaire de Dakar, 2004)

Kane, Omar. "Les Maures et le Futa-Toro au XVIIIe siècle," *Cahiers d'études Africaines* 14:54 (1974), 237-252

Keefer, Katrina. "Marked by Fire: Brands, Slavery and Identity," *Slavery and Abolition* 40:4 (2019), 659-681

Keefer, Katrina. "Group Identity, Scarification, and Poro among Liberated Africans in Sierra Leone, 1808-1819," *Journal of West African History* 3:1 (2017), 1-26

Keefer, Katrina. "Poro On Trial: The 1913 Special Commission Court Case of Rex v. Fino, Bofio and Kalfalla," *African Studies Review* 61:3 (2018), 56-78

Keefer, Katrina. "Scarification and Identity in the Liberated Africans Department Register, 1814-1815," *Canadian Journal of African Studies* 47:3 (2013), 537-553

Kennan, Mary Anne and Lina Markauskaite, "Research Data Management Practices: A Snapshot in Time," *The International Journal of Digital Curation* 10:2 (2015), 69-95

Kenosi, Lekoko. "Managing the Records of Restricted Organizations," *Information Development* 16:2 (2000), 65-69

Kilekwa, Petro. *Slave Boy to Priest: The Autobiography of Padre Petro Kilekwa,* Trans. from Chinyanja by K.H. Nixon Smith (London: Universities' Mission to Central Africa, 1937).

Kirschenbaum, M. G. "Done: Finishing Projects in the Digital Humanities," *Digital Humanities Quarterly* 3:2 (2009) www.digitalhumanities.org:8081/dhq/vol/3/2/000037/000037.html

Knowles, Anne Kelley. "Special Issue: Historical GIS: The Spatial Turn in Social Science History," *Social Science History* 24:3 (2000), 451-470

Koelle, S.W. *Polyglotta Africana*. Reprint, edited, with an introduction, by P. E. H. Hair (Graz, Austria: Akademische Druck- und Verlagsanstalt, 1963)

Kolapo, Femi James. "Military Turbulence, Population Displacement and Commerce on a Slaving Frontier of the Sokoto Caliphate: Nupe c.1810-1857," Ph.D. thesis, York University (1999)

Konadu, Kwasi. *The Akan Diaspora in the Americas* (Oxford: Oxford University Press, 2010)

Labat, Jean-Baptiste. *Nouvelle relation de l'Afrique occidentale* (Paris: Cavelier, tome 1er, 1728)

Ladly, Martha. *Eros, Women, and Technology*. Ph.D. thesis, York University (2013)

Ladly, Martha. "Narrative in Hybrid Mobile Environments" in Lanfranco Aceti, Hana Iverson, Mimi Sheller (eds.), *Leonardo Electronic Almanac*, 21 1; *L.A. Re.Play, Mobile Network Culture in Placemaking* (San Francisco: Leonardo, 2016), 76-96

Ladly, Martha. "Locative Media, Art and Games in the Mobile Space" in James E. Katz, Ellen Lynch, Wayne LaBar (eds.), *Technology and Creativity: Social Media, Mobiles and Museums* (New Brunswick, NJ: Rutgers University Press, 2011)

Ladly, Martha. "Portable and Playful: Affective Devices and Responsive Environments" in Espacio Fundación Telefónica, *Nomadismos Technologicos / Technological Nomadisms* (Buenos Aires: Ariel Publishing, 2010)

Ladly, Martha and Philip Beesley (eds.) *Mobile Nation: Creating Methodologies for Mobile Platforms* (Waterloo: Riverside Architectural Press, 2008)

Ladly, Martha and Penn G., Rudzicz, F., Bakker, T., Chadha K., Farrelly G., Micak, K. "Reality Recalled: Elders, Memory and VR" in *IEEE VSMM 2017, 23rd International Conference on Virtual Systems and Multimedia*, Dublin, 2017

Lahon, Didier. "Inquisição, Pacto com o Demônio e 'Magia' Africana em Lisboa no Século XVIII," *Topoi* 5:8 (2004), 9-70

Landers, Jane. *Black Society in Spanish Florida* (Urbana: University of Illinois Press, 1999)

Landers, Jane. "African 'Nations' as Diasporic Institution-Building in the Iberian Atlantic," in Franklin W. Knight and Ruth Iyob (eds.), "*Dimensions of African and Other Diasporas* (Kingston: University of the West Indies Press, 2014), 105-12

Landers, Jane. "African Ethnic Groups in Florida," in Amanda Carlson and Robin Poyner *Africa in Florida: Five Hundred Years of African Presence in the Sunshine State"* (Gainsville: University Press of Florida, 2013), 73-85

Lara, Silvia Hunold. "Legislação sobre escravos africanos na América Portuguesa." in *Nuevas aportaciones a la historia jurídica de Iberoamérica* (Madrid: Fundación Histórica Tavera, 2000)

Larson, Pier. *Ocean of Letters: Language and Creolization in an Indian Ocean Diaspora* (Cambridge: Cambridge University Press, 2009)

Law, Robin. "Ethnicities of Enslaved Africans in the Diaspora: On the Meanings of 'Mina' (Again)," *History in Africa* 32 (2005), 247-67

Law, Robin. *Ouidah: The Social History of a West African Slaving 'Port' 1727-1892* (Athens: Ohio University Press, 2004)

Law, Robin, and Paul E. Lovejoy. *The Biography of Mahommah Gardo Baquaqua: His Passage from Slavery to Freedom in Africa and America* (Princeton: Markus Wiener Publisher, 2001)

Le Glaunec, Jean-Pierre. "Lire et écrire la fuite d'esclaves dans le monde atlantique : essai d'interprétation comparée et "coopérante" à partir des annonces d'esclaves en fuite, Louisiane, Jamaïque et Caroline du sud (1801-1815) : une histoire culturelle et diplomatique," Ph.D. Thesis: Université de Paris VII (2007)

Le Glaunec, Jean-Pierre. *Esclaves mais Résistants. Dans le Monde des Annonces pour Esclaves en Fuite, États-Unis/Caraïbe* (Paris: Karthala, 2020)

Leitão de Almeida, Marcos Abreu. "Ladinos e Boçais: o Regime de Línguas do Contrabando de Africanos, (1831-C.1850)," M.A. Thesis: Universidade Estadual de Campinas (2012)

Le Page du Pratz. *Histoire de la Louisiane* (Paris: De Bure, 1758), Tome 1, 344-345

Liesegang, Gerhard. "Nguni Migrations between Delagoa Bay and the Zambezi, 1821-1839," *African Historical Studies* 3:2 (1970), 317-337

Liu, Jie, Wei Li, Liming Luo, Jianshe Zhou, Xu Han, Jinsheng Shi, "Linked Open Data Query Based on Natural Language," *Chinese Journal of Electronics* (2017) https://ietresearch.onlinelibrary.wiley.com/doi/abs/10.1049/cje.2016.11.003

Livingstone, David. *Narrative of an Expedition to the Zambesi and its Tributaties and of the Discovery of the Lakes Shirwa and Nyassa* (London: Murray, 1864)

Lord, Phillip, Alison Macdonald, Liz Lyon, and Davis Giaretta. "From Data Deluge to Data Curation," in *Proceedings of the UK e-science All Hands Meeting* (2004), 371-375

Lovejoy, Henry, "The Registers of Liberated Africans of the Havana Slave Trade Commission: Transcription Methodology and Statistical Analysis," *African Economic History* 38 (2010), 107-135

Lovejoy, Henry B. "Redrawing Historical Maps of the Bight of Benin Hinterland, c. 1780," *Canadian Journal of African Studies* 47:3 (2013), 443-463

Lovejoy, Henry B. *Prieto: Yorùbá Kingship in Colonial Cuba during the Age of Revolutions* (Chapel Hill, University of North Carolina Press, 2018)

Lovejoy, Henry B. "Mapping Uncertainty: The Collapse of Oyo and the Trans-Atlantic Slave Trade, 1816–1836," *Journal of Global Slavery* 4 (2019), 127-161

Lovejoy, Henry B. "Who Did What When? Acknowledging Collaborative Contributions in LiberatedAfricans.org," *Slaveries and Post-Slaveries* 3 (2020)

Lovejoy, Henry B., Paul E. Lovejoy, Walter Hawthorne, Edward Alpers, Mariana Candido, Matthew Hopper, Ghyslaine Lydon, Colleen Kriger and John Thornton. "Defining Regions of Pre-Colonial Africa: A Controlled Vocabulary for Linking Open-Source Data in Digital History Projects," *History in Africa* 48 (2021), 1-25

Lovejoy Henry B.; Paul E. Lovejoy; Walter Hawthorne; Edward A. Alpers; Mariana Candido; and Matthew S. Hopper. "Redefining African Regions for Linking Open-Source Data," *History in Africa* 46 (2019), 5-36

Lovejoy, Paul E. *Caravans of Kola: The Hausa Kola Trade, 1700-1900* (Zaria: Ahmadu Bello University Press, 1980)

Lovejoy, Paul E. *Transformations in Slavery: A History of Slavery in Africa* (Cambridge: Cambridge University Press, 1983, 2000, 2012, 2017).

Lovejoy, Paul E. "Background to Rebellion: The Origins of Muslim Slaves in Bahia," *Slavery and Abolition* 15:2 (1994), 151-180

Lovejoy, Paul E. "Biography as Source Material: Towards a Biographical Archive of Enslaved Africans," in Robin Law (ed.), *Source Material for*

Studying the Slave Trade and the African Diaspora (Stirling: Centre of Commonwealth Studies, University of Stirling, 1997), 119-140

Lovejoy, Paul E. "The African Diaspora: Revisionist Interpretations of Ethnicity, Culture and Religion under Slavery," *Studies in the World History of Slavery, Abolition and Emancipation*, 2:1(1997)

Lovejoy, Paul E. "Identifying Enslaved Africans in the African Diaspora," in Paul E. Lovejoy, ed. *Identity in the Shadow of Slavery* (London: Continuum, 2000)

Lovejoy, Paul E. "Methodology through the Ethnic Lens," in Toyin Falola and Christian Jennings (eds.), *Sources and Methods in African History: Spoken, Written, Unearthed* (Rochester: University of Rochester Press, 2003), 105-118

Lovejoy, Paul E. "Autobiography and Memory: Gustavus Vassa and the Abolition of the Slave Trade," *Slavery and Abolition* 27:3 (2006), 317-47

Lovejoy, Paul E. "Transatlantic Transformations: The Origins and Identities of Africans in the Americas," in Boubacar Barry, Livio Sansone, and Elisée Soumonni (eds.), *Africa, Brazil, and the Construction of Trans-Atlantic Black Identities* (Trenton: Africa World Press, 2008), 81-112

Lovejoy, Paul E. "The African Background of Venture Smith," in James B. Stewart (ed.), *Venture Smith and the Business of Slavery and Freedom* (Amherst: University of Massachusetts Press, 2009), 35-55

Lovejoy, Paul E. "Scarification and the Loss of History in the African Diaspora," in Andrew Apter and Lauren Derry (eds.), *Activating the Past Historical Memory in the Black Atlantic* (Newcastle: Cambridge Scholarly Publishing, 2009), 99-129

Lovejoy, Paul E. "The upper Guinea Coast and the Trans-Atlantic Slave Trade Database," *African Economic History* 38 (2010), 1-27

Lovejoy, Paul E. "Les Origines de Catherine Mulgrave Zimmermann: Considérations Méthodologiques," *Cahiers des Anneaux de la Mémoire* 14 (2011), 247-63

Lovejoy, Paul E. "Freedom Narratives of Transatlantic Slavery," *Slavery and Abolition* 32:1 (2011), 91-107

Lovejoy, Paul E. "Mohammed Ali Nicholas Sa'id: From Enslavement to American Civil War Veteran," *Millars: Espai I Història* 42 (2017), 219-32

Lovejoy, Paul E. *Slavery in the Global Diaspora of Africa* (London: Routledge, 2019)

Lovejoy, Paul E. "Ali Eisami's Enslavement and Emancipation: The Trajectory of a Liberated African," in Richard Anderson and Henry B. Lovejoy. (eds.), *Liberated Africans and the Abolition of the Slave Trade, 1807-1896* (Rochester: University of Rochester Press, 2020)

Lovejoy, Paul E., and David V. Trotman (eds.). *Trans-Atlantic Dimensions of Ethnicity in the African Diaspora* (London: Continuum, 2004)

Lyrio Ximenes, Cristina Ferreira. "Joaquim Pereira Marinho: Perfil de um Contrabandista de Escravos na Bahia," M.A. Thesis: Universidade Federal da Bahia (1999)

Mackey, Frank. *Done with Slavery: The Black Fact in Montreal, 1760-1840* (Montréal and Kingston: McGill-Queen's University Press, 2010)

Madan A.C. *Kiungani or Story and History from Central Africa written by Boys in the Schools of the Universities' Mission to Central Africa* (London: George Bell and Sons, 1887)

Mair, Lucille Mathurin, *A Historical Study of Women in Jamaica: 1655-1844* (Kingston: University of West Indies Press, 2006)

Mannix, Daniel P. and Malcolm Cowley. *Black Cargoes: A History of the Atlantic Slave Trade, 1518-1865* (New York: Viking Press, 1962)

Mao Ji-Ye, Karel Vredenburg, Paul W. Smith, and Tom Carey. 2005. "The State of User-Centered Design Practice." Communications of the ACM 48:3 (2005), 105-109. https://doi.org/10.1145/1047671.1047677

Marcílio, Maria Luiza. "Dos Registos Paroquiais à Demografia Histórica no Brasil," *Anais de História* 2 (1971), 81-100

Margo, Robert A. and Richard H. Steckel. "The Heights of American Slaves: New Evidence on Slave Nutrition and Health," Special Issue: Trends in Nutrition, Labor, Welfare, and Labor Productivity, *Social Science History* 6:4 (1982), 516-538

Martin, R. Montgomery. *History of the British Colonies* (London, James Cochrane and Co., 2nd edition, 1835), 5 vols.

Martins, Bruno, Hugo Manguinhas, and Jose Borbinha, "Extracting and Exploring the Geo-temporal Semantics of Textual Rresources," in *2008 IEEE International Conference on Semantic Computing* (2008), 1-9

Mascarenhas de Lima, Valney. "O comércio de escravizados(as) na Bahia na segunda metade do Século XIX," in *Anais Do XXIX Simpósio de História Nacional* (Brasília: Associação Nacional de História, 2017)

Matory, J. Lorand. "Jeje: Repensando Nações e Transnacionalismo," *Mana* 5:1 (1999), 57-80

Maugham R. C. F. *Zambezia. A General Description of the Valley of the Zambezi River, from its Delta to the River Aroangwa, with its History, Agriculture, Flora, Fauna, and Ethnography* (London: John Murray, 1910)

Maya Restrepo, Luz Adriana. *Brujería y Reconstrucción de Identidades entre los Africanos y sus Descendientes en el Nuevo Reino de Granada, Siglo XVII* (Bogotá: Ministerio de Cultura, 2005)

McKnight, Kathryn Joy, "Performing double-edged stories: the three trials of Paula de Eguiluz," *Colonial Latin American Review* 25:2 (2016), 154-174

Médard, Henri. "Introduction" in Médard Henri, Derat Marie-Laure, Vernet Thomas, Ballarin Marie-Pierre (eds.), *Traites et Esclavages en Afrique orientale et dans l'océan Indien* (Paris: Karthala, 2013), 9-28

Melek Delgado, Érika. "Freedom Narratives: The West African Person as the Central Focus for a Digital Humanities Database," *History in Africa* 48 (2021)

Mendes de Almeida, António. "The Foundations of the System: A Reassessment of the Slave Trade to the Spanish Americas in the Sixteenth and Seventeenth Centuries," in David Eltis and David Richardson (eds.), *Extending the Frontiers. Essays on the New Transatlantic Slave Trade Database* (New Haven: Yale University Press, 2008), 63-94

Meirelles, Isabel. "Visualizing Information" in Julia Flanders and Fotis Jannidis (eds.), *The Shape of Data in Digital Humanities: Modeling Texts and Text-based Materials* (Surrey, UK: Ashgate, 2018)

Meirelles, Isabel. *Design for Information: An Introduction to the Histories, Theories, and Best Practices behind Effective Information Visualizations* (Beverly, MA: Rockport Publishers, 2013)

Michel, Joseph. *De l'Esclavage à l'apostolat. Les auxiliaires laïcs du Bienheureux Jacques Laval apôtre de l'île Maurice* (Paris: Beauchesne, 1988)

Migeod, Frederick William Hugh. *The Languages of West Africa* (London: Kegan Paul, Trench,Trubner & Co., 1913), 2 vols.

Milligan, Lan. *History in the Age of Abundance. How the Web Is Transforming Historical Research* (Montreal and Kingston: McGill-Queen's University Press, 2019)

Miranda Ojeda, Pedro. "Amar por voluntad ajena. Los encantamientos sexuales en Yucatán durante el siglo XVII," *Antrópica. Revista de Ciencias Sociales y Humanidades* 4:7 (2018), 89-103

Moradi, Alexander and Joerg Baten. "Inequality in Sub-Saharan Africa: New Data and New Insights from Anthropometric Estimates," *World Development* 33:8 (2005), 1233-1265

Moraes Trindade, Pedro. "Do Lado de Cá da Kalunga: Os Africanos Angolas em Salvador – 1800 1864," M.A. Thesis: Universidade Federal da Bahia (2008)

Moral de Calatrava, Paloma. "Frígidos y Maleficiados. Las Mujeres y los Remedios Contra la Impotencia en la Edad Media," *Asclepio* 64:2 (2012), 353-372

Moreau de Saint-Mery, Mederic Louis Elie. *Description de la Partie française de l'Isle de Saint-Domingue*, Tome 1, B. Maurel and E. Taillemite (eds.) (Paris: Sté de l'Histoire des colonies françaises et Larose, 1958)

Morgan, Philip D. “The Cultural Implications of the Atlantic Slave Trade: African Regional Origins, American Destinations and New World Developments,” *Slavery and Abolition* 18:1 (1997), 122-145

Msamati, B.C. and P.S. Igbigbi. “Anthropometric Profile of Urban Adult Black Malawians,” *East African Medical Journal* 77:7 (2000), 364-368

Mudimbe, Victor Y. *The Invention of Africa: Gnosis, Philosophy, and the Order of Knowledge* (Bloomington: Indiana University Press, 1988)

Myers, Norma. “Servant, Sailor, Soldier, Tailor, Beggarman: Black Survival in White Society 1780-1830,” *Immigrants & Minorities* 12:1 (1993), 47-74

Navarrete, M. C. *Génesis y Desarrollo de la Esclavitud en Colombia Siglos XVI y XVII* (Cali, Universidad del Valle, 2005)

Newell, A.F.P. Gregor, M. Morgan, G., Pullin, and C. Macaulay. “User-sensitive Inclusive Design,” *Universal Access in the Information Society* 10:3 (2011), 235-243

Newitt, Malyn. *A History of Mozambique* (Bloomington: Indiana University Press, 1995)

Newitt, Malyn. “The Portuguese on the Zambezi: An Historical Interpretation of the Prazo System,” *Journal of African History* 10:1 (1969), 67-85

Ngcongco Leonard D. “Le Mfecane et l’émergence de Nouveaux États Africains,” in J. F. Ade Ajayi (ed.), *L’Afrique au XIXe siècle jusque vers les années 1880,* Histoire Générale de l’Afrique vol 6 (Paris: UNESCO, 1996), 117-151

Ngou-Mve, Nicola. “Historia de la población negra en México: Necesidad de un enfoque triangular,” in María Elisa Velázquez Gutiérrez and Ethel Correa Duró (eds.), *Poblaciones y culturas de origen africano en México* (México: Instituto Nacional de Antropología e Historia, 2005), 39-64

Nicolau Parés, Luis. *A Formação do Candomblé: História e Ritual da Nação Jeje na Bahia* (Campinas: Editora da Unicamp, 2006)

Novais Almeida, Kátia Lorena. “Alforrias em Rio de Contas: Bahia Século XIX,” M.A. Thesis: Universidade Federal da Bahia (2006)

Nwokeji, G. U., and David Eltis, “The Roots of the African Diaspora: Methodological Considerations in the Analysis of Names in the Liberated African Registers of Sierra Leone and Havana,” *History in Africa* 29 (2002), 365-379

O'Donnell, James J. “Engaging the Humanities: The Digital Humanities” *Daedalus, Reflecting on the Humanities* 138:1 (2009), 99-104

Ojo, Olatunji. “Beyond Diversity: Women, Scarification, and Yoruba Identity,” *History in Africa* 35 (2008), 347-374

Ojo, Olatunji and Henry B. Lovejoy. “Lucumí, Terranova and the Origins of Yoruba Nation,” *Journal of African History* 56:3 (2015), 353-372

O'Kelly, E. de P. "Map of Sierra Leone (Provisional Issue)," *Intelligence Division, War Office, 1898* (Southampton, 1898 [1901])

Oldendorp, G.C.A. *Geschichte der Mission der Evangelischen Brider auf den Caraibischen Inseln S. Thomas, S. Croix and S. Jan* (Barby, 1777)

Otite, Onigu. *Ethnic Pluralism and Ethnicity in Nigeria* (Ibadan: Shaneson C. I. Ltd., 1990)

O'Toole, Rachel Sarah. "From the Rivers of Guinea to the Valleys of Peru: Becoming a Bran Diaspora within Spanish Slavery," *Social Text 92* 25:3 (2007), www.escholarship.org/uc/item/9pm539xk (accessed 21 August 2021)

Paas, Stephen. *Oxford Chichewa Dictionary* (Cape Town: Oxford University Press, , 5th edition 2018), https://translate.chichewadictionary.org/ [Accessed 2 January 2020].

Paas, Steven. *Johannes Rebmann: A Servant of God in Africa Before the Rise of Western Colonialism* (Eugene, OR: Wipf & Stock, Missiologica Evangelica, 2nd edition, 2018)

Palmer, Colin. "From Africa to the Americas: Ethnicity in the Early Black Communities of the Americas," *Journal of World History* 6:2 (1995), 223-236

Palmie, Stephan. "Ethnogenetic Processes and Culture Transfer in AfroAmerican Slave Populations," in Wolfgang Bider (ed.). *Slavery in the Americas* (Würzburg: Königshausen & Neumann, 1993), 337-363

Paquette, Robert L. "The Drivers Shall Lead Them: Image and Reality in Slave Resistance," in Robert L. Paquette and Louis A. Ferleger (eds.), *Slavery, Secession, and Southern History* (Charlottesville: University of Virginia Press, 2000), 31-58

Park, U. and A. Jain. "Face Matching and Retrieval Using Soft Biometrics," *IEEE Trans. on Information Forensics and Security* 5:3 (2010), 406-415

Peabody, Sue. "Slaves as Witnesses, Slaves as Evidence: French and British Prosecution of the Slave Trade in the Indian Ocean," in Nancy Christie, Matthew Gerber, and Michael Gauvreau (eds.), *Voices in the Legal Archives in the French Colonial World: "The King Is Listening"* (Montreal: McGill-Queens Press, 2021), 281-303

Pedregosa, Fabian, Gaël Varoquaux, Alexandre Gramfort, Vincent Michel, Bertrand Thirion, Olivier Grisel, Mathieu Blondel et al. "Scikit-learn: Machine Learning in Python," *Journal of Machine Learning Research* 12 (2011), 2825-2830

Peerthum Satyendra. "'Voices From the Edge': The Life Histories and Experiences of the Liberated Africans in British Mauritius during the Age of Indenture with Comparative Perspectives (1808-1943)," M.A. Thesis: University of Mauritius (2005)

Peltonen, Matti. "Clues, Margins, and Monads: The Micro-Macro Link in Historical Research," *History and Theory* 40:3 (2001), 347-59

Posner, M. "Here and There: Creating DH Community," in Matthew K. Gold and Lauren F. Klein (eds.), *Debates in the Digital Humanities 2016* (Minneapolis: University of Minnesota Press, 2016).

Prescott, Andrew. "Bibliographic Records as Humanities Big Data," *2013 IEEE International Conference on Big Data* (2013), 55-58

Pruneau de Pommegorge, Antoine Edme. *Description de la Nigritie* (Amsterdam and Paris: Maradan, 1789)

Pustejovsky, James and Amber Stubbs. *Natural Language Annotation for Machine Learning: A Guide to Corpus-Building* (Sebastopol, CA: O'Reilly Media, 2013)

Rattray, R.S. *The Tribes of the Ashanti Hinterland* (Oxford: Clarendon Press, 1932), 2 vols.

Reed, A. "Managing an Established Digital Humanities Project: Principles and Practices from the Twentieth Year of the William Blake Archive," *Digital Humanities Quarterly* 8:1 (2014), 1-16

Reis, João José. *Domingos Sodré, um sacerdote Africano: Escravidão, liberdade e candombl é na Bahia do século XIX* (São Paulo: Companhia das Letras, 2008)

Rodas, G. "Ordenanzas de las minas de Antioquia," in V. Restrepo (ed.), *Estudio sobre las Minas de Oro y Plata de Colombia* (Bogotá: Imprensa de Silvestre y Compañía, 1587 [1988]), 249-262

Rodney, Walter. *A History of the upper Guinea Coast: 1545 to 1800* (New York: Monthly Review Press, 1970)

Rodrigues, Ana Marcía L. "A Teoria dos Arquivos e a Gestão de Documentos," *Perspectivas em Ciência da Informação* 11:1 (2006), 102-117

Rodrigues, Raimundo Nina. *Os Africanos No Brasil* (Rio de Janeiro: Centro Edelstein de Pesquisas Sociais, 2010)

Rogers, Dominique (ed.). *Voix d'Esclaves: Antilles, Guyane et Louisiane Françaises, XVIIIe-XIXe Siècle* (Paris: Karthala, 2015)

Roldán de Montaud, I. "En los Borrosos Confines de la Libertad: El Caso de los Negros Emancipados en Cuba, 1817-1870," *Revista de Indias* 71 (2011), 159-92

Rubin, Arnold (ed.). *Marks of Civilization: Artistic Transformations of the Human Body* (Los Angeles: University of California Press, 1988)

Rudd, J., K. Stern, and S. Isensee. "Low vs. High-Fidelity Prototyping Debate" *Interactions Magazine, Association for Computing Machinery* 3:1 (1996), 76-85

Rugendas, Johann Moritz. *Voyage Pittoresque dans le Brésil* (Paris: Engelmann & Cie, 1835)

Sánchez, Jorge Enrique. "La Hechicería, la Brujería y el Reniego de la Fe," in Anna María Splendiani (ed.), *Cincuenta años de inquisición en el Tribunal de Cartagena de Indias, 1610-1660, De la Roma Medieval a la Cartagena colonial: el Santo Oficio de la* Inquisición, Tomo 1 (Bogotá: Pontificia Universidad Javeriana, 1997), 209-227

Salau, Mohammed Bashir. "Nicholas Sa'id of Borno: American Civil War Veteran," *UNESCO General History of Africa, Global Africa* (Paris: UNESCO, 2019), vol. 10

Sandoval, Alonso de. *Un tratado sobre la esclavitud.* [De instauranda Æthiopum salute] (introdução, transcrição e tradução de Enriqueta Vila Vilar) Madrid: Alianza Editorial, 1987)

Santos de Souza, Daniele. "Da Costa da Mina para a Bahia: escravos e libertos africanos no tráfico de transatlântico c. 1750- c.1770," 6° Encontro Escravidão e Liberdade no Brasil Meridional (Florianópolis: Universidade Federal de Santa Catarina, 2013).

Santos Oliveira, Vanessa. "Donas, Pretas Livres e Escravas Em Luanda (Séc. XIX)," *Estudos Ibero-Americanos* 44:3 (2018), 447-456

Saugnier, M. *Relations de Plusieurs Voyages à la Côte d'Afrique, à Maroc, au Sénégal, à Gorée, à Galam, et.* (Paris: Roux et Compagnie, 1792).

Saunders, A.C. de C.M. *A Social History of Black Slaves and Freedmen in Portugal, 1441-1555* (Cambridge: Cambridge University Press, 1982)

Sauvant, Père. *Grammaire Bambara* (Alger: Maison Carrée, Imprimerie des Missionnaires d'Afrique, 1913)

Saye, F. *Public History: A Practical Guide* (Indiana: Bloomsbury, 2015)

Scarr, Deryck. *Slaving and Slavery in the Indian Ocean* (New York: St. Martin's Press, 1998)

Schwarz, Suzanne. "Extending the African Names Database: New Evidence from Sierra Leone," *African Economic History* 38 (2010), 137-163.

Schildkrout, Enid. "Inscribing the Body," *Annual Review of Anthropology* 33 (2004), 319-344.

Scholes, Robert and Clifford Wulfman. "Humanities Computing and Digital Humanities," *South Atlantic Review, The Changing University and the Humanities* 73:4 (2008), 50-66

Scott, Rebecca and Jean M. Hébard. *Freedom Papers. An Atlantic Odyssey in the Age of Emancipation* (Cambridge, MA: Harvard University Press, 2012)

Sheehan-Dean. Aaron, "Afro-Louisiana History and Genealogy, 1719–1820: Afro-Louisiana History and Genealogy, 1719–1820 <http://www.ibiblio.org/laslave/>," *Journal of American History* 91:1 (2004), 348-349

Shields, Francine. "Palm Oil and Power: Women in an Era of Economic and Social Transition in 19th Century Yorubaland (South-Western Nigeria)," Ph.D. thesis: University of Stirling (1997)

Shimizu, Cogan et al., "The Enslaved Ontology: Peoples of the Historic Slave Trade," *Journal of Web Semantics First Look: Interdisciplinary Semantic Methods & Applications*, 2020 https://papers.ssrn.com/sol3/papers.cfm?abstract_id=3583130

Sidbury, James and Jorge Cañizares-Esguerra. "Mapping Ethnogenesis in the Early Modern Atlantic," *William and Mary Quarterly* 68:2 (2011), 181-208

Sierra Silva, P.M. *Urban Slavery in Colonial Mexico, Puebla de los Ángeles, 1531–1706* (Cambridge: Cambridge University Press, 2018)

Silva Junior, Carlos da. "Ardras, Jejes and Minas, or Slaves of 'First Reputation': African Politics, Slave Trade and Identity in Eighteenth-Century Salvador, Brazil," *Almanack* 12 (2016), 6-33

Soulodre-La France, Renée. "Por el amor! Child Killing in Colonial Nueva Granada," *Slavery and Abolition* 23:1 (2002), 87-100

Southall, Humphrey. "Defining and Identifying the Roles of Geographic References within Text: Examples from the Great Britain Historical GIS Project," in *Proceedings of the HLT-NAACL 2003 Workshop on Analysis of Geographic References* (2003), 69-78.

Sparks, Randy. *The Two Princes of Calabar* (Cambridge, MA: Harvard University Press, 2004)

Spicker, Jessica. "El Cuerpo Femenino en Cautiverio: Aborto e Infanticidio entre las Esclavas de la Nueva Granada 1750-1810," in Luz Adriana Maya (ed.), *Geografía humana de Colombia: los Afrocolombianos*, Tomo 4 (Bogotá: Instituto Colombiano de Cultura Hispánica, 1998), 143-165

Splendiani, A. M., *Cincuenta años de inquisición en el Tribunal de Cartagena de Indias, 1610-1660: Documentos inéditos procedentes del Archivo Histórico Nacional de Madrid (AHMN), Sección Inquisición, Libro 1020 y 1021, años 1610-1660,* Tomo 2 (Bogotá: Javeriana, 1997).

Steckel, Richard H. "Slave Height Profiles from Coastwise Manifests," *Explorations in Economic History* 16:4 (1979), 363-338

Sternfeld, Joshua. "Archival Theory and Digital Historiography: Selection, Search, and Metadata as Archival Processes for Assessing Historical Contextualization" *The American Archivist* 74:2 (2011), 544-575

Stickler, P. J. "Invisible Towns: A Case Study in the Cartography of South Africa," *GeoJournal* 22:3 (1990), 329-333

Stone, Jeffrey C. "Imperialism, Colonialism and Cartography," *Transactions of the Institute of British Geographers* 13:1 (1988), 57-64

Strictrodt, Silke. "Afro-European Trade Relations on the Western Slave Coast, 16th to 19th Centuries" Ph.D. thesis: University of Stirling (2002)

Suárez Pinzón, Ivonne. *Oro y Sociedad Colonial en Antioquia 1575 – 1700* (Medellín: Secretaría de Educación y Cultura, 1993)

Supple, Barry. "Preserving the Past: Creating the Endangered Archives Programme," in Maja Kominko (ed.), *From Dust to Digital: Ten Years of the Endangered Archives Programme* (Cambridge: Open Book Publishers, 2015), xxxix-xliii

Surun, Isabelle. "Du Texte au Terrain: Reconstituer les Pratiques des Voyageurs (Afrique Occidentale, 1790-1880," *Sociétés & Représentations* 1:2 (2006), 213-223

Sweet, James. *Recreating Africa. Culture, Kinship, and Religion in the African-Portuguese World 1441-1700* (Chapel Hill: University of North Carolina Press, 2003)

Sweet, James. *Domingos Álvares, African Healing, and the Intellectual History of the Atlantic World* (Chapel Hill: University of North Carolina Press, 2011)

Tannenbaum, Frank. *Slave and Citizen: The Negro in the Americas* (New York: Random House, 1946)

Tanner, James Mourilyan. *A History of the Study of Human Growth* (Cambridge and New York, Cambridge University Press, 1981)

Tascón, Sonia M. *Human Rights Film Festivals: Activism in Context* (London: Springer, 2015)

Teelock, Vijayalakshmi, "From Mozambique to Le Morne Brabant Mountain: Being Young, Male and Mozambican in Colonial Mauritius," in B. Zimba, E. Alpers, A. Isaacman (eds.), *Slaves Routes and Oral Tradition in Southeastern Africa* (Maputo: Filsom Entertainment Lda, 2005), 279-294

Teelock, Vijayalakshmi and Edward A. Alpers. "Introducing Mozambique," in Vijayalakshmi Teelock and Edward A. Alpers (eds.), *History, Memory and Identity* (Port-Louis: Nelson Mandela Centre for African Culture and University of Mauritius, 2001), 111-155

Telfair, Charles. *Some Account of the State of Slavery at Mauritius since the British Occupation in 1810; in Refutation of Anonymous Charges Promulgated against Government and that Colony* (London: James Ridgway, 2nd ed., 1830)

Texugo, F. Tores. *A Letter on the Slave Trade Still Being Carried on along the Eastern Coast of Africa* (London: A. Redford, 1839)

Thévoz, Michel. *The Painted Body* (New York: Rizzoli International Publications, 1984)

Tillman, Linda C. "Culturally Sensitive Research Approaches: An African-American

Perspective," *Review of Research in Education* 32:9 (2002), 3-12

Tomich, Dale W. and Micheal Zeuske. "Introduction: The Second Slavery: Mass Slavery, World-Economy, and Comparative Microhistories," *Review: A Journal of the Fernand Braudel Center* 31:2 (2008), 91-100

Torralba, A., Fergus, R., Weiss, Y., "Small Codes and Large Image Databases for Recognition," *Computer Vision and Pattern Recognition*, Proceedings of 2008 IEEE Computer Society Conference on Computer Vision, 2008

Torrão, Maria Manuel Ferraz. "Actividade comercial externa de Cabo Verde: organização, funcionamento, evolução," in Luís de Albuquerque and Maria Emília Madeira Santos (eds.), *História Geral de Cabo Verde* (Coimbra: Imprensa de Coimbra, 1991), Vol. 1, 237-345

Trivellata, Francesca, 2011. "Is There a Future for Italian Microhistory in the Age of Global History?" *California Italian Studies,* 2:1 (2011) www.escholarship.org/uc/item/0z94n9hq, accessed 4 January 2021

Usner, Daniel H. "From African Captivity to American Slavery. The Introduction of Black Llaborers in Colonial Louisiana," *Louisiana History* 20 (1979), 25-48

Van Mensch, Peter. "A Structured Approach to Museology," in Peter Van Mensch (ed.), *Object, Museum, Museology, an Eternal Triangle* (Leiden: Reinw, 1987)

Van Someren, M. W., Y.F. Barnard, and J.A. Sandberg. *The Think Aloud Method: A Practical Guide to Modeling Cognitive Processes* (London: Academic Press, 1994)

Vargas Arana, Paola. "Memoria y Libertad: Las insurgencias de la población africana frente a la esclavitud en Antioquia y el sur de Cartagena, Nuevo Reino de Granada (siglos XVI - XVII)," Ph.D. Thesis: Universidad Federal de Río de Janeiro (2019)

Vasconcelos, José. *The Cosmic Race: A Bilingual Edition, trans and annotated by Didier T. Jaén* (Baltimore, 1997; Spanish ed., 1920)

Vaughan, Megan. *Creating the Creole Island: Slavery in Eighteenth-Century Mauritius* (Durham: Duke University Press, 2005)

Véras, Bruno Rafael. "The Slavery and Freedom Narrative of Mahommah Gardo Baquaqua in the Nineteenth-Century Atlantic World," *UNESCO General History of Africa, Global Africa* (Paris: UNESCO, 2019), vol. 10

Verger, Pierre. *Fluxo e Refluxo do Tráfico de Escravos Entre o Golfo do Benin e a Bahia de Todos os Santos dos Séculos XVII a XIX*, Trans. Tasso Gazdanis (São Paulo: Editora Corrupio, 1987)

Verger, Pierre. *Notas Sobre o Culto Aos Orixás e Voduns na Bahia de Todos os Santos, no Brasil, e na Antiga Costa dos Escravos, na África,* Trans. Carlos Eugênio Marcondes de Moura (São Paulo: Editora da Universidade de São Paulo, 2000)

Vieira Ribeiro, Alexandre. "A Cidade de Salvador: Estrutura Econômica, Comércio de Escravos, Grupo Mercantil (c. 1750-1800)," Ph.D. Thesis: Universidade Federal do Rio de Janeiro (2009)

Warner-Lewis, Maureen. *Archibald Monteath, Igbo, Jamaican, Moravian* (Kingston: University of West Indies Press, 2006)

West, Robert. *Colonial Placer Mining in Colombia* (Baton Rouge: Louisiana State University Press, 1952)

Westermann, D. and M. A. Bryan. *Languages of West Africa: Handbook of African Languages*, Part II (London: International African Institute, 1952)

Wheat, David. "The First Great Waves: African Provenance Zones for the Transatlantic Slave Trade to Cartagena de Indias, 1570-1640," *Journal of African History* 52:1 (2011), 1-22

Wheat, David. *Atlantic Africa and the Spanish Caribbean, 1570-1640* (Chapel Hill: University of North Carolina Press, 2016).

Wheat, David. "Biafadas in Havana: West African Antecedents for Caribbean Social Interactions," in Ida Altman and David Wheat (eds.), *The Spanish Caribbean and the Atlantic World in the Long Sixteenth Century* (Lincoln, NE: University of Nebraska Press, 2019), 163-186

Wheat, David. "Tangomãos en Tenerife y Sierra Leona a Mediados del Sigo XVI," *Cliocanarias* 2 (2020): 545-569

Wheat, David. "El Tráfico de Esclavos en los Siglos XVI y XVII: Sierra Leona en los 1560 y la Infraestructura de la Trata," *Seminario de Historia de Cartagena de Indias: Nuevos Trabajos*, Cartegena: Universidad Tecnológica de Bolívar, forthcoming

White, William M. *Journal of a Voyage Performed in the Lion extra Indiaman, from Madras to Colombo and Da Lagoa Bay . . . in the Year 1798* (London, John Stockdale, 1800)

White. Shane and Graham White, "Slave Hair and African American Culture in the Eighteenth and Nineteenth Centuries," *Journal of Southern History* 61:1 (1995), 45-76

Williams, Daryle, "Digital Approaches to the History of the Atlantic Slave Trade," *Oxford Research Encyclopedias* (Oxford: Oxford University Press, 2018)

Williford, J. "Gross Injustice: The Slave Trade by the Numbers," *Humanities: The Magazine for the National Endowment for the Humanities* 31:5 (2010)

Windley, Lathan. *Runaway Slave Advertisements. A Documentary History from the 1730s to 1790*, 4 vol. (Westport, CN / London: Greenwood Press, 1983)

Zimmerman. Z. "Play as Research: The Iterative Design Process," in M. Ladly and P. Beesley, (eds.), *Mobile Nation: Creating Methodologies for Mobile Platforms* (Waterloo: Riverside Architectural Press, 2008), 25-37

Notes on Contributors

Paola Vargas Arana is a British Academy Newton Postdoctoral Fellow at King's College London who works as a collaborator on the Freedom Narratives project. Her research focuses on how the African population combated the enslavement in New Granada during the sixteenth and seventeenth centuries, and how their answers impacted the ongoing historical processes in both Africa and America. She is the author of "Pedro Claver y la labor de evangelización en Cartagena de Indias (siglo XVII). Fuentes para analizar los africanos en el Nuevo Mundo," *Revista de História USP* 155 (2006), 43–81.

Nina Borba is an African-Brazilian undergraduate student in History at York University and a Research Assistant with the *Freedom Narratives* project (www.freedomnarratives.org). She is passionate about studying the African diaspora in Brazil and disseminating historical knowledge through innovative projects in Digital Humanities.

Klara Boyer-Rossol, post-doctoral Fellow, Bonn Center for Dependency and Slavery Studies (BCDSS), University of Bonn. Her doctoral thesis (2015, University Paris 7 Diderot) received the 2016 Thesis Prize of the National Committee for the Memory and History of Slavery (France). She is author of "Makua Life Histories: Testimonies on Slavery and the Slave Trade in the 19th century in Madagascar," in A. Bellagamba, S. E. Greene, and M. Klein (eds.), *African Voices on Slavery and the Slave Trade* (2013). She is the co-director and co-editor of Les esclavages en Afrique (Karthala editions, collection Esclavages).

Kartikay Chadha is the President and CEO of Walk With Web Inc (www.walkwithweb.org). He is also a Ph.D. candidate in the School of Information Studies at McGill University. He holds a MSc. degree from the University of Toronto and a B.Tech. from the Vellore Institute of Technology in India.

Daniel Genkins is a Mellon Assistant Professor of History and Digital Humanities and the Executive Director of the Slave Societies Digital Archive at Vanderbilt University. His 2018 dissertation analyzed imperial competition in the seventeenth-century Caribbean. Since completing his PhD, Genkins has focused on digital work. His research interests include data science as applied to digital archives of historical documents and machine learning techniques to enhance the usefulness and accessibility of these archives.

Gwendolyn Midlo Hall is Professor Emerita of Latin American and Caribbean History at Rutgers University. Born in 1929, Midlo-Hall has been a lifelong civil rights and Black Power essayist and activist, multi award winning historian, digital humanities pioneer and outstanding public intellectual still writing pioneering works as she reaches her 92nd year.

Jerome Handler, an historical anthropologist, is Senior Scholar at Virginia Humanities (formerly, Virginia Foundation for the Humanities) Charlottesville, Virginia. His primary research focus is Barbados, particularly during the period of slavery. He was co-creator and co-director, with Michael Tuite, of "The Atlantic Slave Trade and Slave Life in the Americas: A Visual Record," www.slaveryimages.org today under the direction of Henry Lovejoy.

Katrina Keefer is an Adjunct Professor at Trent University, Ontario, Canada for both the History undergraduate and Cultural Studies graduate programs. She is a digital humanities scholar who specializes in identity, body marking, slavery, and cultural history in West Africa. She leads two large scale digital humanities projects funded by SSHRC on using permanent body marks to better discern origins and birthplace among enslaved Africans. She has previously published on scarification, African representation in games, and cultural identity in Sierra Leone.

Paul Lachance is a retired professor of history at the University of Ottawa where his research focused on colonial and antebellum Louisiana history. Since retirement in 2003 he has been involved in the development of *Slave Voyages*, the website for the trans-Atlantic and intra-American slave trade databases.

Martha Ladly is Professor and Graduate Program Director, Digital Futures, Ontario College of Art and Design (OCAD) University. She is a Principal

Investigator with the Visual Analytics Lab at OCAD University. She is an artist and designer, a noted researcher, a musician, and recipient of Social Sciences and Humanities Research Council of Canada awards.

Jane Landers is the Gertrude Conaway Vanderbilt Professor of History at Vanderbilt University and director of the Slave Societies Digital Archive. Since 2015, she has served as the U.S. member on the UNESCO International Scientific Committee for the Slave Route Project._Landers' award-winning monographs include *Black Society in Spanish Florida* and *Atlantic Creoles in the Age of Revolutions.*

Eric Lehman is a PhD candidate in Canadian Studies at Trent University. His research interests include the study of festivals, culture, and creative labor as well as the relationship between the archive and historiography. Formally, he was a research assistant on *Creating a Visual Language of Marks* project under Keefer and Ladly and is co-editor of a forthcoming book that discusses Black lives in Canada.

Henry B. Lovejoy is an Associate Professor and Director of the Digital Slavery Research Laboratory at the University of Colorado Boulder. His first book, *Prieto: Yorùbá Kingship in Colonial Cuba during the Age of Revolutions*, won the Chief Isaac Oluwole Delano Best Book Prize for Yoruba Studies. He is also co-editor of the volume *Liberated Africans and the Abolition of the Slave Trade, 1807-1896*. In 2021, He was awarded a three-year Andrew W. Mellon Foundation New Directions Fellowship to develop "Africa Historical GIS." He also sits on the board of directors of Walk With Web Inc.

Paul E. Lovejoy is Distinguished Research Professor, Department of History, York University and Fellow of the Royal Society of Canada. His websites include SHADD, "Studies in the History of the African Diaspora Documents" (www.shadd.org), "Freedom Narratives: Testimonies of West Africans in the Era of Slavery" (www.freedomnarratives.org), and "Equiano's World: Gustavus Vassa and the Abolition of the British Slave Trade" (www.equianosworld.org)

Gabriela Mattia is a student at the Federal University of Rio Grande do Sul in Brazi, and was a Mitacs Globalink Research intern with the *Language of Marks* project in , bringing her training in museology and her experience working at both the Museu de Arte Contemporânea do Rio Grande do Sul and the Museu de Porto Alegre Joaquim Felizardo to this project.

Michael McGill holds an M.A. in History from Trent University and worked as a research assistant on the *Creating a Visual Language of Marks* project under Keefer and Ladly, participating in fieldwork in Sierra Leone and the Sierra Leone Public Archives 2019-2020.

Érika Melek Delgado holds a Leverhulme Early Career Fellowship at King's College London. Her research focuses on Liberated African children in Africa and the Americas. She is the principal investigator of *Historical African Childhoods* and Associate Director of *Freedom Narratives*, both digital humanities projects focusing on historical biographies. Formerly she was a Postdoctoral Fellow at The Harriet Tubman Institute for Research on Africa and its Diasporas. She holds a PhD in History from the University of Worcester, UK, an MPhil from Universidade Federal do Rio de Janeiro and BA from Universidade Federal Fluminense.

Susan Peabody is Meyer Distinguished Professor of History at Washington State University. Her prize-winning book, *Madeleine's Children: Family, Freedom, Secrets, and Lies in France's Indian Ocean Colonies* (Oxford UP, 2017) is available in French as *Les enfants de Madeleine* (Karthala, 2019).

Léon Robichaud teaches in the Département d'histoire (Université de Sherbrooke), edits the *Revue d'histoire de l'Amérique française* et co-directs the Laboratoire d'histoire et de patrimoine de Montréal. He specialises in the social history of administration in New France and in digital humanities. His interests focus on the relationship between ordinary people and the authorities as well as the use of geographic information in historical research.

Telma Gonçalves Santos, historian born in Brasília-Distrito Federal, the great-granddaughter of African slaves, defended her thesis, "Tecidos europeus e asiáticos nas rotas portuguesas do tráfico de escravizados africanos centro ocidentais para a Bahia entre os anos de 1695-1750," in 2020. Her study examines the impact of demand of the African leaders on the textile production system of England and Central Europe. She joined the Freedom Narratives team in 2019 and since 2000 has taught public school teacher in basic education.

Jim Schindling is a Postdoctoral Scholar at Vanderbilt University supporting the Trans-Institutional Programs (TIPs) Initiative. He has a B.A. in Anthropology from the University of Colorado, Colorado Springs and a Masters and PhD in Geography from West Virginia University. The focus of his work is the application of digital technologies as a means of advancing humanities scholarship. He has published on a technique for supporting archaeological site prospection using lidar data and has developed a software suite that enables historians to manage and analyze content extracted from historical texts.

Ibrahima Seck is a member of the History department of University Cheikh Anta Diop of Dakar, Senegal. His research is mostly devoted to the historical and cultural links between West Africa and Louisiana with a special interest for religious beliefs, music, foodways, and miscellaneous aspects of culture. He is Director of research of the Whitney Plantation Slavery Museum located in St. John the Baptist Parish in Louisiana. He is the author of a book on this historic site entitled "*Bouki fait Gombo: A History of the Slave Community of Habitation Haydel (Whitney Plantation) Louisiana, 1750-1860*. (2014).

Index

D

E

F

G

H

I

J

K

L